THE EASTERN FRONTIER

THE EASTERN FRONTIER

Limits of Empire in Late Antique and Early Medieval Central Asia

Robert Haug

I.B.TAURIS
LONDON • NEW YORK • OXFORD • NEW DELHI • SYDNEY

I.B. TAURIS
Bloomsbury Publishing Plc
50 Bedford Square, London, WC1B 3DP, UK
1385 Broadway, New York, NY 10018, USA

BLOOMSBURY, I.B. TAURIS and the I.B. Tauris logo are
trademarks of Bloomsbury Publishing Plc

First published in Great Britain 2019
Paperback edition first published 2021

For legal purposes the Acknowledgements on p. vii constitute
an extension of this copyright page.

Cover design: Paul Smith, www.paulsmithdesign.com
Cover image: A fresco from Ancient Sogdian Penjikent at the National Museum of
Antiquities in Dushanbe Tajikistan.

A catalogue record for this book is available from the British Library.

A catalog record for this book is available from the Library of Congress.

ISBN: HB: 978-1-7883-1003-1
PB: 978-0-7556-3852-9
ePDF: 978-1-7867-3614-7
eBook: 978-1-7883-1722-1

Series: Early and Medieval Islamic World

Typeset by Deanta Global Publishing Services, Chennai, India

In memory of my grandfather,
Lloyd George Scheffel (1920–2016)

CONTENTS

List of abbreviations viii
List of maps ix
Acknowledgements x

INTRODUCTION 1

Chapter 1
THE GATE OF IRON: CONCEPTUALIZING THE EASTERN FRONTIER IN MEDIEVAL GEOGRAPHIC LITERATURE 17

Chapter 2
SHAPING THE EASTERN FRONTIER: THE SASANIAN EMPIRE AND ITS EASTERN NEIGHBOURS 43

Chapter 3
THE ARAB-MUSLIM CONQUESTS AND THE LATE ANTIQUE IMPERIAL SHATTERZONE 71

Chapter 4
THE FRONTIER BEYOND THE CALIPHATE: KHURĀSĀN AND THE SECOND FITNA 99

Chapter 5
EXTENDING THE FRONTIER: THE UMAYYADS IN SOGDIANA AND BEYOND 111

Chapter 6
THE UNSETTLED FRONTIER: THE ABBASID AND OTHER REVOLUTIONS AND THE EASTERN FRONTIER 139

Chapter 7
UNIFYING THE FRONTIER: THE FORMATION OF GREATER KHURĀSĀN 169

CONCLUSION: AT THE END OF THE FRONTIER 197

Notes 201
Bibliography 259
Index 282

ABBREVIATIONS

ANS	American Numismatic Society.
Balādhūrī	Aḥmad b. Yaḥyā al-Balādhūrī, *Kitāb futūḥ al-buldān*, M.J. de Goeje [ed.] (Leiden: Brill, 1866).
Bal'amī	Abū 'Alī Muḥammad Bal'amī, *Chronique de-Abou-Djaraf-Mohammed-ben-Yezid Tabari, traduites sur la version persane d'Abou 'Ali Mohammed ben Bel'ami*, Hermann Zotenberg [trans.] (Paris: Oriental Translation Fund, 1867–74).
CHIr	*Cambridge History of Iran.*
Dīnawarī	Abū Ḥanīfa Aḥmad b. Dāwud al-Dīnawarī, *Kitāb al-akhbār al-ṭiwāl*, Vladimir Guirgass and Ignatius Kratchkovsky [eds.] (Leiden, 1888).
EIr	*Encylopaedia Iranica, online edition*, E. Yarshater [ed.], (London: 1982–).
EI[2]	*Encyclopaedia of Islam, second edition*, (Leiden, 1960–2009).
HCCA3	B.A. Litvinsky [ed.], *History of Civilizations of Central Asia: Vol. III The Crossroads of Civilizations: A.D. 250 to 750*, (Paris, 1996).
The History of Bukhara	Abū Bakr al-Narshakhī, *The History of Bukhara*, Richard Frye [trans.] (Cambridge, MA: The Mediaeval Academy of American, 1954).
History of al-Ṭabarī	Abū Ja'far Muḥammad b. Jarīr al-Ṭabarī, *The History of al-Ṭabarī*. Ehsan Yarshater [ed.], 40 volumes (Albany, NY, 1985–99).
Ibn al-Athīr	'Izz al-Dīn Abū al-Ḥassan b. al-Athīr, *al-Kāmil fī 'l-ta'rīkh*, Samīr Shams [ed.] (Beirut, 2009).
Narshakhī	Abū Bakr al-Narshakhī, *Ta'rīkh-i Bukhārā*, Mudarris Raẓavī [ed.] (Tehran, Intishārāt-i Ṭūs, 1363/1984).
Origins	Aḥmad b. Yaḥyā al-Balādhūrī, *The Origins of the Islamic State*, Philip K. Hitti and Francis Clark Murgotten [trans.], (New York: Columbia University Press, 1916–24).
Ṭabarī	Abū Ja'far Muḥammad b. Jarīr al-Ṭabarī, *Ta'rīkh al-rusul wa'l-mulūk*, M.J. de Goeje [ed.] (Leiden, 1879–1901).
Tha'ālibī	Abū Manṣūr 'Abd al-Malik Tha'ālibī, *Ghurar akhbār mulūk al-Furs wa sīyarihim*, Hermann Zotenberg [ed.] (Paris, 1900).

MAPS

Map 1	The Eastern Frontier in Modern Context	8
Map 2	The Chaghāniyān Road According to Ibn Khurradādhbih	18
Map 3	The Topography of the Eastern Frontier	24
Map 4	The Eastern Frontier in Late Antiquity	50
Map 5	The Sasanian Frontier in the Seventh Century	79
Map 6	The Eastern Frontier of the Umayyad Caliphate	122
Map 7	Major Revolts and Campaigns of the Mid and Late Eighth Century (dates in parenthesis)	148

ACKNOWLEDGEMENTS

Writing this book has been a long process with many starts and stops. It began with a PhD dissertation written for the Department of Near Eastern Studies at the University of Michigan and has travelled with me through the first stages of my academic career as a faculty member at the University of Cincinnati. Along the way I have benefitted from the inspiration, guidance, advice and kindness of many people, far too many to thank here in these brief acknowledgements. To anyone I omit, my apologies. To begin with the members of my PhD committee Michael Bonner, Kathryn Babayan, Gottfried Hagen and Rudi Lindner, thank you for shepherding me through the first iteration of this project and for your continued support. Since leaving Ann Arbor, I have been extremely lucky to be part of the University of Cincinnati's Department of History. In particular I would like to thank Elizabeth Frierson, Susan Longfield Karr and especially Willard Sunderland for their feedback and encouragement throughout my writing process. I would also like to thank my colleagues who attended a faculty brownbag several years ago to discuss a very messy draft of a chapter, unrecognizable in the final product – your input is found throughout this manuscript. Outside of the History Department, I would also like to thank fellow Bearcats Craig Perry and Marion Kruse. Over the years, I have presented many aspects of this project at various conferences and I have benefitted greatly from the feedback I have received. I would especially like to thank Alison Vacca, who shared her expertise on the northern frontiers of the Caucasus while commenting on early drafts of this project.

This project has been supported over the years by the Charles Phelps Taft Research Center and the College of Arts & Sciences at the University of Cincinnati through numerous travel and faculty development grants. Speaking of funding, I would be remiss not to thank the History Department's administrators past and present, Hope Earls and Ashely Bone, without whom I could never figure out the paperwork associated with university grants. I would also like to thank everyone at the University of Cincinnati's Langsam and Classics Libraries, especially Sally Moffett. Without the hard-working people of the Ohio-Link and ILL offices, I could not have completed the research behind this book. Amy Koshoffer of UC Library's Research Data and GIS Services provided helpful and timely technical support while I was composing and editing the maps found in this book.

At I.B. Tauris, I would like to thank Prof. Roy Mottahedeh and everyone on the editorial board of this excellent series. My editors Tom Stottor and Rory Gormley have been invaluable as I brought this book to the page and I thank them sincerely for their support and interest in the project. I would also like to thank the two anonymous reviewers who provided thoughtful comments on the manuscript. I hope I have addressed your concerns. As in all things, all mistakes and omissions are my fault alone.

Most importantly, I would like to thank my wonderful wife, Laura, who has been a great inspiration and motivator throughout the writing process and throughout life. I am forever in her debt and extremely fortunate to have her by my side.

INTRODUCTION

The Turks haven't come to us; we have come to them

In his *History of the Prophets and Kings*, the chronicler Ṭabarī (839–923) reported that in 724–5 a messenger came to the Umayyad governor of Samarqand, Ḥasan b. Abī al-ʿAmarraṭah al-Kindī (r. ca. 724–9), warning of an imminent attack against the Muslims of Transoxiana by a force of 7,000 Turks. According to this anecdote presented on the authority of Ḥasan's wife, the messenger announced that 'these Turks have come to you', but Ḥasan corrected him saying, 'They haven't come to us; rather, we have come to them, taken their country from them and enslaved them.'[1] Ḥasan did not dismiss the messenger's concerns, promising that he would still send his troops out to face the Turks. Instead, he recognized the geopolitical realities of Transoxiana in the early eighth century, a region the Muslims had only recently and not quite definitively conquered and removed from the Turkish Khāqānate's sphere of influence. From Ḥasan's view, the Turks were not invading the lands of the Muslims, but the Muslims had invaded the lands of the Turks.

We do not expect such an attitude from a governor overseeing a city on the frontier of the Umayyad Caliphate (r. 661–750) at a time when the Turks were a serious threat to the Muslim presence north of the River Oxus. Ḥasan's contemporaries also found this odd and accused him of shirking his duty to fight the Turks and responding when his wife called but not when Samarqand was threatened by invasion.[2] Beginning in 720, Transoxiana was under seemingly constant threat from the Türgesh Turks, a tribal confederation that seized the reins of the Western Türk Khāqānate in the early eighth century. By the middle of the decade, the Türgesh were on the offensive in Sogdiana – the core of Umayyad Transoxiana centred on the River Zarāfshān and the ancient cities of Samarqand and Bukhara – eventually pushing the agents of the Umayyad Caliphate below the Oxus. One of the worst and most humiliating defeats had come just a year before Ḥasan received the news of the Turks descending on Samarqand at the battle remembered as the Day of Thirst (*yawm al-ʿaṭash*). In 724, during a campaign into the Ferghana Valley, an army under the leadership of the recently dismissed governor of Khurāsān Muslim b. Saʿīd al-Kilābī (r. 722–4) was caught by Turkish forces beyond the River Jaxartes. After making a hasty retreat under constant harassment, covering several stages in a single day and even burning their baggage to stay ahead of the pursuing Turks, Kilābī and his men were blocked at the Jaxartes by the armies of Ferghana and Chāch (Tashkent). The Muslims were forced to fight their way through to the river, resulting in high casualties.[3]

Frontier warfare such as this dominates the story in many of our literary sources for the history of late antique and medieval Central Asia. The eastern frontier of the Islamic world – defined for this study as the area stretching from the eastern shores of the Caspian Sea to the Hindu Kush and from the highlands of the Iranian plateau to the River Jaxartes and beyond towards the Inner Asian steppe – is described as a place for fighting against the Turks.[4] The tenth-century geographers of the so-called Balkhī School are paradigmatic of this. Iṣṭakhrī (writing ca. 951) and Ibn Ḥawqal (d. 973) wrote that there is no region in Islam with a greater portion in jihad than Transoxiana because most of its borders touch the Dār al-Ḥarb or 'Abode of War'.[5] They added that the people of Transoxiana spent profusely on jihad and the defence of the frontier, comparing these expenses and the rewards that come to those of the Hajj. For Muqaddasī (ca. 945–1000) the entire region north of the River Oxus is the Dār al-Jihād or 'Abode of Jihad', a land dedicated to fighting.[6] These geographers placed the eastern frontier at the limits of the Islamic world, imagining it as a dividing line between the Abode of Islam on one side and the Abode of War on the other, but the governor of Samarqand Ḥasan al-Kindī in the opening anecdote understood that no such clear-cut line existed, at least not in the early eighth century, nor could the world be divided so easily into two conflicting realms. Instead, Ḥasan ruled over a complex frontier, a space where the Umayyad Caliphate was still fighting to consolidate its control against local populations and imperial rivals.

This book is a study of the evolution of the eastern frontier of the Iranian and Islamic world from the late antique through early medieval periods, during which empires centred in Iran and lands further west – from the Sasanians (r. 224–651) to the Abbasids (r. 750–1258) – widened the reach of their authority beyond the banks of the River Oxus. I explore the development of this region from a complex zone of overlapping and competing political, social and economic groups to a region that can be imagined by medieval geographers as a clearly delineated border between two well-defined areas. In doing so, the role of the frontier in the development of the medieval Islamic world will be examined. At the same time, by examining the dynamics along this distant frontier, a place far from the centres of imperial power in Iraq, we may develop a better understanding of the nature of late antique and early medieval empire. Due to its physical and human geography, the eastern frontier in the late antique and medieval periods could not be so easily incorporated into the empires that surrounded it. On the one hand, regions like Sogdiana and Ṭukhāristān would always maintain their own identity and a society that relied on movement across the frontier in all directions. On the other hand, the challenge of ruling the eastern frontier was always met by rivals who could neither be eliminated nor co-opted for long, and therefore any authority in the lands between the Murghāb and Jaxartes Rivers represented a precarious balance between competing imperial and local conditions.

In this book, I argue that the dynamics of the frontier, something akin to what Frederick Jackson Turner called the frontier process, was vital to all political decisions as empires advanced into Khurāsān, Ṭukhāristān and Transoxiana and as local populations responded. Such responses were not equal, opposite or reactionary. Instead they sought to meet and maintain an equilibrium; after all a frontier represents the balancing point between a state or other territorially defined entity and its neighbours or the physical limit of its power. Such an equilibrium allowed the frontier – as a meeting of both geopolitical entities such as empires and environmental realms such as the sedentary agrarian world of the river valleys and oases as opposed to the nomadic steppe – to find a certain balance. As we explore the history of the eastern frontier, what we see is that drastic changes on one side of the frontier create a domino effect that shifts this equilibrium dramatically from one direction to the next. For example, a balance developed between two empires who extracted wealth from the oasis cities of Sogdiana through raiding without establishing political superiority, as happened between the Umayyad Caliphate and the Türk Khāqānate in the late seventh century. But once one side pushed forward, established a more permanent occupation in the region and transformed their mode of wealth extraction from raiding to taxation, as the Umayyads did in the early eighth century, the balance of the local order became disrupted. As local lords resisted the changing political and economic dynamic and rivals defended their position more aggressively, conquerors had to remake society to meet the new order, not just rule over the existing one.

The narrative of these dynamics is often lost in our sources – especially those available for late antique and early medieval Central Asia. These sources, such as chronicles and works of descriptive geography, are written from the perspective of the imperial centre. This means that not only do they view the frontier primarily as an extension of the state, but also they view narratives of conquest and settlement as triumphalist, concerning the origins of the empire they are memorializing. Modern historians do much the same by projecting the ideologies, orders and infrastructures of empire out to its limits, expecting states to act coherently and cohesively throughout their borders. This book puts the dynamic of the frontier at the centre of the narrative.

Between the Oxus and the Jaxartes

H. A. R. Gibb opened his 1923 study *The Arab Conquests of Central Asia* with the observation that 'the Oxus is a boundary of tradition rather than of history'.[7] He noted that the famed River Oxus – Jayḥūn in Arabic and Amū Daryā in Persian – never acted as a barrier to imperial ambitions. Neither Alexander the Great (r. 356–23 BCE) nor the Arabs stopped at its banks, but pushed towards its northern twin, the River Jaxartes – Sayḥūn in Arabic and Syr Daryā in Persian – the ancient frontier of the Achaemenid Empire (r. 550–330 BCE) whose borders represent a persistent ambition for later empires of Iran. Nor was it to the Oxus that the Sasanians retreated when the Huns, Hephthalites and Turks descended on Sogdiana and Ṭukhāristān. Rather it was the River Murghāb, closer to the northern face of the Iranian plateau, where they built fortresses and reinforced cities such as Marw, Marw al-Rūd and Herat. Gibb was correct; in none of these cases did the Oxus represent a clear barrier or impediment to conquering armies or the movement of people in general, but, as Gibb suggested, it was certainly a border in the way that people not only imagined Central Asia but how they ruled it.[8] The Oxus played an important role in defining the regions on either side: Khurāsān sat across from Transoxiana or *Mā warā' al-nahr* in Arabic, literally 'that which lies across the river', and they were seen as distinct geographical realms 'even in periods when the two regions came under the sway of one supreme ruler'.[9] Even though both sides of the river shared a great deal of history and culture – Gibb highlighted the continued Iranian-ness of Sogdiana and its Transoxianan neighbours – there were differences that divided them.

Similarly, the Oxus was not the only geographic barrier that defined Central Asian history. Khurāsān and its neighbours, Ṭukhāristān and Transoxiana, were divided by mountains, deserts and rivers while passes, trade routes, pilgrimage sites and river crossings tied them together. Though none of these posed true impediments to imperial expansion, they did influence the way empires took shape. The frontier moulded the Arab–Muslim conquests of Khurāsān, Ṭukhāristān and Transoxiana, the integration of these regions together into the Islamic world and their eventual unification into a Greater Khurāsān most fully realized under the Sāmānid dynasty (r. 819–999). The focus of this book is the role of the frontier as a complex geographic space, in terms of both physical and human geography, in the shaping of Khurāsān and its neighbours to the north and east – the eastern frontier of the Sasanian Empire and the early Islamic caliphate. Throughout I argue that the complexity of the eastern frontier presented a specific set of challenges and opportunities to those who sought to build and expand empires that incorporated Khurāsān, Ṭukhāristān and Transoxiana and that, in the end, instead of any one empire fully subsuming these regions, the experience of the Arab–Muslim conquests and the diffusion of an Islamic imperial identity into the region did more to consolidate a shared local identity – though not one entirely of local provenance – than incorporate the eastern frontier into the larger empire of the caliphate.

This book began as a dissertation with an interest in the rise of the so-called independent eastern dynasties of the ninth and tenth centuries, most importantly the Ṭāhirids (r. 821–73) and Sāmānids. These dynasties ruled Khurāsān, Ṭukhāristān and Transoxiana as an autonomous state while acting nominally as servants of the Abbasid Caliphate. The story of these dynasties is most often told from the perspective of a declining Abbasid Empire with a diminished capacity to keep independence-minded governors in check. I found the simplistic centre–periphery dichotomy to be wanting and sought alternative approaches that could help me explore the rise of these dynasties and the related re-emergence of Persian as a language of literature and the court and the rebirth of a Persianate court culture inspired by the Sasanian shahanshahs. In doing so, I was drawn towards examining these developments through the lens of the frontier for several reasons and realized that the questions I asked could be addressed by concentrating on the frontier. Beyond the centre–periphery question that focused on the relationship between the eastern provinces, the dynasties that ruled them and the political centre in Iraq there were questions about the nature of the Abbasid Empire as a state, the theme of Persian 'nationalism', the intersection between local and imperial cultures and identities and the process of Islamization in Khurāsān, Ṭukhāristān and Transoxiana. Questions related to issues of integration, acculturation and identity are prominent in frontier and borderland studies.

Then there is the eastern frontier itself. Khurāsān, Ṭukhāristān and Transoxiana comprise a frontier that often attracted military interests as empires and states sought to defend themselves from incursions by steppe nomads and expand their territory. Centring the frontier allows us to focus on interactions among different and competing political and social groups to find patterns that may help us understand the political, economic and cultural processes that led to the rise of the Ṭāhirids and Sāmānids. But the origins of the eastern dynasties are no longer the primary objective of this book. Instead, this book is a history of the eastern frontier itself, one that examines Khurāsān, Ṭukhāristān and Transoxiana from the rise of the Sasanians in the third century through the collapse of the Sāmānids at the end of the tenth century.[10] This book seeks to better understand the path of Central Asian history in the late antique and the early medieval periods through its role as a zone of negotiation and competition – a frontier – and to better understand how the geographical context of the region shaped its history.

Given that Khurāsān and its neighbours, Ṭukhāristān and Transoxiana, were long-standing frontiers between not only different states and empires but also different cultural and social spheres and even environmental settings, this book grows from the position that the frontier had a deep impact on the way the region was organized and how its political actors viewed their connections to empires. Instead of this positioning becoming a cause for autonomy from empires, it dictated the manner actors would connect to them. The experience of integration into the early Islamic caliphate, in the end, was more important for the way it knitted Khurāsān and its neighbours together and redefined the frontier – on the one hand pushing it further into Inner Asia while also charging the frontier with new religiously constructed meaning. As the empire of the Abbasids weakened, this new identity also shaped a frontier between Khurāsān and its western neighbours that would become more pronounced as competition grew within the former Abbasid *oikumene*. The frontier was not an open gap or fissure between civilizations. It consisted of networks, political structures and modes of political engagement that persisted across centuries and challenged imperial ambitions in reflexive relationships with imperial structures and actors. Of course, the suggestion of local agency or importance should not strike any historian as novel. This book is an attempt to provide a history of the eastern frontier that details the role of local actors and political structures in conversation with imperial actors and structures.

Frontiers and the history of the Islamic world

Islamic history has previously been examined from the perspective of the frontier, an approach that puts the agency for state and cultural developments in the hands of actors living on the edges of the state or cultural sphere. A variety of scholars have applied such an approach to various aspects of Islamic history, some more directly than others.[11] Some scholars focused on frontiers to understand the larger Islamic world, such as Khalid Yahya Blankinship whose study of the fall of the Umayyad Dynasty, *The End of the Jihād State*, connected the end of the expansionist jihad led by the Umayyad caliphs to the collapse of the regime and the success of the Abbasid Revolution.[12] In Blankinship's analysis, the end of outwardly directed frontier warfare resulted in idle warriors redirecting their attention towards the proper organization and establishment of the centre. Linda Darling made a similar observation that the assassination of the Caliph ʿUthmān (r. 644–56) was the result of frontier interests, namely those of the army of Egypt, filtering back to the centre in Medina.[13] These examples straddle a line between studies of frontiers and studies of the Arab–Muslim conquests, as does this book. Patricia Crone, while not directly addressing frontiers, argued that major political upheavals in early Islamic history were primarily concerned with renegotiating and reorganizing the dynamics of the centre rather than overthrowing, avoiding or doing away with the centre.[14] For both Blankinship and Crone the greater narrative of early Islamic history was based primarily on negotiations that occurred on the frontiers of the Muslim world among the armies of the conquests. Even though we often consider frontiers the very peripheries of states, the experiences of the Arab–Muslim conquests of the seventh century rapidly created an empire that consisted largely of frontiers or at least of territory that had recently been conquered and whose relationship to the caliphate had to be negotiated at a time when territorial expansion was still moving forward at full force. Political centres such as Baṣra and Kūfa in Iraq were founded as garrison cities (*amṣār*) designed to house and coordinate the armies that would conquer Iran. Michael Bonner made the case for viewing the premodern Islamic world as a series of interconnected frontiers and emphasized the role of frontier warfare and jihad in the history of its political and social development.[15]

Taking a less direct political approach, Richard Bulliet made a convincing argument for the pre-eminent role of the frontiers in defining religious doctrine in *Islam: The View from the Edge*.[16] Bulliet argued that too much attention has been paid to the effect of political centres on the development of Muslim belief and that real power of change was located away from the centre among groups of believers brought together by local religious leaders. At its core, Bulliet's argument is similar to that of Frederick Jackson Turner's 'frontier thesis' of American history, which holds that the struggles between people of different backgrounds over economic resources and political power in a receding frontier zone explain the development of a unique American identity.[17] In Bulliet's work, the frontier was where groups of Arab–Muslims and non-Arab converts intermingled and competed and through this process of interaction a new and distinct Muslim identity developed. Bulliet looked east, but a similar dynamic can be seen among volunteer fighters of jihad along the Arab–Byzantine frontier of northern Syria and southeastern Anatolia. Bonner underscored the role played by such frontier fighters and the scholars who inspired (and fought alongside) them in the development of the scholarly and legalistic traditions of Sunni Islam and the strained relationship between the ulema or religious scholars and political authorities.[18] Deborah Tor similarly argued that it was the caliphs' inabilities to effectively lead jihad along the frontiers that allowed authority to transfer from the caliphs to the ulema and the leaders of bands of volunteer fighters of jihad (*mutaṭawwiʿa*).[19]

Other approaches have focused on telling the history of particular frontiers, what some have called *thughūrology* – from the Arabic term for frontier, see Chapter 1.[20] Bonner's work on the *ʿawāṣim*, the region immediately south of the Arab–Byzantine frontier, demonstrated how frontier regions matured and became integrated into imperial networks following conquest. Bonner argued that the *ʿawāṣim* – which modern historians considered a buffer zone between the frontier and the political centres of Syria and Iraq, an area of retreat and a final line of defence beyond the militarized frontier – was a zone of settlement, acting as a space where recently conquered territories were made part of the caliphate.[21] Asa Eger added archaeology to the legalistic perspective rooted in particular textual traditions favoured by Bonner, studying the evidence of settlement and fortification along the Arab–Byzantine frontier in light of the ideological and religious meanings imbued in the frontier by literary sources.[22] These studies of the Arab–Byzantine frontier describe a dynamic zone where not only is expansion possible but the integration of the territory into an imperial sphere was under constant negotiation and involved the intermingling of peoples.

The inhabitants of frontier regions, especially those who fought along the frontier, have also been a focus of study. Linda Darling's study of Ottoman origins, a field rife with examinations of ghazis or holy warriors leading raids across the frontiers of Islamdom, exposed the tension found in literature – particularly epic poems and religious catechisms – between the inhabitants of frontiers and representatives of the central Ottoman authorities.

> The epic celebrated individual heroism that took advantage of the boundarylessness of border society to make friends, converts, and marriages among the putative enemy, extolled the bonds of comradeship and the acquisition and generous disposal of personal wealth, and in general embodied the romantic and individualistic aspects of border warfare. The catechism, on the other hand, sought precisely to set controls on the fluidity of border society, to impose boundaries between warriors identified primarily as Muslims and their unbelieving opponents, and to interpose the state and its demands into the collection of wealth and the disposition of the spoils of campaign.[23]

Darling's case study of frontier warfare in the early Ottoman period demonstrated the tension between the realities of frontier society and the ideals imposed upon it by the constraints of a centralized state. By emphasizing the tensions at play here, she also brought to light the fantasy of a state that shares a homogenous identity from centre to periphery. Similar phenomena have been examined along the frontier between Muslim and Christian Spain where Muslim mercenaries fought their coreligionists under a Catholic banner and vice versa.[24]

The eastern frontier specifically has also been the focus of previous studies. Jürgen Paul examined local elites in eastern Iran and explored the reach of the state in Khurāsān and Transoxiana from the ninth into the thirteenth centuries and the role of intermediaries in negotiating political authority.[25] Paul argued for limited state involvement in local affairs and painted a picture of a region dominated by local lords.[26] Others have focused on the integration of Islamic elites into the local fabric and the development of a hybrid authority. In a recent dissertation, Mark Luce employed the eastern frontier to explore the process of Islamization, not only among the conquered populations but also among the Arabs who replaced tribal identities with urbanized Islamic identities during the Umayyad period.[27] He also argued that the resulting Islamic institutions came to replace the structures of the local kings of Sogdiana and Ṭukhāristān and that these regions were incorporated into the empire of the caliphate. This book complements the interests of Luce's dissertation. Whereas Luce's study is interested in how the arms of empire reached into the frontier and the corresponding institutionalization processes, this study hopes to examine the allure of the frontier from the other direction and the ways in which conqueror and conquered sought a balance that

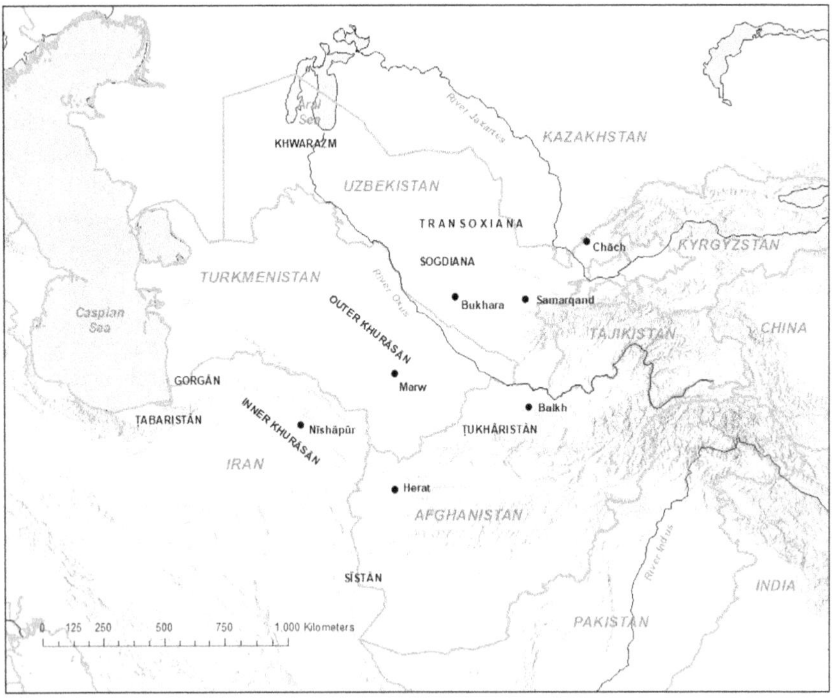

Map 1 The Eastern Frontier in Modern Context.

Sources: Esri, USGS, NGA, NASA, CGIAR, N Robinson, NCEAS, NLS, OS, NMA, Geodatastyrelsen, Rijkswaterstaat, GSA, Geoland, FEMA, Intermap and the GIS user community.

created a new society. The reach of the state has also been of interest to those studying warfare along the eastern frontier. Tor has written on the use of jihad as conducted by *ʿayyār* bands (errant holy warriors) to legitimize the rise of the Ṣaffārid dynasty in Sīstān (r. 861–1003) and their eventual expansion across the Iranian world.[28] In another study, Paul examined the role of volunteer fighters in the Sāmānid military in a similar vein and the difficulties inherent in maintaining the loyalties of their leaders.[29]

For the most part, these studies have focused on the relationship between centre and periphery and the tension between the local and the imperial. In contrast, this book emphasizes the centrality of the frontier region itself as its own actor and a place with its own history and traditions. While the military nature of the frontier is important – and due to the limitations of our sources much of the narrative is told from the perspectives of governors and generals – the focus on frontier warfare emphasizes the oppositional nature of the frontier – the confrontation of two groups who meet at a geopolitical divide. Throughout this book, the frontier is instead examined as a gradient that blends and transitions slowly from one side to the other and from one node of power and authority to another, forming its own unique identity along the way.

The geography of the eastern frontier

The geographic focus of this book is a region that was simultaneously the eastern fringe of the Islamic world and the Iranian world in the late antique and the early medieval periods. In simplest terms, the geographic focus of this book is on the grand province of Khurāsān and its neighbours to the north and east, Transoxiana and Ṭukhāristān, respectively. Under the early Islamic caliphate all three of these territories would often be administered together as a Greater Khurāsān, which could also include Sīstān (Sijistān). From antiquity through the early Islamic period, a broad frontier stretched out from the eastern coast of the Caspian Sea across Transoxiana to the high mountains called 'the roof of the world' of the Tiānshān, Pāmir and Hindu Kush between the Iranian world and the empires that dominated it and the nomadic steppe. This region was often contested between the two groups with the frontier zone falling under the control of nomads who conquered and settled in the region. The division of the Mashriq or 'The East' into distinct regions could be a point of debate and the boundaries between different regions were often contestable. For example, the geographer Muqaddasī defended his decision to use only two divisions, Khurāsān and Transoxiana, leaving Sīstān part of Khurāsān and not even suggesting the possibility of separating Ṭukhāristān in the organization of his geographical work, highlighting conflicting practices among his predecessors.[30] Modern historians have also been challenged by the geographic organization of eastern Iran. Richard Frye, for example, once suggested dividing the region into an Indo-Bactrian zone centred on Ṭukhāristān and a Saka-Bukharan zone that passed from Sogdiana through Khurāsān to Sīstān, each with its own cultural identity.[31] Simultaneously, each of these regions could be further subdivided into multiple zones with their own social, political, cultural and ethnolinguistic characteristics historically. Yet each region also had its own unifying and defining characteristics, as discussed below.

Khurāsān

The name Khurāsān derives from the Middle Persian Khwarāsān meaning 'land of the rising sun'. This name first appeared with the division of the Sasanian Empire into four military-administrative divisions under the Shahanshah Khusrow I Anūshīrwān (r. 531–79).[32] The boundaries of Khurāsān were not geographically fixed and could change with the shifting borders of the empire, growing and shrinking with each military success and failure, thereby leaving its extent open to debate. For consistency, I apply the term Khurāsān to those territories that had regularly fallen under Sasanian rule south of the River Oxus and west of the River Murghāb. Historically Khurāsān, as defined here, had three major urban centres – Marw in modern Turkmenistan which often served as the administrative centre of the province, Nīshāpūr in northeastern Iran which rivalled Marw as the political centre at times and Herat in northwestern Afghanistan – but there were many other smaller cities and districts in Khurāsān such as Marw al-Rūd which commanded the frontier between Khurāsān and Ṭukhāristān along the River Murghāb. The networks of urban centres and their dependent villages and agricultural lands acted as the primary unit for organizing and administering Khurāsān, but other geographical considerations further subdivided the province. Parvaneh Pourshariati suggested a division of Sasanian Khurāsān into an 'Inner' and 'Outer' Khurāsān separated by the Bālkhān, Küren Dāgh, Kopet Dāgh and Bīnālūd mountain ranges and the Khwarazm Desert which lies to the north and east of these ranges.[33] These mountains divided the main urban centres of Marw in 'Outer' Khurāsān – which approximates classical Margiana – from Nīshāpūr in 'Inner' Khurāsān – which approximates classical Parthia. The emphasis of this book is 'Outer' Khurāsān.

Transoxiana

The name of the region both in its more familiar Latin form, Transoxiana, and its Arabic form, *Mā warā' al-nahr*, – 'that which lies beyond the river' – is descriptive of its geography. Transoxiana is the region beyond the River Oxus. The northern and eastern limits of Transoxiana in the Islamic era 'were where the power of Islam ceased and depended on political conditions'.[34] Transoxiana did not have the same history united by empire as Sasanian Khurāsān and the divisions of the region were more pronounced. At the centre of Transoxiana was the area historically known as Sogdiana (Ṣughd in Arabic), the region between the Oxus and Jaxartes rivers along the River Zarāfshān. Dominated by the two great cities of Samarqand and Bukhara, Sogdiana was home to a unique Sogdian culture and people with their own Iranian language, best known for their role throughout late antiquity as traders along the trans-Asian network we today call the 'Silk Road'. Because of their mercantile role, Sogdian colonies were found throughout the region beyond this central core. To the east of Sogdiana laid the region of Usrūshana, in the foothills of the Hissar Mountains, home to an autonomous prince at the time of the Arab–Muslim conquests with the Sogdian title Afshīn. North of Usrūshana, in the Chirchik and Āhangarān Valleys of the western stretches of the Tiānshān Mountains called the Chatkal, were the heavily populated provinces of Chāch or Shāsh and Īlaq. Further east laid Ferghana, a 300-km valley surrounded on the north by the Tiānshān Mountains the east by the Pāmir Mountains and the south by the Alai and Hissar Mountains. Ferghana was the gateway for Sogdian traders to China via the Tarim Basin and was later home to a Sogdian princely line with the title Ikhshīd. To the northwest of Sogdiana, at the point where the River Oxus empties into the Aral Sea was Khwarazm, another region with its own unique Iranian language and history of independent rule. Khwarazm is separated from Khurāsān by the Qara-Qum Desert and from Sogdiana by the Kyzyl-Kum Desert, giving it a sense of isolation and thereby political independence. Khwarazm's place in either Transoxiana or Khurāsān can be debated because it spreads across both sides of the Oxus but, for our purposes, its history is more closely tied to the experiences of Transoxiana than Khurāsān and therefore belongs there.

Ṭukhāristān

Closely approximate to ancient Bactria, Ṭukhāristān can be difficult to define geographically. Some scholars limit its extent to the area between Balkh to the west and Badakhshan to the east, the River Oxus to the north and the Hindu Kush to the south.[35] A more inclusive definition will be employed in this book to recognize the historical connections between the lands east of the River Murghāb, including the mountainous territories of Gūzgān (Jūzjān in Arabic) and Gharshistān (also Gharjistān) and the plains of Ṭālaqān that often acted as the frontier zone between the Sasanian Empire and its eastern neighbours.[36] Ṭukhāristān was centred on the oasis of Balkh, the 'mother of cities' in the Arabic traditions, where many of the Sasanians' eastern rivals made their capital. Some territory north of the upper Oxus such as Chaghāniyān that was separated from Sogdiana by mountains was also connected to Ṭukhāristān. This leaves us with a territory between the Hindu Kush to the south and east and the Hissar Mountains to the north bounded by the River Murghāb and the Qara-Qum Desert to the west.

The name Ṭukhāristān has its origins in the name *Tócharoi*, the name given by the Greeks to the Yuèzhī a nomadic people who entered Bactria from the Tarim Basin in the second century BCE and formed the Kushan Empire in the first century CE. Its etymology is unrelated to the Tocharian language of the Tarim Basin and the *Tócharoi* spoke (or, at least, wrote in) an Iranian language we call Bactrian.[37] Despite its Greek etymology, it was Ṭukhāristān that found its way into Arabic rather than other names of the region such as Kushānshahr or Bactria. As the long history of migration between the Tarim Basin and Ṭukhāristān implies, Ṭukhāristān played an important and strategic role due to its access not only to the

Tarim Basin and thereby China, but also to the passes that crossed the Hindu Kush and connected Khurāsān and Transoxiana to Bāmiyān and Kabul and thereby India and Tibet. Therefore, Ṭukhāristān played a crucial role in linking India to China, making it the lynchpin of not only the 'Silk Road' trade between the two regions but also of the Buddhist pilgrimage routes that helped spread the religion to Central and East Asia. These broader connections can be noted in the role of Balkh as a commercial centre as well as pilgrimage centre for both Buddhists and Zoroastrians in the pre-Islamic period.

Even Greater Khurāsān: Sīstān, Gorgān and Ṭabaristān

Understanding that frontiers are never stable, we cannot bind ourselves to a strictly defined geographical limit at the outset of this book. Invaders – from all directions – did not follow administrative geographies after all. As we follow the development of the eastern frontier, we will also have to turn our attention to areas that neighboured Khurāsān, Ṭukhāristān and Transoxiana and shared an administrative unit with Greater Khurāsān at times but had a history distinct enough to not merit full attention here. Most importantly are Sīstān to the south of Khurāsān and Gorgān and Ṭabaristān to the west. Sīstān, also known as Sijistān, the Arabicized form of Sakāstān or the land of the Sakās or Scythians, was separated from Khurāsān to the north by the Qā'in–Birjand Mountains of Qūhistān, the mountainous region of southern Khurāsān. These mountains, along with the deserts of Kirmān, isolated Sīstān from the rest of Iran while the River Helmand connected Sīstān with the lands south of the Hindu Kush and northern India. These connections with northern India made Sīstān crucial to the economic and political history of the region. Geographically, Sīstān was a place of contrasts. On the one hand, Sīstān centred on great rivers such as the Helmand, which flowed from the Kuh-i Bābā Mountains near Kabul to the south and southwest over 1,000 km through Sīstān and Kirmān. In the Helmand and Arghandāb basin, around the city of Zaranj, rivers feeding from the Hindu Kush formed marshes and lakes including Lake Zarah which measured 160 km long and nearly 50 km wide in late antiquity. On the other hand, Sīstān was bounded by severe deserts, including the Dasht-i Mārgō or 'Desert of Death' between the Helmand and Khwāsh rivers with its summer winds that blew sand at 100 knots covering arable land and making settled life difficult. The frontier of Sīstān against the Zunbīl of Zābulistān and the Kābulshāhs was home to some of the most demanding frontier fighting in the early Islamic period.

At the opposite end of the eastern frontier, Gorgān (Jurjān in Arabic) consisted of the plains to the southeast of the Caspian Sea and roughly corresponded to classical Hyrcania. It was a regular target of invaders from the Inner Asian steppe and was guarded since the Sasanian period by the Great Wall of Gorgān which stretched 195 km from the Alburz Mountains to the Caspian. At times Gorgān was administered from Khurāsān. It held a strategic point on the northern route from Iraq to Marw and was conquered during the Umayyad period by an army from

Khurāsān. Further west was Ṭabaristān, a region consisting of the coastal plains and mountains along the southern shores of the Caspian Sea. The mountains provided protection and isolation for Ṭabaristān which resisted the Arab–Muslim conquests until the Abbasid era and was a regular source of resistance to imperial rule and challenges to the rulers of Khurāsān who, at different historical moments, attempted to claim Ṭabaristān and its revenues as part of their administrative duties. These are frontiers that will not receive a full study in their own right here, but will be reoccurring characters.

Between the steppe and the sown

Our discussion of the geography of the eastern frontier has thus far concentrated on the sedentary populations, focusing on urban centres, agricultural oases and river valleys, but this represents only one aspect of the geography of Khurāsān, Ṭukhāristān and Transoxiana. Throughout the deserts, steppes and even in the mountains – the areas we have used to define the limits of and barriers to each of these geographic zones that are not coincidentally the areas that are less conducive to sedentary agriculture – nomadic and semi-nomadic peoples inhabited the spaces in-between these urban centres and oases. The overlap and interaction between sedentary agrarians and nomadic pastoralists was one of the defining characteristics of Greater Khurāsān that marked it as a frontier zone. The important thing to note is that this was not a dichotomy between two distinct worlds and sedentary and nomadic populations lived together and overlapped with each other. As Nicola di Cosmo described our assumptions when it came to the northern frontier of imperial China, 'The assumption is still with us, reflected in modern notions that the northern frontier has always been characterized by a set of dual oppositions – between pastoral and settled people (steppe and sown), between nomadic and Chinese states, between an urban civilization and a warlike uncivilized society.'[38] To the contrary, these civilizations overlapped and intermingled in both northern China and along the eastern frontier of the Iranian and Islamic world. In many cases, as will be seen in later chapters, the nomadic populations also acted as a ruling class having conquered the region or parts of it and settled into urban populations themselves. We may even think of the armies of the early Arab–Muslim caliphate in such terms.

The deserts, steppes and mountains surrounded urban centres and divided them from each other. The deserts that straddled the Oxus separated the cities along the Murghāb and Zarāfshān rivers. The deserts of Ṭālaqān and the mountains of Gūzgān and Bādhghīs separated Marw al-Rūd and Herat from Balkh. Unlike the European or American frontier experience in which the agriculturalists removed and replaced more mobile neighbours, the Central Asian (as well as the Middle Eastern) experience maintained a frontier between 'dual economies undergoing regular tribal invasions'.[39] Jos Gommans's description of the frontier between nomads and the settled world in South Asia is appropriate to our discussion here for its illustration of such a blended environment.

> This ecological frontier never served as a fixed or closed borderline. Rather, both sides witnessed flourishing mixed economies of wandering pastoralists coexisting with settled peasants. Apart from the seasonal variation, the frontier could be shifted more permanently by the common efforts of peasants to bring wasteland under the plow, often with the help of artificial irrigation. But the roaming pastoralists of the steppes, deserts and jungles of Eurasia were far from being exclusively at the receiving end of the encounter. On the contrary, there was an almost constant eagerness to enjoy – either by plunder or investment – the riches of the settled world. This led to frequent inroads by pastoral nomads, often holding the peasantry to ransom or even replacing agrarian fields with pastures.[40]

Implicit in Gommans's description is an economic interdependence between nomadic and sedentary societies that required some level of interaction if not cooperation. This brings up questions regarding the nature of such interactions between the nomadic and sedentary populations.

The relationship between nomadic and sedentary populations living in close proximity to each other is almost always a relationship driven by economic concerns following a pattern that Gommans referred to as 'plunder or investment' but may also be defined as 'trade or raid'. According to this idea, based upon relative strengths, nomads may choose to raid their settled neighbours and take what they need when they feel they have the stronger position or choose to trade with them when they felt their neighbours had the upper hand.[41] At the two extremes, nomads may conquer cities and establish themselves as a ruling military class and settled empires may advance into the steppes and deserts and by the force of irrigation bring new lands under cultivation. As will become apparent in the chapters that follow, this is not a perfect means to describe the situation in Greater Khurāsān. On the fringes of the region, in Ṭukhāristān and Transoxiana, people who entered the region as nomads often established their own states ruling over the settled populations and settled and urbanized themselves while maintaining their unique identities.[42]

A brief note on organization and sources

This book covers a lot of ground both geographically and chronologically and therefore a few words regarding the organization of the book and the sources employed are in order. For the most part, this book is organized chronologically. Beginning with Chapter 2 in which we examine the 425-year history of the Sasanian frontier and ending with Chapter 7 that situates the independent dynasties of the ninth and tenth centuries in the context of the frontier, each chapter progresses chronologically from the third to the eleventh century. Certain themes pertinent to the condition of the frontier at a particular historical moment will be explored in each chapter. The one exception is Chapter 1. Chapter 1 begins the book with a study of the image of the eastern frontier in the Arabic and Persian geographical literature of the ninth and tenth centuries. These works are considered geographical because they take as their primary focus the description of the world of their time. This first chapter is focused on the different types of spaces that made up the eastern frontier and how medieval authors imagined the frontier as a place. By examining these geographic works we get a picture of a frontier region made up of distinct and varied discrete spaces connected through networks of itineraries to urban nodes that acted as the primary centres of political and economic life. These texts show us a complex frontier with width and depth – not a line of the map – in which the structures of empire were evolving. This chapter also introduces several current theories found in frontier studies that are then employed throughout the rest of the book.

Turning now to our sources, there are many challenges to studying the history of Khurāsān, Ṭukhāristān and Transoxiana in the late antique and early medieval periods, many of which will be discussed in later individual chapters. Across the book, we face a limited number of primary sources written in both the places and times we are studying. Outside of the relatively small caches of documents in Bactrian and Sogdian we have available, we must rely on chronicles and other literary histories that were written either far in geographic space from Khurāsān – most often in Iraq – or distant in time with the largest corpus appearing only in the ninth century and later. Sometimes these later texts include passages and echoes of older historical traditions but channelled through the editorial hand of a later compiler. As students of Sasanian and early Islamic history have become accustomed, we must read these texts across each other critically and with an awareness of the preconceptions that their authors brought to their writings. Sources written from the perspective of the imperial centre are prone to present the frontier as an open hole for the conquering or a place beyond the imperial order (and maybe even beyond the pale of civilization). This is a space where rebellion is natural and enemies hide behind every rocky defile. Any scholar knows to regard these depictions with scepticism. In many places, Chinese sources may supplement the Arabic and Persian texts that will form the core of our source base. The histories of western and eastern Asia have traditionally been separated, notable in the training of historians who may only learn the relevant languages for one of the two halves of the continent. As a result, I will rely heavily on the translations of Édouard Chavannes for engaging these Chinese sources.[43] To fill the gaps left by our textual sources, material culture, most importantly numismatics but also archaeology, will play an important role in providing a firm ground from which to compare and test the more literary accounts we find in our written sources. The dates and places found on coins, for example, often give us solid sounding points from which we can check the veracity of other sources.

Chapter 1

THE GATE OF IRON: CONCEPTUALIZING THE EASTERN FRONTIER IN MEDIEVAL GEOGRAPHIC LITERATURE

Rāsht at the end of Khurāsān

In his *Book of the Routes and Realms*, Ibn Khurradādhbih (d. 911) included a route he called the 'Chaghāniyān Road' (*ṭarīq al-Ṣaghāniyān*).[1] As his readers follow this route, they are directed from the city of Termez on the northern banks of the River Oxus to the northeast through the region of Chaghāniyān in the Surkhān Valley until they reach a town called Rāsht in the Qarātagīn Valley near the modern city of Gharm, Tajikistan.[2] The itinerary of the Chaghāniyān Road places Rāsht at an extreme distance from its closest neighbour, four day's travel from Wāshjird. But Ibn Khurradādhbih went even further in describing Rāsht's remoteness, telling his reader that it is the furthest point of Khurāsān in its direction (*aqṣā Khurāsān min dhālika al-wajh*). Ibn Khurradādhbih stepped away from his usual focus on itineraries and distances to give a description of the town itself. He wrote that it is situated between two mountains and that it was the point from which the Turks used to raid until Faḍl b. Yaḥyā b. Khālid b. Barmak (d. 808) closed the pass with a gate, presumably during his tenure as governor of Khurāsān (792–6).

Writing a couple decades later, the geographer Ibn al-Faqīh (d. after 902) included the same description of Rāsht in his *Book of the Lands*. He mentioned the Chaghāniyān Road without providing a full itinerary, just its beginning at Termez and its end sixty *farāsikh* (approximately 360 km) later in Rāsht. This is, again, the furthest point of Khurāsān in its direction, located between two mountains and the place from which the Turks used to raid until Faḍl b. Yaḥyā built a gate to close the pass.[3] Another Abbasid bureaucrat, Qudāma b. Jaʿfar al-Kātib (d. before 948), provided a similar description of Rāsht minus a few details in his *Book of the Land Tax and the Art of the Secretaries*.[4] At the end of an extended itinerary from Marw to Ṭukhāristān, Qudāma described Rāsht as being four-days travel from Wāshjird, between two mountains, the furthest point of Khurāsān in its direction and the place where the Turks enter Khurāsān to raid. In this version, no gate has been built to end the raiding of the Turks.[5] Variations on this description of Rāsht reappeared in geographical texts until at least the thirteenth century when Yāqūt (d. 1229) noted in his geographical dictionary, *Muʿjam al-buldān*, that Rāsht is 'a land in the furthest point of Khurāsān and its extreme limit (*ākhr ḥudūd Khurāsān*). Between

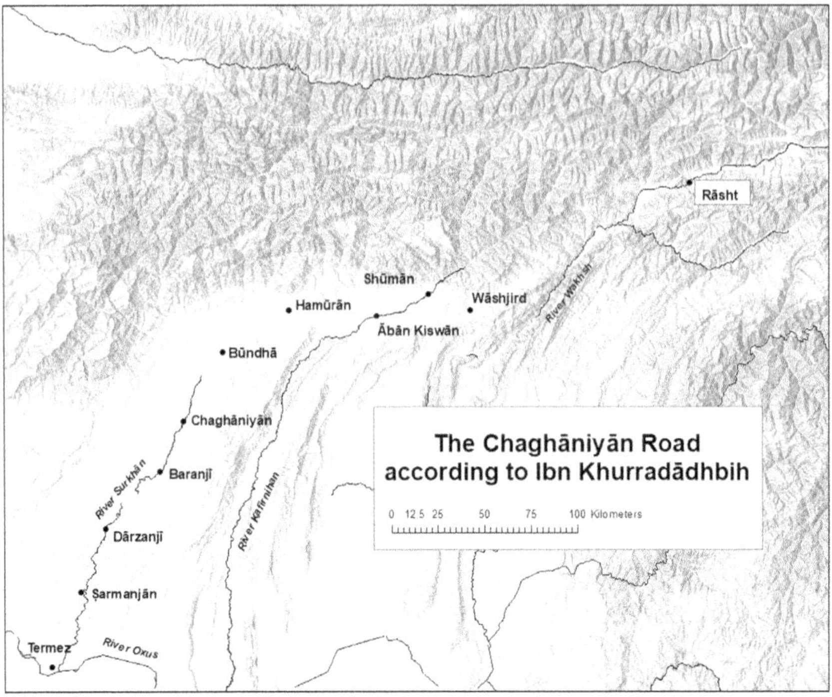

Map 2 The Chaghāniyān Road According to Ibn Khurradādhbih.

Sources: Esri, USGS, NGA, NASA, CGIAR, N Robinson, NCEAS, NLS, OS, NMA, Geodatastyrelsen, Rijkswaterstaat, GSA, Geoland, FEMA, Intermap and the GIS user community.

it and Termez are eighty *farāsikh* (480 km). It is between two mountains and it was from here that the Turks entered the land of Islam (*bilād al-Islām*) to raid them. Faḍl b. Yaḥyā b. Khālid b. Barmak built a strong gate here.'[6]

The descriptions of Rāsht articulated by Ibn Khurradādhbih, Ibn al-Faqīh, Qudāma and Yāqūt are an evocative image of a frontier. Rāsht is a remote outpost positioned between Khurāsān (and by extension the lands of Islam) and the lands of the Turks. It is a frontier in the sense that it sits in a space of transition between the two realms. Most importantly, these descriptions present the narrative of a frontier that a centralizing empire would want to promote. Rāsht was a land of danger, the place from which the Turks entered Khurāsān to raid. But, by building a gate, Faḍl b. Yaḥyā and the Abbasids literally closed the frontier from the Turks and made Khurāsān safe.[7] To what extent does this image represent the reality of Khurāsān's eastern limits in the ninth or tenth centuries, when most of these texts were composed? What does this description tell us about the way these authors and their contemporaries thought about the frontiers of the Islamic world? By extension, what does this indicate to us about the way they imagined the shape and condition of the Islamic world?

This chapter focuses on the conceptual image of the eastern frontier of the early medieval Islamic world in the works of geographers writing in Arabic and Persian during the ninth and tenth centuries. For our purposes, the Islamic world can be understood as synonymous with the Abbasid Caliphate and its successor states such as that of the Sāmānids, the rulers of Khurāsān and Transoxiana during the time most of the geographic sources under study in this chapter were written. This discussion will give us an opportunity to observe how these geographers understood and communicated the presence of a frontier at the edge of Khurāsān and Transoxiana to their readers and how this frontier factored into their image of the broader Islamic world. By concentrating on geographic literature, we may limit our focus to just those sources for whom 'place' is the primary unit of study. Later chapters will address the history and development of the eastern frontier, so here I provide a framework for understanding how contemporary authors viewed the eastern frontier.

Ḥadd *and* Thaghr: *Borders and frontiers in late-antique and early-medieval Central Asia*

As noted, Rāsht is described with a particular terminology. It is called the furthest point of Khurāsān in its direction (*aqṣā Khurāsān min dhālika al-wajh*), identifying its location in comparison to the larger body of Khurāsān and, by extension, the rest of the Islamic world. Only Yāqūt used a more technical geographic term. Besides describing Rāsht as the furthest point of Khurāsān, he also wrote that it is the extreme limit (*ākhr ḥudūd*) of Khurāsān. Yāqūt's term *ḥudūd* can also be translated as border. The choice of *ḥudūd* (sing. *ḥadd*) is notable. *Ḥadd* is most often translated in a geographical context as border, boundary or limit. In more general usage, including the realm of theology, *ḥadd* denotes a limit or finiteness, which by extension means 'definition' in that the limits of a thing define that thing.[8] This definition of *ḥadd* is reminiscent of our modern understanding of border, a dividing line between political and cultural groups. In the sense that a *ḥadd* is a limit, it also represents a border defined by the extent within which a state can effectively wield power. In contexts where a diplomatically negotiated and universally recognized boundary is lacking, borders are defined by the actual power that states can wield over their own societies. A border represents the extent to which a state can, forcibly or not, convince populations that they belong to and should participate in (or, at least, pay taxes to) them as opposed to their neighbour.[9] The border is the physical representation of that limit of power. In the case of Rāsht, the power of the state to exert power up to the border manifests in Faḍl b. Yaḥyā's gate, which is said to have brought an end to Turkish raids into Khurāsān.

In the early medieval geographic literature, an example of the use of *ḥadd* as a geographical limit that defines the whole is found in the anonymous tenth-century Persian geographical text *Ḥudūd al-ʿālam* (translated by Vladimir Minorsky as *The Regions of the World* but more literally *The Limits of the World*).[10] The author of *Ḥudūd al-ʿālam* organized the world into 51 *nāḥiyāt* or regions and, for each of these regions, he begins with a description of its *ḥudūd*, outlining the region and defining it by describing its limits. Other geographers in the so-called Balkhī School of geographers, notably Iṣṭakhrī and Ibn Ḥawqal, likewise began each chapter with a list of 'borders', but in these cases they were describing a map and outlining the edges of a cartographic representation instead of a distinct geographic region.[11]

The Arabic term *ḥadd* should be paired with *thughūr* (sing. *thaghr*), usually translated as frontier. Whereas *ḥadd* has a basic meaning of 'limit', *thughūr* has a basic meaning of 'gaps', 'breaches' or 'openings', but it can also mean 'mouth' or 'teeth', and typically applies to 'points of entry between the Dār al-Islām and the Dār al-Ḥarb beyond it'.[12] As Asa Eger has argued, in the context of frontiers, one can think of *thughūr* as the gaps between the teeth where armies, nomads, merchants or pilgrims could find their way through river gorges, mountain passes and breaches in defences to travel across borders.[13] More specifically, *al-thughūr*, as a definitive or specified noun (i.e. '*the* frontier'), points to one of two major frontier regions of premodern history, the Arab–Byzantine frontier in southeastern Anatolia and the shifting marches between Arab and Christian kingdoms of the Iberian Peninsula. However, Arab and Persian geographers used the term more widely to discuss any point on the fringes of the Dār al-Islām or 'Abode of Islam' from the Mediterranean coast of North Africa to the eastern frontier of Central Asia where invasions from the outside may take place.[14] As gaps or openings, *thughūr* are focused on potential entry points for foreign threats as well as potential exit points for aggressive military action.

Although *ḥadd* and *thughūr* tend to be translated as border and frontier respectively, there is not a one-to-one relationship between the modern meanings of borders and frontiers and the medieval meaning of *ḥudūd* and *thughūr*. The conceptual difference between the meaning of frontier and *thughūr* is important for us to consider. 'Frontier' implies expansion into 'open' or 'empty' territory or, at least, territory that is considered 'open' or 'empty'. This is best illustrated by those frontiers that stand out most clearly in the mind of a modern reader. For example, the American West was imagined as a whole continent that stretched out inviting territorial expansion by a state that pursued a manifest destiny to master the land; or Space, 'the final frontier', is where a whole universe opens to humankind's exploration and exploitation. These are places that call to be conquered. As Walter Prescott Webb described the American West, 'The American thinks of the frontier as lying *within*, and not at the edge of a country. It is not a line to stop at, but an *area* inviting entrance.'[15] Of course, this idea of an 'empty' frontier is almost always fiction. As the anthropologist Igor Kopytoff described frontiers in Africa, 'The definition of the frontier as "empty" is political and made from the intruders' perspective.'[16] We can turn to Frederick Jackson Turner's treatment of indigenous populations in his classic studies of the American frontier for an example of the creation and perpetuation of such a fiction.[17] On the other hand, *thughūr* implies the danger of outside intrusion through the 'openings' or 'gaps', meaning there is someone occupying the opposite side who desires your territory and/or property or whose territory and/or property you desire. Yet both imply the potential for dynamic territorial changes, unlike border and *ḥadd* which have a more static resonance. Ralph Brauer highlighted a similar pattern in which *thughūr* was used almost exclusively for frontiers between Muslims and non-Muslims or between the Dār al-Islām and the Dār al-Ḥarb ('Abode of War') while *ḥadd* was used primarily for internal divisions.[18] He argued that this external frontier is the only territorial division that truly mattered. In contrast to Brauer's argument, Yāqūt describes Rāsht as the *ḥudūd* of Khurāsān despite it being the extreme limit towards the Turks.

With this in mind, what is to be made of Yāqūt's choice of the word *ḥudūd* when describing Rāsht's relationship to Khurāsān? Although Ibn Khurradādhbih, Ibn al-Faqīh and Qudāma all refrained from calling Rāsht a *ḥadd*, they did refer to it as the furthest point of Khurāsān (*aqṣā Khurāsān*), invoking the same concept of limits. All of these geographers were suggesting that Rāsht was the end of Muslim political authority in Khurāsān. But with their narratives of Faḍl b. Yaḥyā and his gate, they were also saying that this was not always the case. Rāsht, sitting at the gap between two mountains, was a *thughūr* through which the Turks could raid but the actions of Faḍl sealed the gap and changed the opening to a limit, from a *thughūr* to a *ḥadd*. How do other geographical writers treat Rāsht and the border that runs through it?

Rāsht as frontier zone

In contrast to the descriptions of Faḍl b. Yaḥyā's gate at the extreme limit of Khurāsān, descriptions of Rāsht by Yaʿqūbī (d. after 905), Ibn Rusta (wrote before 912), Iṣṭakhrī and Ibn Ḥawqal marked it as one of several locations along the frontier of Khurāsān and Transoxiana and made no mention of Faḍl's (or any) gate. In his *Book of the Lands*, Yaʿqūbī (who had served as a secretary to the Ṭāhirids in Khurāsān) included Rāsht not as part of an itinerary but in a list of cities east of Balkh. He wrote, 'A city which is called Munk, it is the border (*ḥadd*) to the Land of the Turks (*bilād al-Turk*) until the place they call Rāsht and Kumād and Pāmir.'[19] In this version, Rāsht does not stand alone as the furthest point of Khurāsān but is one of many settlements sharing a border with the lands of the Turks. Nor is it described as housing a gate which prevents the Turks from raiding. Iṣṭakhrī and Ibn Ḥawqal, who had both travelled in the east while researching their geographies, made a similar connection between Rāsht and Pāmir, but used them to mark the edges of Transoxiana instead of Khurāsān writing, 'As for Mā warā' al-nahr (Transoxiana), it is surrounded from the east by Pāmir and al-Rāsht and what borders (*yutākhimu*) al-Khuttal from the land of Hind along a straight line.'[20] Iṣṭakhrī and Ibn Ḥawqal's association of Rāsht with Transoxiana is not entirely surprising. Rāsht is in the northern reaches of Ṭukhāristān, which crosses the upper Oxus near its source, the traditional border of Transoxiana.[21]

The early-tenth-century geographer and traveller Ibn Rusta presented a similar description of Rāsht in his *Book of the Precious Gems*, connecting it with Kumād and Pāmir in a manner that more clearly shows the relationships between these regions and the frontier. While describing the rivers that feed into the Oxus, Ibn Rusta listed the places along the River Wakhsh (Wakhshāb). Also known as the Surkhāb or Kyzyl-Suu, the Wakhsh joins the River Panj to form the Oxus at the modern border of Tajikistan and Afghanistan just north of Qundūz. Ibn Rusta's list begins in the land (*bilād*) of the Qārlūq Turks (*kharlukhiyya*) before arriving in the land of Pāmir, then the land of Rāsht and the land of Kumād. The river then passes between Wāshjird and Khuttal as it heads towards the River Panj.[22] If we are to follow the River Wakhsh as it passes Rāsht, we might better understand Rāsht as being in a frontier zone or borderland with great depth. Rāsht would be approximately 100 km down the river from the mountains of Pāmir, the Alai Mountain Range on the modern border between Kyrgyzstan and Tajikistan rather than the Pāmir Mountains, meaning that Rāsht would be over 100 km and beyond the mountains from the lands of the Qārlūq Turks.[23] Is it Rāsht that is the frontier with the Turks or is it the entirety of the valley from Pāmir to Chaghāniyān down to the River Oxus 350 km further south? In none of these accounts is Rāsht the singular end of Khurāsān or the symbol of the Abbasids' victory over the frontier. Instead, these accounts presented Rāsht as part of a network of towns that mark the transition from Khurāsān and the lands of Islam to the lands of the Turks. Presumably, there would be a gradation of authority along the valley, with the Turkish presence more pronounced near Pāmir and lesser near Kumād and almost non-existent by the time one reaches Termez, the primary crossing point of the Oxus. A gate at Rāsht may be practical in sealing a defile or narrowing of the valley, but it would neither be the limits of Khurāsān nor an effective defence for all of Khurāsān, only limiting raiding into Ṭukhāristān along this single valley.

This second set of descriptions of Rāsht portrayed an eastern frontier that is geographically broader and deeper, a frontier zone or borderland not easy to control through a single barrier. Frontiers are not linear but have depth. The British geographer Charles Bungay Fawcett, who declared 'all objective frontiers have width', employed the natural metaphor,

> The frontier between sea and land, which is so often spoken and thought of as the coast-line, is really a zone of variable, and constantly varying, width. All round our shores the strip between the high- and low-tide marks, the foreshore, is neither sea nor dry land, but alternatively sea and land. … So that our familiar term coast is, on analysis, found to denote not a line, but a broad zone between land and sea. Such a zone, in which the influences from the two sides mingle so as to lessen the abruptness of the transition between the strongly contrasted regions which it separates, is a true frontier; and such a mingling is the most characteristic feature of a frontier.[24]

Thinking in terms of human geography, the German geographer Friedrich Ratzel proposed at the turn of the twentieth century that national borders were arbitrary when it came to the identification of the people on either side of the border. He proposed instead to think of a borderland (*Grenzraum*) with three distinct parts, two of which were peripheries of the two states that meet at the border while the third is a zone that crosses the political border where elements of both sides have mingled. With this understanding, Ratzel described the border (*Grenzlinie*) as an abstraction of a complex and intermingled borderland.[25] Borders or frontiers as linear phenomenon are largely political constructions. Because the process of defining a border is largely a political negotiation, the intermingling of cultural elements from both sides of the border does not receive pre-eminent consideration. Therefore, the line drawn on a map or described in a geographical text is an abstraction of a complex zone of exchange across the border, the frontier zone or borderland, leaving a mixed population who may have more in common with similar populations living on the other side of the border than with their fellow countrymen. The defining characteristic of a borderland, then, is that it is a zone defined by a border which runs through it. There are shared traits within the borderland found on both sides of the political border, which make the borderland culturally distinct from the political centres lying on either side. Borderlands 'have their own social dynamics and historical developments' which differ from the more centrally located regions of the states found on either side.[26]

Recently Peter Perdue offered a model for frontier zones to discuss conflict and exchange across the Chinese–Mongol frontier that also addresses the questions of core and periphery. Perdue divided the Chinese and Mongol worlds into cores, one of the steppe and one of the sedentary agricultural zone, that never directly interact. These were spaces where a nomad never saw an agricultural peasant and vice versa. The 2,000-km zone where the steppe and agricultural settlements meet along the Chinese frontier became a zone of contact where interaction between pastoralist nomads and sedentary agrarians created their own hybrid frontier culture.[27] In this zone a peasant may take up a horse and become a nomad while a nomad may find some land and settle down. Although the Chinese state was involved in providing for the settlement of the frontier, these exchanges did not happen only at the Chinese border or because of state actions.

The Gate of Iron and the Khurāsānī shatterzone

Yaʿqūbī's description of Rāsht comes at the end of a list of cities located to the east of Balkh, which is immediately followed by a list of cities found to the north of Balkh, the first of which has the Persian name Dar-i Āhanīn. This, Yaʿqūbī tells us, means *bāb al-ḥadīd* in Arabic or the Gate of Iron.[28] Upon reading this name, we may conjure an image like Rāsht and its gate, assuming that a gate of iron means some kind of boundary or barrier and, in a geographic context, a border. In their respective works, *Book of the Routes and Realms* and *Image of the World*, Iṣṭakhrī and Ibn Ḥawqal also mentioned a Bāb al-Ḥadīd, specifying that it is along the road from Bukhara to Balkh.[29] In contrast to Yaʿqūbī's description, neither Iṣṭakhrī nor Ibn Ḥawqal included the Persian name. Likewise, Muqaddasī listed a Bāb al-Ḥadīd along the road from Samarqand to Termez in his *Best Divisions for Knowledge of the Regions*.[30] Unlike the case of Rāsht, the ninth- and tenth-century geographers did not give us any details about this Gate of Iron. Fortunately, it is a

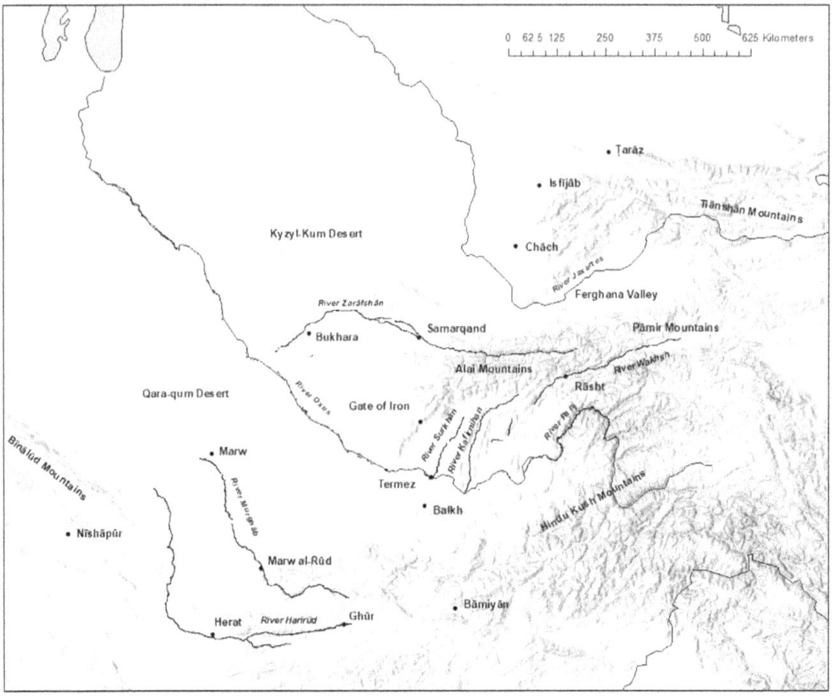

Map 3 The Topography of the Eastern Frontier.

Sources: Esri, USGS, NGA, NASA, CGIAR, N Robinson, NCEAS, NLS, OS, NMA, Geodatastyrelsen, Rijkswaterstaat, GSA, Geoland, FEMA, Intermap and the GIS user community.

well-known place, located in the Buzghāla Pass through the Baisun–Tau Mountain Range between Samarqand and Termez near the modern village of Derbent in southern Uzbekistan.[31]

The Gate of Iron has appeared in literary sources since antiquity and some have identified it with either the Rock of Arimazes or the Rock of Sogdiana, which Alexander the Great successfully captured with the help of his 'alpinists' and from where he kidnapped the Bactrian princess and his future wife Roxana.[32] The seventh-century Buddhist monk Xuanzang (ca. 602–64), who travelled from China to India and back again searching for sacred texts, described the gate in his well-known travelogue, giving much greater detail than our Arabic and Persian sources.

> The pass so called is bordered on the right and left by mountains. These mountains are of prodigious height. The road is narrow, which adds to the difficulty and danger. On both sides there is a rocky wall of an iron colour. Here there are set up double wooden doors, strengthened with iron and furnished with many bells hung up. Because of the protection afforded to the pass by these doors, when closed, the name of *iron gates* is given.[33]

The Gate of Iron also features in the eighth-century Orkhon inscriptions commissioned by Bilgä Khāqān (r. 716–34) of the Türk Khāqānate (r. 552–659) that detail the conquests of the founder of the Türk Empire, Bumïn (d. 552). These inscriptions describe his conquests as reaching the four corners of the world from his homeland in Mongolia, stating that 'to the West I [Bumïn] have made campaigns beyond Yenchü-ügüz ['The Pearl River'] as far as Tämir-kapig ['The Iron Gate'].'[34] It is likely that subduing the Gate of Iron remained an ambition of Bilgä in the eighth century and that is why it was specifically included among Bumïn's conquests. Later, the Gate of Iron appears in the travels of Qiū Chŭjī (1148–1227), the Chinese Daoist monk who had been called to Chinggis Khan's (r. 1206–27) court while the Mongol conqueror was campaigning in the Hindu Kush Mountains.[35] The fifteenth-century Spanish ambassador to the court of Tīmūr (r. 1370–1405), Ruy González de Clavijo (d. 1412), also reported passing through the Gate of Iron, which he describes as the 'Guard House of the Imperial city of Samarqand' where considerable revenue is collected through tolls on merchants travelling to and from India.[36] Clavijo made a special note that there were no physical gates when he travelled through the area, but was assured they had existed in the past. The Gate of Iron appears in several Timurid and early Mughal sources from the fifteenth and sixteenth centuries including Sharaf al-Dīn Yazdī's (d. 1454) *Ẓafarnāma*, the *Bāburnāma* of Ẓahīr al-Dīn Bābur (r. 1483–1530) and Mīrzā Ḥaydar Dūghlāt's (d. 1551) *Ta'rīkh-i Rashīdī*.[37]

The archaeological evidence indicates a history of physical fortifications in the area, including a wall with fortifications and a gate dating back to the fourth century BCE, a second period of construction and occupation during the reign of the Kushan Empire and a third in response to the advancement of the Türk Khāqānate into the region during the sixth century. But none of the Arabic sources indicate that there was an actual gate at the Gate of Iron.[38] Even in chronicles, where the Gate of Iron primarily appears as a landmark during campaigns into Transoxiana, such as those led by the Umayyad governors of Khurāsān Qutayba b. Muslim (r. 705–15) in 710 and Naṣr b. Sayyār (r. 738–48) in 739, we find no indication of whether there was an actual gate.[39] More often than not, chroniclers did not mention it even when it seems logical that a campaigning army travelled through the gate, as when they marched from Termez to Samarqand. Only Xuanzang gave a firm description of the area including a physical gate followed by Clavijo, who was told a gate had existed in the past but was no longer there in his time.

The idea of a Gate of Iron is not limited to this one location in the geographical sources of the ninth and tenth centuries – the most famous being that on the western shores of the Caspian Sea in the Caucasus. It is not even the only Gate of Iron in Transoxiana. Along the road from Chāch to Isfījāb (Sāyrām), Ibn Khurradādhbih listed a Bāb al-Ḥadīd two miles from the silver mines at Īlāq and Balānkank, themselves seven *farāsikh* (42 km) from Chāch.[40] Ibn al-Faqīh described the same Bāb al-Ḥadīd two miles from the silver mines which are then seven *farāsikh* from Chāch, but he claimed the mines are called Fanjahīr.[41] Ibn Ḥawqal named a Bāb al-Ḥadīd as one of the borders (*ḥadd*) of Chāch and Īlāq, between Chāch and Isfījāb. This Bāb al-Ḥadīd is in the steppe and beyond a mountainous region known as Qalās.[42] When comparing the descriptions of these various Gates of Iron, it is important to note that none of them were on the frontier. All of these gates represented barriers within Transoxiana. The most discussed Gate of Iron, on the march through the Baisun–Tau Mountain Range between Termez and Samarqand, was a barrier between Ṭukhāristān and Sogdiana, both under Muslim rule in the ninth and tenth centuries. Even though these gates are internal boundaries, they are still important in developing our understanding of the eastern frontier. We may question the presence of an actual physical gate regarding the various Gates of Iron or even Faḍl b. Yaḥya's gate at Rāsht and we may ask whether the name is figurative or literal. But all of these gates appear in tight mountain passes. These passes and the gates that defend them in our sources highlight the Khurāsānī shatterzone.

The term shatterzone or shatterbelt has been used by geographers in one of two ways, both of which can apply to the area of Khurāsān and Transoxiana. The first is geological. A shatterzone is 'a region of difficult terrain and mountain ranges created by a collision of tectonic plates'.[43] The difficult terrain creates barriers between people and allows for the creation of a variety of ethnic, linguistic, social and ideological differences within a small space. The second usage is geopolitical and anthropological. In this case, the shatterzone refers to regions that are locally divided but are caught in the middle of conflicts between two or more larger powers. As the theory of the geopolitical shatterzone developed in the twentieth century, the most important case study was the Baltic region and the larger East–Central Europe shatterzone which was caught between and fought over by Germany and Russia.[44] In the nineteenth century, these conflicts were expanded to include competitions further south towards the Balkans between the Hapsburg and Ottoman Empires as well.[45] According to political geographers, shatterzones 'consist of states that are fragmented – both internally and between one another – in terms of political ideology, ethnic make-up or religion'.[46] From the perspective of political geographers for most of the twentieth century, it was conflict and the intrusion of larger powers into these conflicts that were the dominant and most important features of the shatterzone.

More recent scholarship has emphasized the geographically and culturally divided nature of shatterzones. Divisions create a greater opportunity for conflicts to develop and attract the attention and intervention of neighbouring powers. In other words, shatterzones are not divided because of conflict, but because they are divided – politically, culturally and/or linguistically – there are more opportunities for conflicts to emerge among competing groups and as more local conflicts emerge it becomes more likely that larger neighbouring powers will be drawn into a conflict.[47] As described by Alfred Rieber in his recent study of the role borderlands played in the decline of Eurasian empires up to the First World War, such processes are exponentially more complicated away from Western Europe – where divisions tended to fall singularly along ethnolinguistic lines – as

> migration, deportation, flight, and colonization … scattered a great variety of culture groups drawn from Germanic, Slavic, Turkic, Mongol, and Chinese

> ethnolinguistic groups, and Christian (Roman Catholic, Orthodox, and Protestant), Judaic, Muslim, and Buddhist believers over vast distances. The result was, in metaphoric terms, a demographic kaleidoscopic of unparalleled variety and complexity rather than a mosaic.[48]

While Rieber was describing empires of the sixteenth through twentieth centuries, his focus is explicitly on 'conquest empires' with moving military frontiers that integrated a variety of subjugated people by force. As addressed in later chapters, the empires that conquered and sprang from late antique and medieval Central Asia encapsulated similar degrees of human diversity and social complexity. Combining these concepts, the geological shatterzone divides people physically and creates barriers between people which allows for internal fragmentation and difference which then sets the groundwork for the geopolitical shatterzone that divides people politically and culturally. Again, quoting Rieber, 'Frontier wars occurred in a geocultural space long characterized by large-scale population movements within varied landscapes, producing shatter zones of highly diverse ethnolinguistic, religious, and socioeconomic groups, kaleidoscopic in their internal rhythms of change.'[49]

From the geological perspective, Khurāsān lies at the middle of a larger Shatterzone known as the Makrān–Pāmir Shatterzone, which runs 'from the Makran Coast on the Arabian Sea to the Pamir Knot and the Karakorum Range in Central Asia'.[50] The Alburz and Hindu Kush Mountain Ranges further divide Khurāsān between the north and south and separate neighbouring regions. The mountain ranges and rivers that dominate the Makrān–Pāmir shatterzone have divided Khurāsān and Transoxiana into multiple zones with their own social, political, cultural and ethnolinguistic characteristics historically. As detailed in the introduction, the shatterzone can account for at least four major zones – Khurāsān, Ṭukhāristān, Transoxiana and Sīstān – each of which can be further subdivided into smaller units such as Quhistān, the mountainous frontier between Khurāsān and Sīstān.

While the geological aspects of the Khurāsānī shatterzone are clear enough to identify by looking at a topographic map, the geopolitical aspects should be examined more closely. The traditional image of Central Asia more generally has been that of a 'crossroads of civilization' where China, India, Iran and the confederacies and empires of the steppes were all drawn together. B. A. Litvinsky and Zhang Guang-da described this imagined arrangement as 'all the great civilizations standing at the crossroads of Central Asia'.[51] At different points in history, each of these powers attempted to assert some form of control or influence over the region. Modern historical imagination of Central Asia tends to lean more towards the picture of 'Silk Road' trade where these civilizations met, interacted and exchanged goods and ideas, but conflict and conquest was as much a part of the construction of Central Asia's 'crossroads civilizations', to borrow a phrase from S. Frederick Starr, as was trade.[52] On the eve of the Arab–Muslim conquests, the region was divided politically between the Sasanian Empire of Iran and the Türk Khāqānate with pockets of Hephthalite authority in Ṭukhāristān and autonomous Sogdian city states in Transoxiana both under nominal Turkish authority. In the mountains and isolated valleys, remoteness allowed even smaller groups to maintain independence. Political and economic rivalries kept the borders dynamic for much of the late Sasanian period, a topic explored in the following chapter.

With this image in mind, we might think of the description of Rāsht that opened this chapter and wonder about its position within the Khurāsānī shatterzone. Even though the medieval geographers wanted to call Rāsht the limit of Khurāsān in its direction, it is perhaps more accurate to call it the limit of northern Ṭukhāristān. Even then, it would be the limit only in one direction, along the Qarātagīn Valley, perhaps protecting Chaghāniyān from invasions from the Pāmirs and beyond but having relatively little influence on the movements of people directly into Sogdiana from the other side of the mountains. Limiting is the proper term here too, as a gate does not necessarily stop movement across a border. Rather, a gate is a sieve not a barrier that controls movement, hopefully stopping invaders while allowing traders through; the Gate of Iron transformed from defensive structure to toll booth depending on historical context. Regardless, Rāsht represents a small sliver of the frontier, separated from the rest by mountains while connected to the regions along the River Wakhsh.

Nūshajān at the frontier of ambition

Our geographic sources so far reflect an interest in identifying borders, but what did the authors know about the political realities of the frontier they are describing? According to Ibn Khurradādhbih, Upper Nūshajān (*Nūshajān al-aʿlā*) is the border (*ḥadd*) of China.[53] It is not clear from this statement if Nūshajān is a border between China and somewhere else or just the limit of China's authority. Likewise, it is not clear who actually had claims to Nūshajān – Tang China (r. 618–907), the Abbasid Caliphate, the Turks or someone else. All we know from this statement is that China ends somewhere near Upper Nūshajān. Ibn Khurradādhbih gave several itineraries leading up to Nūshajān and at no point did he recognize or acknowledge that a border or frontier had been crossed, making one presume that he placed Nūshajān within the realm of Muslim authority in Transoxiana. But all of these itineraries did involve crossing several 'borders' at the same time without any direct recognition from Ibn Khurradādhbih.

The first itinerary starts from Ṭarāz (Ṭalās), the site of the famous battle between the Abbasid and Tang Empires in 751 (see Chapter 6). This is the continuation of an itinerary that connected Ṭarāz to Isfījāb, Chāch and Samarqand, during which no border is explicitly crossed. The second stage on this itinerary from Ṭarāz to Upper Nūshajān, following Lower Nūshajān (*Nūshajān al-suflī*), is Kaṣrī Bās, which is described as the winter camp of the Qārlūq Turks with the winter camp of the Khalaj Turks (*al-khalajiyya*) nearby. Two stages into an itinerary meant to take us to the border, Ibn Khurradādhbih already has his reader travelling through territory which is, for at least part of the year, the pasturage of the Turks and therefore loosely tied, at best, to either Muslim or Chinese authority. Ten stages later is the city of the Khāqān of the Türgesh Turks (*madīna khāqān al-turkishī*), a city under the authority of a Turkish ruler, again without crossing an explicit border. Three more stages follow until we reach Upper Nūshajān, with the final stage lasting fifteen days if you travel as the caravan does through pasturage (*li-l'qawāfil fī al-mar'ā*) but only three if you follow the itinerary of the Turks (*li-barīd al-turk*).[54] Without ever indicating a transition away from the lands of Islam, the Abode of Islam or the territory of any Muslim political authority, Ibn Khurradādhbih took his reader through the lands of multiple Turkish peoples (Qārlūq, Khalaj and Türgesh) to reach the border of China. Another itinerary travels through Ferghana and passes through Ūzkand, the city of Khūrtegīn (*khūrtakīn*), a ruler with a Turkic title, before reaching the mountain pass towards Tibet at Aṭabāsh, and finally Upper Nūshajān six days later.[55] Finally, one could travel three months beyond Nūshajān to the city of the Khāqān of the Tughuzghuz Turks. This route takes you through spacious (*kibār*) and fertile (*khaṣib*) villages inhabited by the fire-worshipping Mazdain Turks.[56] In the end, Ibn Khurradādhbih's itinerary poses questions about Upper Nūshajān: who controls it and who shares this border with China?

Qudāma's geography is more informative about Nūshajān even if complications are added. Qudāma opened with itineraries similar to Ibn Khurradādhbih's. Qudāma first includes the itinerary that starts in Ṭarāz, followed by Kaṣrī Bās that is again associated with the Qārlūq Turks but also near the border of the Kīmāk Turks, and then the village of the Khāqān of the Türgesh before reaching Upper Nūshajān which is still fifteen days of travel from its neighbour as the caravan goes with pasturage and water or three days as the Turks travel.[57] The second is the itinerary that travels through Ūzkand, the city of Khūrtegīn.[58] These itineraries do not clarify any of the questions that Ibn Khurradādhbih left, but later Qudāma provided more concrete information about the status of Nūshajān. At one point, Qudāma included Nūshajān in a list of the regions of Khurāsān under the authority of the Ṭāhirid Governor ʿAbdallāh b. Ṭāhir (r. 828–45). According to Qudāma, this list represents the situation in the year 836, implying that by the early ninth century, Nūshajān was under the domain of the Abbasids (or at least their loyal but autonomous representatives), but this list does not specify whether this is Upper or Lower Nūshajān or the entire district.[59] Qudāma later gave a description of the great frontier (*al-thughūr al-kibār*), the frontier of the Turks that stretches from Gorgān where there is a wall that prevents raids (see Chapter 2) to Nūshajān where the greatest number of Turks are found. From the measurements given, Qudāma was describing Lower Nūshajān here, reporting it is only sixty *farāsikh* (360 km) from Samarqand in the neighbourhood of Chāch and Ferghana.[60] This frontier is threatened by armed bands of Qārlūq Turks up to the border of the Kīmāk Turks.[61] If we assume that Qudāma was referencing Lower Nūshajān in both of these accounts, we are left with the image of a complex frontier over the fifty-two *farāsikh* (312 km) and the additional fifteen days travel that lays between Lower and Upper Nūshajān in the itineraries provided by Ibn Khurradādhbih and Qudāma. Qudāma gave some answers to the questions we initially had about Nūshajān's status; at the least Lower Nūshajān is under Islamic authority (or contributes taxes to Muslim authorities). He was also describing Nūshajān and especially the area between Lower and Upper Nūshajān as being within a pockmarked landscape where authority and control is not uniform.

Yāqūt also provided a description of Nūshajān – citing Ibn al-Faqīh but including information not found in the extant copies of his work – that offers more details without necessarily clarifying the place of Nūshajān itself.[62] He agreed with Ibn Khurradādhbih and Qudāma on many details including the distances between both Upper and Lower Nūshajān and other cities in Transoxiana and the presence of various Turkish groups amid these itineraries while providing us with two new pieces of information to both clarify and complicate the place of Nūshajān. First, he stated that Ṭarāz is 'a city in the boundaries (*tukhūm*) of the Turks along the River Jaxartes', claiming that the starting point of Ibn Khurradādhbih and Qudāma's itineraries to Nūshajān was already in the land of the Turks.[63] Second, he suggested that – despite Nūshajān being the border of China – China itself is over 300 *farāsikh* (1800 km) beyond not only Nūshajān but the city of the Khāqān of the Tughuzghuz making it a remote frontier for China as well as the Islamic world.[64] Put together, Yāqūt widened the frontier between the Islamic world and China greatly. Some of this may reflect the situation during Yāqūt's lifetime when the Khwārzmshāhs (r. 1077–1231) had filled the vacuum left by the Seljuqs (r. 1040–1194) in Iran and Transoxiana, China was split between the Southern Song (r. 1127–1279), Jin (r. 1114–1234) and Western Xia (r. 1038–1227) and the Mongols were on the rise in between. At the same time, Yāqūt cited the ninth-century geographer Ibn al-Faqīh as the source of this information and the disposition of the Turks in the region – as he described it – is closer to the situation in the ninth century than the twelfth or thirteenth. This is not surprising. Despite his first-hand travel experience, Yāqūt's dictionary is primarily archival and encyclopaedic, preserving centuries of geographical knowledge.[65]

Nūshajān's position, ostensibly at the intersection of many frontiers, none of which are securely held, leaves us with questions as to what it means for this place to be described as a border or *ḥadd*. Is Nūshajān some kind of outpost, rather than part of the larger body of Muslim-controlled territories? Its location, according to the available itineraries, is somewhere in or around the Tiānshān Mountains. Was Upper Nūshajān like the Gate of Iron or Rāsht discussed above, controlling access through a remote defile; difficult to access but easy to hold once under one's authority? The designation of *Upper* Nūshajān (*al-aʿlā*) may imply a position in the mountains, elevated above *Lower* Nūshajān (*al-suflī*). It is important to think about the possible intents our sources may have in laying claim to a place like Nūshajān. Are they attempting to aggrandize the extent of Muslim authority? Such questions test our views about what a state should look like.

Do the borders of a state define a homogenous territory within? Much of the territory between Lower and Upper Nūshajān seems largely unfavourable to settlement and therefore less beneficial to a state. This territory is better adapted to a pastoralist lifestyle, hence the grazing grounds of various Turkic people. In his history of modern Afghanistan, Thomas Barfield suggested a model for approaching the political geography of a region whose physical geography includes large swathes of land unsuitable for sedentary agriculture. He called it the 'Tale of Two Cheeses'.

> The modern view of the state is monolithic. … It is a processed American cheese model in which each slice is expected to be uniform in texture and the same as any other (although size and thickness may very). … Such a model does not apply well to those parts of the world such as Turko-Persia where empires were cobbled together with large stretches of sparsely populated territory separating the main centers of agriculture from urban life. Rulers here sought direct control of these centers and the lines of communication among them while ignoring the rest. They employed a Swiss cheese model of the polity that did not assume uniformity across the landscape or their control of it.[66]

At the heart of this 'Swiss cheese' model of rule is an understanding that, from a state's perspective, some land is worth controlling because it can be profitable while other land is less valuable. Easily accessible agricultural lands have higher rewards in the form of legible and taxable produce that is easy to collect and manage. Mountains and deserts offer relatively little in the form of legible produce while challenging anyone wishing to tax and manage them or their inhabitants. This friction of terrain has the power to establish 'relatively inflexible limits to the effective reach of the traditional agrarian state'.[67] In such an environment the state pursues the cheese and ignores the holes.

Such patterns become even more pronounced as we ask ourselves whether the idea of the territorial state even carried that much importance in the late antique and early medieval Islamic world. Ann Lambton most succinctly made the case that it was in the nature of the early Islamic state that territory was secondary to ideology. 'The basis of the Islamic state was ideological, not political, territorial or ethnical, and the primary purpose of government [in Islam] was to defend and protect the faith, not the state.'[68] Lambton took this argument to the point that she claimed, paraphrasing Henry Siegman, 'Political boundaries were unknown to Islam except those that separated the *dār al-Islām*, the area inhabited by Muslims, from the *dār al-ḥarb*, the abode of war inhabited by unbelievers. In its internal aspect it was an assemblage of individuals bound to one another by ties of religion.'[69] In this model, the state's objective was to unite people of similar faith, and territorial extent was dependent on the people the state hoped to bring together. But when it comes to the ideas of borders and frontiers, this model only works if we are examining an 'American-cheese' state. In the 'Swiss-cheese' landscape of the Khurāsānī shatterzone – and much of the broader Middle East and Central Asia – political boundaries as we are accustomed to them are difficult to imagine under any political ideology. Instead of individuals, we should think of the early Islamic state as a network of nodes, sometimes connected by roads and sometimes not. In the case of Upper Nūshajān, for example, the migratory patterns of the pastoralist Turks may result in this node being more closely connected to Islamic Transoxiana for part of the year and less closely connected for another part. This resulted in a state that was neither uniform nor complete and the geographical sources reflect this impression. Such attitudes may be exaggerated by Ibn Khurradādhbih and, to a lesser extent, Qudāma's focus on itineraries and emphasis on getting the reader from point 'a' to point 'b' without much time for whatever may lie off the road.

The result is that our sources describe an eastern frontier that is spotted by what, for lack of a better word, we may call outsiders. Beyond Ibn Khurradādhbih and Qudāma's descriptions of Turks living along the route from Lower to Upper Nūshajān, we have numerous reports of Turks living within the borders of what our sources project to be the lands of Islam. In Ibn Khurradādhbih's accounting of *kharāj* (land tax) collected by the governor ʿAbdallāh b. Ṭāhir, he included 'the Cities of the Turks' (*madāʾin al-turk*) which contribute 46,400 dirhams as well as 1,187 rough cotton robes and 1,300 pieces of iron.[70] *Ḥudūd al-ʿālam* identified groups of peaceful Turks (*jāy-i turkān-i āshtī*), some of whom have converted to Islam, living in and around Sutkand and Isfījāb.[71] Turkish converts are not always integrated members of the Dār al-Islām. According to Muqaddasī, Barūkat and Bālāj, both near Isfījāb, are 'frontiers against' (*thaghrān ʿalā*) the Turkmen who had converted to Islam out of fear.[72] These few areas show a lack of strong and/or uniform political authority in frontier regions, but they might also show a frontier in the process of transforming into something more stable through a long post-conquest process that involves settlement and integration of newly conquered lands. In either case, these examples demonstrate a frontier zone where political authority may neither be easy to identify based on declared borders nor entirely stable.

In attempting to set the limits of the frontier all the way to Upper Nūshajān, the geographers of the ninth and tenth centuries were describing a frontier of ambition, an idealized extent to which Islamic authority reaches. But they were, in a sense, discounting the unevenness and incomplete coverage of authority up to the edge of that frontier. The textual sources that inform our understanding of the geography of early Islamic Central Asia present us with a static geography – and are in fact active participants in determining the boundaries they are describing – but in the messiness of this presentation we may see a geography that is in flux. While discussing natural borders – borders set to natural features such as rivers, mountains or seas that therefore seem innately more legitimate – French historian Lucien Febvre argued that all borders are in fact the unnatural goals of expansion and the limits of men's desire and that they could be violated at any time – citing the Normans' violation of the sea to conquer the Saxons in 1066 as a prime example.[73] Identifying a distant boundary such as Upper Nūshajān, natural or not, motivates and drives people towards an end and therefore understanding the motivations of the people who define boundaries becomes an important part of the study of borderlands and frontiers themselves.

Ghūr, Bāmiyān and the frontier process

We may compare the way Nūshajān was described by Ibn Khurradādhbih and Qudāma with the way Iṣṭakhrī and Ibn Ḥawqal described Ghūr, a mountainous region east of Herat and south of Gharshistān and Gūzgān. In this case, Iṣṭakhrī and Ibn Ḥawqal expressed no claim of Muslim political control or sovereignty over Ghūr. In fact, they clearly stated that Ghūr is part of the abode of infidels (*dār kufr*), but because of the presence of Muslims living in the area, they included it in their description of the Muslim world.[74] This is the case even though, as Iṣṭakhrī later stated, Ghūr is situated in mountains surrounded by the Dār al-Islām, implying the only reason it is still a place under the authority of non-Muslims is that the mountains themselves are insurmountable (*jibāl manīʿa*).[75] According to Ibn Ḥawqal, this is a situation repeated nowhere else in the lands of Islam (*bilād al-Islām*), with the possible exception of certain tribes living in the Maghrib.[76] They recognized that Ghūr lies beyond the reach of Muslim political authority and is therefore outside the geographically defined domains of Islam, but they still considered it part of the Islamic world because of the presence of Muslims within the region and because of its location firmly within the Muslim side of the frontier, surrounded by Muslim-controlled territory. Tying Ghūr to Lambton's ideological definition of the early Islamic state, it is the presence of Muslims in Ghūr that makes Iṣṭakhrī and Ibn Ḥawqal consider it part of the Muslim world. Here we can contrast this with the Christian communities living on the mountains of the Arab–Byzantine frontier, fully surrounded by Muslim-controlled territory and resisting Muslim advancement, as analysed by Eger.[77] In Ghūr, religious and cultural penetration seems to have outpaced military and political advancement and for a long time Ghūr was the target of regular raids, such as the financially profitable but ultimately futile campaigns led by the Umayyad governor of Khurāsān Asad b. ʿAbdallāh al-Qasrī (r. 725–7, 735–8) beginning in 725 (see Chapter 5). Nevertheless, Ghūr presents an interesting challenge to the sources in defining the Islamic world – a challenge that is slightly different from the interest of pushing a frontier to Nūshajān, beyond the point at which political authority could be effective – but they also recognize that this is an anomalous situation.

In grappling with the presence of Ghūr as a land under the authority of non-Muslims, fully within the lands of Islam and home to a Muslim population, the sources must address the question of how the Dār al-Islām, the *bilād al-Islām* or any other corporate identity they want to assign the lands under Muslim authority was defined and the relationship between Muslim political authority, the places where Muslims live and the presence of non-Muslims – especially non-Muslims with political authority over Muslims. These questions are of special importance along a frontier where political and social identities and loyalties are in flux. In the aftermath of conquest and violent upheaval, such as the Arab–Muslim conquests of the seventh and eighth centuries, frontiers were quickly moving and society went through a period of transition in which such issues needed to be worked out. For example, in Chapter 5 we will discuss the tensions created by tax policies in a conquest society that created situations on the ground that allowed landowners from the conquered population to collect taxes from tenants who had come east as conquerors. Is this a case of the conqueror paying tribute to the conquered? How does corporate identity and loyalty impact the nuts and bolts of political and economic administration?

Evident in the ninth- and tenth-century geographers' descriptions of Nūshajān and Ghūr is the slow advance of the 'frontier process'. Originating in Frederick Jackson Turner's 'frontier thesis' that 'the existence of an area of free land, its continuous recession and the advance of American settlement westward, explain American development', a 'frontier process' explains the development over time of a unique frontier identity.[78] Key to Turner's thesis was the idea that the frontier is not a place, but also a 'process' whereby people of different cultures struggled with each other over economic resources and political power across a frontier zone and that these struggles were reflected back upon the political centre, often driving the political and economic development of the centre.[79] For Turner's view of the American West, this process involved the interaction between European immigrants and the wilderness of America, which resulted in an American identity distinct from its European origins. The frontier in which this process occurred was wholly within the state; conquest happened first and then settlement and incorporation of newly won territory followed. While Turner was focused on a specific set of geographic and historical conditions, the Westward expansion of the United States in the nineteenth century, the general model of the frontier is applicable to the Central Asian frontier of late antiquity and the early medieval period.[80] As Jos Gommans put it in his study of premodern frontiers in South Asia,

> Although Turner's idea often has been depicted as relevant only for the young man going west, there are still many similarities to its eastern counterpart that remain instructive. For example, Turner's frontier rightly contains the notion of frequently violent mission and expansion, which so conspicuously determine the identities of all frontier people, whether American cowboys, European crusaders, or Muslim *ghazis*.[81]

Though the names and circumstances may change, the experience of the American West is at once unique and comparable to the experience of people engaging various frontiers throughout time and space. What is of primary interest to this study is the more general notion of a frontier process; that the frontier is a zone of negotiation between conflicting parties over limited resources and that such interactions generate a specific frontier society uniquely different from the society of the centre.

With the application of Turner's definitions and models to our study, first, we may consider the eastern frontier not as a line on the map, but as a zone with great depth. In defining it, we are implicating a band that stretches from the Caspian Sea to the Hindu Kush and from the highlands of the Iranian plateau to the River Jaxartes. We are investigating people living deep within these regions who are experiencing the frontier. Second, when we look at places like Upper Nūshajān and Ghūr, we are seeing frontiers that are not frozen at borders, but rather frontiers of ambition. These are frontiers that reach beyond functional political authority but represent the ambitions of our authors and their audience towards even further expansion. Finally, we may focus on the processes that occur within this frontier zone – those social, political, economic, cultural and religious transformations that take hold as the region moves from pre-Islamic Sasanian, Sogdian, Hephthalite and Turkish rule to Muslim rule and then to autonomy under the rule of local independent dynasties with hybrid Iranian-Islamic identities. This study thus follows a Turnerian frontier process – while considering the many criticisms of Turner, most importantly his disregard for indigenous populations (discussed above) – along the eastern frontier with the hope of mapping the maturing of the frontier over centuries.

This frontier process can create complicated layers of authority and identity as the area transitions from one political authority and cultural milieu to another. Let us take for example the description given by our ninth- and tenth-century geographers of Bāmiyān, famous for the giant standing Buddha statues that were carved into the cliff walls of the Bāmiyān Valley during the sixth century.[82] According to Yaʿqūbī, Bāmiyān is a mountainous city overseen by a *dihqān* (or petty landed gentry, pl. *dahāqīn*) who holds the Persian title of *shīr* (which he mistakenly wants to translate into Arabic literally as *asād* or lion when the term, in this case, is a local royal title). An unnamed *shīr* of Bāmiyān converted to Islam at the hands of Muzāḥim b. Bisṭām during the reign of the Caliph Manṣūr (r. 754–775). It seems that, after his conversion, the *shīr* was allowed a certain level of independence until Faḍl b. Yaḥyā al-Barmakī put Muzāḥim's grandson Ḥasan in charge of the region.[83] In 794–5, Faḍl sent troops under the command of Ibrāhīm b. Jibrīl al-Bajalī, together with the kings of Ṭukhāristān and the *dahāqīn*.[84] Among the kings was Ḥasan who is now identified as the *shīr* of Bāmiyān (the only participant specifically named), against the Kābulshāh whose capital at Jurzabadīn was considered unapproachable and impregnable. They went on to conquer Ghūrawand and its mountain pass, Sārḥūd, Badīlistān and Shāh-Bahār where they destroyed idols.[85] Iṣṭakhrī and Ibn Ḥawqal both noted that the king of Bāmiyān is called *shīr*.[86] *Ḥudūd al-ʿālam* likewise describes Bāmiyān as under the rule of a king called *shīr*.[87] In the narrative provided by Yaʿqūbī we find a remote mountainous region holding on to its own local authority in the form of the *shīr*, but the *shīr* is transformed by Bāmiyān's incorporation into the Islamic world. At first the *shīr* converts to Islam, making himself acceptable to the conquerors as a Muslim ruler. Then, fewer than fifty years after this conquest and conversion, the title *shīr* is given to a descendant of the conquerors. Incorporation into the Islamic world has not changed traditions of local authority, but it has changed the conquerors as they take on local titles in a process of integrating themselves into local traditions of rule.[88] The frontier process is simultaneously changing both the conquered and the conquerors.

While both Ghūr and Bāmiyān illustrate how frontier zones are transformed over time, they also demonstrate how atomized rule may be in a shatterzone. Each of these regions had their own ruler with a complicated relationship to the empire surrounding them. Ghūr is surrounded by the caliphate but impervious to conquest, an island in a sea of Muslim rule. Bāmiyān is conquered but its conquerors are forced to identify with local traditions and they cannot fully import their own identity and ideas. In the bigger picture, Ghūr and Bāmiyān give us a way to understand some of the patterns described above. They ultimately illustrate the effects of the geological shatterzone – regions that are isolated by the mountainous geography surrounding them therefore develop individual traditions and practices. These dynamics create complicated relationship between empire and territoriality. Perhaps it is not just the sources' interest in providing itineraries that make it appear that the Islamic world of the ninth and tenth centuries is little more than cities and the roads between them. What we find is a geography that is extremely localized and nodal.

The walled oases of Balkh and Bukhara: The nodal frontier

In his description of the city of Balkh, Yaʿqūbī described a great wall that encompassed the city and all of its dependent villages and agricultural lands.

> Surrounding the villages of Balkh and its estates (*ḍiyāʿ-hā*) and its arable land (*mazāriʿ-hā*) is a great wall. From one gate of the gates of the wall that surrounds the arable land and the villages to a gate opposite it is 12 *farāsikh* [72 km]. Outside the wall there is not a building nor an estate nor a village, nothing but sand. For this great wall that surrounds the land of Balkh there are 12 gates.[89]

He then described another set of walls around the suburbs (*rabaḍ*) of Balkh, which has four gates and is five *farāsikh* (30 km) away from the great wall, giving it a diameter of two *farāsikh* (12 km). A *farsakh* further is a third wall that surrounds the city itself (*madīna*). This final wall has a one *farsakh* (6 km) diameter. The walls described by Yaʿqūbī would have been massive. With a diameter of twelve *farāsikh* or 72 km, the outer walls of the city would have a circumference of over 225 km and would encompass an area of over 4,000 square km. This is only slightly smaller than the area of the City of Los Angeles. Archaeologists have uncovered traces of these ringed walls and Akhror Mukhtarov confirmed the 72-km diameter.[90] A wall like this could have many possible purposes. For example, it could be for the defence of the agricultural hinterland against predatory raids by the various groups of Turks who threatened Ṭukhāristān in the ninth century when Yaʿqūbī was writing his description of the walls. We may also note Yaʿqūbī's remark that all that lies beyond the wall is sand and consider the role the wall played in preventing desertification.[91] This larger wall encompasses the entirety of the Balkh oasis.[92]

Balkh was not the only city described by our ninth- and tenth-century geographers as having such massive, concentric walls. Iṣṭakhrī described a similar situation in Bukhara, noting that its villages and arable lands are surrounded by a wall with a ten-*farāsikh* (60 km) diameter within which everything is populated (*kulluhā ʿāmara*).[93] Inside this wall, there are buildings, fortified compounds (*quṣūr*) and gardens. Ibn Ḥawqal gave even more detail, describing a series of concentric walls around Bukhara, or, more specifically, the city of Numijkat – the administrative centre or *qaṣaba* of the Bukhara oasis. The first has a diameter of twelve *farāsikh* (72 km) within which are fortified compounds (*quṣūr*), gardens, agricultural lands and villages. Like Yaʿqūbī's description of Balkh, there is no wasteland, ruins or fallow land inside it. A second wall contains fortified compounds, villages and the seat of the Sāmānid dynasty. A final wall surrounds the inner city itself.[94] Muqaddasī also measured Bukhara's outer wall at 12 *farāsikh* (72 km) in diameter and declared that it contains five cities and there is no untilled land within it.[95] If these numbers are to be believed, the walls of Bukhara would equal those of Balkh in size. Richard Frye gave a measurement for Bukhara of 250 km in circumference.[96] The historian and geographer Masʿūdī (896–956) wrote that the middle wall, three *farāsikh* away from the city of Bukhara, was built by one of the kings of Sogdiana and renovated by the Abbasid Caliph al-Mahdī (r. 775–85).[97] *Ḥudūd al-ʿālam* also includes a wall surrounding the whole of Bukhara without any interruptions and all of the city's *ribāṭāṭ* (sing. *ribāṭ*) and villages inside.[98] Narshakhī's (ca. 899–959) local history *Ta'rīkh-i Bukhārā* calls the outer wall *kanpirak* or 'the old lady', reporting that its construction began during the caliphate of Mahdī on the orders of his governor Abū al-ʿAbbās Faḍl b. Sulaymān al-Ṭūsī (r. 783–7) and it took nearly fifty years to complete.[99] The inner wall was built later under the watch of the Ṭāhirids.[100]

Other sources give us some confirmation without directly describing the wall. According to both Ibn Khurradādhbih and Qudāma, the gate of the wall of Bukhara stands two *farāsikh* (12 km) away from Paykand. The itinerary they provide situates the village of Māstīn one and a half *farāsikh* (9 km) inside the gate, then another five *farāsikh* (30 km) to Bukhara itself.[101] If Bukhara was at the centre of the enclosing wall and Ibn Khurradādhbih and Qudāma's itinerary goes directly to the city, these measurements would give the wall a diameter of thirteen *farāsikh* (78 km). While listing the names of the cities of Bukhara, Muqaddasī identified Tawāwīs, Zandana, Khujādā, Mughkān and Numijkat (three of which have their own fortresses while a fourth had a fortress later destroyed) as the cities within the encircling wall.[102] According to Narshakhī, the city of Varakhsha, which is the largest village of Bukhara and had been the seat of the Bukhārkhudā (the king of Bukhara), had walls similar to the wall of Bukhara while also inside the outer walls of Bukhara itself.[103]

Ibn al-Faqīh described the walls of Samarqand in a similar fashion. First, there is a wall with twelve wooden gates twelve *farāsikh* (72 km) in circumference, designed with towers meant for fighting, surrounding 6,000 plots of arable land, developed suburbs and irrigated lands. There is a second wall with four gates that surround 5,000 plots of land. Finally, there is a wall that surrounds the inner city and the *quhandiz* or citadel where the sultan resides.[104] Narshakhī reported that these walls predated the Muslim conquest of Samarqand and that they were the inspiration for the outer wall of Bukhara.[105] Similar cities and towns may also have multiple walls in a similar configuration. According to Muqaddasī, Sawrān – which sits on the frontier against the Oghuz and Kīmāk Turks – has seven fortifications, not necessarily walls, one behind the other, with suburbs within them (*ḥuṣūn sab'a ba'ḍuha khalfa ba'ḍ wa-l-rabaḍ fīhā*).[106] Looking beyond the Arabic and Persian geographical traditions of the ninth and tenth centuries, we find that such wall-building traditions stretch back through antiquity at multiple cities throughout the region. As Richard Frye noted, 'The great walls of Bukhara … were not unique in Central Asia. Antiochus I (r. 281–61 BC) built a wall around the oasis of Merv, according to Strabo, while Samarqand, Shash (near Tashkent), and other oases also had walls.'[107] The walled cities of Bactria were a cultural touchstone as far back as the fifth century BC when the Macedonian playwright Euripides (480–406 BC) commented on them in the *Bacchae*.[108] Such construction projects continued up through antiquity to the Arab–Muslim conquests, as we will see in the following chapter with the construction of the Great Wall of Gorgān on the eastern shore of the Caspian Sea.

Large-scale walls that encircled not just the city but suburbs, dependent villages and agricultural lands provide a holistic approach not just to urban defence, but defence of the entire oasis. The lands on which the city depends for food and other resources require defence just as much as the city, after all. Such defences allow for expanded production without fear of small-scale raids and harassment but may not be practical against a large army.[109] Within the walls, individual landholders built fortified estates to defend themselves, their properties and their dependents. Iṣṭakhrī and Ibn Ḥawqal gave detailed descriptions of the area inside Bukhara's walls, focusing on the properties that lay along the various tributaries of the River Zarāfshān. Along the Nūkandah, Juwaybār Bakār, Kushnah, Rabāḥ, Zaghārkandah and Fashīrdīzah rivers there were thousands of estates (*ḍiyā'*), gardens (*basātīn*) and fortified compounds or fortresses (*quṣūr* and sometimes *ḥuṣūn*) lining each bank.[110] The regular pairing of fortified compounds with agricultural lands implies a relationship between the two, with the fortified compounds in place primarily to secure and protect the agricultural lands. These appear to be private estates with their own personal and, perhaps, privately owned fortifications. The use of the term *qaṣr* further supports this conclusion through the identification of *quṣūr* not only with fortifications but also with palaces and mansions.

It is not surprising to find so many references to fortifications in these texts. As Paul Wheatley pointed out, 'In the medieval Islamic world, fortification was an almost universal attribute of settlement.'[111] It will only be in contexts where defence is the primary service provided by a site that it becomes the primary focus of our geographical sources.[112] There are several terms that might be used for such fortifications including *ḥiṣn*, *qaṣr*, *ribāṭ* and *qal'a*, each with their own meaning and nuance.[113] Of these terms, the one we see most often in Iṣṭakhrī and Ibn Ḥawqal's discussions of the area around Bukhara is *qaṣr*. While the etymology of *qaṣr* has been debated, in comparison to other terms for fortifications, *qaṣr* is often more closely connected to a castle or palace (as in the residence of a government official) and it is more likely that the *qaṣr* developed out of the fortified residential complexes of prominent persons.[114] The close connection in these descriptions between the *quṣūr* and agricultural lands seems to support this idea as it creates an image of agricultural manors dotting the landscape of Bukhara. Narshakhī employed the Persian term *kūshk*, which can similarly mean villa, to describe a preponderance of inhabited fortifications as early as 750 when the Bukhārkhudā Qutayba b. Ṭughshāda (d. before 755) called on the residents of seven hundred fortified estates that surrounded the gates of Bukhara to fight against an Arab Shi'ite rebel who was in the city.[115] According to Narshakhī, these villas were both more populous than the city itself and, unlike the city, absent an Arab population.

The great walled oases of Balkh and Bukhara, encompassing thousands of square kilometres of cities, villages and agricultural lands, demonstrate a political geography that is not in tune with the image of a large-scale, unified empire with clearly defined borders. Instead we see a localized political geography in which larger urban centres act as nodes at the centre of networks of dependent and supporting villages and agricultural hinterlands. In the midst of the Khurāsānī shatterzone and the complex geography of the eastern frontier, political and economic organization was built on these localized networks. Such situations are apparent in the geographical works we have already discussed, even on an imperial level. The itineraries, for example, form a picture of an empire that is made up of urban centres and the roads that connect them to such an extent that the title of many of these geographical works, *al-masālik wa'l-mamālik* or 'routes and realms', make this organization the primary aspect of the geographies they contain. Despite avoiding the use of itineraries, the geographer who most clearly describes the world in such atomized terms is Muqaddasī. Often considered the culmination of geographical writing of this period and an important step towards the development of humanistic geography in the Islamic tradition, Muqaddasī employed a scientific and systematic ordering of the world based on a number of organizing principles.[116] Beyond dividing the realms of Islam (*mamlakat al-Islām*) between the Arab (*mamlakat al-ʿarab*) and non-Arab (*mamlakat al-ʿajam*) provinces, Muqaddasī created a vocabulary for understanding each individual clime (*iqlīm*) – by which he really meant region in a manner closer to the Iranian *keshwar* rather than the Ptolemaic clime – each of which are seen as individual geographic wholes.[117] Each province is centred on a metropolis called the *miṣr* surrounded by several districts called *kūra* which each contain an administrative centre called the *qaṣaba*, which itself is surrounded by other main towns called *madīna*, each of which has their own dependent villages or *quryā* and hinterlands. Muqaddasī employed a metaphor comparing the different ranks of cities to offices in government to explain their different roles. The metropoles are kings (*malūk*), the *qaṣabāt* are chamberlains (*ḥujjāb*), the towns are armies (*jund*) and the villages are the infantry (*rajjāla*).[118] Places like Balkh and Bukhara acted as the urban centres of their own walled-off sub-provinces.[119] These massive walls are a physical representation of this layered political geography dependent on urban nodes and the networks that connect them.

These walled oases and other networks of urban centres surrounded by their interdependent villages and agricultural lands are the nodes at the intersections of a web of routes that make up the empire. In imagining this nodal imperial geography, it may be useful to think in terms of Barfield's 'Swiss-cheese' model but inverted. The holes are under centralized authority and integrated into the empire – represented by the metropoles, administrative centres, towns and villages – while control over the 'cheese' is weak and uneven. As we saw with the region between Lower and Upper Nūshajān, not even the roads that connect these nodes may be fully under a centralized authority. In many ways these nodes may, like the proverbial cheese, stand alone, especially at the edges of the frontier where centralized authority radiating out of the central imperial node at Baghdad is at its weakest. Therefore, within the empire itself, there will be a measure of autonomy and individuality from one node to the next as each urban centre and its dependent regions integrate more or less into the empire and the imperial identity and culture and preserve to a degree their own local identity and traditions. This stands in contrast to more centralized frontiers, such as the Arab–Byzantine frontier which was under regular imperial control and acted as a stage for royal patronage as caliphs and princes personally led campaigns against the Byzantines.

The image of the frontier

What does it mean if the Arabic geographers of the ninth and tenth centuries said Rāsht is the furthest point of Khurāsān in its direction? From their perspective, it demonstrates an interest in presenting a version of Khurāsān that is a solid, unified geographic unit with clear and distinct borders. When we add the narrative surrounding the creation of Faḍl b. Yaḥyā's gate, they are painting a picture of the Abbasid Empire defining and defending these borders. But the geographical sources also show that this image of a clear-cut and well-defined border is not realistic. Instead, they present a frontier of depth and width, even at Rāsht. The border between the Turks and Khurāsān is not at Rāsht alone. Instead the Wakhsh Valley, following the river down from Pāmir all the way through Chaghāniyān to the Oxus, is a deep frontier, a zone of transition from one authority to another. Even if we were to accept a defined and solid external frontier, taking into consideration the academic tradition that the border between the Dār al-Islām and the Dār al-Ḥarb is the only border that matters to the geographical sources, we still would not have a Khurāsān that is a solid and unified geographic unit. Places like the Gate of Iron remind us of the divided nature of the Khurāsānī shatterzone and the many internal boundaries and barriers to travel and communication that have helped isolate parts of greater Khurāsān and its neighbours.

These discussions lead to additional questions about what a border at Rāsht would ultimately define. When a site is identified as a border or limit it is often difficult to identify of what it is a limit. Places like Upper Nūshajān show the impractical nature of the spaces the sources sometimes defined as borders. This is not a place where the sources transition from geographically or spatially defined point '*a*' to geographically or spatially defined point '*b*'. Instead we find that itineraries to Upper Nūshajān force the reader to travel across many boundaries and through a long and deep frontier to reach the location identified as the border, in this case, of China. Sites far from an external limit of the empire can offer similar dilemmas. Ghūr demonstrates the 'Swiss-cheese' nature of political authority in the Khurāsānī shatterzone, the inability to completely consolidate authority in a region beyond which the frontier has clearly advanced. Even if borders are clearly defined, what lies behind them is not necessarily a unified whole and associations among people living on one side of a border or another will develop over time. And when borders are defined by conquest, the transition inherent in the frontier process will change and transform the conquerors as much as the conquered. The story of the *shīr* of Bāmiyān emphasized this transitional nature of the frontier and the frontier process.

In the end, the Arabic and Persian geographical sources of the ninth and tenth centuries describe a greater Khurāsān and Transoxiana that is not easily defined by clear borders. Instead, as we see when we examine large walled oases such as Balkh and Bukhara, this is a geography of nodes and networks. The geography is broken down into smaller and smaller components which may be tied to each other on certain levels but can act as independent units on others. The transition that occurs at the frontier is often described as a waning of central authority. Ralph Brauer argued that the geographers of the Balkhī School understood boundaries as fuzzy, that 'as one progressed in a direction away from the centre of a state, one would sooner or later pass from one sovereignty to another or that one's taxes would flow to different places on either side of such a division.'[120] But he saw this as a progressive weakening from the centre to the periphery 'where the force of sovereignty and identity of that state grew progressively feebler … to be replaced gradually, as one proceeded on a line between the capitals of any two neighbouring states, by the sovereignty and identity of the adjoining state.'[121] Instead, I would argue that when these geographers describe the eastern frontier they are not describing gradations emanating out from the imperial centre. Instead, the mountainous shatterzone combined with the nodal nature of the administrative geography meant that there was never one centre nor one gradient of authority. Instead each geographical subdivision needs to be addressed as an individual entity with its own connections and relationships to the imperial centre. Let us now consider how the eastern frontier interacted with the larger empires that claimed it in a firm historical context by analysing the development of the eastern frontier under the Sasanian Empire and the impact the frontier had on the empire itself.

Chapter 2

SHAPING THE EASTERN FRONTIER: THE SASANIAN EMPIRE AND ITS EASTERN NEIGHBOURS

When Pīrūz dragged the frontier

The history of the Sasanian Empire has long been told from a perspective that favours the western reaches of the empire. Mesopotamia, the administrative heartland of the empire, had a long history of urbanization in a relatively flat land concentrated on the Tigris and Euphrates Rivers that made political centralization that much easier. The west was also where the Sasanians shared a frontier with the Roman and Byzantine Empires whose own historians contributed greatly to our knowledge of Sasanian history. The Sasanian east has been attracting more attention in recent years and there we find a different type of imperial order. Stretched across a shatterzone of mountains, deserts and steppes, in the east the Sasanians faced a series of rivals who originated on the Inner Asian steppes, nomads who sedentarized and urbanized as they entered Ṭukhāristān and Transoxiana. The challenge posed by these eastern rivals required a different kind of response than found in the west. Here, the Sasanians focused their attention on a handful of scattered urban centres – Marw, Marw al-Rūd, Herat and Nīshāpūr – from which the defence of the frontier could be organized and mobilized. Despite evidence of a pseudo-feudal decentralization away from the political centres of the empires, the eastern frontier was an important part of the Sasanian imperial project. It was the site of large-scale imperial construction projects and major military campaigns, some of which threatened the very existence of the empire. In the east, the Sasanians spent heavily in treasure and human capital to shape the frontier. To illustrate this, let us turn to the campaigns of the Shahanshah Pīrūz (r. 459–84) against the Hephthalites.

In the year 484, the Shahanshah Pīrūz marched against the Hephthalite king Akhshunwār for the third and final time. Pīrūz had not always been in conflict with the Hephthalites, a Hunnic people who had recently migrated into Central Asia. In fact, the Hephthalites had been critical allies of Pīrūz in a civil war against his brother Hormozd III (r. 457–9) following the death of their father Yazdgird II (r. 438–57). After Hormozd claimed the throne, Pīrūz fled to the Hephthalites and exchanged control over Ṭālaqān – a region west of Balkh which had only recently been conquered by Yazdgird – for the necessary support to win the crown.[1] Even though this deal made Pīrūz emperor, it also opened up the east to Hephthalite forces and over the course of the next decade they overran Ṭukhāristān – seizing it from the Hunnish kingdom of the Kidarites – and began advancing into Khurāsān. By 469, the Hephthalites had established themselves as the dominant power in the region and Pīrūz found it necessary to march against his former allies. During this first campaign, Pīrūz was defeated, forced to pay a ransom and bow down before the Hephthalite king, an act of humiliation that infuriated the emperor and drove him to seek revenge.[2] During a second campaign, an agent of Akhshunwār led Pīrūz's forces through deserts until they were exhausted and the Hephthalites quickly dispatched them. In the aftermath, Pīrūz promised thirty mule-loads of silver dirhams for his ransom, but the expense of his previous campaign and ensuing ransom had depleted the treasury and he was only able to raise twenty. As a result, his young son Qubād was taken hostage and held by Akhshunwār for two years while the full ransom was collected.[3]

The terms of the peace negotiated between Pīrūz and Akhshunwār following this second battle set the border (*ḥadd* in the Arabic sources) between the Sasanians and the Hephthalites and guaranteed that neither would cross it.[4] In some accounts, the border was marked by a tower along the road from Marw to Bukhara that Pīrūz's grandfather Bahrām V Gūr (r. 420–38) had erected to delimit the border between the Sasanians and the Kidarite Huns following a thwarted invasion.[5] According to one account found in Ṭabarī's *History of the Prophets and Kings*, as Pīrūz marched on Sogdiana that final time in 484, the army came upon this tower and the border it marked. Instead of passing the tower and thereby violating the peace with Akhshunwār, Pīrūz took 50 elephants and 300 men, chained them to the tower and ordered them to drag the tower forward before the Sasanian army. As the elephants and men pulled the tower along the ground, they also figuratively dragged the border. Akhshunwār was not impressed and demanded that Pīrūz honour their treaty. When Pīrūz continued his march, Akhshunwār once again lured him into a trap. The Hephthalites dug a large trench, covered it with branches and earth and drew the Sasanian army directly into it. Pīrūz and his entire army met their demise at the bottom of Akhshunwār's trench.[6] The death of the shahanshah and the bulk of the imperial army on this distant frontier was a disastrous blow to the empire.

Beginning with the reign of Ardashīr I (r. 224–41), the founder of the Sasanian Empire, the Sasanians aspired to an empire that would reach the boundaries of the Achaemenid Empire. These ambitions are expressed in the monumental inscriptions of the third century and even in the title some Sasanian emperors employed, *shāhānshāh Īrān va Anīrān* (the king of kings of Iran and *not* Iran).[7] In the West, this led to a series of wars with Rome and later Byzantium over Mesopotamia, its frontier with Syria and Anatolia and Armenia. In the East, this meant ambitious campaigns into Khurāsān, Ṭukhāristān and Transoxiana that strained the imperial army and treasury with few long-lasting gains and many painful and expensive defeats. Even though not all Sasanian emperors were as brash as Pīrūz, dragging the boundary markers before their army, they were occupied with extending their borders from the start.

This chapter examines the relationship between the Sasanian Empire, its frontiers in Khurāsān, Ṭukhāristān and Transoxiana and its eastern neighbours.

Over four and a quarter centuries of Sasanian rule, this came to include a series of rivals who competed with the Sasanians and among themselves for control over Ṭukhāristān and Transoxiana. Beginning with the Kushan Empire, this list includes the Kushano-Sasanians, Kidarites, Hephthalites and Turks. The literary sources often present these as an undifferentiated barbaric mass, but the lands opposite the Sasanian Empire along the eastern frontier was not a space between or beyond empires. It was home to rival empires in their own right, built out of the tribal confederacies of the steppe who became sedentarized and urbanized as they migrated south and joined the complex mosaic of peoples who inhabited the eastern frontier. Through this exploration, this chapter highlights the place of Central Asia in the world of late antique empire. Emphasis has traditionally been put on the western Sasanian lands and their rivalry with Rome but one must understand the conditions in the east and the Sasanians' rivalries along the eastern frontier in order to get a complete picture of the empire and its history.

In the previous chapter, we discussed the conceptualization of borders as limits that define the whole. By examining the eastern frontier of the Sasanian Empire, the strategies the empire employed to maintain and expand this frontier and the relationship between the Sasanians, their agents in Khurāsān and their neighbours, we can ask questions about how the Sasanians structured their empire, how they understood themselves and how they – and their successors who left us the largest literary record of Sasanian history – defined themselves against their neighbours and rivals. In doing so, this chapter will address current debates regarding the nature of Sasanian political authority and imperial organization between a strong centralized model of imperial authority and a decentralized, confederate model. In the previous chapter, we also discussed the nature of the Khurāsānī shatterzone which created an archipelago of urban centres – the centres of political and economic life – in a sea of steppes, deserts and mountains. Here we will continue this discussion to explore how the Sasanians and their neighbours not only held onto these islands but also attempted to control the bridges between them. As a physically disjointed space remote from the political centres of Mesopotamia but still strategically and politically important to the Sasanian Empire – so much so that the Sasanian shahanshahs were willing to risk both men and treasure in great numbers repeatedly to defend it – the eastern frontier is an interesting place to test models of Sasanian authority against each other. The resources and effort spent along the eastern frontier reinforce its importance to the history of the Sasanian Empire and highlight the extent to which imperial power could be asserted far from Ctesiphon.

Before moving forward, we should note that, of course, the story of Pīrūz moving Bahrām Gūr's tower is fanciful. There is sufficient evidence for Pīrūz's many failures against the Hephthalites, including confirmation in contemporary Byzantine and Armenian sources as well as representations of Pīrūz on Sasanian coins with three different crowns implying at least two disruptions to his rule that match his two moments of captivity under Akhshunwār. But the story of the tower being dragged before the army is an embellishment that found its way into Ṭabarī's history, written nearly four centuries after Pīrūz's death.[8] This should serve as a reminder of the problems inherent in our sources for Sasanian history (to be discussed shortly). Pīrūz's decision to pull the frontier before his army fits the image of a king who is both aggressive and who regularly breaks his word. After violating the treaty with Akhshunwār, Pīrūz was punished with his own death and the destruction of his army, adding a didactic value to the story.[9] Despite these challenges, this narrative can still serve as a reminder of the importance placed on fixing the frontier in the literary tradition. Here we can compare Pīrūz and Bahrām Gūr's tower to Rāsht and the gate of Faḍl b. Yaḥyā al-Barmakī discussed in Chapter 1. As Faḍl closed the frontier with a gate, Pīrūz attempted to drag the frontier forward with elephants both as figurative representations of the state and its role on the frontier.

The organization of the Sasanian Empire

Before turning to the eastern frontier, I would like to discuss some ongoing historiographical debates surrounding the organization of the Sasanian Empire. Until recently, the dominant narrative of Sasanian history had been that of Arthur Christensen's 1944 study *L'Iran sous le Sasanides*. The Christensen thesis, as his analysis of Sasanian political history has been called, argued that the Sasanians had built a highly centralized state in which the shahanshah held ultimate authority. Recently, Christensen's thesis has been critiqued by Parvaneh Pourshariati in her *Decline and Fall of the Sasanian Empire*. Pourshariati argued that the Sasanian Empire was built on a confederacy inherited from the Arsacid Parthians (r. 247 BCE–224 CE) between the Sasanian royal family and a group of powerful Parthian noble families. Together the Sasanians and these Parthian families were 'co-partners' in rule over a decentralized empire.[10] While Pourshariati's thesis is a strong rebuttal to Christensen, it has also met with its own criticisms and some of the strongest have come from the direction of the frontiers. How could an empire that lasted four and a quarter centuries and covered such an extensive territory with long, hostile frontiers on both flanks survive as a loose confederacy? This question is confounded by the presence of large-scale infrastructural projects along the frontiers, some built at moments when the Sasanian Empire appears to be at its weakest, such as the series of large defensive walls built in the midst of Pīrūz's humiliating defeats (to be discussed later in this chapter).[11] St. John Simpson recently argued for something of a compromise position, denying the Christensen model of centralization under the direct authority of the emperor while arguing for a centralized and effective bureaucracy instead. He wrote that the Sasanian Empire 'was not just built on exceptional kingship, feudalism, and faith. Its success lay instead in effective bureaucracy and good management. Integrated planning for economic, military and civilian needs was fundamental, and without it the massive capital projects and military capabilities of the Sasanian state could not have been sustained.'[12] By exploring the eastern frontier of the Sasanian Empire and considering the tradition that borders are the limits that define the whole, this chapter engages in this debate.

To a certain extent, these widely divergent takes on the history of the Sasanian Empire can be attributed to problems with our sources. Christiansen's analysis, for example, relied on state-produced sources – especially third-century monumental inscriptions and a literary tradition formed in the sixth century – which project an image of a strong emperor ruling a centralized empire. The Sasanians left few written sources. Most of the extant literary sources were produced by outsiders – either geographically as in the work of Latin, Greek and Armenian chroniclers who were typically enemies or rivals of the Sasanian state or chronologically as in the works produced after the Arab–Muslim conquests and the collapse of the Sasanian Empire. These later sources tend to claim older traditions as sources, especially an official Sasanian history called the *Khwādaynāma* (*Book of Kings*), which covered the history of Iran from the reign of the legendary First Man Kayūmarth through the last Sasanian shahanshah Yazdgird III (r. 632–51).[13] As an imperial project, this history represents the image the Sasanians wanted to promote of themselves. The *Khwādaynāma* has not survived in its Pahlavi form. Instead we have remnants primarily within the Arabic and Persian historiographical tradition but also in Armenian and Georgian traditions.[14] Beginning with the famous secretary and translator of Pahlavi texts Ibn al-Muqaffaʿ (721–56), the *Khwādaynāma* was translated into Arabic on several occasions and became an important source for Arabic and later New Persian histories of pre-Islamic Iran, including most notably Ṭabarī's *History of the Prophets and Kings* and Firdawsī's (940–1019 or 1025) epic poem, the *Shāhnāma*.[15] As more and more threads of the *Khwādaynāma* tradition are unearthed, it appears increasingly difficult to think of the text as a singular, state-sponsored work that survived in translation and renditions but rather a group of traditions that circulated in a variety of forms simultaneously. Naturally this has led to questions about how to approach the *Khwādaynāma* as a source for Sasanian history.[16]

Contemporary literary sources produced outside of the Sasanian Empire have been used to complement and expand upon the available Sasanian sources. Roman and Byzantine sources tell us much, especially about conflicts between the empires, but contain the inherent problems of sources written by foreign rivals.[17] Armenian sources have been an important window into Sasanian history that often give us a more detailed view of administrative practices, Armenia having been under Sasanian rule – but their ideological perspective emphasizes the place of the Christian church and attempts to separate Armenia from Iran and, therefore, these sources must be read carefully.[18]

All together, these sources tend to focus on the west, generally ignoring Khurāsān and the east. Khodadad Rezakhani described the place of eastern Iran in the historiography of the Sasanian Empire: 'In this context, the history of East Iran was largely left out of narratives or only mentioned when it displayed relevance to the history of the west.'[19] Historians have relied on Chinese sources to fill this gap, but the inconsistent accessibility of these texts in translation and the divide between students of western and eastern Asia have acted as a barrier. Édouard Chavannes's French translations of Chinese documents related to the history of the Turks have been one of the most valuable resources for historians of the Persianate world trying to access Chinese sources for late antique Central Asia.[20] A growing corpus of documents written in Central Asian languages has been invaluable in reconstructing the situation on the ground. Most important for our purposes are the so-called Bactrian documents, a collection of 150 documents written in the Bactrian language primarily from the kingdom of Rōb (modern Rūī on the northern face of the Hindu Kush Mountains), ranging from the third through seventh centuries.[21]

Due to the limits of the written sources for Sasanian history, numismatics – including both coins and seals – and inscriptions have come to the forefront as primary sources for reconstructing Sasanian political history and have acted as proof against unreliable literary sources. Similarly, archaeology has played an increasing role in uncovering the history of late antique Central Asia and the findings of recent excavations will play an important role in this chapter.

The debate about a centralized versus a decentralized empire may also be influenced by the matter of what parts of the empire one focuses on. For example, the Sasanians engaged in many urbanization projects – founding royal cities and building roads and irrigation projects that supported these cities – with the intent of centralizing imperial authority, but this was not a project that was applied evenly across the empire. The focus of these urbanization programmes was Mesopotamia, where a millennium of urbanization predated the emergence of the Sasanians and provided a basis from which independent *poleis* could be transformed into royal cities. Fārs, the Sasanian homeland where royal authority could be best asserted, likewise saw greater attention than the eastern and northern reaches of the empire.[22] From our sources on urban foundations, including the administrative geography *Shahristānīha-i Īrānshahr* which details the foundation of the provincial capitals and major cities of the empire, alongside numismatics and inscriptions, we see that the Sasanians founded new cities in the west and south at a rate that far outpaced similar projects in the rest of the empire throughout their history.[23] Urbanization was an important step towards centralization with urban centres acting as sites for asserting Sasanian imperial authority by appointing governors and collecting taxes. The uneven spread of urbanization meant that there was an equally uneven spread of political and economic centralization. Along the eastern frontier, some of these goals could be achieved through military projects – garrisoning troops in cities and building large defensive infrastructure projects such as walls and forts.

Outside the urban cores, the Sasanian Empire was closer to a 'feudal' society despite the many misgivings over the appropriate application of the term.[24] Iranian feudalism differed from its Western European counterpart in many ways.[25] The Sasanian nobility relied on slaves rather than serfs, emphasized control of irrigation over land and engaged in a limited exchange of rights and obligations between themselves and the monarch. These differences often appear in degrees. For example, legal documents give evidence for slaves who were bound to the land they worked and even alienated with it in a manner similar to European serfs.[26] Richard Bulliet highlighted some of the key contours of Iranian 'feudalism' in his analysis of the connection between investment in the digging of a qanat (underground irrigation canal) and the ownership of the villages and agricultural lands irrigated by the qanat and even the naming of such villages after the investor.[27] Members of the great noble houses did control hereditary lands, along with important military, religious and administrative positions, but there was not a clear exchange of one for the other. Instead of feudalism, Pourshariati suggested we follow Cyril Toumanoff's description of late antique Armenia in his *Studies in Christian Caucasian History* and call the system 'dynastic'. Under the Armenian dynastic system, the *naxarars* controlled hereditary lands and titles, provided military service and advised the king on matters of state, but unlike feudal lords the *naxarars* held sovereignty over their own territories and behaved like tribal organizations.[28] Toumanoff described the dynastic system as a process of 'gradual evolution of tribes into a polity'.[29] In Pourshariati's application, the Parthian noble families, whose own nomadic origins emphasize the tribe to state trajectory, replaced the *naxarars* in the larger Sasanian Empire.[30] The Parthian noble houses, structured as agnatic groups, collectively owned and held authority over large, hereditary landholdings. As such, each family developed a territorial identity along with their shared economic and political identities.[31]

Alongside these noble Parthian houses, the Sasanian confederacy incorporated many vassal kings (*shahrdārs*) during its early years. The monumental inscriptions on the Ka'aba-i Zardusht at Naqsh-i Rustam just outside Persepolis list a series of kings who paid tribute to Ardashīr I and his son, occasional co-emperor and successor Shāpūr I (r. 241–72). Along the eastern frontier, these included the Abarshahrshāh (king of Nīshāpūr), Marwshāh and Sakānshāh (king of Sīstān).[32] Ṭabarī adds the kings of the Kushans (whose territory roughly corresponded with Ṭukhāristān), Tūrān (east-central Baluchistan) and Makrān, who became vassals of Ardashīr after his conquest of Khurāsān.[33] These vassal kings were sometimes members of the Sasanian royal family. The Kab'a-i Zardusht named Shāpūr's son Narseh king of Sind, Sakāstān and Tūrān 'to the edge of the sea' and his eldest son Bahrām the Gīlānshāh (Gīlān is along the southwest coast of the Caspian Sea), while Ṭabarī says the Kirmānshāh was Ardashīr's son Ardashīr.[34]

Between the lands of the Parthian noble houses and the domains of the *shahrdārs*, one can imagine the early Sasanians cobbling together an empire from their own direct possessions in the south and west and the largely autonomous lands of their confederates. Such an arrangement formed an overlapping patchwork of autonomous authorities across the empire. This image of a mixed archipelago of allied but perhaps autonomous domains would be supportive of a decentralized reading of Sasanian authority in which the shahanshah's reign over his royal domains represented just one of many authorities within the empire. While this is the picture modern historians have of the Sasanian Empire overall, it did not look the same way from the frontier. The following sections will overview the history of Sasanian activity along the frontier of Khurāsān from Gorgān on the southeastern shore of the Caspian Sea to the Hindu Kush Mountains from the foundation of the empire through the rise of the Türk Khāqānate to help us understand how the frontiers factor into these debates regarding imperial centralization within the Sasanian Empire and the ways the Sasanian Empire shaped the contours of the frontier.

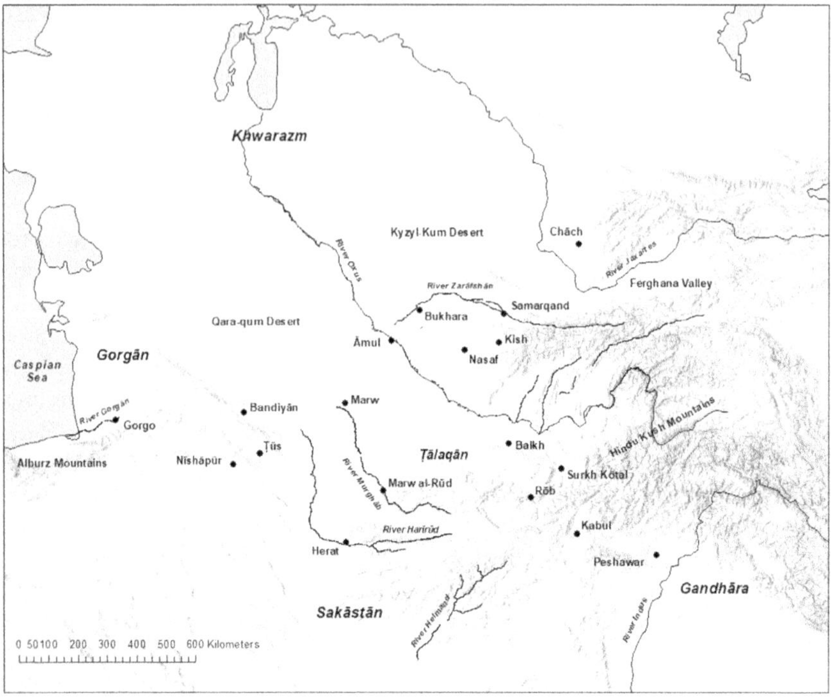

Map 4 The Eastern Frontier in Late Antiquity.

Sources: Esri, USGS, NGA, NASA, CGIAR, N Robinson, NCEAS, NLS, OS, NMA, Geodatastyrelsen, Rijkswaterstaat, GSA, Geoland, FEMA, Intermap and the GIS user community.

Vassal kings and imperial politics in the third century

As the Sasanians rose to power, their empire shared its eastern frontier with the Kushan Empire of Ṭukhāristān. Despite the image of Central Asia as peripheral or marginal, the Kushans were inheritors of a long tradition of state building in Ṭukhāristān, centred on the ancient city of Balkh, known as the 'Mother of Cities' (*umm al-bilād*) in the later Arabic traditions and home to settlements as early as 2000 BCE, and Transoxiana, whose oases were home to the Sapalli Culture as early as 3000 BCE with a tradition of urbanism that developed in the early Iron Age. The Kushans' emergence in the region in the second century BCE and rise to political ascendency in the first century CE pushed the Sakā or Scythians south into the lands which would then become Sakāstān (Sijistān or Sīstān). The Sakā themselves had ruled over a Greco–Bactrian kingdom, the legacy of Alexander the Great's conquests of oasis cities which themselves had been continuously inhabited since the seventh century BCE. Ancient authors such as Strabo and Justin (ca. second century CE) knew Bactria – which for them may have included Sogdiana – as the land of a thousand cities.[35]

This is not the place to give a detailed history of the Kushans, but a few brief comments are valuable for understanding the patterns of empire building along the eastern frontier.[36] The Kushans originated among the Yuèzhī tribes who were driven from Gānsù, China by the Xiōngnú in the second century BCE. During the first century CE, the Kushan tribe consolidated authority over the Yuèzhī and established a kingdom in Ṭukhāristān. The dates for their appearance are extremely rough and the entire chronology of the Kushan Empire remains a point of debate.[37] As mentioned in the introduction, the Greeks named the Yuèzhī *Tócharoi*, the origin of Ṭukhāristān. Despite the paucity of detailed information available to us about the Kushans, we know that at their height they extended their authority across both sides of the Hindu Kush into northern India where they established cities at Peshawar and Mathurā and to the northeast up to the Tarim Basin. In doing so, the Kushans secured the trade routes between China, India and Iran that we today call the Silk Road and acted as intermediaries between Rome and China through the ports of Makrān. It has been proposed that the Sogdian merchants of Transoxiana first travelled to China during the Kushan period.[38] Through these networks, the Kushans also promoted the expansion of Buddhism throughout Central Asia and into China.

As early as 233, Ardashīr I led campaigns into Greater Khurāsān conquering territories from Gorgān to Abarshahr, Marw and as far eastward as Balkh while extending his influence to Khwarazm in the north and Sīstān in the south. During Ardashīr's reign Marw and Sīstān were already important Sasanian mints.[39] It may be the case that by the time the Sasanians emerged the Kushans had entered a period of decline opening these regions up for quick conquest.[40] The inscriptions of the Kaʿaba-i Zardusht claim that Shāpūr I was the ruler of Kushānshahr – the lands of the Kushans or, roughly, Ṭukhāristān – as far as Peshawar.[41] A relief at Rāg-i Bībī on the northern face of the Hindu Kush between Balkh and Kabul near the Kushan temple of Surkh Kōtal depicts a king identified as Shāpūr. He hunts rhinoceros attended by men in Kushan dress, evidence for the emperor's eastern expansion.[42] As the Sasanians conquered Kushānshahr, they appointed junior members of the royal family as autonomous rulers with the title Kushānshāh.

Much like the Kushan Empire itself, little is known about the Kushano-Sasanians, as the dynasty of Sasanian vassal kings was called.[43] Written sources are lacking and much of their history must be reconstructed from coins, limiting us essentially to debates over the chronology of kings. Even their relationship to the main line of the Sasanian royal family can be difficult to disentangle at times with a lack of certainty whether they represented a true dynasty or whether the Kushānshāhs were appointed by the reigning shahanshah from his own family. Some have claimed that every heir to the Sasanian throne across the third century was first the Kushānshāh but this is not plausible.[44] Similar questions can be asked about the Sasanians' relationship with other vassal kings such as the kings of Armenia or the Sakānshāh of Sīstān. The best-documented moments in Kushano-Sasanian history, even if sparsely so, are those in which they were in conflict with the main line of the Sasanian family such as the rebellion of the Kushānshāh

Hormozd (r. ca. 270–ca. 300) against his brother the Shahanshah Bahrām II (r. 274–93) beginning around 283.[45] Even here the evidence is thin – so thin that some question whether or not it was even the Kushānshāh who revolted[46] – and the only textual sources come from scattered Roman texts primarily concerned with the opportunities this rebellion made for the Romans to attack the Sasanian capital at Ctesiphon.[47]

Although the details of his rebellion are unclear, the questions it raises about the relationship between the Sasanian emperor and his vassals are relevant to this chapter. Numismatic evidence may lead us to believe this was not a simple provincial uprising but rather an attempt to either overthrow Bahrām II or establish a rival empire in the east.[48] Some coins give Hormozd the title Kushānshāhānshāh or the 'Kushan king of kings', borrowing older Kushan royal titulature that mirrored the titles of the Iranian emperors.[49] Hormozd gained the support of the peoples of the east in his rebellion with one source, a birthday oration for the Roman Emperor Maximian (r. 286–305), listing the Sakā (Saci), Kushans (reading Rufii as a corruption of Cussis meaning Kushan) and Gēlānī (Geli, a tribe living between the River Murghāb and Ṭālaqān on the frontier between Khurāsān and Ṭukhāristān) among the forces that marched against Bahrām.[50] The Sakānshāh is the only participant in this revolt whose fate is clear as, some time before his death in 293, Bahrām II led a campaign into Sīstān and replaced him with his son and successor, the future Bahrām III (r. 293).[51] This revolt is most often viewed through the lens of competition within the Sasanian royal family. Such competition had become so fierce that in 293 the nobility revolted against Bahrām III – only four months into his reign – in the name of his great uncle Narseh (r. 293–302) to remove kingship from a toxic branch of the royal family.[52] In this revolt, Narseh – who had previously been the Sakānshāh and the king of Armenia – had the support of the Kushānshāh (still Hormozd according to the numismatic evidence) and the kings of Khwarazm, Pārdān (southeast Sīstān), Makrān, Tūrān and Gorgān, along with nobles from Herat and Dihistān.[53] He also had the support of Parthian nobles with roots in Khurāsān including Ardashīr Sūren, Hormozd Varāz and a member of the Qārin family whose first name is corrupted.[54] In the revolts of Hormozd Kushānshāh and Narseh, we see an early Sasanian Empire composed of the territories of several local kings whose loyalties needed to be earned and who acted to shape the empire, first supporting a rebellious Kushānshāh and then an ambitious prince.

In the fourth century, a long period of stability at the top during Shāpūr II's seventy-year reign (r. 309–79) and the arrival of the Chionite Huns appear to have brought these eastern lords more directly under Sasanian authority. A pair of inscriptions on door posts in the ruins of Persepolis describe the Sakānshāh Shāpūr – the brother of Shāpūr II and specified in the inscriptions as the ruler of Sind, Sīstān and Tūrān – coming to Persepolis with several nobles from Sīstān to pay tribute to the Shahanshah.[55] The reach of Shāpūr II was also recognized by the Roman soldier and historian Ammianus Marcellinus (330–95) who listed Bactriani (Ṭukhāristān), Sogdiana, Sīstān and Scythia to the foot of the Himalayas as part of the emperor's domains.[56] Shāpūr minted coins at Marw, Sīstān and Kabul alongside Kushano-Sasanian issues and he may even have struck coins at Gandhāra south of the Hindu Kush.[57] Bactrian documents from Rōb dating to Shāpūr's reign mention a satrap and even a specifically Persian satrap indicating some form of direct Sasanian rule in Ṭukhāristān.[58] In 359, Ammianus Marcellinus saw the Kushānshāh Varahrān (r. ca. 325–ca. 360) fighting and leading troops alongside Shāpūr's forces at the siege of Amida (Diyarbakr) along the upper Tigris. Ammianus thought he saw Shāpūr himself but he described a commander 'wearing in place of a diadem a golden image of a ram's head set with precious stones' that matches the image of Varahrān on his coinage rather than the image of Shāpūr on his coins.[59] Even though none of this is clear evidence for direct Sasanian rule in Kushānshahr, it is evidence for increasing Sasanian authority over their vassals during Shāpūr's reign.

This early period already highlights the tension between a centralized and decentralized model of rule. Whereas the establishment of a Sasanian prince or princes over frontier provinces implies direct Sasanian rule, signs of autonomy from the minting of coins with local titles to the revolts of Hormozd and Narseh with the support of eastern nobles demonstrate that such loyalty was not always assured. As such, the Kushānshāhs are reminiscent of the European margraves or march lords, rulers of the marchlands whose position on the edges, distant from the royal centre, granted them great autonomy and opportunity.[60] While the participation of the Kushānshāh in the siege of Amida may demonstrate the Kushano-Sasanians fighting in service to the emperor, it also came at a time when Kushānshahr was under threat from new Hunnic invaders (to be discussed shortly) and Varahrān may in fact be a refugee at Shāpūr's court. At the least, the Kushano-Sasanians inspire us to expand the dynastic and feudal umbrellas of the decentralization model to include vassal kings and cadet branches of the Sasanian family acting autonomously.

The individualized identities of the regions along the eastern frontier would also encourage a level of decentralization. Kushānshahr had its own language (Bactrian using the Greek script) and distinct religious identities (Buddhist along with Zoroastrian) challenging integration within a Persian and Zoroastrian Sasanian Empire. The Kushano-Sasanians could attempt to imprint their identity in the region by establishing fire temples, including Zoroastrian iconography on their coins, shifting from gold to silver issues and possibly even persecuting Buddhists. Yet there would always be a palimpsest of the pre-existing cultures which would shape the way a Sasanian imperial identity was employed – Mithra was preferred to Ahura Mazda and his image on coins evolved out of representations of the Hindu god Shiva, for example.[61] The Bactrian documents reflect this kind of mixed identity whereby people with Pahlavi names use Bactrian month names and engage in social practices against Sasanian norms such as polyandry.[62] As Rezakhani observed, 'The Kushano-Sasanians developed their own particular style in art and architecture, drawn from sources other than Iran, which included India, and formed an independent identity from the Sasanians.'[63] Even if there is some truth to Roman Ghirshman's often-repeated refrain that state-sponsored

Zoroastrianism checked Buddhism on the Helmand, Ṭukhāristān remained an important Buddhist centre and key link between Indian and Chinese practitioners from the Kushano–Sasanian era up through the Arab–Muslim conquests.[64] Analysis of toponyms indicated that Buddhism had spread across Iran as far west as Hamadān, but the rise of the Sasanians saw the closure of all Buddhist monasteries in their domains with the exception of the famous Naw Bahār or *nava vihāra* meaning new Buddhist monastery in Balkh.[65] Despite the Kushano–Sasanian attempt to bring Kushānshahr under Sasanian authority, it would remain firmly 'not Iran', or what Richard Frye called a 'Kushan-Bactrian sphere of influence' whose impact was seen long after the fall of the Sasanians.[66]

Shifting balances along the Hunnic frontier of the fourth century

The fourth century brought new migrations of Iranian Huns into Ṭukhāristān and Transoxiana that re-shuffled the dynamics of the eastern frontier. The complex relationship between each wave of newcomers is often a point of contention among modern scholars and it can be difficult to tell where an older inhabitation ended and a newer one began.[67] It is likely that each of these groups had some connection to the Xiōngnú who had been dominating the Inner Asian steppes since at least the fourth century BCE. Much of the debate surrounding the identity of these groups focused not only on the relationship between the Huns and the Xiōngnú but also between the Iranian Huns and the Huns who arrived in Europe in the late fourth century.[68] One challenge inherent in this debate is the lack of textual evidence from the Xiōngnú or the Huns and the reliance on texts in multiple languages from Latin in the West to Chinese in the East and every language in between, each with its own terminology for these peoples. Another problem is that we too often assume the identity of these newcomers is an ethnicity when it is more accurate to see the Xiōngnú, Huns and their affiliates as part of a larger political coalition of steppe peoples.[69] It may in fact be more accurate to think of the term 'Hun' as a catch-all for a variety of unrelated Iranian- and Altaic-speaking nomads.[70] Peter Golden described the ethno-genesis of another confederacy of steppe nomads, the Turks, in these terms: 'In reality these communities were always polyethnic and political in character. Its members consisted of both those who were, indeed, born into it and those who joined it. Thus, it became a community of "descent through tradition" as well as through recognition of political leadership of a charismatic clan.'[71] Finally, in constructing a political history of the region we may write as if one group dislodged and replaced another when, on the ground, there is really a layering, mixing and re-mixing of peoples. In general, as various Hunnic groups 'distinguished themselves with particular ethnonyms and political symbols on their coinage' they seem to have also participated in a form of 'collective sovereignty' in a way that 'provided a measure of political and economic unity … from the late fourth through the sixth centuries'.[72] Regardless, the introduction of Hunnic peoples during the fourth and fifth centuries drastically changed the dynamic of the eastern frontier and began a period when the Sasanian emperors needed to regularly defend and reinforce the frontier with large investments of men and treasure.

The first wave of Hunnic migrants to Ṭukhāristān and Transoxiana who received attention from our sources were a group of Iranian-speaking nomads known as the Chionites.[73] The earliest record of the Chionites came in 350 when Shāpūr II received news of invasions in the east and promptly turned away from the siege of the Roman fortress of Nisibis to attend to the matter.[74] Shāpūr campaigned in the east from 356 to 358 against the Chionites, the Gelānī and a people called the Euseni, who were presumably the Cuseni or Kushans but could also be the Kushano–Sasanians or the Kidarites who adopted the title Kushānshāh and were called Kushans by some contemporary sources.[75] Shāpūr made peace with the Chionites and their allies and in 359 the Chionites and Gelānī fought alongside the emperor and the Kushānshāh Varahrān in Mesopotamia (perhaps evidence that the aforementioned Euseni were the Kushano–Sasanians).[76] Ammianus Marcellinus detailed the death of the son of the Chionite King Gurambad during the battle and the seven days of feasting that accompanied his cremation.[77] The appearance of the Chionites, Gelānī and Kushānshāh in Mesopotamia and their allegiance to Shāpūr may be the result of increased Sasanian influence in the east, but it may also be a response to the rise of the Kidarite dynasty who drove them from Ṭukhāristān.

Thanks to the numismatic evidence, we can track the decline of the Kushano–Sasanians and Sasanian authority in the east against the rise of the Hunnic Kidarites in Ṭukhāristān and Alkhans along the southern face of the Hindu Kush.[78] Both of these dynasties, identified based on their coin issues, may have branched off from the Chionites or they may represent separate Hunnish migrations. Kushano–Sasanian coin production declined noticeably under Varahrān and came to a complete end after 360, implying a loss of political authority when he appears in Mesopotamia. This was followed by a period of more direct Sasanian rule in the east during which the imperial mint itself may have moved from Ctesiphon to Kabul, something that might occur if the emperor was campaigning in the region for an extended period.[79] The fifth-century Armenian historian Pʿawstos Buzand provided accounts of two such campaigns against the king of the 'Kushans'– likely the Kidarites – who made his capital at Balkh, the first dated sometime between 363 and 368 and the second around 375.[80] This second campaign resulted in a tragic defeat for the Sasanians that effectively ended Sasanian control in Ṭukhāristān though they were able to hold onto mints further east including Kabul and Taxila in Gandhāra.[81] This situation lasted until approximately 384 when Kabul was captured along with its mint and the Alkhan dynasty began striking coins using not only captured and modified Sasanian dies but also gold and silver looted from the Sasanian treasury.[82] By the end of the fourth century, coins similar in style to the Kushano–Sasanian issues appeared featuring the name Kidara marking the beginning of a recognizable Kidarite dynasty.

After several waves of Hunnish invasions, Ṭukhāristān would, with brief exceptions, fall out of the Sasanian sphere of influence and the eastern limits of the empire would be increasingly situated along the River Murghāb between the administrative regions of Harēy (Herat) and Marw. The Huns entered Ṭukhāristān as nomads, but upon their arrival they established their own states ruling over the settled populations and largely settled and urbanized.[83] The relationship between the Sasanians and their neighbours, including the shape of the frontier itself, was then determined by relative strengths of the two parties and from this point forward the Sasanians' frontier policy would need to focus on preventing and minimizing the damage from invasions and raids.

The apparent stabilization of the frontier between the Kidarites and the Sasanians allowed the Huns to consolidate authority over Ṭukhāristān and expand into Sogdiana. A half-century gap in Sasanian coinage found at Chinese markets between the reigns of Shāpūr III (r. 383–8) and Bahrām Gūr and the appearance of Kidarite coinage at the same markets indicates that they also consolidated authority over the 'Silk Road' trade into China and excluded the Sasanians.[84] Large-scale building projects and the flourishing of the arts in Sogdiana during the Kidarite period may be connected to their control over this trade in which the Sogdian merchants were important players.[85] As Étienne de la Vaissière reminded,

> Contrary to the commonly held opinion that the Hun invasions created a series of economic, demographic and political disasters, the Hunnic period, from 350 to the second half of the fifth century, was, after the invasions themselves, a time of rapid development in Sogdiana, thanks to significant contributions of population and to a certain political stability over the course of three generations.[86]

This was not necessarily a universal experience and there is evidence that the Hunnic migrations resulted in serious economic decline further north in Khwarazm.[87] Similarly, limited excavations in Ṭukhāristān have shown the abandonment of many settlements and irrigation systems and the movement of populations into the mountains.[88]

Much of the building undertaken by the Kidarites had a military purpose and was matched by similar projects on the Sasanian side of the frontier. Based on the available archaeological evidence, we see that the frontier became increasingly fortified with 'city fortresses' constructed on both sides.[89] Paykand, remembered in the Arabic tradition as the 'city of merchants', was founded in the Bukhara oasis at this time. Most likely with a defensive purpose, it secured the frontier between the Kidarites and Sasanians near the Oxus crossing at Āmul (Türkmenabat) between Marw and Bukhara.[90] On the Sasanian side the cities of Khurāsān were expanded and migrations of people (sometimes forced) arrived in the east to settle the frontier. As early as Shāpūr II's campaigns against the Chionites, the shahanshah directed large-scale construction projects at Nīshāpūr, perhaps founding the city itself but certainly building the *quhandiz* or citadel that formed the centre of the city.[91] From Nīshāpūr, a garrison could respond to incursions from Gorgān to Sīstān and, throughout the Sasanian period, Nīshāpūr would remain a small but heavily fortified and politically and economically significant city.[92] There may have been similar projects at Marw that stood much more directly on the frontier with the Huns and the city appears to have hosted an army during Shāpūr's campaigns.[93] It may also have been during Shāpūr's campaigns that the prominent Christian community in Marw was established through the forced relocation of Christians away from the Byzantine frontier and towards areas in need of increased population and labour.[94]

The ensuing campaigns brought more projects to the east. While much of the literary evidence for the campaign of Bahrām Gūr is problematic, echoing later conflicts between the Sasanian royal family and the Parthian nobility, we know of some important building projects associated with it. The circumstances of his border tower are unclear, as discussed at the beginning of this chapter, but it was built near Kushmayhan between Marw and Āmul. The *Shahristānīha-i Īrānshahr* reports that Bahrām also founded the important frontier city of Marw al-Rūd (riverine Marw) along the River Murghāb towards the frontier of Ṭukhāristān during his campaigns.[95] Regardless of the relationship between the Sasanian royal family and the provinces under normal circumstances, campaigns such as these brought increased imperial attention and created opportunities for the shahanshah to assert his direct authority in the east. According to Ṭabarī, Bahrām Gūr appointed a *marzbān-i Kushān* – a warden of the Kushan marches – who may have been his brother Narseh who Ibn Qutayba (828–89) claimed was named governor of Khurāsān.[96] Bahrām's victory over the Kidarites was celebrated both in contemporary artwork, including the stucco panels found at Bandiyān near Darreh Gaz, southeast of modern Ashgabat on the Iran–Turkmenistan border, and in later literary accounts that celebrate the jewels and pearls from the 'khāqān's' diadem that Bahrām donated to the fire temple of Ādur-Gushnasp in Azerbaijan.[97]

Bahrām's son and successor Yazdgird II led numerous campaigns to regain control of Ṭukhāristān from the Kidarites with varying levels of success. He resided in the east for seven years, between 442 and 449, making his base at Nīshāpūr and commanding nobles from across the empire to come and fight along the frontier in two-year cycles.[98] Yazdgird also founded the city of Shahristān-i Kūmis (Shahr-e Qūmis) approximately 450 km west of Nīshāpūr.[99] In 450, he led another campaign that captured Ṭālaqān and chased the Kidarites into their supposedly impregnable desert fortresses.[100] During a subsequent campaign in 453 or 454, he brought a large number of Armenian nobles and clergy who had been imprisoned following a revolt in 450 to Nīshāpūr, but after a humiliating defeat at the hands of the Kidarites, he had them executed.[101] In the aftermath of this loss, the Sasanians were forced to pay the Kidarites tribute, which they did until 456 when Yazdgird led a successful assault that came close to ending Kidarite rule in Ṭukhāristān.[102] On the precipice of victory, the emperor suddenly died. Yazdgird had not left a clear line of succession and fighting broke out between two of his sons, Hormozd III and Pīrūz. As described at the beginning of the chapter, Pīrūz, who was the Sakānshāh at the time of his father's death, defeated his brother with the assistance of another group of Iranian Huns, the Hephthalites, to whom Pīrūz had promised Ṭālaqān.[103]

The Kidarite period was important in defining the eastern frontier of the Sasanian Empire, developing a contested zone between the Sasanians on the

River Murghāb and their neighbours in Sogdiana and Ṭukhāristān. Migrations of people from the Inner Asian steppe led to conflicts on the frontiers of the empire that forced redefinitions of the extent of the empire. Early instances of the Chionites fighting against the Romans as part of the Sasanian army indicate that the Sasanians tried to incorporate their new neighbours into their imperial networks as vassals, perhaps even replacements for the Kushano-Sasanians, but such arrangements were not long lived and conflict across the frontier was more common. Ṭukhāristān fell out of the Sasanian sphere of influence with Balkh becoming the centre of Kidarite and later Hephthalite authority. Meanwhile, Herat, which we know from numismatic evidence had been more closely associated with the Kushano-Sasanians, became more integrated into the empire and played an increasingly strategic role in maintaining the frontier against the Kidarites and their successors.[104] The expansion of the Kidarite kingdom into Sogdiana stretched the frontier between themselves and the Sasanians to the west as well with Bahrām Gūr's campaign against his eastern neighbours focused on the region around Marw. The frontier as it developed between the Sasanians and Kidarites in the early fifth century would, with minor changes, hold after the Kidarites were replaced by newer arrivals from the steppe.

With the rise of the Kidarites as a formidable rival in the east, the Sasanians found themselves invested in large-scale and long-term campaigns on the eastern frontier. These campaigns involved the movement of the court to the east where the shahanshah would reside sometimes for years. Populations from the western reaches of the empire were likewise permanently relocated to the east and settled in the growing cities of the frontier such as Nīshāpūr, Marw and Marw al-Rūd. The foundation and expansion of cities and the construction of forts and other infrastructure related to the defence of the frontier clearly involved some form of centralized imperial authority. From our literary sources, it appears that during this period the Sasanian state took direct responsibility for the maintenance of the frontier in a way that questions the image of a western-focused Sasanian state. The attention the eastern frontier received from the Sasanians would only increase as the Kidarites were replaced by new Hunnic invaders, the Hephthalites.

Pīrūz and the Great Wall of Gorgān: Building the frontier

In the mid-fifth century, the Hephthalites emerged as the next Hunnic migrants to Central Asia.[105] Whereas the appearance of the Kidarites had altered the shape of the frontier and pushed Ṭukhāristān out of Sasanian reach, the Hephthalites threatened Sasanian authority in Khurāsān. Their arrival challenged Kidarite power early on and partially instigated the conflicts that began with Yazdgird II as the Hephthalites unsettled Ṭukhāristān and Sogdiana and pressured the Kidarites to expand outward. As is common with such migrations, developments in Mongolia sent the Hephthalites west and set off a chain reaction that pushed the Kidarites towards war with Yazdgird. In the decade after Pīrūz's initial alliance with the Hephthalites, detailed at the beginning of the chapter, the latter conquered Ṭukhāristān and began to push into Sogdiana, likely in an alliance with the Sasanians who thought themselves the beneficiaries of the destruction of the Kidarite kingdom. The Sasanians are credited with military victories over the Kidarites in some of our sources, or at least credited with boasting about them 'in barbaric fashion … since they wished to advertise the very large force which they had present', but it was the Hephthalites who achieved territorial gains in the long run.[106] In some instances, the rulers who filled the void of the collapsed Kidarite kingdom in Ṭukhāristān bridged a gap between the Sasanians and their neighbours. For example, in the Bactrian documents we find 'Mēyam, the king of the people of Kadag, the governor of the famous and prosperous king of kings Pīrūz', identifying him as both an autonomous king and a Sasanian governor.[107] Mēyam most likely ruled from the Badakhshan Valley of eastern Ṭukhāristān as a member of the Alkhan dynasty but his relationship to Pīrūz may signal the type of alliances the shahanshah had formed during his struggle against his brother.[108] The dating of the document to 461–2, early in Pīrūz's reign, also points to a period during which the emperor was still on good terms with his eastern allies. The Kidarite capital near Balkh was captured in 467 and the Kidarites were then pushed south into Gandhāra where they maintained a smaller state for at least another decade. As noted, the balance of power between the Sasanians and Hephthalites was not as stable or peaceful as Pīrūz may have hoped when he first allied with these newcomers against his brother Hormozd, and Pīrūz led up to three failed campaigns against the Hephthalites, leaving the Sasanians to pay tribute to their neighbours to prevent further invasions.

The impact of Pīrūz's losses was great, resulting in the payment of tribute and eventually the death of the shahanshah and the destruction of the Sasanian army. But in contrast to this image of total failure on the eastern frontier, there may also be evidence of territorial expansion and large-scale construction projects along the frontier. It was most likely during Pīrūz's reign that the 195-km Great Wall of Gorgān (also known as the Sadd-i Iskandar or Wall of Alexander, Sadd-i Pīrūz and Sadd-i Anūshīrwān) was built between the Caspian coast and the Alburz Mountains just north of the River Gorgān. Various dates have been suggested for the construction of the wall, from the time of Alexander the Great through the late Sasanian period with many arguing for a Parthian origin, but recent archaeological excavations have somewhat settled this debate, dating the wall to the mid-fifth century, in line with Pīrūz's reign.[109] This wall and the thirty-six forts built along it blocked access to the plains of Gorgān along the Caspian Sea, denying one path by which invaders from the steppes arrived in Iran. The area north of the wall has been suggested by the Byzantine diplomat Priscus (d. after 472) as the site of a campaign by Pīrūz against the Kidarite king Kunkhas.[110]

The construction and garrisoning of the wall and its forts, as well as the fortifications on the western shore of the Caspian at Derbent known as Bāb al-Abwāb or the Gate of Gates, were partially financed by the Byzantines who saw the Sasanians as an important buffer between themselves and the Central Asian steppe empires.[111] Byzantine contributions towards a shared defence of the Caucasian frontier, presented as a Sasanian service to the defence of the Byzantine

Empire, had been formalized by treaty in 363 and renewed regularly through Pīrūz's reign.[112] In 465, Pīrūz had sent delegates to Constantinople to ask the Emperor Leo I (r. 457–74) for financial support in his war against the Huns, expanding the existing policy of shared defence to the east as well. The Emperor Zeno (r. 474–5, 476–91) continued to make regular contributions to the Sasanians for these purposes during Pīrūz's reign, helping finance the shahanshah's campaign against the Hephthalites and even paying part of his ransom after he was captured.[113] Not only was the defence of the frontiers against the Huns a centralized project of the Sasanian Empire but it also required formal support from their Byzantine rivals.

We often assume that walls such as these were entirely defensive, built to prevent the incursion of foreign raiders, but if we look more holistically at the campaigns of Pīrūz, we may be able to identify offensive origins for the wall. In all of our sources, Pīrūz is portrayed as an aggressive emperor. In each of his campaigns, it is his desire to push forward without thinking or heeding advice – running into a mountain valley, pursuing a wild goose chase through endless deserts and eventually riding head first into a ditch – that led to his defeat. These actions and the story of him dragging Bahrām Gūr's tower before his army do not sound like the actions of a man who would sit back on the defensive. Even though elements of each of these narratives are fictional and mythologizing, they show an image of Pīrūz as an emperor with an aggressive personality that has been passed down over centuries and across numerous historiographical traditions. The Armenian chronicler Łazar P'arpec'i, a contemporary of Pīrūz, was particularly harsh on this account, describing Pīrūz as a tyrant whose campaigns against the Hephthalites showed no concern for the lives of his soldiers. P'arpec'i went as far as saying the blood of those who died on these campaigns was on Pīrūz's hands.[114] Although the general impression is of a hot-headed emperor rushing from one defeat to the next, one source does credit Pīrūz with victories. In the sixth century, Pseudo-Joshua the Stylite wrote that 'Peroz subdued the Huns, seized many places within their territory, and added them to his kingdom before he was eventually taken prisoner'.[115] This account of Pīrūz's reign then continues with his final two defeats and death. Pseudo-Joshua's description of Pīrūz's territorial gains can be tied to his campaign against the Kidarites at Gorgān and the area around the great wall and we may want to consider the construction of the wall in the context of a momentarily victorious Pīrūz rather than a Pīrūz whose domain was under threat.

Recent scholarship on the Great Wall of China has emphasized the potential offensive nature of walls and other linear barriers in not only protecting recently captured territories but also in laying claim to them and building an association between the conquerors and the conquered lands. The wall, in such a situation, is not just to keep the invaders out but to keep the territory and its inhabitants in.[116] If we follow Pseudo-Joshua despite the fact he gives no specifics about these successful campaigns, we can imagine Pīrūz achieving some early victories against the Kidarites along the shores of the Caspian, pushing them north beyond the plains of Gorgān where he then builds a wall to consolidate his successes before attempting to advance further in a campaign that ended in failure. Procopius (ca. 500–ca. 554) described Gorgo, near the modern city of Gonbad-e Kāvus, as the city of the Hephthalites (likely meaning Kidarites) at the time of Pīrūz's first disastrous campaign, but, notably, Gorgo lies immediately to the south of the wall.[117] Therefore, Pīrūz must have had some success in pushing the Kidarites back before building the wall. Pīrūz is also remembered for other building projects in Gorgān, including the possible foundation of a city between the wall and the plains of Gorgān, which would indicate a plan to settle and further integrate the plains of Gorgān into the Sasanian Empire.[118]

In general, maintaining, garrisoning and provisioning a wall of this magnitude, not to mention its three dozen forts, would have been a major investment only possible if the agricultural lands south of the River Gorgān saw increased production and/or increased provisions were brought from elsewhere in the empire. Raising domesticated animals – especially sheep and goats – must be included in this equation as archaeological evidence has shown a reliance along the wall on these herd animals as a food source unevenly complemented by fish and water fowl at sites closer to the Caspian Sea.[119] Estimates based on archaeological evidence and comparisons to similar sites place a garrison of around 22,500 men at the Wall of Gorgān.[120] The need for increased agricultural production would still be the case if, as some have argued, the real strength of the Sasanian army was a cavalry force kept at a centralized location such as Nīshāpūr, which could respond to the appearance of a threat anywhere from Gorgān to Sīstān with a minimal garrison at the wall itself.[121] It would also still be the case if the wall was built by the Sasanian emperor but regular maintenance and garrisoning was the responsibility of local elites, as may also be the case. In the end, the very existence of such a massive building project clearly dated to the fifth century complete with barracks for a garrison numbering in the tens of thousands should make us consider the question of just how centralized or decentralized the Sasanian state really was.[122] At least at the frontiers, it appears that money and men could be found to maintain large defensive infrastructure on a scale that must have required some form of centralized authority. Similarly, those projects that have been excavated – not just in the east but around the empire – show a homogeneity of style that implies some form of centralized coordination, meaning that frontier fortifications were not entirely the purview of local lords.[123]

Qubād and the Sasanian–Hephthalite alliance

The death of Pīrūz and the ascendency of the Hephthalites constituted major challenges to the Sasanian state. The destruction of the Sasanian army left Iran open and the total conquest of the empire by the Hephthalites appeared to be a real possibility. Procopius stated that the Sasanian Empire was made subject and tributary of the Hephthalites who ruled over them for two years.[124] Similarly, the tribute paid by Pīrūz and continued by his son Qubād (r. 488–96, 499–531) and grandson Khusrow I Anūshīrwān was a substantial portion of the Sasanian monetary supply, so much so that Sasanian coins with Hephthalite counter-stamps still commonly appear in Afghan markets today.[125] The appearance of countermarked Sasanian coins in Chinese hordes further indicates that they were used for trade between the Hephthalites and China.[126] It is likely that, during this period, Sasanian silver channelled through the Hephthalites reached Sogdiana and underwrote the expansion of their merchant networks connecting the region to China.[127] The Hephthalites also became important players in the court politics of the Sasanian Empire with a proposed pro-Hephthalite faction among the nobility jockeying for control of the throne.

Pīrūz's brother Bīlāsh (r. 484–8) succeeded the deceased shahanshah with the support of the Qārinid noble Parthian family under the leadership of a man named Sūkhrā (d. 493) who is portrayed as the real power behind the throne. Sūkhrā is credited with leading a reprisal campaign against Akhshunwār that recovered many captives and much of the loot that had been lost – most likely a reflection of a campaign that re-established Sasanian authority in Khurāsān.[128] Much as his father had done, Pīrūz's son Qubād, who had lived for at least two years as a hostage at the court of Akhshunwār, contested Bīlāsh's claims and fled to the Hephthalites who promised him military support against his uncle, which was slow to materialize, most likely because Qubād was around ten years old at the time of his father's death.[129] When Qubād did achieve the throne four years later, it is portrayed in our sources as the result of Sūkhrā's activities and his reign was dominated by conflicts between the Sasanian royal family and the Parthian noble families.[130] By 496, these tensions fed a coup that resulted in Qubād's imprisonment and the ascension of his brother Zāmāsp (r. 496–8). Qubād's turn in fortune is often associated with his support for a heretical priest named Mazdak (d. 528) who preached a populist interpretation of Zoroastrianism that has been called proto-communist and antagonistic towards the nobility who turned on the shahanshah.[131] With the aid of a female relative and Zarmihr, the son of Sūkhrā (d. 558), Qubād escaped prison and fled once again to the Hephthalites with whom he resided for three years.[132] In return for ceding control of Chaghāniyān in northern Ṭukhāristān and tribute in the form of Sasanian dirhams with Hephthalite counter-stamps, the Hephthalites gave Qubād a force of 30,000 men with which he retook the throne.[133] The grant of Chaghāniyān opened up Sogdiana to the Hephthalites and in 509 they were able to capture Samarqand, as evidenced by the switch from Sogdian to Hephthalite embassies at Chinese courts.[134]

The connections between the Hephthalites and Sasanian and Parthian nobility are notable. Qubād had spent at least a decade of his life at the Hephthalite court, first as a hostage during his father's reign and then twice as a refugee during the reigns of his uncle Bīlāsh and brother Zāmāsp. He married a Hephthalite princess who was his own niece, the daughter of his sister Pīrūzdukht who was captured during one of Pīrūz's failed campaigns and made one of Akhshunwār's wives.[135] Some have even seen competition between a pro-Hephthalite faction and a pro-Roman faction within the Sasanian Empire led by the Qārinid and Mihrānid Parthian families, respectively.[136] The Kanārangīyān Parthian family, whose territories in Ṭūs put them directly on the Hephthalite frontier, appear to have had special animosity and concern for Qubād's relationship with their Hunnish neighbours. When Qubād was deposed, the Kanārang Gushnāspdād (d. 488) argued that it would be best to kill Qubād instead of imprisoning him. He told the conspiring nobles, 'You see this knife, how extremely small it is; nevertheless it is able at the present time to accomplish a deed which, be assured, my dear Persians, a little later two myriads of mail clad men could not bring to pass.'[137] Upon regaining the throne, Qubād had Gushnāspdād killed and replaced as the Kanārang.[138] The Hephthalites not only helped Qubād against his domestic rivals, but there is also evidence of Hephthalite troops marching with Qubād during the Anastasian War (502–6) against the Byzantines, specifically at Qubād's siege of Theodosiopolis (Erzurum) then in Western Armenia and Amida and Edessa in Mesopotamia.[139]

Any alliance between the Sasanians and the Hephthalites benefitted both sides. Besides the monetary tribute the Hephthalites earned, the apparent stabilization of the frontier allowed them to engage in campaigns of expansion in both Sogdiana and to the northeast towards the Tarim Basin where they conquered several cities that had been within the Chinese sphere of influence.[140] The strength of the Hephthalites, it can be argued, came from their ability to extract wealth from their sedentary subjects and tributary neighbours and distribute it among the nomadic military elite. The Hephthalites were not mere nomadic raiders and they established and organized a sophisticated state on the Sasanians' frontier. In the words of Procopius,

> The Ephthalitae are of the stock of the Huns in fact as well as in name; however they do not mingle with any of the Huns known to us. … For they are not nomads like the other Hunnic peoples, but for a long period have been established in a goodly land. … It is also true that their manner of living is unlike that of their kinsmen, nor do they live a savage life as they do; but they are ruled by one king, and since they possess a lawful constitution, they observe right and justice in their dealings both with one another and with their neighbours, in no degree less than the Romans and Persians.[141]

The Bactrian documents confirm such a picture, with economic documents referencing a specific Hephthalite tax collected as tribute as well as Hephthalite scribes.[142] The Hephthalites were able to adapt and incorporate pre-existing economic and political institutions and build a state in Ṭukhāristān and Sogdiana that resembled what had come before it, incorporating both Sasanian institutions and the administrative apparatus of the Sogdian city states. The Bactrian documents give local lords Iranian titles while seals show them in Iranian dress as they acted as agents of the Hephthalites, such as the '*kadagbid* of the famous (and) prosperous *yab*[*ghu*] of Hephthal' who acted as an intermediary between the nobility of Kadagistān and the Hephthalites.[143] In doing so, the Hephthalites were continuing a tradition of rule established by the Xiōngnú and repeated by the Huns and Turks who integrated nomadic military elites with agrarian systems of surplus extraction to effect maximum social and economic power.[144]

The Hephthalites were the culmination of the Hunnic advance into Central Asia. They were not 'barbarian' hordes as our sources both medieval and modern want to dismiss them. Instead they established a state that was capable of extracting wealth in the form of taxation and tribute and plying political influence over Iran. It is for this reason that Frantz Grenet has referred to the period from 470 to 560 as the period of the *Imperial* Hephthalites.[145] Hephthalite dominance did not last and, much as they had pushed aside the Kidarites, it took the rise of another Inner Asian steppe power to dislodge them. From Pīrūz's wall to Qubād's employment of the Hephthalites against his internal and external rivals, the eastern frontier was again the site of a strongly centralized imperial presence and a region that required a great deal of investment in money as well as manpower and time from the shahanshah.

The coming of the Turks and the eastern frontier at the end of the Sasanian Empire

The dynamic across the eastern frontier shifted again during the reign of Khusrow, partially not only due to changes the shahanshah pursued within the Sasanian Empire that will be addressed in the following chapter, but also due to the arrival of the Türk Khāqānate. The Turks, an Altaic-speaking people from Mongolia, first emerged as their own power in 552 when, under the leadership of Bumïn Khāqān, they overthrew the Róurán Khāqānate, a nomadic confederation that had ruled Mongolia from the mid-fourth until the mid-sixth century and whose rise to power may have initiated the Hunnic migrations of the fourth century.[146] The Türks emerged from the Āshǐnà clan, of probable Xiōngnú descent, part of the military nobility of the Róurán.[147] The destruction of the Róurán by one of its confederate members, often referred to as the Róuráns' slaves, demonstrates the fragility of steppe coalitions and the possibility for rivals within the coalition to change the character of the association quickly. As with the Huns, discussed earlier in this chapter, the largely political nature of the confederations that formed on the steppe often leave us confused about the specific identities of and relationships between its members. To what extent did the Turks represent a new movement and to what extent did they represent a changing of the guard within an existing organization? Because we have a clearer history of Turk origins, it does not seem as confused as the blurred lines between various Hunnic groups discussed earlier, but we should imagine that similar dynamics had existed among earlier waves of migrants and invaders.

Bumïn died shortly after taking power and the Türk Khāqānate was divided between his son Mùqǎn who ruled the east and his brother Istämi (r. 553–75) who ruled the west. Under Istämi, the Western Turks moved to challenge the power of the Hephthalites, winning a major victory against them at a site called Gol-Zarriūn in Transoxiana, and, eventually, the Sasanians.[148] According to our literary sources, as early as 557 Istämi, known as Sinjibū Khāqān in Arabic sources and Silziboulos in Greek sources, made an alliance with Khusrow against the Hephthalites, including a diplomatic marriage between the shahanshah and a Turkish princess.[149] The Hephthalites were crushed between the Turks and

Sasanians, with Khusrow conquering Ṭukhāristān, including Zābulistān, Kabul and Chaghāniyān, while Istämi conquered Chāch, Ferghana, Samarqand, Kish (Shahr-i Sabaz), Nasaf (also known as Nakshshab and Qarshi since the thirteenth century) and territories down to Bukhara.[150] Ṭabarī adds that Istämi killed the Hephthalite king, while Masʿūdī wrote that Khusrow killed him in revenge for his grandfather Pīrūz.[151] Despite the seemingly overwhelming nature of this victory, it did not in fact mean the end of Hephthalite authority, at least not in the territories claimed by the Sasanians. By the 580s our literary sources show the Hephthalites again ruling Ṭukhāristān, but this time as the vassals of the Turks. Michael Jackson Bonner has argued that this transition appears messy because the Sasanians did not actually participate in the conquest of the Hephthalite Empire but used its destruction for propaganda purposes.[152] Regardless, the transition from the Hephthalite rule was complicated and control was contested throughout the sixth century. The Bactrian documents tell of local lords who were forced to pay tribute to both the Hephthalites and the Sasanians at the same time, most likely stuck in a position that neither side could effectively hold but both could threaten.[153] Numismatic evidence similarly shows spotty Sasanian rule in Balkh and elsewhere that does not line up neatly with the narrative presented by our literary sources.[154] What may likely be the case is a situation like the one described in the previous chapter in which the major urban centre of Ṭukhāristān, Balkh, along with some isolated regions such as the province of Kadagistān, which is known only from the Bactrian documents and administrative seals, retained a connection to the Sasanian Empire while the Hephthalites held the lands around them.[155]

The collapse of the Hephthalite domains made neighbours of the Türk Khāqānate and the Sasanian Empire, both sharing a border that ran the length of the River Oxus. Further Turkish expansion to the west and around the Caspian Sea saw them dominate the western steppes and its people and extend this frontier down to the Caucasus where they also shared a border with the Sasanians. Khusrow is noted at the time for improving the fortifications on either side of the Caspian, Bāb al-Abwāb at Derbent and the Great Wall of Gorgān.[156] Combined with older system of fortifications in Mesopotamia and the Wall of the Arabs (*War-i Tāzigān* in Pahlavi and *Khandaq Sābūr* in Arabic) stretching from the Persian Gulf to the site of Baṣra – both founded by Shāpūr II – these fortifications formed what some have called a *limes sasanicus* that shielded the empire from its neighbours.[157] This project could be considered akin to the *bianqiang* or 'border barriers' of the Ming Empire (r. 1368–1644) which connected and reinforced pre-existing walls to form what we call today the Great Wall of China.[158]

The rivalry that developed along the Oxus between the Sasanians and Turks can be understood largely in economic terms. Turkish expansion was not necessarily about territory but about gaining access to wealth and the produce of settled empires. In this the Western Turks were attempting to copy the success of their eastern brethren who received tribute from multiple Chinese states. Ṭabarī illustrates this relationship between the Turks and the Sasanians as a continuation of the tributary relationship between the Sasanians and their neighbours during the reigns of Pīrūz and Qubād. In his account the people of the Caucasus who had come under Turkish authority, namely the Abkhāz and Balanjar, tell Istämi about the tribute the Sasanians had previously paid them to prevent incursions. Upon learning of this, Istämi raised a force of an exaggerated 110,000 warriors with the intention of forcing similar tribute. His attacks in the Caucasus and Gorgān were frustrated by the walls Khusrow had reinforced and garrisoned.[159] Other accounts make it seem that there were possibilities for friendly trade between the two powers, mostly focused on the Sogdian silk trade.

The Eastern Turks were receiving large amounts of raw silk as tribute from the Northern Zhou (r. 557–81) and Northern Qin (r. 550–77) of China and they needed a market where they could sell it.[160] According to the sixth-century Byzantine soldier and historian Menander Protector, the Sogdian merchants who had fallen under Turkish authority asked Istämi to send an embassy to the Sasanians requesting that they open up their markets to them so that the Sogdians could sell the silk in Iran.[161] De la Vaissière has portrayed this approach towards the Sasanians in terms of the Sogdian merchants employing Turkish military might to force their way into the Sasanians markets under a Turco–Sogdian alliance.[162] Richard Payne sees this as an extension of a larger trade network through which 'the security nomadic imperial structures afforded Sogdian merchants minimized what practitioners of New Institutional Economics call transaction cost, the obstacles to efficient, low-risk, and profitable trade.'[163] Khusrow refused and even burnt the silk the merchants brought with their first embassy. Khusrow's refusal was multilayered; there was an economic interest in preserving Sasanian monopolies over trade with Byzantium but there were also political considerations in limiting the Sogdians' access to the empire and their ability to spy for the Turks. The burning of the silk also showed contempt for the Turks and the spoils they had gained from their Chinese tributaries – presumably using the silk would have been a public sign of their rival's successes.[164] When the Sogdians and Turks then turned to Byzantium, with their first embassy arriving in Constantinople in 568, looking to open a northern trade route to the capital, a trade war kicked off between the Byzantines and Sasanians. It was in this context that the Sasanians conquered Yemen, allowing them to monopolize the maritime trade between the Byzantine Empire and India as well.[165] Unfortunately for the Sogdians and Turks, by this time the Byzantines had developed their own silk industry and were establishing price controls to protect local silk merchants and manufacturers.[166]

While the Huns had been a threat to the Sasanian and Byzantine Empires simultaneously, encouraging cooperation in frontier defence, the Turks were able to insert themselves into the inter-imperial rivalry as a third player who could be used to tilt the balance towards either side. As a result, diplomacy and trade between the Turks and Byzantines was of great concern to the Sasanians and there are reports of the Sasanians attempting to intercept Turkish embassies travelling to Constantinople.[167] The Turks similarly tried to interfere with Sasanian diplomats. Menander Protector reported that the Turks humiliated Sasanian envoys in front of their Byzantine counterparts, for example.[168] This does not mean that the relationship between the Byzantines and Turks was always easy, as seen in the embassy of Valentinos in 576 when the Turks accused the Byzantines of being lax in their obligations to attack the Sasanians and duplicitous in their alliance with the Avars whom the Turks had subjugated and thought of as their slaves.[169]

In other cases, this alliance was rather effective, as in the campaign of 588 when the Turks, Byzantines, the Byzantines' Arab allies and the Turks' Khazar and Hephthalite allies coordinated attacks against the Sasanians.[170] In the east, the Turks' Hephthalite vassals attacked Khurāsān from Ṭukhāristān, reaching Bādhghīs in northwestern Afghanistan and Herat before the Sasanians could respond. The Shahanshah Hormozd IV (r. 579–90), who was coincidentally the son of Khusrow and a Turkish princess, appointed Bahrām Chōbīn (d. 591) of the Mihrānid Parthian family satrap or military governor of Khurāsān and gave him an army of 12,000 trained and hand-chosen cavalrymen to turn back the Hephthalites.[171] Bahrām succeeded in pushing the Hephthalites out of Herat and Bādhghīs and then went further conquering Ṭukhāristān. The political situation in Ṭukhāristān at this moment was complex. Whereas chronicles and other literary sources make it appear that Ṭukhāristān had fallen out of Sasanian control, the numismatic evidence contradicts this. As the Hephthalites attacked Herat, Sasanian coins reappeared at Khulm from 582 through 584 and Balkh in the years 587–591 while they disappeared from Herat from the year 583 to 589.[172] This would imply that when the Hephthalites attacked Herat, the Sasanians controlled Balkh, while they lost control of Herat perhaps as early as five years before the invasion that called Bahrām Chōbīn to action. The Bactrian documents and bullae impressed with official seals hint at further Sasanian control in pockets of Ṭukhāristān at this time.[173] Bahrām then pushed across the Oxus as far as Paykand in the Bukhara oasis.[174] Coins minted in the name of Hormozd at Samarqand and Chāch but dated to the years 582–4 and 585 respectively, must have some relation to these campaigns, despite the dates inscribed on them.[175] An earlier Sasanian presence this deep in Sogdiana is highly improbable. According to Ṭabarī, Bahrām killed the Khāqān Shābah or Sāvah Shāh – to add a literary flourish, this was achieved by a single arrow shot that was remembered as one of the three greatest arrow shots in the history of the Persians.[176]

Even though Bahrām's campaign against the Hephthalites and Turks was a success, it led to a political crisis in the Sasanian Empire. Hormozd grew suspicious of Bahrām's popularity and removed him from office and publicly insulted him. In response, Bahrām revolted, leading his army to Ctesiphon in 590. The story of Bahrām's revolt is most often presented in terms of a conflict between the shahanshah and the nobility but it may be more appropriate to view this in the context of Bahrām, a charismatic and popular general, leading a professional army, an issue we will return to in the following chapter.[177] The necessity of defending the frontier against the Hephthalites and Turks gave Bahrām the tools he needed to overthrow Hormozd. Hormozd's son Khusrow II Parvīz (r. 590, 591–628) was able to retake the throne with support from the Byzantine Emperor Maurice (r. 582–602), to whom Khusrow ceded portions of Armenia. Bahrām Chōbīn, now Bahrām VI (r. 590–1), fled Ctesiphon and headed east to either Balkh or the court of the Turkish khāqān, who reportedly supported Bahrām's revolt with warriors.

Bahrām even issued coins from Balkh.[178] There he was killed by either the khāqān or an agent of Khusrow.[179]

The chaos sown by Bahrām's revolt in the Sasanian Empire was matched within the Türk Khāqānate itself, making it difficult for them to take advantage of their neighbour's weakened position. The Türk Khāqānate was largely organized as a steppe confederation and rivalries among members could run high. As the Sui Dynasty (r. 581–618) chronicle *Suí Shū* described the situation: 'The Türks prefer to destroy each other rather than to live side-by-side. They have a thousand, nay ten thousand clans who are hostile to and kill one another.'[180] The last decade of the sixth century and the first decade of the seventh were a period of political division and power struggles within the larger Türk Khāqānate as Tardu (r. 575–603), Istämi's son and successor in the west, attempted to unify the steppe under his authority.[181] These conflicts were exacerbated by the Sui and Tang dynasties of China both of whom brought greater unification to China, increasing pressure on their northern neighbours and interfering in steppe politics. Along the Sasanian frontier, the Western Türk Khāqānate acted much more as a coalition of peoples instead of a unified polity and the Turks had a rather small footprint in both Ṭukhāristān and Sogdiana.[182] They only maintained a large enough presence to prevent rebellions and to defend the territories under their authority when they were under direct threat. Otherwise, much like the Hephthalites before them, the Turks relied on local institutions to manage their domains and insure that tribute and taxes continued to flow, even if they did possess a stronger sense of group identity than the earlier Hunnic invaders.[183] What intermingling we see occurred within the ruling class, where intermarriage and blending of court cultures helped bring the Turks and their subjects together.[184] The localized identities of Ṭukhāristān, Sogdiana and Khwarazm could still prevail under this environment. In such a decentralized condition, it also meant that the possibilities for an effective attack on Sasanian Khurāsān would be limited. Adding to this was the general strength of the empire under Khusrow II. It was in the early seventh century that the Sasanian Empire reached its largest territorial extent after a successful campaign against the Byzantines from 602 to 628 brought Syria, Palestine and even Egypt under Sasanian authority.

Major raids still occurred into Sasanian Khurāsān and archaeological evidence implies that the defensive infrastructures of the eastern frontier, most notably the Gorgān Wall, remained garrisoned in the early seventh century.[185] The contemporary Armenian historian Sebēos described raids 'over the face of the whole country' that eventually travelled as far west as Isfahan in 616 or 617.[186] Smaller raids may have hindered Sasanian rule in Khurāsān even earlier with disruptions in coin production from the mints of Sakāstān, Herat and Marw occurring in 600, 601 and 603, respectively. Minting resumed in Sakāstān by 610 and Marw by 613.[187] In response to these raids, Khusrow sent the Armenian prince Smbat IV Bagratuni (d. 617) who defeated the Hephthalites near Nīshāpūr, but then the Hephthalites were able to call upon support from the Turks who sent an army reported at the exaggerated size of 300,000 in support of their vassals.[188] Smbat was defeated somewhere between Nīshāpūr and the Oxus. A second battle went better for the Sasanians and Smbat and his army travelled as far as Balkh, allowing him to plunder all of Ṭukhāristān and destroy Hephthalite fortresses before retiring to Marw and Marw al-Rūd.[189] By the seventh century, the Hephthalites and other peoples across the frontier were no longer the organized threat they had been in the previous centuries. Instead they could raid Khurāsān but would melt away when counter measures were organized. In a situation where the Turks were available to provide support, perhaps they could push the raids further (it is only after the Turks joined the Hephthalites and defeated Smbat that they travelled as far as Rayy and Isfahan), but without such support a concentrated counter assault could put the Sasanians back in Ṭukhāristān. It is also clear that despite successful campaigns under Khusrow I, Hormozd IV and Khusrow II into Ṭukhāristān, Sasanian control was never long-lasting nor secure beyond the frontiers as they had been defined in the fifth century and this remained a territory under Hephthalite authority.[190]

The Türk Khāqānate was successful in asserting its authority over the peoples of the frontiers of the Sasanian Empire, from the Caucasus to Ṭukhāristān, but they treated these domains as part of a confederation. They allowed the local populations, such as the Hephthalites and Sogdians, much autonomy while remaining available to provide support and protection when their vassals were faced with a challenge. This coupled with efforts taken by Sasanian shahanshahs to construct and reinforce military infrastructure such as the Great Wall of Gorgān also limited their ability to expand into the territory of the Sasanian Empire beyond raids – albeit large and destructive raids. The Sasanians were able to maintain the frontier that had been established in earlier centuries along the Oxus and the Murghāb rivers. For the most part, this was the situation that held until the end of the Sasanian Empire and through the early decades of the Arab–Muslim conquests. Although there had been moments of ambition during which the Sasanians attempted to expand their territory or incorporate lands beyond this frontier into their sphere of influence, especially in the third century, the eastern frontier remained relatively stable through the reigns of the Kushans, Kushano-Sasanians, Kidarites, Hephthalites and Turks. Despite whatever temporary gains may have been made, the frontier would return to this equilibrium.

Change and continuity along the eastern frontier

This chapter began with Pīrūz figuratively dragging the frontier forward with elephants chained to a boundary marker, but the image we get of the eastern frontier during the Sasanian period after taking these four centuries as a whole may better be that of generals like Bahrām Chōbīn and Smbat Bagratuni propping up a dam, what James Howard Johnston has called 'aggressive defence'.[191] Early victories against a faltering Kushan Empire sent the Sasanians into Ṭukhāristān and Sogdiana where they established vassal kings who remained tenuously allied to the larger empire. Hunnic invasions pushed the Sasanians back to the River Murghāb and the empire invested heavily in the fortification of the frontier from the foundation and expansion of cities such as Marw, Marw al-Rūd and Nīshāpūr as places that could garrison armies to the building and garrisoning of the Great Wall of Gorgān. The Kidarites matched this construction along the River Zarāfshān in Sogdiana and the contested frontier zone on either side of the Oxus became increasingly hedged in. New migrations brought new opportunities and challenges. Newcomers could become allies as Pīrūz used the Hephthalites against both his brother and the Kidarites, and Khusrow I used the Turks against the Hephthalites, but they could also become dangerous enemies and rivals as Pīrūz lost his life and almost the empire to the Hephthalites and the Turks led several invasions of Khurāsān that endangered the Sasanian heartland. But this was not the wild east. The Kidarites, Hephthalites and Turks all belonged to a history of state and empire building in Central Asia and the Sasanians were forced to respond to them as such.

Because this chapter provided only a brief overview of the conflicts across the eastern frontier between the Sasanian Empire and its neighbours, covering four centuries of Sasanian rule, it has highlighted only some of the themes that will be important moving forward. First, the frontier was ever changing as new peoples moved into the frontier zone who posed different challenges to Sasanian authority; but in many ways the challenges remained consistent as did the shape of the frontier with the Sasanians increasingly entrenched on the River Murghāb. Second, the construction of large-scale defensive infrastructure from the foundation and expansion of cities to the building of massive walls demonstrates a high level of imperial investment along the eastern frontier throughout the Sasanian period. Such projects need to be discussed in light of current debates about the nature and structure of the Sasanian Empire on the macro level. These were not the projects of nobles and local lords, but projects that required the full investment of the empire (and sometimes the Byzantine Empire as well). This is not to diminish the very real power of the nobility, but it is to say that in spaces like the eastern frontier we can see a balancing of noble power within a larger imperial frame. The large armies raised by the shahanshah to defend the frontier and placed under the leadership of generals such as Bahrām Chōbīn and Smbat Bagratuni – even if under the immediate leadership of noblemen – demonstrate another avenue of imperial investment into the defence of the frontier. Third, such projects also shaped the geography of the frontier and helped define the regions of Khurāsān, Ṭukhāristān and Transoxiana in ways that would mould how they each interacted with the Arab–Muslim conquests and integrated themselves into the Islamic world, as we will discuss in the following chapters. Now, let us leave the Sasanian frontier and turn towards the Arab–Muslim conquests with an image of the eastern frontier that had a legacy as a militarized imperial zone where the Sasanians did not face the wild east of steppe nomads but complex states and imperial rivals for control over the frontier and beyond.

Chapter 3

THE ARAB–MUSLIM CONQUESTS AND THE LATE ANTIQUE IMPERIAL SHATTERZONE

The Marzbān *of Marw al-Rūd*

In the mid-seventh century, the armies of the Arab–Muslim conquest first entered Khurāsān and quickly spread up to and beyond the borders of the Sasanian Empire. As they headed east, they encountered at least three distinct zones representing different forms of political order. In Khurāsān, the lands that had traditionally fallen under the authority of the Sasanian Empire, they found a society centralized around urban centres – including Marw, Marw al-Rūd, Herat and Nīshāpūr – where representatives of the Sasanian military class, primarily the *marzbāns*, still held sway. Here the Arabs were able to negotiate and come to terms with these established authorities. In Ṭukhāristān, the Arabs found the domains of the Hephthalites who ruled from their mountainous holdfasts. Beyond the River Murghāb, the Arabs were able to raid but faced resistance that made permanent gains difficult. Across the Oxus, the Sogdian city states made for plump targets, willing to pay tribute to avoid prolonged military confrontations, but here the Arabs had to compete with the Turks who saw Sogdiana as within their domain. In each case, Arab advancement was limited by their own ambitions – a desire to raid and then return to the political centres of Iraq rather than conquer, settle and rule – and the ambitions of competing imperial powers, including the Türk Khāqānate, Tang Empire of China and remnants of the Sasanian royal family who sought to rebuild their empire. This is a very different story from the traditional narrative of the Arabs attacking, conquering and supplanting the Sasanian Empire. This chapter looks at the complexity of the eastern frontier at the end of the Sasanian Empire, during a period in which the armies of the Arab–Muslim caliphate sought to raid but not necessarily conquer and rule. To begin, let us turn to a fairly typical encounter with a former agent of the Sasanian military.

In his *History of the Prophets and Kings*, Ṭabarī gives an account of the Arab general Aḥnaf b. Qays's (d. 686) conquest of Marw al-Rūd. According to this account, told on the authority of Madā'inī (d. 843), the author of the lost *Conquests of Khurāsān*, Aḥnaf besieged the Sasanian frontier garrison city on the shores of the River Murghāb in the year 652–3.[1] The defenders of Marw al-Rūd sallied out and engaged the Arabs but were routed back into their fortress. The following morning, the *marzbān* or march lord of the city and Sasanian military governor of the frontier with Ṭukhāristān, Bādhān, sent his nephew out to the Arab camp with a letter outlining terms of surrender. As recorded by Ṭabarī, Bādhān's letter read,

> To the commander of the army: We praise God, in whose hand are the turns of fortune, who transfers kingship as He pleases, who lifts up whomever He wishes after abasement and brings down whoever He wishes after exaltation. Verily He has called upon me to arrange peace terms with you on the [same] line as my grandfather's submission and with the marks of honor and rank that your master (*ṣāḥibkum*) think appropriate. So welcome to you and rejoice. I summon you to peace between you and us, based on [the following conditions]: (1) that I render you a tribute (*kharāj*) of 60,000 dirhams, (2) that you confirm me in the possession of what Kisrā, King of Kings [the Sasanian Shahanshah Khusrow II], conceded (*aqṭaʿa*) to my great-grandfather, when he killed the serpent that was feeding on the people and cutting the roads that connected the lands and villages along with their inhabitants; (3) that you take no tribute whatever from any member of my house, (4) that the office of *marzbān* not be taken from my house and given to any other. If you do all this for me, I will come forth to you.[2]

Aḥnaf agreed to these terms on the condition that Bādhān and his *asāwira* (cavalry, presumably from the local nobility) provide military service to the Muslims when necessary.[3]

Bādhān's letter and the terms of his surrender to Aḥnaf reveal several interesting themes regarding the way the Arab–Muslim conquests were recorded and remembered by later historians and how the process of conquest has been understood by modern historians. First, this document shows a concern for administrative and legal terms, promising Bādhān and the people of Marw al-Rūd certain rights and obligations vis-à-vis the Arabs. Conquest narratives found in the Arabic literary tradition, including both traditions focused on the conquests themselves known as *futūḥ* literature and more general works of history, often included an administrative element. These texts emphasized the precedents of taxation, tribute and land tenure set by the conditions under which a region was conquered. This primarily involved a distinction between conquest by force (*ʿanwa*), which meant a city was sacked and tribute rates set higher, and conquest by treaty (*ṣulḥ*), which tended to mean a more lenient arrangement was made.[4] The precedents set at the time of conquest had bearing on issues such as the taxes owed by future generations and land tenure and, as such, accounts of the conquests had a legal and administrative role in defining the rights of the conquered peoples.[5]

The administrative element of conquest narratives could be such that even when multiple accounts of a single event differ, the details pertinent to administration agree. For example, Balādhūrī (d. 892) reported in his *Conquests of the Lands* that when Aḥnaf b. Qays besieged Marw al-Rūd, an unnamed *marzbān* invoked his ancestor Bādhām (the *marzbān* describes himself as *min walad Bādhām*) who was the master (*ṣāḥib*) of Yemen and who had converted to Islam during the time of the Prophet Muhammad. This account is in contrast to Ṭabarī's snake-slaying great-grandfather, but when a deal is struck the tribute is the same 60,000 dirhams.[6] In this manner, *futūḥ* narratives are often meant to explain the status of a place at the time the account was written, not necessarily at the moment of conquest. It has been noted that 60,000 dirhams is rather small in comparison to the tribute paid by the other cities of Khurāsān who typically paid at least ten times that amount, and some have argued that this is a sign of the fierceness with which Bādhān and his warriors fought in the initial battle against the Arabs, forcing the invaders to accept such favourable terms to avoid further fighting.[7]

The second point of interest in Bādhān's letter was his demand that Aḥnaf acknowledge his family's status and position in local politics. Bādhān does not declare his loyalty to the Sasanian dynasty or make declarations of resistance against a foreign invader – which should seem odd coming from a governor-general charged with defending the Sasanian frontier – just a question about whether the Arabs would acknowledge the rights and privileges granted by Khusrow II to his great-grandfather. It is interesting in this context to note that in Ṭabarī's account Bādhān emphasizes the Sasanian origins of his family's authority while in Balādhūrī's account the allusion to Bādhām of Yemen (d. ca. 632), sometimes Bādhān well known as the Sasanian envoy to the Prophet Muhammad during the reign of Khusrow II and an early non-Arab convert to Islam, connects his claim of authority to prophetic history instead. In Bādhān's concern for preserving his ancestral rights over Marw al-Rūd, the *marzbān*'s response to the Arabs appears typical of the dominant image of the Arab–Muslim conquests of the Sasanian realm: the Arabs invaded the realms of the Sasanians and the local authorities chose to surrender and pay tribute in return for preserved status.

To complicate this picture, this chapter explores the Arab–Muslim conquests of Khurāsān during the seventh century within the context of the eastern frontier, specifically examining the place of the Arab incursions into the east within the imperial shatterzone that formed as the Sasanian Empire collapsed and gave way to the early Arab–Muslim caliphate.[8] The story of the Arab–Muslim conquests has been told many times, including histories of the conquest of Central Asia specifically.[9] There are certain patterns that emerge in narratives of the Arab–Muslim conquests to which this chapter responds. The first and most basic of these is that the Arab–Muslim conquests were, in fact, conquests. In the east, this would mean they were campaigns intended to overthrow and succeed the Sasanian Empire. In many ways, this is a fabrication of our sources, the majority of which were written during the Abbasid era from the perspective of an imperial court that saw itself in part the inheritor of the Sasanian legacy. In contrast, this chapter argues that, up until the Marwānid period (684–750) of the Umayyad Caliphate and perhaps not before the governorship of Qutayba b. Muslim, the Arabs were engaged only in incursions, that is, military adventures with the goal of capturing spoils and extracting tribute, rather than formal conquest.[10] A second, related point to be examined is that the progression of the conquests in Greater Khurāsān followed a pattern of 'capture–rebellion–recapture' in which Arab gains were regularly overturned by rebellious locals.[11] In following the first point, I argue that one cannot rebel if there was not first an honest conquest. What we see instead are repeated campaigns that make only slow and incremental progress towards establishing imperial control over Khurāsān and then Ṭukhāristān and Sogdiana with warriors returning to Iraq between campaign seasons. Perhaps a model of 'raid–abandon–raid again' is more appropriate.

A third pattern focuses on the state of Greater Khurāsān in the seventh century. Historians both medieval and modern have portrayed Greater Khurāsān as decentralized and ruled by a variety of petty lords concerned first and foremost with their local authority, much like Bādhān is portrayed in the account detailed above. In Sasanian Khurāsān two models of political authority emerge. One, focused on the reform movement of Khusrow I, argues that the shahanshah had instigated a series of reforms meant to weaken the power of the great noble houses by creating a standing army that did not rely on the military service of the nobles and their retainers in part by strengthening the role of the landed gentry or *dahāqīn* as tax collectors and military recruiters.[12] According to this pattern, the *dahāqīn* submitted to Arab authority in return for protection of their rights. More recently, Parvaneh Pourshariati has argued that the great Parthian noble houses had weathered Khusrow's reforms and it was they who enabled the Arab–Muslim conquest by negotiating away the empire in return for protection of their status.[13] Beyond the Sasanian frontier, Sogdiana and Ṭukhāristān were dominated by, in the words of Vasily Bartold, 'numerous small principalities constantly at war with one another … with the brave, warlike, but utterly unorganized class of knights'.[14] This model is reinforced by our medieval sources including our ninth- and tenth-century geographical sources that include lists of kings of Khurāsān and al-Mashriq (the East), such as the list found in Ibn Khurradādhbih's *Book of the Routes and Realms*.[15] In the model of 'capture–rebellion–recapture', these lords are seen as agents of resistance and rebellion to Arab rule and, in the analysis of H. A. R. Gibb, even self-consciously nationalistic in their anti-colonial attitudes.[16]

In this chapter, I describe a more nuanced relationship between the local lords of the eastern frontier and the Sasanian Empire and the armies of the Arab–Muslim conquest, while also complicating the relationships between these local lords themselves. In part, this is achieved through shifting the focus from 'conquest' to 'incursion', understanding the Arabs to be an ephemeral presence for the first half-century of their involvement in Khurāsān – semi-nomadic warriors making long-distance raids in search of loot and trade – and analysing their interactions with local lords through this context. Likewise, greater emphasis is placed on the interactions between various local lords independent of the Arabs. The eastern frontier in the seventh century was a complex space geopolitically and emphasis on the bilateral relationships between Arab–Muslim conquerors and their local subjects limits our understanding. This chapter therefore addresses not only the armies of the Arab–Muslim conquests and their interactions with the post-Sasanian nobility including the *marzbāns* or frontier governor-generals and *dahāqīn* or landed gentry; it also addresses their interactions with the Hephthalites who continued to dominate the highlands of Ṭukhāristān, the local kings of the Sogdian city states and the Turks whose weakened and disorganized khāqānate continued to influence the dynamics of the frontier, especially in Sogdiana. This chapter also looks beyond the immediate frontier to discuss the fate of the Sasanian royal family and the activities of the Sasanians-in-exile who attempted to regain their lost empire and even temporarily succeeded in reasserting authority in parts of east Iran. I also compare the Arab–Muslim approach to empire with the Area Commands established by the Tang Empire of China in Ṭukhāristān.

As an example of such interactions, we may return to the case of Bādhān and Marw al-Rūd. After Aḥnaf b. Qays received Bādhān's submission, he marched approximately one day's travel up the River Murghāb and secured a fort that was then renamed Qaṣr Aḥnaf.[17] With this, Aḥnaf and the Arabs had secured the Khurāsānī side of the Murghāb, the former Sasanian frontier. As Aḥnaf and his forces attempted to cross the river, the people of Ṭukhāristān, including the people of Gūzgān, Ṭālaqān, Fāryāb and Chaghāniyān – the Hephthalite-dominated domains between Marw al-Rūd and Balkh – came together in a force reportedly between 30,000 and 40,000 to attack Aḥnaf and his 4,000 Arab fighters, in some accounts accompanied by 1,000 non-Arab allies.[18] Despite having agreed to terms with Aḥnaf that included a promise to provide military support, Bādhān acted tentatively as this force descended upon the Murghāb. Bādhān held back his tribute, waiting for news of the coming battle – one account even includes warriors from Marw al-Rūd joining Aḥnaf's opponents. Upon defeating the Hephtalites, Aḥnaf sent two men to arrest Bādhān and collect the tribute from him.[19] As the *marzbān* of Marw al-Rūd, Bādhān was familiar with this kind of warfare and familiar with the Hephthalites. Marw al-Rūd, after all, was the first line of defence against the many Hephthalite raids into Sasanian Khurāsān discussed in the previous chapter. Regardless of their treaty, Bādhān waited for the outcome of Aḥnaf's first test along the frontier of Ṭukhāristān, knowing whatever tribute was collected would not be worth paying had the Arabs lost. On the other hand, accounts of Marwazis fighting alongside the Hephthalites should make us question Bādhān's relations with his neighbours and his relative comfort with them in contrast to the newly arrived Arabs. This in-between status would continue for over sixty years when, in the year 709, a descendant of Bādhān joined the Hephthalite lord Nīzak Ṭarkhān in an uprising against Arab rule (to be discussed in Chapter 5). Bādhān's position is not determined solely by his relationship to the Arabs, but by the dynamics across the frontier as well.

The opening of the frontier: Military adventures and the Arab–Muslim conquests

Before going further, some notes on terminology and our sources are required. The word used in Arabic for conquest is *futūḥ*, literally 'openings'. As we turn to the Arab–Muslim conquests, we should recollect our discussion in Chapter 1 on the terms for frontiers in both modern English and classical Arabic and the deeper meanings of these terms. The use of the word *futūḥ* projects an image of conquest that fits a certain understanding of frontiers as empty spaces or open spaces inviting expansion. Even in comparison to the term *thughūr*, *futūḥ* evokes an opening of the gaps. *Futūḥ* narratives were one of the first genres of Arabic historical writing – first as texts that specifically dealt with reports of the conquest of specific regions such as

Madā'inī's *Futūḥ Khurāsān*, then in works that compiled accounts of the conquests across the caliphate such as Balādhūrī's *Futūḥ al-buldān* or *Conquests of the Lands* and finally as reports included in universal chronicles such as Ṭabarī's *History of the Prophets and Kings*. Despite the early place of *futūḥ* literature in Islamic historiography, it still developed long after the events these works describe. This means that, from the perspective of our sources, the conquests were completed and successful and, in many cases, these sources attempt first and foremost to explain the world as it was at the time the sources were composed as a result of the conquests rather than as it was at the time of the conquests themselves. Both the concept of *futūḥ*, conquest as openings, and the literature that commemorated them contains an optimistic and triumphalist attitude that glorifies the achievements of the early caliphate. As mentioned above, *futūḥ* narratives developed into the form we have them today largely in an imperial context, around the Abbasid court, that saw itself as the inheritor of many intertwined imperial legacies including those of both the conquerors and the conquered and the *futūḥ* narratives are an important part of constructing this image.[20]

Futūḥ narratives are often literary in nature, even if they do contain administrative and economic data. The conquests, as they are described in *futūḥ* narratives, played an important role in the foundation and development of the Islamic world that is being commemorated by the texts. The early, regionally specific *futūḥ* works often acted much like the later local histories in that they sought to glorify the region under study and attempted to elevate its status and that of its inhabitants and conquerors within an Islamic world view.[21] The conquest narratives integrated into texts with a scope broader than the conquests themselves often presented the conquests as an important formative moment in the development of the Islamic community, setting the conditions by which different regions were integrated into the Islamic world. This is not just a feature of historical writing but also geographical writing. Authors such as Yaʿqūbī included the conditions under which a place or region was conquered as a regular element of his geographical descriptions alongside more contemporary and specifically geographic information. For example, in his entry on Marw, Yaʿqūbī reported between details of the routes to Marw and the demographics of the city that 'Ḥātim b. al-Nuʿmān al-Bāhilī conquered it and he was under the authority of ʿAbdallāh b. ʿĀmir during the caliphate of ʿUthmān, but some say that al-Aḥnaf b. Qays participated in its conquest. This was in the year 31 (651–2)'.[22] The conditions of the conquest were an essential part of a place's identity.

As works of literature, the *futūḥ* narratives are interwoven with literary themes and topoi that must be separated from the narrative itself when mining these accounts for historical content.[23] The authors and compilers of our sources looked to create a narrative of the birth of the Islamic caliphate and in doing so they fictionalized, romanticized and sanitized numerous aspects of the history of the conquest. One example of such polishing of the narrative involved the simplification of complex events that unfolded over long periods of time into more digestible units such as the reign of an individual caliph or a single year, thereby breaking up and/or collapsing narratives often in an artificial manner.[24] We can see these problems at play in an account of what would have been, if we choose to accept the dating, the earliest Arab incursions into Khurāsān. Ṭabarī provides an account partially on the authority of an unnamed group of *akhbārī* (people who traded in historical reports called *khabar*) and partially on the authority of the controversial informant Sayf b. ʿUmar (d. 796).[25] According to this report, Aḥnaf b. Qays conquered all of Khurāsān and Ṭukhāristān, chasing the last Sasanian shahanshah Yazdgird III into Transoxiana, in a single pass during the year 642–3, nearly a decade earlier than any other report.[26] There are numerous red flags regarding the veracity of this account. First, it is not confirmed in any other source. Even the later chroniclers who either translate or reproduce large parts of Ṭabarī's work, including Balʿamī (d. ca. 992–7) and Ibn al-Athīr (1160–1233), directly questioned this account.[27] Second, the second half of the account, the portion transmitted on the authority of Sayf b. ʿUmar, is, in the words of Albrecht Noth, 'nothing more than a hotchpotch of well-known narrative motifs, anecdotes, and legends'.[28] What is the purpose of such an account? On the one hand, by placing the conquest of Khurāsān earlier, during the reign of the Caliph ʿUmar (r. 634–44), it may elevate the status and standing of the conquest and of Khurāsān. We find examples of this in local histories as well. While not including any details, Waʾīẓ al-Balkhī (d. after 1214) briefly mentions that Aḥnaf conquered Balkh during the reign of ʿUmar in his local history *The Merits of Balkh*.[29] Accounts such as these also elevate the status of the conquerors. Certain literary aspects, such as the poetry Aḥnaf recites in praise of himself, are indications of origins in the oral histories of the Banū Tamīm, the tribe of both Aḥnaf and Sayf.[30] The account was meant to aggrandize the heroics of Aḥnaf and the Banū Tamīm.

Not one of these aforementioned accounts resulted in a permanent conquest. In each version, Aḥnaf's campaigns are followed by 'rebellion' in which the people of Khurāsān threw off Arab rule which could only be reasserted during the caliphate of ʿUthmān and the return of Yazdgird. We have much more reliable evidence for campaigns into Khurāsān and Ṭukhāristān during ʿUthmān's reign, which are corroborated across multiple sources and traditions. But even in these cases, it would be difficult to refer to these events as anything more than incursions or military adventures. In most cases, the resulting 'rebellions' that give the histories of the conquest of Khurāsān its pattern of 'capture–rebellion–recapture' are nothing more than the disappearance of Arab authority from Khurāsān as the warriors migrated back to Iraq.

The Rāshidūn (r. 632–61) and Sufyānid Caliphs (r. 661–84) did not rely on standing armies for their conquests. Instead, individuals were given command over provinces and frontiers and were then responsible for raising troops themselves and paying them a stipend (*ʿaṭāʾ*) from the spoils.[31] Even though our literary sources present this as an organized imperial enterprise leading to conquest and incorporation of territories into the caliphate, it may be more appropriate to think of these early incursions in terms of 'adventure capitalism', a Weberian term coined to describe disconnected raids under charismatic leadership whose primary focus was treasure.[32] These campaigns were focused around charismatic leaders who simultaneously held positions of leadership within their own tribes – such as Aḥnaf

b. Qays of the Banū Tamīm and his overlord, the governor of Baṣra ʿAbdallāh b. al-ʿĀmir (r. 649–56, 661–4) of the Banū ʿAbd Shams whose father was the maternal uncle of the Caliph ʿUthmān. Such leaders recruited fighters with spoils from brief military adventures. In the early years, this system benefitted from a general population consisting of experienced warriors with few barriers between warriors and the rest of Arab society. In his study of the Arab–Byzantine frontier, Asa Eger proposed that these early conquests even on more central frontiers like those of northern Syria and Mesopotamia were long-distance trading (or raiding) expeditions that only slowly involved settlement and integration of 'conquered' regions into an imperial framework as the Arabs were themselves sedentarized.[33]

Khurāsān was administered from Baṣra and it was from there that armies were sent out to conquer and police the province. The first settlement of Arabs in Khurāsān was at Marw. The treaty signed between Ibn ʿĀmir and Māhawayh, the *marzbān* of Marw and assassin of Yazdgird III, required the Marwazis to quarter Arab fighters in their homes (*fī manāzilihim*).[34] Marw quickly became an administrative centre with Arab–Sasanian coins minted there as early as 651.[35] These coins were modelled on Sasanian coins of Yazdgird III with the Arabic phrase *jayyid* or 'excellent' inscribed on the obverse in Kufic script. As early as 652, Arab–Sasanian coins were being struck at Marw including the *bismillāh* (in the name of God).[36] This garrison may have held as few as 4,000 fighters, the number most often given for the size of the Arab armies in Khurāsān at this time, and it did not involve permanent settlement – the fighters did not bring their families and they were rotated between Khurāsān and Baṣra. Not long after the initial incursions into Khurāsān the First Fitna or civil war broke out following the assassination of the Caliph ʿUthmān in Medina. This conflict, which lasted through the caliphate of ʿAlī (r. 656–61), pitted Iraq against Medina first and then Syria and necessarily acted as a distraction for the Iraqi troops stationed throughout Iran with many returning west. The light presence of Arabs in Khurāsān during this time, if there was any at all, is often associated with rebellion by the Arabic literary sources, but is it accurate to call what was essentially Khurāsānīs refusing to pay tribute to non-present Arabs a rebellion?

During ʿAlī's contested caliphate, Arab governors sent to Khurāsān were barred from entering the cities by the local populations without the use of force, as in the case of Khulayd b. Qurra al-Yarbūʿī (r. ca. 657–9) who was sent to Khurāsān in 657–8.[37] ʿAlī even faced challenges employing local supporters to maintain some semblance of caliphal authority in Khurāsān. In one report, the *marzbān* of Marw, Māhawayh, met with ʿAlī in Kūfa and the caliph gave him a letter encouraging the *dahāqīn*, *asāwira*, *dihsālārīn* (village headmen similar to *dahāqīn*) and *jundsālārīn* (military officers) to pay the *jizya* or poll tax but the Khurāsānīs refused.[38] At least one account reports that Sasanian tax collectors re-emerged in Nīshāpūr during the fitna while another says that Khulayd had been opposed in Nīshāpūr by a Sasanian princess.[39] O. G. Bol'shakov has attempted to tie Māhawayh's trip to Kūfa with Pīrūz b. Yazdgird's (d. 679) attempts to rebuild the Sasanian Empire (which will be discussed later) arguing that he was seeking support against the son of the emperor he had killed just a few years prior.[40] While Pīrūz's campaigns appear to come later, some attempt to reassert Sasanian authority was occurring as early as 657. The First Fitna was likewise accompanied by a fifteen-year break in minting at Marw, which had consistently struck coins from 651 to 657.[41] The interest in portraying these early incursions as effective conquest shades the way our sources discuss these events and an increasing number of scholars have recognized a lack of a real Arab presence in many of the provinces of the caliphate before the reign of ʿAbd al-Malik (r. 685–705) or his son and successor Walīd (r. 705–15).[42]

None of this is sufficient reason to throw out the Arabic literary sources for the conquests entirely. It is important to note that at each step of the development of *futūḥ* literature both as a genre and as a topic of historical writing earlier texts were subsumed by newer texts. For example, Madāʾinī's history may be lost to us, but large portions of it survive in both Balādhūrī's and Ṭabarī's accounts of the conquests of Khurāsān.[43] This does not mean that we have Madāʾinī's unadulterated text by any means, as edits were certainly made by later redactors, but our available literary sources do provide a link back to earlier traditions. Also, case studies including those on the conquests of Sogdiana have shown sufficient convergence between literary histories in Arabic and the available documentary

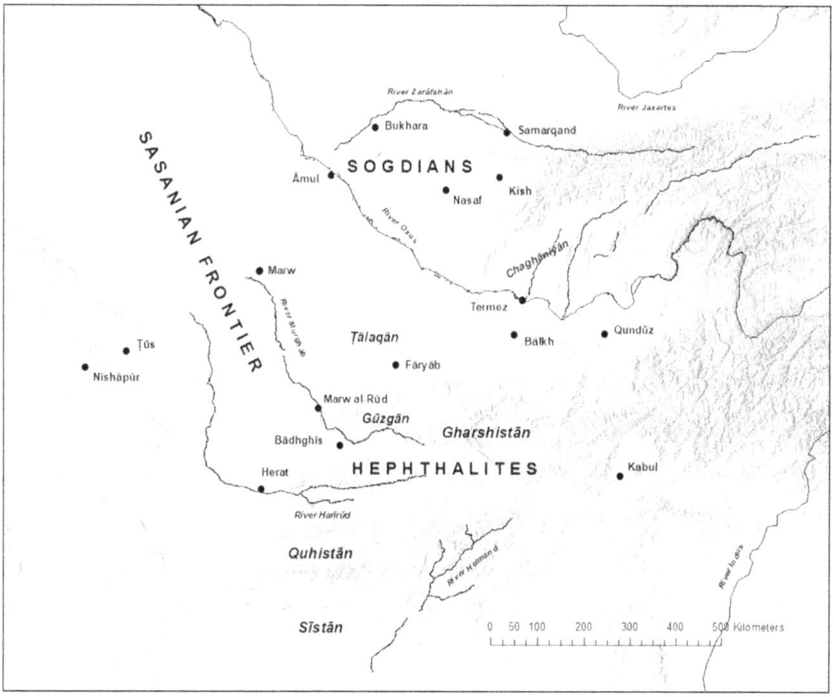

Map 5 The Sasanian Frontier in the Seventh Century.

Sources: Esri, USGS, NGA, NASA, CGIAR, N Robinson, NCEAS, NLS, OS, NMA, Geodatastyrelsen, Rijks waterstaat, GSA, Geoland, FEMA, Intermap and the GIS user community.

evidence.[44] We may continue to rely on the literary sources but must read them critically and, where possible, in line with other available contemporary evidence. Most importantly here for our study of the eastern frontier at the time of the Arab–Muslim conquests, we need to read them against the grain of the imperial metanarrative that seeks to portray the conquests as a formal imperial project from the outset.

Parthian nobility and Sasanian generals on the frontiers of Khurāsān

The chapter opened with a discussion of the submission of the *marzbān* or frontier governor-general of Marw al-Rūd, Bādhān, to Aḥnaf b. Qays and placed his surrender in the context of the late Sasanian political environment as described by our literary sources. The political environment of the late Sasanian Empire is most often defined by the reforms of Khusrow I, a programme meant to break the strength of the nobility that had begun as early as the reign of Khusrow's father Qubād who was temporarily removed from the throne and forced to flee to the Hephthalites over his treatment of the nobility. The *Khwādaynāma* tradition, especially in its Islamic rendition, portrays the reforms of Khusrow I as extremely successful in limiting the power of the Parthian nobility. As a result, from the perspective of the conquests and *futūḥ* narratives (many of which appear in the same Arabic sources that also preserve the *Khwādaynāma* traditions, making them all part of a shared literary tradition in the Islamic era), the Sasanian Empire with which the armies of the Arab–Muslim conquest engaged was dominated by the *dahāqīn* who held autonomous authority on the local level and were willing to deal with the Arabs to preserve the status quo. According to these sources, Khusrow's reforms had four major parts: the reform of the land tax that involved a new land survey and established fixed rates determined by type of agricultural produce, reform of the poll tax, the rehabilitation of agricultural lands including restoring lands to small farmers and providing them with financial assistance in times of drought to prevent the consolidation of agricultural lands into the large estates of the nobility, and the professionalization of the military under the direct command of the emperor and his officers – the commander-in-chief or Erānspābed, the four *spāhbeds* each overseeing one quarter of the empire and the *marzbāns* who acted as military governors of the frontier provinces.[45] Although the general image presented by many of our sources is that these reforms resulted in power shifting from the great noble families to the *dahāqīn*, these reforms were more likely focused on stabilizing the imperial treasury with the goal of maintaining a professional standing army, objectives especially important to a Sasanian Empire still suffering the aftershocks of Pīrūz's defeats at the hands of the Hephthalites, discussed in the previous chapter, that destroyed the army and left the Sasanians paying a massive tribute in silver to their neighbours. Furthermore, the division of the army into four commands under the four *spāhbeds* would give the Sasanian army better flexibility to deal with simultaneous threats on multiple and distant frontiers.[46]

The historical traditions based in the *Khwādaynāma* portray Khusrow's reforms as successful in centralizing authority under the shahanshah and elevating the *dahāqīn*. Ṭabarī, for example, presents the *dahāqīn* as overseeing the peasantry in their work on the roads, bridges, markets and agriculture.[47] Michael Morony described the situation in Iraq as a 'pyramidal system' with the *dahāqīn* acting as the administrative authority on the lowest level.[48] Richard Frye claimed 'the *déhkān* class, the knight who owned a village' were 'the backbone of Iranian society'.[49] Like all images of the Sasanians as a centralized empire under a strong shahanshah, this is to an extent a trick of the sources reinforced in modern historiography by works such as Arthur Christensen's *L'Iran sous les Sassanides* which notably overemphasized Khusrow's reforms, but more recent studies including the work of Zeev Rubin, Pourshariati and Michael Jackson Bonner have all shown in one way or another that these reforms were less than successful in effectively bringing the empire together under a centralized authority or in weakening the great noble houses.[50]

Although the *dahāqīn* may have seen an increased authority as tax collectors on the local level, their military role has been overstated, supposedly being responsible for conscripting peasants on their lands for military service. There are some cases in which people have gone so far as to translate *dihqān* as professional soldier or, as Frye is quoted as saying above, 'the knight who owned a village'.[51] Instead members of the great noble Parthian houses still retained much of their authority and could sometimes even increase it through the reformed military. For example, a recent study by Touraj Daryaee on the revolt of Bahrām Chōbīn emphasized the authority he was able to derive as a general within a professional military over the more traditional understanding of Bahrām revolting in the name of the Mihrānid Parthian household in a bid to renew Parthian kingship. Here Bahrām is presented as just the first in a series of generals to challenge Sasanian authority with the support of the army in the empire's final, post-reform decades.[52] Rubin and Jackson Bonner have emphasized that the post-Khusrow armies still relied heavily on nomadic mercenaries, meaning that even after these reforms predictable recruitment was problematic.[53] Local conscriptions by the *dahāqīn* were not providing a substantially sized or reliable force. When we look to the eastern frontier at the time of the Arab–Muslim conquests, it is apparent that power was still in the hands of the generals, many of whom but not all were from the Parthian noble families, and there was still a tradition of relying on Turkish and Hephthalite military support.

The narrative of the Arab–Muslim conquest of Iran that is most commonly told is the one based in the image of autonomous *dahāqīn* who were willing to exchange guarantees of their status and property for submission to Arab rule. Whereas this might hold for the more central regions of the empire such as Iraq, it is not so clearly the case in Khurāsān and especially not 'Outer Khurāsān' or the lands along the old Sasanian frontier.[54] The sources for the Arab–Muslim conquest of Sasanian Khurāsān focus almost entirely on the major urban centres that had been associated with the defence of the frontier. The garrisoning of troops and the individuals who speak and negotiate with the Arabs are rarely called *dihqān*, but hold military titles, most notably *marzbān* – margrave or march lord. In cases where they are called *dihqān* it is one of many titles. For example, in one account of the death of Yazdgird III, Māhawayh is called both the *marzbān* and the *dihqān* of Marw, among other titles.[55] The rulers of Sarakhs, Ṭūs, Marw and Marw al-Rūd were all named *marzbāns*.[56] Nīshāpūr is said to have had four quarters at the time of its conquest, each with its own master (*ṣāḥib*), one of whom was the *marzbān*.[57] Nasā was under the rule of a *ṣāḥib* who negotiated with the Arabs but it is also described as being under the authority of the *marzbān* of Ṭūs.[58] Abīward was under a grandee (*ʿaẓīm*) named Bahmana.[59] There are some places where it appears leadership was divided. Balādhūrī describes a grandee (*ʿaẓīm*) of Herat negotiating a peace agreement with Ibn ʿĀmir, including a letter outlining the surrender of Herat, Bādhghīs and Būshanj, but this is immediately followed by an account of the *marzbān* of Herat fighting against and then making new terms with Ibn ʿĀmir.[60] It is not clear if these are the same or different people. Perhaps the grandee is a civil leader of the urban population while the *marzbān* is a military commander or a misidentified Hephthalite lord who dominated the highlands such as the Nīzak Ṭarkhān of Bādhghīs or the Barāzān Ibn Khurradādhbih lists as the king of Herat, Bādhghīs and Būshanj.[61] For all but Nasā and Abīward, both dependents of Nīshāpūr, the overlord of the city who negotiated with the Arabs was referred to as a *marzbān*, meaning that these were not a batch of decentralized rural lords but military officers who had been, at least in theory, sanctioned by the Sasanian state. Some have brushed over the differences in terms used for the local rulers of Khurāsān in Arabic texts, claiming that later authors were confused or that *marzbān* and *dihqān*, as used in later Arabic sources, were close enough to be synonymous, but the named officials in our sources hold authority over much larger territories than any one *dihqān*.[62] This is not to say that the Sasanians were able to form a strong, centralized standing army in Khurāsān in the face of the Arab-Muslim conquests, but it does highlight the fact that these lords were connected to the larger politics of the empire and entrusted with the defence of its frontiers.[63] They were not petty rural lords, but most likely the immediate overseers of the rural *dahāqīn* for whom they appear to speak and masters of the fortified and garrisoned cities that defended the Sasanian frontier.

Perhaps more compromising of the idea that local economic and military authority had been decentralized among the *dahāqīn* and other local notables in a meaningful manner is the lack of any long-term resistance in Sasanian Khurāsān. This point is central to Pourshariati's analysis of the conquests as well, in which she argues that some of the Parthian noble families enabled the Arab–Muslim conquests through their refusal to fight in support of the Sasanian family and their occasional active support for them.[64] After Yazdgird III arrived in Marw, he discharged his general, the Parthian Ispahbud Farrukhzād (d. 665), under whose protection the shahanshah had fled east. In many accounts, Farrukhzād became angered with Yazdgird's decision to trust his eventual assassin Māhawayh, choosing to stay in Marw instead of fleeing to the mountains of Ṭabaristān, the ancestral lands of the Ispahbudān. As a result, Farrukhzād and his army mutinied and offered their support to the Arabs in the conquest of Rayy.[65] This is the last one hears of a Sasanian army in Khurāsān in our sources. In the aftermath, with the retreat of the standing army of the Sasanians, Khurāsān fell quickly to the Arabs.[66] Had the *dahāqīn* played a more prominent role in organizing the army and recruiting troops from the local population, one would imagine seeing more forms of organized resistance within Khurāsān itself following the departure of Farrukhzād and the death of Yazdgird.

When we can identify an individual local ruler across multiple sources they are integrated into the larger networks of the empire. For example, the *marzbān* of Ṭūs named Kanār by Ṭabarī and Kanāzak by Balādhūrī is most certainly the Parthian Kanārang.[67] Kanārang was a hereditary title, the Pahlavi translation of the Kushan *karālang*, similar to *marzbān*, and the family that possessed it was known as the Kanārangīyān.[68] Besides governing Ṭūs, the Kanārang was also one of the four masters of Nīshāpūr and the master of half of both Abarshahr and Nasā.[69] M. A. Shaban had identified the Kanārang as the governor-general of all of Khurāsān, overseeing the *marzbāns*.[70] By pulling all accounts of the divided rule of Nīshāpūr and the Kanārang's support for the Arabs against his local rivals, Pourshariati demonstrated that the progression of the conquests in the region was dictated by competition between the Kanārangīyān noble family and their local rivals, the Parthian Qārins, over control of Nīshāpūr.[71] The rivalry between Māhawayh of Marw and the Ispahbud Farrukhzād highlighted above similarly involved rivalries between Māhawayh, the Ispahbudān and Kanārangīyān, all of whom presumably sought the privilege of sheltering the shahanshah.[72] One of the more interesting aspects of the tale of Māhawayh and Yazdgird is that, according to certain accounts of Yazdgird's death, Māhawayh came from humble beginnings and was not a member of one of the great Parthian noble houses, instead owing his title and position to Yazdgird personally, and this is one of the reasons the shahanshah preferred to seek shelter in Marw rather than Ṭabaristān with the Ispahbudān or Ṭūs with the Kanārangīyān, both of whom had inherited their titles.[73]

Based upon the accounts we have available to us, in the territories that had been under Sasanian authority on the eve of the Arab–Muslim conquests, the authorities who treated with the Arabs appear to be representatives of the great Parthian noble families or the *marzbāns* and therefore representatives of the Sasanian military. In some cases, they were both. For those figures who are identifiable, they could take advantage of the Arab–Muslim conquests to reassert their rights to local authority and to settle local scores. For the rulers of Marw al-Rūd, Ṭūs and Marw, the Arab–Muslim conquests were perhaps more of an opportunity than not. If we think about the larger political narrative of the late Sasanian Empire, there was a great deal of decay and disorder at the political centre on the eve of the conquests. In the four years between the death of Khusrow II and the ascension of Yazdgird III there were upwards of ten people who claimed the Sasanian throne including at least two members of the Parthian noble households and two daughters of Khusrow.[74] The first Arab incursions into the Sasanian Empire occurred in the second year of Yazdgird's reign according to the Arabic sources, though some have argued they may have begun even before he took the throne.[75] The end result was that, for at least the last twenty-three years of nominal Sasanian rule in Khurāsān, there was no strong imperial authority and it would not be hard to imagine local authorities feeling comfortable exchanging one imperial master for another, especially when one appears noticeably stronger, given protections and reassurances for their wealth and authority. It may be that during this quarter century the position of many generals and *marzbāns* on the frontiers became something more like warlords who could use the loyalty of their troops to carve out their own fiefdoms. In such a context, these *marzbān* warlords gravitated towards the urban centres of the shatterzone – Marw, Marw al-Rūd, Herat, Nīshāpūr, and so forth.

The historiography on the Arab–Muslim conquest of Sasanian Khurāsān has focused on the decentralized nature of the province on the eve of the conquests and tied this situation to larger transformations across the Sasanian Empire. When the available accounts of the earliest incursions to Khurāsān are analysed, two patterns emerge. First, the lowest agents of local authority, the *dahāqīn*, are barely present. Instead, the emphasis is on the governor-generals of the major frontier outposts, the *marzbāns*, individuals tied to the Sasanian military. The emphasis on the frontier cities matches a later pattern of Arab settlement that focused on 'Outer' Khurāsān as well.[76] Second, even among the *marzbāns* there is not a unified response to the Arab presence. The direction of the conquests often appears to be dictated by conflict and competition among the *marzbāns* and the noble Parthian houses, many of whom may have become warlords leading remnants of the Sasanian army during the quarter century of declining Sasanian political authority. While many of these local lords took advantage of the arrival of the Arabs to secure their own positions, it was often done within the context of competition against local rivals. As we look beyond the River Murghāb into the Hephthalite-dominated lands of Ṭukhāristān we will see that the limits of this conflict and competition did not end at the frontiers of the Sasanian Empire. Rather the *marzbāns* often worked in cooperation with their Hephthalite rivals and it is to these interactions across the frontier that we now turn.

Conflict and cooperation along the Sasanian–Hephthalite frontier

In the introduction to this chapter, we briefly discussed the Hephthalite forces from Gūzgān, Ṭālaqān, Fāryāb and Chaghāniyān that attacked Aḥnaf b. Qays and the Arabs as they crossed the River Murghāb into Ṭukhāristān. Certain elements of this account resonate as familiar. In part, this is because the reports of this battle are filled with topoi familiar to the *futūḥ* literature, many of which parallel the earlier account of a strikingly similar battle between Aḥnaf and the Hephthalites found in Sayf b. ʿUmar's questionable report of the conquest of Khurāsān and Ṭukhāristān during the reign of the Caliph ʿUmar also discussed above. Among these topoi, Aḥnaf is said to have walked through the camp the night before the battle in disguise, listening to the talk among his troops, when a man either tending to a stew or kneading bread suggested that, instead of marching into the mountains to face the enemy directly, the Arabs should set themselves with the mountains to their backs at a point where the mountains came close to the river, denying the enemy the advantage of their numbers. Aḥnaf took this advice and the Arabs were victorious.[77] The Arabs fighting with their backs to a mountain is a topos that appears in many conquest narratives and is connected to the Battle of Uḥud (625) during which the Prophet Muhammad chose to fight with his back to the mountains.[78] That this advice came from a wise but presumably low ranking man, a camp cook, may be meant to signal a kind of divine intervention or inspiration further connecting Aḥnaf and the conquests back to the campaigns of the Prophet and a salvific history.

In all accounts, the Arabic sources describe this confrontation as the prelude to the conquest of Ṭukhāristān. The people of Ṭukhāristān rallied together to keep the Arabs from moving beyond the Murghāb, maintaining the traditional Sasanian frontier, and once they failed Ṭukhāristān opened up to the Arabs. Aḥnaf was able to march across the region only facing resistance in Gūzgān.[79] Balkh fell rather quickly, signing a treaty for either 400,000 or 700,000 dirhams.[80] The pattern of large-scale raids from Ṭukhāristān followed by reprisal campaigns that quickly penetrated deep into the region sounds familiar because it follows a pattern discussed in the previous chapter when Bahrām Chōbīn in 588 and Smbat Bagratuni in 616–17 marched Sasanian armies deep into Ṭukhāristān and even across the River Oxus. Likewise, it was noted in the previous chapter that these reprisal campaigns rarely resulted in the Sasanians consolidating authority over Ṭukhāristān. After each victory, they were pushed back again behind the Murghāb.

Even though the details of Aḥnaf's battle against the Hephthalites appear suspect, the various reports of Balkh's response to the arrival of the Arabs all tie to the patterns dictated by Balkh's place on the frontier between the Sasanian and Hephthalite worlds, ranging from accommodationist to defensive. In the previous chapter we discussed the difficulties of identifying the position of Balkh within the geopolitics of the Sasanian Empire. As a city in the plains of Ṭukhāristān it was a tantalizing target for armies marching east, but surrounded by the mountainous homes of the Hephthalites it was often the target of their raids; Balkh's status at any given moment is often debatable. On the one hand, some reports show the Balkhīs accommodating the Arab conquerors. In the aftermath of Aḥnaf's campaign against Balkh, he left his nephew Asīd b. al-Mutashammis in charge of collecting the tribute while the army moved on, marching for Khwarazm. While the tribute was being gathered, the festival of Mihragān, the Zoroastrian Autumn harvest festival, occurred and the people of the city brought Asīd many gifts not included in the tribute as was traditional to give the ruler during the festivities. Madā'inī, on whose authority Ṭabarī relates this report, turned this narrative into a commentary on the licitness of the gifts, fitting it into the general theme of administration and taxation but also acting as a prelude to later legal challenges regarding gifts offered on Zoroastrian holidays during the caliphate of ʿUmar II (r. 717–20), including specifically Mihragān.[81] Here the Balkhīs were accommodating of the Arabs and treated them as they would any ruler who could assert their power over the city by offering them the gifts of Mihragān.

On the other hand, the decision to engage the Arabs turned out poorly for the people of Balkh in an account originating in Kirmānī's (d. ca. mid-ninth century) lost *History of the Barmakids* preserved in Ibn al-Faqīh's and Yāqūt's geographical works. According to this account, when Balkh was conquered hostages were taken to Medina as guarantors for the tribute (*kānū ḍamanū mālān min al-balad*) including the Barmak, the custodian of the Naw Bahār (*nava vihāra*) Buddhist monastery, and a group of *dahāqīn*.[82] While in Medina, the Barmak converted to Islam taking the name ʿAbdallāh. This conversion angered the Balkhīs, the people of Ṭukhāristān in general and the Nīzak Ṭarkhān in particular. He attacked Balkh after Barmak had returned, killed Barmak and ten of his sons and chased his last remaining heir to Qashmīr.[83] This account was designed to glorify the Barmakids who would rise to great power under the Abbasids, though it also demonstrates the difficult position of Balkh between the Arabs and the Hephthalites and the complex political environment of Ṭukhāristān with the Balkhīs and particularly the Barmak, whose role in the political life of Balkh and Ṭukhāristān is often debated, stuck between the Arabs who had successfully attacked the city and demanded tribute and the Hephthalites who could strike once the Arabs had returned to Khurāsān or even Iraq.[84] Looking back to the previous chapter where some Ṭukhārian lords paid tribute to both the Sasanians and the Hephthalites in the same year, we can say that this condition was nothing new.

As the Arabs first advanced into Ṭukhāristān and beyond the cities of the Sasanian frontier in general, the western reaches of the region were still dominated politically by the Hephthalites likely under nominal Turkish overlords based in Qundūz. Even though these lands were difficult to control, certain patterns of rule and relationships between the Hephthalites and their neighbours had developed over the centuries. In the earliest Arab excursions beyond the River Murghāb, the most important figure to emerge was the ruler of Bādhghīs, the Nīzak Ṭarkhān. *Ṭarkhān* is a Turkish title and many (but not all) Arabic sources refer to the Nīzak Ṭarkhān as the leader of a Turkish force, but it is clear that he was a Hephthalite vassal of the Turks.[85] The name Nīzak first appears as a dynastic title on late fifth-century silver coins from Kāpiśā (Bagram).[86] Inscriptions on these coins indicate a Hephthalite dynasty that survived the initial Turkish conquest of Ṭukhāristān and migrated into and south of the Hindu Kush.[87] The connections between the older line of Kāpiśian Nīzaks and the Nīzak Ṭarkhāns of Bādhghīs is not absolutely clear, but Shoshin Kuwayama has identified the latter Nīzaks with the *Yida Taihan* or Hephthalite Ṭarkhāns found in Chinese sources confirming at least their Hephthalite origins.[88] The Arabic sources associate the Nīzak with Bādhghīs but Kuwayama locates their centre of power further east at the ancient fortress of Surkh Kōtal on the River Surkhāb. In either case, the Nīzak Ṭarkhāns who appear in the Arabic sources until 710 asserted their authority over Ṭukhāristān from its mountainous fringes. The Nīzak was only one of several Hephthalite lords in Ṭukhāristān at the time as indicated by the use of the title *barāz* and derivatives by several local notables.[89] Ibn Khurradādhbih gives the Hephthalite title *barāz* to the kings of Nasā (Abrāz), Gharshistān (Barāz Bandah) and Herat, Bādhghīs and Būshanj collectively (Barāzān).[90]

When thinking about the relationships of the eastern frontier, we should focus on the dynamics between the Hephthalite lords of Ṭukhāristān and the *marzbāns* of the Sasanian frontier. We have already mentioned the possible participation of Bādhān of Marw al-Rūd in the Hephthalite-led attacks on Aḥnaf or, at the very least, the *marzbān*'s hesitant stance between Aḥnaf and the Hephthalites, but in other contexts the cooperation across the frontier is much clearer. For example, the Nīzak Ṭarkhān first appears in the Arabic and Persian literary sources as an ally of Māhawayh, the *marzbān* of Marw, in 651 during his conflict with Yazdgird III. In these reports, Māhawayh called upon the Nīzak to aid him in ridding Marw of the shahanshah, making the Nīzak an important player in his murder.[91] The relationship between Māhawayh and the Nīzak is complicated. Ṭabarī gives Māhawayh a son named Barāz, which may be a signal of deeper ties between the *marzbān* and his eastern neighbours, perhaps even a sign that he himself was of Hephthalite background.[92] Dīnawarī (815–96) claims that Māhawayh and the Khāqān of the Turks were joined by marriage, but in the context of other reports it is more likely he was related to the Nīzak Ṭarkhān instead.[93] Such a marriage alliance, for example, would help us understand why the *marzbān*'s son held a Hephthalite title. These reports show that Māhawayh was apparently closer to the Hephthalites than the Sasanians. In one of Balʿamī's accounts of Yazdgird's death, the shahanshah is portrayed as a burden, travelling with 4,000 persons including slaves, cooks, servants, his wives and concubines and the elderly and children of the Sasanian household without a single warrior and expecting Māhawayh to provision this entourage.[94] According to Balādhūrī, Māhawayh's decision to turn on Yazdgird was inspired by the shahanshah's demands to see the *marzbān*'s accounts. In response, Māhawayh wrote to the Nīzak, who had already been slighted by the shahanshah when he asked to marry a Sasanian princess, saying Yazdgird was 'the one who came here as a runaway fugitive'.[95] In a couple accounts, Ṭabarī likewise had Yazdgird arrive in Marw looking for money.[96] Yazdgird arrived in Marw as a foreign ruler with his hand out rather than an ally of the Khurāsānī lords.

Returning to Firdawsī's report mentioned earlier in which Māhawayh was singled out for not being of Parthian noble blood, we may find it attractive to conjecture that the *marzbān* was of Hephthalite descent himself and an example of the continued reliance upon Hephthalite and Turkish mercenaries highlighted by Rubin and Jackson Bonner cited above. At the very least, reliance on said mercenaries had improved relations between some frontier governors and their neighbours and presumptive rivals. Much like the 'barbarians' on the northern frontier of the Roman Empire, participation in the military may have created bonds between Hephthalites and Sasanian military men. Firdawsī does give a slightly different impression though with the Nīzak playing Māhawayh to his advantage and even invading Marw and killing the *marzbān* following Yazdgird's murder.[97] In this account, the Nīzak acts as if he sought revenge or justice for Yazdgird against the faithless Māhawayh.

The position of Bādhghīs and the Nīzak Ṭarkhān or the Hephthalite mountain lords in general within the larger networks of Sasanian Khurāsān was complicated. In theory, Herat itself was under a Sasanian *marzbān* who held authority over Bādhghīs and Būshanj and the three are regularly tied together in conquest narratives, but in practice the Herat Valley was dominated by the Hephthalites who likely migrated between the highlands and valley seasonally. When Aḥnaf first entered Khurāsān he was attacked by Hephthalites from either Herat or Quhistān who he routed. There is no narrative of Aḥnaf attempting to conquer the area, instead he marched more directly on Nīshāpūr, pursuing the urban centres in the flatlands of Khurāsān, after escaping this initial conflict.[98] As Ghirshman highlighted, Ṭabarī's account here is one of the rare instances where the Arabic sources specifically name the Hephthalites instead of their typical use of 'Turk' to describe all non-sedentary inhabitants of greater Khurāsān.[99] It was only after the initial campaign against Balkh that Khulayd b. ʿAbdallāh al-Ḥanafī was sent to capture the area, at which time he made a treaty with the *marzbān* or *ʿaẓīm* of Herat covering not just Herat but also Bādhghīs and Būshanj, but it is not clear exactly who Khulayd fought and with whom he made peace.[100] Herat reneged on their treaty shortly after the Arabs left, and it is also unclear whether it was the *marzbān* or *ʿaẓīm* who turned on the Arabs or if there was a general lack of control over the region.

The Herat Valley continued to be a site of resistance against the Arabs. After failing to stop the Arabs at Nīshāpūr where they held out in the *quhandiz* or citadel, the Qārinid Parthian family turned to Herat to stage a second resistance. In Madāʾinī's account preserved by Ṭabarī, Qārin gathered a host of 40,000 from Ṭabasayn, Bādhghīs, Herat and Quhistān and advanced against the Arabs.[101] These were the mountainous, Hephthalite-dominated fringes of Khurāsān and Qārin's ability to bring these regions together under his leadership is perhaps further evidence for a Qārinid–Hephthalite alliance proposed in the previous chapter and a sign of deeper connections between the Qārinids and Hephthalites.[102] ʿAbdallāh b. Khāzim (d. 691–2), one of Ibn ʿĀmir's generals who would play an important role in the politics of Islamic Khurāsān up to his death, usurped the governorship of Khurāsān at this time either in response to Qārin's revolt or the assassination of the Caliph ʿUthmān in Medina, and organized a counter-force that attacked the Qārinid–Hephthalite forces in the middle of the night.[103] The Arabs were victorious and Qārin was killed. At both Nīshāpūr and Herat, we see the Qārinids retreating from the advancing Arabs and organizing resistance at the fringes of Khurāsān. More importantly, in this instance we see cooperation across the Sasanian frontier between Parthians and Hephthalites to oppose Arab expansion.

In the Hephthalite raids along the Murghāb and the coming together of Māhawayh and the Nīzak and the Qārinids and Hephthalites to resist Arab advances, what we are seeing is not something new but rather the continuation of a dynamic that had been alive and well during the Sasanian period. The Hephthalites had been able to maintain control on the fringes of Khurāsān. When opportunities arose, they could unite to raid deep into Khurāsān but faced difficulties holding territories beyond the Murghāb. An organized military could not only turn them back but temporarily advance into Ṭukhāristān with ease while the Hephthalites regrouped in the mountains and beyond the Oxus. In the shatterzone of the frontier and the competition within the Sasanian Empire, the Hephthalites could also act in alliance with the Parthian noble families and the *marzbān* warlords as seen in the alliances with Māhawayh and Qārin. The mountains played an important role in the dynamic as they provided sanctuary from the advancing Arab armies. For example, the Nīzak Ṭarkhān was able to control Bādhghīs from an inaccessible mountain stronghold until 703–4 when the governor Yazīd b. al-Muhallab (672–720) was able to capture it, not by strength but guile, waiting for the Ṭarkhān to leave it undefended.[104] Even then, Yazīd's brother and successor Mufaḍḍal (d. 720) needed to lead a second campaign into Bādhghīs the following year but even that did not finish the Nīzak who was only eliminated by Qutayba b. Muslim in the year 710, as discussed in Chapter 5.[105]

The first Arab incursions into Sogdiana

Arab interest in Sogdiana grew as their presence in Khurāsān became more stable. According to many of our literary sources, the first adventures across the Oxus occurred during the caliphate of Muʿāwiya (r. 661–80) when the governor of Baṣra Ziyād b. Abīhi (d. 673) sent the *ṣaḥaba* or Companion of the Prophet Ḥakam b. ʿAmr al-Ghifārī (d. 670) as his governor in Khurāsān.[106] Ghifārī led a raid into Ṭukhāristān in the year 670 that captured a large amount of booty and slaves, but the reports emphasize a brief moment when Ghifārī crossed the River Oxus and became the first Muslim to lead prayers in Transoxiana.[107] These reports are more focused on placing Ṭukhāristān and Transoxiana within an Islamic cosmography rather than accurately depicting the Arab presence in either region. By attaching one of the *ṣaḥaba* to Transoxiana, expansion across the river became, in a sense, blessed by the first generation of Muslims.

Real change to Arab rule came after Ghifārī's death in Marw, where he succumbed to injuries received during his campaign east. Ziyād appointed Rabīʿ b. Ziyād al-Ḥārithī (d. 673) governor of Khurāsān. Rabīʿ established the first permanent Arab presence in the region, settling 50,000 Arab warriors along with their families in and around Marw in the year 671.[108] It has been estimated that the total number of Arabs who migrated to Khurāsān at this time, including the wives and children of the fighters, was between 200,000 and 250,000. These numbers originate with Julius Wellhausen's calculation that each warrior would bring four family members with him, but this figure is not without its critics.[109] This force was able to reassert Arab authority in many places that had fallen out of Arab reach including Balkh which is described by Khalīfa b. Khayyāṭ (ca. 776–855) and Ṭabarī as having 'closed' (*ūghliqat* or *āghlaqūhā*) since Aḥnaf's conquests, the literal opposite of *futūḥ* or 'open'.[110] It is of great consequence that this settlement was purposeful and planned.[111] It demonstrated a centralized effort to settle the frontier with an Arab population and the garrison at Marw acted as a base from which the Arabs could advance into Transoxiana.

Both Ziyād and Rabīʿ died in 672 and Muʿāwiya eventually named Ziyād's son ʿUbaydallāh (r. 673–83) governor of Khurāsān. ʿUbaydallāh continued the process of expanding and strengthening Arab authority in Khurāsān.

Coins with his name were struck at Herat as early as 672, posthumously in the name of his father at Nīshāpūr in 673 and as far east as Balkh by 681.[112] In 674, ʿUbaydallāh led the first serious and well-documented Arab incursion across the Oxus in a campaign that reached Bukhara, most likely travelling directly from Marw and crossing the river at Āmul before marching up the River Zarāfshān. When ʿUbaydallāh arrived at Bukhara, the oasis was under the authority of Khātūn, the widow of the recently deceased Bukhārkhudā (king of Bukhara) Bīdūn and mother and regent to his infant heir Ṭughshāda (d. 739).[113] The Bukhārkhudās are primarily known from the local history of Bukhara written by Narshakhī and a series of coins recognized by modern numismatists as 'Bukhārkhudā'. These coins are modelled on Sasanian issues of Bahrām V Gūr which gives us our presumed *terminus post quem* for the advent of the dynasty, but identifying individual rulers or a solid chronology from either of these sources is difficult.[114] Under ʿUbaydallāh, the Arabs raided the cities of Paykand and Rāmithān and then marched on Bukhara itself. These two cities played an important role in the economic and political life of the oasis. Paykand, founded by the Kidarites likely as an outpost against the Sasanian frontier as discussed in Chapter 2, had become a central part of the Sogdian trade networks and was dubbed the City of Merchants.[115] Rāmithān, near Paykand, had been home to the Bukhārkhudāh's winter palace.[116] In response, Khātūn reportedly called on the support of the Turks who arrived and fought against the Arabs, but were defeated. The Türk Khāqānate held nominal authority over Sogdiana as the Arabs made their first incursions across the Oxus, but, in reality, the Turks were in a weakened state in the late seventh century having been subdued by the Tang Empire of China in 659.[117] Even at their strongest, the Turks maintained a light footprint in the region with military men being the only Turkish presence in Sogdiana, perhaps acting as mercenaries employed by the local rulers as proposed by Sören Stark.[118]

The focus of this incursion was spoils and the Arabs left the Bukhara oasis with arms, robes, gold and silver vessels and prisoners/slaves. Our sources are almost universally interested in a single jewel-encrusted stocking that Khātūn dropped in flight said to be worth 200,000 dirhams alone. It is details like this that have led many to refer to these early portions of Narshakhī's *History of Bukhara* as a kind of Khātūn romance, though it does reinforce the lure of spoils in these earliest incursions over formal conquest. Khātūn agreed to pay an additional tribute of 1,000,000 dirhams if the Arabs stopped pillaging and destroying the agricultural lands of the oasis.[119] Included among the prisoners the Arabs captured was a group of either 2,000 or 4,000 archers ʿUbaydallāh took with him to Baṣra and employed as a personal retinue.[120] The *Bukhāriyya* as they became known will be discussed in more detail below. Our sources focus primarily on the spoils, perhaps because there was little else achieved during this campaign. The Arabs did not remain in Bukhara and returned to Marw.[121] Narshakhī described the activities of the Arabs towards Bukhara succinctly: 'Every time a Muslim army came to Bukhara it raided in the summer and departed in the winter.'[122] As Gibb has argued, it is likely that the early Arab adventures into Sogdiana did not look any different than early

Turkish 'plundering raids' and the Bukharans and others presumed that once the Arabs were paid they would simply go away.[123]

Under such circumstances, the Bukhara oasis was a contested frontier zone caught between the Arab and Turkish spheres of influence. In the seventh century neither could be said to represent formal territorial states in Central Asia but both sought access to the wealth of the region. The geography of the Bukhara oasis, isolated from the world around it by the Kyzyl-Kum Desert but connected to both the Oxus at the Āmul crossing and Samarqand by the River Zarāfshān, furthered this situation. Throughout the rest of the seventh century, the pattern of Arab incursion and Turco–Sogdian counter-attack continued.

When ʿUbaydallāh was made governor of Baṣra in 675–6, Muʿāwiya sent Saʿīd b. ʿUthmān (d. ca. 678), son of the third Rāshidūn Caliph, to Khurāsān.[124] In this position, Saʿīd also led a campaign into Sogdiana.[125] When Saʿīd approached Bukhara, Khātūn requested peace on the same terms as her peace with ʿUbaydallāh, as if the treaty had been an agreement between two individuals, not between Bukhara and the Umayyad Caliphate, or as if peace with ʿUbaydallāh had not established a more permanent relationship.[126] It was then that an army made up of an exaggerated 120,000 fighters from Samarqand, Kish and Nasaf, along with Turks, arrived to challenge the Arabs. Khātūn threw off her allegiance and attempted to side with the Sogdians and Turks, but the Arabs were victorious, chasing away their rivals and leaving Khātūn forced to again pay tribute to them.[127] Despite the fact that Khātūn repeatedly broke faith with the Arabs, she was not removed from power nor was an Arab overseer stationed in Bukhara. As Saʿīd pushed further, marching on Samarqand, he demanded eighty hostages from the princes and *dahāqīn* of Bukhara to guarantee they would not attack his rear.[128] In Balādhūrī's account, Khātūn was instead forced to assist Saʿīd with troops.[129] Saʿīd was successful in collecting tribute from Samarqand and then moved against Termez, the Oxus crossing into Ṭukhāristān. Yet again the Arabs did not remain in Sogdiana following their victories. In fact, Saʿīd took his spoils including several hostages from the families of the Sogdian nobility back to Medina where he reduced the hostages to slaves, confiscating their finery and forcing them to perform manual labour until they finally rose up and killed him.[130] The enslaved nobles then killed themselves.

Salm b. Ziyād b. Abīhi (r. 680–3) may have been the first governor of Khurāsān with intentions to winter across the Oxus. There are two competing traditions on Salm's Sogdian campaigns. One, found in Yaʿqūbī and Narshakhī, focuses on Bukhara and follows the pattern above. The Arabs arrive in Bukhara, Khātūn calls upon the support of Ṭarkhūn (d. 710), the Ikhshīd or king of Samarqand, offering him her hand in marriage, but Ṭarkhūn failed to stop the Arabs who once again collected spoils and returned to Marw, leaving Khātūn in power over Bukhara.[131] A competing tradition found in Balādhūrī and Ṭabarī on the authority of Madāʾinī says that Salm prepared to winter in Transoxiana following a campaign that first attacked Khwarazm and then Samarqand. Salm even brought his pregnant wife Umm Muḥammad bt. ʿAbdallāh al-Thaqafī on the campaign; she was noted as the first Arab woman in Transoxiana, and she gave birth to a son while in Samarqand who was named al-Ṣughd, the Arabicized form of Sogdiana.[132] Despite Salm's intentions, it was during his campaigns that Arab unity shattered and the Second Fitna broke out. This internal conflict put the conquests on hold and resulted in fierce factional fighting in Khurāsān, to be discussed in the following chapter.

The first decade of Arab involvement in Sogdiana was made possible by the establishment of a permanent garrison in Marw but these incursions never established an Arab presence in Sogdiana itself. Instead, the Sogdian cities, especially the cities of the Bukhara oasis, were targets for Arab raids with the goal of extracting spoils before returning to Marw. As such, the Arabs followed a pattern close to that of the Western Türk Khāqānate and resistance to the Arab incursions often came from the Turks, perhaps looking to preserve their hold over the same sources of wealth. The Second Fitna temporarily derailed campaigns into Sogdiana but, as will be discussed in Chapter 5, the aftermath opened the door for more permanent conquest.

The Sasanian dynasty after Yazdgird III

As it is most commonly understood, the Sasanian Empire came to an end with the murder of Yazdgird III in Marw, but members of the Sasanian royal family and their supporters survived after 651 and several of them even attempted to retake control of Iran. In many instances, this continuation of the Sasanian dynasty from exile was supported by the Hephthalites, Turks and the Tang Empire of China. From the beginning of his flight eastwards, Yazdgird reached out to foreign allies. Chinese sources tell us that Yazdgird sent an embassy to the Tang court seeking aid against the Arabs as early as 638.[133] Ṭabarī reports that, upon arrival in Marw, Yazdgird wrote to the kings of China, Ferghana, Kabul and the Khazars seeking assistance.[134] None of these calls came to fruition and, in the case of the Nīzak Ṭarkhān, Yazdgird's foreign saviour became a factor in his demise.

Yazdgird's death was not the end of the Sasanian line. The shahanshah is reported to have been survived by two sons, one of whom appears in both Arabic and Chinese sources for another quarter century. Following Yazdgird's murder, his son Pīrūz was captured by the Turks and taken to Ṭukhāristān, likely Qundūz. According to Balādhūrī, Pīrūz was given a Turkish wife and settled down, but Chinese reports show he was seeking aid from the Tang Empire to claim his father's throne.[135] During the First Fitna, when the Arabs appear to have abandoned Khurāsān, Pīrūz was able to seize control of Sīstān with the support of the Turkish Yabghu, the nominal overlord of Ṭukhāristān, and establish himself in Zaranj.[136] Subsequently, in the year 661, the Tang recognized Pīrūz as the commander of Bosi, the Area Command of Persia (the system of Area Commands will be discussed shortly) and, in the following year, the king of Persia.[137] The Arabic and Persian sources do not make direct reference to Pīrūz, the Sasanians or the Tang Empire but do discuss the temporary loss of Sīstān attributing it to the disruptions of the First Fitna. The anonymous *History of Sīstān* tells us that the Sīstānīs rejected their governor at this time due to concern that they should have a representative of the true Imam as their governor.[138] Pīrūz did not remain in Zaranj long and the Arabs returned sometime before 664 when ʿAbd al-Raḥmān b. Samura (d. 670) reconquered Sīstān.[139] Following the loss of Sīstān, Pīrūz fled again to the Yabghu in Ṭukhāristān and then travelled to the Tang court at Cháng'ān on at least two occasions, once in 673 and again in 675, where he was received by the Emperor Gāozōng (r. 650–83).[140] A statue of Pīrūz at the entrance to the tombs of Gāozōng and his wife, the Empress Wǔ (r. 684–705), includes an inscription referring to Pīrūz as 'king of Persia, grand general of the right courageous guard and commander-in-chief of Persia.'[141]

Pīrūz's son Narseh (d. after 708) was given his father's titles upon his death with the charge to pacify and govern the Arabs.[142] In 679 he accompanied the minister Pei Xingjian (d. ca. 682) when he travelled west with the goal of uniting the Turks against the Tibetans.[143] After Pei Xingjian took the city of Sūyāb (Ak-Beshim in Kyrgyzstan) from the Turks, Narseh was left to complete his journey west without Chinese support.[144] Tibet's conquest of the Tuyuhun, nomads inhabiting Qinghai on the eastern reaches of the Tibetan Plateau and their advance into the Tarim Basin and northwestern China in the 660s and 670s turned the Tang's focus away from Ṭukhāristān and Sogdiana except as a possible source of warriors to fight in Tibet.[145] Narseh spent at least twenty years with the Yabghu in Ṭukhāristān, fighting to earn back his hereditary throne before he returned to China sometime before 708.[146] The eleventh-century Chinese chronicle *New History of Tang* remembers Narseh's two decades at Qundūz with pity, reporting that 'Ninieshi [Narseh] remained for 20 years as a guest in Tuhulou (Tokhāristān). His people gradually apostatized from him and dispersed.'[147] According to a report based on the authority of Ibn al-Kalbī (d. 819) found in the geography of Ibn al-Faqīh, Narseh fought and lost a battle against Qutayba b. Muslim early in Qutayba's governorship in Ṭukhāristān. In the aftermath of this battle, Narseh's daughter Shāhfirind was captured, given to the Caliph Walīd and then became the mother of the Caliph Yazīd III (r. 744).[148] It was likely Qutayba's successes (to be discussed in Chapter 5) that forced Narseh to give up on his ambitions and retire to Cháng'ān where he died. A community of Sasanian nobles continued to live in China throughout the eighth century, though their position significantly weakened after the An Lushan Revolt of 755–6 and the consequential restrictions placed on foreign nobles living at Cháng'ān.[149] By the beginning of the eighth century, attempts to mount a Sasanian counter-strike from Ṭukhāristān had come to an end.

Pīrūz and Narseh were not the only Sasanians to attempt to reclaim the empire, according to our sources. Dīnawarī reports that, during the caliphate of ʿAlī, around the same time Pīrūz established himself in Sīstān, a daughter of Khusrow II named Bāmān who had sought refuge among the Hephthalites in Kabul travelled to Nīshāpūr and instigated an insurgency against the Arabs.[150] Bāmān's uprising or a similar event around 657 is a more likely instigator for Māhawayh's visit to ʿAlī at Kūfa, as discussed above, than an attack by Pīrūz. Bāmān was captured by the governor Khulayd b. Qurra and sent to ʿAlī who encouraged her to marry his son Ḥasan (624–70). She refused and ʿAlī freed her. During his campaigns in the Bukhara oasis, Qutayba b. Muslim faced the Vardānkhudā who, according to Narshakhī, was the son of Shāpūr, an exiled son of Khusrow II who had sought refuge with the Bukhārkhudā, possibly after his father had been overthrown by his brother Qubād Shirūy (r. 628).[151] Qubād's coup was accompanied by a violent purge of his siblings during which Qubād had seventeen of his brothers killed – a seemingly appropriate time for Shāpūr to flee across the Oxus.[152] The Vardānkhudā did not appear interested in reconstructing the Sasanian Empire, but he was involved in the power struggles of the Bukhara Oasis and may have usurped the title of Bukhārkhudā by the early eighth century.[153] Recently Domenico Agostini and Sören Stark have identified a possible Sasanian court-in-exile in Zābulistān and Kābulistān on the southern face of the Hindu Kush that lasted until 747 on the basis of Chinese sources, Zoroastrian apocalyptic texts that predict the coming of a Sasanian saviour from the east and a small sample of coins with Pahlavi inscriptions.[154] It may be possible in this context that Pīrūz is the Fayrūz Ibn Khurradādhbih identified as the king of Zābulistān.[155]

The death of Yazdgird III was not the end of the Sasanian dynasty and, in the context of the eastern frontier, various members of the Sasanian family could find not only shelter from the Arabs but also support for attempted counter-conquests. Although none of these were ultimately successful, their existence, minor successes and perseverance over decades demonstrate the opportunities to oppose the Arabs, especially in this period of small incursions. The interactions between the Sasanians-in-exile and Tang Empire also present us with an alternative means by which an empire may play an ephemeral role in Central Asia. Rather than leading incursions with the goal of extracting spoils, the Tang attempted to establish a series of 'loose-rein' prefectures that handed management of their frontiers to the people living along the frontiers. It was under such a structure that both the Sasanians-in-exile and the Yabghu and the Turks were connected to the Chinese empire.

The 'loose-rein' prefecture and the Tang model of frontier imperialism

Many empires asserted a remote and ephemeral presence along the eastern frontier in the mid-seventh century. Not only did the Western Türk Khāqānate claim a light presence in Sogdiana and in western Ṭukhāristān, as mentioned above, but the Tang Empire of China was attempting to advance its authority in Central Asia in the late seventh century as well. The seventh century was a period of expansion for the Tang Empire with a focus on subduing the Turks on their northern and northwestern frontiers. By 630 the Tang had been able to defeat their northern neighbours, the Eastern Türk Khāqānate, in part thanks to a winter of heavy snows that killed livestock and disrupted agriculture in Mongolia, but mostly through exploiting political disunity among the Turks that even led to the Western Turks supporting the Tang in these campaigns.[156] As the Eastern Turks were conquered by the Tang, the Western Turks also became divided. Following the assassination of the Western Turk ruler Tŏng Yabghu Khāqān (r. 619–30) by his uncle, the Western

Turks dissolved into ten tribes known as the 'Ten Arrows'.[157] The Tang attempted to co-opt these divided tribes individually until the Khāqān Ashina Ho-lu organized them against the Chinese in 649 and successfully pushed the Tang out of Kashgar and the Tarim Basin. The Tang responded with force, capturing Ashina Ho-lu who was taken to Cháng'ān in 657 where he died. By 659, the Tang had reasserted control over the territory of the Western Turks.[158]

The Chinese approach towards the Western Turks and the territories under their authority including the frontiers of Ṭukhāristān, Sogdiana and Sīstān was rather different from that of the Arabs. Instead of extracting tribute, they attempted to integrate these regions into the Chinese imperial world through the establishment of *jimi fuzhou* or 'loose-rein' prefectures, a title meant to imply indirect Chinese control. The *jimi fuzhou* of the Tang consisted of 856 non-Chinese states and tribes who inhabited China's frontiers on all sides and who were brought into a tributary relationship as vassals of the Tang.[159] The *jimi fuzhou* were recognized as part of the Tang administrative geography as Area Commands and the rulers of each *fuzhou* were given titles and honours from the Chinese emperor, but it is unlikely they received any real military support from the Tang.[160] Although the area commanders were themselves tributaries to the Tang, they were also given a variety of responsibilities related to maintaining border security for the empire beyond acting as a simple buffer. These duties included receiving and vetting foreign emissaries heading to the Chinese court and even inspecting tribute sent to the Tang.[161] The *jimi fuzhou* should be seen within the Chinese imperial tradition of 'using barbarians to control barbarians'.[162]

In Ṭukhāristān, the Tang established two protectorates – each with their own subdivisions – that oversaw territories south of the Hindu Kush and north into Sogdiana as well.[163] The most important of these protectorates for our purposes was centred on Qundūz, under the command of the Turkish Yabghu who oversaw territory from the Gate of Iron to the Hindu Kush.[164] While the Arabs were distracted by the fitna and had failed to commit serious resources to Khurāsān, the Tang integrated large parts of Transoxiana, Ṭukhāristān and even Sīstān into the *jimi fuzhou*, deepening the connections between these regions and China at the time we presume the Arabs were seeking to tie them more closely to Iran, Iraq and the larger caliphate. The economic connections were perhaps the most important aspect of this system with Chinese records from the period showing regular embassies to Cháng'ān from across the region bearing gifts of local products.[165] The most significant of these with regard to Arab ambitions in Khurāsān was the Area Command of Bosi under the authority of Pīrūz b. Yazdgird which was able to reassert Sasanian authority in at least Sīstān. According to Chinese administrative geography, the Area Command of Bosi was one of eight Area Commands designated at this time under the authority of the Anxi protectorate in the Tarim Basin.[166]

The effectiveness of the Area Commands and the extent to which the Tang offered real support is questionable. Hans Bielenstein called the whole thing preposterous while Agostini and Stark referred to the Area Command of Bosi as 'fictional'.[167] Are these 'loose-rein' prefectures any more imaginary than the idea of Arab conquest in Khurāsān in the seventh century? As forms of empire, both are ephemeral and do not involve real control over territories that they claim, but while the Arabs were extracting spoils through their 'conquests', the Tang were building bonds with their neighbours and defining a place for them within their imperial cosmography. The Tang may not be supplying Pīrūz, for example, with material military support, but by granting him a title and acknowledging him at the Tang court, the Sasanians have been brought into the Tang sphere of influence with hopes that they would benefit from any potential successes without an equal outlaying of resources. We do know that officials were sent from Cháng'ān to Ṭukhāristān such as Wang Minyuan who delivered a report to the emperor that is unfortunately lost.[168] Other official delegations from the Tang court do show how self-interested these relationships were. When Narseh b. Pīrūz was sent back to Ṭukhāristān in 679 with the support of a Chinese military complement under the leadership of Pei Xingjian, the Chinese were primarily concerned with campaigning against the Tibetans and Turks and stopped after taking the city of Sūyāb, leaving Narseh without the promised support.[169]

Resistance to the Arab–Muslim conquests continued to be connected to China in the Arabic literary tradition. In 706–7, there are reports that the army of Qutayba b. Muslim met a force of Turks and Sogdians under the leadership of Kūrbaghānūn al-Turkī who is alleged to be the nephew of the Tang emperor, the son of his sister.[170] Whether this army was truly under the command of a Tang prince is debatable. Édouard Chavannes suggested that, because there is no evidence of a Chinese mission to Transoxiana at this time, the Arabic sources must be confusing the emperor of China with the supreme ruler of the Turks.[171] This would better fit with his *nisba* al-Turkī which also appears as al-Turqishī or the Türgesh, the Turkic people who seized control of and reconstituted the Türk Khāqānate at the beginning of the eighth century. A diplomatic marriage between a Turkish leader and a Tang princess may also explain Kūrbaghānūn's background.

The Tang and the Arabs had two rather different approaches to Central Asia as well as two distinct objectives in advancing into the region. The concept of 'loose-rein' prefectures was based in the idea of turning potentially dangerous neighbours into allies and a defensive buffer zone. Essentially the Tang outsourced a certain amount of their frontier defence and management to their neighbours instead of attempting to directly conquer and control the frontier regions, hence 'loose rein'. This scheme could not only provide for the defence of the frontier, but it also had the potential to strengthen economic ties and trade with China. Although Hans Bielenstein declared the *jimi fuzhou* and frontier Area Commands a fabrication, his study of Chinese diplomacy and trade includes summaries of numerous emissaries and trade delegations arriving at the Tang court from these very regions. The reality is that they did not need to be fully incorporated into the administrative and military hierarchy of the empire to be effective; they simply needed to define a bond between the Tang and their neighbours. At least one tradition in the Arabic sources shows these exchanges travelling in both directions. In Kirmānī's account of the Naw Bahār Buddhist monastery in Balkh, the kings of

India, China and Kabul (also vassals of the Tang) would make pilgrimage to Balkh and pay respect to the Barmak custodian of the temple.[172] Such pilgrimages, even if we want to question whether or not the actual emperor of China ever travelled to Ṭukhāristān, worked to integrate these frontier zones into the royal cosmography of the empire and thereby gave Balkh a place in China and India and China and India a place in Balkh.

As will be discussed in more detail in the following chapters, as the Arabs arrived in Khurāsān, Ṭukhāristān and Sogdiana, they did not build such networks based on local networks of power and authority. Instead, they forced individuals to join their own Arab–Muslim networks. Converts to Islam became clients or *mawālī* (sing. *mawlā*) of an Arab tribe. Even more monodirectional were the massive movement of slaves taken as spoils during the conquests. Conquered populations were forced into Arab–Muslim social categories instead of integrating into the newly formed empire with their own existing social networks. The distinction between this process and the 'loose-rein' prefectures is important for thinking about not only the progress of the conquests themselves but also the way the empire would be organized as it matured and grew.

The Arab–Muslim incursions and the imperial shatterzone

The Arabic literary sources written under the Abbasid Empire and later present a picture of the Arab–Muslim conquests in which the early caliphate conquered and succeeded the Sasanian Empire. This conquest was achieved with the support of the Parthian nobility and the *dahāqīn* or petty landed gentry who exchanged imperial masters for guarantees of status and protection of their property. The reality though was that, throughout the seventh century, Arab campaigns into Khurāsān and beyond were little more than armed incursions intent on extracting spoils. Furthermore, this narrative focused on the caliphate defeating and replacing the Sasanian Empire ignores the complexity of the eastern frontier. The most prominent figures who emerge on the Sasanian side of the conquest are largely military figures responsible for the defence of the frontier but, in the context of the collapse of the Sasanian Empire, they may have turned to warlordism and many of them developed strong ties to the Hephthalites and cooperated with them against both the Sasanians as in the case of Māhawayh and the Nīzak Ṭarkhān and against the Arabs as in the case of Qārin. Under these circumstances, we cannot think about the conquests involving a 'capture–rebellion–recapture' pattern. Instead the Arabs led raids into Khurāsān, returned to Iraq and then raided again and the people of the eastern frontier were left to negotiate their position among themselves. The nature of the shatterzone meant that without a strong centralizing imperial presence, these former general turned Khurāsān into a patchwork of petty kingdoms.

The examples of the Tang Empire, the Türk Khāqānate and the early caliphate and their interactions with Khurāsān, Ṭukhāristān and Transoxiana draw us towards questions of the nature and purpose of empire. The Tang and the *jimi fuzhou* demonstrate the concept of Zhōngguó or Middle Kingdom.[173] While this view separated the central lands of China, the lands of the Huaxia tribes, from the surrounding 'barbarians', the *jimi fuzhou* brought those 'barbarians' into a Chinese imperial cosmography that allowed the Tang to benefit via tribute and security while still maintaining their status as *axis mundi* at the centre. In contrast, both the Türk Khāqānate and the Arabs in the seventh century viewed the frontier zone primarily as a source of wealth, extracting what they could without establishing particularly close or deep ties to Khurāsān, Ṭukhāristān or Transoxiana. This relationship is in part a by-product of the structures of empire employed by both the Turks and Arabs who organized their empires around tribes. Similar to the non-territorial state discussed in Chapter 1, the Arabs who first 'conquered' Khurāsān did not focus on territory as much as people and resources and the management of both was conducted by Arab tribes and later the regiments of individual Arab commanders. This organizing principle trickled down to the lowest tiers of interaction as non-Arabs who sought to convert or join the Arab–Muslims were required to become the *mawālī* or clients of an Arab tribe. Much as the Western Turks collapsed into the 'Ten Arrows', these networks also proved to be the system's undoing as Arab unity fell apart, most notable during the Second Fitna which will be discussed in the following chapter, with serious consequences for the expansion of the caliphate across the former Sasanian frontier into Sogdiana and the establishment of Arab–Muslim rule in Greater Khurāsān.

Chapter 4

THE FRONTIER BEYOND THE CALIPHATE: KHURĀSĀN AND THE SECOND FITNA

The flight of Mūsā b. ʿAbdallāh b. Khāzim

In the previous chapter, we outlined the diversity of the eastern frontier as the armies of the Arab–Muslim conquest first entered Khurāsān and beyond in the context of early campaigns that would be better called incursions, campaigns with little interest in permanent conquest and occupation. During this period, our sources give us the impression of a fairly cohesive Muslim presence in Khurāsān with the conquests acting as a uniting experience, bringing together the warriors of the caliphate, but any such comradery, if it had existed at all, was short lived. By 680, the armies of the caliphate began to break down along both political and tribal lines and this had a detrimental impact on the advancement of the conquests. In Khurāsān, Ṭukhāristān and Transoxiana, this created an opportunity for some Arab tribes to seek a kind of autonomy on the frontier, distant from the political centres of Iraq and Syria. This chapter will look at the activities of a few such actors in the context of the frontier as they staked out their own independent kingdoms. Let us begin by looking at the formation of the most successful of these breakaway Arab kingdoms in the east.

As the Second Fitna (680–92) or civil war came to a close, the victorious caliph ʿAbd al-Malik wrote to the acting governor of Khurāsān, the man who had seized control of the province as the empire descended into civil war, ʿAbdallāh b. Khāzim al-Sulamī. ʿAbd al-Malik invited Ibn Khāzim to remain as governor, but now under Umayyad authority, sending him a patent for seven years. During the war, Ibn Khāzim had been a supporter of the failed counter-caliph ʿAbdallāh b. al-Zubayr (r. 680–92) and subsequently refused to acknowledge the Umayyads or accept ʿAbd al-Malik's offer. The writing had been on the wall and Ibn Khāzim planned for this eventuality. He sent his son Mūsā (d. 704–5) across the River Oxus and into Sogdiana with the treasury of Marw to prepare an exit when Ibn Zubayr was finally defeated and the Umayyads reasserted their authority in Khurāsān. At this point Ibn Khāzim attempted to flee Khurāsān in hopes of reaching his son, but his own lieutenant Bukayr b. Wishāḥ al-Saʿdī (d. 696–7) took the governorship for himself and then chased down and killed his former patron.[1]

Unlike his father, Mūsā successfully escaped Khurāsān but found himself adrift among the kingdoms of Sogdiana. According to our accounts of Mūsā's adventures, he first sought shelter with the master (*ṣāḥib*) of Bukhara who turned him away, accusing him and his followers of being murderers (*fātik*) and evil (*sharr*). By some accounts, Mūsā had attracted brigands and robbers (*qawm min al-ṣaʿālīk*) to his side during his flight, but what else would one expect from a band of fugitives?[2] Underlying this is an image of Mūsā as the extreme 'adventure capitalist', abandoning even the veneer of imperial conquest for personal gain beyond the River Oxus. Because he fought the Arabs previously, it should be no surprise if the Bukhārkhudā did not want to antagonize his new neighbour by inviting in a rebel. Mūsā did find temporary shelter from the *dihqān* of Nūqān, an otherwise unattested locality in the Bukhara oasis.[3] He then turned to the Ikhshīd Ṭarkhūn of Samarqand who welcomed the wayward Arabs into his kingdom and feasted them until one of Mūsā's men challenged the 'Cavalier of Sughd' (*fāris al-ṣughd*) to a duel by eating from the plate of honour set aside for the champion. Mūsā's man got the better of the cavalier and killed him.[4] Consequentially Ṭarkhūn chased Mūsā out of town. At this point Mūsā attempted to found his own kingdom, leading a campaign against Kish, but its lord contacted Ṭarkhūn who did not want to see his neighbour fall into Mūsā's hands, perhaps because he felt Kish was within his own sphere of influence – the king of Samarqand was often referred to as the king of Sogdiana – but perhaps because he was still sore over the death of his champion.[5] From his later actions, it seems that Mūsā made a powerful enemy out of Ṭarkhūn. Finally, Mūsā turned towards Termez, an important crossing point along the River Oxus connecting Upper and Lower Ṭukhāristān. Here he met a disgruntled *dihqān* who had grown tired with the weak Termezshāh and saw in Mūsā a means to remove the king. The *dihqān* taught Mūsā how he could trick the king into letting him and his supporters into the city and even into the palace for a feast, at which point the Arabs simply refused to leave and Mūsā declared himself the new lord of the city.[6] Obviously, the Termezshāh was much too reliant on his walls to protect him.

By taking Termez Mūsā was the first Muslim to settle across the Oxus, even if it was for the specific purpose of fleeing the Umayyads and their supporters. To be certain, other major crossing points had surely been secured by the Arabs by this point, including Āmul the nearest crossing to Marw which led to Paykand and the Bukhara Oasis, but Mūsā's rebel kingdom in Termez was the first Arab state across the river. Not only did he capture Termez, but Mūsā then held it for fifteen years, staving off attacks from both the Umayyads and the Sogdians under Ṭarkhūn and forces of Hephthalites and even Tibetans – if our sources are to be trusted, that is. Certainly, there is a level of fantasy to Mūsā's adventures with accounts of him and his supporters facing and defeating an Arab army in the morning and a Sogdian army in the evening, but, behind the strong walls of Termez, Mūsā's kingdom survived for a decade and a half as a refuge for those escaping the growing authority of the Umayyad Caliphs.

In many ways, the story of ʿAbdallāh b. Khāzim and his son Mūsā are the stories of Khurāsān and the eastern frontier at the end of the seventh century. Despite decades of Arab incursions and the settlement of some garrisons at places such as Marw, Khurāsān was loosely connected to the caliphate if at all, and disturbances at the centre resulted in de facto autonomy. This was in part due to distance. By modern highways, the trip from Baṣra, from where the caliphs tried to administer Khurāsān, to Marw is over 2,000 km, taking a path that cuts diagonally through Iran and runs along the southern face of the Alburz Mountains through Gorgān. But a path such as this was unavailable before 715 when Arabs finally subjugated the Turks of Gorgān (see Chapter 5). Instead, travel between Khurāsān and Iraq followed a more southerly route that passed through the provinces of Fārs and Kirmān before travelling north through Qūhistān. This was the path taken by the forces of ʿAbdallāh b. ʿĀmir when they first campaigned in Khurāsān. This distance meant that governors sent to Khurāsān had great leeway to act independently and could only be reined in at great effort from Baṣra. At moments when Baṣra was distracted by more pressing concerns closer to home, such as the civil war, there were even fewer controls on the Arabs of Khurāsān.

Most importantly, the story of Ibn Khāzim, his seizure of power and the adventures of his rebel son paint a picture that makes Khurāsān and the eastern frontier out to be the 'Wild Wild East'. In this brief chapter, I will explore Khurāsān and the eastern frontier during the Second Fitna and its aftermath. This was an important period of transition. Following the initial incursions, this was when Arabs had become settled and established in Khurāsān but before this distant province was fully integrated into the empire. In part, this was because, as the fitna so plainly revealed, the empire of the caliphate was not itself fully formed yet. While certain trappings of empire were present in Khurāsān, such as the minting of coins in the Arab–Sasanian style of the early caliphate, the actual practice of governance and the role of the empire along the frontier was dictated by the men on the ground such as Ibn Khāzim who could often treat Khurāsān as their own fiefdoms. More importantly, the eastern frontier was a dynamic place where overlapping populations competed for power in ways that blurred ethnic and religious lines. In the adventures of Mūsā we see the role of the frontier as a sanctuary and refuge for different people fleeing powers on both sides of the frontier and the intermingling of opposition movements beyond the reach of empires. For these few decades the frontier became a zone where people like the Banū Khāzim could grab power for themselves in the absence of strong imperial structures before a reinvigorated Umayyad caliphate reasserted its own authority.

The Second Fitna in Khurāsān

The Second Fitna covers an overlapping series of challenges to caliphal authority that highlight the divisions among the Arab conquerors that defined much of Umayyad rule not only in Khurāsān but across the empire, most notably the conflicts between the tribal confederations of Qays/Muḍar, Yaman and Rabīʿa.[7] These confederations nominally represented divisions among the Arabs based on geographical origins within the Arabian Peninsula with Qays/Muḍar consisting of the northern Arabs, Yaman, the southern Arabs, and Rabīʿa, the eastern Arabs. As will be discussed further in the following chapter, these divisions grew over time to act in a manner that some have seen as more akin to political parties than tribes.[8] In this, they acted much like the tribal confederacies that dominated the Inner Asian steppe discussed in Chapter 2 where membership and the meaning of membership was only ever partially hereditary. The changing nature of the caliphate as the first generations of Muslims died off created fractures that allowed these divisions to further split and for violence to break out between them. The surface catalyst for this outbreak of violence was the appointment of the Caliph Muʿāwiya's son Yazīd (r. 680–3) as his successor and the transformation of the caliphate into a hereditary office. These developments were met with resistance on multiple fronts that lasted into the reign of ʿAbd al-Malik.[9] After the death of Yazīd, closely followed by the death of his own son and successor Muʿāwiya II (r. 683–4), there was no clear successor within the Sufyānid line of the Umayyad dynasty and the entire enterprise came close to collapse with fighting within the Umayyad family dominating Syria and the counter-caliph ʿAbdallāh b. al-Zubayr gaining support from his base in the Ḥijāz across Iraq and Iran. The tribal confederacies of Qays/Muḍar and Yaman asserted themselves directly into the conflict, choosing sides against each other.

During the Second Fitna, Khurāsān quickly dissolved into tribal warfare. According to our literary sources, the governor Salm b. Ziyād b. Abīhi – who, we are told, was so beloved 20,000 children born in Khurāsān during his tenure had been named after him – attempted to conceal the deaths of both Yazīd and Muʿāwiya II and the conflicts unfolding in the west. When news did find its way east, Salm lost control of Khurāsān and fled to the Ḥijāz where he joined Ibn Zubayr.[10] Muhallab b. Abī Ṣufra (d. 702) was named his successor by Ibn Zubayr, but he was detained fighting Khārijites around Baṣra and did not return to Khurāsān until after the fitna and then as a Umayyad governor.[11] Instead, the province became divided between Muḍar and Rabīʿa. The literary sources have Salm being accosted as he tried to flee west by members of the two confederacies, upset that the governorship was given to Muhallab of the Yamani tribe of Azd. In response, Salm assigned parts of Khurāsān to his petitioners. Sulaymān b. Marthad (d. ca. 683–4) and Aws b. Thaʿlaba b. Zufar (d. ca. 683–4) of the Bakr b. Wāʾil tribe of Rabīʿa were given authority over Marw al-Rūd (along with the frontier towards Ṭukhāristān including Fāryāb, Ṭālaqān and Gūzgān) and Herat respectively. As Salm approached Nīshāpūr, he was met by ʿAbdallāh b. Khāzim of the Banū Sulaym of Qays/Muḍar who demanded the commission for all of Khurāsān, which he was granted.[12]

Although the story of Salm divvying up Khurāsān as he fled feels fabricated, it is likely that these divisions reflected pre-existing conditions on the ground. Bakr b. Wāʾil was associated with Qūhistān along the southern flank of Khurāsān from the earliest conquest accounts and Salm granted them the neighbouring eastern flank, while Ibn Khāzim participated in the conquest and governance of Nīshāpūr beginning with the caliphate of ʿUthmān.[13] Balādhurī simplified the whole situation as a conflict between Sulaymān b. Marthad and Ibn Khāzim.[14]

The literary sources portray Ibn Khāzim as the aggressor in the ensuing conflicts, continuing the image of him as an opportunist we saw in the previous chapter when he seized control over Khurāsān during the First Fitna. He killed

Sulaymān b. Marthad and his sons at Marw al-Rūd, pursued their supporters to Ṭālaqān where they took to the desert forts – the traditional refuge of the Huns and Hephthalites – and then chased the remaining Bakr to Herat which he besieged for over a year before finally taking the city.[15] It is reported that Ibn Khāzim killed 8,000 men from Bakr at Herat, which would have constituted up to one-sixth of the pre-fitna garrison in Khurāsān and likely near the entire contingent of Bakr, creating a further disruption to the Arabs' ability to govern the province.[16] In 685–6 Ibn Khāzim turned against his previous allies from the Banū Tamīm, also of Muḍar, and defeated them as well.[17] From the perspective of the local populations, these conflicts must have looked similar to the conflicts that had previously torn apart the Western Türk Khāqānate. The accounts of the conflict between Ibn Khāzim and his rivals make it seem as if tribes of partially sedentarized Arabs were fighting ongoing battles among themselves over control of taxable spoils.

Whereas the literary sources provide us with this fairly coherent (if fanciful) narrative, the numismatic evidence is not so straightforward. This is not unusual during the Second Fitna with similar problems appearing in the issues of Isfahan.[18] As demonstrated in the table below (Table 4.1), Salm and Ibn Khāzim's names appear on competing coins struck throughout Khurāsān during the decade of fitna, which is also the most productive period for Arab–Sasanian coins in

Table 4.1 Mints operating in Khurāsān during the Second Fitna[19]

Year AH (CE)	Abarshahr (Nīshāpūr)	Marw	Marw al-Rūd	Herat	Balkh
63 (682–3)	Salm b. Ziyād	Salm b. Ziyād Ibn Khāzim	Salm b. Ziyād		
64 (683–4)	Salm b. Ziyād	Salm b. Ziyād Ibn Khāzim	Salm b. Ziyād	Salm b. Ziyād	
65 (684–5)	Ibn Khāzim	Salm b. Ziyād Ibn Khāzim			
66 (685–6)		Salm b. Ziyād (?) Ibn Khāzim		Salm b. Ziyād	
67 (686–7)	Ibn Khāzim	Salm b. Ziyād Ibn Khāzim	Salm b. Ziyād	Salm b. Ziyād Muḥammad b. ʿAbdallāh b. Khāzim	Salm b. Ziyād (?) Ibn Khāzim
68 (687–8)	Ibn Khāzim	Salm b. Ziyād[20]			Ibn Khāzim
69 (688–9)	Ibn Khāzim	Salm b. Ziyād Ibn Khāzim	Ibn Khāzim	Salm b. Ziyād	
70 (689–90)		Salm b. Ziyād Ibn Khāzim	Salm b. Ziyād Ibn Khāzim		
71 (690–1)		Ibn Khāzim	Salm b. Ziyād		
72 (691–2)		Ibn Khāzim			
73 (692–3)		Ibn Khāzim			

Khurāsān with 95 per cent of all known coins appearing between 682 and 690.[21] From the coins we can identify some distinct patterns. First, before the deaths of Yazīd and Mu'āwiya II, Salm enjoyed support from the four major urban centres of Khurāsān with coins struck in his name at Marw, Abarshahr (Nīshāpūr), Marw al-Rūd and Herat as late as 684, confirming his image as a popular governor but also implying fairly uniform rule across Khurāsān.[22] While Marw is the only Arab settlement in Khurāsān before the eighth century for which we have evidence, it is apparent that Arab warriors travelled out in tribally organized units to, at the very least, police and collect tribute from other urban centres. Therefore, we have the above-mentioned associations of Ibn Khāzim with Nīshāpūr and the Bakr with Qūhistān. The numismatic evidence shows that these other cities also minted coins in a uniform style, most likely to pay the tribute. Second, as early as 682, before even the Caliph Yazīd's death, coins were also minted at Marw in Ibn Khāzim's name implying first that Salm and Ibn Khāzim were not necessarily allies as the literary sources would imply and, second, that the rivalry between them began before the full outbreak of the Second Fitna in Khurāsān.[23] Ṭabarī, for example, has Ibn Khāzim acting as Salm's intermediary with Yazīd, delivering spoils from the campaigns against Khwarazm and Samarqand discussed in the previous chapter at the time these competing coin issues were struck in Marw.[24] Ibn Khāzim was returning from Syria when he met Salm at Nīshāpūr and demanded the governorship. This pattern of competing issues coming from the centre of Arab authority in Khurāsān continued for eight years and implies a contested governorship. They also demonstrate some form of continued support and claim to authority for Salm well after his flight west.[25] Third, the mint to most consistently strike coins in Ibn Khāzim's name is Abarshahr, implying this was his centre of power.[26] As mentioned above, Ibn Khāzim had a long history in Nīshāpūr and our literary sources centre his authority in that city as well.[27] Fourth, the eastern reaches of Khurāsān and Ṭukhāristān, where Salm is said to have given Bakr authority and where Bakr staged their resistance to Ibn Khāzim, continued to acknowledge Salm with coins appearing in his name as late as 691 at Marw al-Rūd, 689 at Herat and, perhaps, even Balkh in 686–7.[28] As a result, we may argue that either Bakr was more supportive of Salm or that Salm remained the default governor for those not fully immersed in these conflicts or those who were opposed to Ibn Khāzim. These coins may simply represent the local mint officials' understanding of the political situation or the use of older, muled or counterfeit dies during a period of political instability.[29]

A coin struck in the name of Muḥammad b. 'Abdallāh b. Khāzim at Herat, where he served as his father's governor until the Banū Tamīm attacked the city and killed him, helps us date some of the events surrounding the fitna.[30] Although Ṭabarī condensed these complex events to two years (64–5 AH/683–5 CE), he also gave a vague sense of time passing declaring that certain sieges and battles were drawn out over years. Muḥammad b. 'Abdallāh's coin from Herat dated 67 AH (686–7) gives us a *terminus ante quem* for Ibn Khāzim's defeat of Bakr and a *terminus post quem* for the Banū Tamīm's victory over Muḥammad, a window for Muḥammad's rule in Herat that falls two years later than Ṭabarī dates these events.

Issues in the name of Salm from Marw, Marw al-Rūd and Herat also issued in 67 AH, may point us towards this as the year Ibn Khāzim achieved his victories over Bakr and secured control over (the majority of) Khurāsān.

The intertribal conflicts of the Second Fitna pull us back to the question of territoriality and the nature of the early caliphate that arose in Chapter 1 and the question of the nature of the early conquests discussing in Chapter 3. At this point the empire was not about land even though, as discussed in the previous chapter, the conquest narratives are organized spatially and it was the conquest of land that made the empire wealthy. Instead the Umayyad Empire of the Sufyānids and the Zubayrid counter-caliphate were organized in the late seventh century around networks of people in the form of tribes and tribal confederacies, or at least that is how our literary sources chose to portray them, and therefore the fighting that took place occurred along these tribal lines. One of the most interesting factors here is that, in the midst of an imperial civil war, the fighting in Khurāsān appears rather localized. Both Salm and Ibn Khāzim were supportive of Ibn Zubayr, so the competing coin series do not clearly represent opposing sides in the larger conflict. Ibn Khāzim and the Banū Tamīm were both from Muḍar so this fighting likewise breaks the traditional Qays/Muḍar versus Yaman paradigm. The real fight was over local authority first and foremost and these larger conflicts were perhaps retrojected onto smaller conflicts by later historians in an attempt to make sense of the chaos. The fighting in Khurāsān was not about who would become caliph but rather who would be governor and which tribe would reap the benefits of raiding and taxing along the eastern frontier. Distant Khurāsān was home to its own conflicts related to but separate from the larger civil war.

The Hephthalites and the Second Fitna

Inter-Arab fighting also had a clear impact on the frontier. Not only did the Second Fitna slow conquest, with the campaigns into Sogdiana coming to a temporary end, it also created opportunities for opponents along the frontier. It is reported that while Ibn Khāzim was laying siege to Herat for the first time, the Hephthalites (called Turks) raided Khurāsān reaching as far as Nīshāpūr.[31] Attacks by Hephthalites such as this may be connected to the Arab–Hephthalite coin series that emerged in the late 680s. These coins are identical to Arab–Sasanian issues of the time but include Bactrian legends alongside the standard Pahlavi and Arabic inscriptions and countermarks. Many of the Arab–Hephthalite coins include the mint name Anbīr, a city in mountainous Gūzgān, as well as the name Zhulād Gūzgān, King of Ghar. These coins may represent tribute paid to the Hephthalites, much like the counter-stamped Sasanian coins discussed in Chapter 2, though their origins and purposes remain uncertain. It is also possible they are Hephthalite struck imitations.[32] As Stephen Album and Tony Goodwin have noted, the coins of Salm and Ibn Khāzim are much more likely than contemporary coins struck in the west to include such countermarks and are much less likely to have circulated outside of Greater Khurāsān. Over 85 per cent of the coins of these two governors in the collection of the British Museum, for example, include a countermark.[33] The implication is that many of the coins of Salm and Ibn Khāzim may in fact be Hephthalite imitations or, at least, circulated primarily among the Hephthalites, and rarely found their way to Iraq or points west. Not only were the politics of Khurāsān, in a sense, separated from Iraq during the fitna, but apparently so was the economy.

Tying these coins back to the raids reported in the literary sources, two known coins list both the mints of Anbīr and Marw and are dated to 68 and 69 AH (687–9), corresponding to a disruption in minting in the names of both Salm and Ibn Khāzim.[34] These coins have led many to speculate that the Hephthalites under the king of Gūzgān took advantage of the chaos in Khurāsān, seized control of Marw in 687–8 and issued coins from its mint.[35] This could be the event recorded as a raid on Nīshāpūr but it could just as easily be a second Hephthalite raid. The date corresponds with the period when the Banū Tamīm organized their offensive against Muḥammad b. ʿAbdallāh at Herat, based upon the dates of Muḥammad's coins from Herat, and Ibn Khāzim organized a punitive counter-attack against his former allies. Considering the small number of Arabs in Khurāsān and their division into warring factions, it can be argued that both of Ibn Khāzim's campaigns against Herat, first against Bakr and then against Tamīm, were noticed by the Hephthalites – who may have come into Khurāsān from points as close to Herat as Bādhghīs where the Nīzak Ṭarkhān continued to be a thorn in the Arabs' side – and resulted in successful Hephthalite raids against the urban centres of Khurāsān. Considering Bakr b. Wā'il's connection to the Hephthalite-dominated lands of Qūhistān, these may have even been coordinated with Bakr who may have built relationships with the Hephthalites as we earlier conjectured that some of the Parthian noble families of the Sasanian era had done. Ibn Khāzim's focus on Herat at these two moments opened the doors for the Hephthalites to attack his centres of power, Marw and Nīshāpūr, and this may have been done in coordination with Ibn Khāzim's Arab rivals to preserve some type of order or relationship along the frontier.

The rebel kingdom of Termez

As discussed in the introduction to this chapter, following the victory of ʿAbd al-Malik over Ibn al-Zubayr, the caliph offered the governorship of Khurāsān to Ibn Khāzim for seven years but Ibn Khāzim refused to acknowledge Umayyad authority. Instead, Ibn Khāzim's deputy Bukayr b. Wishāḥ accepted the governorship, chased down Ibn Khāzim and killed him as the deposed governor attempted to reach his son Mūsā who had fled to Sogdiana with the treasury of Marw and established himself as the ruler of Termez.[36] The adventures of Mūsā b. ʿAbdallāh were already noted in this chapter including his struggles to find safe harbour among the lords of Sogdiana and his conquest of Termez. Here I would like to discuss Mūsā's rebel kingdom of Termez in the context of the continued rebellion and conflict along the eastern frontier following the formal end of the Second Fitna in the west. This case study shows that in the aftermath of the civil war Khurāsān and the eastern frontier continued to remain only loosely integrated into the larger empire, that governors acted with greater autonomy responding to local conditions on the ground rather than commands from the imperial centre and that this created conditions attractive to those who had run afoul of the caliphate and sought sanctuary from the Umayyads. The larger reforms instituted by ʿAbd al-Malik and the Marwānid dynasty will be discussed in the following chapter.

In the aftermath of the Second Fitna, Khurāsān and the eastern frontier remained a place for those fleeing the re-established power of the Umayyads under the Marwānid line. Although Mūsā is the most successful rebel best remembered by our sources, there are clear indications that his practice or at least concern for it was more widespread. Despite Bukayr's claim to the governorship, ʿAbd al-Malik placed his cousin Umayya b. ʿAbdallāh b. Khālid b. Asīd (r. ca. 693–7) in charge of Khurāsān in 693–4 hoping a governor from the tribe of Quraysh would help soothe tensions. Umayya offered Bukayr the governorship of Ṭukhāristān and Bukayr spent a substantial amount of money preparing to campaign in the region, evidence that Ṭukhāristān had fallen out of Arab control during the Second Fitna if not sooner, but Umayya rescinded the offer after one of Bukayr's rivals suggested he would throw off his allegiance once he was established there.[37] In 696–7, Umayya again asked Bukayr to campaign into Sogdiana. This time, Bukayr and his ally ʿAttāb al-Liqwa al-Ghudānī took out loans from a group of Sogdian merchants to finance the campaign, but, again, Umayya was convinced to rescind his offer out of fear that Bukayr would rebel once he was beyond the Oxus.[38] Étienne de la Vaissière has suggested that these Sogdian merchants had economic interests in Iran and they hoped the Arab conquest of Sogdiana would result in more favourable trading rights and fewer tariffs and that they may have formed the core of a community of Sogdians living at Marw.[39] The spaces beyond the old Sasanian frontier were associated with rebellion and governors feared that anti-Umayyad Arabs would seek their independence beyond the frontier. As will be seen in the following chapter, this is a pattern that would continue, but in later instances it would involve governors afraid of being replaced who fled further and further beyond the frontier in hopes of raising a rebellion.

In the cases of Mūsā and Bukayr, these were both Arabs who had deep connections to Khurāsān and the eastern frontier. The Banū Khāzim including ʿAbdallāh and his six sons had been associated with Khurāsān since the initial Arab incursions and, over the decades, they had become integrated to an extent within the local community. Mūsā's mother, for example, was the daughter of the ruler of Āzādawār in the district of Abarshahr or Nīshāpūr.[40] Whereas his father was a conqueror, Mūsā was a child of Khurāsān. Bukayr had been a part of Ibn Khāzim's administration from the start of the Second Fitna, serving as the head of his police force and had defended Herat against the Banū Tamīm alongside Muḥammad b. ʿAbdallāh. Perhaps a résumé that includes serving as deputy to a rebellious former governor involved in factional violence and then killing him for a chance at self-promotion would place one's actions under suspicion. Regardless, the eastern frontier also became a refuge for Arabs fleeing Umayyad authority in Iraq. In 702–3 after the failed revolt of ʿAbd al-Raḥmān b. Muḥammad b. al-Ashʿath (d. 704), some members of his 'Peacock Army' (*jaysh al-ṭawāwīs*), so called for the finery the nobles wore as they left Baṣra for Sīstān, fled east from the governor of Iraq Ḥajjāj b. Yūsuf (r. 694–714). They tried to take control of Herat where they collected taxes (*jibāya*), or more likely shook down the local population for money, and then sought sanctuary with Mūsā in Termez.[41] As Umayyad authority was reasserted in Iraq, the loose reins of the eastern frontier made a tempting destination.

Legacies of the Second Fitna and the alliances that formed during the civil war also affected the way Umayyad governors in Khurāsān responded to such rebellions. Umayya was replaced in 697 by Muhallab b. Abī Ṣufra. Muhallab also had deep connections to Khurāsān and had participated in the conquests under Ibn ʿĀmir as well. He had also supported Ibn Zubayr during the fitna but, unlike Ibn Khāzim, had come around to the Umayyads after ʿAbd al-Malik's victory. Still, Muhallab's role in the Second Fitna may have created bonds of loyalty between him and his supporters and some of the rebels who now sought sanctuary on the frontier. It is noticeable, for example, that throughout Muhallab's five-year governorship he never once campaigned against Mūsā in Termez. When he decided to campaign in Sogdiana and besieged Kish, he secured a separate crossing point at Zamm instead of confronting Termez.[42] Similarly, when the remnants of the 'Peacock Army' attacked Herat in 702–3 and even killed his lieutenant, Muhallab's son and successor Yazīd practically refused to fight against them saying that he does 'not like [the idea of] fighting you' and instead accepted their promises that they were simply resting and would soon carry on until they decided to collect taxes, thereby forcing the governor's hand.[43] M. A. Shaban proposed that the uncharacteristic timidity of the Muhallabids in such cases is a hang-over from a time when their family had fought on the side of Ibn Zubayr with the Banū Khāzim and the Baṣran nobles of the 'Peacock Army'.[44] This would be a concern not just for the governors but for the soldiers they may be asking to fight against one-time allies and possibly even tribemates.

In spaces like Termez, alliances were built between Arabs and locals over concerns of both the Umayyads and other local rulers. Mūsā is portrayed in most sources as being caught between the Muhallabid governors of Khurāsān and Ṭarkhūn of Samarqand. The rebels pulled towards Termez included prominent *mawālī* or non-Arab clients such as the Ibn Quṭba brothers, clients of the Banū Khuzāʿa. In 700, Ḥurayth b. Quṭba (d. 704) had threatened Muhallab after the governor beat him for failing to follow his orders and he fled to Termez with his brother Thābit (d. 704) seeking safety.[45] It should be noted that the designation of the Ibn Quṭba brothers as clients/*mawālī* undermines their prestige. They led troops against Bukayr when he revolted with Ḥurayth striking a blow against the former governor.[46] When they fled to Termez, they brought a force of 300 *čākira* – a personal bodyguard which would not be out of place in the entourage of two prominent Sogdians – as well as a contingent of Arabs who were reportedly loyal to them. More likely, these Arabs had compounded interests in turning against the Muhallabids. They also left families and financial interests in Marw. When Yazīd b. Muhallab became governor following his father's death in 702, he confiscated the Ibn Quṭba brothers' property, seized their female relatives and killed their half-brother Ḥarith b. Munqidh (d. ca. 702) and Thābit's son-in-law. News of Yazīd's actions spurred Thābit to action. He rallied Ṭarkhūn, the Nīzak Ṭarkhān of Bādhghīs, Sabal the ruler of Khuttal and the people of Bukhara and Chaghāniyān to join together with Termez and remove Yazīd from Khurāsān.[47] H. A. R. Gibb even proposed that the Sasanian prince Narseh had been involved in this uprising.[48] Thābit successfully organized an awkward alliance between Sogdians, Hephthalites and Arabs united around a common goal of limiting Umayyad – perhaps more specifically Muhallabid – authority beyond the River Oxus. The Arabs among the rebels recognized Mūsā as the lord of Sogdiana at this point – or at least that is how the Arabic historical tradition remembers these events – but the real power was with Ḥurayth and Thābit. In spite of their conflicts with the Umayyads, Mūsā and his Arab supporters refused to back an attack against the Muhallabids, fearing that victory would hand Khurāsān over to Ḥurayth and Thābit and that Arab rule would end in the east.[49] They turned on their Sogdian allies in an attempt to preserve Arab rule, but these actions weakened the rebels' position and Termez was eventually retaken and Mūsā killed in 704–5.

It may be attractive to think of Termez in terms of Turner's model of the frontier process, discussed in Chapter 1. The group we find at Termez was a mixture of people brought together through struggles for economic and political resources along the frontier. From the end results, it is clear this was an alliance of convenience and the fault lines between Muslims and non-Muslims and Arabs and non-Arabs seemed too powerful to overcome at this time. Rather than a true frontier melting pot, Termez was a place of refuge beyond the reach of empire. This was not the only case of Arabs and non-Arabs uniting in rebellion. Returning to Bukayr b. Wishāḥ, twice bitten by the governor of Khurāsān, when Umayya personally led a campaign into Sogdiana, Bukayr turned back and initiated a revolt from Marw. An essential element of his revolt was recruitment among the Marwazis, which he achieved by promising an exemption to the *kharāj* for anyone who fought on his side. According to his ally Aḥnaf b. ʿAbdallāh al-ʿAnbarī, such a promise would bring 50,000 Marwazis to his cause.[50] These Marwazis were not being drawn to Bukayr on any political or ideological grounds. To the contrary, they were lured by pure financial self-interest, escape from imperial taxation.

Again, the eastern frontier was a dynamic place with overlapping populations with their own interests. Ethnic and religious lines were often blurred and did not signal clear political associations. A dichotomy between Arabs and non-Arabs or Muslims and non-Muslims is not sufficient to understand the dynamics at work. Likewise, Mūsā's Termez questions the power of the Umayyad Caliphate to control the frontiers and complicates the question of who held legitimate authority over the eastern frontier.[51] From the beginning of the Second Fitna until the Umayyad conquest of Termez, the Arabs of Khurāsān seem driven by their own interests, disconnected from a distant political centre in Syria which was rebuilding itself. These interests, at times, aligned with those of local populations who themselves had a variety of concerns from preserving political independence to economic ties and modes of imperial taxation.

The autonomous governorships of the eastern frontier

Separated from the central authority in Iraq by long distances, the governors of Khurāsān had great leeway to act independently through the Second Fitna and its aftermath. Although it is impossible not to read the actions of Ibn Khāzim in Khurāsān within the larger context of the empire-wide civil war, there are many ways in which his actions do not match the general narrative of the Second Fitna; the conflicts that roiled Khurāsān do not fit into the easy divisions of the larger civil war. Khurāsān was beyond the effective control of the caliphate, especially during a period of crisis, and this created opportunities for the Khurāsānī Arabs. As we will see in the following chapter, this did not end with the Umayyad victory in Syria. The Muhallabids, for example, continued to treat Khurāsān largely as an autonomous fiefdom while the Umayyads worked to consolidate their authority. It was only when the governor of Iraq Ḥajjāj b. Yūsuf sent his protégé Qutayba b. Muslim east in 705 that the rule of Khurāsān truly became integrated within the larger caliphate.

Under such circumstances, the governors of Khurāsān were largely focused on maintaining their authority, and expansion was a slow process. Challenging Arab and Muslim rebels who had sought security beyond the reach of the caliphate may not have been the most efficient use of their limited human and financial resources. This is even more noticeable when we consider that a Muhallabid attack on Mūsā's kingdom in Termez would likely require people to fight against their former allies, friends and even relatives. Loyalties in the frontier region were complex, multifaceted and overlapping. The generally divided nature of the frontier shatterzone created spaces where such rebels could establish themselves successfully, potentially for long periods of time as in the case of Mūsā's fifteen-year tenure as the lord of Termez, and the fear that other rebels would follow their lead was a constant threat to those governors hoping to reassert caliphal authority after the civil war.

In the previous chapter, we explored the variety of opponents the Arabs faced as they sought to conquer Sasanian Khurāsān and extend the frontier into Ṭukhāristān and Sogdiana. This chapter has reinforced the idea that despite the rhetoric of the conquest narratives and the unifying language of Islam, the Arabs themselves were not united and were becoming the real threat to Arab authority in Khurāsān. While such disunity has long been acknowledged, it has been understood through the larger frame of the Second Fitna and the tribal conflicts that arose from this conflict, but in Khurāsān Arab disunity did not clearly follow the political or tribal factions that dominate this larger narrative. Similar divisions existed among the local populations and several powers were competing for influence on the edges of Khurāsān spreading this conflict beyond the Arabs. In the frontier zone, these multiple layers of division had opportunities to overlap and create new alliances that could work to advance individual interests. In the following chapter, we will turn the focus to the concerted effort in the eighth century to conquer Sogdiana and integrate it into the Umayyad Empire. As the frontier advanced, even more people were brought into the empire with their own interests, further complicating these imperial relationships. The challenge of integration of distant frontiers into the empire created further inspirations and opportunities for rebellion.

Chapter 5

EXTENDING THE FRONTIER: THE UMAYYADS IN SOGDIANA AND BEYOND

Qutayba b. Muslim in Samarqand

In the eighth century, the Umayyad presence along the eastern frontier moved from incursions by armies from Iraq and the wild east of rebellious tribesmen fleeing the reach of the imperial authorities to a regularized and centralized mission of conquest that sought to integrate not only Khurāsān but also Ṭukhāristān and Transoxiana into the empire. As these forces moved further north and east, they could not simply conquer and supplant local political orders, instead they had to remake the eastern frontier. This involved not only changing the political, economic and social structures of places like Sogdiana to meet imperial needs – sometimes even physically by seizing property and building garrisons to support Arab troops – but also changing the political, economic and social order of the conquerors as well. In both cases the Umayyads and their governors in the east faced push back. This chapter examines the process by which the eastern frontier was formally conquered by the Umayyad Empire and brought into the imperial sphere. In doing so, the Umayyads faced many struggles from the revolts of the Hephthalites and Sogdians to invasions by Turkish rivals and intertribal conflict among the conquerors themselves. In the end, the eastern frontier of the Umayyads was not stable in the early eighth century, but it pushed forward a process of integrating the region into the empire. To begin, let us look at the response to the first formal attempts at a permanent conquest of Sogdiana.

In many ways, the year 709 was a watershed moment for Umayyad expansion into Sogdiana and Ṭukhāristān. Following a protracted series of four campaigns, Qutayba b. Muslim – the Umayyad governor of Khurāsān renowned for his conquests of Transoxiana that established an Arab presence in both Bukhara and Samarqand and pushed Umayyad authority, momentarily, to the River Jaxartes – finally conquered the Bukhara oasis. But in the aftermath he lost two important allies. First was the Ikhshīd Ṭarkhūn of Samarqand. Upset that Ṭarkhūn had 'been satisfied with humiliation and … deemed the [paying of tax agreeable]', the Samarqandīs deposed their king out of anger and replaced him with a man named Ghūrak (r. 710–38) who promised a firmer hand against the Muslims.[1] Ṭarkhūn did not survive the coup and may have chosen to fall on his sword while imprisoned rather than face the executioner's blade.[2] Qutayba had considered

Ṭarkhūn his personal *mawlā* or client and took his disposal as an affront against him.[3] Before Qutayba could respond though, the Nīzak Ṭarkhān – the Hephthalite ruler of Bādhghīs who had fought alongside Qutayba during the conquest of Bukhara – abandoned Qutayba, returned to Ṭukhāristān and organized a revolt against Umayyad rule.

The Nīzak's revolt was also inspired by Ṭarkhūn's negotiation with Qutayba or, more accurately, Qutayba's willingness to treat with Ṭarkhūn so recently after the two had fought. The Nīzak reportedly described Qutayba as a dog, saying, 'If you beat him, he barks, and if you feed him, he wags his tail.'[4] The revolt in Ṭukhāristān, discussed below, was far more pressing but eventually Qutayba returned to Samarqand to avenge Ṭarkhūn. In 712 following a campaign against Khwarazm, Qutayba marched on Samarqand with the support of warriors from both Khwarazm and Bukhara. He was intent on removing Ghūrak. Instead, once the walls of the city had been breached, Ghūrak offered to make peace with Qutayba, offering 1,200,000 dirhams and an annual tribute of 30,000 slaves neither too young (*ṣabīy*) nor too old (*shaykh*). Furthermore, Ghūrak agreed to build a mosque in Samarqand and then empty the city so the Muslims could pray, but once inside Qutayba refused to leave.[5] Balādhūrī offered an alternative account in which Ghūrak made peace for 700,000 dirhams, but despite the agreement the Muslims plundered the idols from Samarqand's temples.[6] Ṭabarī provided a similar report on the authority of Madā'inī that Ghūrak made peace for 100,000 slaves and then the Muslims looted the temples.[7]

Qutayba acted harshly in transforming Samarqand into a Muslim space, effectively barring non-Muslims from remaining in the city. In one account, any non-Muslims entering the city had a clay seal placed on their hands and if the clay dried before they left the city – a sign they had overstayed their welcome – they were to be killed. If any non-Muslims were found carrying weapons in the city, they were to be killed. And if any non-Muslims were found in the city after nightfall, they were to be killed.[8] Despite Ghūrak's invitation into the city and offers of a peace treaty, Qutayba behaved as if Samarqand had been conquered by force. Even Ghūrak himself was forced to leave the city, transferring his palace to Ishtīkhan seven *farāsikh* (42 km) northwest of Samarqand.[9] The Samarqandīs offered Qutayba a peace agreement but he looted the temples and barred the locals from returning to their homes anyway.

The ninth- and tenth-century chroniclers on whom we rely presented Qutayba's conquests as a duplicitous affair. According to Balādhūrī, on the authority of the philologist Abū ʿUbaydah Maʿmar b. al-Muthannā (728–825), the people of Samarqand had not broken the treaty they had made with the governor Saʿīd b. ʿUthmān when he came to Samarqand three decades earlier, yet Qutayba had disregarded this treaty when he conquered the city.[10] The same is said of Khwarazm which Qutayba had subdued immediately before his campaign against Samarqand.[11] Ṭabarī included an anecdote from Madā'inī in which a messenger was sent to inform Qutayba's overlord, the governor of Iraq Ḥajjāj b. Yūsuf of the victory in Samarqand. Ḥajjāj then sent ʿUmar on to Syria to share the news with the Caliph Walīd. Upon arriving in Damascus before sunrise, the messenger visited the mosque where he engaged a blind man in conversation. When he recounted the news from Sogdiana, the blind man scolded him saying, 'By Him Who sent Muḥammad with the truth, you have only conquered it by perfidy. You, O people of Khurāsān, are those who will strip the Banū Umayya of their dominion and pull Damascus down stone by stone.'[12] The blind man – and by relaying this narrative Madāʾinī and then Ṭabarī as well – associated Qutayba's conquest of Samarqand with violations of the proper order. Through his allusion to the Abbasid Revolution, he also tied Qutayba's behaviour to those who would eventually bring down the entire Umayyad dynasty.

Chapters 3 and 4 focused on the political landscape of the eastern frontier in the mid- to late-seventh century, as the initial Arab incursions into Khurāsān, Ṭukhāristān and Transoxiana occurred and as the Second Fitna fractured Arab unity. It was argued in Chapter 3 that in its early phase the Arab–Muslim conquests were not true campaigns of conquest but rather incursions and that the dynamics of the frontier were not entirely dictated by the collapse of the Sasanian Empire and its replacement by an imperial caliphate. Instead, it was argued that the frontier needed to be analysed in the context of the Turkish, Hephthalite and Chinese players in Sogdiana and Ṭukhāristān as well. Chapter 4 focused on the autonomy of the Arab governors of Khurāsān and the role of the eastern frontier as a refugee for those fleeing the political dramas of the west. In this chapter, I focus on the next phase of the conquests, Arab expansion into Sogdiana and the incorporation of the east into the imperial structures of the empire. While the first incursions into the Zarāfshān Valley may have come as early as 654, it was not until the governorship of Qutayba that permanent settlements and Arab–Muslim rule were established beyond the Oxus.

The decision to settle and establish formal rule in Sogdiana and elsewhere along the eastern frontier shifted the dynamics of the frontier and created a complex set of changing relations between not only the conquerors and the conquered but also among factions within each side. These transformations have been primarily studied through the lens of the Abbasid Revolution – discussed in the following chapter – and the formation of a pro-Abbasid or anti-Umayyad constituency that marched west from Khurāsān to transform the caliphate. These studies have often focused on demographics and the formation of factions among the Arabs – in many ways committing the same mistakes of Frederick Jackson Turner by focusing on the settlers while ignoring the indigenous population – but the frontier was a much more complex place. In this chapter, I will focus on the ever-changing dynamics of the eastern frontier as the Umayyads attempted to integrate Sogdiana and, to a lesser extent, Ṭukhāristān into the caliphate and the resistance and support they received from an array of frontier populations from the Arabs and Sogdians to the Hephthalites and Turks. As such, this chapter examines Sogdiana as a meso-imperial space caught between and desired by both the Umayyad Caliphate and the Western Türk Khāqānate. The story that unfolds is not just one of conquest and rebellion, as it is often described, but one driven by the fluctuating fortunes of the two empires that surrounded the region. Beginning with the governorship of Qutayba b. Muslim, the Umayyads broke free of the Sasanian frontier and actively expanded and settled Sogdiana, campaigning to the River Jaxartes and beyond. These campaigns were planned and directed by imperial authorities who asserted their authority over the frontier and brought the Umayyads into direct competition with the Turks over the wealth of Sogdiana.

The conquests of Qutayba b. Muslim

The conclusion of the Second Fitna gave the Umayyads an opportunity to reshape and strengthen their hold over the empire under the Marwānid line. Along the eastern frontier, this included a coordinated series of campaigns that would bring Sogdiana under caliphal authority, establishing the foundation of Muslim-ruled Transoxiana and extending the reach of the frontier far beyond the River Oxus. In Iraq and the east, the consolidation of Umayyad authority was led by the governor Ḥajjāj b. Yūsuf who had risen through the ranks of ʿAbd al-Malik's *shurṭa* or police and had led the final assault against the counter-caliph Ibn Zubayr in Mecca. After the war Ḥajjāj was named governor of both Baṣra and Kūfa with authority over Khurāsān and Sīstān, making him the effective ruler of the east. As governor, Ḥajjāj systematically broke the tribal nobility of Iraq, most infamously by instigating and then crushing the revolt of Ibn al-Ashʿath and his 'Peacock Army' in 701. Ḥajjāj replaced the Iraqis with Syrian forces and even founded a new city, Wāsiṭ, between Baṣra and Kūfa from which he and his Syrian troops could police Iraq. In this context, Ḥajjāj is often put forward as paradigmatic of the Marwānid reliance on violence when ideological justifications for their rule failed to materialize.[13]

Following the death of ʿAbd al-Malik and the succession of his son Walīd, Ḥajjāj sent Qutayba b. Muslim to Khurāsān to replace the Muhallabid governors whose Azdite tribesmen were becoming too numerous in the east. The Muhallabids stoked fears that they could cultivate an independent power base and entrench themselves in the distant province. In his biography of the Muhallabid family, Salama b. Muslim al-ʿAwtabī (ca. late eleventh to early twelfth century) reported that, at the time of Muhallab b. Abī Ṣufra's death in 702, he rode with 350 sons, grandsons, brothers and nephews and we presume his own son Yazīd inherited a similar number of Azdite backers along with his father's office.[14] In contrast, Qutayba's tribe of Bāhila, though of the Qays or northern faction, was considered politically neutral vis-à-vis the tribal conflicts that had engulfed the early years of Umayyad rule or, at least, numerically insignificant enough in Khurāsān as to not sway the conflict alone. More importantly, Qutayba had proven his personal loyalty to Ḥajjāj during the civil war. While the Muhallabids were Azdites and could be accused of building a family power based in Khurāsān, Qutayba was Ḥajjāj's man. The hope was that Qutayba could stabilize some of the factional rivalries that had dominated Khurāsān for decades. Upon his arrival, Qutayba imprisoned any Muhallabids who remained in Khurāsān and confiscated their wealth.[15] Ḥajjāj had Yazīd b. al-Muhallab imprisoned in Iraq as well, but the former governor escaped and found refuge with the caliph's brother and eventual successor Sulaymān

(r. 715–17). With Qutayba replacing the Muhallabids, Khurāsān was firmly under Ḥajjāj and Iraq's authority.

More consequentially, Qutayba was sent to Khurāsān with instructions to extend the frontier. From Iraq, Ḥajjāj directed and organized campaigns in Ṭukhāristān, Transoxiana and even against the Zunbīl in the Hindu Kush, a campaign coordinated with the army of Sīstān.[16] Qutayba's campaigns across the eastern frontier were not simply adventures seeking spoils as many of his predecessors had done. Instead he reshaped the political, economic and social landscape of the region by removing local leaders antagonistic to Umayyad expansion and establishing Arab garrisons beyond the River Oxus. Throughout his governorship, Qutayba worked to solidify alliances with friendly local rulers, including the incorporation of large numbers of *mawālī* or non-Arab converts into his army often under the leadership of the Daylamite *mawlā* Ḥayyān al-Nabaṭī (d. 720–1), while also fighting brutally against those who opposed his goals.[17] When Qutayba first arrived in Khurāsān in 705, he immediately travelled to Ṭukhāristān where he received the loyalties of the *dahāqīn* of Balkh and the king of Chaghāniyān Tish al-Aʿwar (the One-Eyed Tish) and he defeated the lords of Akharūn and Shūmān on Tish's behalf.[18] His victories secured the passages from Ṭukhāristān to Sogdiana through the Gate of Iron. Through the *mawlā* Sulaym al-Nāṣiḥ (the Counsellor), Qutayba secured a peace treaty with the Hephthalite lord of Bādhghīs the Nīzak Ṭarkhān that included the release of an unspecified number of Muslim prisoners.[19] One set of conditions included in this arrangement was that Qutayba would never enter Bādhghīs and the Nīzak would campaign alongside Qutayba in Sogdiana.

After securing Ṭukhāristān, Qutayba turned his attention towards the Bukhara oasis which he transformed not only politically but also physically. The political situation in Bukhara is not clear in the early eighth century and the evidence does not clearly coincide with the Khātūn legends and the rule of her son Ṭughshāda as it is described by Narshakhī's *History of Bukhara*, an account which likely has its origins in the family histories of the Bukhārkhudās. Instead, it appears that Paykand, the famous 'City of Merchants', was autonomous and ruled by a council of merchants while the Vardānkhudā named Kh.n.k was acting as the Bukhārkhudā, ruling the oasis from around 689.[20] As mentioned in Chapter 3, the Vardānkhudā was the son of Shāpūr, an exiled son of the Sasanian Shahanshah Khusrow II who had sought refuge with the Bukhārkhudā.[21]

Qutayba led a series of four annual campaigns into the Bukhara oasis.[22] The first focused on Paykand, the closest Sogdian city to Marw as one crosses the Oxus at Āmul. After receiving the city's submission, Qutayba left a small garrison and marched deeper into the oasis, but the Paykandīs rose up and killed the encamped Arabs. Qutayba's response was brutal. He besieged Paykand, refusing all peace terms and offers of tribute. When they finally breached the walls, the Arabs killed all of Paykand's warriors (*muqātila*) and looted the city before returning to Marw with so much plunder it caused inflation in the markets.[23] The size of the spoils were perhaps notable due to the wealth of Paykand and its merchant community, but, as Étienne de la Vaissière suggested, they may also be notable because this was the first instance of plundering to have occurred in the east, the cities of Khurāsān having submitted by treaty, and the first conquests and opportunities for spoils following the internal dramas of the Second Fitna.[24] In Narshakhī's account, many of the merchants of Paykand were on a trading mission to China when Qutayba arrived and, upon their return, they ransomed the women and children who had been taken captive and rebuilt the city which had been destroyed.[25]

As Qutayba marched up the Zarāfshān in subsequent years, he faced further resistance. In 706–7, Qutayba took the villages of Tumushkath and Karmīniyya before fighting and defeating an army of Turks and Sogdians (presumably the army of Samarqand) under the leadership of Kūrbaghānūn al-Turkī. Our sources claim Kūrbaghānūn was the nephew of the Tang emperor, but it is more likely he was instead a relative of the supreme commander of the Turks – though diplomatic marriages between the Chinese royal family and Turkish rulers could explain the confusion.[26] The following year, Qutayba was under orders from Ḥajjāj to remove the Vardānkhudā – and thus establish Ṭughshāda as the Bukhārkhudā – but he was defeated.[27] Symbolic of the manner in which Khurāsān was now being administered from Iraq, Ḥajjāj gave Qutayba specific tactical instructions for the next year, ordering him to capture Kish and Nasaf before moving on Vardān. Ḥajjāj's instructions are presented as a pun on the name of these cities. 'Reduce Kish (*kis bi-Kish*), raze Nasaf (*ansif Nasaf*) and oppose Vardān (*wa ridd Wardān*).'[28] The fourth campaign defeated a force of Sogdians and Turks supporting the Vardānkhudā, captured Vardān and established Ṭughshāda, the son of Khātūn, as the Bukhārkhudā.[29] Through this campaign we can identify a layering of political authority in Sogdiana as outside powers supported competing claimants to the throne of Bukhara. The Vardānkhudā was supported by his neighbours in Samarqand who are often called the kings of Sogdiana and their overlords, the Turks, while Ṭughshāda was backed by the new imperial rival, the Umayyads, a choice that seems to come all the way from Iraq. It was at this point Qutayba also made his treaty with Ṭarkhūn, discussed above. This treaty and the resulting deposal and death of Ṭarkhūn must be read in the context of competing Umayyad and Turkish spheres of influence in Sogdiana.

When Qutayba conquered Bukhara, he did not simply seek tribute from the Bukharans. He transformed the oasis. According to Narshakhī, following his fourth campaign into the oasis, Qutayba became tired of the need to continuously reassert his authority in Bukhara and decided to establish a garrison, which would have the added advantage of facilitating regular campaigns against Samarqand. Qutayba forced the Bukharans to give half of their homes and estates (*khan-hā va ẓiyā-hā*) to the Arabs and supply them with fodder for their horses and firewood.[30] These were the responsibilities of those living both in the city and outside of it (*bīrūn shahr*). Narshakhī specifies one group of Bukharans for displacement by Qutayba, a group of high-ranking, wealthy and foreign merchants called the Kashkatha. The Kashkatha gave up all their houses to the Arabs and built 700 villas (*kūshk*) outside the city where they lived as *dahāqīn*, presumably meaning they stopped being merchants and instead became agriculturalists.[31] In general, the establishment of an Arab garrison in Bukhara resulted in the transfer of local elites from the city to the countryside, including the court of the Bukhārkhudā which shifted at some point in the early eighth century to the palace of Varakhsha, approximately 45 km to the west.[32]

The confiscation of so much property and the forced resettlement of large parts of the population may feel odd to anyone familiar with traditions that the Arab–Muslim conquests preserved the property rights of the conquered – to maintain a tax base – but these traditions became codified long after the conquests were completed as jurists attempted to harmonize historical practice with religiously inspired theory.[33] Therefore we should not be surprised by behaviours that would later be considered illegal. As a result, we find several references to people later contesting the confiscations when legal opinions had turned in their favour. During the caliphate of ʿUmar II, for example, the people of Samarqand petitioned the caliph directly for the return of property confiscated by Qutayba. When a judge was sent to investigate their grievances Sulaymān b. Abī al-Sārī, a *mawlā* of the Banū ʿUwāfah who held various posts in Umayyad Sogdiana including fiscal administration and military commissions, outmanoeuvred the caliph and made it known that if the judge found in the Samarqandīs' favour, he would simply reconquer the city by force and establish a new, harsher treaty with the people. For good reason, the Samarqandīs balked at this.[34] Land confiscated by Qutayba was still contested half a century later. Narshakhī reported that the district in which Qutayba's amirs lived was called 'the palace quarter' (*kūy-i kākh*) and that this quarter belonged to a *dihqān* named Khīna who had changed his name to Aḥmad after converting to Islam. In this quarter there had been a palace where the *dahāqīn* and amirs of Bukhara would reside. In 767, a descendant of Khīna named Kadra-i Khīna pleaded before the Abbasid Caliph Manṣūr, bringing a deed for the whole quarter of the city including 1,000 shops (*dukkān*) and seventy-five private villages (*dīha-i khāṣṣ*). Manṣūr surrendered all the properties to him.[35] It is unclear if Khīna was one of the Kashkatha but, regardless, when Qutayba settled an Arab garrison in Bukhara, it displaced a substantial number of the city's residents and claims against confiscated property could carry on for generations.

In the accounts of the Kashkatha and Khīna we also see how permanent conquest could impact the livelihood of the Bukharans. The Kashkatha are specifically described as foreign merchants while Khīna's properties included 1,000 shops. Both were involved in trade. Narshakhī's phrasing implies that the Kashkatha had been merchants, not *dahāqīn*, but by giving up their properties in the city and establishing themselves in the countryside, building villas for themselves and their servants, they became *dahāqīn*. The switch from merchants to agriculturalists may be a result of the changing geopolitical realities that accompanied Qutayba's conquests. The Sogdian merchants who helped finance Arab campaigns into Sogdiana were briefly discussed in the previous chapter in the context of Bukayr b. Wishāḥ's failed revolt and it was proposed that they may have been looking to improve trade relations with the caliphate and lower the duties on their merchandise, perhaps being more inclined towards trade in Iran. Other merchants, such as those who lost their homes in Paykand and perhaps the Kashkatha, may have had an eastern orientation, trading primarily with China.

A more permanent conquest of Bukhara by the Arabs could pose a challenge to those attempting to trade in the east, encouraging some merchants to pivot and settle on agricultural estates instead.[36] M. A. Shaban made a similar argument, seeing a pro-Arab party among the Sogdians with commercial interests in Khurāsān including a Sogdian community living in Marw and an anti-Arab party with commercial interests in China.[37] Disruptions among the Turks, discussed below, may also have contributed to the strains placed on the Sogdian trade with China as the pathways of the so-called 'Silk Road' became less secure.[38]

The question of trade with China features in many aspects of Qutayba's conquests. It may very well be the case that the Paykandīs' decision to massacre the Arab garrison was tied to their economic relationship with China; an act of resistance against incorporation into the Umayyad economic sphere when their primary trade partner was the Tang. In some accounts, Qutayba attempted to seize control of the trade with China for the Arabs. According to some sources, Qutayba captured the trade routes towards the Tarim Basin, the gateway for Central Asian trade into China, going as far as Kashgar in the year 715.[39] Madā'inī claimed that Qutayba then sent a delegation to the Chinese court that so impressed Emperor Xuánzōng (r. 712–56) they returned with tokens of his submission including soil from China for Qutayba to tread upon and Tang princes to act as hostages.[40] Chinese accounts tell of an Arab embassy that arrived at the Tang court a year earlier, but they focus on the Arabs' refusal to perform the kowtow before the emperor, claiming such obeisance was reserved for God alone, though they eventually relented under pressure.[41] The Arab reports of these eastern campaigns are highly suspect with Gibb believing them to be an echo of later Arab participation in a raid on Kashgar by the Türgesh Turks, unreported by the Arabic and Persian sources but perhaps involving the vestiges of Qutayba's army that remained in Ferghana after the governor's death and joined the Turks.[42] That these accounts survive alongside those of the disruption and destruction of Sogdian merchant communities points towards at least the hope of Arab domination of the lucrative trade.

Qutayba attempted to transform the religious outlook of Bukhara as well. Again, according to Narshakhī, each time the Bukharans made peace with the Arabs, they would convert to Islam and then immediately apostatize once the Arabs left. In 712–13, four years after his last campaign against Bukhara and the settlement of Arabs in the city, Qutayba took efforts to reverse this trend. He built a congregational mosque in the citadel (*ḥiṣār*) on the site of an existing temple and, to encourage participation, he paid the locals two dirhams if they attended Friday prayers.[43] Qutayba tried other unorthodox approaches to converting the people as well including allowing them to read the Qur'an in Persian and employing a prayer leader who would call out instructions in Persian, perhaps meaning Sogdian.[44] This would be extremely early for a translated Qur'an – the first Persian work of *tafsīr* or Qur'anic exegesis would not come until the tenth century – and would presumably be forbidden in the early eighth century, but again, Qutayba is acting far from the political and theological centre and at a time before many of these norms were codified. In Narshakhī's time, this mosque still retained much of its pre-Islamic form, including carvings of idols (with their faces scratched off) on wooden doors which had been taken from the villas (*kūshk*) of the notables (*tuwāngarān*) who had refused to attend the mosque (and did not need the weekly two dirham bribe).[45] It may be the case that included among these were the Kashkatha, whose villas were known as the Villas of the Magians (*kūshk-i Mughān*) and were home to many fire temples. Narshakhī described gates on their villas decorated like those hung in the mosque.[46] Nasafī (1067–1142) described the conversion of the village of Kurjan in the Bukhara oasis during Qutayba's conquest in his biographical dictionary, *The Sweet in Remembering the Ulema of Samarqand*. In this instance, the *dihqān* of the village sent out a Zoroastrian priest (*ʿālim al-majūs*) named Khushtiyār to learn about Islam and, when he decided it was true, the *dihqān* and the whole village converted on his recommendation.[47] Even though this conversion narrative feels like a formulaic trope, it highlights the autonomy of individual villages with not only independent leadership in the form of the *dihqān* but their own religious institutions and clerics as well.

The rebellion of the Nīzak Ṭarkhān

As discussed in the introduction to this chapter, the Ikhshīd Ṭarkhūn's willingness to make peace with Qutayba was not well received, resulting in his ouster by Ghūrak and death, but it also, in part, inspired the revolt of the Hephthalite lord of Bādhghīs, the Nīzak Ṭarkhān. The Nīzak Ṭarkhān had participated in the conquest of Bukhara as a condition of his earlier peace agreement with Qutayba, but in 709 he took to his mountain holdfasts and organized a rebellion against Umayyad rule. Protected by the mountains, Bādhghīs had been the target of campaigns in the years leading up to Qutayba's governorship. As mentioned briefly in Chapter 3, the brothers Yazīd and Mufaḍḍal b. al-Muhallab had led consecutive campaigns against the Nīzak between 703 and 705, but the fortress high in the mountains continued to provide refuge to the Hephthalites.[48] The Azdite poet and companion of the Muhallabids Kaʿb b. Maʿdān al-Ashqarī described Bādhghīs as impenetrable in a poem celebrating Yazīd's conquest.

> Bādhghīs – which [is such that] he who occupies its upper part
> overcomes kings and, if he wishes, may act tyrannically and oppressively-
> Is well fortified: No king before [Yazīd] has taken it by guile;
> [it can be taken] only when it is faced by a vast army of his.
> Its fires, viewed from a distance, could be imagined to be
> stars, in the first third of the night.
> When [Yazīd] circled round it, their hearts sank
> until they left it to him to judge, and he decided.
> He humbled its inhabitant (that is, Nīzak) after his [previous] greatness
> [by making him] pay poll tax, [he thereby] acknowledging abasement and oppression.
> …

He expelled Nīzak from Bādhghīs, and Nīzak was in a position which was too
difficult for kings to snatch from him,
[a position] soaring beneath the sky, like
a white summer cloud from which the rain clouds have passed away.
Not even the mountain goats reach its uppermost parts,
nor birds, save its eagle and osprey.
The children of its people have not been frightened by the wolf,
nor have its dogs barked at anything save the stars.[49]

The position of Bādhghīs in the mountains gave the Nīzak a certain level of immunity from conquest. The specifics of the treaty between Qutayba and the Nīzak negotiated in 705 forbade Qutayba from entering Bādhghīs, thereby leaving the mountains and its fortress in the hands of the Hephthalites and, when the Nīzak chose to turn on Qutayba, it was to these mountains that he returned.

As the Nīzak returned to Marw alongside Qutayba at the end of the campaign of 709, he asked for and received permission to return to Ṭukhāristān where he rallied the Ispahbud of Balkh, the kings of Ṭālaqān, Fāryāb and the Gūzgān as well as the *marzbān* of Marw al-Rūd Bādhām – likely a son or grandson of the Bādhām who made peace with Aḥnaf b. Qays nearly sixty years earlier (see Chapter 3) – for a spring revolt. He also came to an agreement with the Kābulshāh to send his treasury south, away from his force, attempting to lure the Arabs away from him believing their priority would be the spoils.[50] In the face of Qutayba and the Umayyads' strengthened position in Sogdiana, Ṭarkhān brought together the lords of Ṭukhāristān in an effort to preserve local autonomy. Despite references to the Turkish Yabghu as the nominal king of Ṭukhāristān, the Nīzak acted as the de facto ruler and even imprisoned the Yabghu, simultaneously recognizing that he was but the Yabghu's slave (*min ʿabīdi-hi*), before initiating his revolt.[51] In doing so, the Nīzak was playing a part similar to that of the kings of Bukhara and Samarqand, caught between the Umayyads and the Turks, able to turn from one side to the other when it seems beneficial but also able to use his strategic strength at times to express his autonomy.

Qutayba learnt of the revolt when his governor, Muḥammad the son of Sulaym the Counsellor – the *mawlā* who had negotiated the earlier peace between Qutayba and the Nīzak – was expelled from Ṭukhāristān but was unable to organize a response until the spring. That Sulaym's son acted as Qutayba's lieutenant in Balkh may be another indication of Ṭukhārian origins for this family as well as a prior relationship with the Nīzak and the Hephthalites. Presumably the army of Khurāsān was still largely a campaign army that disbanded in the autumn. A force of 12,000 was sent immediately to Barūqān, the garrison two *farāsikh* (12 km) outside of Balkh, under Qutayba's brother ʿAbd al-Raḥmān (d. 715). By our best estimates, this constituted more than a quarter of the Arab troops in Khurāsān during Qutayba's governorship.[52] As spring neared Qutayba called upon the lords of Nīshāpūr, Abīward, Sarakhs and Herat who joined him.[53] Qutayba's campaign against the Nīzak and his allies was notably violent. Bādhān fled from Marw al-Rūd to Gharshistān, leaving two sons behind who were killed and crucified.[54] At Ṭālaqān, one account tells us that Qutayba faced brigands (*luṣūṣ*) or wretches (*ṣaʿālīk*) whom he defeated and crucified, while an earlier report adds details that two parallel rows of crucified bodies stretched four *farāsikh* (approximately 24 km).[55] The terror of this slaughter was enough that the king of Fāryāb, the people of Gūzgān and the Ispahbud of Balkh all surrendered without a fight, though the king of Gūzgān did flee to the mountains.[56] As for the Nīzak, he fled to the Khulm Valley where he barricaded himself in a strong fortress (*qalʿa ḥaṣīna*) called Kurz that was inaccessible until the Rōb Khān – ruler of the kingdom of Rōb well known from the Bactrian documents – showed Qutayba how to circumvent the pass and approach the fortress from the rear. In the end, Qutayba had Sulaym the Counsellor trick the Nīzak into abandoning his fortress without promises of safe conduct.[57] Qutayba killed the Nīzak with his own hands and exiled the Yabghu to Syria replacing him with his young son – demonstrating an ongoing practice of dismissing individual lords but leaving local traditions of rule in place. Seven hundred of the Nīzak's supporters were killed along with him.[58]

The rebellion of the Nīzak Ṭarkhān and Qutayba's response highlight two challenges facing the Umayyads on the eastern frontier. First was the relationship between the caliphate and local lords. With the Nīzak Ṭarkhān, Ṭarkhūn of Samarqand and Ṭughshāda of Bukhara, Qutayba attempted to incorporate local authorities into the structures of Umayyad Khurāsān but their loyalties could not always be trusted. As we shall see, this is a theme that will carry on throughout Umayyad and into Abbasid rule as local lords and populations vacillated between support for the Arabs and support for their rivals, most notably the Turks whose lighter footprint must have felt more like independence but whose inconsistent ability to provide security against the Arabs left them exposed. This tension resulted in occasional violent purges of former allies, as in the case of the Nīzak. Displacing a portion of the urban populations and establishing garrisons allowed the Arabs to create a 'military archipelago' of disjointed garrisons in the major urban centres across the frontier.[59] Such garrisons may have provided a more stable long-term solution in the cities, but the true military threat came from the mountains, deserts and steppes. Thinking back to Barfield's 'Swiss-Cheese' frontier described in Chapter 1, Qutayba's campaigns were focused on controlling the urban centres and the agricultural oases – the centres of legible and taxable wealth or 'the cheese' – but, to hold these positions, the deserts, steppes and mountains that surrounded them also needed to be subdued. While Qutayba could establish a garrison in Balkh and even built a mosque there, the Hephthalites could cut off the whole of Ṭukhāristān from their mountain holdfasts, much as they had done to the Sasanians as discussed in Chapter 2. The brutal violence of Qutayba's campaign and the mass execution of the Nīzak's followers reflect the necessity of not only defeating the semi-nomadic peoples of the deserts, steppes and mountains but preventing them from returning to these territories from which they could again strike at or cut off Balkh. Without control of the mountains, control of Balkh and Ṭukhāristān in general was ephemeral. Following another metaphor, to possess the islands, the seas needed to be tamed.

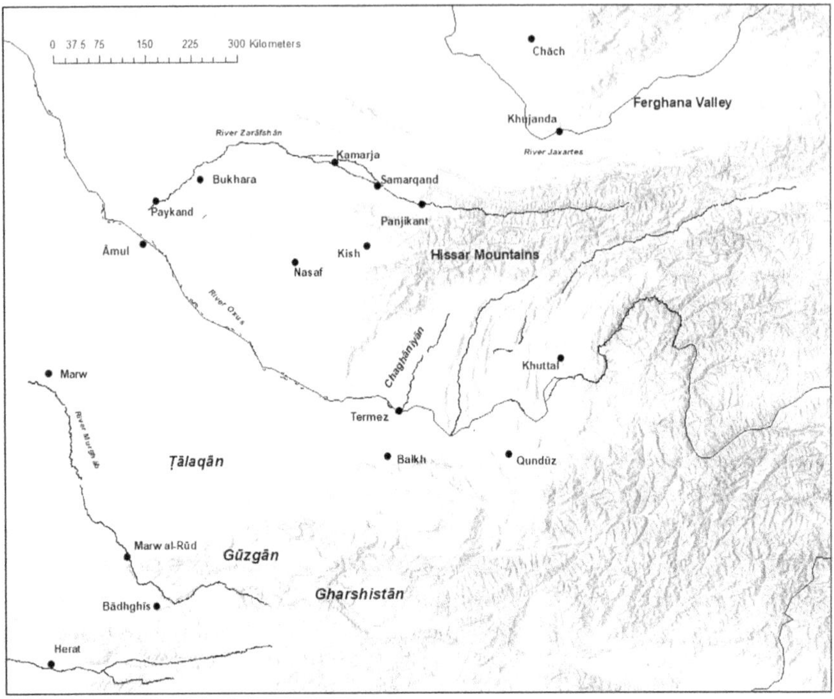

Map 6 The Eastern Frontier of the Umayyad Caliphate.

Sources: Esri, USGS, NGA, NASA, CGIAR, N Robinson, NCEAS, NLS, OS, NMA, Geodatastyrelsen, Rijkswaterstaat, GSA, Geoland, FEMA, Intermap and the GIS user community.

The eastern frontier after Qutayba

Qutayba b. Muslim continued to campaign beyond Samarqand, leading campaigns into the Ferghana Valley and Chāch to reach as far as the River Jaxartes. In these campaigns he was often joined by forces from Bukhara, Samarqand and Khwarazm, integrating both imperial, largely Arab armies with local warriors. These conquests were not nearly as permanent as those discussed above. The death of Ḥajjāj in 714 followed by the Caliph Walīd the following year drove tensions between Khurāsān, Iraq and Damascus. Ḥajjāj and Qutayba had actively supported Walīd's son ʿAbd al-ʿAzīz (d. 728–9) as his successor but it was his brother Sulaymān who would rise to the throne. Further complicating matters, when Ḥajjāj had arrested Yazīd b. al-Muhallab, it was Sulaymān who sheltered the fugitive after he escaped his imprisonment. As caliph, Sulaymān ordered the removal of Qutayba from Khurāsān, installing Yazīd in his place, but the governor instead organized a revolt. Upon learning of the death of Walīd, Qutayba marched his troops to Ferghana and attempted to rally them to his cause, hoping his men would stand with the governor who had led them to so many lucrative victories far beyond the reach of the Syrian troops of the Umayyads. Instead, with few exceptions, Qutayba's troops, both Arab and non-Arab, turned on Qutayba and killed him along with several of his brothers.[60] The eleventh-century Chinese chronicle *Comprehensive Mirror to Aid in Government* by Sima Guang (1019–86) reports that the Tang Empire had sent 10,000 Turkish soldiers to Ferghana in 715 to support their vassal against Qutayba but the assassination of the governor and the retreat of his troops delayed the confrontation between the caliphate and China by another thirty-five years.[61]

Yazīd b. al-Muhallab attempted to expand the frontier during his second governorship, focusing his attention along the Caspian coast in Gorgān and Ṭabaristān. Attempts had been made to conquer this region since the earliest excursions east but none had succeeded and the Turkish presence in Gorgān blocked the more direct northernly route to Marw from Iraq. By the early eighth century, the Turks had even taken hold of the fortifications along the Great Wall of Gorgān, or what remained of them at least.[62] Yazīd reportedly downplayed Qutayba's conquests beyond the Oxus, arguing that, while Ferghana was so remote no one could verify Qutayba's claims, Gorgān was more pressing and immediately valuable to the caliphate.[63] Yazīd led a mixed force into Gorgān including Iraqis from both Kūfa and Baṣra, Syrians and Khurāsānīs as well as *mawālī*, slave soldiers (*mamālik*) and volunteer fighters (*mutaṭaww ʿīn*).[64] Further accounts include a group of *čākir* or a personal bodyguard under the leadership of a Khurāsānī Persian (*rajul min ʿajam Khurāsān*), perhaps what was meant by *mamālik* in other accounts but certainly indicative of the role local notables with their own private retinues played in this campaign.[65] Like many of Qutayba's campaigns, Yazīd's conquest of Gorgān is remembered for its bloodthirstiness, perhaps indicative of an anti-Muhallabid bias in our sources.[66] At Dihistān he killed 14,000 Turkish prisoners in fetters (*ṣabrān*).[67] He later lined a distance of two to four *farāsikh* (12–24 km) with the crucified bodies of his victims and the entire campaign is reported to have culminated in Yazīd washing the blood of 12,000 prisoners down the River Anda or Andarhaz so that the blood powered a mill. Yazīd used the grain from the mill to bake bread which he then ate.[68]

The death of the Caliph Sulaymān in the year 717 cut these campaigns short as well. Sulaymān's successor ʿUmar II threw Yazīd back into prison, ostensibly for failing to pay the proper fifth of the spoils earned in Gorgān and Ṭabaristān. Yazīd would again escape from prison to lead an unsuccessful revolt against ʿUmar's successor, Yazīd II (r. 720–4), and was killed. ʿUmar was adverse to conquest, ordering his governors in Khurāsān 'not to undertake raids' and 'hold on to what you already have in your possession' and his caliphate marked a slowing of expansion across the frontiers of the Umayyad Empire.[69] Qutayba b. Muslim and Yazīd b. al-Muhallab had pushed the eastern frontier further than it had ever gone on multiple fronts but ʿUmar's actions then slowed this momentum to a halt and the Umayyads began to take a more defensive stance. The final decades of Umayyad rule in Khurāsān were dominated by two ongoing conflicts. The first was the continued feud among the Arabs between the Qays/Muḍar and Yaman tribal confederacies. These conflicts challenged stable Umayyad rule with governors representing each faction favouring their confederates and opposing their rivals. As the governorship fluctuated between the two groups, the fortunes of each faction swayed accordingly. The second conflict involved the arrival of the Türgesh Turks who by 716 had emerged victorious out of the strife that had earlier divided the Türk Khāqānate. As early as 720, the Türgesh were attacking Muslim held territory in Transoxiana and by 728 they had reached as far as Bukhara and Paykand, putting the Umayyads in Sogdiana on the defensive. A result and contributing factor to both crises was a lack of stable governance in Khurāsān. Governors were changed frequently and increasingly on demand from the caliph rather than the governor of Iraq in response to ongoing factional fighting and Turkish victories. Such frequent changes weakened the Umayyads' ability to respond efficiently to these challenges.

Caught in the middle of both conflicts were the *mawālī*, especially those living in the recently conquered territories of Sogdiana, who tried to find either an optimal position for themselves within the structures of the Umayyad Caliphate or remove themselves from the caliphate entirely. Such choices could be influenced by these other conflicts. For example, within the conflict between Qays/Muḍar and Yaman, the Yaman or southern Arabs were considered more closely allied with and supportive of the *mawālī* with greater interests in settlement and assimilation compared to the Muḍar or northern Arabs who were more supportive of continued conquest, but this was neither universal nor absolute.[70] At the same time, internal strife coupled with a reinvigorated Turkish alternative to Arab imperialism led to a series of Sogdian revolts, attempts to reposition the place of Sogdiana caught between the Umayyad and Türgesh rivals. It is to these conflicts we now turn.

Divided Arabs and divided Sogdians

Earlier in this chapter, a case was discussed in which a group of Samarqandīs approached the Caliph ʿUmar II with grievances about the manner in which Qutayba confiscated their land during his conquest of the city in 712. According to this account, the Samarqandīs first brought these complaints to Sulaymān b. Abī al-Sārī, himself a *mawlā* but also an agent of the imperial administration, and he granted them permission to petition the caliph.[71] Upon hearing their complaints, ʿUmar sided with the Sogdians and ordered that a judge be appointed to hear their case and, if that judge found in their favour, the Arabs should be expelled from Samarqand, forced to live in their camps (*muʿskarahum*) and everything returned to as it was before Qutayba's conquest of the city.[72] In response, Sulaymān made it known that if the judge should find in the Samarqandīs' favour, the Arabs would return to their camps at which time they would reconquer the city and establish a new (and presumably less favourable) peace treaty. The threat of another conquest deterred the Samarqandīs who noted that the Arabs had already intermixed with them (*khālaṭanā*) and they retracted their complaints, happy to leave things as they were avoiding renewed conflict.[73] This account highlights the great challenge facing the Umayyads after conquest: how to integrate conquered territories and populations into their empire. Central to this were questions of how one should treat converts, how to tell a sincere from insincere convert and how the imperial finances could shift from conquest and spoils to management and taxation in a balanced manner. The answers were not clear to either the conquerors or the conquered. For example, it may be the case that the decision to not pursue grievances over confiscated land was made by the agriculturalists of Samarqand who had not lost property in the city during Qutayba's conquest against the interests of the merchants of the city who had been expelled to make way for Qutayba's troops. Regardless, ʿUmar was not happy with this result and ordered all Muslims to leave Transoxiana with their women and children and resettle in Marw but, when the order was relayed by the military governor ʿAbd al-Raḥmān b. Nuʿaym al-Ghāmidī (r. 719–20), the Muslims refused saying that Marw was not sufficient for them. In turn, ʿUmar responded by barring any further campaigns in Transoxiana, cutting off the spoils and thereby the warriors' incomes.[74]

Beginning with the reign of ʿUmar II, the politics of the eastern frontier shifted away from conquest and focused increasingly on the integration of Sogdiana into the caliphate and the negotiation between the Umayyad governors and their Sogdian subjects, especially on issues of the collection of taxes from converts. For example, ʿUmar dismissed his own governor Jarrāḥ b. ʿAbdallāh al-Ḥakamī (r. 717–19) when he was accused by the *mawlā* Abū al-Ṣaydā' Ṣāliḥ b. Ṭarīf of continuing to collect the *jizya* – a poll tax theoretically levied only on non-Muslims – from converts, forcing the *mawālī* to participate in campaigns without receiving their stipends (*ʿaṭā'*) and generally ruling by the sword and whip.[75] When Abū al-Ṣaydā' expressed similar concerns during the governorship of Ashras b. ʿAbdallāh al-Sulāmī (r. 727–30), he was arrested and replaced as financial administer of Samarqand with Sulaymān b. Abī al-Sārī who, despite being a *mawlā* himself, did not have the same qualms.[76] The central question that challenged Umayyad governors was how to encourage conversion – and sometimes whether to encourage conversion – and thus how to integrate the local populations into the empire while maintaining revenues. Taxation in early Islamic Khurāsān was based on the terms of tribute and functioned, to an extent, like the *kharāj* or land tax because the collection of the taxes fell largely on the land holders, namely the *dahāqīn*. The *dahāqīn* adjusted this system to meet certain Sasanian traditions – including the exclusion of the nobility, soldiers and priests from taxation – and passed the cost on to their peasants and tenants, in many ways transforming it into a poll tax akin to the *jizya*.[77] In order to ensure sufficient revenues that provided for both the tribute as well as a profit for the tax collectors and landowners, taxes were collected from both non-Arab and Arab, non-Muslim and Muslim tenants alike in a manner that went against the spirit if not the letter of the law, blurred the lines between conquerors and conquered and stoked anger and resentment against the Umayyad regime.

ʿUmar, for one, attempted to protect the *mawālī* from taxation, but this opened the system up to abuse in which the sincerity of conversion came into question. When Jarrāḥ al-Ḥakamī attempted to institute a circumcision test on converts seeking tax relief, ʿUmar reportedly chastised him saying, 'God sent Muhammad in order to summon people to Islam, not to circumcise them.'[78] Such sentiments could, at times, speak beyond the question of circumcision to address the broader tension between the mission of spreading Islam and the necessity of funding the empire. As G. R. Hawting highlighted, orthographically, 'The word for "as a circumciser" (*khatinan*) is only distinguishable by a few dots from "as a tax-collector" (*jabiyan*), and one more frequently finds the saying "God sent Muhammad to call men to Islam, not as a tax-collector" attributed to ʿUmar.'[79] Circumcision tests were also meant as acts of humiliation and subjugation, even for converts to Islam. Freeing converts from taxation en masse threatened to wreak havoc on the revenues of Sogdiana as expressed by Ṭabarī, quoting the *dahāqīn* of Bukhara who, in the year 728–9, asked the governor Ashras b. ʿAbdallāh al-Sulāmī, 'Who will you take the *kharāj* from, now that all the people have become Arabs?' meaning converts to Islam.[80] Even the terminology in this instance is interesting as the *dahāqīn* speak of the land tax (*kharāj*) which is traditionally understood to be payable by all landowners regardless of religious or ethnic affiliation while Ashras's response and Ṭabarī's commentary focuses on the *jizya*, the poll tax paid only by non-Muslims. As Daniel Dennett has argued, this passage is likely an artefact of a moment of transition, when conquest-based tribute was stabilizing into the more familiar systems of land tax and poll tax.[81] As Hawting described the predicament the Umayyads found themselves in, they could choose to either free the *mawālī* of taxation or support the local lords on whom they relied for tax collection.[82] More broadly, how could the Umayyads balance the economic incentives of imperial expansion with the successful integration of conquered peoples into the religious and social networks of the empire?

Questions about tax were followed by questions about what should be done with the money once it was collected, with many accusations of corruption flying between Marw and Iraq. When Yazīd II's first governor of Khurāsān Saʿīd b. ʿAbd al-ʿAzīz (r. 720–1) – better known as Khudhayna or the 'Mistress', a nickname he reportedly received from a group of Sogdian *dahāqīn* who found his yellow robes and hairstyle feminine[83] – first arrived in the east, his immediate concern in Sogdiana was the arrest of several lieutenants appointed by Yazīd b. al-Muhallab and the governors of ʿUmar II accused of stealing the money of the Muslims. These men were imprisoned in the *quhandiz* or citadel of Marw. They were tortured and at least three killed at the hands of vengeful members of the Banū Bāhila who were caught up in factional animosity.[84] The remainder of these prisoners gained their freedom when the Türgesh threated an Arab outpost called Qaṣr Bāhiliyya and they were needed to fight.

Misappropriated tax revenues became a regular accusation flung across factional lines during these years of conflict. In one of the more descriptive rebuttals to such charges recorded by Ṭabarī, a warrior from Khurāsān explained to the governor of Iraq ʿUmar b. Hubayra al-Fazārī (r. 721–4), a notorious and abusive Qaysite partisan, that these funds were spent defending the frontier and were better used to that end than in Iraq.

> We live on a frontier where we fight against an enemy that is constantly at war. We wear iron so often that the rust sticks to our skin; indeed, the smell of

> iron causes a female servant to turn her face away from her master and from other men that she serves. You, on the other hand, stay at home, adorning yourselves in fine clothes dyed in saffron. Now, the men who have been accused of appropriating those revenues – the leaders of the army of Khurāsān and the army of the provinces – undertake enormous expenses in order to carry out military expeditions.[85]

The collection of taxes caused tensions not only between the Arabs seeking revenues from Sogdiana and the Sogdians who found their dues excessive, but also between the governors of Iraq where the imperial coffers demanded to be filled and the warriors on the frontier who expected a share of the revenue for themselves and for the financing of their campaigns.

Under Khudhayana, Sogdiana erupted into open revolt. As early as 719, Chinese records report a combined embassy from the Bukhārkhudā Ṭughshāda, the Ikhshīd Ghūrak and the kings of Kumād (in the Qarātagīn Valley) and Chaghāniyān (the latter, Tīsh, acting as an emissary for the Yabghu of Ṭukhāristān) informing the Tang that they had been attacked by the Arabs and requesting support – that never did materialize.[86] These were all rulers who had previously found some accommodation with Qutayba, but less than five years after his death they were turning to their former patrons seeking to improve their situation. By 721 and with support from the Türgesh, Sogdian resistance had grown so powerful that Khudhayna, perceived as weak and ineffective by the Sogdians and Arabs alike, was replaced with Saʿīd b. ʿAmr al-Ḥarashī (r. 721–2). Facing a stronger governor and seeing Türgesh support retreat, the Sogdians changed tactics in a manner that illustrated splits within their community as well. At this point Ghūrak appears to have become supportive or, at the least, resigned to Muslim rule. As Gibb noted, during these uprisings the Umayyads made their camp at Ishtīkhan where Ghūrak had established his court since Qutayba's conquest of Samarqand, implying some coordination between the two – but not necessarily friendliness.[87] Despite this, the army of Ishtīkhan, along with those of Qiyy, Bārkath and Sabaskath, each a territory in or around Samarqand, abandoned Sogdiana under their own commanders for Ferghana, whose king, called Ṭār, promised to clear a district for them.[88] Interestingly, the district offered to them was held by a lieutenant of Qutayba's named ʿIṣām b. ʿAbdallāh al-Bāhilī, who may have held out in Ferghana following his master's death and the return of the king of Ferghana. The Sogdians had a long history of colonizing along the trade routes towards China and this type of retreat fits the pattern. More importantly, this scenario shows the Sogdians did not speak with a single voice on their relationship to the Umayyads. Some left and others remained.

Ḥarashī pursued the Sogdians – encouraged by the king of Ferghana who promised not to interfere if he could reach his quarry within forty days, at which time Ṭār had promised the refugees his protection – and besieged them at Khujanda, on the River Jaxartes at the mouth of the Ferghana Valley. Ḥarashī was ultimately successful and the campaign ended in the slaughter of the captured Sogdians.[89] The economic incentives to bring the Sogdians back home are clear in our sources. Ibn Khayyāṭ, for example, emphasized the collection of the *jizya* whose revenues necessitated a taxable population as a prime motivation for Ḥarashī.[90] Ṭabarī, on the other hand, emphasized the safety granted to a group of merchants returning from China. When Ḥarashī ordered the execution of the Sogdian prisoners, he spared a group of 400 merchants bearing wares from China and included their goods in the spoils.[91] As de la Vaissière has pondered, it is unclear whether this was because Ḥarashī was supportive of trade or because these merchants were supportive of the Umayyads or had no relation to the rebels.[92]

A second group of Sogdians had travelled to Panjikant, approximately 70 km up the River Zarāfshān from Samarqand, ruled by the local lord Dīwāshtīch.[93] The conditions in Panjikant leading up to 722 are better known than the conditions in other districts of Sogdiana, thanks to a collection of contemporary documents in both Arabic and Sogdian found in 1932 on nearby Mount Mugh, where the rulers of Panjikant maintained a citadel called Abghar.[94] These documents, as they pertained to the conquest of Panjikant and the fall of Dīwāshtīch, have also been the subject to detailed study by Frantz Grenet and Étienne de la Vaissière.[95] According to a letter between Dīwāshtīch and the governor Jarrāḥ al-Ḥakamī dated to 719 – the same year other lords of Sogdiana were sending a joint embassy to China seeking aid against the Arabs – the lord of Panjikant referred to himself as the *mawlā* of the governor and claimed to have with him two sons of the former king of Samarqand Ṭarkhūn whom he was willing to hand over.[96] Ṭabarī refers to Dīwāshtīch as the *dihqān* of Samarqand.[97] When matched with his claims to the title of Ikhshīd, king of Sogdiana, it has been assumed that Dīwāshtīch was a rival of Ghūrak who would happily side with the Arabs when they opposed the king of Samarqand and against the Arabs when Ghūrak was their ally.[98] Wall paintings at the palace of Panjikant depict a coronation ceremony and the reception of an Arab embassy, both of which may be associated with Dīwāshtīch's claim to the throne and demonstrate that the Arabs, at least at one point, acknowledged or entertained his claims over Sogdiana.[99] By 722, the situation had changed, presumably as Ghūrak became closer to the Arabs, and Dīwāshtīch was attempting to coordinate the lords of Sogdiana and the Türgesh against Ḥarashī. One letter addressed to the *khuv* or lord of Khākhsar in Dargham, a fertile district south of Samarqand, concerns a message Dīwāshtīch had asked the *khuv* to send to the Türgesh via a Chinese page.[100] A second letter, dated to sometime after Ḥarashī had made peace with Usrūshana as he marched on Khujanda in pursuit of the rebellious Sogdians, has Dīwāshtīch's agent in Chāch declaring Türgesh support a lost cause, writing that 'the *khuv* [… and…] *tudun* [a Turkish title for a resident or colonial administrator] [of Chāch], on account of the agreement with the Arabs, has withdrawn, and … the report concerning the Turks (is that) suddenly they have disappeared, as they have gone up and until now not one has come (back)'.[101] Ḥarashī's march on Khujanda had either caused or been facilitated by a retreat of the Türgesh, leaving the Sogdian rebels on their own. From this correspondence, we see Dīwāshtīch wavering back and forth between the Arabs and the Türgesh, seeking aid from whoever may best support his claim against Ghūrak for the throne of Samarqand and Sogdiana. We also see the desperation as Türgesh support dissolved during the Sogdian uprising.

Upon conquering Khujanda, Ḥarashī sent a force under Sulaymān b. Abī al-Sārī to Panjikant, accompanied by both Arab and Transoxianan forces including the Khwārazmshāh and the lord of Akharūn and Shūmān. They besieged Dīwāshtīch, who settled on peace terms with Sulaymān. A defeated Dīwāshtīch was then sent to Kish where Ḥarashī was leading another siege against rebellious Sogdians while the governor dispatched agents to Panjikant to liquidate Dīwāshtīch's assets.[102] After receiving submission from Kish, Ḥarashī took Dīwāshtīch to Rabinjan, halfway between Bukhara and Samarqand on the River Zarāfshān, and crucified him before cutting off his head, which he sent to Iraq, and his hand, which he sent with Sulaymān b. Abī al-Sārī to Ṭukhāristān.[103] Archaeologists have uncovered evidence that temples, Dīwāshtīch's palace and several homes at Panjikant were burnt around this time as well.[104]

Throughout the conquest of Sogdiana, the Umayyads – more specifically the Marwānids who relied more heavily on systemic violence to maintain their rule – engaged in a programme of calculated frightfulness and violent attacks, including attacks against those who had already surrendered such as the Nīzak Ṭarkhān and his supporters, the Turks of Gorgān, the Sogdians at Khujanda and Dīwāshtīch. Such public performances of violence were designed to induce fear and encourage submission from others. As Sean Anthony argued regarding the widespread use of crucifixion across the caliphate, 'Crucifixion in all its diversity, most importantly, must be understood as a public and ritualized form of violence intended to conjure up an amorphous array of polyvalent symbols that, in the first instance at least, serve to the legitimizing efforts of the Umayyad polity.'[105] In these contexts, crucifixion is both eliminating and embarrassing local rulers while expressing the ultimate authority of the caliph.

Such violent displays did not end with Dīwāshtīch either. When the lord of Khuzār, a fortress near Wakhsh in Ṭukhāristān, surrendered, Ḥarashī had him crucified.[106] Ṭabarī tells us of a *dihqān* who met a similar fate, granted a guarantee of safe conduct only to be crucified by Ḥarashī.[107] When the governor of Iraq ʿUmar b. Hubayra dismissed Ḥarashī from his office, the official explanation was his treatment of Dīwāshtīch, but Ṭabarī makes it seem that this was just the straw that broke the camel's back with Ibn Hubayra already angered by Ḥarashī's larger pattern of insubordination.[108]

The death of the Caliph Yazīd II and the succession of his brother Hishām (r. 724–43) brought another wave of tribal fighting among the Arabs. When Ḥarashī's successor Muslim b. Saʿīd al-Kilābī attempted a campaign into Ferghana shortly after Yazīd's death, many held back in Balkh, perhaps understanding that Muslim's time in office was limited as the imperial office changed hands. The governor was forced to send his lieutenant, the future governor of Khurāsān, Naṣr b. Sayyār accompanied by the army of Chaghāniyān to force the reticent troops across the Oxus. The Arabs divided themselves between Muḍar in support of Naṣr and Rabīʿa with the Banū Azd against him, claiming that it was Muslim's intention to lead them into revolt once they were on the frontier *à la* Qutayba. The fighting only ceased when news arrived that the Yamanite Asad b. ʿAbdallāh al-Qasrī had been named the new governor of Khurāsān.[109] It should be acknowledged that, in contrast to the simplified image of Yaman being more closely allied with the *mawālī*, in this instance we have the Hephthalite force of Chaghāniyān fighting alongside Muḍar against Yaman. The news of Muslim's cashiering reached the governor while he was in Bukhara making his way towards Ferghana, but he was encouraged by Khālid al-Qasrī (r. 724–38), the new governor of Iraq and brother of Asad, to complete his campaign before returning west. This campaign, which has come to be remembered as the 'Day of Thirst' (*yawm al-ʿaṭash*), was largely a failure. Muslim's army was undermanned with 4,000 Azdites defecting when news of Muslim's dismissal arrived at Bukhara. When a Türgesh relief force met the Muslims in Ferghana, they were forced to make a quick retreat covering several stages in a day and even to burn their baggage so as to increase their speed and escape the constant harassment of the Turks. Their path was blocked at the Jaxartes by the armies of Ferghana and Chāch, whom they were forced to assault to reach a source of fresh drinking water, resulting in many casualties.[110]

A sign of the Umayyads' continuing struggles in Transoxiana was that Asad al-Qasrī began to focus his attention on Ṭukhāristān, albeit with little success. In 725–6, he campaigned against Gharshistān and secured the conversion of its king Namrūn.[111] According to Ṭabarī, the kings of Gharshistān were still the *mawālī* of the Yaman in his own day. Asad followed this with a raid against Ghūr that captured a great deal of booty that had been hidden in mountain caves.[112] These were campaigns into the mountainous territories of Ṭukhāristān that remained and would remain outside of Muslim authority. As discussed in Chapter 1, Ghūr was within the *Dār Kufar* or Abode of the Infidels and, therefore, outside of Muslim authority two centuries later according to the geographers Iṣṭakhrī and Ibn Ḥawqal.[113] Asad also attempted to campaign across the Oxus, marching on Khuttal, but he was turned back by the Türgesh who apparently had been able to advance this far south.[114] It should be noted that Asad – a champion of Yaman who are often portrayed as less enthused about conquest – did not shun conquest, he just was not very successful at it. Yet his impact on Ṭukhāristān is notable in reports of an emissary from the Yabghu to the Tang court in which the Turks complain of heavy taxes and fear that their kingdom would be destroyed by the Arabs unless the emperor sent the forces he had promised both the Yabghu's father and grandfather.[115] In his letter, the Yabghu believes the Türgesh are agents of the Chinese emperor who would ride to his assistance at the command of the Tang, but this was far from the reality. Even though the Tang felt the domains of the Western Türk Khāqānate should remain within their sphere of influence and had previously wielded such authority, the Türgesh as they formed under the leadership of the Khāqān Suluk (r. 716–38) fought fiercely against Chinese interference.

In the end, Asad's first governorship was marred by factional fighting among the Arabs and in 728–9 the Caliph Hishām ordered his removal due to his Yamanite partisanship and replaced him with Ashras al-Sulamī of Muḍar. By doing so Hishām essentially separated the rule of Khurāsān from Iraq as he dismissed the governor of Khurāsān without the consent of the governor of Iraq, Asad's brother Khālid, and ensured that the two provinces were the domains of different tribal factions.

Ashras attempted to bring the Sogdians back into the Umayyad fold by offering to lift the *jizya* from anyone who converted, but this had a drastic negative effect on revenues, as alluded to above. Even Ghūrak turned on Ashras on this point, complaining that conversions for base financial purposes had resulted in severe declines in revenue which hurt the Umayyads' local allies charged with collecting revenues for the caliphal coffers.[116] Narshakhī included a similar story involving Ṭughshāda who accused his fellow Bukharans of dishonestly converting to Islam to avoid taxation, asking permission to punish the false converts during the governorship of Asad al-Qasrī.[117] When Ashras attempted to address the situation by placing the *jizya* back on the *mawālī*, the Sogdians refused to pay with many apostatizing and calling upon the Türgesh for aid. Ashras forced them into submission with a group of the *dahāqīn* being publicly humiliated by tearing their garments and tying their belts around their necks – clear signs of submission – as punishment for this behaviour.[118] In the end, the people of Bukhara and Samarqand again turned to the Türgesh who temporarily pushed the Arabs south of the River Oxus. In contrast to the revolts in Sogdiana, Ashras's policies may have had greater financial benefits in Ṭukhāristān. It is during the years 729–30 that we see coins minted in Balkh (labelled as Madīna Balkh al-Bayḍā or the Shining City of Balkh) for the first time in over thirty years.[119]

The rise of the Türgesh and the defensive frontier

The Türgesh emerged out of the internal conflicts that had plagued the Türk Khāqānate in the late seventh and early eighth centuries, establishing themselves in the Ili Basin in modern Kazakhstan by 716 when the Khāqān Suluk was able to unify leadership among various factions. The internal fighting among the Turks and intervention by the Tang had helped open Transoxiana up to Qutayba, but under Türgesh leadership, the Turks were able to reassert their authority and threaten Sogdiana once again.[120] In the Arabic sources, the Türgesh first appeared in 720 during the siege of Qaṣr Bāhliyya and at this point they already had a frightening reputation. Four thousand volunteers were organized in Samarqand to relieve the siege and rescue the 100 families trapped in the fortress. But when one of the warriors, Musayyab b. Bishar al-Riyāḥī, gave a speech warning that they were heading into the arena (*ḥalba*) of the Turks and the khāqān where Paradise would be their reward and Hellfire the punishment for those who fled, 1,300 men promptly abandoned the march. At intervals. more and more men peeled off from the army until only 700 fighters remained as they approached the fortress.[121] In the end, this was enough to rescue those trapped inside the fortress, but Qaṣr Bāhliyya itself had to be abandoned to the Turks.[122] The Türgesh continued to advance until they were at the walls of Samarqand by the end of 721, where they supported the revolting Sogdians. However, it appears they were not prepared to besiege Samarqand itself and retreated, being pursued by Khudhayna to Waraghsar or 'the head of the dam', the limits of Sogdiana's irrigation system.[123] By not pursuing this victory, Khudhayna was accused of supporting the Türgesh and allowing them the opportunity to regroup and prepare another attack. From the letters of Dīwāshtīch, discussed above, this first Türgesh wave appears to be exploratory in nature and had left Sogdiana entirely by 722 when the lord of Panjikant was informed that Turkish support would not be arriving. It was not until 724 that a Türgesh force re-emerged, resulting in the disaster known as the 'Day of Thirst' described above and within two years they were as far south as Khuttal along the banks of the River Oxus in Upper Ṭukhāristān where they turned back Asad al-Qasrī.

The defence of the frontier against the Türgesh became a primary concern for the governor Ashras al-Sulamī. In 727–8, he established *rābiṭa* in Sogdiana. The *rābiṭa* (different from but etymologically related to *ribāṭ* or frontier forts) were cavalry garrisons placed along the frontier or, as Khalid Yahya Blankinship translated the term, a 'mobile frontier force'.[124] But they were not sufficient for turning back the advancing Türgesh – in fact the leaders of the *rābiṭa* would soon find themselves hostages of Suluk. When the Sogdians called on Türgesh support in 728–9, they quickly pushed the Umayyads south of the River Oxus, forcing Ashras to fight a long campaign to regain control. These campaigns started at Āmul where the Arabs were unable to cross the river for three months due to Turkish bands on the northern bank, some of whom even made raids into Khurāsān itself.[125] They then fought a battle at Paykand where the Arabs were cut off from supplies of water until a relief force from the tribes of Qays and Tamīm relieved them.[126] Another two-month siege took place at Kamarja, a fort seven *farāsikh* (42 km) west of Samarqand, that ended in a truce with the khāqān and the evacuation of the Muslims.[127] Throughout this siege, noted by Ṭabarī as one of the noblest days of Khurāsān (*min āshraf āyyām Khurāsān*), there were attempts by Suluk to lure the Muslims to his side. One attempt was made by someone claiming to be Khusrow b. Pīrūz b. Yazdgird, the grandson of the last Sasanian shahanshah, who said the Türgesh had come to restore his grandfather's kingdom.[128] In another instance, the Khāqān offered to pay any warriors who crossed the lines twice what they earned fighting for the Muslims.[129] In the midst of this fighting, the Caliph Hishām decided to replace Ashras with Junayd b. ʿAbd al-Raḥmān al-Murrī (r. 730–4), supposedly because he had bribed the caliph with jewellery for his wife. Junayd's arrival in Sogdiana during this siege was fraught with danger highlighting the range of Türgesh control. The new governor was afraid to cross the Oxus without sufficient support and he requested an escort from Ashras. This force had to fight its way from Bukhara to the Oxus and back again before Junayd could take control and lead a battle against the Khāqān at Zarmān near Kamarja, demonstrating that even when victories could relieve a particular city, the Türgesh still threatened the countryside across the breadth of Sogdiana.[130] Ashras and Junayd could hold the islands but the spaces in-between remained outside of their authority. In 731, these conflicts with the Türgesh over Sogdiana would culminate in one of the largest disasters the Umayyads faced at the Battle of the Pass (*yawm al-shiʿb*).

The Battle of the Pass was precipitated by the divided nature of the eastern frontier, both geographically and politically, and the challenges of maintaining authority in both Sogdiana and Ṭukhāristān when both rose in opposition simultaneously.[131] At the beginning of 731, Junayd was forced to march on Ṭukhāristān with 28,000 men presumably due to some form of uprising, though details are few. He sent these troops in multiple directions while forces were maintained at Herat and Ṭālaqān, implying widespread disruptions to Umayyad rule. While campaigning in Ṭukhāristān, word came from Sawra b. al-Ḥurr (d. 731), Junayd's lieutenant in Samarqand, that Suluk had returned and Junayd quickly set off to relieve the city. His approach was too rapid, though, and despite warnings from Mujashshir b. Muzāḥim al-Sulamī – a veteran of Qutayba's conquest of Samarqand – that he should never cross the Oxus with fewer than 50,000 men (interpreted as a sign of the Arabs' fear of the Turks' military prowess), Junayd went forward with the troops on hand and made camp at Kish. From Kish, Mujashshir convinced Junayd to take a shortcut over a steep pass but Suluk – leading a force of Turks along with the armies from Sogdiana, Chāch and Ferghana – met him four *farāsikh* (24 km) from Samarqand. The khāqān and his forces nearly wiped out Junayd's army, so he sent to Samarqand for a relief force and Sawra, after much prodding, marched out with 12,000 warriors. Sawra also took a shortcut and found himself trapped by the khāqān one *farsakh* (6 km) from Junayd's forces, blocked from water and in the heat of the day as the Turks set fire to the grass around them (presumably dry from drought). The heat, smoke and dust forced Sawra and the army from Samarqand to charge the Turks directly pushing both armies into the fires which killed all but one or two thousand of the Muslims, including Sawra. Junayd still had to fight his way to Samarqand, which he eventually reached. The total Muslim casualties were likely close to 20,000.[132]

The rough geography through the mountains between Ṭukhāristān and Sogdiana played as much a role in Junayd's downfall at the Battle of the Pass as either the Turks or his own hubris. The mountains allowed the Turks to trap both Junayd and Sawra's forces while preventing them from meeting despite their close proximity. The isolation and distances between Samarqand and the centres of Umayyad authority in Khurāsān presented similar challenges. In the end, it appears that Junayd planned to abandon Samarqand. After residing there for four months he evacuated the families of those who had died with Sawra, leaving behind only a minimal garrison of 800 men, too few to effectively defend the city. The remainder of Samarqand's garrison and the survivors of the Battle of the Pass went on to face Suluk who was then attacking Bukhara. Junayd won a pair of victories at Karmīniya and Ṭawāwīs before retiring to Chaghāniyān where he was joined by 20,000 reinforcements from Iraq sent by the Caliph Hishām. Junayd was also given permission to enlist 15,000 soldiers from Khurāsān, perhaps one of the first clear indications that there was a substantial Arab population in Khurāsān that was not in military roles, and Hishām granted him 30,000 shields and lances to supply these new recruits.[133] Junayd's successors fought multiple campaigns against Samarqand across the 730s, implying that the city was abandoned to Ghūrak with or without Türgesh patronage after the disaster of the Battle of the Pass.[134] It was not until 739 when Naṣr b. Sayyār made three campaigns into Sogdiana that Samarqand seems to have finally fallen back under Muslim authority.

The attacks of the Türgesh into territory that had previously been held by the Umayyads transformed the nature of warfare along the eastern frontier. Whereas the earlier campaigns into Sogdiana had involved great spoils and the advancement of territory, the Arabs were now fighting to regain what had previously been theirs against an enemy, the Türgesh, who did not carry the wealth of the Sogdian merchants or even possess cities or lands that could be properly conquered and taxed. In comparison to the Sogdians, the Türgesh could not become fiscally legible from the state's perspective, meaning they could always flee further beyond the reach of the empire and possessed little wealth that could be easily transformed into recordable and taxable income for the state. Nor did they possess substantial booty with which the Muslim warriors could reward themselves, a point Blankinship highlighted through contemporary poetry commemorating the Battle of the Pass.[135] Specifically, he quotes the poet Sharʿabī al-Ṭāʾī who stated that there was nothing 'we covet from the enemy'. Rather he had seen 'many a fleshy young woman / Whom an ugly, fat-faced, small-eared Sughdī was driving along (as a captive)', and that he fears the Muslims will be 'divided up (as booty)' and that the 'Khāqān and his soldiers [are] greedy for [them]'.[136] When Asad al-Qasrī – who was reinstated as governor by Hishām – initially faced Suluk near Khuttal in 737, the battle came down to a defence of the Muslims' baggage train as they retreated back across the Oxus and further to Balkh.[137] There was no wealth to be gained, only spared. In fact, the meagreness of rewards was thought to impact even the Umayyads' ability to wage war; at the outset of this battle the king of Khuttal claimed that the country had been stripped bare so that the Turks, who were better suited for fighting under deprived conditions, would certainly triumph over Asad.[138]

Aside from herds of sheep mentioned often in the context of engagements with the Türgesh, perhaps the only thing that could consistently be gained by fighting the Turks was slaves. Slaves had been an important commodity from the beginning of the conquests of Khurāsān and the earliest excursions across the Oxus. The spoils of many conquests include thousands of nameless slaves whose origin and fate often go unreported by our sources. From those exceptional cases in which their fate is told, we know that some were sent west as labourers while others were soldiers (most famously the Bukhāriyya discussed in Chapter 3) and female slaves became concubines. The truck in Turkish slaves would become increasingly important in the ninth century as Turkish slave soldiers formed a central part of the Abbasid army.

Like all steppe confederacies, the Türgesh's ability to organize lasted only as long as their ability to win. When Suluk attempted to invade Ṭukhāristān for a second time in 737, he was met by organized resistance from Asad al-Qasrī that eventually led to the khāqān's death. Suluk marched into Ṭukhāristān with the support of the Yabghu, the princes of Ṭukhāristān and their *čākir*. He was also supported by Sogdians from Samarqand, Chāch, Usrūshana and Khuttal – which may have been under Hephthalite control at this point – as well as the Arab rebel Ḥārith b. Surayj (d. 746) whose movement will be discussed in the following chapter. On the advice of Ḥārith, who was confident that Asad was too weak to face such a large army, the khāqān's forces were scattered into raiding parties that were sent against numerous Muslim fortifications. But when these garrisons held their ground, most notably at Khulm and Jazza, Asad was able to rally his troops into an attack on the Turkish forces at Kharīstān in the region of Gūzgān. The show of force was enough to bring the lord of Gūzgān to Asad's side, immediately weakening the Turks' position and adding numbers to Asad's forces which consisted of armies from both Khurāsān and Syria. Following the initial conflict, the Umayyad forces were able to make off with 155,000 sheep and beasts of burden and when they caught Suluk's camp they captured many women including Arab and *mawālī* women who had previously been taken as booty by the Turks as well as silver vessels and other spoils.[139] The khāqān was forced to retreat while his divided troops were defeated individually across Ṭukhāristān. Ṭabarī tells us that after their failure and retreat, tensions rose among the Turks and, eventually, Suluk found himself in an open fight against the Türgesh prince Kūrṣūl (r. 738–9). According to this account, the conflict began over a game of backgammon and the wager of a partridge and escalated until Kūrṣūl killed Suluk. In the aftermath, the Türgesh and their allies scattered with the Turks returning to fighting among themselves and the Sogdians returning to their homes.[140]

Asad's successes against Suluk and the Türgesh were so unexpected following so many setbacks and failures that when the news reached the Caliph Hishām it is reported that he did not believe it.[141] The inhabitants of Ṭukhāristān shared the caliph's surprise. At a Mihragān festival – the Zoroastrian harvest festival during which gifts were traditionally bestowed upon the governor – held in Balkh the *dihqān* of Herat named Khurāsān praised Asad for his victory and plundering the camp of the khāqān.[142]

Conquest and the frontier process

In Khurāsān, the Umayyads were able to adopt and co-opt existing imperial structures that made for a smoother transition once the last remnants of the Sasanian Empire were removed, as seen in Chapter 3. Expanding beyond the frontiers of the Sasanian Empire posed new challenges. The conquest of Sogdiana and Ṭukhāristān meant the integration of peoples with less direct historical connection to empire and a greater sense of autonomy. The incorporation of these peoples into the caliphate posed a serious set of challenges that would continue to plague Umayyad rule in the east until the collapse of the dynasty – not coincidentally through a revolution that began in Khurāsān, as will be discussed in the next chapter – these included the integration of local populations, including local lords and warriors, into the empire in a manner that proved economically beneficial to the caliphate in terms of tax revenues while also attractive enough to the conquered population as to reduce unrest as well as the threat of military rivals from across the frontier, namely the Turks.

As the Umayyads extended their rule across the River Oxus, the eastern frontier became a zone of negotiation not only between the Arabs, Muslims and the Sogdians but also with the Turks and, on occasion, the Tang Empire of China, each of which could claim parts of the region within their historical sphere of influence. Qutayba b. Muslim and his successors were not advancing into empty space, nor were they advancing against truly isolated and autonomous petty rulers. Rather, they were advancing into complex spaces caught in their own political dynamics and, like the geopolitical shatterzones described in Chapter 1, local conflicts and competitions often drew in larger neighbours. Qutayba's conquest of Bukhara, for example, was not just about Qutayba and the Umayyads against the Bukhārkhudā. Instead we see the Bukhārkhudā Ṭughshāda allied with the Umayyads, the merchants of Paykand who were connected to the Tang through trade and the Vardānkhudā with the support of Samarqand and the Turks. Each of these parties had an interest in the outcome of the conquests. Even supporters of Qutayba like the Nīzak Ṭarkhān had a vested interest in how the Umayyads extended their authority into Sogdiana and switched sides when he saw the direction the winds were blowing.

As will be discussed further in the next chapter, the successes and failures of the Umayyads tended to be the result of a balance between Arab unity and Turkish unity, as the two groups most immediately pressing onto Sogdiana experienced cycles of violent and disruptive internal factionalism. Sogdian resistance to Umayyad expansion – both active in the form of military resistance and passive in the form of flight to Ferghana – was dictated by this balancing act between the availability of Türgesh support and the presence of Arab enforcers of imperial control. The position and status of a frontier is often a sign of the balance between the relative strengths of the powers situated on either side and this was no less the case for the eastern frontier in the Umayyad period.

The integration of the Sogdians into imperial structures, particularly the question of taxation and conversion and the larger implication these policies had for the economics of empire, has similarly been portrayed as a simple dichotomy between the Umayyad conquerors and the Sogdian conquered but, as we should see by now, the frontier was a more complex space than this. The native inhabitants of the eastern frontier – considering the long history of migration and conquest, this was a difficult group to identify with an easy label – were not a uniform body that spoke with a single voice. The tensions between various factions among the Sogdians, Hephthalites and Turks and subgroups among them were also driven by the relative balances of power along the frontier. It often seems, for example, that modern scholarship treats the *mawālī* as a monolithic group that is assumed to be part of the local, native population, but the *mawālī* who play the most prominent roles in Umayyad Khurāsān, Ṭukhāristān and Sogdiana were not so closely tied to local populations nor did they clearly act purely for the benefit of local populations against the imperial invaders. Many like Ḥayyān al-Nabaṭī and Abū al-Ṣaydā' Ṣāliḥ b. Ṭarīf were actually outsiders who travelled to the east with their Arab patrons. In a rather telling moment, when Ashras al-Sulamī tried to send Abū al-Ṣaydā' to Sogdiana to missionize, he claimed not to know Persian and required a translator. Ashras sent him with an Arab interpreter, one Rabīʿ b. ʿImrān al-Tamīmī.[143] In this case, the *mawlā* was less connected to the local population – not even proficient in Persian – than an Arab who had been born and raised in Khurāsān, a son of one of the original Arab conquerors of the region. Which of the two represents a local identity? Rather than being local, they were parts of a mobile imperial elite. Some like Sulaymān b. Abī al-Sārī acted as imperial agents against the local populations. More generally, it was often the local landlords collecting the taxes who Sogdians so often called oppressive. As the empire matured, the dichotomy between conqueror and conquered became more complex, creating a continuum of actors, as subject populations became active participants in imperial life.

As the reach of the Umayyad Caliphate extended across the River Oxus, Sogdiana went through a frontier process, akin to that described and discussed in Chapter 1. This process involved a conflict between different actors over access to political and economic resources that resulted in a hybrid frontier identity unique from those that contributed to it. Creating such an identity required a reshaping on the frontier region itself into a uniquely Muslim Central Asia. It should be noted that this was not a single process either. We see conflict and competition among Arab migrants and their clients, most notably in the conflicts between Qays/Muḍar and Yaman. These conflicts are probably the most comparable to those described by Frederick Jackson Turner in his own work which negligently focused only on the dynamics among the settlers. The competitions among the Arabs in the east helped shape a frontier identity that would become important during the Abbasid Revolution. There were then further negotiations and competitions between a newly arrived imperial elite and the local population as Sogdiana was integrated into the empire of the caliphate as well as conflicts among competing groups of locals as they sought an advantageous position in this new order. As local populations entered the political, economic and social world of the caliphate, they also changed and changed the identity of the caliphate. Now, let us shift the focus to a series of revolts that resulted in but did not end with the Abbasid Revolution and the transformation of the empire of the caliphs into a new system that better incorporated the populations of the frontier.

Chapter 6

THE UNSETTLED FRONTIER: THE ABBASID AND OTHER REVOLUTIONS AND THE EASTERN FRONTIER

Ḥārith b. Surayj at the intersection of revolutionary Islam and Turkish invaders

The conquest and integration of Ṭukhāristān and Transoxiana into the Umayyad Caliphate brought regions that had long been outside any form of direct imperial control – if ever – into the empire of the caliphate. This drastic change to the local order along the eastern frontier caused political, social and economic disruptions that were expressed through a series of revolts in the mid-eighth century. These disruptions did not just affect the local populations but also the conquerors themselves. The competition and conflict among various parties along the frontier, the web of actions and activities we have called the frontier process, inspired revolutionary movements with distinct, complex characteristics. The result was that these revolts did not involve only one population with a clear set of grievances rising against imperial authority – as in the previous chapter when Sogdians resisted conquest with the aid of the Turks. Instead these movements crossed many different factional lines, involving both the conquerors and conquered, in ways that did not easily match the larger political divisions of the time. The most famous and consequential of these revolts was the Abbasid Revolution which broke out in Khurāsān in 747 and ultimately overthrew the Umayyad Caliphate in 750. This was far from the only instance, however. The large-scale and long-term impact of the Abbasid Revolution has caused historians to focus primarily on this singular revolt and to read the warning signs of the revolution into other movements, but it was only one of many movements that took hold in Khurāsān, Ṭukhāristān and Transoxiana in the mid-eighth century. It was not the last either. In the aftermath of conquest and the difficult integration of Ṭukhāristān and Transoxiana, the political and social orders of the eastern frontier were in disarray. Many different groups held grievances against the Umayyads and then Abbasids that expressed themselves in revolutionary terminologies. This chapter will examine some of these movements and their aftermath in terms of the eastern frontier.

Let us consider an example from the movement of Ḥārith b. Surayj, an Arab of the Banū Tamīm. Ḥārith instigated a revolt in the name of 'the Book of God and the Sunnah of His Prophet', calling on the Umayyads to live up to the promise of the caliphate that stretched across Ṭukhāristān and into Khurāsān and

Transoxiana. Ḥārith's revolt began in 734 in northern Ṭukhāristān in the town of Nakudh near Fāryāb where he gathered 4,000 men and marched on Balkh. From the leadership named in the chronicles, the nucleus of Ḥārith's movement at this early stage was his fellow tribemates from the Banū Tamīm, though other prominent Arabs with deep familial ties to Khurāsān and the eastern frontier were mentioned among his ranks. For example, after successfully conquering Balkh, Ḥārith placed Sulaymān b. ʿAbdallāh b. Khāzim – brother of Mūsā, the rebel who had ruled Termez for over a decade (see Chapter 4) – in charge of the city.[1] From Balkh, Ḥārith marched west, conquering Gūzgān, Ṭālaqān and Marw al-Rūd before arriving at the provincial capital of Marw. As Ḥārith marched, his numbers swelled and, by the time he reached the city, his army is reported to have grown to 60,000 men including the cavalry of Tamīm and Azd (crossing the Qays/Muḍar and Yaman divide), some of the *dahāqīn* of Gūzgān, Fāryāb and even Marw itself and the prince of Ṭālaqān, Suhrab.[2] Ḥārith's successes across Ṭukhāristān and his message targeting the oppression of Marwānid rule attracted a broad spectrum of society, but it remains unclear whether his followers were attracted to Ḥārith and his specific religious message or if he was capitalizing off a more general anti-Marwānid or anti-Umayyad sentiment.

The makeshift army that gathered around Ḥārith failed to breach the walls of Marw and was defeated by the forces of the newly appointed governor of Khurāsān ʿĀṣim b. ʿAbdallāh al-Hilālī (r. 734–5). Many of Ḥārith's troops drowned in the canal of Marw and in the River Murghāb as they confronted the governor and his forces, while the *dahāqīn* who had fought alongside him dispersed and returned to their homes.[3] In the aftermath, ʿĀṣim sent a delegation to Ḥārith's camp to negotiate a peace between the two sides. Included among the delegates was Muqātil b. Ḥayyān al-Nabaṭī, son of the famous *mawlā* commander from Daylam who had led the non-Arab troops under Qutayba b. Muslim. In one account, Muqātil gave a speech hoping to unify the Muslims of Khurāsān behind an idealized image of the frontier. 'O people of Khurāsān, we used to be the equivalent of one household, our frontier was one and our hand against our enemy was one.'[4] These words highlight a sense of disunity among the Muslims of Khurāsān that had only been growing and the challenge it posed to imperial authority in the east. At the same time, it imagines frontier fighting and the defence of the frontier against the Turks as a unifying purpose for the Muslims of Khurāsān, a common goal that would bring them together across tribal and ethnic lines. Interestingly, this call for unification under the Umayyads came from one of the *mawlā*. Granted he was a *mawlā* of high status in the Umayyad administration, his father had also been betrayed and murdered by the Umayyad governor Khudhayna, which made him a victim of Umayyad oppression as well.[5] In many ways, this challenges some of the key assumptions regarding Ḥārith and his revolt as it continued for another dozen years.

The motivations of Ḥārith's revolt are not nearly as clear as some modern accounts may have us think. Ḥārith and his rebellion have often been associated with the Murji'ite religious movement that promoted equality among Arab and non-Arab believers in Islam. As it has been understood, Murji'ism in Khurāsān,

Ṭukhāristān and Transoxiana attracted support from a variety of non-Arabs including Iranians, Turks and Hephthalites.[6] Therefore, it is presumed that Ḥārith, as a Murji'ite, was concerned with protecting the interests of the *mawālī* through an emphasis on the bonds of Islam rather than ethnic and tribal identities, but such a singular attitude is not fully supported by the sources.[7] Nor does Murji'ism appear prominently in the available sources. Ḥārith's initial call to revolt was dominated by religious rhetoric and slogans, but of a more generic tenor calling for the application of the Qur'an and the Sunna of the Prophet to governance, perhaps wanting to hold rulers responsible for their un-Islamic behaviours. His initial followers were largely Arabs of the Banū Tamīm. Unfortunately, we must rely on accounts from Ḥārith's rivals in order to understand his initial demands, such as a poem satirizing his movement credited to the governor of Khurāsān, Naṣr b. Sayyār, who had commanded the forces at Balkh that Ḥārith defeated in his first major victory.[8] At least one coin has been connected to Ḥārith's revolt that includes a religious slogan that some have tied to the Murji'ites; a dirham struck in Balkh in 116 AH/734–5 CE, early in the revolutionary movement, that reads, 'God commanded justice for one triumphant' (*amara Allāh bi-l-ʿadl li-manṣūr*).[9] Ḥārith's Murji'ism and his dedication to a Murji'ite religious programme has also been read from his association with the Murji'ite theologian Jahm b. Ṣafwān (d. 746), himself a *mawlā* from Mesopotamia who had been appointed a toll collector in Termez, but he may have only become involved in Ḥārith's movement later, first appearing in the sources as the revolutionary's spokesman in 744, the same year Naṣr welcomed Ḥārith back to Marw.[10] Therefore, it is not clear to what extent Jahm or his theology helped inspire or motivate Ḥārith or his supporters.

Perhaps most important was Ḥārith's general message of opposition to Marwānid oppression rather than any religious message. It was this rallying cry that attracted Arabs from both Qays/Muḍar and Yaman to his movement, making it a movement that crossed the major sociopolitical divisions of Umayyad Khurāsān. Illustrative of this, we can turn to the governor ʿĀṣim b. ʿAbdallāh himself. Despite his early victory against Ḥārith, the governor was unable to regain control of Khurāsān, holding onto only the cities of Marw and Nīshāpūr with even the strategic Oxus crossing at Āmul falling outside of his reach.[11] As a result, the Caliph Hishām sacked him and ordered Asad b. ʿAbdallāh al-Qasrī to return for a second term as governor of Khurāsān. When ʿĀṣim received the news, he contemplated joining Ḥārith to oppose Asad before ultimately deciding against such an unexpected alliance.[12] There is little doubt that ʿĀṣim looked to Ḥārith in hopes of holding onto his authority in Khurāsān, not because of his theology. The interests of multiple parties converged on a set of issues related to Umayyad rule in the east, resulting in complicated and overlapping expressions of anti-Umayyad sentiments that did not always fit together so neatly. The easy accusation of religious heterodoxy is not consistent in the descriptions of the movement.

When Asad al-Qasrī arrived in Khurāsān he was able to quickly drive Ḥārith back to Ṭukhāristān and then across the Oxus where he joined the Türgesh Turks who had pushed Umayyad forces out of Transoxiana during the previous decade, as discussed in the previous chapter. It is notable how quickly Ḥārith's support in Khurāsān and Ṭukhāristān melted away once faced with the threat of an army from Syria. As H. A. R. Gibb observed, 'The weakness of [Ḥārith's] hold over his temporary followers is much more striking than his transient success.'[13] Asad was able to retake Ṭukhāristān and even moved his capital to Balkh from where he could build better relationships with those *dahāqīn* who had initially rallied to Ḥārith.[14] A four-year gap in coinage from Balkh following the unusual issues mentioned above may be an indication that Asad's reintegration of Balkh did not go so smoothly, though eventually Asad's court became a centre for the Ṭukhārian *dahāqīn*.[15] The re-emergence of coins from Balkh in 737 coincided with Asad's first campaigns north of the Oxus against the Türgesh Khāqān Suluk, as discussed in the previous chapter, implying that Umayyad authority had stabilized in Ṭukhāristān by this point.

The fact that Ḥārith joined the Khāqān of the Türgesh and campaigned alongside him against the Muslims on several occasions gave our sources fodder to question his religious sincerity as well. They describe him as 'God's enemy' who brought the Khāqān to 'put out God's light and change His religion'.[16] Naṣr b. Sayyār accused Ḥārith of passing his time 'in the land of idolatry' and raiding 'the Muslims with the idolaters'.[17] We may question Ḥārith's intentions. Not only did he attract a variety of unrelated peoples and factions with a variety of grievances to his cause, but his beliefs were apparently flexible enough that he could quickly change sides to join the Türgesh. From accounts of Asad al-Qasrī's campaigns against the Türgesh it appears that Ḥārith played an important military role with the Türgesh but not an ideological one. He is described as fighting in the vanguard alongside the Sogdians and, when Asad's forces were victorious, Ḥārith was charged with defending Suluk's retreat.[18] When Asad descended on the Turks' camp, the Khāqān and his horse sank into the mud, and it was Ḥārith who stood over and defended him, acting as Suluk's bodyguard rather than the commander of his own religious movement.[19]

The supposed popular appeal and widespread nature of Ḥārith's revolt has led people to identify it as a precursor to the Abbasid Revolution that followed Ḥārith's death. On the one hand, Ḥārith's revolt demonstrated the appeal of religiously tinged anti-Umayyad rhetoric in Khurāsān and shows that the east was fertile ground for a revolutionary movement. On the other hand, it has been argued that the chaos that was strewn in Marw and throughout the east by Ḥārith and his supporters – alongside the continued tribal conflicts between the Muḍarite governor Naṣr b. Sayyār and his Yamanite rival Judayʿ b. ʿAlī al-Kirmānī (d. 747) of the Banū Azd, to be discussed shortly – paved the way for Abbasid success by weakening the hold the state had on the region. Along the frontier, the interests of multiple parties converged on a set of issues related to Umayyad rule, resulting in complicated and overlapping expressions of anti-Umayyad sentiments that did not always fit together so easily.

Studies of Umayyad and particularly Marwānid Khurāsān, Ṭukhāristān and Transoxiana often take the Abbasid Revolution as the ultimate outcome – the region is studied first and foremost to understand how it was that the Abbasid

Revolution came to be. But these studies often neglect to fully explore the Abbasid Revolution in the context of a series of revolts both before and after the critical movement that brought Umayyad rule to a close. To an extent, this is the result of the available sources which were primarily written in the Abbasid era when the authors understood the Abbasid Revolution to be successful in overturning Umayyad authority and essential to understanding the world as their authors knew it. From their perspective, other revolts such as that of Ḥārith b. Surayj were failures that did not substantially change the direction of the caliphate. As explored below, attention in studies of the Abbasid Revolution is often placed on diametric conflicts such as the tribal feuding between the Qays/Muḍar and Yaman confederacies or on competition between Arabs and non-Arabs. In this chapter, the Abbasid Revolution is explored within a broader narrative of reactions to conquest and settlement along the eastern frontier that complicates nearly every one of these dichotomies.

The Abbasid Revolution and Umayyad Khurāsān

Conquest and settlement brought together different people across the eastern frontier. Their differences were religious – Muslims and non-Muslims including Zoroastrians and Buddhists – and ethnolinguistic – Arabs, Iranians and Turks. The competition among these groups for economic and political power within the frontier zone could be viewed as an example of the 'frontier process' discussed in Chapter 1. There we described an image of a frontier based on but distinct from Frederick Jackson Turner's studies of the American West that was not just a place but an activity and a process.[20] The frontier process involved the struggles among people of different cultures and backgrounds over economic resources and political power that created a distinctive, hybrid frontier identity that could be reflected back upon the political centre, driving political, economic and social developments there. As Khurāsān, Ṭukhāristān and Sogdiana were incorporated into the caliphate, a frontier process took hold in each region that shaped the politics, culture and identity of Greater Khurāsān. For example, as the Arab Ḥārith b. Surayj led a revolt against the caliph's governor, he employed Muslim rhetoric and centred his movement within his tribe while attracting a mix of Arab (from both Muḍar and Yaman) and non-Arab and, presumably, Muslim and non- or nominally Muslim supporters and even seeking out the Muslims' presumptive enemies, the Türgesh, as a source of protection and military support. His revolt was constructed, at least as it was remembered in our sources, as a Muslim movement, but in the environment of the eastern frontier it attracted a variety of actors creating a movement unique to the frontier.

With this in mind, I would like to discuss some major trends in the historiography of the Abbasid Revolution and how this scholarship incorporates Greater Khurāsān and the eastern frontier into its analysis. Although there are many common features among arguments about the conditions in Khurāsān that inspired the Abbasid Revolution, there has also been a great amount of variety with several schools of thought emphasizing certain aspects over others. Parvaneh Pourshariati discussed some of the points of agreement: the social structures of Khurāsān changed very little from Sasanian to Arab rule (a clear difference from Transoxiana and Ṭukhāristān, I might add), the Arabs established a series of protectorates that allowed the native rulers to remain in power in return for tribute and Arab migration resulted in assimilation with the local populations. As a result, 'the interests of the various strata of the Iranian and Arab population of Khurāsān converged.'[21] Finally, due to the concentration of Arab settlement and activity in and around Marw, there has been a similar emphasis on Marw in the historical record and in modern scholarship. Revolutionary activities were centralized in Marw, as were the conflicts that flared up in the years before the outbreak of the Abbasid Revolution between the last Umayyad governor of Khurāsān Naṣr b. Sayyār and his rivals Juday' b. 'Alī al-Kirmānī who led the Banū Azd in a fight motivated by tribal factionalism and the Kharijite Shaybān b. Salama (d. 747–8). These events in Marw dominate our sources on late Umayyad Khurāsān as much as they do the attention of modern scholars.

On the other hand, we find debates surrounding the level of assimilation and the identification of the primary actors in the revolutionary movement. Gerlof van Vloten, writing at the end of the nineteenth century, placed most of the agency on the local Iranian populations, arguing that the Abbasid Revolution was fuelled by local hatred of foreign dominance that found voice in the messianic universalism of Shi'ism as employed by Abbasid propagandists including Abū Muslim (ca. 718–755).[22] Writing a decade later, Julius Wellhausen popularized the argument that the Abbasid Revolution was successful thanks to disgruntled Iranians drawn towards the universalist message of Shi'ism against an Arab chauvinist Umayyad dynasty.[23] Key to both of these arguments was the identification of Iranian converts as the aggrieved victims who felt oppressed by the Arabs who did not welcome them as equal partners in Islam and therefore turned on the Umayyads, an explanation similar to that given for Ḥārith b. Surayj's revolt. By the mid-twentieth century, Daniel Dennett argued that the exploitation of the *mawālī* in Khurāsān, particularly the economic exploitation that came from continued taxation of converts – meant to preserve state coffers in the face of growing conversion – was meted out by fellow Iranians, not the Arabs, challenging the anti-Arab component of Wellhausen's thesis and replacing the ethnic conflict with class conflict based in Sasanian socio-economic traditions. As discussed briefly in the previous chapter, it was Dennett's argument that the Sasanian system of taxation excused the nobility, soldiers and priests and, so that they became the collectors of tribute for the Arab–Muslims, they continued to pass the burden down to the peasantry.[24] Abd al-Aziz Duri similarly made an economic argument. According to Duri, taxation in early Islamic Khurāsān focused on the *kharāj* almost exclusively but the *dahāqīn* who were both the landowners and the group charged with collecting the taxes in the villages and countryside passed this cost on to their peasants and tenants – both Arab and non-Arab, Muslim and non-Muslim – transforming it into a poll tax similar to *jizya* in a manner that stoked anger and resentment against the Umayyad regime.[25]

Economic arguments such as Dennett's opened the door for others to see the Abbasid Revolution and the politics of early Islamic Khurāsān as something other than an ethnic conflict between Iranians and Arabs. M. A. Shaban gave Arabs the active role in the revolution, arguing that the armies of the Abbasid Revolution were made up of Arabs who felt they had lost their status as members of the ruling class – particularly those who settled in Khurāsān, assimilated and then found themselves paying taxes to non-Arab aristocracy and landowners in the name of the Umayyads.[26] According to Shaban's analysis, tensions in Khurāsān focused on the proper relationship between conquerors and conquered and the protection of the conqueror's elite status. From Shaban's perspective, the *mawālī* did play a role in the revolution, but the number of converts to Islam in the mid-eighth century was most likely very low, in contrast to Dennett's assumption that conversion and the subsequent economic impact was high, and the *mawālī* would not have been a significant factor in the revolution. Richard Bulliet's landmark study of conversion to Islam pushed significant conversion in Iran forward to the tenth century, long after the Abbasid Revolution.[27] The meaning of conversion in Khurāsān and Sogdiana is also a tricky issue with multiple references in the sources to converts attracted by more favourable tax incentives than true belief so that even if these converts did drive the revolutionary movement, we may still argue that they were motivated by economic rather than social or religious concerns.[28] To add to this confusion, the vast majority of the population – perhaps upwards of 90 per cent across the region – were peasants and their voice is the quietest in our sources, including the data used by Bulliet who relied on biographical dictionaries focused on educated, urban religious scholars and their social circles. Saleh Said Agha made the counterargument that Arab settlement in Khurāsān was likewise too small and too dedicated to fighting along the frontier to have engineered a successful revolution, arguing instead for a generally Iranian character for the revolutionary movement and even suggesting that a sizeable percentage of the participants converted to Islam late and perhaps only during the revolution itself.[29] It is interesting to note that the Turks play a minimal role, if any, in these analyses.

The most important factor in Shaban's analysis was the dividing line between pro-expansionist Arabs from the Qays/Muḍar confederation, who were supported by the late Umayyad state and the Muḍarite governor Naṣr b. Sayyār in the lead-up to the revolution, and the pro-settlement and assimilationist Arabs from the Yaman confederation, who were politically on the outs and in open revolt against Naṣr's regime. There is a certain irony here in that Naṣr was chosen by the Caliph Hishām because his tribe, the Banū Kināna, was weak in Khurāsān and Hishām assumed he would therefore be more loyal to the state, repeatedly declaring that Naṣr would have Hishām as his tribe. Similar arguments had been made about Qutayba b. Muslim thirty years earlier. Instead Naṣr favoured his wife's tribe, the Banū Tamīm, who were close to Kināna.[30] Some accounts put this favouritism on Hishām himself who is said to have turned away whenever a governor from Yaman or Rabīʿa was suggested – declaring that 'the frontiers will not be blocked with Rabīʿa' – but it was ultimately Naṣr who appointed only Muḍarites for the first four years of his governorship.[31] This is also one of the more controversial elements of Shaban's analysis and Patricia Crone has written a detailed rebuttal to it.[32] Crone questions the possibility that 'non-militancy [could] flourish in a frontier province under constant invasion' while pointing out that the divisions between Qays/Muḍar and Yaman were never so neat or clean on either genealogical or political lines.[33] As we have already seen, Ḥārith b. Surayj was able to attract support from both Muḍar and Yaman, who came to his movement with largely the same motivations. Also, as we will discuss shortly, in the conflicts between Naṣr b. Sayyār and Muḍar against Juday' al-Kirmānī and Yaman, Ḥārith and his supporters vacillated between the two sides frequently. A middle ground existed in practice. On the question of frontier fighting, intertribal violence peaked once Naṣr had defeated the Türgesh and the Turks retreated beyond the Jaxartes. In Khurāsān, tribal conflicts had long simmered, perhaps kept in check by frontier warfare, but the dissolution of the Türgesh allowed the rivalries to boil over.

Some have seen the *mawālī* in similar terms as a united faction intertwined in these tribal conflicts, but recently Elizabeth Urban convincingly argued for an equally complex set of overlapping identities among both the *mawālī* and *'ajam* or non-Arabs/foreigners, a term most often used for Persians, that betrays their identity as a cohesive faction.[34] The blurring of these two terms not only complicates their identification but also the role conversion played in defining the *mawālī* versus other kinds of political and social affiliations. As discussed in the previous chapter, the identification of the *mawālī* as a unified faction also tends to speak of them in terms that emphasize their native identity, even though many of the prominent *mawālī* with leadership positions in Umayyad Khurāsān were neither of Khurāsānī origins nor permanently settled in the east. Many of them were just as transient a presence on the eastern frontier as the Arabs and travelled to Khurāsān as part of an Arab tribe and an Arab–Muslim imperial network. Chapter 5 included the case of the *mawlā* Abū al-Ṣaydā Ṣāliḥ b. Ṭarīf, for example, who needed an interpreter to proselytize among the Sogdians and was therefore sent with an Arab who had been raised in Khurāsān and knew Persian. The example of Abū al-Ṣaydā may cause us to question who represented a native population in this context. The complex backgrounds of the *mawālī* who supported the Abbasid movement was also addressed by Kevin van Bladel who has argued, based on a new reading of a tradition from the famous secretary and translator Ibn al-Muqaffa', that the Khurāsānīs who marched in the army of the Abbasids were more specifically Ṭukhārians who spoke Bactrian.[35]

Elton Daniel elaborated on the question of class in the revolutionary movement. He argued that a local 'feudal' structure survived the conquest but now fell under the authority of a political system rooted in the Arab tribe.[36] The legal and economic regime established by the Arabs was not suited towards agriculture, with the Arabs who settled in the cities relying upon rural populations for their sustenance. This is perhaps most noticeable in moments of drought and other economic and ecological stresses when the system broke down, as in the summer of 733 when food became so dear that a loaf of bread cost a dirham and the governor Junayd b. 'Abd al-Raḥmān commanded the rural districts to increase their shipments to Marw.[37] The largest burden fell on the aristocratic landholders who had an abundance of both productive land and peasants who could be taxed through both the *kharāj* and *jizya* respectively.[38] This resulted in a larger transfer of wealth from the countryside to the cities. The preservation of pre-existing political and economic systems within a new imperial framework eventually blurred the lines between conquerors and conquered. For Daniel, Khurāsānī society therefore came to be dominated by parallel and allied social groups that shared horizontal socio-economic status – Iranian and Arab tribal nobility who collectively ruled the province and whose presence is best felt in our sources, along with *dahāqīn* and upper-class Arab landowners who felt the strain of Umayyad fiscal policy as well as the peasantry and urban proletariat who saw oppression and injustice in the system.[39] This last category was almost entirely Iranian and made up the majority of the population. Of course, outliers existed such as pastoralists nomads including Turks, Iranians and Arabs.

The emphasis on Marw as the centre of revolutionary activity has been another topic of focused study. Marw was the centre of Abbasid propaganda activity and home to most of the propagandists as well as the place where the revolution first openly manifested.[40] It was also importantly the primary garrison in Khurāsān, the provincial capital having been brought back from Balkh following Asad al-Qasrī's death and the ascension of Naṣr b. Sayyār. While Arab warriors travelled out in tribally organized units to, at the very least, police and collect taxes from other urban centres, evidence for settlement outside of Marw is weak and inconsistent. Saleh Said Agha collected the evidence for Arab migration outside of Marw before the Abbasid Revolution, identifying what he calls a 'military archipelago' of disconnected communities spread throughout Khurāsān, Ṭukhāristān and Transoxiana, but none of these come close to Marw in size or importance.[41] Yury Karev has argued for a greater role for Sogdiana and Ṭukhāristān in the revolutionary movement than previously understood, pointing to a unique passage in Dīnawarī that lists places from which people came to support Abū Muslim, tying these locations to Shi'ite activities both before and after the revolution.[42] Hugh Kennedy suggested that the separation of different tribal groups in different parts of Khurāsān, Ṭukhāristān and Transoxiana helped keep tribal identities and rivalries strong – a situation that was already apparent in the Second Fitna as discussed in Chapter 4.[43] The 'Swiss-Cheese' frontier or shatterzone, as described in Chapter 1, kept the 'islands' of this 'archipelago' separate and distinct, intensifying any sense of distance between groups.

Many of these arguments regarding the origins of the Abbasid Revolution and the place of Khurāsān in the revolutionary movement focused on dichotomies such as those between 'Arabs' and 'Persians' writ large or between Qays/Muḍar and Yaman and have situated the background of the revolution in these contentious dialogues. This chapter situates the Abbasid Revolution within a broader series of revolts along the eastern frontier both before and after the rise of the Abbasids and considers the different dynamics seen across these revolutionary movements to understand the Abbasid Revolution in the context of the frontier. The eastern frontier, as a shatterzone, was a much more diverse space than these dichotomies will allow, resulting in complex identities and relationships as well as overlapping interactions. While the interests of many of these groups converged, they never merged, as we saw at the outset of this chapter with the revolt of Ḥārith b. Surayj who attracted support from diverse sources but could not mould them into a movement that could speak with a single voice or survive a military setback. Once Asad al-Qasrī came to Balkh and repaired relations with the *dahāqīn*, Ḥārith's movement began to look much more like a band of rebellious Arabs seeking protection among the Turks rather than a religious movement with mass appeal across ethnic or regional lines. There was not a singularity of anti-Umayyad protest but the historiography of the Abbasid Revolution, both medieval and modern, has relied on the voice of the victorious to dictate the concerns of not just the revolutionaries but also the people of Khurāsān, Ṭukhāristān and Transoxiana as a whole. Viewing these revolts through the frontier and the legacy of conquest and the warfare against the Türgesh should help us bring different voices forward and understand how they competed and collaborated with each other.

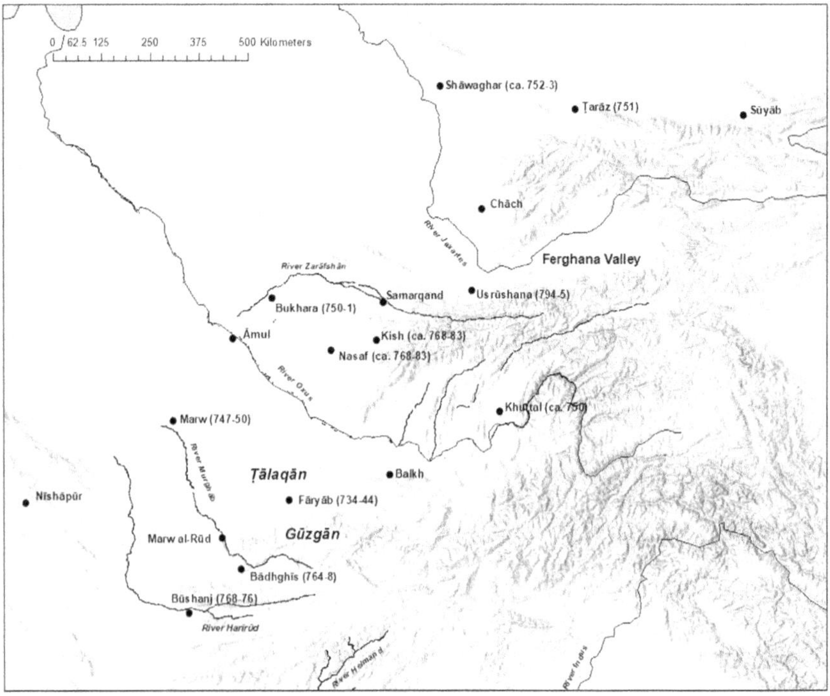

Map 7 Major Revolts and Campaigns of the Mid- and Late-Eighth Century (dates in parenthesis). Sources: Esri, USGS, NGA, NASA, CGIAR, N Robinson, NCEAS, NLS, OS, NMA, Geodatastyrelsen, Rijkswaterstaat, GSA, Geoland, FEMA, Intermap and the GIS user community.

Naṣr b. Sayyār and the breakdown of Umayyad Khurāsān

Naṣr b. Sayyār was a veteran of warfare along the eastern frontier, having participated in major campaigns beginning with Qutayba's conquests of Sogdiana before he became governor of Khurāsān at the age of seventy-four.[44] His age is noteworthy – Wellhausen highlighted Naṣr and the Caliph Muʿāwiya who died at the age of seventy-eight as the rare statesmen of the Umayyad era to successfully reach such advanced age.[45] During his tenure, imperial authority was challenged on multiple levels and, from the perspective of our sources, Umayyad rule in Khurāsān was unravelling. The rebel Ḥārith b. Surayj was still a concern despite his exile among the recently defeated Türgesh. The governor of Iraq, Yūsuf b. ʿUmar al-Thaqafī (r. 738–44), a second cousin of Ḥajjāj b. Yūsuf, commanded Naṣr to pursue Ḥārith in Chāch and his expulsion from the city in 741 was part of the peace agreement between Naṣr and the lord of Chāch.[46] Ḥārith was not captured though, and he fled south to Fāryāb where his revolt began. He remained there until 744 when Naṣr enticed him to Marw with a caliphal pardon and the return of confiscated properties so that he could join forces with his fellow Muḍarites against Judayʿ b. ʿAlī al-Kirmānī and Yaman.[47] Back in Marw, Ḥārith continued to preach his message of adherence to 'the Book of God and the Sunnah of His Prophet' and act as a pious dissident selling any gifts brought to him by Naṣr, distributing the proceeds among his supporters and refusing official appointments including the governorship of Transoxiana.[48] In the end, Ḥārith and his supporters were an important swing vote in the intertribal factionalism of late Umayyad Khurāsān, thanks to their mixed background. They fought at times for both sides until 25 April 746 when Ḥārith was killed by Kirmānī. His decapitated body was displayed in Marw, and his supporters were absorbed by the Abbasid revolutionary movement.[49] Whatever religious message Ḥārith's movement began with, he died a victim of inter-Arab factionalism.

Naṣr also inherited a Sogdiana that had been mostly outside of Umayyad authority for almost a decade – though control had been tenuous at best for at least a decade before that thanks to the Türgesh invasions. Beginning in 739, Naṣr led at least three campaigns into Sogdiana.[50] The first of these saw Naṣr march from Balkh through the Gate of Iron and then return to Marw. A second campaign reached Samarqand, which had been beyond Umayyad reach for the better part of the decade, and the third, Chāch. This final campaign ended in a confrontation between Naṣr and the Türgesh prince Kūrṣūl along the River Jaxartes. Kūrṣūl was captured and crucified along the banks of the river resulting in a total collapse of the Türgesh, who had now lost two supreme leaders in seven years.[51] The disarray was so great that groups of Turks either switched sides or were captured and joined the ranks of the Umayyad military. As early as 741, Muqātil b. ʿAlī al-Sughdī introduced himself to the Caliph Hishām as the master (*ṣāḥib*) of the Turks who had come to Damascus with 150 Turks for his service.[52] In 743, in preparation for a battle, Naṣr asked his lieutenants to gather the Turks, as if they were a contingent of his forces.[53] A reference found just a few pages earlier in Ṭabarī's chronicle to Naṣr gathering slave soldiers (*mamlūk*) may be evidence that these

Turks were in fact enslaved prisoners of war.[54] It was at this time that Naṣr also appointed Muqātil al-Sughdī over the river crossing at Āmul and if he continued to be a conduit for Turkish warriors entering into the Umayyad military, they were certainly now involved in policing this strategic point. According to Kirmānī's lost *History of the Barmakids*, the Barmak – whose precise identity in this case is contentious – arrived at the court of Hishām in Damascus with 500 *čākira*, which has been interpreted to mean Turkish slaves taken from Ṭukhāristān, due to the Barmak's connection to Balkh, but could also be a private retinue considering his prominent standing as the guardian of the Naw Bahār Buddhist monastery.[55] Étienne de la Vaissière has highlighted these passages as the earliest references to Turks in the service of the caliphate, arguing that they must be prisoners of war.[56] I might suggest that with the destruction of the Türgesh leadership at this time they may have simply joined with the victorious Muslims, something that would have felt natural as the Türgesh confederacy unravelled and warriors sought new patrons. Either way, despite the general view of the caliphate of Hishām as a period of declining engagement along the frontiers, Naṣr's campaigns resulted in successes and an influx of Turkish warriors into the caliphate.[57] By the close of the century, Turkish military commanders will appear in the service of the Abbasids in Greater Khurāsān.

With the Türgesh defeated, Naṣr offered the Sogdians peace on lighter terms than any previous governor if they were to return to their homes and accept Umayyad rule. These terms included the lifting of punishments against apostates, forgiveness of debts and tax arrears and a more restrictive process for the return of Muslim prisoners, which required the decree of a *qāḍī* and the testimony of witnesses, presumably to make it more difficult for slaves to gain their freedom through either heartfelt or disingenuous conversion.[58] These concessions covered all the standard concerns that had caused tensions to rise between the Umayyads and their Sogdian subjects over the first half of the eighth century. It should be noted that Naṣr, as a Muḍarite partisan, is here working to ingratiate himself with the *mawālī* in contrast to the general view that it was the Yaman who were in alliance with the local populations. Naṣr did receive some pushback on these provisions and complaints were made against him all the way to the Caliph Hishām, but the governor was able to silence his critics by invoking the ferocity the Sogdians had previously shown in battle. Much as we saw in the conquests of Qutayba b. Muslim in the previous chapter, Naṣr found himself negotiating a position between different factions in Sogdiana, between the local lords and their subjects as well as Naṣr's own agents. In one of the more notable cases, Naṣr's lieutenant in Bukhara, Wāṣil b. ʿAmr al-Qaysī, and the Bukhārkhudā Ṭughshāda were simultaneously assassinated in 739 by two of the *dahāqīn* of Bukhara. In Narshakhī's account, Ṭughshāda and Wāṣil conspired to confiscate the property of these two *dahāqīn*, despite the fact they were relatives of the Bukhārkhudā and Muslims having converted to Islam under the guidance of Naṣr himself – therefore, theoretically, being the governor's *mawālī*. Considering that Ṭughshāda was himself not a practising Muslim – the assassination occurred while he was neglecting communal prayers in the mosque – the *dahāqīn* found this move to be a betrayal of both blood and faith and, therefore, decided to assassinate the two rulers of Bukhara, seeing no other possibility for justice.[59] Although they were successful in executing their quarries, the *dahāqīn* were also killed in the process and Ṭughshāda's son Qutayba (d. ca. 751), named for the conqueror of Bukhara who had secured the Bukhārkhudā's throne for him, succeeded his father. Despite being Muslims, the *dahāqīn* were hard-pressed to seek justice from Naṣr's lieutenant against a non-Muslim king and felt forced to use violence.

Naṣr's own position was saved by the devolution of the Umayyad Caliphate into a final bout of civil war following the death of Hishām. Also known as the Third Fitna, this conflict within the Umayyad family and between the Arab tribal confederacies saw four caliphs from three different branches of the Umayyad family come to power in less than two years between 743 and 744, including one assassination and one fearful abdication. By the end of Hishām's reign, the governor of Iraq Yūsuf b. ʿUmar sought to replace Naṣr, reattach Khurāsān more directly to Iraq and hand power to Qays. During the brief reign of Hishām's successor Walīd II (r. 743–4), Naṣr, much like Qutayba under similar circumstance, prepared his lieutenants to set out on a campaign in Transoxiana if rumours of his dismissal reached them so that he may use the fighting as an excuse not to attend to Yūsuf in Iraq.[60] News of Walīd II's assassination and the conflicts that broke out in Syria over the succession of the caliphate came to Naṣr as he was slowly meandering towards Iraq to attend to Yūsuf, and he instead turned back to Khurāsān, refusing to step down from his governorship and distributing the lavish tribute that had been collected for the caliph among his close companions.[61]

Eventually the tribal tensions in Khurāsān exploded into open conflict as Judayʿ b. ʿAlī al-Kirmānī, the leader of the Banū Azd in Khurāsān, led the Yamani in open revolt against Naṣr.[62] Naṣr became concerned that inter-Arab fighting would endanger the frontier (*thaghr*) and give the upper hand to the non-Arabs (*al-aʿājim*).[63] These developments did not occur within a vacuum. The conflict between Muḍar and Yaman did not come fully out into the open until several years after Naṣr's victory over the Türgesh, the reconquest of Sogdiana and the defeat of Ḥārith b. Surayj that forced him into hiding in Fāyrāb. It also occurred over a backdrop of conflict in Syria. By 747, the activities of the Kharijite Shaybān b. Salama of the Rabīʿa could be added to Naṣr's troubles while, in that same year, the Abbasid propagandist and general Abū Muslim brought the revolutionary movement out into the open. Naṣr attempted to unite the various factions against Abū Muslim but failed.[64] In the end, it was Kirmānī's son and the Banū Azd who handed Marw over to Abū Muslim and the Abbasids.[65] In early 748 Naṣr abandoned the citadel of Marw and fled the city for Nīshāpūr. From there he continued west, first to Gorgān where he was met with Syrian reinforcements but was again defeated by the Abbasids. Naṣr died on the run at the age of eighty-five as he tried to reach Hamadān in western Iran. It should be noted that Naṣr's dream of a united front against Abū Muslim did briefly materialize in Ṭukhāristān when Muqātil b. Ḥayyān raised an army including representatives of Muḍar, Yaman, Rabīʿa and the *mawālī*. Muqātil was placed in charge of this force because, as a *mawlā*, he was considered a neutral arbiter between the Arab tribal divisions against the 'black-clad warriors' as the Abbasid troops were known.[66]

It is interesting to note that, despite the importance placed on Naṣr's campaigns into Sogdiana at the beginning of his tenure and the threat the Türgesh seemed to pose at the outset of the fighting between Naṣr and Kirmānī, the frontier largely disappeared from the equation in reports of the inter-Arab conflicts and the rise of the Abbasids. Instead, the narrative plays out as a conflict within Marw and between Marw and Nīshāpūr before the focus then shifted west – aside from the Abbasid campaigns into Ṭukhāristān to track down remaining Umayyad loyalists. On the one hand, the chaos of intertribal fighting opened the door for the Abbasid revolutionary movement but, at the same time, the decline of the Türgesh and the lack of a real danger across the frontier perhaps prevented the people of Khurāsān, Ṭukhāristān and Transoxiana from coming together against an outside foe as they had during earlier periods of communal disturbance, opening the door to increased civil strife and a successful revolution. I do not want to devote much space to detailing the Abbasid Revolution itself; there are many useful studies that have covered this material from several perspectives as detailed above. Instead, I would like to now shift to the aftermath of the revolution and examine how the Abbasids addressed the challenges of the frontier.

The shaping of the Abbasid frontier

Even though the Abbasid Revolution began in and gathered its base of support from Khurāsān, there was much work to be done in the aftermath of their victory over the Umayyads to solidify their rule in the east. In part this may be because many of the Abbasids' strongest supporters moved west with the revolution and established themselves in the new imperial centre of Iraq. Immediately following the success of the revolution, the governorship of Khurāsān was given to Abū Muslim, the propagandist who had instigated the revolution and led its armies to victory. Known by a nom de guerre, Abū Muslim's background remains mysterious with some sources attempting to give him a noble lineage, tying him to either powerful figures of the Sasanian period or the Abbasid and even ʿAlid families. It is likely he was of Persianate background – both Marw and Isfahan have been suggested as his birthplace – while most agree that he grew up in Kūfa, and it was from that hotbed of anti-Umayyad activity that he first entered the service of the Abbasids. As the first governor after the revolution, it was Abū Muslim's duty to establish Abbasid rule in Khurāsān and secure the empire's eastern frontier. In both instances, Abū Muslim faced unique challenges. Unlike all prior Muslim governors, he was not part of the Arab tribal system, not even as a *mawlā* or client, nor did he have experience within the army of Khurāsān fighting on the frontier despite his important role in leading the armies of the revolution. At the same time, he was not attached to the local networks of Khurāsān outside of those of the revolutionary movement even though he will be forever associated with the province. As such, he was paradigmatic of the new men of the Abbasid regime who owed their position to the dynasty and its supporters.

Resistance to the early Abbasids in the east is often discussed in terms of the rhetoric and realities of Abbasid rule, but on the ground, these conflicts often reflected older tensions related to the expansion and settlement of the frontier under the Umayyads. For example, we may turn to the revolt of Sharīk b. Shaykh al-Mahrī (or Fihrī), which broke out at Bukhara in 750–1.[67] Sharīk was an Arab and a supporter of the ʿAlids who had participated in the revolution but became disillusioned when the Shi'ite rhetoric of the revolutionary movement resulted in the ascension of Abū al-ʿAbbās al-Saffāḥ (r. 749–54) as caliph rather than someone with a more solid connection to the family of the Prophet, in whose name the revolution had been fought.[68] He was supported in this revolt by an unnamed amir of Bukhara, an Arab from the Banū Azd, and a large segment of the Arab population of the city. Abū Muslim sent his lieutenant Ziyād b. Ṣāliḥ (d. 752–3) to Bukhara to put down Sharīk and his followers, naming Ziyād his governor of Transoxiana. Ziyād received support from the Bukhārkhudā Qutayba b. Ṭughshāda who raised an army to fight against the rebels. The Bukhārkhudā's support for the Abbasids seems to have little to do with Sharīk or his movement – or the Abbasid regime for that matter – but rather it was tied to the legacies of the conquest of the oasis under Qutayba b. Muslim – the Bukhārkhudā's namesake – discussed in the previous chapter.

According to Narshakhī's account, Sharīk, his supporters and the Arabs held the city while the Bukhārkhudā and the local notables resided in the rural villas (*kūshk*), where not one Arab resided, and it was from this rural population that the Bukhārkhudā recruited his army. During the conquest of Bukhara by Qutayba forty years prior, a large segment of the local population was forced out of the city to make way for an Arab garrison. As discussed in the previous chapter, many of those who were chased out of Bukhara established estates for themselves outside of the city and this resulted in changes to their lifestyle and economic activities. By siding with the Abbasids against Sharīk, the Bukhārkhudā organized the rural notables who had been removed from the city against the Arab newcomers who occupied the city. Their participation had less to do with questions of Abbasid versus ʿAlid legitimacy and more to do with the immediate political and economic life of the oasis and the place, quite literally, of the local population vis-à-vis the Arab–Muslim newcomers.[69] This did not necessarily mean that the situation changed after the defeat of Sharīk and twenty years later the seat of the Bukhārkhudā was still at Varakhsha.[70] As evidence that the Bukhārkhudā's fight against Sharīk did not signal a particularly strong or long-lasting alliance with the Abbasids, it was not long after this that Qutayba b. Ṭughshāda, an unnamed brother and a number of his followers were killed by Abū Muslim for apostasy.[71] Another brother, Bunyāt, was then named Bukhārkhudā and a balance was maintained between supporting and repressing the local lords. Despite the revolutionary rhetoric of the Abbasids or of their Shi'ite rivals, the people of Bukhara seem to be primarily concerned about their immediate local concerns.

While such rebellions continued, Abū Muslim also oversaw expansion into Transoxiana that took caliphal authority further beyond the River Jaxartes than ever before. Perhaps one of the more widely known events in the history of early Abbasid Central Asia is the famed Battle of Ṭalās – also known as Ṭarāz or Aṭlakh – an engagement between armies of the Abbasid and Tang Empires that took place in July 751 along the River Ṭarāz 12 km southeast of the city of the same name at a place called Aṭlakh. This confrontation, often seen as a battle for control over western Central Asia, resulted in a victory for the Abbasids and began the retreat of the Tang from Central Asia. Following the outcome of the battle, it would be over 1,000 years before the Qing Dynasty (r. 1644–1912) would bring Chinese rule back to Central Asia.[72] As Karev has argued, this was not some accidental meeting of the two empires but the direct result of the ambitions of Abū Muslim, committed to asserting Muslim control over Transoxiana in the aftermath of the Abbasid Revolution, and the Tang general Gao Xianzhi (d. 756).[73] Gao, himself of Korean (Goguryeo) descent, commanded the Anxi protectorate in the Tarim Basin – discussed in Chapter 3 – and was famous for leading successful campaigns against the Tibetan Empire that briefly reasserted Chinese influence in Central Asia.[74]

Following the death of the Türgesh rulers Suluk and Kūrṣūl, the Chinese once again involved themselves directly in the conflicts among the Turks and invaded the Türgesh capital at Sūyāb, 320 km east of Ṭarāz and 50 km east of Bishkek. These advances were not entirely the result of the declining fortunes of the Türgesh, though the Tang took advantage of the situation, and the wars against Tibet continued to be the most important factor in dictating China's western policy. By 748 the Tang had taken Sūyāb and built a temple there.[75] Near the end of 750, General Gao marched further west against the king of Chāch who was accused of not performing the proper duties of a frontier subject and clashing with the king of Ferghana, another Tang vassal.[76] Chāch, approximately 700 km southwest of Sūyāb, was conquered, and its king, called Chebishi in the Chinese sources, was taken to the Tang capital where he was executed.[77] Ibn al-Athīr provided a unique account of these events from the Muslim perspective, describing the hostility between the king of Chāch and the Ikhshīd or king of Ferghana who requested support from China. The Tang responded with 100,000 troops, surrounded Chāch and forced the king's submission.[78] The presence of a Chinese army so far west was a shock to the lords of Sogdiana but also Abū Muslim and the Abbasids who claimed Chāch as part of their sphere of influence – even if only aspirationally – and, in response, Abū Muslim organized a retaliatory expedition.[79]

The outcome of the Battle of Ṭarāz itself was dictated by the shifting alliances and relationships between different communities along the frontier.[80] We lack an accurate description of the composition of either forces and many questions remain, especially in regard to the participation of Sogdians among the Abbasid forces, but it would appear that both armies numbered between 20,000 and 30,000, with the Chinese army supported by troops from Ferghana and the Qārlūq Turks who hoped to fill the void left by the Türgesh.[81] The deciding factor after five days of battle was a change of heart among the Qārlūq. They joined the Abbasids. The numbers were further swung in the Muslims' favour when the Ferghanian troops abandoned the cause at the sedition of their Turkish allies and Gao was forced to retreat with the remaining Chinese soldiers, cutting down some of his recent allies as the Feghanians blocked his escape through a narrow pass.

As the Battle of Ṭarāz unfolded, Abū Muslim was likewise in the process of cementing Abbasid authority in Sogdiana. Following the defeat of Sharīk b. Shaykh at Bukhara, Ziyād b. Ṣāliḥ was sent to Samarqand, again, as the new governor of Transoxiana.[82] Few details are given about Ziyād's time in Samarqand. It is reported that fighting took place and a wall was built, but it can be assumed that, in the aftermath of a revolt at the other major urban centre of the Zarāfshān Valley, Ziyād's mission was to project Abbasid strength at Samarqand. Ṭabarī reported in an off-handed manner that, before returning to Marw from Samarqand – likely after the Battle of Ṭarāz which the chronicler omits – Abū Muslim killed some people in Samarqand and Bukhara.[83] Maqdisī, the tenth-century chronicler of the Sāmānid court, gave the impression that noble families were targeted with properties confiscated and children taken to Marw as hostages.[84] It may have been in this context that the Bukhārkhudā Qutayba was killed for apostasy. Based on circumstantial evidence, the Ikhshīd of Samarqand Tūrghar b. Ghūrak may have been killed and replaced with his brother Yazīd at this time too.[85]

We know of other campaigns against local lords in greater detail. Abū Muslim's lieutenant in Ṭukhāristān, Abū Dāwud Khālid b. Ibrāhīm (d. 757–8), led campaigns into Khuttal and Kish against local lords who had previously offered their loyalty to the Abbasids. The king of Khuttal, Ḥanash b. Subul, is said to have not instigated a revolt but had his hand forced by the leading men among the *dahāqīn* who took to the forts and mountain passes to resist the Abbasids. When Abū Dāwud pressured Ḥanash, the king fled under the cover of night with his *dahāqīn* and *čākira* for Ferghana, then to the Turks and finally China.[86] There are Chinese reports of an embassy from Khuttal bringing slaves and horses in 750, but they do not specifically reference any threat to the kingdom or a fugitive king.[87] At Kish, Abū Dāwud killed the ruler Ikhrīd, replacing him with his brother Ṭārān and confiscating a number of Chinese goods of exceptional quality, including ornamented vessels, saddles, furnishings and brocade, which he gave to Abū Muslim.[88] Ikhrīd's relationship to the caliphate is difficult to ascertain. Abū Dāwud was ordered to specifically target him and the literary sources emphasize the Chinese goods in his possession. We also know of aniconic copper *fulūs* struck at Kish in the name of 'Ikhrīd the *dihqān* of Kish' that use Arabic inscriptions in contrast to the coins struck by other Sogdian lords who still followed pre-Islamic models.[89] Does the change in the coins of Kish imply a pivot, at least economically, towards the caliphate? If so, what does it mean that Abū Dāwud was sent to kill him? In both incidents, China appears as an alternative to the Abbasids, placing the Battle of Ṭarāz within the longer dynamic of Chinese competition for influence in Sogdiana. Despite the Chinese loss at Ṭarāz, some Sogdian lords sought more direct support from the Tang, a sign that this defeat was not widely understood as definitive. An embassy from the Afshīn, the Sogdian title for the king of Usrūshana, arrived at the Tang court in 752 and suggested a coordinated attack against the Arabs in 'black robes' or the Abbasids.[90] In response, the Emperor Xuánzōng asked the Afshīn to help keep the peace.[91] We do not know of any direct response against the Afshīn but, according to Nasafī, Ziyād b. Ṣāliḥ was sent by Abū Muslim against Bārkath, which he calls a village of Usrūshana, where he killed the *dihqān*, but it is not clear if these events are related.[92]

From both Abū Muslim and Gao's actions, we see a changing political dynamic in Central Asia in the mid-eighth century. Following the collapse of the Türgesh, the Turks were temporarily not a serious threat to imperial ambitions in the region. Naṣr b. Sayyār's victories appear to have brought an end to Turkish raids during the final years of Umayyad rule and through the Abbasid Revolution. Even the rebel Ḥārith b. Surayj left the Turks, returned to Marw from Transoxiana and involved himself in the intertribal feuds of the Arabs. Both the Abbasids and Tang took advantage of this vacuum to assert their authority in Transoxiana, and the conflict between them was the balancing of the two sides. Though the Qārlūq Turks participated in the battle, it was in support of first the Tang and then the Abbasids, not as independent players. The defeat of the Tang and their reluctance to march in support of the Sogdian lords opened the door further for Abū Muslim to assert his authority in a stronger manner than his predecessors at a time when there was no Turkish counterbalance or alternative to which the Sogdian lords could turn, placing new obligations on the local rulers of Sogdiana. For example, Abū Muslim executing the Bukhārkhudā for apostasy is in sharp contrast to Naṣr b. Sayyār supporting a non-Muslim ruler of Bukhara against Muslim *dahāqīn*, as described above. The local kings were not expecting such a drastic change to the conditions under which they had previously ruled in the name of the caliphate but they may have prompted this change themselves by encouraging the Abbasids to act as a counterbalance to the Tang following Gao's attack on Chāch.

With the collapse of the Türgesh and Abū Muslim's purges in Sogdiana, the Abbasids attempted to assert their imperial authority between the Oxus and Jaxartes rivers. The Abbasids made several attempts to integrate Sogdiana into the imperial structures. This could be done forcefully. In some instances, the sons of vanquished rebels were enrolled in the Abbasid military while their daughters were sent to the royal harem.[93] A more congenial version of this movement can be seen in the organization of the new capital of Baghdad, founded by the Caliph Manṣūr in 762, and the settlement of peoples from Khurāsān, Ṭukhāristān and Transoxiana in a special quarter near the Gate of Syria. Yaʿqūbī provided a list of people who were granted land in this quarter, including people who would seemingly live on the fringes and even beyond the reach of Abbasid authority such as the people of Isfījāb and Kabul.[94] At Baghdad, Manṣūr attempted to pull these populations physically to the centre and create a somewhat mobile elite community that circulated between the capital and the provinces. Something similar may have been happening along the Arab–Byzantine frontier as early as the caliphate of Mahdī but certainly by the caliphate of Hārūn al-Rashīd (r. 786–809) when groups from Khurāsān, Ṭukhāristān and Transoxiana appear in lists of fighters. One account originating in the tenth-century judge Ṭarsūsī's *Way of the Frontier* speaks of warriors arriving at Ṭarsūs or Cilicia in south-central Anatolia during the reign of Mahdī from Balkh, Khwarazm, Herat, Samarqand, Ferghana and Isfījāb under the leadership of Ḥasan b. Qaḥṭaba al-Ṭā'ī (d. 797), a son of an Abbasid *naqīb*.[95] The methods of recruitment or motivations of such warriors are not clear.

Construction projects further demonstrated the early Abbasids' commitment to integrating Sogdiana into the empire. Reports of the wall Abū Muslim built around Samarqand describe a massive undertaking measuring 60 km in circumference, including 360 towers and encompassing 450 manors (*jawāsiq*).[96] Archaeological excavations have also uncovered a palace that has been dated to Abū Muslim's governorship, indicating a commitment to the city and perhaps plans to establish a provincial capital for Sogdiana matching Marw, which Abū Muslim also renovated with a new congregational mosque, palace and markets.[97] A firm seat in Samarqand could also serve as a staging ground for campaigns deeper into Transoxiana. Karev identified a pair of buildings located 40 km from Ṭarāz. He suggested that they is an outpost built by Abū Muslim in the aftermath of the Battle of Ṭarāz to defend the extreme frontier, which would demonstrate a commitment to such expansion.[98] Ṭabarī reported that Abū Muslim sent a force under Ibn Najāḥ – likely of Turkish descent himself – to Shāwaghar, modern Türkistān in Kazakhstan located 230 km north of Chāch and 160 km northwest of Isfījāb, which he conquered from its Ispahbud.[99]

The assertion of a stronger caliphal presence in Sogdiana still balanced imperial authority with local traditions and was clearly not uniform. For example, under Abū Muslim's successor, Abū Dāwud Khālid b. Ibrāhīm (r. 755–7), there was a small reformation of the coinage of Sogdiana, visible in the coins of Bukhara. Instead of eliminating the traditional Bukhārkhudā issues, modelled off the coins of the Sasanian Shahanshah Bahrām Gūr, and replacing them with Abbasid issues, Abū Dāwud simply added his name, 'Khālid', to the existing local coinage, something akin to the Arab–Sasanian coins of a century prior.[100] In doing so, Abū Dāwud simultaneously asserted his authority over Bukhara while preserving local traditions and political and economic practices. The Bukhārkhudā dirhams would continue, parallel to locally struck 'Islamic' coins, until at least the reign of the Caliph Ma'mūn (r. 813–33) but maybe as late as the Qarākhānid period (eleventh to thirteenth century).[101] By 760, more noticeably Abbasid-style *fulūs* emerged at several mints in Ṭukhāristān and Transoxiana, reflecting a stronger presence beyond Khurāsān proper. *Fulūs* featuring the names of governors, the caliph and Abbasid slogans appeared at Termez, Balkh and Chaghāniyān in 759 and Samarqand and Bukhara the following year.[102] Even though these coins more closely met the standards for Abbasid issues, it should be noted that they were not uniform with a large variety of types appearing, including different inscriptions and even titles for the caliph, his son and his governors and their lieutenants.[103]

The early years of Abbasid rule along the eastern frontier involved an effort to consolidate and expand imperial authority, especially in Transoxiana, with military campaigns pushing Abbasid rule far beyond the limits achieved by the Umayyads and large construction projects and administrative reforms tying the region more closely into the imperial networks. But the Abbasids still faced many of the problems their predecessors did trying to rule the distant reaches of their empire. Notable among these challenges was the problem of maintaining control over their own representatives as the caliphs consolidated their authority with numerous rebellions arising among the governors of Khurāsān and their lieutenants, many growing from the ill-treatment Abū Muslim received at the hands of the Caliph Manṣūr. The first Abbasid caliphs feared the charismatic governor could recruit his own army and build his own kingdom in the east. There was the impression that the Abbasids owed their victory to Abū Muslim, and when Saffāḥ died the general led his Khurāsānī forces against the caliph's uncle ʿAbdallāh b. ʿAlī (ca. 712–64) to secure the title for his brother and successor Manṣūr, which reinforced the idea that the Abbasids ruled at Abū Muslim's pleasure. As early as 752, the Caliph Saffāḥ had attempted to replace Abū Muslim with his lieutenant Ziyād b. Ṣāliḥ, an event remembered in our sources as a failed revolt by Ziyād.[104] When Abū Muslim appeared to be moving towards sedition, refusing the caliph's orders to appear before him, Manṣūr offered the governorship to Abū Dāwud and he counselled Abū Muslim to obey his master.[105] In the end, when Abū Muslim finally agreed to Manṣūr's summons, the caliph had the governor of Khurāsān killed, sparking off a series of revolts among his supporters across Iran.[106] Abū Dāwud, similarly connected to the revolutionary movement as one of the twelve *nuqabā'* or missionaries sent to spread the Abbasid message in Khurāsān, was named Abū Muslim's successor. He continued the policy of appointing individuals whose standing was determined by their relationship to the Abbasid family.

Muqannaʿ and the eastern frontier

The fear that the governor of Khurāsān was beyond the authority of the caliph did not die with Abū Muslim. Following Abū Dāwud's death – suspiciously described as an accident in which he fell from the parapet of his palace in Marw while addressing a group of disgruntled troops – he was replaced by ʿAbd al-Jabbār b. ʿAbd al-Raḥmān al-Azdī (r. 757–8), the commander of Manṣūr's *shurṭa* or police. ʿAbd al-Jabbār was ordered to eliminate commanders with Shi'ite tendencies as part of Manṣūr's purge of his ʿAlid rivals, but Manṣūr soon grew suspicious that his governor was using this order as a pretence to eliminate his own rivals and prepare for a revolt. According to one account, the caliph requested ʿAbd al-Jabbār to bring the army of Khurāsān west for a campaign against the Byzantines, to which ʿAbd al-Jabbār claimed that attacks by the Turks made it too dangerous to abandon Khurāsān.[107] When Manṣūr offered to send him reinforcements, ʿAbd al-Jabbār claimed that there was a shortage of food and he would not be able to supply the caliph's troops. In the end, Manṣūr sent his son Muḥammad, the future Caliph Mahdī, at the head of a force that captured and killed ʿAbd al-Jabbār.[108] In other accounts, ʿAbd al-Jabbār is said to have joined the Shi'ite cause himself, promoting an ʿAlid pretender to the throne and openly denouncing Manṣūr.[109] He may have also reached out to Muḥammad Nafs al-Zakiyya (the Pure Soul; d. 762), a great-grandson of the second Shiʿite Imam Ḥasan b. ʿAlī who was not so secretly plotting an ʿAlid revolt.[110]

The Arab governor of Ishtīkhan, Ashʿath b. Yaḥyā al-Ṭāʾī, is reported to have resisted when his overlord ʿAbd al-Jabbār rebelled.[111] Although we have little information about Ashʿath's resistance, the information we do have about Ishtīkhan and a couple of coins struck in Ashʿath's name in the years after ʿAbd al-Jabbār's rebellion might point us in some interesting directions. First, as discussed briefly in the previous chapter, since Qutayba b. Muslim's conquest of Samarqand, the kings of Samarqand had relocated their court to Ishtīkhan. This was likely a result of the disruptions caused by the foundation of an Arab garrison in the city. Second are the interesting titles found on copper *fulūs* minted in Ashʿath's name at Bukhara in 143 AH/760–1 CE and Samarqand in 144 AH/761–2 CE, two years after ʿAbd al-Jabbār's revolt. The coins minted at Bukhara are the earliest known use of the title Mahdī for the third Abbasid Caliph Muḥammad b. ʿAbdallāh.[112] The coins minted at Samarqand also employ the title Mahdī but include the *tamgha* of the Ikhshīd of Samarqand as well.[113] Piecing this evidence together, we may see a comparable situation to the developments that occurred during the revolt of Sharīk b. Shaykh in Bukhara. In both cases an Arab governor rebelled in the name of the ʿAlids and people connected to the local lords resisted and helped stop the rebellion. Ashʿath's position in Ishtīkhan and the appearance of the *tamgha* on his coins tie him to the Ikhshīds while his early use of the title Mahdī with its messianic meanings for Muḥammad b. ʿAbdallāh – it is important to note that this was before even Manṣūr had taken his regnal title or *laqab* – implies he was an advocate for Abbasid claims to power over more directly ʿAlid lineages. As Jere Bacharach argued, the choice of the title Mahdī – literally the 'guided one', a name associated with an eschatological redeemer – by Muḥammad b. ʿAbdallāh may have itself been a challenge to ʿAlid claims, particularly those of the other Muḥammad b. ʿAbdallāh, the Pure Soul, who ʿAbd al-Jabbār may have been trying to contact.[114]

The most famous and longest lasting revolt by a former member of the Abbasid military was that of Hāshim b. Ḥākim al-Jāḥiẓ (d. ca. 783), better known as Muqannaʿ or 'the Veiled One'. According to Narshakhī's *Taʾrīkh-i Bukhārā* – the most detailed account of the background of Muqannaʿ, his movement and revolt – he served as a captain (*sarhang*) in the army of Khurāsān during the Abbasid Revolution through the caliphate of Manṣūr and had been an adviser to ʿAbd al-Jabbār.[115] Although it is likely he served the Abbasids during this period, it is unlikely he was highly ranked. With the downfall of ʿAbd al-Jabbār, Hāshim was discharged from the military and may have spent time in prison, perhaps for participating in ʿAbd al-Jabbār's revolt, before he returned to the village of Kāza near Marw. At some point he claimed prophethood, preaching a syncretic religion that borrowed from the many traditions present in Central Asia, including Islam, Christianity, Zoroastrianism and, especially, Buddhism. At the heart of his message was the idea that God could enter the body of men as a divine incarnation, that He had entered Adam, Noah, Abraham, Moses, Jesus, Muhammad and Abū Muslim and that He had now entered Muqannaʿ in order to spread his message among the people.[116]

Copper *fulūs* minted in the name of Muqannaʿ confirm this religious programme with obverse inscriptions reading 'by the order of Hāshim, the executor of the will of Abū Muslim (*waṣī Abī Muslim*)', related to a traditional Shi'ite formulation that named ʿAlī as the executor of the will of the Prophet Muhammad.[117]

Muqannaʿ sent out missionaries, including his own father-in-law who proselytized in Sogdiana.[118] The missionary activities across the River Oxus were successful and at some point his supporters became militarized – perhaps in response to threats against their leader in Marw – and they captured several fortresses around Kish and Nasaf. A group known as the 'Wearers of White-Clothes' (*mubayyiḍa* in Arabic and *sapid jāmagān* in Persian), which predated Muqannaʿ, gravitated towards him as well, appearing as a militant wing of his movement. Sometime between 768 and 773 Muqannaʿ led a group of his followers from Marw to the fortress of Nawākit in the Siyām Mountains near Kish where he entrenched himself.[119] From Nawākit, Muqannaʿ's supporters conquered villages in the districts of first Kish and Nasaf and then Bukhara and Samarqand, spreading their influence across the breadth of Sogdiana. Balʿamī even attributed failed campaigns below the Gate of Iron into Chaghāniyān and northern Ṭukhāristān to them.[120] Ṭukhāristān was facing its own disturbances at this time. A man named Ustādhsīs led an uprising originating in the silver mines near Bādhghīs that lasted from 764 until 768. Yūsuf al-Barm led a revolt that stretched from Būshanj west of Herat to Marw al-Rūd, Ṭālaqān and Gūzgān, which began as early as 768 and ran until 776.[121] The high point of Muqannaʿ's revolt came around 775 – near the deaths of both the governor of Khurāsān Ḥumayd b. Qaḥṭaba (r. 769–75) and the Caliph Manṣūr – when his supporters attacked the Bukhara oasis and, in conjunction with a Turkish force, conquered Samarqand itself, after which Muqannaʿ claimed the title King of Sogdiana.[122] Muqannaʿ's hold on Samarqand was perilous and he had to conquer the city twice but the Abbasid reconquest of Sogdiana was similarly slow, lasting until 779–80 when the Turkish military commander Saʿīd al-Ḥarashī successfully besieged Nawākit and starved out Muqannaʿ's supporters, leaving only his wives – up to 100 in number – and his closest servants and confidants to collectively drink poison while Muqannaʿ burnt himself alive.[123]

Muqannaʿ's movement seems to have had broad appeal across the villages of Sogdiana, but, like the revolt of Ḥārith b. Surayj, the exact character of that support is not precisely clear due to a lack of sources from the perspectives of Muqannaʿ or his supporters. According to Narshakhī, the movement first took hold in Sūbakh, a village of Kish, where a man named ʿUmar Sūbakhī led a revolt against the Arab amir, likely the commander of a fort, and killed him.[124] Actions such as these paint the movement as a locally inspired anti-Abbasid uprising. The same can be said of the wearing of 'White-Clothes' in contrast to black, the official colour of the Abbasid regime. Some of Muqannaʿ's supporters are specified as *dahāqīn*, but of smaller locations not well known, leaving the general impression that he had greater appeal in the lower class.[125] Support for Muqannaʿ was not universal among the villagers of Sogdiana though and some turned to the Abbasids for support. At Numijkat (or Bumijkath), the old centre of the Bukhara oasis, the 'Wearers of White-Clothes' faced resistance and killed an entire village, including its muezzin. This spread fear to other villages and the people went to the amir of Bukhara Ḥusayn b. Muʿādh who took government troops to the village of Narshakh in an attempt to hold back Muqannaʿ's advance, but he failed when the 'Wearers of White-Clothes' reneged on their agreement and seized control of the fortress (*ḥiṣār*) and the local food supply after the government troops dispersed.[126] In these earliest outbreaks of violence, there may be a connection between resistance to Muqannaʿ and the presence of mosques, as indicated in the account of Numijkat and its muezzin, implying that his movement was more successful in places without a substantial Muslim population or religious infrastructure, but this is speculative.[127] Similarly, Numijkat was extremely close to the city of Bukhara itself, only four *farāsikh* (24 km), implying it was better integrated into the political structures of the oasis than outlying villages.

The Abbasids also received local support. When Muʿādh b. Muslim was sent as the new governor of Khurāsān in 777 a large group of *dahāqīn* and warriors met him at Bukhara, some of whom were put to work building siege engines, essential for facing an enemy who had taken numerous fortresses throughout Sogdiana.[128] According to Balʿamī, the people of Nasaf resisted an attack by 3,000 of Muqannaʿ's followers. This is portrayed as a communal decision made by the people both small and great (*khard va buzurg*). Muqannaʿ's troops became discouraged and instead attempted to take the village of Tamūdar where a wealthy *dihqān* named Aḥmad was said to live, but Aḥmad also resisted, overcame the attackers and killed them all.[129] Nasaf was supposedly a stronghold of support for Muqannaʿ from his first missionary activity in Transoxiana. The same can be said of Kish where one of the notables (*mihtar*) convinced a reported 30,000 men, women and children hiding in the fortress of Bawkat to reject Muqannaʿ and surrender to Saʿīd al-Ḥarashī instead.[130] This number would seem exaggerated unless it included large numbers of people who had been displaced by Muqannaʿ and the 'Wearers of White-Clothes' who had gathered together at this fortress.[131]

The position of the local lords during this rebellion is not always clear. Narshakhī claims that the Bukhārkhudā Bunyāt supported Muqannaʿ and apostatized for which Mahdī had him executed.[132] Again, we might be able to tie this to a rural community allied with the Bukhārkhudā against an urban community allied to the Arab amir as in the case of Sharīk b. Shaykh's revolt, but with the positions reversed and the rural population now the ones revolting against Abbasid authority. After Muqannaʿ and the Turks had taken Samarqand, the Ikhshīd Yazīd b. Ghūrak minted copper *fulūs* that simply stated the location (Ishtīkhan) and date (160 AH/776–7 CE) of minting in Arabic on one side and his family *tamgha* on the other.[133] The meaning of this coin has been debated by Aleksandr Naymark and Luke Treadwell who found a certain level of restraint in its expression of local identity through the *tamgha* but lack of religious inscription which could tie Ibn Ghūrak to either the Abbasids or Muqannaʿ. These characteristics make it appear that the Ikhshīd was biding his time between the two options, perhaps with hopes of regaining his independence. Karev argued that Muqannaʿ's difficulties in holding Samarqand – losing control of the city at least once and requiring support from the Qārlūq Turks to regain it – and the lack of evidence of a difficult siege when the Abbasids retook the city imply that support for Muqannaʿ was especially weak in the largest city of Sogdiana.[134] Some have used the presence of the Ikhshīd among the kings who paid tribute to Mahdī in a unique passage in Yaʿqūbī as a sign he had something to ask forgiveness for and, due to the timing of this event, it is assumed to be participation in the revolt of Muqannaʿ. However this list includes kings from Ṭabaristān to China who had no connection to the revolt of Muqannaʿ and therefore seems to be very weak evidence that Ibn Ghūrak had joined the rebellion.[135]

As in the story of Narshakh above, Muqannaʿ's warriors are often described as duplicitous, reneging on agreements with the Abbasid forces. Narshakhī describes them as a bunch of riff-raff, using terms such as *ʿayyār* (errant fighters), *ṭarrār* (pickpockets), *mubāriz* (fighters) and *dāvanda* (runners) but, as Patricia Crone pointed out, many of these terms could have double meanings.[136] While *ʿayyār* can mean something close to a brigand – at least in sources written from the central government's position – it also meant a kind of volunteer fighter for the faith or a fighter for a religious or political cause and that latter definition was developing in Khurāsān at the time of Muqannaʿ's revolt.[137] *Mubāriz* and *dāvanda* could both mean either people who fought or ran for public entertainment (perhaps involving gambling) or it could mean a soldier or runner for the postal relay. Given the context of a revolt led by a former soldier in a frontier region that recently saw a major political upheaval, the idea that Muqannaʿ's followers included other disenfranchised former soldiers and state functionaries seems not at all unlikely. The antagonism of former soldiers and their families towards the Abbasids is found in accounts of the revolt, including among people who did not openly support Muqannaʿ. The head of the village of Narshakh, for example, is said to be the widow of a soldier who had served under Abū Muslim but who Abū Muslim had killed. When she insulted Abū Muslim, asking how the killer of her husband could be 'father to the Muslims', the Abbasid military commander Jibra'īl b. Yaḥyā al-Bajalī had her executed.[138]

When Muqannaʿ turned towards Samarqand, he sought the help of the Turks, promising them the spoils of the Muslims.[139] These are most likely the Qārlūq attempting to consolidate their authority over the former Türgesh domains. The Turkish leader who was called in to support Muqannaʿ is named Khallukh Khāqān by Balʿamī, which is probably a misspelling of Kharlukh, the Arabic form of Qārlūq.[140] By 777, the Qārlūq were the major opponents to the Abbasids with Turkish forces found throughout the breadth of Sogdiana and the Abbasid army focused on retaking Samarqand from them while the 'Wearers of White-Clothes' appear sparingly.[141] The Qārlūq are portrayed as being attracted by spoils and, much like the Türgesh fighting alongside Ḥārith b. Surayj, uninterested in the religious message of the uprising. Despite this, there were most likely, as argued by Patricia Crone, some Türgesh and other Turks who found themselves disenfranchised as the political environment shifted on the steppes and became attracted to Muqannaʿ and his message.[142] The Turks would continue to be a problem after the end of Muqannaʿ's revolt. The people of Bukhara went to the governor Faḍl b. Sulaymān al-Ṭūsī (r. 782–7) seeking protection from Turkish raids, and he built the large encircling wall described in Chapter 1.[143] In 792 the governor Ghiṭrīf b. ʿAṭā al-Jurashī (r. 792–3) led a campaign against the Qārlūq in Ferghana.[144]

It is important to note that just a couple decades removed from the Abbasid Revolution, several descendants of Naṣr b. Sayyār, the last Umayyad governor of Khurāsān who had been chased west by the revolutionary forces until he died, are listed among the fighters on the Abbasid side. Three members of Naṣr b. Sayyār's family are listed as fighting against the 'White-Clothed Ones' in Bukhara, including two sons Layth and Muḥammad and a grandson Ḥassān b. Tamīm b. Naṣr.[145] A Naṣr b. Layth mentioned by Balʿamī may be a fourth. The presence of Naṣr's descendants speaks to the continuing transition into Abbasid rule where a family so closely tied to the former regime remained in positions of authority. Their presence will seem more noticeable as we turn towards the revolt of another descendant of Naṣr, his grandson Rāfiʿ b. Layth, whose father was one of the opponents of Muqannaʿ. The revolt erupted at Samarqand at the beginning of the ninth century and will be discussed in the following chapter.

What these revolts show is that the challenges facing Sogdiana and Ṭukhāristān as they were integrated into the caliphate were not solved by the Abbasid Revolution. A subset of these revolts focused on political and religious disappointments with the direction of the revolution. They were fought by revolutionaries who were still seeking to achieve unfulfilled aims, as in the case of Sharīk b. Shaykh and ʿAbd al-Jabbār b. ʿAbd al-Raḥmān, who rebelled in the name of an ʿAlid imam. In contrast, the variety of people supporting Muqannaʿ including Sogdians, the 'White-Clothed Ones' and Turks came with different concerns. For the Sogdians and 'White-Clothed Ones' their hopes were likely the result of disruptions to local communities and society brought on by the cycle of conquest, invasion, revolution and continued revolts that had been occurring since the beginning of the eighth century. We see these concerns in the aftermath of the revolt as various governors attempted to institute reforms in Khurāsān, Ṭukhāristān and Sogdiana to meet the needs of the people and better integrate the region as a productive part of the caliphate.

Settling the Abbasid frontier

For the half-century following the Abbasid Revolution, Khurāsān, Ṭukhāristān and Transoxiana were sites of near-constant revolt. For the first half of that period, the governors, amirs and soldiers of the Abbasid Empire themselves were some of the most dangerous threats to stability along the frontier and cooperation between the east and Iraq. Following the revolt of Muqannaʿ, measures were taken by a series of governors to settle the situation in Greater Khurāsān and address the long-simmering concerns of the local population. The first governor associated with such a policy was Faḍl b. Sulaymān al-Ṭūsī, a native of Khurāsān, Abbasid propagandist and revolutionary general. According to Gardīzī (d. ca. 1061), Ṭūsī embarked on a series of reforms focused on land use and the *kharāj* meant to protect the rights of the people against the chiefs and headmen of the cities and villages, especially those who abused their position and profited from excessive tax collection. These reforms included a renovation of the irrigation system of Marw and a review of land tenure and tax rates.[146] Two of Faḍl's predecessors – ʿAbd al-Jabbār b. ʿAbd al-Raḥmān and Musayyab b. Zuhayr al-Ḍabbī (r. 780–2) – are remembered for increasing the *kharāj* to the point of disrupting the local populations and, according to Ṭabarī, Faḍl was specifically appointed at a time when Musayyab's behaviour had 'agitated' the populace against him.[147]

Chapter 1 began with the story of another Faḍl who engaged in building projects along the eastern frontier, that being Faḍl b. Yaḥyā al-Barmakī who was named governor of Khurāsān by the Caliph Hārūn al-Rashīd in 792. There we focused on a gate built in a defile near Rāsht on the road from Chaghāniyān that blocked the Turks from raiding. The gate was attributed to Faḍl by several geographical texts, but the history of his governorship is filled with numerous other projects. He is noted generally for constructing mosques and *ribāṭāt* (sing. *ribāṭ*) or frontier garrisons expanding the reach of Islamic institutions and strengthening the frontier.[148] Perhaps most importantly, Faḍl al-Barmakī organized the local population (*ʿajam*) into an army called the ʿAbbāsiyya or the 'partisans of the Abbasids'. This force was reported to number upto an exaggerated 500,000 according to Ṭabarī and its members were placed on the caliph's payroll.[149] Some 20,000 of these soldiers were sent west and were perhaps related to the eastern troops stationed at Ṭarsūs during the caliphate of Mahdī mentioned above. The ʿAbbāsiyya appeared in armies as far west as North Africa. It should be noted that this army is distinguished from the Khurāsānī forces found in the armies of the caliphs since the Umayyad period by the enlistment of Iranians rather than Arabs who had been settled in Khurāsān. The formation of a regular army in the east recruited from local populations and paid a salary contributed to the security of the region but also tied locals directly to the caliphate through employment. Even though local forces had been employed by the Umayyads and Abbasids since the governorship of Qutayba b. Muslim, if not sooner, these had been forces that were joined to the armies of the caliph by alliances with the local lords. The kings of Khwarazm, Bukhara or Samarqand would supply troops under their own commanders and, at the end of the campaign, they would return to their lords. Their participation was dependent on the whim of the local kings and, as often as not, they could quickly change and become enemies of the Muslims. The foundation of the ʿAbbāsiyya created a force that was directly under the command of the caliph or his governor who could then serve beyond Khurāsān, Ṭukhāristān and Transoxiana or neighbouring regions.[150]

While Faḍl b. Yaḥyā and the entire Barmakid family were natives of Balkh, having been the guardians of the Naw Bahār Buddhist monastery, Faḍl's governorship was based in his personal relationship to the Abbasid household. Much like the governors before him, Faḍl was one of the new men, elevated by the

Abbasid regime. His father Yaḥyā b. Khālid (d. 803) became attached to the Caliph Mahdī when the latter was stationed in Rayy as governor during the caliphate of Manṣūr. He then became tutor to a young Hārūn who grew up alongside Faḍl and his brother Jaʿfar. As such, Faḍl's authority in Khurāsān was not derived from the position of his ancestors, though it certainly helped him in making connections with local notables and may have inspired his more open-minded policies. His position came from a personal relationship to the Abbasid caliph and as a member of the extended imperial household. It was perhaps such a personal relationship that made it possible for Hārūn to cut off the Barmakids in 803, executing Jaʿfar and imprisoning Yaḥyā and Faḍl, without much local resistance in the east when the political necessities changed.

Faḍl b. Yaḥyā is also credited with two major campaigns that expanded Abbasid authority along the frontier. The first was against Usrūshana during which the Afshīn Khārākhara submitted to Abbasid authority.[151] Khārākhara's grandson is the famous general Afshīn Ḥaydar b. Kāwūs (discussed in the following chapter), who is best known for his service in the Caucasus. The second campaign was discussed in Chapter 1 briefly. This was a campaign against the Kābulshāh during which Ibrāhīm b. Jibrīl b. Yaḥyā al-Bajalī – whose father had commanded troops against Muqannaʿ – led an army including the kings and *dahāqīn* of Ṭukhāristān with the *shīr* of Bāmiyān into the Hindu Kush.[152]

The reforms implemented during the governorships of the two Faḍls were important steps towards fully integrating Khurāsān, Ṭukhāristān and Transoxiana into the Abbasid Caliphate. These reforms began breaking down a political, economic and social structure in which local lords ruled as intermediaries between a conquered, subject population and a foreign empire. These reforms focused on the major points of exchange between the Abbasids and their eastern subjects, the collection of taxes and the recruitment of the military with the channels between the caliph's agents and the people becoming streamlined and more direct in both cases. Unfortunately, this was not the end of instability and revolt in the region. Faḍl b. Yaḥyā was succeeded by ʿAlī b. ʿĪsā b. Māhān (r. 796–808), the son of an Abbasid propagandist in Marw and a *mawlā* who later mutinied and was killed by Abū Muslim. Ibn Māhān is more closely associated with the *abnāʾ al-dawla* or 'the sons of the dynasty', the name given to the veterans of the Khurāsānī army who were settled in Baghdad following the Abbasid Revolution. As governor, Ibn Māhān became infamous for extorting the people of Greater Khurāsān and bribing the Caliph Hārūn al-Rashīd.[153] There were many disturbances across the region during his governorship, including uprisings led by the governors of sub-regions who were perhaps unable to collect the increased levels of taxes expected by Ibn Māhān, but the most dangerous was the revolt of Rāfiʿ b. Layth that practically brought an end to caliphal rule in the east and precipitated major reforms in the governorship of the region, which will be addressed in the following chapter. In some reports Ibn Māhān's greed and oppression are explained through a rivalry with the Barmakids and a desire to undo the work of Faḍl b. Yaḥyā, who had advised Hārūn al-Rashīd not to send him east.

The cycle of revolt

Qutayba b. Muslim completed his conquest of Sogdiana before his death in 715 but by 720 the Sogdians were up in arms and attempting to cast off Arab–Muslim rule with the support of the Türgesh, as discussed in the previous chapter. This was a revolt that would only be fully overturned when the governor Naṣr b. Sayyār was able to defeat the Türgesh and reassert Umayyad rule in Samarqand twenty years later. In 734 Ḥārith b. Surayj instigated a revolt that attracted both Arabs and *mawālī* as well as support from the Türgesh, who saw their coalition destroyed in the process, but it is clear that these groups did not come together with the same goals or with the same motivations. Even though this revolt lasted until 746, it was only in the first couple of years that Ḥārith posed a serious threat to Umayyad rule in Khurāsān or Ṭukhāristān. In later years Ḥārith and his diehard supporters appear to be ancillaries to campaigns by the Türgesh khāqān or the tribal violence that engulfed the Arabs of Khurāsān. By 748, Abū Muslim had openly proclaimed the Abbasid Revolution and taken Marw, attracting enough support to overthrow the Umayyad Caliphate *en totale* and replace them with a new dynasty. But it is still unclear who exactly supported the Abbasids in their revolution and when. Sharīk b. Shaykh revolted at Bukhara in the name of the ʿAlid family against the pseudo-Shiʾism of the Abbasids just a couple years after the revolution while ʿAbd al-Jabbār b. ʿAbd al-Raḥmān – a veteran of the revolution who had served the Abbasid Caliph Manṣūr – did the same in 759. Muqannaʿ's movement began less than a decade after that and lasted until 780, attracting a wide array of people from across Sogdiana and beyond the Jaxartes through his syncretic religious doctrine. As will be covered in the following chapter, twenty-five years later Rāfiʿ b. Layth, grandson of Naṣr b. Sayyār, organized a revolt that threatened Abbasid rule in the east entirely. In between there were plenty of small-scale disturbances tamed by the policies of capable governors like Faḍl b. Sulaymān and Faḍl b. Yaḥyā. Despite the different approaches taken by each of these revolutionaries and the different ways in which they legitimized their revolts, for the most part they were dealing with the same set of problems that had carried over from the conquests and through the Umayyad period – problems related to the integration of a far-flung and diverse region into a larger empire. Even though many of these revolts attracted a broad base of support, none of them addressed or could hope to remedy the concerns of all participating parties at the same time.

Much like the Arab–Muslim conquests themselves, the Abbasid Revolution did not change the face of the eastern frontier overnight. Abū Muslim attempted to simultaneously advance the frontier beyond the River Jaxartes and prune untrustworthy local rulers from the region. Although he gained many supporters in the region, as visible through the near messianic status he was given by some of his followers and as evidenced in the doctrine of Muqannaʿ, he was not able to bring all the people of Khurāsān, Ṭukhāristān and Transoxiana together. Nor was he able to maintain the trust of his masters in Iraq. Revolts by former Abbasid agents can be understood within the narratives of the collapsing 'big tent' of the revolutionary movement which tried to attract the attention of anyone with a grievance against the Umayyads, but neither the revolution nor its outcome addressed the concerns of people on the ground. These issues combined kept Greater Khurāsān in a constant state of flux for the century following Qutayba b. Muslim's rapid expansion of the frontier beyond the limits of the Sasanian Empire. Many saw what came in response to this disorder as a return to local traditions of rule, the rise of nativist dynasties under the Abbasid imperial umbrella, but the rulers of Greater Khurāsān who emerged in the ninth century did not grow directly from the local kings or nobility. Instead they were the products of the Abbasid imperial system, new men of the frontier as much as those who came before them. To these dynasties we now turn.

Chapter 7

UNIFYING THE FRONTIER: THE FORMATION OF GREATER KHURĀSĀN

The Ṭāhirids, the Sāmānids and the frontier process

In 1953, Vladimir Minorsky coined the term Iranian Intermezzo to describe the period of Iranian history that fell between the era of direct rule by the Arab caliphs of the Rāshidūn, Umayyad and Abbasid Caliphates and the era of Turko-Mongol rule that began with the invasion of the Seljuq Turks in the eleventh century and lasted until the fall of the Turkmen Qājār Dynasty (r. 1789–1925) in the twentieth century.[1] Implicit in this phrase and its application to the history of ninth- and tenth-century Iran is the idea that, somehow, the Iranian Intermezzo was a return to 'native rule'. In such thinking Khurāsān and the eastern frontier were central to this process. It was in Khurāsān that the Ṭāhirids – an Iranian dynasty who ruled autonomously as vassals of the Abbasid caliphs from 821 until 873 – emerged as the first independent local dynasty of Iran when the Caliph Ma'mūn granted Ṭāhir b. al-Ḥusayn (ca. 776–822) virtual independence as governor and the right to bequeath his title to his sons. It was in Transoxiana that the Sāmānids – first ruling as vassals of the Ṭāhirids and then establishing their own dynasty and becoming the rulers of Greater Khurāsān for most of the tenth century – pushed the idea of 'native' rule further by reintroducing Persian as the language of court and administration, patronizing New Persian written in the Arabic script with great influence from the language of Islam, all while encouraging a mode of kingship modelled on and inspired by the pre-Islamic rulers of Iran.

Modern historians most often portray this as the story of the rise and triumph of nationalist local Persian dynasties, groups driven away from the imperial centre by centrifugal forces to seize power for themselves as the strength and reach of the caliphate waned during the ninth century.[2] Such arguments promote the idea that somehow the Sāmānids – and to a lesser extent their Ṭāhirid forbearers – represented a return to an older, local model of kingship based largely in the Sasanian past and that by developing an independent state across both banks of the Oxus the Sāmānids, in some manner, undid the long Arab conquests. There are several problems with such an analysis. First, by this point we hopefully understand that the eastern frontier was a complicated space and that Khurāsān, Ṭukhāristān and Transoxiana – the regions that were united in the ninth century into a Greater Khurāsān under the Ṭāhirids and Sāmānids – did not have a shared history or identity they could collectively fall back upon, nor was their history particularly tied to a singularly Sasanian or even Iranian past. During the Ṭāhirid and Sāmānid periods, Greater Khurāsān coalesced into a recognizable autonomous unit under a shared administrative structure and, eventually, an independent state of its own. For example, Rocco Rante pointed to the spread of uniform Ṭāhirid coinage – most importantly copper *fulūs*, the currency of daily life – from their capital in Nīshāpūr as far north and east as Chāch as a sign of the administrative joining of Transoxiana to Khurāsān in the ninth century.[3] The Ṭāhirid and Sāmānid projects represented something new that developed out of the experience of Abbasid rule in the east rather than a return to something old.

In this chapter, I argue that the rise of the independent local dynasties drastically changed the shape of the eastern frontier in ways even the Arab–Muslim conquests had not achieved. First, most importantly the formation of both the Ṭāhirid and Sāmānid states resulted from imperial networks of personal clientage and vassalage centred on the caliph. The formation of these networks began under the Abbasids, particularly those caliphs who began their political careers in Khurāsān including Mahdī, as discussed in the previous chapter, and Ma'mūn who turned Khurāsān into the base for a successful civil war against his brother Amīn (r. 809–13) and the formation of a renewed Abbasid regime.

Second, the frontier process, the conflict and competition among different groups along the frontier, did not end with one party triumphing over the other *en totale*. The conqueror did not wipe away all traces of the conquered and supplant them with an imported identity and culture. Neither did successful resistance mean that local populations walled themselves off from the influences of their attackers. Instead, the process created something new that integrated aspects of both sides. I argue that rather than a return to 'native rule', the Ṭāhirids and Sāmānids are the products of such a frontier process. Maintaining control over Greater Khurāsān and preserving the eastern frontier were vital to the caliphate, and authority was granted to those who were part of the caliph's personal networks of loyalty and clientage. As Abbasid power waned, these same individuals asserted their own autonomous power over the region. Though their initial claims to authority were not based on the local identity, these independent dynasties constructed a local identity to justify their positions while also creating new political, social and cultural realities in the region.

Dynasties such as the Ṭāhirids and Sāmānids came to power through imperial networks, situating themselves as the intermediaries between the frontier and the centre, nodes within a network of personal relationships that spread out from the imperial centre in Iraq to the local lords of Greater Khurāsān.[4] While certain aspects of their rule reflected local cultures and orientations, their position was derived almost entirely from the structures of the Abbasid Caliphate and Iraq's desire to better manage these distant provinces. In doing so, the Ṭāhirids and Sāmānids redefined the region, bringing Khurāsān, Ṭukhāristān and Transoxiana together in a way that had not been achieved before, but they also helped bring about a new Khurāsānī identity that was steeped as much, if not more, in notions of Islamic kingship as the Iranian notions with which they are typically associated.

The frontier process did not allow purely Iranian identities to survive. It also did not allow an Arab–Muslim identity to completely overtake Greater Khurāsān. Instead it created a new Greater Khurāsān both politically and culturally.

The origins of the Ṭāhirids and the revolt of Rāfiʿ b. Layth

The Ṭāhirid family was of Iranian origins but had been tied to the Arab tribe the Banū Khuzāʿa since the early years of the Arab incursions into Khurāsān. Ṭāhir's great-grandfather Ruzayq became a *mawlā* of Ṭalḥa b. ʿAbdallāh al-Khuzāʿī (d. 685), known as the 'incomparable Ṭalḥa' (Ṭalḥa al-Ṭalaḥāt).[5] This likely occurred during Ṭalḥa's governorship over Sīstān (r. 680–5), but little is known of the circumstances. Due to the important role the Ṭāhirids played in the development of autonomous Iranian kingship during the Iranian Intermezzo, one can expect to find their origins in the east, but there is no explicit evidence to be confident that this is indeed the case. Some sources indicate that Ruzayq travelled to Khurāsān from elsewhere, perhaps during the governorship of Muhallab b. Abī Ṣufra and that he had been one of the *asāwira*, the Sasanian cavalry, who was either captured by or defected to the Arabs during the conquests.[6] If this was the case, then he likely joined the Banū Khuzāʿa in western Iran. The background that mattered most for the audience of our medieval chronicles was the connection to the Banū Khuzāʿa rather than their pre-Islamic history because it was this relationship that situated the Ṭāhirids in the larger narrative of early Islamic history.[7] It was not until the Abbasid Revolution that the family appeared again and even then it was still their attachment to the Banū Khuzāʿa that dictated their role and their transition into clients of the Abbasids. Ṭāhir's grandfather Muṣʿab and his brother Ṭalḥa b. Ruzayq were secretaries to the propagandist Sulaymān b. Kathīr al-Khuzāʿī (d. ca. 750). Ṭalḥa was more prominent in the revolution as a propagandist himself and a close confidant of Abū Muslim. Abū Muslim even chose Ṭalḥa to administer the oath of allegiance to the revolutionary troops after the capture of Marw.[8] As a reward for his service, Muṣʿab was given the governorship of Būshanj and, possibly, Herat. He was still in Būshanj in 776–7 – where Ṭāhir had been born a year earlier – when the rebel Yūsuf al-Barm chased him out of the city.[9]

In many ways the Ṭāhirids were exemplars of the powerful families of Khurāsān who rose to positions of prominence in the ninth century, even if more successful than most, having associated themselves as *mawālī* with the Arab tribes of the conquest and then having attached themselves to the Abbasid *daʿwa* or propaganda mission. But it was not this long history of service to the Banū Khuzāʿa that brought them to the heights of power. Rather it was the direct associations they were able to make with the caliph himself during the revolt of Rāfiʿ b. Layth – the grandson of the last Umayyad governor of Khurāsān, Naṣr b. Sayyār – and then the Abbasid civil war between the sons of Hārūn al-Rashīd – Amīn and Maʾmūn – known as the War of the Two Brothers. Under the early Abbasids the term *mawlā*, especially the title *mawlā amīr al-muʾminīn* or Client of the Commander of the Faithful – the title of the caliph – came to mean something more than convert and tribal client.

Instead, it meant something like honorary kinsman of the caliph and was granted to high-ranking servants linked personally to the caliph and the Abbasid family.[10] It was a term used not only for members of the Abbasid administration such as governors, generals and secretaries, but also for local lords who had submitted to Abbasid authority. In practice, it represented the shift away from an empire constructed through tribal linkages towards one in which status was gained via a personal network with the caliph at the centre, and it was such a network which the Ṭāhirids used to gain and expand their authority in the ninth century.

Over the years 806–9, Sogdiana was engulfed by the revolt of Rāfiʿ b. Layth. Rāfiʿ's revolt came at an auspicious moment, ending shortly after the death of the Caliph Hārūn al-Rashīd when his son Maʾmūn inherited rule of the empire east of Rayy (near modern Tehran) as an autonomous principality from which he staged a successful revolt against his brother Amīn. The bonds built between Maʾmūn and the people who fought against Rāfiʿ and then Amīn helped form a new imperial elite for Maʾmūn's reborn Abbasid Caliphate, the impact of which shaped Greater Khurāsān through the elevation of the Ṭāhirid family in both Khurāsān and Iraq. As mentioned briefly in the previous chapter, despite the opposition to the Abbasid Revolution from Rāfi's grandfather Naṣr b. Sayyār, less than two decades after the fall of the Umayyads his family had found their way into the service of the new dynasty. Someone called Layth, who was a *mawlā* of the Caliph Manṣūr and who we presume to be Naṣr's son and Rāfi's father, led a campaign against Ferghana that reportedly reached Kashgar at the mouth of the Tarim Basin in the early 760s, according to a unique report from Yaʿqūbī.[11] Later one Layth, now a *mawlā* of the Caliph Mahdī, was listed among the warriors sent to fight against Muqannaʿ alongside the governor Muʿādh b. Muslim in the year 777–8.[12] A more explicitly named Layth b. Naṣr was listed among those who fought against the 'White-Clothed Ones' in Bukhara along with a brother Muḥammad and nephew Ḥassān b. Tamīm b. Naṣr.[13] In the context of Muqannaʿ's revolt, the family of Naṣr b. Sayyār may have simply been living in Sogdiana and answered the call when warriors were needed to stop the revolt.[14] Despite the fall of the Umayyads, the family probably maintained an elevated status as members of the old Arab elite with deep ties to the region.

The reasons for Rāfiʿ's revolt, if not the immediate context, are rather clear. It began as a rejection of an abusive governor – ʿAlī b. ʿĪsā b. Māhān – who was enriching himself at the expense of the people of Khurāsān, Ṭukhāristān and Transoxiana, as mentioned briefly in the previous chapter. Some of our sources include more salacious rationales for the revolt that speak clearly to the relationship of the frontier to Baghdad in the early ninth century. In these accounts, Rāfiʿ stole the wife of Yaḥyā b. Ashʿath b. Yaḥyā – most probably the son of the governor of Samarqand known from the copper *fulūs* featuring the earliest use of the title Mahdī for the third Abbasid caliph, discussed in the previous chapter. This account, found in Ṭabarī, revolves around Ibn Ashʿath moving to Baghdad for an extended period, abandoning his wife in Samarqand and taking up with concubines with whom he fathered children.[15] This is an interesting reflection on the problems of Abbasid agents migrating to Iraq and highlights some of the tensions underlying Rāfiʿ's revolt against Ibn Māhān. The latter was a governor of Khurāsānī roots who travelled to Baghdad as part of the *abnā' al-dawla* or 'sons of the dynasty' and was known for mistreating the people of his home province, extracting money in the form of excessive taxes which were then sent to Iraq instead of being spent in Khurāsān, as represented by the abandoned wife. If we were to believe that the Abbasid Revolution would address the concerns of the people of Greater Khurāsān, a mere half-century later there remained a divide between the east and the imperial centre.

Rāfiʿ's rebellion began in Samarqand. When Rāfiʿ killed the local governor Sulaymān b. Ḥamīd and Ibn Māhān sent his son ʿĪsa to punish Rāfiʿ, the people of the city rose up and gave their support to a man named Sibāʿ b. Masʿada. Sibāʿ imprisoned Rāfiʿ and the people in turn imprisoned Sibāʿ, released Rāfiʿ and made him their chief.[16] By 807 both Nasaf and Chāch were in open revolt behind Rāfiʿ. The *ṣāḥib* or master of Chāch – unclear if he was a local lord or an Abbasid administrator – allied himself with the Turks or maintained a Turkish personal guard who attacked ʿĪsā b. ʿAlī and killed him at their master's insistence.[17] Following his son's death, Ibn Māhān left Balkh – where he had established himself – for Marw, concerned that Rāfiʿ would make a move against the provincial capital. When he departed his palace, his slaves uncovered a hidden treasure that the people of Balkh raided, at which point Hārūn al-Rashīd dismissed Ibn Māhān, citing his negligence with a vast treasury while still requesting additional funds to support his campaign against the Transoxianan rebels.[18] Ibn Māhān was replaced with Harthama b. Aʿyan (d. 816–17), who had risen high during Hārūn's caliphate, having served previously as governor of Palestine, Egypt, North Africa and Mosul and as the head of Hārūn's *ḥaras* or personal guard. He had also led armies of Khurāsānīs along the Arab–Byzantine frontier.[19] Ṭabarī included copies of Hārūn's letters appointing Harthama and dismissing Ibn Māhān and it is interesting to note the caliph's emphasis on Ibn Māhān's mistreatment of the population rather than Rāfiʿ's revolt as the larger disturbance in Khurāsān.[20] This characterization is important in that Rāfiʿ's revolt was understood as anti-Ibn Māhān rather than anti-Abbasid at its outset, but it did not remain as such. Under Hārūn's command, Harthama wrote to the people of Chāch, Ferghana, Balkh (evidence the revolt had spread to Ṭukhāristān) and Samarqand advising them to abandon Rāfiʿ now that Ibn Māhān had been dismissed, but he was ignored.[21] Harthama took an army into Sogdiana in 808 and won a victory against Rāfiʿ at Bukhara.[22]

Rāfiʿ's revolt was serious enough that Hārūn al-Rashīd travelled east to supervise Harthama personally – a first for a reigning caliph – but he fell ill while travelling and died in Ṭūs on 24 March 809. The death of the caliph had a dramatic impact on the dynamics within the empire and in Khurāsān in particular. In 802, Hārūn had made two of his sons, Amīn and Ma'mūn, sign a succession agreement known by modern scholars as the Mecca Protocol, which declared Amīn his immediate successor but granted the elder Ma'mūn autonomous control of Khurāsān including all territories east of Rayy and a place in the succession as the heir to his brother.[23] Although this scheme was deployed in the wake of Hārūn's death, it was unsustainable and by 811 a civil war had broken out between Amīn and his supporters in Baghdad led by the *abnā' al-dawla* and Ma'mūn and his supporters in Khurāsān. In the lead-up to this war, the resolution of Rāfiʿ b. Layth's revolt played an important role in building a support base around Ma'mūn.

Ma'mūn was already connected to Khurāsān before he came to Marw. His mother was a slave named Marājil from Bādhghīs, perhaps of Hephthalite background though typically described as Persian or generally Iranian. He was tutored by Faḍl b. Sahl (d. 818), a Zoroastrian convert whose father had entered the service of the Barmakids in Iraq and converted along with his father at the powerful family's urging. These personal connections are important for understanding Ma'mūn's career in Khurāsān. Following the dismissal of Ibn Māhān – whose excesses had been the initial rationale for the revolt – it was expected that those in revolt would return to the Abbasid fold, but not all did. Those who joined Ma'mūn's camp had the opportunity to tie themselves and their families to the Abbasid regime as clients and servants of the prince and heir to the caliphate. One notable example of this was Ḥusayn b. Muṣʿab b. Ruzayq, the father of Ṭāhir, the founder of the Ṭāhird dynasty. Ḥusayn was one of the two 'most prominent of the Khurasanians and their nobles' Ṭabarī identified as being treated especially harshly and humiliated by Ibn Māhān. In this anecdote, Ibn Māhān accused Ḥusayn of getting drunk and spreading rumours that he got word from Baghdad that Ibn Māhān was being dismissed. For this, Ibn Māhān punished Ḥusayn publicly, calling him the heretical son of a heretic (*mulḥid b. mulḥid*).[24] In this confrontation, Mongi Kaabi saw a rivalry between two important families of Khurāsān, the Ruzayqids (proto-Ṭāhirds) and Māhānids, who were both *mawālī* of the Banū Khuzāʿa and who had competed for positions of authority within the Abbasid regime.[25] The anecdote from Ṭabarī ends with Ḥusayn making the pilgrimage to Mecca where he sought out Hārūn al-Rashīd and asked for his protection from Ibn Māhān. Here, Kaabi argued, Ḥusayn walked away from the revolt of Rāfiʿ before it became openly anti-Abbasid to seek out a personal relationship of clientage with the caliph.[26] Ṭāhir b. Ḥusayn then first appeared in the sources in the army of Harthama b. Aʿyan as Rāfiʿ b. Layth surrendered to Ma'mūn at the end of 809.[27]

According to Narshakhī, the Sāmānids made a similar alliance with Ma'mūn in this context. Ma'mūn is reported to have written to the four sons of Asad b. Sāmānkhudā – Nūḥ, Aḥmad, Yaḥyā and Ilyās – when Rāfiʿ's uprising became serious and they fought alongside Harthama at Samarqand. Narshakhī reported that the Sāmānids made marriage alliances with Rāfiʿ as part of his surrender, implying that the Sāmānids were already a known entity of some standing in the region with whom a diplomatic marriage was valuable.[28] The details read like the invention of a local historian seeking to praise his patron, but from the Sāmānids' appearance among the supporters of Ma'mūn shortly after the revolt, their participation seems likely.

The death of Hārūn al-Rashīd did not slow Harthama's campaign against Rāfiʿ, which continued to march from Bukhara to Samarqand. According to Yaʿqūbī, Rāfiʿ gathered a vast array of supporters from Chāch, Ferghana, Khujanda, Usrūshana, Chaghāniyān, Bukhara, Khwarazm and Khuttal along with the districts (*kūr*) of Balkh, Ṭukhāristān, Sogdiana and Transoxiana. The Qārlūq and Tughuzghuz Turks and the army of Tibet were also listed among his supporters.

All of them gathered at Samarqand, whose fortifications Rāfiʿ had reinforced, with intentions to fight the authorities.[29] The reinforcements of both manpower and urban defences were not enough and in 809 Harthama entered the massive walls of Samarqand – which, once again, were not effective against a larger, organized army, only raiding nomads – forcing Rāfiʿ to take refuge in the inner city (*madīna dākhila*). From there he sent for aid from the Turks hoping they would squeeze Harthama against the walls of the city, but the Turks withdrew.[30] According to Yaʿqūbī, the Yabghu of the Qārlūq had converted at the hand of the Caliph Mahdī and this explains his withdrawal. In the end, Rāfiʿ surrendered and joined Ma'mūn who treated him kindly.[31] It is likely Ma'mūn was gathering any supporters he could with the growing tensions between himself and his brother the Caliph Amīn. According to a tradition originating with Sallāmī (d. ca. 961), Rāfiʿ was executed instead in 810–11.[32] The most important lasting result of Rāfiʿ's revolt was the bonding between Ma'mūn and the local notables of Khurāsān, Ṭukhāristān and Transoxiana. These relationships were to play an important role in the upcoming civil war between Ma'mūn and Amīn as well as in Ma'mūn's reconfiguring of the empire following his victory.

The caliph on the frontier and the Ṭāhirid dynasty

As war broke out in 811, Ṭāhir b. al-Ḥusayn was selected to lead Ma'mūn's forces, largely made up of Khurāsānīs and especially Iranians, against a Baghdad-based army under the leadership of Ibn Māhān that had been sent east by Amīn. The first battle of the civil war took place outside of Rayy where Ṭāhir won a surprising victory, earning himself the nickname Dhū al-Yamīnayn (literally 'the possessor of two right hands' or 'the ambidextrous'). Following this victory, Ṭāhir led a rapid march west until he reached Baghdad, which he besieged for a year alongside a second army led by Harthama b. Aʿyan. Ṭāhir's forces eventually won when he stormed the city, captured Amīn and executed the deposed caliph. In the aftermath, Ma'mūn remained in Marw, making his capital in the east until unrest in Iraq forced him to return in 819, and Ṭāhir was named governor of Syria and the Jazīra or Upper Mesopotamia where he was charged with putting down anti-Ma'mūn rebels including members of the Abbasid royal family. Eventually he gathered various positions in Baghdad to his family including the chief of police or *ṣāḥib al-shurṭa*. Support for Ma'mūn was a family affair. One of Ṭāhir's cousins served as his sub-commander and another was an adviser to Ma'mūn.[33]

Ma'mūn's victory transformed the Abbasid Caliphate. Not only did the political centre of the empire shift east literally, if only temporarily, the nature of Abbasid authority shifted with it. In Baghdad, the descendants of the Khurāsānī army that had brought the dynasty to power, the *abnā' al-dawla*, had been a dominant political force but as supporters of Amīn they were swept away in the aftermath of the civil war. They may not even have coalesced around a united identity before the civil war as the party of Amīn, but they did not survive the conflict.[34] Ma'mūn created a new base of support, one that was again found in Khurāsān, Ṭukhāristān and Transoxiana, but this time it had a decidedly less Arab composition.[35] At the centre of many of these plans was Faḍl b. Sahl, now Ma'mūn's vizier known by the nickname Dhū al-Riy'āsatayn or 'possessor of the two responsibilities', meaning the civil and military administration. Faḍl had been accused of goading Ma'mūn into war against his brother, convincing him to abandon the *abnā'* and tying him to the Khurāsānī elites, but, in the aftermath of the war, Faḍl and his brother Ḥasan were largely responsible for affairs in Iraq while Ma'mūn remained in Khurāsān.

In order to build this new network, Ma'mūn accepted many local notables as his *mawlā*. Some of these arrangements had obviously begun before the outbreak of the civil war. In one case, Faḍl b. Sahl convinced Ma'mūn to make peace with the neighbouring lords of Transoxiana and Ṭukhāristān before engaging his brother in the west. These included the Yabghu (likely of the Qārlūq), the Afshīn of Usrūshana and the Kābulshāh who the Muslims had been attacking and to whom Ma'mūn now promised security.[36] If you cannot beat them, network. Some of these lords were sent west during and after the civil war to fill roles in the centre of the empire, like the Ṭāhirids and Sahlids. ʿAbbās b. Bukhārkhudā appears among Ṭāhir's army in Iraq.[37] Dāwūd b. Bānījūr of the Bānījūrid dynasty of Khuttal in northern Ṭukhāristān was made governor of Baṣra, Yamāma and Baḥrayn in 821–2.[38] The Sāmānids likewise became clients of the Abbasid regime at this time. During the governorship of Ghassān b. ʿAbbād (r. 817–21), Ma'mūn ordered him to appoint the four sons of Asad b. Sāmānkhudā to governorships in Transoxiana. According to Narshakhī, this was in return for their service during the revolt of Rāfiʿ but Luke Treadwell suggested this arrangement was the working of Faḍl b. Sahl, a cousin of Ghassān, based on evidence that the Sahlids remained close to the Sāmānids after their fall from grace in the west.[39] Others came to Ma'mūn without noticeable family or dynastic affiliations. For example, Ḥasan b. ʿAlī al-Ma'mūnī, a native of Bādhghīs and later governor of Armenia, took the caliph's name as his *nisba* and personal identifier much as earlier *mawlā* would take their *nisba* from their patron tribe.[40]

Following Ma'mūn's return to Baghdad, these bonds of patronage became more complicated and layered as the caliph became more removed from the centre of the networks in Greater Khurāsān. In 821, Ma'mūn named Ṭāhir b. al-Ḥusayn governor of Khurāsān, among other titles that made him the effective ruler of all lands from Baghdad to the east, and as governor he and his successors became the new de facto node of these relationships in the east, connecting the local lords to the caliph. The appointment of Ṭāhir has been understood in the past as the beginning of a period of autonomous rule in Khurāsān when 'centrifugal forces' drove the governors of distant provinces away from a caliphate in decline, unable to directly control their agents. The Ṭāhirids were seen as independent and almost rebellious in their rule of Khurāsān. C. E. Bosworth's description of the rise of the Ṭāhirids as a breakaway from the Abbasids is typical:

> Soon after his arrival in the east, Ṭāhir began leaving al-Ma'mūn's name out of the <u>kh</u>utba [the Friday sermon] and certain coins minted by him in 206/821–2 also omit the caliph's name; both of these actions were virtual declarations of

> independence from Baghdad. However, at this point he died in Marv (207/822). It is obviously difficult to gauge Ṭāhir's motives, since we do not know how events might have turned out.[41]

Such an assessment seems at odds with the fact that the Ṭāhirids maintained powerful positions of authority in Baghdad and beyond concurrent with their governorships in Khurāsān and remained role models of ideal governors. For example, when Ṭāhir's son ʿAbdallāh was appointed governor of Raqqa in northern Syria, Ṭāhir wrote him a letter which has been preserved in Ṭabarī as a model of advice to governors and administrators.[42] According to Ṭabarī, people fought to get their hands on a copy when it was first written and Ma'mūn made sure a copy was sent to every one of his governors. The omission of Ma'mūn's name from Ṭāhir's coins seems less incriminating once they are compared to the coins minted elsewhere throughout the empire, including coins minted by Ṭāhir while he was governor of Egypt before he was sent to govern Khurāsān, which also left off the caliph's name while including his own.[43] The issue of the *khuṭba* or Friday sermon, which would have had a more immediate impact than coins that needed to be minted and circulated before anyone could read the message they were conveying, is also unclear with the event in question occurring the evening before Ṭāhir's sudden death of a fever at age 46.[44] Over time, the Ṭāhirids' image has certainly improved in scholarship. In contrast to Bosworth above, Hugh Kennedy referred to Ṭāhirid rule in Khurāsān as 'effectively a partnership between the ʿAbbasids and Tahirids. ... the most successful solution the ʿAbbasids ever devised for integrating the province into the caliphate.'[45] Central to this argument in Kennedy's estimation was the alliance between the Ṭāhirids and the local magnates, the role the Ṭāhirids filled as a node in the networks connecting the east to Iraq.

Ṭāhir did not last long after becoming governor, dying in the year 822, and he was succeeded by his son Ṭalḥa (r. 822–8) while his son ʿAbdallāh, who appears to have been the preferred and better candidate, continued to serve the Abbasids in the west. Ṭalḥa was not as forceful a figure as his father and it is reported that the army of Khurāsān rose up upon Ṭāhir's death and looted the treasury until a eunuch named Sallām al-Abrash took control and paid the soldiers six months' pay.[46] Ma'mūn felt it necessary to send his vizier Aḥmad b. Abī Khālid (d. 823) to lead a campaign against Usrūshana which captured the Afshīn Kāwūs b. Khārākhara (d. after 822) and his son Faḍl, named after Faḍl b. Yaḥyā to whom the Afshīn had submitted in 794. Both father and son were brought back to Ma'mūn. Kāwūs converted to Islam (again), presumably becoming a *mawlā* of Ma'mūn, and was confirmed as king of Usrūshana.[47] Another son of the Afshīn, Ḥaydar, would become an important general in Ma'mūn's army and a rival of the Ṭāhirids. Ṭalḥa died in 829 and was replaced by his brother ʿAbdallāh who was given a choice between governing Khurāsān or the Jazīra and Caucasus, a region that was then facing the revolt of Bābak Khurramdīn (795–838).[48]

As ʿAbdallāh solidified Ṭāhirid authority and unified Greater Khurāsān under their rule – and pushed the boundaries of what constituted Greater Khurāsān into Sīstān and even Ṭabaristān – they faced challenges from the local lords who were concerned about their relative position within the Abbasid Caliphate. Illustrative of these conflicts is the challenge to ʿAbdallāh's authority made by the Qārinid Ispahbud of Ṭabaristān Māzyār b. Qārin (d. 840). Sometime in the mid-830s, the Caliph Muʿtaṣim (r. 833–42) requested that Māzyār deliver the *kharāj* of Ṭabaristān to ʿAbdallāh b. Ṭāhir, thereby placing Ṭabaristān and the Qārinid dynasty under the authority of Khurāsān and the Ṭāhirids, but Māzyār refused, declaring he would deliver the taxes to Muʿtaṣim but not to ʿAbdallāh.[49] Both Māzyār and his father had been named *mawlā* of Ma'mūn after joining the caliph's court at Baghdad, converting to Islam at his hand and fighting alongside the Abbasids on the Arab–Byzantine frontier, and Māzyār's refusal to give the *kharāj* to an intermediary was a reflection of the feeling that, as *mawlā amīr al-mu'minīn*, he had a direct and personal connection to the caliph.[50] For a time, Muʿtaṣim pursued a kind of workaround for this situation, having an agent meet the Qārinid representative carrying the *kharāj* at Hamadān, in Jibāl province of northwestern Iran, who would then pass the monies to an agent of the Ṭāhirids, who would then take the *kharāj* of Ṭabaristān back to Khurāsān where it could be given to ʿAbdallāh.[51] The Afshīn Ḥaydar convinced Māzyār to hold back the *kharāj* entirely, himself competing with the Ṭāhirids for authority in Greater Khurāsān, hoping to pull ʿAbdallāh into a campaign in mountainous Ṭabaristān in which he would be humiliated and therefore deposed.[52] This was not just a conflict over the position of Ṭabaristān vis-à-vis Khurāsān, but also a competition between ʿAbdallāh and the Afshīn over authority in Khurāsān and relative status in the court of Muʿtaṣim. The network of personal relationships also affected the administrative geography in the east. The Ṭāhirids ultimately triumphed over Māzyār, resulting in the Ispahbud's capture and presentation to the caliph at the new imperial capital of Sāmarrā' where he testified against the Afshīn before being flogged on Muʿtaṣim's orders.[53] Perhaps unintentionally, Māzyār died of his wounds and his body was crucified publicly alongside Bābak – the leader of the twenty-year-long Khurramdīnī revolt in Azerbaijan – and the Afshīn – who had successfully defeated and captured Bābak but died a prisoner of the caliph – and Ṭabaristān fell under the Ṭāhirids' authority.[54] Despite this victory, Ṭabaristān does not seem to have become a permanent part of Greater Khurāsān, retaining its political autonomy and individual identity and the Qārinids' rivals, the Bāvandids, re-emerged as local lords following Māzyār's defeat.[55]

Despite this image of autonomy, the Ṭāhirids were important agents of the Abbasid caliphs, maintaining the network of personal relationships between the caliphs and the local lords and acting as a critical node in the imperial administration. Authority passed out from Baghdad (and later Sāmarrā') to the Ṭāhirids in their capital at Nīshāpūr and from them to their representatives further afield while tax revenues flowed back in the opposite direction. The authority of the Ṭāhirids and many of their lieutenants was not based in their local identities, but in their connection to these imperial networks and, in fact, in many cases these supposed local rulers seemed little concerned about the existing local networks that had survived since the Arab–Muslim conquests. To explore this, let us turn to the Sāmānids.

The Sāmānids and a new frontier elite

For the most part, the Ṭāhirids focused on the core regions of Khurāsān and relied on local rulers to maintain the fringes. This may be illustrated in the shift of capitals under ʿAbdallāh from Marw in 'Outer Khurāsān' – the original Arab garrison from which the conquests of Ṭukhāristān and Transoxiana were organized – to Nīshāpūr in 'Inner Khurāsān' whose status was greatly increased by the appearance of the governor's court. Exemplary of this is, of course, the Sāmānid family who had been reconfirmed in their positions under the Ṭāhirids. Much like the Ṭāhirids themselves, the background of the Sāmānids is unclear with various accounts placing their ancestors in Ferghana and perhaps even among the Turks.[56] The eponymous ancestor, the Sāmānkhudā – a title indicating lordship over a place called Sāmān – first appears during the governorship of Asad b. ʿAbdallāh al-Qasrī when he is described by Narshakhī as the ruler of Balkh, which is highly unlikely.[57] In this account the Sāmānkhudā converted to Islam at the hands of Asad, consequentially naming a son after the governor, and was reconfirmed in his post as a local lord, a typical story of conversion under an Arab governor. Gardīzī gave a similar narrative during the reign of Ma'mūn, which would be problematic for the rise of the Sāmānkhudā's grandchildren (discussed above), not to mention the identification of his son Asad.[58] An anonymous history of Termez called *Nasabnāma* associates the Sāmānkhudā with a village near Termez.[59] While the rest of the *Nasabnāma*'s story is questionable – involving a family of *asyād* (sing. *sayyid*) or descendants of the Prophet Muhammad – the location near Termez bridges a gap with Narshakhī's by at least placing his origins in Ṭukhāristān and within the sphere of Balkh. The predominance of Hephthalite rulers in the region may again point us in an interesting direction for the Sāmānids' ancestry. The most often reported background for the Sāmānids – and the one found in their own propaganda – links the family to the rebel Parthian general who briefly ruled the Sasanian Empire as Bahrām VI, Bahrām Chōbīn (see Chapter 2). Bahrām's flight to the Turks after he was ousted by Khusrow II tied him to the territories from which the Sāmānids emerged, but the connection is still unlikely.[60]

Regardless of their family origins, the Sāmānids quickly earned positions across the breadth of Transoxiana and Khurāsān. When Ghassān b. ʿAbbād appointed the four sons of Asad b. Sāmānkhudā to positions of authority, they were each granted a different territory: Nūḥ in Samarqand, Aḥmad in Ferghana, Yaḥyā in Chāch and Usrūshana and Ilyās in Herat. The location of these appointments is not universally agreed upon with Narshakhī only identifying Nūḥ in Samarqand and Aḥmad in Ferghana while Gardīzī and Ibn al-Athīr – writing one and three centuries after Narshakhī respectively – listed all four.[61] Copper *fulūs* appeared in Samarqand, Ferghana and Chāch naming Nūḥ, Aḥmad and Yaḥyā respectively, but no coins appeared naming Ilyās at Herat and coins struck in Herat in the year 206 AH/821–2 CE name a Shukr b. Ibrāhīm instead.[62] Likewise, the continued presence of the Afshīn in Usrūshana sheds serious doubts on Yaḥyā's claims there. Nūḥ is the only one of the four Sāmānid brothers for whom coins are known close to the date of appointment with coins appearing at Samarqand as early as 820 whereas coins for Aḥmad are not known before 842 and Yaḥyā before 847, both after the death of Nūḥ who played the pre-eminent role as governor of Samarqand.[63] Despite this, Ilyās appears to be the brother who was the closest to the Ṭāhirids, being employed as a military commander and governor sent to problematic regions to help suppress revolt. According to the anonymous *Tārīkh-i Sīstān*, Ilyās was sent to Sīstān on at least three occasions – once in 823 and twice in the 830s – to help subdue the Khārijite rebels who were a constant threat.[64] In 826 he was in Egypt fighting alongside ʿAbdallāh b. Ṭāhir against the rebellious governor ʿUbaydallāh b. al-Sarī (r. 821–6) and his Andalusian mercenaries.[65] The reigns of these four brothers were long, lasting until their deaths: Nūḥ in 842, Aḥmad in 864, Yaḥyā in 855 and Ilyās in 856.

Authority in Sāmānid Khurāsān, Ṭukhāristān and Transoxiana was channelled through layers of dynastic rulers tied to the Sāmānid amirs as vassals and clients, modelled off not only the traditions of the pre-Islamic Sogdian city states but also the developments of the Abbasid era discussed earlier – including their own relationship to the Ṭāhirids. This was especially the case along the furthest northern and eastern reaches of the frontier, far from the centre of political authority in Bukhara.[66] Examples of these relationships are found in the geographers of the ninth and tenth centuries who described mass levies of warriors during times of invasion and crisis. Iṣṭakhrī informs us that every village under the Sāmānids supplied one infantryman and one cavalryman.[67] According to Muqaddasī, Chaghāniyān alone was able to raise 10,000 warriors from its 16,000 villages.[68] These levies were part of a mixed force that include Turkish slaves and the peasants of the *dahāqīn*.[69] In many ways, this reflects the idealized Sasanian model based on the reform movements of Khusrow I described in Chapter 3 better than any system found in our sources earlier (or in territories that had actually been a part of the Sasanian Empire). Jürgen Paul used these passages to argue that there was no direct state authority over the Sāmānid military, that this was a decentralized peasant and volunteer militia.[70] This comes close to echoing Soviet scholarship that saw in the Sāmānid peasant armies as evidence of a popular movement supported by the 'working classes'.[71] Considering the nodal networks of authority and personal relationships, this may just be the way the state best functions in a shatterzone, in an atomized and almost feudal structure. The local lords associated with the Sāmānids tend not to be the ones who had held authority in the first two centuries of Muslim rule along the eastern frontier, instead they are the lower ranking *dahāqīn*, and the Sāmānids inserted themselves instead as the legitimate local lords. This is most noticeable, thanks to the work of Narshakhī, in and around Bukhara. Here we have several instances of the Sāmānids confiscating lands that belonged to local elites to use for state functions. Most prominent among these is the seizure of the palace at Varakhsha from the last Bukhārkhudā, Ibrāhīm b. Khālid b. Bunyāt by Ismāʿīl b. Aḥmad (r. 892–907) – the first Sāmānid amir to unify authority over Transoxiana and even expand the Sāmānid domains with the conquest of Bukhara in 892. In this instance, Ismāʿīl declared that the palace 'is the property of the ruler and [the Bukhārkhudā] is not really the ruler' before seizing it for himself.[72] Ismāʿīl offered to rebuild the palace as a grand mosque but the people of Varakhsha refused, saying a mosque was unnecessary and it remained in disuse until Ismāʿīl's great-great-grandson Aḥmad b. Nūḥ – who may be the amir Manṣūr b. Nūḥ (r. 961–76) – dismantled the palace and used the wood to build a new palace in Bukhara.[73] The Varakhshans' rejection of Ismāʿīl's mosque may not represent a total rejection of either Islam or the Sāmānids. The geographer Muqaddasī notes that there were no mosques in many of the villages of Bukhara because the people adhered to the Ḥanafī *madhhab* which requires appropriate authorities to lead prayers in a mosque, which they lacked.[74]

The most important role of the Sāmānid brothers was to govern and protect the frontiers in the name of the Ṭāhirids. Beyond the campaigns of Ilyās in Sīstān, we have very limited details about the Sāmānids' actions in this regard. In 839 Nūḥ conquered Isfījāb where he built a wall around the vineyards and cultivated fields, presumably to prevent Turkish raiding.[75] Ibn al-Athīr also reports that during the same campaign Nūḥ reached Kāsān and Ūrast in Ferghana. In the same year, according to Ṭabarī, ʿAbdallāh b. Ṭāhir sent Nūḥ b. Asad to arrest Ḥasan b. Ḥaydar, son of the Afshīn whose father was imprisoned in Sāmarrā' under orders from the Caliph Muʿtaṣim. Interestingly, ʿAbdallāh is said to have used a ruse in which he simultaneously gave Nūḥ orders to arrest Ḥasan in Usrūshana and Ḥasan a letter that he had been named governor of Samarqand and should remove Nūḥ from his office. A battle took place and Nūḥ was victorious.[76] This stratagem of throwing two frontier governors against each other in hopes of eliminating one may demonstrate an inability on the part of ʿAbdallāh to control his vassals entirely – deciding that if Nūḥ were to disobey and not arrest Ḥasan, at least Ḥasan would preemptively punish Nūḥ – or a desire to hedge his bets and make sure that he backed the winner – if Nūḥ failed to capture Ḥasan, at least Ḥasan would think ʿAbdallāh had always meant to elevate him. A similar strategy was used between the Sāmānids and the Ṣaffārids in 900 when the Caliph Mu'taḍid (r. 892–902) gave both the Sāmānid amir of Transoxiana Ismāʿīl b. Aḥmad and the Ṣaffārid amir of Sīstān ʿAmr b. Layth (r. 879–901) the governorship of Khurāsān and Transoxiana. A battle ensued which Ismāʿīl won. Considering the similar dates, it is possible that Nūḥ attacked Usrūshana and then travelled to Isfījāb further beyond the Jaxartes and Kāsān in the Ferghana Valley as part of the same campaign. The Ṭāhirids are credited with one undated campaign of their own. ʿAbdallāh sent his son and heir Ṭāhir II (r. 844–62) on a campaign against the Oghuz Turks, presumably with Sāmānid support.[77] According to Balādhurī, this campaign went further into the steppe than any Muslim army before.

Campaigning on the frontier produced one of the most valuable commodities to the Abbasid Caliphs in the ninth century, Turkish slaves. While slaves had been a top commodity coming from the eastern frontier since the first Arab–Muslim incursions of the seventh century, in the mid-ninth century Turkish slaves came to fill a much more important position in Abbasid society. Upon ascending to the throne, Muʿtaṣim had reformed the Abbasid military around a core of Turkish slave soldiers known as either *mamlūk* (pl. *mamālīk*) or *ghilmān* (pl. *ghulām*), even founding a new capital at Sāmarrā' in 836 to house them away from Baghdad.

These slaves served alongside a cadre of Transoxianan lords including the Afshīn before his fall, making Sāmarrā' the centre of a new network of eastern imperial elites.[78] Not only was the trade in slaves from the eastern frontier not new, neither was their employment in the military. In Chapter 3 we discussed the *Bukhāriyya*, the group of Bukharan slaves who were archers and served as police in Baṣra. Some have argued that Muʿtaṣim's army was simply an extension of the Iranian practice of *čākir* or personal bodyguards made up of professional mercenaries, questioning their position as slaves while still emphasizing their eastern origins.[79] The process by which Turkish slaves made it to the capital is not always entirely clear but they certainly came through the domains of the Sāmānids who likely profited off this trade. As Matthew Gordon wrote,

> The sources fail to provide information even on such basic matters as identity of its participants (who were the traders? who were the captives – prisoners of war, tribute, orphans cast off to those willing to feed them?), the mechanics of the trade (how were the slaves transported, fed, housed?), and the levels of profit.[80]

One source of slaves for the Abbasid court discussed in our sources is a tribute from the Ṭāhirids and Sāmānids. Ibn Khurradādhbih reported that during the reign of ʿAbdallāh b. Ṭāhir, Kabul contributed 1,000 slaves annually valued at 600,000 dirhams as part of their tribute.[81] During the caliphate of Muʿtaṣim, Nūḥ b. Asad sent 3,000 Turkish slaves to Iraq a year.[82] Upon the ascension of the Caliph Mutawakkil (r. 847–61), the Ṭāhirids sent him 200 slaves of both sexes as a gift.[83]

Despite the economic benefits the caliphs received from the Ṭāhirids and Sāmānids, the relationship was largely a one-way street and the caliphs felt limited responsibility to their distant vassals. For example, in 841–2 when the people of Chāch needed resources to dredge a canal, Muʿtaṣim resisted sending any money asking his chief qāḍī Ibn Abī Duwād (776–854), 'What concern is it of mine or yours that you should take my money for the people of al-Shāsh and Farghānah?'[84] This sense of disassociation between the caliph and the east certainly encourages the image of a waning caliphate unable to hold onto the distant provinces that have therefore fallen under the sway of autonomous dynasties. The Ṭāhirids kept very close ties to the Abbasids through their positions in Baghdad where they remained in power after they had lost control of Khurāsān to the Ṣaffārids. The Sāmānids were more remote but relied heavily on official recognition from the caliphs as their representatives as part of their legitimation. This was especially important when it came to sanctioning their control over the judicial system and in their employment of jihad to help rally troops to their cause along the frontier.[85] Both of these functions were essential to the stability of the Sāmānid state as they could justify their rule through their defence of Islam and the frontier with a patent from the Abbasid caliph, but they were not the first to use such tactics to legitimate their rule. In return the Sāmānids did not send regular tribute as the Ṭāhirids had but they did police the frontiers and took on rebels such as the Afshīn Ḥaydar and the Ṣaffārids in the name of the caliph.

The frontier as legitimation

One of the greatest concerns of the Ṭāhirids throughout their rule in Khurāsān was unrest in Sīstān, which fell under their political authority. There the Khārijites gathered support among rural populations against the Ṭāhirid tax collectors in the city, spreading general unrest throughout the region. The Ṭāhirids' inability to gain control over this problem eventually led to their downfall when a coppersmith by the name of Yaʿqūb b. Layth (r. 861–79) organized bands of *ʿayyār* in the name of Sunni Islam to defend the people of Sīstān. When Yaʿqūb turned these forces against the local governors, seizing control of the provincial capital of Zaranj, his movement evolved into a political dynasty, the Ṣaffārids or the 'coppersmiths', who would quickly conquer much of Iran, reaching into Iraq, for a brief moment.[86] The Ṣaffārids emphasized the responsibility of the state to defend the Muslims and the caliphate's frontiers, gaining fame through campaigns into the Hindu Kush that overcame such intractable rivals as the Zunbīl. Despite their humble and rebellious beginnings, the Ṣaffārids could justify their actions, including their march on Baghdad, through their dedication to the jihad, the defence of Islam, and their accusation that the Ṭāhirids were negligent in this responsibility. When Yaʿqūb b. Layth conquered the Ṭāhirid capital at Nīshāpūr in 873, Ṭāhirid rule over Khurāsān came to an end.

Defence and expansion of the frontier could be a powerful tool of legitimation for rulers who came from outside the traditional positions of power.[87] As Deborah Tor put it,

> The battleground with infidelity in Central Asia gave legitimation to what was a wholly new and unprecedented political phenomenon in the Mashriq: the breaking of Muslim political unity by the establishment of usurping dynasties, for which no place yet existed in proto-Sunni theology.[88]

It had a populist appeal and the perceived dereliction of frontier warfare by the Abbasid caliphs had already driven a wedge between the caliphs and the ulema as early as the caliphate of Hārūn al-Rashīd.[89] As the bonds of clientage between local lords, governors and, ultimately, the caliph weakened and collapsed on multiple levels, new methods of explaining and justifying one's rule came to the forefront focused on the role of the amir as a defender of the Dār al-Islām.

Controlling one of the largest and most active frontiers of the Islamic world, the Sāmānids were able to employ the frontier as a tool to legitimize their rule and attract supporters to fill their armies. Although the Sāmānids had already commanded the eastern frontier for almost three quarters of a century when their Ṭāhirid patrons collapsed, from the stingy reports of activities along the frontier found in our sources it would appear they had mostly done so in a defensive capacity, maintaining the walls and *ribāṭāt* that defended the population centres loyal to them. The geographers of the tenth century praise the people of Sāmānid Transoxiana for their dedication to fighting jihad, maintaining *ribāṭāt* and defending the frontier.[90] Under Ismāʿīl b. Aḥmad, a combination of Sunni piety and frontier warfare became a legitimation strategy for a dynasty that could no longer rely on ties to the fallen Ṭāhirids. In 893, Ismāʿīl conducted the largest campaign of any Sāmānid amir when he conquered Ṭarāz, described by Ṭabarī as the capital of the Turks, meaning the Qārlūq. The prisoners, including the king of the Qārlūq and his queen, numbered 10,000. The spoils included an uncountable number of horses. In the end, every horseman among the Sāmānid forces received 1,000 dirhams.[91] By 900, when Ismāʿīl faced the Ṣaffārid ʿAmr b. Layth who had been granted a competing governorship over Transoxiana and Khurāsān by the Caliph Mut'aḍid, Ismāʿīl's frontier bone fides were substantive enough that he could convince the warriors and even the generals of the Ṣaffārids, the innovators of frontier warfare as a legitimizing tool, to switch to his side.[92]

As Jürgen Paul argued, the Sāmānids were able to take what had been a very loosely organized and individualized experience – outside of large state-organized campaigns with professional armies, frontier fighting was often associated with ascetics in the early Islamic period who chose to deprive themselves on the frontier – and provide it a level of organization under the state. This organization seems to have grown over time. People with official-seeming titles related to organization and training of ghazis or holy warriors appear in texts like the *Qandiyya* of Nasafī, but they seem primarily to be dated to the eleventh century, after the collapse of the Sāmānid state. Sometimes these campaigns got out of control, as in a case described by Paul in which 200 ghazis were killed attacking Shāvdār, a Christian community near Samarqand.[93] Paul questioned the legitimation of such a campaign against people who would theoretically be under the protection of the amir as *dhimmi*, especially considering how close they resided to a major city.

The defence of the frontier was also achieved through the practice of *ribāṭ*, frontier forts often associated with a form of holy war and ascetics.[94] The maintenance and provisioning of the thousands of *ribāṭāt* found across the Sāmānid domains in the geographical works of the ninth and tenth centuries certainly required a mixture of state and private sponsorship. Iṣṭakhrī, for example, reports that 'the majority of the people of property in Transoxiana direct their expenses towards the *ribāṭāt* and the buildings along the roads and the way stations in the path of jihad'.[95] He adds that the agricultural estates of Transoxiana provide for over 10,000 *ribāṭāt* and that people come from across the region to stay at the *ribāṭāt* in order to repair and improve them and that during their stay their provisions are provided. As the Sāmānids replaced the Bukhārkhudā and other local notables, they also dedicated newly gained lands towards frontier fighting. For example, Ismāʿīl b. Aḥmad bought the village of Chargh (located across the river from Iskijkat) that had been home to a prosperous market along with all its fields and estates (*ḍayāʿāt va ʿaqārāt*) and donated them as an endowment (*waqf*) for the construction of *ribāṭāt*.[96] The practice of endowing *ribāṭāt* via *waqf* spread over the course of the Sāmānid period. According to Muqaddasī, *ribāṭāt* endowed by *waqf* include the *ribāṭāt* of Qarātagīn (d. 932) in Isfījāb and Kharākharāf in Yakānkath near Isfījāb, both of which also housed the tombs of these military commanders.[97]

New challenges came with this form of legitimation though – most importantly, the expectation that one continue to dutifully conduct frontier warfare and maintain a righteous leadership. As we will see below, this was easier said than done and the eventual end of the Sāmānids came from peoples beyond the frontier who had been successfully converted to Islam and who could present themselves to religious authorities and local populations as more righteous rulers. A similar thing can be said about the assumption that the Sāmānids represented a form of 'native rule' as part of their claim to authority. Competition over such an authentic identity also pushed rivals to Sāmānid rule.

The Shāhnāma *of Abū Manṣūr Maʿmarī*

In the mid-tenth century, Abū Manṣūr Muḥammad b. ʿAbd al-Razzāq Ṭūsī (d. 961), who claimed descent from the Kanārang of Ṭūs, asked his minister (*dastūr*) Abū Manṣūr Maʿmarī to gather together Zoroastrian scholars and *dahāqīn* from around Khurāsān and compile a *Book of Kings* or *Shāhnāma* in Persian prose based on a translation of the *Khwādaynāma*, the supposed Sasanian court history discussed in Chapter 2. He gathered together the *dahāqīn*, along with the learned men (*farzāngān*) and the men of experience (*jahān dīd gān*), naming four specifically from Herat, Sīstān, Nīshāpūr and Ṭūs who compiled a book based on their knowledge of the kings and their deeds from the first king to Yazdgird III.[98] The book, which was completed in 957, is lost to us but the introduction has survived attached to numerous manuscripts of Firdawsī's much more famous and later verse *Shāhnāma*, completed fifty years after Maʿmarī's. From this introduction we learn a lot about the patron Abū Manṣūr Ṭūsī and his motivations for commissioning a work on the pre-Islamic kings of Iran and about how the author Maʿmarī understood this work to sit in the historiography of pre-Islamic Iran. What we see when we put Maʿmarī's introduction into the context of Ibn ʿAbd al-Razzāq's life and the political events surrounding him is the story of a frontier zone undergoing yet another transformation and the use of literature to stake political claims in a time of transition.

From Maʿmarī's perspective, his work was part of a chain of historical writing reaching back to the Sasanian past and beyond. He claimed as his inspiration for the project first and foremost the kings of India who patronized the writing of *Kalīla wā dimna* (a collection of animal fables originally known as *Panchatantra* in Sanskrit), the writings of the Indian physician Shānāq and the Hindu epic the *Ramāyana*.[99] Maʿmarī saw these kings as role models for rulers who should patronize scholarship in order to leave a lasting vestige of their good deeds and right kingship in the form of books. He saw a similar benefit for kings who patronize the translation of texts. Here he followed the path by which *Kalīla wa dimna* made its way from Sanskrit to Pahlavi through a translation prepared by Borzūya the legendary physician to the Sasanian Shahanshah Khusrow I, which was then translated into Arabic by the famous translator and secretary to the

Umayyad caliphs Ibn al-Muqaffaʿ, and then into New Persian with a translation by the Sāmānid vizier Abū Faḍl Muḥammad Balʿamī (d. 940).[100] Maʿmarī tried to tie these translations to great kings, arguing that at each junction there was a wise adviser who convinced his lord that translating texts will provide him with immortality. Borzūya immortalized Khusrow with his translation. Ibn al-Muqaffaʿ was said to have made his translation at the behest of the Caliph Ma'mūn – which is impossible considering that Ma'mūn was born a quarter century after Ibn al-Muqaffaʿ's death. Maʿmarī was conflating the most famous translator of Pahlavi literature and one of the most famous patrons of translations into Arabic, the founder of the legendary Bayt al-Ḥikma or House of Wisdom in Baghdad. The text then reached New Persian by way of Abū Faḍl Balʿamī – also known as Balʿamī-i Buzurg or Balʿamī the Elder – for the Sāmānid amir Naṣr II b. Aḥmad (r. 914–43).[101] Balʿamī's translation is lost but his son Abū ʿAlī Muḥammad, a contemporary of Maʿmarī, would begin his famous *Tārīkhnāma*, a translation of Ṭabarī's *History of the Prophets and Kings* revised to such an extent by Balʿamī it is considered an original work in its own right, for the Sāmānid amir Manṣūr b. Nūḥ in 963.[102] Here Maʿmarī compared himself and his work as a translator to Borzūya, Ibn al-Muqaffaʿ and Balʿamī-i Burzurg while comparing his patron Abū Manṣūr b. ʿAbd al-Razzāq to the great kings from the ancient kings of India to Khusrow, Ma'mūn and Naṣr. Maʿmarī's history of *Khaīila wa dimna* does not stop with these translations as he reminds his audience that the Persian poet Rūdakī (858–941) put the stories to verse and that Chinese painters illustrated manuscripts of the stories to entertain a wider audience.[103]

As Maʿmarī imagined his *Shāhnāma*, his project fits into our understanding of the *Shāhnāma* as a literary tradition and, especially, our understanding of the poetic work by Firdawsī that credits Maʿmarī's text as an important source. Regarding the scholarly understanding of Firdawsī's *Shāhnāma*, Julie Scott Meisami explained, 'Since the nineteenth century in particular, it has often been read as a lament for the past glories of Iranian monarchy and as a monument to the Iranian national spirit'.[104] By writing a *Shāhnāma*, Maʿmarī placed himself in a line of scholars and his patron in a line of kings tying them both back to the past glories of the Sasanian Empire and beyond through a chain of both textual transmission and royal duty to preserve and disseminate knowledge. But this is not the only history Maʿmarī invoked. Besides the *Khwādaynāma* tradition and the wise men of Khurāsān he consulted, he also cited a series of Islamic historians – all of Iranian origins as well – whose books he read in the libraries of Ma'mūn.[105] From these sources, Maʿmarī established two parallel patterns, one featuring cycles of kings divided by interregnums filled with disturbances, which is the major organizing principle of Firdawsī's *Shāhnāma* as well, while the second is a cycle of prophets with long centuries between them during which religion deteriorates.[106] It is not clear at what point on either of these cycles Maʿmarī imagined himself, but as we shall see shortly, it is likely in one of the periods of dangerous transition.[107] This intertwining of the histories of Iranian kings with Muslim prophets implies that Maʿmarī was not necessarily lamenting a distant past but is part of a project of creating a new hybrid history and hybrid Iranian–Muslim identity, something similar to the project of Ṭabarī with his *History of the Prophets and Kings* and Balʿamī with his *Tārīkhnāma*.

From the text, it would seem that Abū Manṣūr b. ʿAbd al-Razzāq had another history he wanted to invoke in this work as well, a personal and family history. Maʿmarī provided genealogies for himself and his patron that meet at the Kanārang of Ṭūs under the Sasanian Shahanshah Khusrow II.[108] The remainder of the introduction then focuses on the stories of the Kanārang, including campaigns against the Byzantines during which the Kanārang reportedly captured the emperor and presented him to the Shahanshah and a campaign against the Hephthalites (called Turks) as a result of which Khusrow named him ruler (*pādshāh*) of Ṭūs.[109] Maʿmarī then wrote that when Ibn ʿĀmir first marched on Khurāsān during the caliphate of ʿUthmān, the Kanārang sent his son to Nīshāpūr to receive the Arabs and offer their support. Ibn ʿĀmir then asked the Kanārang for a loan and granted him rule over Nīshāpūr as security.[110] This seems like a story we have heard before – thinking back to Bādhān the *marzbān* of Marw al-Rūd at the beginning of Chapter 3 – and it fits the general narrative we have of the Kanārang of Ṭūs during the original Arab incursions, including a shared but contested stake in the control of Nīshāpūr (again, see Chapter 3). There are some minor changes; what the Arabic sources might call tribute or taxation, Maʿmarī called a loan, for example.

What purpose did Abū Manṣūr b. ʿAbd al-Razzāq have in invoking this 300-year-old narrative of his ancestor, the honours bestowed upon him by Khusrow II and reconfirmed by Ibn ʿĀmir? Maʿmarī concluded his introduction with a notice that control of Ṭūs had fallen out of the hands of the descendants of the Kanārang when the city was taken by the Abbasid governor Ḥumayd b. Qaḥṭaba al-Ṭāʾī, but that Abū Manṣūr Ṭūsī had recaptured it.[111] With that, Maʿmarī ended the introduction to his prose *Shāhnāma*. The story of the Kanārangīyān family's fall from grace also fits the known narrative. Ḥumayd did remove the Kanārang from power but it is unclear if this was during the governorship of Abū Muslim as part of a purge of the local Parthian nobility who had been in opposition to the Abbasids, as argued by Paravaneh Pourshariati, or if it was during Ḥumayd's own governorship in Khurāsān, during the reign of Manṣūr and at the outbreak of Muqannaʿ's revolt discussed in Chapter 6.[112] The return of Abū Manṣūr to power also fits the wider history of his career as we understand it. Abū Manṣūr had served Abū ʿAlī Chaghānī (d. 955), the hereditary ruler of Chaghāniyān, as his lieutenant in Nīshāpūr and Ṭūs when Chaghānī was the Sāmānid governor of Khurāsān (r. 939–45, 952–3) and during his revolts against the Sāmānids and, more directly, their Turkish generals.

In the introduction to Maʿmarī's prose *Shāhnāma* we have two stories, one focused on the author and his interests in the Iranian past and the other focused on the patron and his interests in his family's past. More importantly, Abū Manṣūr b. ʿAbd al-Razzāq's story is focused on a particular claim to authority in his ancestral home based in narratives of the Sasanian past and the Arab–Muslim conquests being deployed at a time when he was trying to reassert those rights after they had been stripped from his ancestors. There are questions asked about the purpose of such narratives and the re-emergence of the Persian language and Persian kingship in the tenth century, many of which focus on tensions between local Iranian populations and agents of an Arab and Islamic empire in the form of the Abbasid Caliphate. These questions seek to understand to whom the purveyors of New Persian were responding: Arabs, Muslims or the Abbasids? In the story of Abū Manṣūr Ṭūsī we may have another option, one based in the collapse of the eastern frontier under the Sāmānids and the spread of Turks beyond the frontier, into Iran, and their rise to power at the end of the Iranian Intermezzo.

Iranians and Turks in the service of the Sāmānids

As Abū Manṣūr b. ʿAbd al-Razzāq claimed authority based on his own lineage and the hereditary authority of his ancestors, his career was tied closely with the Muḥtājid ruler of Chaghāniyān Abū ʿAlī Chaghānī. The background of the Muḥtājid dynasty is mysterious but they were likely descendants of the Chaghānkhudās, the hereditary rulers of Chaghāniyān whom we have encountered throughout the book. The Muḥtājids rose to prominence again as military commanders and administrators for the Sāmānids.[113] Abū Bakr Muḥammad b. Muẓaffar (d. 941), the first of the Muḥtājids to appear prominently in the sources, was briefly governor of Ferghana following his defeat of Ilyās b. Isḥāq, a Sāmānid prince who attempted on three occasions to seize the throne from his cousin Naṣr b. Aḥmad (r. 914–43).[114] For our discussion of the frontier, it should be noted that on one occasion Ilyās marched on Samarqand with an army of 30,000 Turks. When he was defeated he sought refuge at Kashgar, which was then under the authority of the Turkish Qarākhānids. It was when Ilyās attempted to invade Ferghana from Kashgar that Ibn Muẓaffar led the Sāmānid resistance. In the aftermath of this revolt, Naṣr stopped appointing relatives to key positions including governorships, fearing they may use their offices as launch pads for revolts against him and his family line. Instead Naṣr granted these positions to his generals, including a mix of both Turkish *mamlūk* slave soldiers and Iranian nobles, Ibn Muẓaffar being one of the latter.[115] This decision created a division within the Sāmānid military elite between the Turks, the Iranian nobles and the Sāmānid family that strained Sāmānid rule as each party jockeyed for position against the others. This strain was not something new to Naṣr's reign; his grandfather Ismāʿīl who had consolidated Sāmānid authority under a single line already began the process of replacing vassal retainers with military commanders personally loyal to the amir.[116] As notices sprinkled throughout Narshakhī's *History of Bukhara* also attest, he also broke up the power of many of the local lords, buying up their estates around the Bukhara oasis. Ibn Muẓaffar's son Abū ʿAlī first came to notice in 929–30 when three Sāmānid princes under the leadership of Yaḥyā b. Aḥmad staged a revolt against their brother Naṣr. While his father subdued Yaḥyā in Ṭukhāristān, Abū ʿAlī oversaw Chaghāniyān, which remained loyal while the rest of the region opened into revolt. In return for his support, Naṣr named Ibn Muẓaffar governor of Khurāsān following the defeat of Yaḥyā.[117]

Khurāsān was in a difficult position in the 930s as the Ziyārid Dynasty spread across northern Iran from Gīlān under its founder Mardāvīj b. Ziyār (r. 930–5) and his brother and successor Vushmgīr (r. 935–67) who made his capital at Rayy. As the Ziyārids and Sāmānids clashed, Khurāsān regained its status as a frontier, fought over by the two Muslim powers. The Ziyārids advanced onto Gorgān and Khurāsān and pushed the Muḥtājids out of Nīshāpūr on two occasions in 935 and 936. Ibn Muẓaffar became ill at this time and the governorship passed to his son Abū ʿAlī.[118] In 940 Abū ʿAlī led a campaign against Vushmgīr, who had allied with Mākān b. Kāki, a Daylamite general who had thrown off his allegiance to the Sāmānids. During this campaign Abū ʿAlī occupied Rayy and chased the Ziyārids into Ṭabaristān.[119] In the aftermath, Abū ʿAlī was able to reach as far west as Kurdistān, the furthest conquests ever made by a Sāmānid force, but he returned to Nīshāpūr in March 943, just one month before the death of the Amir Naṣr b. Aḥmad.[120] His return east opened Rayy up to the Būyid Rukn al-Dawla (r. 947–77), and Sāmānid control in central Iran disappeared. The new Sāmānid Amir Nūḥ b. Naṣr (r. 943–54) ordered Abū ʿAlī to retake Rayy, which required two campaigns. The first in 944 failed when large portions of his army defected to the Turkish general Manṣūr b. Qarātigīn (d. 952) and his Kurdish troops chose to join the Būyids (r. 934–1062), but a second in 945 re-established Sāmānid authority in Rayy.[121] This conflict over Rayy was part of a larger conflict between the Sāmānids and Būyids not only for political control of Iran but also to be the standard bearer of Iranian cultural identity and kingship.

The Iranian lords of Khurāsān were caught between the two sides, asked to fight on behalf of the Sāmānids for control of central Iran but also pushed towards the Būyids by the Sāmānid policy of pitting their governors and generals against one another. Nūḥ tried to restrain Abū ʿAlī's power while he was campaigning against Rayy, first by appointing military overseers to monitor his army's pay and then by handing the governorship of Khurāsān to the Turkish general Abū Isḥāq Ibrāhīm b. Sīmjūr (d. 948), which pushed Abū ʿAlī to revolt against Nūḥ.[122] The ensuing conflict put the various agents and vassals of the Sāmānids at odds with each other as Abū ʿAlī sought to put Nūḥ's uncle Ibrāhīm b. Aḥmad on the Sāmānid throne with the backing of the Abbasid Caliph Rāḍī (r. 934–40) and possibly the Būyids. Throughout this entire conflict, the most pressing concern was the loyalty of the army to both their immediate commander and the Sāmānid amir, a loyalty that was often bought and paid for with cash. By the mid-940s it seemed that the Sāmānids were losing control of the army and, as a result, of the state itself.

The story of Abū Manṣūr b. ʿAbd al-Razzāq began during this rebellion. When Abū ʿAlī reconquered Nīshāpūr from Ibn Sīmjūr and marched on Marw, he left the Kanārang of Ṭūs in charge of the city. As Abū ʿAlī's revolt collapsed, Ibn ʿAbd al-Razzāq fought to maintain his position in Nīshāpūr, repelling an attack by Abū ʿAlī's brother who had remained loyal to Nūḥ before finally fleeing to the Būyids once Nūḥ's new military governor of Khurāsān Manṣūr b. Qarātigīn arrived.[123] But in the messiness of the Sāmānid–Būyid frontier, no good general was left on the outs for too long and following Ibn Qarātigīn's death in 951, Abū ʿAlī was pardoned and reinstated as governor of Khurāsān. Ibn ʿAbd al-Razzāq was pardoned along with him and returned to Nīshāpūr.[124] Many of our sources portray the situation as Ibn Qarātigīn unable to control the army of Khurāsān and the Sāmānids needing Abū ʿAlī, who was trusted and respected by the soldiers. But it should also be noted that most of our sources rely on the lost *History of the Governors of Khurāsān* written by Sallāmī, who had been employed by the Muḥtājid court by Abū ʿAlī's father, and therefore was biased towards the lords of Chaghāniyān.[125] Three years later, in 954, Abū ʿAlī was again removed from the governorship of Khurāsān by first Nūḥ and then, after the amir's death, his son and successor ʿAbd al-Malik (r. 954–61). Abū ʿAlī died a year later of the plague, a refugee at the Būyid court of Rayy. His son died along with him.[126]

By 960, Ibn ʿAbd al-Razzāq was elevated to governor of Khurāsān, but his ties to the Būyids, built during his years in exile alongside Abū ʿAlī, made him suspect – especially as the Būyid Amir Rukn al-Dawla invaded Gorgān – and he was replaced with the Turkish general Alptigīn (d. 963). Ibn ʿAbd al-Razzāq again fled to the Būyids.[127] Then ʿAbd al-Malik suddenly died and was succeeded by his brother Manṣūr who reappointed Ibn ʿAbd al-Razzāq with orders to remove Alptigīn by force.[128] Although Abū Manṣūr took Nīshāpūr, he failed to capture Alptigīn. The Turkish amīr fled east with several allied Sāmānid generals and their troops and conquered Ghazna for himself, setting the foundations for the Ghaznavid Sultanate (r. 977–1186). For his failure, Abū Manṣūr was removed from office. He was killed in battle against a Sāmānid army sent to capture him as he attempted to flee yet again to his Būyid allies.[129]

This was the context in which Abū Manṣūr b. ʿAbd al-Razzāq commissioned Maʿmarī to compose his prose *Shāhnāma*. The text was completed at a time when the governorship was in the hands of the Turkish general Muḥammd b. Ibrāhim b. Sīmjūr (r. 957–60), between the death of Abū ʿAlī and Ibn ʿAbd al-Razzāq's appointment as governor. Its composition came in a period of chaos, when Ibn ʿAbd al-Razzāq's position was unclear and the politics of Sāmānid Khurāsān were increasingly violent. With this in mind, it is clear that Ibn ʿAbd al-Razzāq's intentions when he asked Maʿmarī to write a history of pre-Islamic Iran with an introduction that placed his and his family's authority over Ṭūs in the ancient past was to solidify and justify his own position in the midst of this scrum. We can read the *Shāhnāma* as a text about the competition for political authority in a broken Khurāsān, not as a text that is necessarily anti-Arab, Muslim or Abbasid, but one that is lashing out against the Sāmānid preference for Turkish generals over Iranian hereditary rulers, the people they supposedly represented with their return to 'native' Iranian kingship.

The Shāhnāma *and a broken frontier*

As discussed above, a central question asked about the formation of New Persian and the writing of pre-Islamic Iranian history in texts such as the *Shāhnāma* is, to whom are these authors and their audiences responding? Of course, this is a question that assumes that Persian did not re-emerge of its own cultural milieu. Typically one of two answers is given: either Arab–Muslim society as a whole or the Abbasid Caliphate in particular. Such a description sees the development of this literature in a nationalist, anti-colonial framework. It is an argument that places the formation of New Persian on the offensive, as in the 'linguistic Shu῾ūbiyya' arguments of Lutz Richter-Bernburg that the future of Islam as a monolingual civilization was at stake as writers in Persian tested the limits to see where Persian could replace Arabic's legal standing.[130] The problems with such an understanding are twofold. First, New Persian flourished as a literary language during the reign of the Sāmānid amir Naṣr b. Aḥmad at a point when the presence of the caliphate or Arabs, or at least Arabs who were not speakers of Persian in their day-to-day life, was already extremely light in Khurāsān, Ṭukhāristān and Transoxiana. The second problem is the idea of an offensive characteristic to the project. As discussed above, the content of New Persian literature was not explicitly anti-Arab or anti-Muslim and, in fact, it often spoke quite clearly in dialogue with both traditions; the authors and patrons of New Persian works were also familiar with Arabic literature of both religious and secular natures.[131] At a site like the Sāmānid court, perhaps authors were attempting to test the limits of Persian's place in legal discourses, but how would that explain the *Shāhnāma* of Ma῾marī? The court of Abū Manṣūr b. ῾Abd al-Razzāq was not a place to go on the offensive against social and cultural norms, at least not if the goal was to change larger patterns of behaviour. Throughout his political career and as expressed in the introduction to the *Shāhnāma*, Ibn ῾Abd al-Razzāq was mostly on the defensive, concerned about his position in Khurāsān and preserving his hereditary status. Rather than remembering the glories of old, Ibn ῾Abd al-Razzāq was holding on to the remnants of the present.

The more pressing concern for an author or patron of Persian texts of the standing of Ma῾marī or Ibn ῾Abd al-Razzāq in the mid-tenth century was more likely the growing numbers of Turks in the military and administration of the Sāmānid state and the impact of these newcomers on their own positions in the lands they felt were their ancestral possessions. Ibn ῾Abd al-Razzāq commissioned his *Shāhnāma* at a time when his centuries-old claim to Ṭūs was in flux. At first his fortunes rose along with Abū ῾Alī Chaghānī under Naṣr b. Aḥmad, who patronized the Iranian nobility, but then they fell with his son and successor Nūḥ, who favoured the Turkish generals. A glimmer of hope rose again under Manṣūr only to be crushed by Ibn ῾Abd al-Razzāq's inability to defeat the Turkish general Alptigīn. It is no surprise that the *Shāhnāma* was completed at such a low point in his career, during the period following the death of his former patron Abū ῾Alī in exile at the Būyid court – the Sāmānids' chief rivals for the claim to Persian kingship – when Ibn ῾Abd al-Razzāq's hereditary domains were under the authority of the Turkish military governor Muḥammad b. Ibrāhīm b. Sīmjūr. Even though we do not have the body of Ma῾marī's *Shāhnāma*, it is listed by Firdawsī as one of his sources and, therefore, we may presume the existence of certain similarities in content and that a regular conflict throughout the narrative of the *Shāhnāma* is the rivalry between Irān and Turān – between the Iranians and the Turks – the very rivalry Ibn ʿAbd al-Razzāq and his fellow Iranian lords living under Sāmānid authority were experiencing.

The careers of Ibn ʿAbd al-Razzāq and Abū ʿAlī Chaghānī demonstrate the nature by which the frontier shifted in the tenth century. Frontier warfare to the north and east played an important role in legitimizing the Sāmānid state, but its presence as an activity organized by the state declined sharply in the mid-tenth century. Some scholars, such as Treadwell, took this to be an actual 'cessation of hostilities' with a decline in both fighters, many of whom transferred to the Byzantine and Indian frontiers, and in defensive outposts.[132] Tor, on the other hand, has argued that the sources are simply ignoring frontier warfare because the Sāmānids are just not winning anymore and the authors of our sources, especially those employed by the Sāmānid court, want to avoid embarrassing topics.[133] Perhaps the state had become less involved as frontier warfare became the purview of volunteer fighters of the jihad organized locally. Alongside this there is a changing dynamic along the frontier itself as Turks converted to Islam and became more connected to the people of Sogdiana and beyond and as the Sāmānids and other Muslim dynasties increasingly invited the Turks into the Dār al-Islām to serve in their militaries. In the case of the Sāmānids, they had invited the Turks in and made them rulers over the Iranian nobility. In a bit of a reversal from the passage that opened this book, instead of Ḥasan b. Abī al-ʿAmarraṭah al-Kindī declaring that the Turks were not coming to the Muslims, rather, the Muslims had come to the Turks, Ibn ʿAbd al-Razzāq was stating through Maʿmarī that the Turks had come to the Iranians and that he was prepared to fight for his claim. With the shift in the political geography of Iran in the tenth century, we may think of the direction of the frontier as having shifted as the Sāmānids placed most of their military attention towards the west, against their Būyid rivals. It was towards Rayy that Abū ʿAlī Chaghānī fought most of his wars, in contrast to his father who began his career chasing rebel princes in Ferghana.

It is important to note that Ibn ʿAbd al-Razzāq was not the only figure in this situation to commission works of history in Persian and many local Iranian lords patronized Persian literature. The historian Abū ʿAlī Husayn al-Sallāmī, author of the lost *History of the Governors of Khurāsān* – an important source for both Gardīzī and Ibn al-Athīr who have preserved a large portion of his text – wrote in the service of the Muḥtājids, having worked for both Abū ʿAlī and his father Abū Bakr. The Muḥtājids were also patrons of Arabic works, including Shaʿyā b. Farighūn's encyclopaedia *Comprehensive Work on the Sciences*. The same Ibn Farīghūn may also be the author of the anonymous geographical work *Ḥudūd al-ʿālam*, written in Persian and patronized by the Farīghūnid rulers of Gūzgān, vassals of the Sāmānids to whom Ibn Farīghūn may have been related.

The Qarākhānids and the end of the eastern frontier

The ultimate collapse of the Sāmānid state came precisely from this dynamic. Simply put, in late 999 an army of the Qarākhānids arrived at the gates of the

Sāmānid capital at Bukhara and the people of the city opened their doors to them. By the late tenth century, the Sāmānid house was in disarray with the dynasty facing an ongoing cycle of revolt from their supposed vassals. The most successful of these in the long run were the Ghaznavids, former Turkish generals who had inaugurated their own dynasty on the southern face of the Hindu Kush in the region of Ghazna in 977, but it was the Sīmjūrids who now challenged the Sāmānids for control of Khurāsān south of the Oxus. Increasingly the Sāmānids' rivals looked beyond the frontier and sought help from the Turks, the most important source of which was Bughrākhān Abū Mūsā Hārūn b. Īlak (d. 992), co-founder of the Qarākhānid confederacy. By the mid-tenth century the Qarākhānid Turks had converted to Islam without integrating into a Muslim polity directly. They retained Turkic titles and continued to live in the lands on the frontiers of the Sāmānid state. The historian of Maḥmūd of Ghazna's reign, ʿUtbī (d. after 1020) tells us that it was the *dahāqīn* of Transoxiana who first invited the Qarākhānids into the Sāmānid realm because they had grown tired of the Sāmānid regime.[134] Rebels including the Turkish general Abū ʿAlī Sīmjūrī (d. 997) and Fāʾiq (d. 999) soon followed.[135] Sīmjūrī's plan involved dividing the Sāmānid realm with his neighbour, the Sīmjūrids taking Khurāsān while the Qarākhānids remained north of the Oxus. As the Qarākhānids slowly made their way across Ferghana, the Sāmānid Amir Nūḥ II b. Manṣūr (r. 976–97) tried to stop them unsuccessfully. The Qarākhānids first took Bukhara in 992 when the general in charge of its defence simply let the city fall, but Nūḥ convinced the Sīmjūrids to retake the city in return for Khurāsān.[136] Abū ʿAlī Sīmjūrī demanded that Nūḥ call him *mawlā amīr al-muʾminīn* – the title and the status still meant something even if the Abbasids had no power in Khurāsān by this point.[137] It was Īlak Khān's decision to leave Bukhara at this time, unaccustomed to the climate and extremely unpopular with the population, opening the way for Nūḥ to reclaim his capital.

War continued between the Sāmānids and their Turkish generals, with Nūḥ now turning to the Ghaznavids for support, but the constant warfare across the Sāmānid realms was draining on the population. When Īlak Khān returned in 999, the preachers of Bukhara tried to rally the people of the city against the Qarākhānids but the people refused. Instead, they turned to the jurists, the masters of Islamic law, and asked how they should respond, to which they were told that they should not take up arms against their fellow Muslims.[138] The people were tired of the incessant fighting and had lost respect for a weakened Sāmānid state being torn apart by its own generals. They chose to open the doors of the city to the Turks, who were, although foreign invaders, at least Muslims. With this defeat not only did the Sāmānid state collapse but the Iranian Intermezzo came to a close and more than a millennium of Turkish rule in Iran began. The destruction of the Sāmānid state was not just the end of a dynasty but also the end of the eastern frontier. The bulwark that had stood for centuries between, first, the Iranian and, then, the Islamic worlds and the steppes of the Turks fell in upon itself. In the process, the Sāmānids had done much to weaken and even eliminate many of the smaller lords who had ruled over the frontier for this period, but the victory of the Turks brought a definitive end to historical patterns that had been alive since the Sasanian period.

The formation of Greater Khurāsān

As early as the caliphate of Mahdī but no later than the rise of Ma'mūn, the Abbasids situated themselves at the centre of a web of vassals or clients that radiated out from the capital to the frontiers. Even though this may give the impression of a breakdown of caliphal authority, as powerful local and provincial players were able to establish their own networks and exert authority without the direction of the caliph, in many ways this created an elegant solution to troublesome regions such as Khurāsān, Ṭukhāristān and Transoxiana. Direct rule in such cases was not always cost effective. The need to send armies off to far-flung frontiers to defend against encroaching enemies or put down internal revolts and turmoil could consume the entire tax return. Farming these responsibilities out to more local actors was a solution that allowed the caliph to focus on problems closer at hand. This pattern travelled from the caliph to provincial governors like the Ṭāhirids to their sub-governors such as the Sāmānids all the way down to the village headman. The fitting of all these layers of authority into a single network became a delicate balancing game, as seen in the conflicts between the Ṭāhirids and Māzyār or the Sāmānids and Ibn ʿAbd al-Razzāq. The caliph played a role in dictating these relationships, creating a hierarchy of political relationships, and remained a figure who local lords could turn for redress, even if this only came in the form of statements of legitimation.

The decentralization of authority also created an increasing number of places where authority could be questioned for any number of legitimate or illegitimate reasons. There were squabbles among peers placed in a hierarchical relationship such as Māzyār's rivalry with ʿAbdallāh b. Ṭāhir or Abū ʿAlī Chaghānī's competition against the Turkish generals for control of Khurāsān. At the same time, others could claim that the responsibilities they had encumbered better legitimized their authority over their patrons. In the case of the Ṣaffārids, the Ṭāhirids were accused of neglecting their duties on the frontiers and, consequentially, Yaʿqūb b. Layth found it appropriate to usurp that authority. Similarly the people of Bukhara recognized the Qarākhānids as better representing their interests than the Sāmānids and therefore surrendered. A final concern in these networks of relationships is the balance between effectiveness and loyalty. Jürgen Paul argued that such equations matter in the organization of the army and that it was for this reason slave soldiers increasingly became a part of the militaries of the Islamic world from the Abbasid court in Iraq to the Sāmānids in Transoxiana.[139] Similar calculations must be made when considering retainers in general and, as we will see in the conclusions, the choices made may have devastating effects on the balance of the state.

Over the course of the ninth and tenth centuries, Khurāsān, Ṭukhāristān and Transoxiana were united together as a Greater Khurāsān that, over time, turned into an independent state under the Sāmānids. This was not a total rejection of the rule of the caliphate or a return to some form of 'native rule', a reversal of the Arab–Muslim conquests. Instead it was an outgrowth of the imperial politics of the Abbasid Caliphate, built on a hierarchy of networks reaching out from the person of the caliph at the centre to the farthest reaches of the empire. In many ways, it was the Sāmānids who best brought the local lords of the eastern frontier under the authority of the caliphate, but it was also the Sāmānids who broke down their authority, chasing after loyal and efficient vassals. Eventually this meant the introduction of Turkish generals as administrators of Greater Khurāsān, a change which essentially broke down the old frontier and eventually led to the conquest of the Sāmānid state by Inner Asian Turks.

CONCLUSION: AT THE END OF THE FRONTIER

By the end of the tenth century, with the Qarākhānid Turks conquering Sāmānid Central Asia and ushering in a millennium of Turkic rule across Iran and much of the Islamic World, the dynamic of the frontier had changed qualitatively. No longer was the eastern frontier the bulwark against the invasion of Inner Asian nomads into Iran and beyond. Rather, it became the conduit by which these same nomads came to rule. Over time, the nomadic population of Iran itself would increase as first Turks, then Mongols and then Turks again migrated south and west. Yet, many of the conditions we used to define the eastern frontier remained until the age of premodern empires when the Timurids gave way to the Safavids (r. 1501–1736) and Mughals (r. 1526–1857) – the latter being descendants of Timur – followed by the expansion of the Russian and British empires. These later invaders brought new ideas and technological means to build their empires. The topography still formed a shatterzone that shaped the new empires that came to Central Asia and it remained the river valleys and oases where these empires centred their power and wealth – often in the same cities covered in this book. We may think of the splendour of Timurid Samarqand and Clavijo's descriptions of the Gate of Iron as the tollbooth that taxed the merchants heading into Sogdiana. Compare this to the guerilla fighting of the mountains of Afghanistan. There, despite all forms of modern technology that aim to eliminate the variances of geography – whether satellite communication, air transportation or hi-tech weaponry that can be deployed remotely – the reach of even the most powerful empires could not go far enough. In doing so, we may be reminded of the struggles governors and generals faced in the late antique and medieval periods in controlling these same territories.

As the later Turko-Mongol migrations passed through Greater Khurāsān, it was the culture of the eastern frontier, the courtly Persian with praise for the kings of pre-Islamic Iran, that shaped the cultural identity of the states they would build. The *Shāhnāma* became a staple of Turkic kingship. Sultans commissioned elaborately illuminated manuscripts as a sign that they understood what it meant to be a proper ruler. If Ibn ʿAbd al-Razzāq commissioned his prose *Shāhnāma* in response to the threats Turkish generals made on his hereditary position, as argued in Chapter 7, then there is a certain irony that Firdawsī's much more famous prose *Shāhnāma* was delivered to the Turkish Ghaznavid Sultan Maḥmūd (r. 998–1030). The Turks became the vehicle by which the culture that had been formulated on the frontier made its way to the centre. But these long-term effects were not what this book was about.

In managing the study of a frontier that stretched geographically from the shores of the Caspian Sea to the Hindu Kush Mountains and from the highlands of the Iranian Plateau beyond the River Jaxartes and chronologically over seven centuries, we employed certain geographic concepts, detailed in Chapter 1, to provide some order. The most prominent of these was the concept of the 'shatterzone'. In geological terms, the mountains, deserts and steppes of the eastern frontier created isolated political and economic centres that allowed for the growth of diverse political and social identities among its populations. In order to rule the eastern frontier, empires needed to find ways to bring these centres together. The urban centres of Khurāsān, associated with an imperial military presence since antiquity, were easily networked with the larger empires of Iran. As the Islamic caliphate spread eastwards these were the cities most easily conquered and integrated into the new imperial order. In Sogdiana, the merchant cities thrived off trade that took advantage of their location between great imperial and cultural zones, taking advantage of the stability these empires could bring to facilitate and protect long-distance trade while using their autonomy to move between imperial zones. As the caliphate expanded north beyond the River Oxus, they faced local resistance that was often economic in its outlook – not only concerned about the payment of taxes to an empire based in far-off Iraq but also fearful for the future of their commercial networks. Their advance was also contested by rival empires that had benefitted from this exchange, most notably the empires of the Turks. The Hephthalite-dominated mountains and steppes of Ṭukhāristān barred entry to the region and divided the empire from the easternmost urban centres such as Balkh. Eastern expansion required excessive force to bring these fringes in line. Each of these geographic units and their isolated subdivisions required their own approach and attention if they were to be integrated into the empire.

The concept of the 'shatterzone' helped us move beyond the large-scale, monolithic narrative of imperial conquest favoured by sources produced at the centre. Such sources saw the caliphate as conquering, supplanting and succeeding the Sasanian Empire. Instead, we get a narrative in which an Arab–Muslim caliphate, which itself was not united behind a single mission – engaged with a plurality of rivals, none of which appear to be the grand Iranian empire whose defeat the chroniclers praise. As the conquests moved forward and the caliphate matured, the 'shatterzone' also limited the extent to which the Umayyads or Abbasids could incorporate the eastern frontier into a grand imperial order. The region maintained a unique and localized identity that needed to be shaped into the empire. In Chapter 1, we borrowed a metaphor from Charles Bungay Fawcett to describe borderlands. There, Fawcett compared the frontier to a shoreline, emphasizing the depth found between the lines of high and low tide. Continuing this metaphor, we may think of conquest like a wave striking the shoreline. While it looks like the water overcomes and covers the sand, the wave also breaks on the sand and parts of it sink into the nooks and crevices between the grains, rocks and shells. The water finds every space it can fill, moving around those objects it cannot budge. The wave moves and rearranges the sand on the surface but below the upper layer, the beach maintains its shape. Similarly, when the wave pulls away, it takes some of the sand back to the ocean with it and the water may become cloudy. Both water and beach are changed by the process just as both the conquered and the conqueror are changed by the conquest.

Though much of this book took the shape of a chronological narrative, each part contributed to a larger argument about the nature of empire at the frontiers. The experiences of the Sasanians in Chapter 2 set a baseline for imperial management of the frontier. Despite ongoing attempts to expand beyond the Oxus and Murghāb Rivers, the empires could not maintain control outside the urban centres that were connected to the larger empire – namely Marw, Herat, Nīshāpūr, Marw al-Rūd and sometimes Balkh – and these became the centre of a defensive military strategy along with a handful of large infrastructure projects, the Great Wall of Gorgān being the most noticeable. When we turn to the larger debate about the nature of the Sasanian Empire, the eastern frontier shows how the empire could be centralized at specific points where imperial resources – both money and manpower – were concentrated but decentralized as one travelled further away allowing for an uneven application of imperial authority – a variant of the 'Swiss-Cheese' frontier discussed in Chapter 1. The collapse of the Sasanian Empire and the arrival of Arab–Muslim armies, first leading incursions to seek financial gain but not the creation of a permanent imperial presence – much like the Turks and the Hephthalites before them – allowed the eastern frontier to break down into its individual 'shatterzone components', as detailed in Chapter 3. Each part allied with others or outside powers as it was advantageous. As the Arabs began to more consciously migrate into the region in greater numbers, they maintained their tribal identities and, still largely nomadic themselves, looked to divide the region along the tribal lines they overlaid upon the 'shatterzone'. This reorganization and application of a new Arab political and social order upon the frontier resulted in fierce conflict and incredible violence during the Second Fitna, as seen in Chapter 4, but continued well after as the caliphate struggled to get beyond tribal politics. As the Umayyad Caliphate began to coalesce around a stronger imperial framework in the eighth century, the new challenge became the integration of conquered populations into this new imperial framework. This process was often complicated by both Arab factionalism and the active presence of a Turkish rival, as seen in Chapter 5. The Umayyads could neither adopt whole cloth the pre-existing structures of the conquered territories nor import their own without alteration, and the negotiations on all sides led to often violent struggles that challenged the reach of empire into Transoxiana and Ṭukhāristān. The revolts that engulfed the frontier in the eighth century, including the Abbasid Revolution, were reactions to the process by which the empire of the caliphate was shaping itself to fit the challenges of the frontier, as detailed in Chapter 6. Though many of our sources want to see these conflicts as extensions of the larger political dramas of the eighth-century caliphate, the lines drawn between allies and enemies across the empire were never so neat on the ground and only became messier the further one moved away from the political centres of Syria and Iraq. As seen in Chapter 7, it was only when networks that connected individual representatives of the caliphate – including the caliph himself – to individual local authorities that the system began to click and Khurāsān, Ṭukhāristān and Transoxiana united into a single geopolitical unit, a Greater Khurāsān, under somewhat stable Muslim leadership. Eventually the struggle to control these networks and the subsequent importation of a Turkish military elite who pushed aside and replaced the local Iranian lords caused the system to break down. In the end, the Sāmānids were replaced by Muslim Turks who migrated from the steppe into Sogdiana. The challenge of building an imperial network and extending rule into the 'shatterzone' of the eastern frontier was never truly overcome.

This book has attempted to bring in new sources to complement those literary sources with an overly centralized, imperial perspective we must so heavily rely upon for this period of history, but more can certainly be done, especially as ongoing archaeological digs bring more evidence to light. As the study of late antique and medieval Central Asia moves forward, archaeology will be at the centre of new discoveries and the synthesis of archaeological and textual evidence will continue to bring exciting new discoveries. Most importantly, material culture can help us get beyond the narrative of governors and generals and open up the social history of the frontier in ways our literary sources do not allow. As it stands, we only know of what is happening on the ground when things are broken – when revolts and protest are brought to the level that they are noticed by chroniclers such as Ṭabarī or seen as consequential enough that they deserve a place in the larger imperial narrative. Greater access to material culture will help us understand how the frontier functioned when it was in its proper order.

This book was about a frontier as a place and a process, as a space of conflict and competition. It was also a book about a frontier as the limit of empire and imperial reach in the first millennium CE. By examining the behaviour of imperial agents far from the political centre, working towards personal goals – both individual and tribal or communal – and the ambitions of the empire, we have seen some of the strategies and mechanics of empire in the late antique and early medieval period exposed in a manner that helps us understand how these empires functioned even at their centre. By examining the people of the frontier as they engage and respond to these agents of empire, we get a look into society beyond the imperial propagandistic lens of our sources. For these reasons, we need to keep looking beyond the centre and spend more time on the frontiers.

NOTES

Introduction

1 Ṭabarī, vol. 2, p. 1485; *The History of al-Ṭabarī*, vol. 25, p. 22.
2 Ṭabarī, vol. 2, p. 1486; *The History of al-Ṭabarī*, vol. 25, p. 22.
3 On the Day of Thirst, see Chapter 5.
4 A southeastern frontier extends south of the Hindu Kush along the frontiers of Iran and India. Its history is connected to that of the eastern frontier, but the experiences are distinct and peripheral to this book.
5 Abū Isḥāq Iṣṭakhrī, *al-Masālik wa'l-mamālik*, Muḥammad Jābir ʿAbd al-ʿĀl al-Ḥīnī [ed.] (Cairo, 1961), p. 163; Abū al-Qāsim Ibn Ḥawqal, *Kitāb ṣūrat al-ard*, J. H. Kramers [ed.] (Leiden, 1939), pp. 466–8.
6 Shams al-Dīn Abū ʿAbdallāh Muḥammad Muqaddasī, *Aḥsan al-taqāsīm fī maʿrafa al-aqālīm*, M. J. de Goeje [ed.] (Leiden, 1906), p. 261, n. e; Shams al-Dīn Abū ʿAbdallāh Muḥammad Muqaddasī, *The Best Division for Knowledge of the Regions*, Basil Anthony Collins [trans.] (Reading, 1994), pp. 237–8.
7 H. A. R. Gibb, *The Arab Conquests in Central Asia* (London, 1923), p. 1.
8 Perhaps the most famous and influential expression of this comes from the introduction to the lost prose *Shāhnāma* of Abū Manṣūr Maʿmarī (d. 961) who set the limits of Iran at the Oxus. Vladimir Minorsky, 'The Older Preface to the Shāh-Nāma', in *Studi Orientalistici in Onore Di Giorgio Levi Della Vida* (Rome, 1956), vol. 2, p. 172.
9 Andreas Wilde, *What Is Beyond the River? Power, Authority, and Social Order in Transoxania (18th-19th Centuries) Volume 1* (Vienna, 2016), p. 9. See also Bert G. Fragner, 'The Concept of Regionalism in Historical Research on Central Asia and Iran (A Macro-Historical Interpretation)', in Devin DeWeese [ed.], *Studies on Central Asian History. In Honor of Yuri Bregel* (Bloomington, IN, 2001), pp. 345–53; Christine Noelle-Karimi, *The Pearl in Its Midst: Herat and the Mapping of Khurāsān (15th-19th Centuries)* (Vienna, 2014), p. 6.
10 This is not the first study to locate the origins of the eastern dynasties, most importantly the Sāmānids, in the Sasanian past. For example, see Khodadad Rezakhani, *ReOrienting the Sasanians: East Iran in Late Antiquity* (Edinburgh, 2017), pp. 7–8.
11 For an overview of major themes in the study of Islamic frontiers, Robert Haug, 'Frontiers and the State in the Medieval Islamic World: Jihād Between Caliphs and Volunteers', *History Compass* 9, no. 8 (2011), pp. 634–43.
12 Khalid Yahya Blankinship, *The End of the Jihād State: The Reign of Hishām Ibn ʿAbd Al-Malik and the Collapse of the Umayyads* (Albany, NY, 1994).
13 Linda Darling, 'Contested Territory: Ottoman Holy War in Comparative Context', *Studia Islamica* 91 (2000), p. 141.
14 Patricia Crone, *God's Rule: Government and Islam* (New York, 2004), pp. 36–9.
15 Michael Bonner, *Jihad in Islamic History: Doctrines and Practices* (Princeton, NJ, 2006), pp. 118–56.

16 Richard Bulliet, *Islam: The View from the Edge* (New York, 1995).
17 Frederick Jackson Turner, 'The Significance of the Frontier in American History', in *The Frontier in American History* (New York, 1953), pp. 1–38.
18 Michael Bonner, 'The Naming of the Frontier: ʿAwāṣim, Thughūr, and the Arab Geographers', *Bulletin of the School of Oriental and African Studies* 57 (1994), pp. 17–24; Michael Bonner, *Aristocratic Violence and Holy War: Studies in the Jihad and the Arab-Byzantine Frontier* (New Haven, CT, 1996).
19 Deborah Tor, 'Privatized Jihad and Public Order in the Pre-Seljuq Period: The Role of the Mutatawwiʿa', *Iranian Studies* 38 (2005), pp. 555–73.
20 A. Asa Eger, 'Ḥiṣn, Ribāṭ, Thaghr or Qaṣr? Semantics and Systems of Frontier Fortifications in the Early Islamic Period', in Paul M. Cobb [ed.], *The Lineaments of Islam: Studies in Honor of Fred McGraw Donner* (Leiden, 2012), p. 427; Alison Vacca, 'Past the Mediterranean and Iran: A Comparative Study of Armenia as an Islamic Frontier, First/Seventh to Fifth/Eleventh Centuries', in Kathryn Babayan and Michael Pifer [eds], *An Armenian Mediterranean: Words and Worlds in Motion* (Cham, Switzerland, 2018), p. 40.
21 Bonner, 'The Naming of the Frontier', pp. 23–4.
22 A. Asa Eger, *The Islamic-Byzantine Frontier: Interaction and Exchange among Muslim and Christian Communities* (London, 2015).
23 Darling, 'Contested Territory', p. 141. The debates surrounding ghazis and Ottoman origins begin with the Wittek Thesis – the motivating force and raison d'etre of the Ottoman state was holy war – and response to it. Paul Wittek, *The Rise of the Ottoman Empire* (London, 1938), pp. 18, 20; Colin Imber, 'What Does "Ghazi" Actually Mean?', in Çiĝdem Balim-Harding and Colin Imber [eds], *The Balance of Truth: Essays in Honor of Professor Geoffrey Lewis* (Istanbul, 2000), pp. 165–78; Rudi Paul Lindner, *Explorations in Ottoman Prehistory* (Ann Arbor, MI, 2007).
24 Hussein Fancy, *The Mercenary Mediterranean: Sovereignty, Religion, and Violence in the Medieval Crown of Aragon* (Chicago, 2016).
25 Jürgen Paul, *Herrscher, Gemeinwesen, Vermittler: Ostiran und Transoxanien in vormongolischer Zeit* (Beirut, 1996).
26 Paul has recently applied this model across Iran in the twelfth century. Jürgen Paul, *Lokale und imperiale Herrschaft im Iran des 12. jahrhunderts: Herrschaftspraxis und konzepte* (Wiesbaden, 2016).
27 Mark Luce, 'Frontier as Process: Umayyad Khurāsān' (PhD, University of Chicago, 2009).
28 Deborah Tor, *Violent Order: Religion Warfare, Chivalry, and the* ʿayyār *Phenomenon in the Medieval Islamic World* (Würzburg, 2007), Chapter 5.
29 Jürgen Paul, *The State and the Military: The Samanid Case* (Bloomington, IN, 1994), pp. 13–23.
30 Muqaddasī, *Aḥsan al-taqāsīm fī maʿrafa al-aqālīm*, p. 260; Muqaddasī, *The Best Division for Knowledge of the Regions*, pp. 236–7.
31 Richard Frye, 'Kushans and Other Iranians in Central Asia', in *Reşid Rahmeti Arat İçin* (Ankara, 1966), p. 245.
32 Khurāsān or the concept of an administrative division called the east may have a precedent from the Alkhans, a dynasty of Iranian Huns who ruled south of the Hindu Kush in the fifth and sixth centuries. Rezakhani, *ReOrienting the Sasanians*, pp. 117–23.
33 Parvaneh Pourshariati, *Decline and Fall of the Sasanian Empire: The Sasanian-Parthian Confederacy and the Arab Conquest of Iran* (London, 2008), pp. 417–20.

34 Vasily Bartold, 'Mā warā' al-nahr', *EI*[2].
35 C. E. Bosworth, 'Ṭukhāristān', *EI*[2].
36 Sasanian control east of the River Murghāb was temporary, ephemeral and subject to debate. In using this more inclusive definition, I am attempting to reflect this geopolitical reality following the example of Luce, 'Frontier as Process', p. 37.
37 N. Sims-Williams, 'Bactrian Language', *EIr*.
38 Nicola Di Cosmo, *Ancient China and Its Enemies: The Rise of Nomadic Power in East Asian History* (Cambridge, 2002), p. 2.
39 Jos Gommans, 'The Silent Frontier of South Asia, C. A.D. 1100-1800', *Journal of World History* 9 (1998), p. 2. For further discussion of the ecological divide between pastoral nomads and sedentary agrarians in Central Asia and the Middle East, Owen Lattimore, *Inner Asian Frontiers of China* (New York, 1940), pp. 151–69; Ernest Gellner, 'Tribalism and State Formation in the Middle East', in Philip S. Khoury and Joseph Kostiner [eds], *Tribes and State Formation in the Middle East* (Berkeley, CA, 1990), pp. 109–27.
40 Gommans, 'The Silent Frontier of South Asia', p. 2.
41 Peter B. Golden, *An Introduction to the History the Turkic Peoples: Ethnogenesis and State Formation in Medieval and Early Modern Eurasia and the Middle East* (Wiesbaden, 1992), pp. 6–11; Anatoly M. Khazanov, *Nomads and the Outside World*, Julia Crookenden [trans.] (Cambridge, 1984); Sechen Jagchid, 'Patterns of Trade and Conflict between China and the Nomadic Peoples of Mongolia', *Zentralasiatische Studien* 11 (1977), pp. 177–204; Sechen Jagchid and Van Jay Symons, *Peace, War and Trade along the Great Wall* (Bloomington, IN, 1989).
42 Golden, *An Introduction to the History the Turkic Peoples*, pp. 10–11.
43 Édouard Chavannes, *Documents sur les Tou-Kiue (Turcs) occidentaux* (Paris, 1903).

Chapter 1

1 ʿUbayd Allāh b. ʿAbdallāh Ibn Khurradādhbih, *Kitāb al-masālik wa'l-mamālik*, M.J. de Goeje (ed.), (Leiden, 1889), pp. 33–4. Ibn Khurradādhbih was director of posts and intelligence (*ṣāḥib al-barīd wa'l-khabar*) under the Caliph Muʿtamid (r. 870–92). His geographical work presumably represents the postal routes of the Abbasid Empire and was either written during his time in office or was informed by it. Travis Zadeh, *Mapping Frontiers across Medieval Islam: Geography, Translation, and the ʿapping Empire* (London, 2011), pp. 17–20.
2 For a full description of the area, Vasily Bartold, *Turkestan Down to the Mongol Invasion*, fourth edition (Oxford, 1977), pp. 70–4.
3 Abū Bakr Aḥmad Ibn al-Faqīh, *Mukhtaṣar kitāb al-buldān*, M.J. de Goeje (ed.), (Leiden, 1885), pp. 324–5. A *farsakh* or farsang is a unit of distance approximately 6 km in length. W. Hinz, 'Farsakh', *EI*[2].
4 Qudāma was a lifelong bureaucrat and served in several offices of the Abbasid administration including the office of control and audit (*majlis al-ziman*) in the Divan of the East (*dīwān al-mashriq*). For more on Qudāma, his career and his book, see Paul Heck, *The Construction of Knowledge in Islamic Civilization: Qudāma b. Jaʿfar and His* Kitāb al-Kharāj wa-ṣināʿat al-kitāba (Leiden, 2002), pp. 22–5.
5 Besides the omission of Faḍl b. Yaḥyā's gate and a few word choices that differ from Ibn Khurradādhbih and Ibn al-Faqīh, Qudāma includes one new piece of

information. He writes that Rāsht borders Ferghana (*mimma yalī Farghāna*), expanding the frontier in his view further to the north. Qudāma, *Kitāb al-kharāj wa-ṣināʿat al-kitāba*, Muḥammad Ḥusayn al-Zubaydī (ed.) (Baghdad, 1981), p. 109.

6 Yāqūt, *Muʿjam al-buldān*, Muḥammad ʿAbd al-Raḥman al-Murʿashlī (ed.), (Beirut, 1997), vol. 4, pp. 380–1.

7 As such, we may compare the story of Faḍl b. Yaḥyā and his gate to the popular legend of the Wall of Alexander which held back the denizens of Gog and Magog and was a popular theme in the geographic literature under examination here – most famously in Ibn Khurradādhbih's account of Sallām the Interpreter (*al-tarjumān*) who went on a mission to inspect the wall on behalf of the Caliph Wāthiq (r. 842–7). For two recent studies of Alexander's Wall and Sallām's mission, Emeri Van Donzel and Andrea Schmidt, *Gog and Magog in Early Christian and Islamic Sources: Sallam's Quest for Alexander's Wall* (Leiden, 2010); Zadeh, *Mapping Frontiers across Medieval Islam*.

8 B. Carra de Vaux, 'Ḥadd', *EI*[2].

9 Michiel Baud and Willem van Schendel, 'Toward a Comparative History of Borderlands', *Journal of World History* 8 (1997), pp. 211, 215. Here Baud and van Schendel discuss the formation of borders in a modern, specifically post-colonial, context, but this element of their definition may be applied to premodern states as well.

10 While the author of *Ḥudūd al-ʿālam* is unknown, he dedicated the work to Abū 'l-Ḥārith, the Farīghūnid ruler of Gūzgān and vassal of the Sāmānids. The dates of Abū 'l-Ḥārith's rule are not clear and there were two successive Farīghūnid rulers with this kunya who were themselves father and son. The text was completed in 982–3. On the translation of the title, Minorsky says *ḥudūd* may more precisely be defined as 'regions within definite boundaries' but also acknowledges that *nāḥiyat* as used by the author of *Ḥudūd al-ʿĀlam* is closer to regions. Bartold included a similar debate in his preface. *Ḥudūd al-ʿālam: 'The Regions of the World'*, Vladimir Minorsky (trans.), second edition (Cambridge, 1970), pp. xli n. 2, 30–1.

11 On the Balkhī School, Gerald R. Tibbetts, 'The Balkhī School of Geographers', in J.B. Harley and David Woodward (eds.), *The History of Cartography, Vol. 2, Book 1: Cartography in the Traditional Islamic and South Asian Societies* (Chicago, 1992), pp. 108–36.

12 J.D. Latham and C.E. Bosworth, 'Thughūr', *EI*[2].

13 A. Asa Eger, *The Spaces Between the Teeth: A Gazetteer of Towns on the Islamic–Byzantine Frontier* (Istanbul, 2012); A. Asa Eger, *The Islamic–Byzantine Frontier: Interaction and Exchange among Muslim and Christian Communities* (London, 2015), p. 8.

14 It is important to note here that the geographical sources rarely use the phrase Dār al-Islām to describe the object of their study. For a discussion of the terms that were used under different circumstances, Zadeh, *Mapping Frontiers across Medieval Islam*, pp. 87–9.

15 Walter Prescott Webb, *The Great Frontier* (Boston, 1952), pp. 2–3. Emphasis not added.

16 Igor Kopytoff, 'The Internal African Frontier: The Making of African Political Culture', in Igor Kopytoff (ed.), *The African Frontier: The Reproduction of Traditional African Societies* (Bloomington, IN, 1987), p. 25. Quoted in Eger, *The Islamic–Byzantine Frontier*, p. 9.

17 Turner, 'The Significance of the Frontier in American History', pp. 1–38. See the many critiques of Turner's 'frontier thesis' for largely ignoring or downplaying the role of indigenous populations in the shaping of the American West. Allan G. Bogue, *Frederick Jackson Turner, Strange Roads Going Down* (Norman, OK, 1998), p. 202. In the imaginative sphere, despite claims to the contrary, while exploring 'the final frontier' Captain Kirk rarely seemed to find himself truly 'where no man has gone before'.
18 Ralph W. Brauer, 'Boundaries and Frontiers in Medieval Muslim Geography', *Transactions of the American Philosophical Society*, New Series, 85 (1995), pp. 12–16.
19 Aḥmad b. Abī Yaʿqūb al-Yaʿqūbī, *Kitāb al-buldān*, M.J. de Goeje (ed.), (Leiden, 1892), p. 290.
20 Iṣṭakhrī, *al-Masālik wa'l-mamālik*, p. 161; Ibn Ḥawqal, *Kitāb ṣūrat al-ard*, p. 459. Ibn Ḥawqal presents his work as an improvement and expansion on Iṣṭakhrī's text, which he claims was done at the behest of the older geographer after they had met and compared their work while travelling in Sind, so it is common to see identical passages in the two texts. Ibid., pp. 329–30.
21 See the discussion of Ṭukhāristān's geography in the Introduction.
22 Aḥmad Ibn Rusta, *Kitāb al-a'lāq al-nafīsa*, M.J. de Goeje (ed.), (Leiden, 1882), p. 92.
23 On the location of Pāmir, Bartold, *Turkestan Down to the Mongol Invasion*, p. 70.
24 Charles Bungay Fawcett, *Frontiers: A Study in Political Geography* (Oxford, 1918), pp. 17–18.
25 Friedrich Ratzel, *Politische Geographie*, second edition (Munich and Berlin, 1903), p. 538.
26 Baud and van Schendel, 'Toward a Comparative History of Borderlands', pp. 211–12.
27 Peter Perdue, 'From Turfan to Taiwan: Trade and War on Two Chinese Frontiers', in Bradley J. Parker and Lars Rodseth (eds.), *Untaming the Frontier in Anthropology, Archaeology, and History* (Tucson, AZ, 2005), pp. 30–7; Jonathan Karam Skaff, 'Survival in the Frontier Zone: Comparative Perspectives on Identity and Political Allegiance in China's Inner Asian Borderlands during the Sui-Tang Dynastic Transition (617–630)', *Journal of World History* 15 (2004), pp. 121–2.
28 Yaʿqūbī first gives the Persian name, then translates it to Arabic. Yaʿqūbī, *Kitāb al-buldān*, p. 290. A note for the non-Arabist, *ḥadīd*/iron and *ḥadd*/border do share a common root, but there are no reasons to interpret this as the 'Gate of the Border.' These are two separate words that happen to share a linguistic root.
29 Iṣṭakhrī, *al-Masālik wa'l-mamālik*, p. 188; Ibn Ḥawqal, *Kitāb ṣūrat al-ard*, p. 517.
30 Muqaddasī, *Aḥsan al-taqāsīm fī ma'rafa al-aqālīm*, p. 342; Muqaddasī, *The Best Division for Knowledge of the Regions*, p. 302.
31 Richard Frye, 'Dar-i Āhanīn', *EI*².
32 The details of the siege of the Rock of Sogdiana are found in Arrian's *Anabasis*, 4:18–19. For the identification of the Rock of Sogdiana with the gorges between Derbent and Samarqand, see John Atkinson's notes in Arrian, *Alexander the Great: The* Anabasis *and the* Indica, Martin Hammond (trans.) (Oxford, 2013), p. 304. For a fuller discussion of the identification of the various rocks besieged by Alexander in Sogdiana, Claude Rapin, 'On the Way to Roxane: The Route of Alexander the Great in Bactria and Sogdiana (328-327 BC)', in Gunvor Lindströn, Svend Hansen, and Alfried Wieczorek (eds.), *Zwischen Ost und West: Neue Forschungenzum antiken Zentralasien* (Darmstadt, 2013), pp. 43–82.
33 Hsüsan-tsang, *Si-Yu-Ki: Buddhist Records of the Western World*, Samuel Beal (trans.) (London, 1884), p. 36.

34 E. Denison Ross and Vilhelm Thomsen, 'The Orkhon Inscriptions: Being a Translation of Professor Thomsen's Final Danish Rendering', *Bulletin of the School of Oriental Studies* 5 (1930), p. 862. Yenchü-ügüz or Pearl River is an older Turkish name for the Jaxartes.

35 Li Chi Ch'ang, 'The Travels of Ch'ang Ch'un to the West, 1220-1223', in E. Bretschneider (ed. and trans.), *Mediaeval Researches from Eastern Asiatic Sources* (New York, 1888), pp. 81–3.

36 Ruy González de Clavijo, *Historia del gran Tamorlan, e itinerario y enarracion del viage* (Madrid, 1782), pp. 140–1; Ruy González de Clavijo, *Embassy to Tamerlane, 1403-1406*, Guy Le Strange (trans.) (New York, 1928), pp. 204–6.

37 Sharaf al-Dīn Yazdī, *Ẓafarnāma*, M. ʿAbbāsī (ed.) (Tehran, 1957), vol. I, pp. 38, 40, 45; Ẓahīr al-Dīn Muḥammad Bābur, *Bāburnāma: Chaghatay Turkish Text with Abdul-Rahim Khankhanan's Persian Translation*, Wheeler Thackston (trans.) (Cambridge, MA, 1993), pp. 52–3, 254–5; Mīrzā Haydar Dūghlāt, *Ta'rīkh-i rashīdī*, Wheeler Thackston (ed.) (Cambridge, MA, 1996), pp. 17, 20, 135, 207.

38 Claude Rapin, 'Les Portes de Fer près de Derbent: Sur la route de Bactres à Samarkand', *UMR8546 CNRS/ENS-Paris, Archéologie & Philologie Orient & Occident*, http://www.archeo.ens.fr/spip.php?article374&lang=fr; Claude Rapin, Aymon Baud, Frantz Grenet, and Sh. A. Rakhmanov, 'Les recherches sur la region des Portes de Fer de Sogdiane: bref état des questions en 2005', *Istorija Material'noj Kul'tury Uzbekistana (IMKU, The History of Material Culture of Uzbekistan)* 35 (2006), pp. 91–112.

39 Ṭabarī, vol. 2, pp. 1228–9, 1688; *History of al-Ṭabarī*, vol. 23, p. 175, vol. 26, p. 24.

40 Ibn Khurradādhbih, *Kitāb al-masālik wa'l-mamālik*, p. 27.

41 Fanjahīr should not be confused with the famous silver mines at Panjhīr which is closer to Balkh. Ibn al-Faqīh, *Mukhtaṣar kitāb al-buldān*, p. 327.

42 Ibn Ḥawqal, *Kitāb ṣūrat al-ard*, p. 507. The reference to Qalās may tell us that this is not the same Bāb al-Ḥadīd that Ibn Khurradādhbih and Ibn al-Faqīh described. Bartold, *Turkestan Down to the Mongol Invasion*, p. 175.

43 Mark Luce, 'Frontier as Process', p. 4.

44 For a history of theories related to the East–Central Europe shatterzone and, geopolitical theory on shatterzones in general, Paul R. Hensel and Paul F. Diehl, 'Testing Empirical Propositions about Shatterbelts, 1945-76', *Political Geography* 13 (1994), pp. 33–6.

45 Omer Bartov and Eric D. Weitz (eds.), *Shatterzone of Empires: Coexistence and Violence in the German, Habsburg, Russian, and Ottoman Borderlands* (Bloomington, IN, 2013).

46 Hensel and Diehl, 'Testing Empirical Propositions about Shatterbelts, 1945-76', p. 39.

47 Ibid., pp. 47–9.

48 Alfred J. Rieber, *The Struggle for the Eurasian Borderlands: From the Rise of Early Modern Empires to the End of the First World War* (Cambridge, 2014), pp. 8–9.

49 Ibid., p. 615.

50 Joseph Arlinghaus, 'The Transformation of Afghan Tribal Society, Tribal Expansion, Mughal Imperialism and the Roshaniyaa Insurrection 1450-1600' (PhD, Duke University, 1988), p. 6. Cited by Luce, 'Frontier as Process', p. 5.

51 B.A. Litvinsky and Zhang Guang-da, 'Central Asia: The Crossroads of Civilizations', in *HCCA3* (Paris, 1996), p. 476. For a recent critique of one of the more extreme variations on this theme, see Marshall Hodgson's description of Central Asia existing in a 'civilizational cleavage', Khodadad Rezakhani, 'From the "Cleavage" of Central

Asia to Greater Khurasan: History and Historiography of Late Antique East Iran', *Iranian Studies* 49 (2016), pp. 205–15.

52 Starr suggests the term 'crossroads civilization' to represent a Central Asia that combines elements of those civilizations around it into a wholly new civilization with its own distinct features in contrast to a 'crossroads of civilization' model in which neighbouring civilizations overshadow and overtake Central Asia's own unique culture and identity. S. Frederick Starr, *Lost Enlightenment: Central Asia's Golden Age from the Arab Conquest to Tamerlane* (Princeton, NJ, 2013), p. 69.

53 Ibn Khurradādhbih, *Kitāb al-masālik wa'l-mamālik*, p. 29. Nūshajān al-aʿlā could also mean Nūshajān the elevated, as in Nūshajān of elevated status as the term is used for the frontiers of al-Andalus which were divided between *thaghr al-aʿlā* or *al-aqṣā* for the frontline, distant frontier and *thaghr al-awsaṭ* or *al-adnā* for the near frontier.

54 Ibid., pp. 28–9.

55 Ibid., p. 30. Ibn Khurradādhbih goes on to say that Nūshajān and Tibet form the centre of the East (*al-mashriq*).

56 Ibid., pp. 30–1. On Nūshajān, Ibn al-Faqīh says that Upper Nūshajān is three months from the city of the Khāqān of the Tughuzghuz. Ibn al-Faqīh, *Mukhtaṣar kitāb al-buldān*, p. 328. Qudāma gives a similar itinerary, but says the place of the Tughuzghuz Khāqān, who he specifies is the king of the Tughuzghuz (*tughuzghuz khāqān malik al-tughuzghuz*), is only six days travel from Nūshajān. Qudāma, *Kitāb al-kharāj wa-ṣināʿat al-kitāba*, p. 105. Yāqūt gives a truncated form of Ibn Khurradādhbih's itinerary in his description of the city of the Khāqān of the Tughuzghuz, but credits it to Ibn al-Faqīh. Yāqūt, *Muʿjam al-buldān*, vol. 8, p. 407.

57 Qudāma, *Kitāb al-kharāj wa-ṣināʿat al-kitāba*, pp. 101–3.

58 Ibid., pp. 104–5. In Qudāma's version, Khūrtegīn is called the *dihqān*.

59 Ibid., p. 172. Nūshajān does not appear in Ibn Khurradādhbih's longer and more detailed version of this list. Ibn Khurradādhbih, *Kitāb al-masālik wa'l-mamālik*, pp. 34–9.

60 Qudāma, *Kitāb al-kharāj wa-ṣināʿat al-kitāba*, p. 195.

61 Ibid. Assuming that *kharlanjiyya* is a misspelling or alternative spelling for *kharlajiyya*.

62 For the preserved portion of Ibn al-Faqīh's brief comments on Nūshajān, see Ibn al-Faqīh, *Mukhtaṣar kitāb al-buldān*, p. 328.

63 Yāqūt, *Muʿjam al-buldān*, vol. 8, p. 407.

64 Ibid.

65 On Yāqūt's place in the discourse of memory and place, see Zayde Antrim, *Routes & Realms: The Power of Place in the Early Islamic World* (Oxford, 2012), pp. 145–6.

66 Thomas Barfield, *Afghanistan: A Cultural and Political History* (Princeton, NJ, 2010), pp. 67–8.

67 James C. Scott, *The Art of Not Being Governed: An Anarchist History of Upland South Asia* (New Haven, CT, 2009), p. 43.

68 Ann K.S. Lambton, *State and Government in Medieval Islam* (Oxford, 1981), p. 13. In arguing this point, Lambton is following a line of mid-twentieth-century historians who wrote on the relationship between Islam and politics in the early Islamic period and argued for a disconnect between the state and territoriality in the Islamic world. H. A. R. Gibb, 'The Evolution of Government in Early Islam', *Studia Islamica* 4 (1955), pp. 5–17; Henry Siegman, 'The State and the Individual in Sunni Islam', *The Muslim World* 54 (1964), pp. 14–26. This debate was first brought to my attention in Brauer, 'Boundaries and Frontiers in Medieval Muslim Geography.'

69 Lambton, *State and Government in Medieval Islam*, p. 13; Siegman, 'The State and the Individual in Sunni Islam', p. 14. Such arguments can be taken up to the twentieth century and the collapse of the Ottoman Empire. 'People identified themselves as Muslims (or members of a minority "millet"), and as inhabitants of some sub-state "little community". They were regarded by the rulers as ra'aya (flocks) to be both protected and fleeced, not politically active citizens ready to defend a nation.' Raymond Hinnebusch, *International Politics of the Middle East* (Manchester, 2003), p. 16.

70 Ibn Khurradādhbih, *Kitāb al-masālik wa'l-mamālik*, p. 38.

71 Minorsky translates the term *āshtī* as 'trucial' while I have chosen 'peaceful'. The term implies a sense of peace due to a state of reconciliation or concordance. *Ḥudūd al-ʿālam*, Manūchihr Sutūdih, (ed.), (Tehran, 1962), pp. 117–8; *Ḥudūd al-ʿālam: 'The Regions of the World'*, p. 118.

72 Muqaddasī, *Aḥsan al-taqāsīm fī maʿrafa al-aqālīm*, p. 274; Muqaddasī, *The Best Division for Knowledge of the Regions*, p. 245.

73 Lucien Febvre, *La terre et l'évolution humaine; introduction géographique à l'histoire* (Paris, 1922), pp. 374–5.

74 Iṣṭakhrī, *al-Masālik wa'l-mamālik*, p. 157; Ibn Ḥawqal, *Kitāb ṣūrat al-ard*, p. 444.

75 Iṣṭakhrī, *al-Masālik wa'l-mamālik*, p. 157.

76 Ibn Ḥawqal, *Kitāb ṣūrat al-ard*, p. 444.

77 Eger, *The Islamic–Byzantine Frontier*, pp. 294–9.

78 Turner, 'The Significance of the Frontier in American History', p. 1. It has been noted that this thesis has become so familiar in studies of the American West that 'even to summarize it is to engage in ritual'. William Cronon, 'Revisiting the Vanishing Frontier: The Legacy of Frederick Jackson Turner', *The Western Historical Quarterly* 18 (1987), p. 157.

79 Turner, 'The Significance of the Frontier in American History', pp. 30–8.

80 For an example of a similar dynamic of expansion and settlement along the Abbasid–Byzantine frontier, Bonner, 'The Naming of the Frontier', pp. 17–24.

81 Gommans, 'The Silent Frontier of South Asia', p. 1. For an example of Turner's thesis applied to Ottoman history, Gábor Ágoston, 'A Flexible Empire: Authority and Its Limits on the Ottoman Frontiers', *International Journal of Turkish Studies* 9 (2003), pp. 15–31.

82 These statues are probably best known today for their destruction at the hands of the Taliban in March, 2001. *Ḥudūd al-ʿālam* is the only one of our geographic sources that makes a direct reference to these giant Buddhas referring to them as the Red Idol and White Idol (*surkh-but* and *khing-but*). *Ḥudūd al-ʿālam*, pp. 99–100; *Ḥudūd al-ʿālam: 'The Regions of the World'*, p. 109.

83 Yaʿqūbī, *Kitāb al-buldān*, p. 289.

84 On the career of Ibrāhīm b. Jibrīl, see Patricia Crone, *Slaves on Horses: The Evolution of the Islamic Polity* (Cambridge, 1980), pp. 179–80.

85 Yaʿqūbī gives the date 792–3 for these conquests, but Ṭabarī and others date this conquest to 794–5. Yaʿqūbī, *Kitāb al-buldān*, pp. 290–1; Ṭabarī, vol. 3, p. 634; *The History of al-Ṭabarī*, vol. 30, p. 147. This conquest is reflected in later geographical sources which place Kabul under Bāmiyān's authority. Iṣṭakhrī, *al-masālik wa'l-mamālik*, pp. 156–7; Ibn Ḥawqal, *Kitāb ṣūrat al-ard*, p. 447.

86 Iṣṭakhrī, *al-Masālik wa'l-mamālik*, p. 156; Ibn Ḥawqal, *Kitāb ṣūrat al-ard*, 449.

87 *Ḥudūd al-ʿālam*, pp. 99–100; *Ḥudūd al-ʿālam: 'The Regions of the World'*, p. 109.

88 It is interesting to note here that the *shīr* of Bāmiyān later appears as the Abbasid governor of Aleppo, the *jund* or military district of Qinnasrīn and the ʿAwāṣim (the region immediately behind the Arab–Byzantine frontier in northern Syria and Iraq) during the reign of the Caliph al-Mutawakkil (r. 847–61). Kamāl al-Dīn ʿUmar b. Aḥmad Ibn al-ʿAdīm, *Zubda al-ḥalab min ta'rīkh Ḥalab*, Khalīl Manṣūr (ed.) (Beirut, 1996), pp. 43–4.
89 Yaʿqūbī, *Kitāb al-buldān*, p. 288.
90 Akhror Mukhtarov, *Balkh in the Late Middle Ages*, R.D. McChesney (trans.), (Bloomington, IN, 1993), p. 13.
91 Robert Haug, 'The Gate of Iron: The Making of the Eastern Frontier' (PhD, University of Michigan, 2010), pp. 122–3.
92 Bartold questions whether this wall still existed in the ninth century when Yaʿqūbī was describing it. Bartold, *Turkestan Down to the Mongol Invasion*, p. 78. Abū al- Fidā' (1273–1331) also mentions Balkh's villages and agricultural lands are surrounded by a single wall. Abū al- Fidā', *Kitāb taqwīm al-buldān*, Joseph Toussaint Reinaud and William McGuckin de Slane (eds.) (Paris, 1840), p. 461.
93 Iṣṭakhrī, *al-Masālik wa'l-mamālik*, p. 165.
94 Ibn Ḥawqal, *Kitāb ṣūrat al-ard*, pp. 482–3. Abū al-Fidā' cites Ibn Ḥawqal when describing a wall with a twelve-*farāsikh* diameter surrounding Bukhara's villages and agricultural lands. Abū al- Fidā', *Kitāb taqwīm al-buldān*, p. 489.
95 Muqaddasī, *Aḥsan al-taqāsīm fī ma'rafa al-aqālīm*, pp. 266–7; Muqaddasī, *The Best Division for Knowledge of the Regions*, p. 240.
96 Richard Frye, *Bukhara: The Medieval Achievement*, second edition (Costa Mesa, CA, 1996), p. 10.
97 Abū al-Ḥasan ʿAlī b. al-Ḥusayn Masʿūdī, *Kitāb al-tanbiyya wa'l-āshrāf*, M.J. de Goeje (ed.), (Leiden, 1893), p. 65.
98 *Ḥudūd al-'ālam*, p. 106; *Ḥudūd al-'ālam: 'The Regions of the World'*, p. 112.
99 Narshakhī, pp. 46–8; *The History of Bukhara*, pp. 33–4.
100 Narshakhī, pp. 48–9; *The History of Bukhara*, pp. 34–5.
101 Ibn Khurradādhbih, *Kitāb al-masālik wa'l-mamālik*, p. 25; Qudāma, *Kitāb al-kharāj wa-ṣināʿat al-kitāba*, p. 98.
102 Muqaddasī, *Aḥsan al-taqāsīm fī ma'rafa al-aqālīm*, p. 281; Muqaddasī, *The Best Division for Knowledge of the Regions*, p. 250.
103 Narshakhī, p. 24; *The History of Bukhara*, p. 17.
104 Ibn al-Faqīh, *Mukhtaṣar kitāb al-buldān*, pp. 325–6.
105 Narshakhī, p. 47; *The History of Bukhara*, p. 34.
106 Muqaddasī, *Aḥsan al-taqāsīm fī ma'rafa al-aqālīm*, p. 274; Muqaddasī, *The Best Division for Knowledge of the Regions*, p. 245.
107 Frye, *Bukhara*, p. 10. Strabo's reference to Marw (or Margiana) and its wall, which he measures at 1,500 stadia or over 250 km, is to be found in Book XI, Chapter 10 of his geography.
108 Euripides, *Bacchae, Iphigenia at Aulis. Rhesus*, David Kovacs (trans.) (Cambridge, MA, 2003), p. 13. Kovacs writes fortifications but I am following the translation suggested by Peter Frankopan here instead. Peter Frankopan, *The Silk Roads: A New History of the World* (New York, 2015), p. 5.
109 Yury Karev, *Samarqand et le Sughd à l'époque ʿAbbāsside: Historie politique et sociale* (Paris, 2015), pp. 244–5.
110 Iṣṭakhrī, *al-Masālik wa'l-mamālik*, pp. 172–3; Ibn Ḥawqal, *Kitāb ṣūrat al-ard*, pp. 484–5. The term *bustān* may also imply orchards or at least a larger agricultural

enterprise than a decorative or kitchen garden. In this and the following instances, *bustān* (pl. *basātīn*) should probably be thought of in such terms. G. Marçais, 'Bustān', *EI*².

111 Paul Wheatley, *The Places Where Men Pray Together* (Chicago, 2001), p. 256.

112 See Wheatley's comments on places with a primarily defensive role in Khurāsān and Transoxiana. Ibid., pp. 179, 185.

113 Haug, 'The Gate of Iron', pp. 97–101.

114 It is speculated that *qaṣr* was a loanword from the Latin *castrum*, which itself came from the Greek *kastron*, J.P. Van Staël, 'Ḳaṣr', *EI*². Lawrence Conrad has argued that it is an original Arabic word, the *maṣdar* or verbal noun of *qaṣara*, giving it a 'basic connotation … of enclosure, confinement, or restriction'. Lawrence Conrad, 'The Quṣūr of Medieval Islam: Some Implications for the Social History of the Near East', *al-Abhāth* 29 (1981), p. 9. For a response and refutation to Conrad's philological arguments, see Irfan Shahīd, *Byzantium and the Arabs in the Sixth Century, Vol. 2, Part 1* (Washington, DC, 2002), pp. 67–75. For Conrad's argument that the *quṣūr* developed from the residences of prominent persons, Conrad, 'The Quṣūr of Medieval Islam', pp. 15ff.

115 Narshakhī, p. 87; *The History of Bukhara*, p. 63.

116 On Muqaddasī's place in the pantheon of Arab geographers, André Miquel, *La géographie humaine du monde musulman jusqu'au milieu du 11e siècle: Géographie et géographie humaine dans la litérature arabe des origins à 1050* (Paris, 1967), pp. 322–30.

117 The Arab and Persian geographers of the ninth and tenth centuries often invoke the Ptolemaic concept of clime as their system for organizing the text. They use the term *iqlīm* and call upon the Greek tradition even though they are more often than not using a system that is closer in usage to the Iranian *keshwar* which divides the world into a series of countries radiating out from Īrānshahr, the central lands of the Iranian empires.

118 Muqaddasī, *Aḥsan al-taqāsīm fī ma'rafa al-aqālīm*, p. 47; Muqaddasī, *The Best Division for Knowledge of the Regions*, pp. 50–1.

119 Under al-Muqaddasī's classification schema, Samarqand is the metropole of al-Mashriq (the East) but Bukhara is a district with its *qaṣaba* at Numijkat while Balkh is the name of both the district and its capital. Muqaddasī, *Aḥsan al-taqāsīm fī ma'rafa al-aqālīm*, pp. 47–8, 266–7, 295–6; Muqaddasī, *The Best Division for Knowledge of the Regions*, 51, 240, 261.

120 Brauer, 'Boundaries and Frontiers in Medieval Muslim Geography', pp. 5–6.

121 Ibid.

Chapter 2

1 Abū Muḥammad ʿAbdallāh b. Muslim Ibn Qutayba, *Kitāb al-ma ʿārif*, Saroite Okacha (ed.) (Cairo, 1960), p. 661; Dīnawarī, p. 60; Yaʿqūbī, *Tārīkh* (Beirut, 2010), vol. 1, p. 163; Ṭabarī, vol. 1, pp. 871–3; *History of al-Ṭabarī*, vol. 5, pp. 107–10; Balʿamī, vol. 2, pp. 127–8; Abū 'l-Qāsim Firdawsī, *Shāhnāma*, Y.A. Birtils (ed.) (Moscow, 1960), vol. 8, pp. 7–8; Abū 'l-Qāsim Firdawsī, *The Shāhnāma of Firdausī*, Arthur George Warner and Edmond Warner (trans.) (London, 1905), vol. 7, pp. 157–8; Ibn al-Athīr, vol. 1, p. 193.

2 Procopius, *History of the Wars*, H.B. Dewing (trans.) (London, 1914), 1.3.1ff.
3 Joshua the Stylite, *The Chronicle of Pseudo-Joshua the Stylite*, Frank R. Trombley and John W. Watt (trans.) (Liverpool, 2000), pp. 10–11; Ibn Qutayba, *Kitāb al-maʿārif*, pp. 661–2; Ṭabarī, vol. 1, pp. 874–5; *History of al-Ṭabarī*, vol. 5, pp. 113–15; Balʿamī, vol. 2, pp. 132–6; Thaʿālibī, pp. 578–9; Ibn al-Athīr, vol. 1, p. 193.
4 Ṭabarī, vol. 1, p. 876; *History of al-Ṭabarī*, vol. 5, p. 115; Balʿamī, vol. 2, pp. 136–7.
5 For Bahrām Gūr's battle with the Kidarites, Ibn Qutayba, *Kitāb al-maʿārif*, p. 661; Dīnawarī, pp. 57–9; Ṭabarī, vol. 1, pp. 863–5; *History of al-Ṭabarī*, vol. 5, pp. 94–6; Abū al-Ḥasan ʿAlī b. al-Ḥusayn Masʿūdī, *Les prairies d'or*, C. Barbier de Meynard and A. Pavet de Courteille (trans.) (Paris, 1861), vol. 2, pp. 190–1; Balʿamī, vol. 2, pp. 119–21; Firdawsī, *Shāhnāma*, vol. 7, pp. 386–93; Firdawsī, *The Shāhnāma of Firdausī*, vol., 7, pp. 84–92; Thaʿālibī, pp., 558–60; Abū Saʿīd ʿAbd al-Ḥayy Gardīzī, *Ta'rīkh-i Gardīzī*, ʿAbd al-Ḥayy Ḥabībī (ed.) (Tehran, 1984), pp. 76–7. Many of the details in the accounts of Bahrām Gūr's campaign may be anachronistic, reflecting instead the seventh-century conflicts between Khusrow II and Bahrām Chōbīn. Pourshariati, *Decline and Fall of the Sasanian Empire*, p. 68, n. 323.
6 Ṭabarī, vol. 1, pp. 878–9; *History of al-Ṭabarī*, vol. 5, pp. 118–9. Dīnawarī has Pīrūz destroy the tower instead of drag it. Dīnawarī, pp. 61–2. Firdawsī includes Bahrām Gūr's tower but has Pīrūz simply march past it without moving or destroying it. Firdawsī, *Shāhnāma*, vol. 8, pp. 11–17; Firdawsī, *The Shāhnāma of Firdausī*, vol. 7, pp. 164–9. The Armenian chronicle Łazar Pʿarpecʿi does not include Bahrām Gūr's tower, but he does depict the Sasanian army becoming distraught when Pīrūz asks them to cross the border and violate the peace treaty. Łazar Pʿarpecʿi, *The History of Łazar Pʿarpecʿi*, Robert W. Thomson (trans.) (Atlanta, GA, 1991), pp. 214–5. Other sources describe Pīrūz's death in the trench, sometimes in great and graphic detail mentioning that the pearl earring he wore as a sign of his kingship and that even his body could not be found. Only Ṭabarī describes the tower being pulled by elephants and men. Joshua the Stylite, *The Chronicle of Pseudo-Joshua the Stylite*, p. 11; Procopius, *History of the Wars*, 1.4.1ff.; Agathias, *The Histories*, Joseph D. Frendo (trans.) (Berlin, 1975), 4.4; Sebēos, *The Armenian History Attributed to Sebeos*, Robert W. Thomson (trans.) (Liverpool, 1999), vol. 1, p. 5; Addaï Scher, 'Historie Nestorienne (Chronique de Séert), seconde partie, Fasc. 1', *Patrologia Orientalis* 7 (1911), pp. 107–8; Ibn Qutayba, *Kitāb al-maʿārif*, p. 662; Yaʿqūbī, *Tārīkh*, vol. 1, p. 163; Masʿūdī, *Kitāb al-tanbiyya wa'l-āshrāf*), p. 101; Thaʿālibī, pp. 579–82; Ibn al-Athīr, vol. 1, pp. 193–4. In the *Murūj al-dhahab*, Masʿūdī claims that Akhshunwār killed Pīrūz in Marw al-Rūd, which would move this combat from the border of Sogdiana to the border of Ṭukhāristān. Masʿūdī, *Les prairies d'or*, vol. 2, p. 195.
7 M. Rahim Shayegan, *Arsacids and Sasanians: Political Ideology in Post-Hellenic and Late Antique Persia* (Cambridge, 2011), p. 21.
8 On Pīrūz's coins, Nikolaus Schindel, *Sylloge Nummorum Sasanidarum: Paris-Berlin-Wien: Band III/1L Shapur II-Kawad I/2. Regierung* (Wien, 2004), pp. 390–2.
9 Pourshariati sees in most accounts of Pīrūz's reign a commentary on kings who break oaths. Pourshariati, *Decline and Fall of the Sasanian Empire*, pp. 380–5.
10 Ibid., p. 3.
11 Such questions are being brought to the fore by archaeologists working along the frontiers of the Sasanian Empire. Eberhard W. Sauer, Hamid Omrani Rekzavandi, Ton J. Wilkinson and Jebrael Nokandeh, *Persia's Imperial Power in Late Antiquity: The Great Wall of Gorgān and Frontier Landscapes of Sasanian Iran* (Oxford, 2013), pp. 616–19.

12 St John Simpson, 'Sasanian Cities: Archaeological Perspectives on the Urban Economy and Built Environment of an Empire', in Eberhard W. Sauer (ed.), *Sasanian Persia: Between Rome and the Steppes of Eurasia* (Edinburgh, 2017), pp. 21–2.

13 For an overview of the Iranian national historical tradition under the Sasanians, Ehsan Yarshater, 'Iranian National History', *CHIr Vol. 3(1)* (Cambridge, 1983), pp. 359–477; A. Shahpur Shahbazi, 'On the Xwadāy-Nāmag', *Acta Iranica* 16 (1990), pp. 208–29. One should not ignore the classic study by Theodor Nöldeke, *The Iranian National Epic*, L. Bogdanov (trans.) (Philadelphia, 1979).

14 I would like to thank Alison Vacca for her advice on the Armenian and Georgian historical traditions. Timothy William Greenwood, 'Sasanian Echoes and Apocalyptic Expectations: A Re-Evaluation of the Armenian History Attributed to Sebeos', *Le Muséon* 115 (2002), pp. 323–97; Stephen H. Rapp Jr., *The Sasanian World through Georgian Eyes: Caucasia and the Iranian Commonwealth in Late Antique Georgian Literature* (Surrey, 2014), pp. 357–62.

15 On Firdawsī's sources, Dick Davis, 'The Problems of Ferdowsī's Sources', *Journal of the American Oriental Society* 116 (1996), pp. 48–57; Kumiko Yamamoto, *The Oral Background of Persian Epics: Storytelling and Poetry* (Leiden, 2003), pp. 60–109. Khodadad Rezakhani has recently made a strong argument for an eastern origin of the *Shāhnāma* tradition. Rezakhani, *ReOrienting the Sasanians*, pp. 194–8.

16 Greenwood, 'Sasanian Echoes and Apocalyptic Expectations', p. 330.

17 For a list of Greek and Latin sources for Sasanian history, G. Widengren, 'Sources of Parthian and Sasanian History', *CHIr Vol. 3(2)* (Cambridge, 1983), pp. 1273–4.

18 Timothy William Greenwood, 'Sasanian Reflections in Armenian Sources', *e-Sasanika* 3 (2008), pp. 1–28.

19 Rezakhani, *ReOrienting the Sasanians*, p. 13. For a brief overview of the sources for East Iran under the Sasanians, Ibid., pp. 23–6.

20 Chavannes, *Documents sur les Tou-Kiue (Turcs) occidentaux.*

21 For an excellent overview of the Bactrian documents, Khodadad Rezakhani, 'The Bactrian Collection: An Important Source for Sasanian Economic History', *E-Sasanika* 13 (2008), pp. 1–14.

22 Pourshariati, *Decline and Fall of the Sasanian Empire*, pp. 37–41. It should be noted that some recent scholars have pointed towards the east as the real homeland of the Sasanians. Marek J. Olbrycht, 'Dynastic Connections in the Arsacid Empire and the Origins of the House of Sāsān', in Vesta Sarkhosh Curtis, Elizabeth J. Pendleton, Michael Alram and Touraj Daryaee (eds.), *The Parthian and Early Sasanian Empires: Adaptation and Expansion* (Oxford, 2016), pp. 23–35; Rezakhani, *ReOrienting the Sasanians*, pp. 44–5.

23 S.H. Nyberg, *A Manual of Pahlavi, Part I: Texts* (Wiesbaden, 1964), pp. 113–17; Touraj Daryaee, *Šahrestānīhā Ī Ērānšahr: A Middle Persian Text on Late Antique Geography, Epic and History* (Costa Mesa, 2002); Rika Gyselen, *La Géographie administrative de l'empire Sassanide: Les témoignages sigillographiques* (Paris, 1989).

24 For an overview of the debate on the use of the term feudal, Mohsen Zakeri, *Sāsānid Soldiers in Early Muslim Society: The Origins of* ʿayyārān *and* Futuwwa (Wiesbaden, 1995), pp. 13–22.

25 For a general comparison, Richard Frye, 'Feudalism in Sasanian and Early Islamic Iran', *Jerusalem Studies in Arabic and Islam* 9 (1987), pp. 13–18.

26 Maria Macuch, 'Barda and Barda-Dāri ii. In the Sasanian Period', *EIr*. On the use of slaves over serfs, Pourshariati, *Decline and Fall of the Sasanian Empire*, pp. 63–4.

27 Richard Bulliet, *Cotton, Climate, and Camels in Early Islamic Iran: A Moment in World History* (New York, 2009), pp. 17–27.

28 Cyril Toumanoff, *Studies in Christian Caucasian History* (Washington, DC, 1963), pp. 34–40.
29 Ibid., p. 36.
30 Pourshariati, *Decline and Fall of the Sasanian Empire*, pp. 53–6.
31 Anahit Perikhanian, 'Iranian Society and Law', *CHIr Vol. 3(2)* (Cambridge, 1983), pp. 642–3.
32 Philip Huyse, *Die dreisprachige Inschrift Šābuhrs I. an der Ka'ba-i Zardušt (ŠKZ)* (London, 1999), vol. 1, p. 54.
33 Ṭabarī, vol. 1, pp. 819–20; *History of al-Ṭabarī*, vol. 5, p. 15.
34 Huyse, *Die dreisprachige Inschrift Šābuhrs I. an der Ka'ba-i Zardušt (ŠKZ)*, vol. 1, pp. 47, 50; Ṭabarī, vol. 1, p. 817; *History of al-Ṭabarī*, vol. 5, p. 10.
35 Strabo, *The Geography*, H.L. Jones (trans.) (Cambridge, MA, 1932), Book 15.1.3; Marcus Junianus Justinus, *Epitome of the Philippic History of Pompeius Trogus*, Rev. John Selby Watson (trans.) (London, 1853), Book 41.1.8.
36 For an overview of the Kushan Empire, Rezakhani, *ReOrienting the Sasanians*, pp. 46–71; A.D.H. Bivar, 'Kushan Dynasti i. Dynastic History', *EIr*; A.K. Narain, 'Indo-Europeans in Inner Asia', in Denis Sinor (ed.), *The Cambridge History of Early Inner Asia* (Cambridge, 1990), pp. 159–73.
37 Rezakhani, *ReOrienting the Sasanians*, p. 49; H. Falk, 'Kushan Dynasty iii. Chronology of the Kushans', *EIr*.
38 Étienne de la Vaissière, 'The Rise of Sogdian Merchants and the Role of the Huns: The Historical Importance of the Sogdian Ancient Letters', in Susan Whitfield and Ursual Sims-Williams (eds.), *The Silk Road: Trade, Travel, War, and Faith* (Chicago, 2004), p. 21.
39 János Harmatta, 'Minor Bactrian Inscriptions', *Acta Antiqua Academiae Scientiarum Hungaricae* 13 (1965), pp. 186–94; Michael Alram, 'Ardashir's Eastern Campaign and the Numismatic Evidence', in Joe Cribb and Georgina Herrmann (eds.), *After Alexander: Central Asia before Islam* (Oxford, 2007), p. 233; Nikolaus Schindel, 'The 3rd-Centruy "Marw Shah" Bronze Coins Reconsidered', in Henning Börm and Josef Wiesehöfer (eds.), *Commutatio et Contentio: Studies in the Late Roman, Sasanian, and Early Islamic Near East, in Memory of Zeev Rubin* (Düsseldorf, 2010), p. 24; Daniel T. Potts, 'Sasanian Iran and Its Northeastern Frontier: Offense, Defence, and Diplomatic Entente', in Nicola Di Cosmo and Michael Maas (eds.), *Empires and Exchanges in Eurasian Late Antiquity: Rome, China, Iran, and the Steppe, ca. 250-750* (Cambridge, 2018), p. 287.
40 This may have been precipitated by a smallpox epidemic which had come to northern India with Roman merchants. A.D.H. Bivar, 'Hāritī and the Chronology of the Kuṣaṇas', *Bulletin of the School of Oriental and African Studies* 33 (1970), pp. 10–21.
41 Huyse, *Die dreisprachige Inschrift Šābuhrs I. an der Ka'ba-i Zardušt (ŠKZ)*, vol. 1, pp. 23–4.
42 Frantz Grenet, Jonathan Lee, Philippe Martinez, and Françpis Ory, 'The Sasanian Relief at Rag-i Bibi (Northern Afghanistan)', in Joe Cribb and Georgina Herrmann (eds.), *After Alexander: Central Asia before Islam* (Oxford, 2007), pp. 243–67.
43 For an overview of the Kushano-Sasanian Dynasty, Rezakhani, *ReOrienting the Sasanians*, pp. 72–86; A.H. Dani and B.A. Litvinsky, 'The Kushano-Sasanian Kingdom', *HCCA3* (Paris, 1996), pp. 107–22.
44 Ernst Herzfeld, 'New Light on Persian History from the Pahlavi Inscriptions', *Journal of the K.R. Cama Institute* 7 (1926), p. 111. Quoted in Ursula Weber, 'Wahrām II., König der Könige von Ērān und Anērān', *Iranica Antiqua* 44 (2009), p. 571.

45 For the Kushānshāh Hormozd, A. Shahpur Shahbazi, 'Hormozd Kušānšāh', *EIr*. For an overview of the revolt which places these events within the family dynamics among the descendants of Shāpūr I, Ursula Weber and Josef Wiesehöfer, 'Der Aufstand des Ormies und die Thronfolge im frühen Sasanidenreich', in Henning Börm, Norbert Ehrhardt, and Josef Wiesehöfer (eds.), *Monumentum et instrumentum inscriptum: Beschrifete Objekte aus Kaiserzeit und Spätantike als historische Zeugnisse: Festschrift für Peter Weiss* (Stuttgart, 2008), pp. 217–25.

46 Nikolaus Schindel, 'The Beginning of Kushano-Sasanian Coinage', in Michael Alram and Rika Gyselen (eds.), *Sylloge Nummorum Sasanidarum Paris-Berlin-Wien. Band II: Ohrmazd I. - Ohrmazd II* (Wien, 2012), p. 73; Alexander Nikitin, 'Notes on the Chronology of the Kushano-Sasanian Kingdom', in Michael Alram and Deborah E. Klimburg-Salter (eds.), *Coins, Art, and Chronology: Essays on Pre-Islamic History of the Indo-Iranian Borderlands* (Wien, 1999), pp. 260–1. More recently, Khodadad Rezakhani has declared with no explanation that 'the suggestion that the Sasanian prince *Ormis* rebelling against his brother Wahram II, referred to by *Panegyrici Latini* 2.17, is the same as this Hormizd I Kushanshah … must now be dismissed'. Rezakhani, *ReOrienting the Sasanians*, p. 81.

47 C.E.V. Nixon and Barbara Saylor Rodgers, *In Praise of Later Roman Emperors: The Panegyrici Latini* (Berkeley, CA, 1994), pp. 68–9, 101; Flavius Vopiscus, *Scriptores Historia Augusta*, David Magie (trans.) (Cambridge, MA, 1961), vol. 3, pp. 427–9; Flavius Eutropius, 'Abridgment of Roman History', in Rev. John Selby Watson (trans.), *Justin, Cornelius Nepos, and Eutropius, Literally Translated* (London, 1886), Book 9.15.

48 For an overview of the numismatic evidence, Joe Cribb, 'Numismatic Evidence for Kushano-Sasanian Chronology', *Studia Iranica* 19 (1990), pp. 151–93; David Jongeward, Joe Cribb and Peter Donovan, *Kushan, Kushano-Sasanian, and Kidarite Coins: A Catalogue of Coins from the American Numismatic Society* (New York, 2015), pp. 210–16.

49 Cribb, 'Numismatic Evidence for Kushano-Sasanian Chronology', pp. 156, 183; Jongeward, Cribb and Donovan, *Kushan, Kushano-Sasanian, and Kidarite Coins*, pp. 211, 213; Rezakhani, *ReOrienting the Sasanians*, p. 81.

50 Nixon and Rodgers, *In Praise of Later Roman Emperors*, p. 101. On the identification of the Saci, Rufii and Geli, János Harmatta, 'Chionitae, Euseni, Gelani', *Acta Antiqua Academiae Scientiarum Hungaricae* 31 (1985–88), p. 46.

51 Agathias, *The Histories*, Book 4.24.6–8. This report makes no mention of Hormozd's revolt but describes the naming of Bahrām III Sakānshāh as a consequence of conquest. Bahrām III is identified as the Sakānshāh elsewhere, most notably the Paikuli inscriptions.

52 Weber and Wiesehöfer, 'Der Aufstand des Ormies und die Thronfolge im frühen Sasanidenreich'.

53 Helmet Humbach and Pods Skjærvø, *The Sassanian Inscription of Paikuli: Part 3.1: Restored Text and Translation* (Munich, 1983), pp. 71–3.

54 Ibid., pp. 33–4, 42–3.

55 Richard Frye, 'The Persepolis Middle Persian Inscriptions from the Time of Shapur II', *Acta Orientalia* 30 (1966), pp. 84–5.

56 Ammianus Marcellinus, *The Roman History*, C.D. Yonge (trans.) (London, 1894), Book 33.6.14.

57 Cribb, 'Numismatic Evidence for Kushano-Sasanian Chronology', p. 178.

58 Nicholas Sims-Williams, 'The Sasanians in the East: A Bactrian Archive from Northern Afghanistan', in Vesta Sarkhosh Curtis and Sarah Stewart (eds.), *The Sasanian Era* (London, 2008), pp. 91–2; Nicholas Sims-Williams, *Bactrian Documents from Northern Afghanistan, II* (Oxford, 2007), pp. 158, 166.
59 Marcellinus, *The Roman History*, Book 19.1.3.
60 Robert Bartlett, *The Making of Europe: Conquest, Colonization, and Cultural Change, 950-1350* (Princeton, NJ, 1993), pp. 31–9.
61 Dani and Litvinsky, 'The Kushano–Sasanian Kingdom', pp. 113–14; Richard Payne, 'The Making of Turan: The Fall and Transformation of the Iranian East in Late Antiquity', *Journal of Late Antiquity* 9 (2016), pp. 6–7.
62 Sims-Williams, 'The Sasanians in the East', p. 91.
63 Rezakhani, *ReOrienting the Sasanians*, pp. 84–5; Nikitin, 'Notes on the Chronology of the Kushano-Sasanian Kingdom', pp. 261–2.
64 Roman Ghirshman, *Iran: From the Earliest Times to the Islamic Conquest* (Harmondsworth, 1954), p. 318.
65 Richard Bulliet, 'Naw Bahār and the Survival of Iranian Buddhism', *Iran* 14 (1976), p. 144.
66 Frye, 'Kushans and Other Iranians in Central Asia',p. 245.
67 It is possible that a single wave of migration occurred around the 350s from which all subsequent Iranian Hun dynastic and ethnic groups emerged. Rezakhani, *ReOrienting the Sasanians*, pp. 87–8.
68 On European historians' scepticism regarding these connections and their refusal 'to be drawn into Central Asian wastes', Walter Goffart, *Barbarian Tides: The Migration Age and the Later Roman Empire* (Philadelphia, 2006), pp. 17–18.
69 Étienne de la Vaissière, 'Huns et Xiongnu', *Central Asiatic Journal* 49 (2005), pp. 3–26.
70 Daniel T. Potts, *Nomadism in Iran: From Antiquity to the Modern Era* (Oxford, 2014), pp. 128–9.
71 Golden, *An Introduction to the History the Turkic Peoples*, p. 2. For a more general critique of the idea that tribes are constructed of blood relations, Rudi Paul Lindner, 'What Was a Nomadic Tribe?', *Comparative Studies in Society and History* 4 (1982), pp. 689–711.
72 Payne, 'The Making of Turan', pp. 8–9. On the concept of 'collective sovereignty, David Sneath, *The Headless State: Aristocratic Orders, Kinship Society, & Misrepresentations of Nomadic Inner Asia* (New York, 2007), pp. 178–9.
73 For an overview of the Chionites, Wolfgang Felix, 'Chionites', *EIr*; Roman Ghirshman, *Les Chionites–Hephtalites* (Cairo, 1948).
74 Vague references to these events are made in the histories of both Ammianus Marcellinus, a contemporary historian, and the twelfth-century historian John Zonaras. Marcellinus, *The Roman History*, Book 14.3.1; John Zonaras, *The History of Zonaras: From Alexander Severus to the Death of Theodosious the Great*, Thomas M. Banchich and Eugene N. Lane (trans.) (London, 2009), Book 13.7.
75 Marcellinus, *The Roman History*, Books 16.9.4, 17.5.1. On the identity of the Euseni, Rezakhani, *Re Orienting the Sasanians*, p. 89, n. 4.
76 For the treaty, Marcellinus, *The Roman History*, Books 17.5.1.
77 Marcellinus calls him Grumbates. Ibid., Books 19.1.7–19.2.1.
78 For an overview of the Kidarites, Frantz Grenet, 'Kidarites', *EIr*; E.V. Zeimal, 'The Kidarite Kingdom in Central Asia', *HCCA3* (Paris, 1996), pp. 123–37; Ghirshman, *Les Chionites–Hephtalites*. There is much debate around the chronology of the

Chionites and Kidarites. Here I will be following the rough chronology set out by Robert Göbl, *Dokumente zur Geschichte der Iranischen Hunnen in Baktrien und Indien* (Wiesbaden, 1967), vol. 2, pp. 52–5. On the Alkhans, Rezakhani, *ReOrienting the Sasanians*, pp. 104–24.

79 Potts, *Nomadism in Iran*, p. 130; Michael Alram, 'Alchon und Nēzak. Zur Geschichte der iranischen Hunen in Mittleasien', in Istituto italiano per il Medio ed Estremo Oriente and Accademia nazionale dei Lincei (eds.), *La Persia e l'Asia centrale da Alessandro al X secolo* (Rome, 1996), pp. 521–2.

80 Buzandats'i P'awstos, *The Epic Histories Attributed to P'awstos Buzand*, Nina G. Garsoïan (trans.) (Cambridge, MA, 1989), pp. 197–8, 217–18; Potts, *Nomadism in Iran*, pp. 130–1.

81 Frantz Grenet, 'Crise et sortie de crise en Bactriane-Sogdiane au IVe-Ve siècles: de l'héritage antique a l'adoption de modèles sassanides', in Istituto italiano per il Medio ed Estremo Oriente and Accademia nazionale dei Lincei (eds.), *La Persia e l'Asia centrale da Alessandro al X secolo* (Rome, 1996), p. 371; Potts, *Nomadism in Iran*, pp. 132–3.

82 Potts, *Nomadism in Iran*, p. 132.

83 This was not unusual, at least not for the ruling class of nomadic conquerors. Golden, *An Introduction to the History the Turkic Peoples*, pp. 10–11.

84 Xiang Wan, 'A Study of the Kidarites: Reexamination of Documentary Sources', *Archivum Eurasiae Medii Aevi* 19 (2012), p. 280.

85 Étienne de la Vaissière, *Sogdian Traders: A History*, James Ward (trans.) (Leiden, 2005), pp. 107–10.

86 Ibid., p. 107.

87 E.E. Nerazik, 'Khwarizm: Part One: History and Culture of Khwarizm', *HCCA3* (Paris, 1996), p. 215.

88 Rezakhani, *ReOrienting the Sasanians*, p. 99.

89 Rocco Rante and Annabelle Collinet, *Nishapur Revisited: Stratigraphy and Ceramics of the Qohandez* (Oxford, 2013), p. 204.

90 Rocco Rante and Abdisabur Raimkulov, 'Les fouilles de Paykend: nouveaux éléments', *Cahiers d'Asie centrale* 21/22 (2013), pp. 253–5.

91 Recent French excavations of the *quhandiz* have confirmed its dating to Shāpūr II's campaigns. Rante and Collinet, *Nishapur Revisited*, pp. 10, 204.

92 The small size of the Sasanian city was first noted by Richard Bulliet, 'Medieval Nishapur: A Topograhic and Demographic Reconstruction', *Studia Iranica* 5 (1976), p. 87. Its economic significance, based in its many dependent villages, was noted by Peter Christensen, *Decline of Iranshahr: Irrigation and Environment in the Middle East, 500 B.C. - A.D. 1500* (London, 2016), p. 194.

93 While I am not aware of direct evidence for building projects in Marw during Shāpūr II's reign, archaeologists have uncovered large numbers of coins from his reign which would indicate the presence of an army in the city at that time, though the increased numbers may also be a residue of Shāpūr's long 70-year reign. Gabriele Puschnigg, *Ceramics of the Merv Oasis: Recycling the City* (Walnut Creek, CA, 2006), p. 24.

94 'It is only from the middle of the 4th century, around AD 360, that there are conclusive indications of Christians in Merv.' Ian Gillman and Hans-Joachim Klimkeit, *Christians in Asia before 1500* (Ann Arbor, MI, 1999), p. 209. It is important to note that it was during Shāpūr II's reign that the Roman emperor Constantine (r. 306–31) converted to Christianity and began the process of converting the empire. This made Christianity an element of the rivalry between the

Byzantines and Sasanians and led to persecutions of Sasanian Christians, including forced relocations. By 424 there were Nestorian bishoprics in three major cities of Khurāsān – Nīshāpūr, Marw and Herat – with Marw acting as the metropole over all of Khurāsān. A.V. Williams, 'Zoroastrians and Christians in Sasanian Iran', *Bulletin John Rylands Library* 78 (1996), p. 40; Wilhelm Baum and Dietmar W. Winkler, *The Church of the East: A Concise History* (London, 2003), pp. 10–11. According to the *Chronicle of Seert*, the Christian community in Marw began when a sister of Shāpūr who converted to Christianity was married to the *marzbān* of Marw. Addaï Scher, ed., 'Histoire Nestorienne (Chronique de Séert), premiere partie, fasc. 2', *Patrologia Orientalis* 5 (1910), pp. 254–8.

95 Daryaee, *Šahrestānīhā ī Ērānšahr*, pp. 18, 37.

96 Ṭabarī, vol. 1, p. 864; *The History of al-Ṭabarī*, vol. 5, p. 96; Ibn Qutayba, *Kitāb al-ma ʿārif*, p. 661.

97 For the stucco panels, Mohammad Rahbar, 'The Discovery of a Sasanian Period Fire Temple at Bandiyān, Dargaz', in D. Kennet and P. Luft (eds.), *Current Research in Sasanian Archaeology, Art and History* (Oxford, 2008), pp. 15–40; Mohammad Rahbar, 'Découverte d'un monument d'époque sassanide à Bandian, Dargaz (Nord Khorassan): Fouilles 1994 et 1995', *Studia Iranica* 27 (1998), pp. 213–50; Mohammad Rahbar, 'Découverte de panneaux de stucs sassanides', *Dossiers d'archólogie* 243 (1992), pp. 62–65; Philippe Gignoux, 'Le site de Bandiān revisité', *Studia Iranica* 37 (2008), pp. 163–74; Philippe Gignoux, 'Les inscriptions en moyen-perse de Bandiān', *Studia Iranica* 27 (1998), pp. 251–8. For the literary accounts, Ṭabarī, vol. 1, pp. 865–6; *History of al-Ṭabarī*, vol. 5, pp. 96–9; Balʿamī, vol. 2, pp. 120–1; Firdawsī, *Shāhnāma*, vol. 7, pp. 386–93; Firdawsī, *The Shāhnāma of Firdausī*, vol. 7, pp. 92–6; Thaʿālibī, pp. 559–60.

98 Ełišē, *History of Vardan and the Armenian War*, Robert W. Thomson (trans.) (Cambridge, MA, 1982), pp. 63–6.

99 Daryaee, *Šahrestānīhā ī Ērānšahr*, p. 18.

100 Ełišē, *History of Vardan and the Armenian War*, p. 72.

101 The Armenian sources for this campaign mention very little about the actual fighting, only enough to set up the martyr narratives. Ibid., pp. 192–4; Pʿarpecʿi, *The History of Łazar Pʿarpecʿi*, p. 133.

102 Historians had read the relevant passages from Priscus as the Kidarites stopping payment of tribute to the Sasanians but Robert Blockley has convincingly reversed this relationship. The reports of Yazdgird's humiliating defeat two years earlier would make it more likely that the Sasanians were paying tribute to the Kidarites. Roger Blockley, *The Fragmentary Classicising Historians of the Later Roman Empire: Eunapius, Olympiodorus, Priscus and Malchus* (Liverpool, 1983), vol. 2, p. 349.

103 Ibn Qutayba, *Kitāb al-ma ʿārif*, p. 661; Dīnawarī, p. 60; Yaʿqūbī, *Tārīkh*, vol. 1, p. 163; Ṭabarī, vol. 1, pp. 871–3; *History of al-Ṭabarī*, vol. 5, pp. 107–10; Balʿamī, vol. 2, pp. 127–8; Firdawsī, *Shāhnāma*, vol. 8, pp. 7–8; Firdawsī, *The Shāhnāma of Firdausī*, vol. 7, pp. 157–8; Ibn al-Athīr, vol. 1, p. 193.

104 Political control over Herat is always difficult to identify. Our literary sources make Herat an important part of Sasanian campaigns to the east, but there is less evidence this translated into actual control over the city. For example, Nestorian synodal records say a bishop was placed over Herat during the reign of Bahrām Gūr, but it's unclear if one actually arrived. Christensen, *Decline of Iranshahr*, p. 197.

105 For an overview of the Hephthalites, A.D.H. Bivar, 'Hephthalites', *EIr*; B.A. Litvinsky, 'The Hephthalite Empire', *HCCA3* (Paris, 1996), pp. 136–65; Ghirshman, *Les*

Chionites-Hephtalites, pp. 82–104. More recently, it has been argued on the basis of Chinese sources that the Hephthalites were of Turkic origins and later adopted the Bactrian language after settling in Ṭukhāristān. Étienne de la Vaissière, *Samarcande et Samarra: élites d'Asie Centrale dans l'Empire Abbasside* (Paris, 2007), pp. 120–2.

106 Priscus in Blockley, *The Fragmentary Classicising Historians of the Later Roman Empire*, vol. 2, p. 361.

107 Sims-Williams, *Bactrian Documents from Northern Afghanistan, II*, pp. 108–9, 114–15. Mēyam is also known from a pair of seals. Judith Lerner and Nicholas Sims-Williams, *Seals, Sealings and Tokens from Bactria to Gandhara (4th to 8th Century CE)* (Vienna, 2011), pp. 82–3.

108 Rezakhani, *ReOrienting the Sasanians*, pp. 117–21.

109 Sauer, Rekzavandi, Wilkinson, and Nokandeh, *Persia's Imperial Power in Late Antiquity*, pp. 594–5; Jebrael Nokandeh, Eberhard W. Sauer, Hamid Omrani Rekavandi, Tony J. Wilkinson, Ghorban Ali Abbasi, Jean-Luc Schwenninger, Majid Mahmoudi, David Parker, Morteza Fattahi, Lucian Stephen Usher-Wilsom, Mohammad Ershadi, James Ratcliffe, and Rowena Gale, 'Linear Barrier of Northern Iran: The Great Wall of Gorgan and the Wall of Tammishe', *Iran* 44 (2006), pp. 158–62. See also János Harmatta, 'The Wall of Alexander the Great and the Limes Sasanicus', *Bulletin of the Asia Institute, New Series* 10 (1996), pp. 79–84. There is only one literary source that directly attributes the wall to the reign of Pīrūz. Bahā' al-Dīn Muḥammad Ibn Isfandiyār, *Ta'rīkh-i Ṭabaristān*, ʿAbbās Iqbāl (ed.) (Tehran, 1320), p. 71.

110 Blockley, *The Fragmentary Classicising Historians of the Later Roman Empire*, vol. 2, p. 349.

111 Nokandeh, Sauer, Rekavandi, Wilkinson, Abbasi, Schwenninger, Mahmoudi, Parker, Fattahi, Usher-Wilsom, Ershadi, Ratcliffe, and Gale, 'Linear Barrier of Northern Iran', p. 166.

112 For an overview of this relationship, Roger Blockley, 'Subsidies and Diplomacy: Rome and Persia in Late Antiquity', *Phoenix* 39 (1985), pp. 62–74.

113 Joshua the Stylite, *The Chronicle of Pseudo-Joshua the Stylite*, pp. 9–10. The fragmentary history of Priscus tells us that such requests were not always received favourably and sometimes the Sasanian requests for aid were rejected. Blockley, *The Fragmentary Classicising Historians of the Later Roman Empire*, vol. 2, p. 347.

114 Pʿarpecʿi, *The History of Łazar Pʿarpecʿi*, pp. 214–5, 220, 223, 226–7. The later Armenian chronicler Movsēs Dasxurancʿi makes the Hephthalites the agents of God's wrath against Pīrūz for his abuse of Christians. Moses Kałankatuạci, *The History of the Caucasian Albanians by Movsēs Dasxuranci*, C.J.F. Dowsett (trans.) (London, 1961), pp. 25–6.

115 Joshua the Stylite, *The Chronicle of Pseudo-Joshua the Stylite*, p. 10.

116 Nicola Di Cosmo, *Ancient China and Its Enemies*, pp. 139–49; Julia Lovell, *The Great Wall: China Against the World, 1000 BC-AD 2000* (New York, 2006), p. 43. Cited in Nokandeh, Sauer, Rekavandi, Wilkinson, Abbasi, Schwenninger, Mahmoudi, Parker, Fattahi, Usher-Wilsom, Ershadi, Ratcliffe, and Gale, 'Linear Barrier of Northern Iran', p. 167.

117 Procopius, *History of the Wars*, Book 1.3.2.

118 Ṭabarī calls this city Rūsham Pīrūz but that identification is questionable. Ṭabarī, vol. 1, p. 874; *History of al-Ṭabarī*, vol. 5, pp. 112–13; Balʿamī, vol. 2, p. 131. The closest city to Gorgān built by Pīrūz according to Dīnawarī or Firdawsī was Rām Pīrūz near Rayy which is also described by Ṭabarī and Balʿamī. Dīnawarī, p. 61; Firdawsī, *Shāhnāma*,

vol. 8, p. 11; Firdawsī, *The Shāhnāma of Firdausī*, vol. 7, p. 163. According to Tha'ālibī, Rām Pīrūz was between Gorgān and the wall. Tha'ālibī, p. 578. Gardīzī credits Pīrūz with building the *qaṣaba* (administrative centre) of Gorgān as well as adding to the irrigation canals of Marw and founding the city of Fāryāb on the River Oxus. Gardīzī, *Ta'rīkh-i Gardīzī*, p. 79. Pīrūz also released a group of Armenian nobles who had been held prisoner since the revolt of 450 with orders for them to settle in Herat 'with their cavalry, and carry out whatever task' they were given, most likely with regard to frontier defence. P'arpec'i, *The History of Łazar P'arpec'i*, p. 159.

119 Marjan Mashkour, Roya Khazaeli, Homa Fathi, Sarieh Amiri, Delphine Decruyenaere, Azadeh Mohaseb, Hossein Davoudi, Shiva Sheikhi and Eberhard W. Sauer, 'Animal Exploitation and Subsistence on the Borders of the Sasanian Empire: From the Gorgan Wall (Iran) to the Gates of the Alans (Georgia)', in Eberhard W. Sauer (ed.), *Sasanian Persia: Between Rome and the Steppes of Eurasia* (Edinburgh, 2017), pp. 77–8.

120 Sauer, Rekzavandi, Wilkinson, and Nokandeh, *Persia's Imperial Power in Late Antiquity*, pp. 230–4.

121 James Howard Johnston, 'The Two Great Powers of Late Antiquity: A Comparison', in Averil Cameron (ed.), *The Byzantine and Early Islamic Near East, Vol. 3: States, Resources and Armies* (Princeton, NJ, 1995), p. 195.

122 Sauer, Rekzavandi, Wilkinson, and Nokandeh, *Persia's Imperial Power in Late Antiquity*, pp. 613–19.

123 Ibid., pp. 616–17.

124 Procopius, *History of the Wars*, Book 1.4.28–9.

125 de la Vaissière, *Sogdian Traders*, p. 111.

126 Michael Alram and Matthias Pfisterer, 'Alkhan and Hephthalite Coinage', in Michael Alram, Deborah E. Klimburg-Salter, Minoru Inaba, and Matthias Pfisterer (eds.), *Coins, Art and Chronology II: The First Millennium C.E. in the Indo-Iranian Borderlands* (Vienna, 2010), pp. 30–2.

127 de la Vaissière, *Samarcande et Samarra*, p. 111; Rezakhani, *ReOrienting the Sasanians*, p. 153.

128 Ibn Qutayba, *Kitāb al-ma'ārif*, p. 662; Dīnawarī, p. 62; Bal'amī, vol. 2, pp. 142–4; Tha'ālibī, pp. 582–3. Ṭabarī's account places Sūkhrā's reprisal campaign after Pīrūz's first defeat. Ṭabarī, vol. 1, pp. 873, 877–8; *History of al-Ṭabarī*, vol. 5, pp. 110–11, 116–17.

129 Ṭabarī, vol. 1, pp. 883–4; *History of al-Ṭabarī*, vol. 5, pp. 129–30; Bal'amī, vol. 2, pp. 145–6; Tha'ālibī, p. 583. Firdawsī's account has Sūkhrā place Qubād on the throne directly following his reprisal campaign. Firdawsī, *Shāhnāma*, vol. 8, pp. 18–28; Firdawsī, *The Shāhnāma of Firdausī*, vol. 7, pp. 173–82.

130 On these conflicts and the rivalries between the Parthian families, Pourshariati, *Decline and Fall of the Sasanian Empire*, pp. 75–83.

131 On the relationship between Qubād and Mazdak and the problems with our sources for the Mazdakian movement, Patricia Crone, 'Kavād's Heresy and Mazdak's Revolt', *Iran* 29 (1991), pp. 21–42; Patricia Crone, *The Nativist Prophets of Early Islamic Iran: Rural Revolt and Local Zoroastrianism* (Cambridge, 2012), pp. 22–3; Khodadad Rezakhani, 'Mazdakism, Manichaeism and Zoroastrianism: In Search of Orthodoxy and Heterodoxy in Late Antique Iran', *Iranian Studies* 48 (2015), pp. 55–70. For a critique of Crone's analysis, Michael Richard Jackson Bonner, *Al-Dīnawarī's* Kitāb al-aḫbār al-ṭiwāl: *An Historiographical Study of Sasanian Iran*, Res Orientales 23 (Leuven, 2015), pp. 86–90.

132 Procopius, *History of the Wars*, Book 1.6.1–11; Agathias, *The Histories*, Book 4.28.3; Scher, 'Histoire Nestorienne (Chronique de Séert), Seconde Partie, Fasc. 1', pp. 127–8; Dīnawarī, p. 67; Yaʿqūbī, *Tārīkh*, vol. 1, p. 164; Ṭabarī, vol. 1, p. 887; *History of al-Ṭabarī*, vol. 5, pp. 135–6; Balʿamī, vol. 2, pp. 149–51; Ibn al-Athīr, vol. 1, p. 196.

133 Joshua the Stylite, *The Chronicle of Pseudo-Joshua the Stylite*, pp. 21–2; Procopius, *History of the Wars*, Book 1.6.11–18; Agathias, *The Histories*, Book 4.28.6–7; Dīnawarī, *Kitāb al-akhbār al-ṭiwāl*, pp. 67–8; Ṭabarī, vol. 1, p. 887; *History of al-Ṭabarī*, vol. 5, p. 136, note 348; Balʿamī, vol. 2, pp. 151–2; Firdawsī, *Shāhnāma*, vol. 8, pp. 38–41; Firdawsī, *The Shāhnāma of Firdausī*, vol. 7, pp. 198–201; Thaʿālibī, pp. 590–4. For the counter-stamped coins, Göbl, *Dokumente zur Geschichte der iranischen Hunnen in Baktrien und Indien*, vol. 1, pp. 193–4; Robert Göbl, *Sasanian Numismatics*, Paul Severin (trans.) (Braunschweig, 1971), p. 70.

134 de la Vaissière, *Sogdian Traders*, p. 110–11.

135 Joshua the Stylite, *The Chronicle of Pseudo-Joshua the Stylite*, p. 21; Procopius, *History of the Wars*, Book 1.6.11; Agathias, *The Histories*, Book 4.28.4.

136 Jackson Bonner, *al-Dīnawarī's* Kitāb al-aḫbār al-ṭiwāl, pp. 83–4.

137 Procopius, *History of the Wars*, Book 1.5.6.

138 Ibid., Book 1.6.19.

139 Joshua the Stylite, *The Chronicle of Pseudo-Joshua the Stylite*, pp. 50–1, 57, 66, 69, 81; Procopius, *History of the Wars*, Book 1.8.12–16.

140 Denis Sinor, 'The Establishment and Dissolution of the Türk Empire', in Denis Sinor (ed.), *The Cambridge History of Early Inner Asia* (Cambridge, 1990), p. 299.

141 Procopius, *History of the Wars*, Book 1.3.2–6. On Procopius's analysis of the Hephthalites, Anthony Kaldellis, *Ethnography after Antiquity: Foreign Lands and Peoples in Byzantine Literature* (Philadelphia, PA, 2013), pp. 17–19.

142 Sims-Williams, *Bactrian Documents from Northern Afghanistan, II*, pp. 44–9, 164–5; Nicholas Sims-Williams, 'From the Kushan-Shahs to the Arabs: New Bactrian Documents Dated in the Era of the Tochi Inscriptions', in Michael Alram and Deborah E. Klimburg-Salter (eds.), *Coins, Art and Chronology: Essays on the Pre-Islamic History of the Indo-Iranian Borderland* (Vienna, 1999), p. 255.

143 Gyselen, *La géographie administrative de l'empire Sassanide*, pp. 28–9; Rika Gyselen, 'Le kadag-xwadāy Sassanide: quelques réflexions à partir de nouvelles données sigillographiques', *Studia Iranica* 31 (2002), pp. 61–69; Lerner and Sims-Williams, *Seals, Sealings and Tokens from Bactria to Gandhara (4th to 8th Century CE)*, pp. 100–1; Sims-Williams, *Bactrian Documents from Northern Afghanistan, II*, pp. 124–5.

144 Payne, 'The Making of Turan', pp. 10–11. Payne cites the work of numerous archaeologists working in Mongolia including recent surveys by J. Daniel Rogers, 'Inner Asian States and Empires: Theories and Synthesis', *Journal of Archaeological Research* 20 (2012), pp. 205–56; William Honeychurch, 'The Nomad as State Builder: Historical Theory and Material Evidence from Mongolia', *Journal of World Prehistory* 26 (2013), pp. 283–321.

145 Frantz Grenet, 'Regional Interaction in Central Asia and Northwest India in the Kidarite and Hephthalite Periods', in Nicholas Sims-Williams (ed.), *Indo-Iranian Languages and Peoples* (Oxford, 2002), p. 209.

146 Golden, *An Introduction to the History the Turkic Peoples*, pp. 115–54; Denis Sinor, 'The First Türk Empire', *HCCA3* (Paris, 1996), pp. 322–30; Sinor, 'The Establishment and Dissolution of the Türk Empire.'

147 Sneath, *The Headless State*, pp. 24–5.

148 Rezakhani, *ReOrienting the Sasanians*, p. 142.

149 Ṭabarī, vol. 1, p. 899; *History of al-Ṭabarī*, vol. 5, p. 160; Thaʿālibī, p. 611. According to Firdawsī Khusrow's marriage to one of the khāqān's daughters came later as part of a peace treaty following the destruction of the Hephthalites. Firdawsī, *Shāhnāma*, vol. 8, pp. 166–90; Firdawsī, *The Shāhnāma of Firdausī*, vol. 7, pp. 339–63.

150 Dīnawarī, p. 69. According to Ṭabarī, Khusrow conquered all the territories that Istämi did not but no specific territories are mentioned. Ṭabarī, vol. 1, p. 895; *History of al-Ṭabarī*, vol. 5, p. 152. See also Ibn Qutayba, *Kitāb al-maʿārif*, p. 664; Balʿamī, vol. 2, pp. 161–2; Firdawsī, *Shāhnāma*, vol. 8, pp. 156–64; Firdawsī, *The Shāhnāma of Firdausī*, vol. 7, pp. 328–37; Thaʿālibī, pp. 610–11.

151 Ṭabarī, vol. 1, p. 895; *History of al-Ṭabarī*, vol. 5, p. 152; Masʿūdī, *Les prairies d'or*, vol. 2, p. 203; Ibn al-Athīr, vol. 1, pp. 207–8.

152 Jackson Bonner, *al-Dīnawarī's* Kitāb al-aḫbār al-ṭiwāl, p. 111.

153 Sims-Williams, 'The Sasanians in the East', p. 96; Nicholas Sims-Williams, *Bactrian Documents from Northern Afghanistan, I* (Oxford, 2001), p. 164.

154 Rika Gyselen, 'La reconquête de l'est iranien par l'empire sassanide au VIe s. d'après les sources «iraniennes»', *Arts asiatiques* 58 (2003), pp. 162–7.

155 For a full overview of the evidence for Kadagistān, Sims-Williams, 'The Sasanians in the East', pp. 98–9.

156 Ṭabarī spends much more time describing the Bāb al-Abwāb's effectiveness as a deterrent to the Turks and only mentions Gorgān in passing while Firdawsī focuses entirely on Gorgān. Ṭabarī, vol. 1, pp. 895–6; *History of al-Ṭabarī*, vol. 5, p. 153; Firdawsī, *Shāhnāma*, vol. 8, pp. 68–72; Firdawsī, *The Shāhnāma of Firdausī*, vol. 7, pp. 236–9; Ibn al-Athīr, vol. 1, p. 207.

157 On the *limes sasanicus*, Richard Frye, 'The Sasanian System of Walls for Defence', in M. Rosen-Ayalon (ed.), *Studies in Memory of Gaston Wiet* (Jerusalem, 1977), pp. 7–15. For a new study of the conceptual meaning of these walls, Touraj Daryaee, 'If These Walls Could Speak: The Barrier of Alexander, Wall of Darband and Other Defensive Moats', in Stefano Pellò (ed.), *Borders: Itineraries on the Edges of Iran* (Venice, 2016), pp. 79–88.

158 Arthur Waldron, *The Great Wall of China: From History to Myth* (Cambridge, 1990), p. 27; Carlos Rojas, *The Great Wall: A Cultural History* (Cambridge, MA, 2010), p. 31.

159 Ṭabarī, vol. 1, pp. 895–6; *History of al-Ṭabarī*, vol. 5, p. 153.

160 de la Vaissière, *Sogdian Traders*, pp. 209–10.

161 Menander Protector, *The History of Menander the Guardsman*, Roger Blockley (trans.) (Liverpool, 1985), pp. 111–13.

162 de la Vaissière, *Sogdian Traders*, p. 228.

163 Richard Payne, 'The Silk Road and the Iranian political economy in late antiquity: Iran, the Silk Road, and the problem of aristocratic empire', *Bulletin of SOAS* 81 (2018), p. 229.

164 de la Vaissière, *Sogdian Traders*, pp. 228–32. Before the arrival of the Turks, Persian merchants had settled in Central Asia and had established networks connecting them to India, China and points beyond as far as Indonesia. E.H. Schafer, 'Iranian Merchants in T'ang Dynasty Tales', in Walter Joseph Fischel (ed.), *Semitic and Oriental Studies* (Berkeley, CA, 1951), pp. 403–22; Payne, 'The Silk Road and the Iranian political economy in late antiquity'.

165 de la Vaissière, *Sogdian Traders*, pp. 228–30.

166 Nicolas Oikonomidès, 'Silk Trade and Production in Byzantium from the Sixth to the Ninth Century: The Seals of Kommerkiarioi', *Dumbarton Oaks Papers* 40 (1986),

pp. 33–4. Procopius provides us with a story of a pair of monks smuggling silk worms into the empire to begin local production. Procopius, *History of the Wars*, 8.17.1–8.

167 Menander Protector, *The History of Menander the Guardsman*, pp. 125–7; Golden, *An Introduction to the History the Turkic Peoples*, p. 129.

168 Menander Protector, *The History of Menander the Guardsman*, pp. 121–3.

169 Ibid., pp. 173–7.

170 Ṭabarī, vol. 1, p. 991; *History of al-Ṭabarī*, vol. 5, pp. 298–301; Balʿamī, vol. 2, pp. 248–50. Menander Protector mentions an earlier coordinated attack around 570 when Turkish envoys encouraged the Byzantine Emperor Justin II (r. 565–78) to attack the Sasanians while the Turks attacked from the north and east. Menander Protector, *The History of Menander the Guardsman*, p. 147.

171 On Hormozd's parentage, Sebēos, *The Armenian History Attributed to Sebeos*, vol. 1, p. 14; Dīnawarī, p. 76; Yaʿqūbī, *Tārīkh*, vol. 1, p. 165; Ṭabarī, vol. 1, p. 988; *History of al-Ṭabarī*, vol. 5, p. 295; Masʿūdī, *Les prairies d'or*, vol. 2, p. 211; Balʿamī, vol. 2, p. 247; Thaʿālibī, p. 636; Ibn al-Athīr, vol. 1, p. 223. Hormozd's Turkish blood is said to have made him bad intentioned and led him to attack and insult the nobility. Ṭabarī, vol. 1, p. 990; *History of al-Ṭabarī*, vol. 5, p. 297.

172 Klaus Vondrovec, *Coinage of the Iranian Huns and Their Successors from Bactria to Gandhara: 4th to 8th Century CE* (Vienna, 2014), p. 525; Gyselen, 'La reconquête de l'est iranien par l'empire sassanide au VIe s. d'après les sources «iraniennes»', pp. 164–5.

173 Sims-Williams, 'The Sasanians in the East', pp. 96–9.

174 Sebēos, *The Armenian History Attributed to Sebeos*, vol. 1, p. 15; Ibn Qutayba, *Kitāb al-maʿārif*, p. 664; Dīnawarī, pp. 81–4; Yaʿqūbī, *Tārīkh*, vol. 1, p. 166; Ṭabarī, vol. 1, pp. 991–3; *History of al-Ṭabarī*, vol. 5, pp. 298–303; Masʿūdī, *Les prairies d'or*, vol. 2, pp. 212–14; Thaʿālibī, pp. 642–55; Ibn al-Athīr, vol. 1, pp. 23–4. Balʿamī and Firdawsī offer accounts of Bahrām Chōbīn, his campaign against the Hephthalites and Turks and his rebellion that stand out from the majority. This is because they were written in the context of the Sāmānid court and the Sāmānids claimed descent from him. Balʿamī emphasizes Hormozd's mistreatment of Bahrām while Firdawsī uses these events to reflect on the proper relationship between kings and their subjects. For an overview of these changes, A.C.S. Peacock, *Mediaeval Islamic Historiography and Political Legitimacy: Balʿamī's Tārīkhnāma* (London, 2007), pp. 118–23.

175 Vondrovec, *Coinage of the Iranian Huns and Their Successors from Bactria to Gandhara*, p. 525; Rezakhani, *ReOrienting the Sasanians*, pp. 176–8.

176 Ṭabarī, vol. 1, pp. 992–3; *History of al-Ṭabarī*, vol. 5, p. 302. The identity of Shābah/Sāvah is contested. In his translation of Ṭabarī, C.E. Bosworth argues that this 'supreme ruler of the Turks' was actually a Hephthalite vassal, but Peter Golden believes he was the grandson of Istämi and the son of the Khāqān Tardu. Regardless, the politics of the Turk Khāqānate were complicated at this moment due to internal power struggles making the interpretation of a single Arabicized Turkic name rather difficult. Golden, *An Introduction to the History the Turkic Peoples*, p. 132.

177 Touraj Daryaee, 'Wahrām Čōbīn the Rebel General and the Militarization of the Sasanian Empire', in Anna Krasnowolska and Renata Rusek-Kowalska (eds.), *Studies on the Iranian World I: Before Islam* (Krakow, 2015), pp. 193–202.

178 Vondrovec, *Coinage of the Iranian Huns and Their Successors from Bactria to Gandhara*, p. 525.

179 Sebēos, *The Armenian History Attributed to Sebeos*, vol. 1, pp. 15–23; Addaï Scher and Robert Griveau, 'Histoire Nestorienne (Chronique de Séert), Seconde Partie, Fasc.

2', *Patrologia Orientalis* 13 (1919), pp. 443–4, 465–7; Ibn Qutayba, *Kitāb al-ma'ārif*, p. 664; Dīnawarī, pp. 84–105; Ya'qūbī, *Tārīkh*, vol. 1, pp. 167–71; Ṭabarī, vol. 1, pp. 993–1001; *History of al-Ṭabarī*, vol. 5, pp. 303–17; Mas'ūdī, *Les prairies d'or*, vol. 2, pp. 214–24; Tha'ālibī, pp. 658–65, 672–83; Ibn al-Athīr, vol. 1, pp. 224–6.

180 Quoted by Sinor, 'The Establishment and Dissolution of the Türk Empire', p. 307.

181 For the various conflicts among the Turks in Inner Asia, Golden, *An Introduction to the History the Turkic Peoples*, pp. 131–4; Sinor, 'The First Türk Empire', pp. 329–30.

182 Jonathan Karam Skaff, 'Western Turk Rule of Turkestan's Oases in the Sixth through Eighth Centuries', in Halil Inalcik (ed.), *The Turks* (Ankara, 2002), pp. 364–72.

183 Payne, 'The Making of Turan', pp. 23–4.

184 de la Vaissière, *Sogdian Traders*, pp. 200–2.

185 Sauer, Rekzavandi, Wilkinson, and Nokandeh, *Persia's Imperial Power in Late Antiquity*, p. 600.

186 Sebēos, *The Armenian History Attributed to Sebeos*, vol. 1, pp. 50–3.

187 Gyselen, 'La reconquête de l'est iranien par l'empire sassanide au Vie s. d'après les sources «iraniennes»', pp. 164–5; Rika Gyselen, 'Realia for Sasanian History: Mint Networks', in Anna Krasnowolska and Renata Rusek-Kowalska (eds.), *Studies on the Iranian World I: Before Islam* (Krakow, 2015), pp. 220–1.

188 On Smbat IV Bagratuni, Scott McDonough, 'The "Warrior of the Lords": Smbat Bagratuni at the Center and Periphery of Late Sasanian Iran', *Iranian Studies* 49 (2016), pp. 233–45.

189 Sebēos, *The Armenian History Attributed to Sebeos*, vol. 1, pp. 50–3.

190 In the final instance, it may be the case that troops were progressively siphoned away from the eastern frontier as they were needed to defend against Byzantine incursions that eventually threatened Ctesiphon under the Emperor Heraclius (r. 610–41).

191 James Howard Johnston, 'The Late Sasanian Army', in Teresa Bernheimer and Adam Silverstein (eds.), *Late Antiquity: Eastern Perspectives* (Exeter, 2012), p. 123.

Chapter 3

1 As will be discussed in more detail later, as historical literature developed in the Islamicate world, older texts were subsumed by newer histories. Therefore, while Madā'inī's *Futūḥ Khurāsān* has been lost to us with no known copies surviving, large portions of it have been preserved in the work of Ṭabarī and other later historians such as Balādhūrī in his *Conquests of the Lands* (*Futūḥ al-buldān*). On this process, see Chase Robinson, *Islamic Historiography* (Cambridge, 2003), pp. 34–5.

2 Ṭabarī, vol. 1, p. 2898; *The History of al-Ṭabarī*, vol. 15, pp. 102–3.

3 Ṭabarī, vol. 1, pp. 2898–9; *The History of al-Ṭabarī*, vol. 15, pp. 103–4. The Banū Tamīm, of which Aḥnaf was a member and eventually the leader, were well-known for their employment of *asāwira* with members of the Sasanian cavalry joining the Banū Tamīm as clients as early as 638. Khalil 'Athamina, 'Non-Arab Regiments and Private Militias during the Umayyād Period', *Arabica* 45 (1998), pp. 348–55.

4 Tarif Khalidi, *Arabic Historical Thought in the Classical Period* (Cambridge, 1994), pp. 65–8.

5 Albrecht Noth, *The Early Arabic Historical Tradition: A Source-Critical Study*, Michael Bonner (trans.) (Princeton, NJ, 1994), pp. 48–9. For an example of the long-term

influence of conquest narratives on the administration of conquered territories, turn to Nīsābūrī's (d. 1014) *History of Nīshāpūr*. In one account, the people of Nīshāpūr turned to conquest narratives to contest the *kharāj* or land tax a deputy of the Ṭāhirid governor ʿAbdallāh b. Ṭāhir was trying to collect from the people of the city. The conquest account they cited was considered sound and therefore the taxes were lifted nearly two centuries after the initial conquest. Muḥammad b. ʿAbdullāh Ḥākim al-Nīsābūrī, *The Histories of Nishapur*, Richard Frye (ed.) (Cambridge, MA, 1965), folio 61–2; Muḥammad b. ʿAbdullāh Ḥākim al-Nīsābūrī, *Ta'rīkh-i Nīshābūr*, Muḥammad Riẓā Shafīʿī Kadkanī (ed.) (Tehran, 1996), pp. 206–7.

6 Balādhūrī, p. 406; *Origins*, vol. 2, pp. 164–5. This is the account that also appears in Ibn al-Athīr, vol. 3, p. 63.

7 Zakeri, *Sāsānid Soldiers in Early Muslim Society*, pp. 108–9. Any such numbers reported by medieval chroniclers should be treated with suspicion. What matters most here is the comparison between similar numbers recorded in the same text.

8 I am employing the hyphenated Arab–Muslim designation for the conquests in recognition that neither truly captures the nature of the conquests on its own, especially not, as we shall see, in places like Khurāsān, Ṭukhāristān and Transoxiana where the lines of cooperation and conflict rarely followed ethnic/linguistic or sectarian lines. For a thorough breakdown of the problems inherent in the terminology, Fred McGraw Donner, 'Book Review: Robert Hoyland, *In God's Path: The Arab Conquests and the Creation of an Islamic Empire*', *al-ʿUṣūr al-Wusṭā* 23 (2015), pp. 136–40.

9 For studies of the overall Arab–Muslim conquests, Fred McGraw Donner, *The Early Islamic Conquests* (Princeton, NJ, 1981); Hugh Kennedy, *The Great Arab Conquests: How the Spread of Islam Changed the World We Live In* (Philadelphia, PA, 2007); Robert G. Hoyland, *In God's Path: The Arab Conquests and the Creation of an Islamic Empire* (Oxford, 2014). For the history of the conquest of the Sasanian Empire, see the controversial account of Pourshariati, *Decline and Fall of the Sasanian Empire*, pp. 161–285. The most complete studies of the Arab–Muslim conquests of Central Asia remains Bartold, *Turkestan Down to the Mongol Invasion*; Gibb, *The Arab Conquests in Central Asia.*

10 The reign of the Umayyad Caliphate is divided into two periods, the Sufyānid during which the descendants of Abū Sufyān b. Ḥarb (560–650) held the caliphate and the Marwānid when Marwān b. al-Ḥakim (r. 684–5) and his descendants ruled.

11 The phrase 'capture–rebellion–recapture' originates with Donald Hill's discussion of the conquest of Fārs, but the sentiment is seen throughout the scholarship on the conquest of Greater Khurāsān. Donald R. Hill, *The Termination of Hostilities in the Early Arab Conquests, A.D. 634-656* (London, 1971), p. 135. As highlighted by Mark Luce, 'Frontier as Process',p. 114.

12 For overviews of Khusrow's reforms, Zeev Rubin, 'Ḳosrow I ii. Reforms', *EIr*; Zeev Rubin, 'The Reforms of Khusro Anushirwān', in Averil Cameron (ed.), *The Byzantine and Early Islamic Near East III. States, Resources, and Armies* (Princeton, NJ, 1995), pp. 225–97.

13 Pourshariati, *Decline and Fall of the Sasanian Empire*, pp. 5–6.

14 Bartold, *Turkestan Down to the Mongol Invasion*, pp. 180–2.

15 Ibn Khurradādhbih, *Kitāb al-masālik wa'l-mamālik*, pp. 39–41.

16 Gibb, *The Arab Conquests in Central Asia*, pp. 10–11.

17 Balādhūrī, p. 406; *Origins*, vol. 2, p. 164; Ṭabarī, vol. 1, p. 2900; *The History of al-Ṭabarī*, vol. 15, p. 104. Later geographers say the fort was named in honour of Aḥnaf's ghazi activities in Ṭukhāristān. Yāqūt, *Muʿjam al-buldān*, vol. 7, p. 55.

18 Again, all such reports of numbers should be taken with a grain of salt. Khalīfa b. Khayyāṭ, *Ta'rīkh*, Akram Ḍiyā' ʿUmarī (ed.) (Damascus, 1977), p. 165; Balādhūrī, pp. 406–7; *Origins*, vol. 2, pp. 165–6; Ṭabarī, vol. 1, pp. 2900–2; *The History of al-Ṭabarī*, vol. 15, pp. 104–6; Ibn al-Athīr,vol. 3, pp. 63–4.

19 Ṭabarī, vol. 1, pp. 2901–2; *The History of al-Ṭabarī*, vol. 15, p. 105; Balʿamī, vol. 3, p. 572.

20 While the Abbasids grew from the imperial legacies of the Rāshidūn and Umayyad Caliphates which preceded them, it was the Sasanian legacy that permeated Abbasid imperial identity. Gaston Wiet, for example, referred to the Abbasids as 'neo-Sasanians' while Dimitri Gutas saw the Abbasid translation movement as a conscious effort to emulate the Sasanians. Gaston Wiet, 'L'Empire néo-byzantin des omeyyades et l'empire néo-sassanide des Abbasides', *Cahiers d'histoire mondiale* 9 (1953), pp. 63–71; Dimitri Gutas, *Greek Thought, Arabic Culture: The Greco-Arabic Translation Movement in Baghdad and Early ʿAbbāsid Society (2nd-4th/8th-10th Centuries)* (London, 1998).

21 See Tarif Khalidi's analysis of Ibn ʿAbd al-Ḥakam's *Futūḥ Misr*. Khalidi, *Arabic Historical Thought in the Classical Period*, pp. 65–7.

22 Yaʿqūbī, *Kitāb al-buldān*, p. 279.

23 Noth, *The Early Arabic Historical Tradition*, pp. 31–3.

24 Ibid., pp. 40–8.

25 For an overview of the criticisms of Sayf and some words of rehabilitation, Ella Landau-Tasseron, 'Sayf Ibn ʿUmar in Medieval and Modern Scholarship', *Der Islam* 67 (1990), pp. 1–26.

26 Ṭabarī, vol. 1, pp. 2682–93; Ṭabarī, *The History of Ṭabarī*, vol. 15, pp. 53–63.

27 Balʿamī, vol. 3, pp. 503–4; Ibn al-Athīr, vol. 3, pp. 19–21.

28 Noth, *The Early Arabic Historical Tradition*, pp. 214–15.

29 Abū Bakr ʿAbdallāh b. ʿUmar Wāʿiẓ Balkhī, *Faḍā'īl-i Balkh*, ʿAbd al-Ḥayy Ḥabībī (ed.) (Tehran, 1971), p. 30.

30 Boaz Shoshan, *The Arabic Historical Tradition and the Early Islamic Conquests: Folklore, Tribal Lore, Holy War* (Abingdon, 2015), p. 32.

31 For the organization of the army in general during the conquests and early Umayyad periods, Hugh Kennedy, *The Armies of the Caliphs: Military and Society in the Early Islamic State* (Abingdon, 2001), pp. 2–12, 18–23. For issues specific to Khurāsān, Donner, *The Early Islamic Conquests*, pp. 221–45.

32 On 'adventure capitalism', H.H. Gerth and C. Wright Mills, 'Introduction: The Man and His Work', in *From Max Weber: Essays in Sociology* (Oxford, 1946), pp. 66–7; Frank Parkin, *Max Weber*, Revised (London, 2002), p. 41.

33 Eger, *The Islamic-Byzantine Frontier*, pp. 232–41.

34 Balādhūrī, p. 405; *Origins*, vol. 2, p. 106; Yaʿqūbī, *Tārīkh*, vol. 2, p. 167; Gardīzī, *Ta'rīkh-i Gardīzī*, pp. 229–30.

35 John Walker, *A Catalogue of the Arab-Sassanian Coins*, Reprint (Oxford, 1967), p. 3.

36 Ibid., p. 5.

37 Dīnawarī, p. 163; Ṭabarī, vol. 1, pp. 3349–50; *The History of al-Ṭabarī*, vol. 17, p. 99; Balʿamī, vol. 3, p. 670.

38 This account is also of interest for its list of Sasanian titles still employed by local authorities in Khurāsān including military titles. Balādhūrī, p. 408; *Origins*, vol. 2, p. 169; Yaʿqūbī, *Tārīkh*, vol. 2, p. 184; Yaʿqūbī, *Kitāb al-buldān*, p. 296; Ṭabarī, vol. 1, p. 3249; *The History of al-Ṭabarī*, vol. 16, pp. 190–1; Balʿamī, vol. 3, p. 670. Gardīzī has ʿAlī write a letter for Burāz b. Māhawayh the *dihqān* of Marw. Gardīzī, *Ta'rīkh-i Gardīzī*, pp. 232–3.

39 Dīnawarī, pp. 163–4; Naṣr b. Muzāḥim Minqarī, *Waq'at Ṣiffīn*, 'Abd al-Salām Muḥammad Hārūn (ed.) (Qum, 1962), p. 12.
40 O. G. Bol'shakov, *Istorija Xalifata, III* (Moscow, 1998), p. 45. Cited by Frantz Grenet and Étienne de la Vaissière, 'The Last Days of Panjikent', *Silk Road Art and Archaeology* 8 (2002), p. 185, n. 4.
41 For the early years, Marw is the only mint with 'a continuous series of authentically dated early coins'. Stephen Album and Tony Goodwin, *Sylloge of Islamic Coins in the Ashmolean, I: The Pre-Reform Coinage of the Early Islamic Period* (Oxford, 2002), pp. 7, 15.
42 Besides the work of Asa Eger cited above, Chase Robinson, *Empire and Elites after the Muslim Conquest: The Transformation of Northern Mesopotamia* (Cambridge, 2000), pp. 39–40; Arietta Papaconstantinou, 'Between Umma and Dhimma. The Christians of the Middle East under the Umayyads', *Annales Islamologiques* 42 (2008), p. 141; Alison Vacca, *Non-Muslim Provinces under Early Islam: Islamic Rule and Iranian Legitimacy in Armenia and Caucasian Albania* (Cambridge, 2017), p. 1, n. 1.
43 Robinson, *Islamic Historiography*, pp. 34–5.
44 Richard Frye, 'Ṭarxūn-Türxūn and Central Asian History', *Harvard Journal of Asiatic Studies* 14 (1951), p. 114; Chase Robinson, 'The Conquest of Khūzistān: A Historiographical Reassessment', *Bulletin of the School of Oriental and African Studies* 67 (2004), pp. 14–39; Étienne de la Vaissière, 'Historiens arabes et manuscrits d'Asie centrale: quelques recoupements', *Revue des mondes musulmans et de la Méditerranée* 129 (2011), http://remmm.revues.org/7112.
45 Rubin, 'Ḵosrow I ii. Reforms'. For sigillographic evidence for the four *spāhbeds*, Rika Gyselen, *The Four Generals of the Sasanian Empire: Some Sigillographic Evidence* (Rome, 2001).
46 Howard Johnston, 'The Late Sasanian Army', p. 124.
47 Ṭabarī,vol. 1, p. 2470; *The History of al-Ṭabarī*, vol. 13, p. 50.
48 Michael G. Morony, *Iraq after the Muslim Conquest* (Princeton, NJ, 1984), pp. 128–9.
49 Richard Frye, 'The Political History of Iran under the Sasanians', *CHIr Vol. 3(1)* (Cambridge, 1983), p. 154.
50 Rubin, 'The Reforms of Khusro Anushirwān'; Pourshariati, *Decline and Fall of the Sasanian Empire*; Jackson Bonner, *al-Dīnawarī's* Kitāb al-aḫbār al-ṭiwāl.
51 Frye, 'The Political History of Iran under the Sasanians', p. 154; Christensen, *Decline of Iranshahr*, pp. 146, 296.
52 Daryaee, 'Wahrām Čōbīn the Rebel General and the Militarization of the Sasanian Empire', pp. 193–202.
53 Rubin, 'The Reforms of Khusro Anushirwān', p. 285; Michael Richard Jackson Bonner, *Three Neglected Sources of Sasanian History in the Reign of Khusraw Anushirvan* (Leuven, 2011), pp. 85–8.
54 See the many references to *dahāqīn* as the agents of surrender and the administrators of conquered lands in Iraq in Morony, *Iraq after the Muslim Conquest*, especially chapter three 'Administrative Geography'.
55 Ṭabarī,vol. 1, pp. 2876, 2879; *The History of al-Ṭabarī*, vol. 15, pp. 83, 85; Ibn al-Athīr, vol. 3, p. 61.
56 Khalīfa b. Khayyāṭ, *Ta'rīkh*, p. 165; Balādhūrī, pp. 405–6; *Origins*, vol. 2, pp. 162–5; Ṭabarī, vol. 1, pp. 2888, 2897; *The History of al-Ṭabarī*, vol. 15, pp. 93, 102; Ibn al-Athīr vol. 3, p. 63.

57 Ibn al-Athīr calls all four *aṣḥāb marzbāns*. Balādhūrī, p. 404; *Origins*, vol. 2, p. 161; Ibn al-Athīr, vol. 3, p. 63.
58 Balādhūrī, p. 404; *Origins*, vol. 2, p. 162; Ṭabarī, vol. 1, p. 2886; *The History of al-Ṭabarī*, vol. 15, p. 91.
59 Murgotten translated *ʿaẓīm* as mayor. Balādhūrī, p. 404; *Origins*, vol. 2, p. 162.
60 Balādhūrī, p. 405; *Origins*, vol. 2, p. 163.
61 Ibn Khurradādhbih, *Kitāb al-masālik wa'l-mamālik*, pp. 39–40.
62 Zakeri, *Sāsānid Soldiers in Early Muslim Society*, pp. 109–10.
63 Philippe Gignoux, 'L'organisation administrative sasanide: Le cas du marzbān', *Jerusalem Studies in Arabic and Islam* 4 (1984), p. 26.
64 Pourshariati, *Decline and Fall of the Sasanian Empire*, pp. 5–6.
65 For a complete analysis of Farrukhzād's mutiny, Ibid., pp. 260–5.
66 Such a collapse is reminiscent to the fall of Roman North Africa to the Vandals following the defeat of the professional, imperial army in the early fifth century. Goffart, *Barbarian Tides*, pp. 28–9.
67 Balādhūrī, p. 405; *Origins*, vol. 2, pp. 162–3; Ṭabarī, vol. 1, p. 2886; *The History of al-Ṭabarī*, vol. 15, p. 91.
68 Sims-Williams, 'The Sasanians in the East', p. 93.
69 While Abarshahr is an older name for Nīshāpūr, in any context where both names are employed, it is likely that Abarshahr refers to the region while Nīshāpūr means the city.
70 M.A. Shaban, *The ʿAbbāsid Revolution* (Cambridge, 1970), p. 5.
71 Pourshariati, *Decline and Fall of the Sasanian Empire*, pp. 271–6.
72 Ibid., pp. 257–78. Ispahdudhān also derived from a military title, *spāhbed* or *ispahbud*.
73 Firdawsī, *Shāhnāma*, vol. 9, p. 334; Firdawsī, *The Shāhnāma of Firdausī*, vol. 9, p. 87.
74 The largest number is given by Ṭabarī. Ṭabarī, vol. 1, pp. 1045–67; *The History of Ṭabarī*, vol. 5, pp. 381–409.
75 For a chart of alternative dates for the Arab conquests into Iraq, Pourshariati, *Decline and Fall of the Sasanian Empire*, pp. 468–9.
76 Pourshariati, 'Iranian Tradition in Ṭūs and the Arab Presence in Khurāsān' (PhD, Columbia University, 1995), pp. 153–61.
77 Khalīfa b. Khayyāṭ, *Ta'rīkh*, p. 165; Balādhūrī, pp. 406–7; *Origins*, vol. 2, pp. 165–6; Ṭabarī, vol. 1, pp. 2900–2; *The History of al-Ṭabarī*, vol. 15, pp. 104–6; Ibn al-Athīr, vol. 3, pp. 63–4.
78 Noth, *The Early Arabic Historical Tradition*, pp. 142–3.
79 Balādhūrī, p. 408; *Origins*, vol. 2, p. 167; Ṭabarī, vol. 1, p. 2903; *The History of al-Ṭabarī*, vol. 15, p. 106; Ibn al-Athīr, vol. 3, p. 64. The martyrs at Gūzgān are commemorated by poems from either Ibn Ghurayza or Ibn Kuthayyir al-Nahshalī.
80 Khalīfa b. Khayyāṭ, *Ta'rīkh*, p. 165; Balādhūrī, p. 408; *Origins*, vol. 2, p. 167; Ṭabarī, vol. 1, p. 2903; *The History of al-Ṭabarī*, vol. 15, p. 106; Balʿamī, vol. 3, p. 573; Ibn al-Athīr, vol. 3, p. 64.
81 In this account, Asīd is uncertain whether or not it was permissible for him to accept the gifts. He asked Aḥnaf who was likewise uncertain, so he asked Ibn ʿĀmir who declared them licit. The story ends with Aḥnaf performing an act of modest piety saying he has no need for the gifts himself which then allowed for another to jump up and take them for himself. Ṭabarī,vol. 1, pp. 2903–4; *The History of al-Ṭabarī*, vol. 15, pp. 106–7; Balʿamī, vol. 3, pp. 573–4; Ibn al-Athīr, vol. 3, p. 64.

82 For a detailed description of the Naw Bahār complex, Arezou Azad, *Sacred Landscape in Medieval Afghanistan: Revisiting the Faḍā'il-I Balkh* (Oxford, 2013), pp. 77–86.
83 Ibn al-Faqīh, *Mukhtaṣar kitāb al-buldān*, pp. 323–4; Yāqūt, *Mu'jam al-buldān*, vol. 8, p. 405. Kevin van Bladel has compiled the different versions of this report and translated the text. Kevin van Bladel, 'The Bactrian Background of the Barmakids', in Anna Akasoy, Charles Burnett, and Ronit Yoeli-Tlalim (eds.), *Islam and Tibet – Interactions along the Musk Routes* (Surrey, 2011), pp. 62–6.
84 The Barmakids' prominent role in the Abbasid Revolution and empire has been interpreted as a sign of their broader regional authority, their ability to turn local sentiment in favour of the Abbasids. This has then been further interpreted that the Naw Bahār acted as a kind of religio-political centre that asserted authority over Buddhist Central Asia.
85 The Arabic literary sources often generalize all non-sedentary populations along the frontier as Turks. The primary proponent of a Turkish identity for the Nīzak Ṭarkhān is Emel Esin, 'Tarkhan Nīzak or Tarkhan Tirek? An Enquiry Concerning the Prince of Bādhghīs Who in A.H. 91/A.D. 709-710 Opposed the 'Omayyad Conquest of Central Asia', *Journal of the American Oriental Society* 97 (1977), pp. 323–32. For criticisms of Esin's conclusions, Frantz Grenet, 'Nēzak', *EIr*. On the title Ṭarkhān, Peter B. Golden, 'Ṭarkhān', *EI*[2].
86 On the early emergence of the Nīzak Shāhs, Vondrovec, *Coinage of the Iranian Huns and Their Successors from Bactria to Gandhara*, p. 453; Rezakhani, *ReOrienting the Sasanians*, p. 160.
87 On the Nīzak Shāhs of Kāpiśā, Michael Alram, 'Alchon und Nēzak. Zur Geschichte der iranischen Hunen in Mittleasien', pp. 517–54; Shoshin Kuwayama, 'Historical Notes on Kāpiśī Kābul in the Sixth-Eighth Centuries', *Zinbun* 34 (1999), pp. 25–77; Shoshin Kuwayama, 'The Hephthalites in Tokharistan and Gandhara', in *Across the Hindukush of the First Millenium: A Collection of Papers* (Kyoto, 2002), pp. 107–39; Grenet, 'Nēzak'. For a detailed study of the coins of the Nīzak Shāhs, Klaus Vondrovec, 'Coinage of the Nezak', in Michael Alram, Deborah E. Klimburg-Salter, Minoru Inaba, and Matthias Pfisterer (eds.), *Coins, Art and Chronology II: The First Millennium C.E. in the Indo-Iranian Borderlands* (Wien, 2010), pp. 169–90.
88 Kuwayama, 'The Hephthalites in Tokharistan and Gandhara', pp. 130–5.
89 Some have argued for a Pahlavi origin for the term, from *abrāz* meaning high or elevated. C.J. Brunner, 'Abrāz', *EIr*. Following the numismatics, *barāz* is attested on Hephthalite coins and is given by Ṭabarī as the name of the last Hephthalite king before their defeat at the hands of the Turks. Ghirshman, *Les Chionites-Hephtalites*, pp. 22–3; *The History of al-Ṭabarī*, vol. 5, p. 152, n. 393; M.A. Shaban, *The 'Abbāsid Revolution*, p. 11.
90 It should be noted here that Ibn Khurradādhbih lists Nīzak as the name of one of the minor Turkish kings. Ibn Khurradādhbih, *Kitāb al-masālik wa'l-mamālik*, pp. 39–41.
91 Dīnawarī, p. 148; Balādhūrī, pp. 315–16; *Origins*, vol. 2, pp. 491–2; Ṭabarī, vol. 1, pp. 2872–3, 2877–9; *The History of al-Ṭabarī*, vol. 15, pp. 78–80, 83–5; Firdawsī, *Shāhnāma*, vol. 9, p. 349; Firdawsī, *The Shāhnāma of Firdausī*, vol. 9, p. 96; Tha'ālibī,pp. 744–8; Ibn al-Athīr, vol. 3, pp. 60, 61.
92 This argument is put forward by Shaban, *The 'Abbāsid Revolution*, pp. 11, 19. References to Māhawyah's son Barāz are found in Ṭabarī, vol. 2, pp. 2876–9, 2881–2, 2888; *The History of al-Ṭabarī*, vol. 15, pp. 83–5, 88, 93.

93 The place of Dīnawarī's account vis-à-vis other accounts of Yazdgird's death can be tricky. For example, not only does Dīnawarī insist that it was the Khāqān, king of the Turks who Māhawyah called upon but that the Turks arrived at Marw from the north and crossed the River Oxus at Āmul. These details are not confirmed by and stand in contrast to other accounts. Dīnawarī, p. 148.
94 Bal'amī, vol. 3, p. 504.
95 In this account, the Nīzak had spent one month with Yazdgird in Marw before leaving. Balādhurī, pp. 315–16; *Origins*, vol. 1, p. 491.
96 Ṭabarī, vol. 1, p. 2872; *The History of al-Ṭabarī*, vol. 15, p. 78.
97 Firdawsī, *Shāhnāma*, vol. 9, pp. 373 ff.; Firdawsī, *The Shāhnāma of Firdausī*, vol. 9, pp. 115 ff.
98 Khalīfa b. Khayyāṭ, *Ta'rīkh*, pp. 164–5; Balādhurī, p. 403; *Origins*, vol. 2, p. 160; Ṭabarī, vol. 1, pp. 2885, 2904; *The History of al-Ṭabarī*, vol. 15, pp. 91, 107; Ibn al-Athīr, vol. 3, pp. 62–3.
99 Ghirshman, *Les Chionites-Hephtalites*, p. 98.
100 Balādhurī, p. 405; *Origins*, vol. 2, p. 163; Ibn al-Athīr, vol. 3, p. 63.
101 Ṭabarī, vol. 1, p. 2905; *The History of al-Ṭabarī*, vol. 15, p. 108.
102 On the Qārinid–Hephthalite alliance, see the previous chapter as well as Jackson Bonner, *al-Dīnawarī's* Kitāb al-aḫbār al-ṭiwāl, pp. 83–4.
103 Khalīfa b. Khayyāṭ, *Ta'rīkh*, pp. 167, 179; Ṭabarī, vol. 1, pp. 2905–6; *The History of al-Ṭabarī*, vol. 15, pp. 108–10; Ibn al-Athīr, vol. 3, p. 68. This is most likely the event Balādhurī is referencing when he writes that the Turks gathered together but Ibn Khāzim defeated them. Balādhurī, p. 408; *Origins*, vol. 2, p. 168. In a different account, Ṭabarī has Ibn Khāzim again usurp the governorship a decade later in 663–4 but still in the context of an uprising from Ṭukhāristān. Ṭabarī, vol. 2, pp. 65–6; *The History of al-Ṭabarī*, vol. 18, pp. 68–70. An earlier account on the authority of Sayf b. 'Umar sets this usurpation to the death of 'Uthmān when Ibn Khāzim tricked his cousin, then governor of Khurāsān Qays b. al-Haytham, to return west. Ṭabarī, vol. 1, pp. 2832–3; *The History of al-Ṭabarī*, vol. 15, p. 37. These accounts primarily emphasize Ibn Khāzim's ambition and duplicitous character, a theme that will continue until his death. Bal'amī gives a rather different account in which Qārin is the *marzbān* of Qumis and Gorgān, northwest of Khurāsān, from where he leads an army against Nīshāpūr. Many of the details are the same as Ṭabarī's account of a revolt near Herat, including Ibn Khāzim leading his troops on a nighttime raid during which they dip their spears in oil and light them on fire that ends in the defeat of Qārin. Bal'amī, vol. 3, pp. 574–5.
104 Ṭabarī, vol. 2, pp. 1129–31; *The History of al-Ṭabarī*, vol. 23, pp. 74–6; Bal'amī, vol. 4, p. 148; Ibn al-Athīr, vol. 4, p. 249.
105 Ṭabarī, vol. 2, p. 1144; Ṭabarī, *The History of al-Ṭabarī*, vol. 23, pp. 88–9; Bal'amī, vol. 4, pp. 150–1; Ibn al-Athīr, vol. 4, p. 252.
106 There are reports of earlier campaigns across the Oxus, but these seem farfetched. 'Umayr b. 'Uthmān b. Sa'd is reported to have led a campaign as far as Ferghana in 649–50, securing tribute before returning to Khurāsān. Ṭabarī, vol. 1, pp. 2828–9; *The History of al-Ṭabarī*, vol. 15, p. 34. Envoys reached the Tang court from Samarqand concerned about Arab advances around this same time, so the fear was real even if it is hard to believe that organized campaigns were occurring. Hans Bielenstein, *Diplomacy and Trade in the Chinese World, 589-1276* (Leiden, 2005), p. 341. Chinese sources also indicate a raid into Sogdiana at a place called Mi or Māymargh as early as 654 that may connect to a raid mentioned by Balādhurī.

Chavannes, *Documents sur les Tou-Kiue (Turcs) occidentaux*, p. 144; Balādhūrī, p. 408; *Origins*, vol. 2, p. 167; De la Vaissière, *Sogdian Traders*, p. 265. This region may correspond with the area southeast of Samarqand, centred on Panjikant. Grenet and de la Vaissière, 'The Last Days of Panjikent', pp. 165–6.

107 Yaʿqūbī, *Tārīkh*, vol. 2, p. 222; Balādhūrī, p. 410; *Origins*, vol. 2, pp. 170–1; Ṭabarī, vol. 2, pp. 81, 84–5, 109–11; *The History of al-Ṭabarī*, vol. 18, pp. 86–7, 92, 119–21; Ibn al-Athīr, vol. 3, pp. 230–1, 232

108 Balādhūrī, p. 410; *Origins*, vol. 2, p. 171; Ṭabarī, vol. 2, pp. 81, 156; *The History of al-Ṭabarī*, vol. 18, pp. 87, 163; Gardīzī, *Taʾrīkh-i Gardīzī*, p. 235; Ibn al-Athīr, vol. 3, p. 249.

109 Julius Wellhausen, *The Arab Kingdom and Its Fall*, Margaret Graham Weir (trans.) (Calcutta, 1927), p. 427, n. 3. Saleh Said Agha has summarized the competing theories while proposing a number between 115,000 and 175,000 based on statistical modelling. Saleh Said Agha, 'The Arab Population in Ḫurāsān during the Umayyad Period: Some Demographic Computations', *Arabica* 46 (1999), p. 217.

110 Khalīfa b. Khayyāṭ, *Taʾrīkh*, p. 211; Khalīfa b. Khayyāṭ, *Khalifa Ibn Khayyat's History on the Umayyad Dynasty (660-750)*, Carl Wurtzel (trans.) (Liverpool, 2015), pp. 64–5; Ṭabarī, vol. 2, p. 156; *The History of al-Ṭabarī*, vol. 18, p. 163. According to Shaykh al-Islām al-Waʿīẓ al-Balkhī Arab control did not return until the governorship of Saʿīd b. ʿUthmān. Balkhī, *Faḍāʾīl-i Balkh*, p. 30.

111 Saleh Said Agha, *The Revolution Which Toppled the Umayyads: Neither Arab nor ʿAbbāsid* (Leiden, 2003), p. 178.

112 Walker, *A Catalogue of the Arab-Sassanian Coins*, pp. 36, 54, 73.

113 Narshakhī, p. 12; *The History of Bukhara*, p. 9.

114 On the Bukhārkhudāh coins, Richard Frye, *Notes on the Early Coinage of Transoxiana* (New York, 1949), pp. 24–31.

115 Narshakhī, pp. 25–6; *The History of Bukhara*, pp. 18–19. Paykand is called the City of Merchants in both geographic sources and chronicles. Ibn Khurradādhbih, *Kitāb al-masālik waʾl-mamālik*, p. 25; Ibn al-Faqīh, *Mukhtaṣar kitāb al-buldān*, p. 325; Ṭabarī, vol. 2, p. 1186; *The History of al-Ṭabarī*, vol. 23, p. 135.

116 Narshakhī, p. 23; *The History of Bukhara*, pp. 16–17.

117 Pan Yihong, *Son of Heaven and Heavenly Qaghan: Sui-Tang China and Its Neighbours* (Bellingham, WA, 1997), pp. 195–6; Golden, *An Introduction to the History the Turkic Peoples*, p. 136.

118 Skaff, 'Western Turk Rule of Turkestan's Oases in the Sixth through Eighth Centuries', pp. 364–72; Sören Stark, 'Mercenaries and City Rulers: Early Turks in Pre-Muslim Mawarannahr', in Laura M. Popova, Charles W. Hartley, and Adam T. Smith (eds.), *Social Orders and Social Landscapes* (Newcastle, 2007), pp. 307–34.

119 Khalīfa b. Khayyāṭ, *Taʾrīkh*, pp. 222–3; Khalīfa b. Khayyāṭ, *Khalifa Ibn Khayyat's History on the Umayyad Dynasty (660-750)*, pp. 80–1; Balādhūrī, p. 410; *Origins*, vol. 2, p. 172; Yaʿqūbī, *Tārīkh*, vol. 2, p. 236; Ṭabarī, vol. 2, pp. 169–70; *The History of al-Ṭabarī*, vol. 18, pp. 178–9; Aḥmad Ibn Aʿtham, *al-Futūḥ*, Suhayl Zakkār (ed.) (Beirut, 1992), vol. 2, p. 35; Narshakhī, pp. 52–3; *The History of Bukhara*, pp. 37–8; Balʿamī, vol. 4, p. 19; Gardīzī, *Taʾrīkh-i Gardīzī*, p. 238; Ibn al-Athīr, vol. 3, p. 253.

120 Balādhūrī, p. 376; *Origins*, vol. 2, p. 111; Ibn al-Faqīh, *Mukhtaṣar kitāb al-buldān*, p. 191; Yāqūt, *Muʿjam al-buldān*, vol. 2, p. 283.

121 Ṭabarī, vol. 2, p. 394; *The History of al-Ṭabarī*, vol. 19, p. 187. According to Ibn Aʿtham, ʿUbaydallāh quit Khurāsān entirely after this and returned to Muʿawiya's court. Ibn Aʿtham, *al-Futūḥ*, vol. 2, p. 36.

122 Narshakhī, pp. 65–6; *The History of Bukhara*, p. 47.
123 Of course, our constantly improving understanding of the politics of the Türk Khāqānate may make us reconsider such dismissive terms as ‘plundering raid’. Gibb, *The Arab Conquests in Central Asia*, p. 23.
124 More to the point, Sa῾īd shamed Mu῾āwiya into appointing him, reminding the caliph of the role his father had played in advancing Mu῾āwiya’s career.
125 In his geography, Ya῾qūbī declares Sa῾īd the first to cross the Oxus. Ya῾qūbī, *Kitāb al-buldān*, pp. 297–8.
126 Ya῾qūbī, *Tārīkh*, vol. 2, p. 237; Balādhūrī, p. 411; *Origins*, vol. 2, p. 172; Gardīzī, *Ta’rīkh-i Gardīzī*, p. 239; Narshakhī, p. 53; *The History of Bukhara*, p. 38.
127 Balādhūrī, p. 411; *Origins*, vol. 2, pp. 172–3; Narshakhī, p. 53; *The History of Bukhara*, p. 38.
128 Narshakhī, p. 54; *The History of Bukhara*, pp. 38–9.
129 Balādhūrī, p. 411; *Origins*, vol. 2, p. 173.
130 Ya῾qūbī, *Tārīkh*, vol. 2, p. 237; Balādhūrī, pp. 412–3; *Origins*, vol. 2, p. 175; Ṭabarī, vol. 2, p. 179; *The History of al-Ṭabarī*, vol. 18, pp. 189–90; Ibn al-Athīr, vol. 3, p. 259. Ibn A῾tham gives a version of Sa῾īd’s campaign, but places it during Ziyād b. Abīhi’s governorship, including the enslavement of twenty sons of the ‘kings of Bukhara’ (*abnā’ mulūk Bukhārā*). Ibn A῾tham, *al-Futūḥ*, vol. 2, pp. 27–8. Narshakhī also writes that the prisoners Sa῾īd took to Medina were from Bukhara. He also says that an additional 30,000 slaves were taken from Samarqand. Narshakhī, pp. 56–8; *The History of Bukhara*, pp. 40–1. In Nasafī’s account, the slaves are the sons of the *dahāqīn* given by Khātūn as a security and after they killed Sa῾īd they were chased up a mountain where they died of thirst. ῾Umar b. Muḥammad Nasafī, *al-Qand fī dhikr ῾ulamā’ Samarqand*, Naẓar Muḥammad Fāryābī (ed.) (Riyad, 1991), p. 71.
131 Ya῾qūbī, *Tārīkh*, vol. 2, p. 252; Narshakhī, pp. 57–60; *The History of Bukhara*, pp. 41–3.
132 Balādhūrī, p. 413; *Origins*, vol. 2, p. 176; Ṭabarī, vol. 2, pp. 394–5; *The History of al-Ṭabarī*, vol. 19, pp. 187–8; Ibn al-Athīr, vol. 4, p. 51. The birth of al-Ṣughd is followed by stories of Umm Muḥammad borrowing jewellery (*ḥilyahā*) from the wife of the master of Samarqand, presumably to adorn her infant with, which she does not return.
133 Yazdgird sent a live ferret as a gift with this embassy. Chavannes, *Documents sur les Tou-Kiue (Turcs) occidentaux*, pp. 171–2, 256; Bielenstein, *Diplomacy and Trade in the Chinese World, 589-1276*, p. 353.
134 Ṭabarī, vol. 1, pp. 2683, 2876; *The History of al-Ṭabarī*, vol. 14, p. 54, vol. 15, p. 83; Bal῾amī, vol. 3, pp. 503–4; Ibn al-Athīr,vol. 3, pp. 19, 61.
135 Balādhūrī, p. 316; *Origins*, vol. 1, p. 493. There are two competing Chinese accounts of these events found in the *Old History of the Tang* and *New History of the Tang*. The *Old History of the Tang* make the Tang seem more proactive in the establishment of Pīrūz while the *New History of the Tang* gives a more active role to the Yabghu. More historians prefer the *New History*’s account. Matteo Compareti, ‘Chinese-Iranian Relations xv. The Last Sasanians in China’, *EIr*; Domenico Agostini and Sören Stark, ‘Zāwulistān, Kāwulistān and the Land Bosi – On the Question of a Sasanian Court-in-Exile in the Southern Hindukush’, *Studia Iranica* 45 (2016), p. 18.
136 On the Yabghu, Sören Stark, *Die Alttürkenzeit in Mittel- Und Zentralasien: Archäologische Und Historische Studien* (Wiesbaden, 2008), pp. 211–14.
137 Yihong, *Son of Heaven and Heavenly Qaghan*, p. 283; Matteo Compareti, ‘The Last Sasanians in China’, *Eurasian Studies* 2 (2003), p. 206; Compareti, ‘Chinese-Iranian Relations xv. The Last Sasanians in China’.

138 *Ta'rīkh-i Sīstān*, Ja'far Mudarris Ṣādiqī (ed.) (Tehran, 1994), p. 48; *The Tārikh-e Sīstan*, Milton Gold (trans.) (Rome, 1976), pp. 71–3.

139 Khalīfa b. Khayyāṭ, *Ta'rīkh*, p. 205; Balādhūrī, p. 396; *Origins*, vol. 2, p. 146; Ibn al-Athīr, vol. 3, p. 223. Interestingly, *Ta'rīkh-i Sīstān* does not include a reconquest narrative. Instead, the author simply states that Mu'āwiya's victory brought the question of the rightful caliph to a close and the conflict was over. *Ta'rīkh-i Sīstān*, pp. 48–9; *The Tārikh-e Sīstan*, p. 73.

140 Chavannes, *Documents sur les Tou-Kiue (Turcs) Occidentaux*, pp. 172–3, 256–8, 279; Bielenstein, *Diplomacy and Trade in the Chinese World, 589-1276*, p. 354.

141 Antonino Forte, 'On the So-Called Abraham from Persia: A Case of Mistaken Identity', in Paul Pelliot and Antonino Forte (eds.), *L'inscription nestorienne de Si-Ngan-Fou* (Kyoto and Paris, 1996), p. 404; Hassan Rezai Baghbidi, 'New Light on the Middle Persian-Chinese Bilingual Inscription from Xi'an', in Mauro Maggi and Paola Orsatti (eds.), *The Persian Language in History* (Wiesbaden, 2011), p. 105.

142 Chavannes, *Documents sur les Tou-Kiue (Turcs) Occidentaux*, p. 74.

143 Ibid., p. 258.

144 Compareti, 'Chinese-Iranian Relations xv. The Last Sasanians in China'.

145 For the conflicts between the Tang and Tibet, Yihong, *Son of Heaven and Heavenly Qaghan*, pp. 239–43; Christopher Beckwith, *The Tibetan Empire in Central Asia* (Princeton, NJ, 1987).

146 Chavannes, *Documents sur les Tou-Kiue (Turcs) Occidentaux*, pp. 74, 135–6, 172–3, 258; Bielenstein, *Diplomacy and Trade in the Chinese World, 589-1276*, pp. 354–5.

147 Agostini and Stark, 'Zāwulistān, Kāwulistān and the Land Bosi', p. 19.

148 Ibn al-Faqīh, *Mukhtaṣar kitāb al-buldān*, p. 209. Muqaddasī included an odd version of this story in which Shāhfirind (called Shāhīn in the text) was in possession of a basket when she was captured by Qutayba that contained a treatise by the Sasanian Shahanshah Qubād (r. 488–96, 498–531) on the best places to build cities in the Sasanian Empire. Muqaddasī, *Aḥsan al-taqāsīm fī ma'rafa al-aqālīm*, pp. 257–8; Muqaddasī, *The Best Division for Knowledge of the Regions*, pp. 233–4. The marriage of Sasanian princesses to both caliphs and Shi'ite Imams appears in several places as a literary trope meant to tie Islamic regimes to the Sasanian legacy.

149 Bielenstein, *Diplomacy and Trade in the Chinese World, 589-1276*, p. 355; Compareti, 'The Last Sasanians in China', p. 211. On the impact of the An Lushan Revolt on Iranians in China, Étienne de la Vaissière and Éric Trombert, 'Des Chinois et Des Hu: Migrations et intégration des Iraniens orientaux en milieu chinois durant le Haut Moyen Âge', *Annales. Histoire, Sciences Sociales* 59 (2004), pp. 961–3.

150 Dīnawarī, pp. 163–4. Minqarī (ca. 738–827) does not discuss a Sasanian princess in his history of the First Fitna, but does say that governors of Khusrow arrived in Nīshāpūr from Kabul. Minqarī, *Waq'at Ṣiffīn*, p. 12.

151 Narshakhī, pp. 44–5; *The History of Bukhara*, pp. 31–2.

152 Ṭabarī, vol. 1, pp. 1060–1; *The History of al-Ṭabarī*, vol. 5, p. 398; Pourshariati, *Decline and Fall of the Sasanian Empire*, pp. 274–8.

153 Aleksandr Naymark, 'Coins of Bukharan King Kunak/Khanuk', in Madhuvanti Ghose and Lilla Russel-Smith (eds.), *From Nisa to Niya: Studies in Silk Road Art and Archaeology* (London, 2004).

154 Agostini and Stark, 'Zāwulistān, Kāwulistān and the Land Bosi', pp. 30–2.

155 Ibn Khurradādhbih, *Kitāb al-masālik wa'l-mamālik*, p. 39.

156 For an overview of these conquests, David A. Graff, 'Strategy and Contingency in the Tang Defeat of the Eastern Turks, 629-630', in Nicola Di Cosmos (ed.), *Warfare in Inner Asian History (500-1800)* (Leiden, 2002), pp. 33–71; Yihong, *Son of Heaven and Heavenly Qaghan*, pp. 176–9.
157 Golden, *An Introduction to the History the Turkic Peoples*, pp. 135–6.
158 Yihong, *Son of Heaven and Heavenly Qaghan*, pp. 195–6; Golden, *An Introduction to the History the Turkic Peoples*, p. 136. It should be noted that the period from the rise to the fall of Ashina Ho-lu covers the first period of Arab incursions into Khurāsān and Ṭukhāristān and we may want to consider Arab successes in the context of a Western Türk Khāqānate at war with the Tang.
159 Yihong, *Son of Heaven and Heavenly Qaghan*, pp. 197–202; Tansen Sen, *Buddhism, Diplomacy, and Trade: The Realignment of Sino-Indian Relations, 600-1400* (Honolulu, HI, 2003), p. 29. For more information on individual *jimi fuzhou*, see the entries in Bielenstein, *Diplomacy and Trade in the Chinese World, 589-1276*, pp. 323–54. Bielenstein declares all of these vassal states imaginary but does give information about names and the dates they were founded.
160 Yihong, *Son of Heaven and Heavenly Qaghan*, p. 200.
161 Sen, *Buddhism, Diplomacy, and Trade*, p. 29.
162 Yihong, *Son of Heaven and Heavenly Qaghan*, p. 198.
163 The southern division was focused on Zābulistān or ancient Kāpiśā on the southern face of the Hindu Kush. Zābulistān, along with the Zunbīls and Kābul Shāhs, resisted Arab expansion and contested the frontiers of Sīstān until the late third/ninth century. For Zābulistān, the Zunbīl and Kābul Shāhs, André Wink, *Al-Hind: The Making of the Indo-Islamic World* (Leiden, 1990), vol. 1, pp. 112–28.
164 This division matches the situation in 630 when the Chinese Buddhist monk Xuanzang travelled through the region and remarked on a Turkish king who ruled all the territories south of the Gate of Iron from Qundūz. Hsüsan-tsang, *Si-Yu-Ki: Buddhist Records of the Western World*, pp. 287–8.
165 These embassies are summarized by Bielenstein, *Diplomacy and Trade in the Chinese World, 589-1276*.
166 Bielenstein, *Diplomacy and Trade in the Chinese World, 589-1276*, p. 336.
167 Ibid., p. 354; Agostini and Stark, 'Zāwulistān, Kāwulistān and the Land Bosi', p. 18.
168 Yihong, *Son of Heaven and Heavenly Qaghan*, p. 85.
169 Chavannes, *Documents sur les Tou-Kiue (Turcs) occidentaux*, p. 258; Compareti, 'Chinese-Iranian Relations xv. The Last Sasanians in China'.
170 Khalīfa b. Khayyāṭ, *Ta'rīkh*, p. 301; Khalīfa b. Khayyāṭ, *Khalifa Ibn Khayyat's History on the Umayyad Dynasty (660-750)*, p. 172; Ṭabarī, vol. 2, p. 1195; *The History of al-Ṭabarī*, vol. 23, pp. 143–4; Ibn Aʿtham, *al-Futūḥ*, vol. 3, p. 109; Narshakhī, pp. 63–5; *The History of Bukhara*, pp. 45–7; Balʿamī, vol. 4, pp. 162–3; Ibn al-Athīr, vol. 4, p. 265.
171 Chavannes, *Documents sur les Tou-Kiue (Turcs) Occidentaux*, p. 289.
172 Ibn al-Faqīh, *Mukhtaṣar kitāb al-buldān*, p. 323; Yāqūt, *Muʿjam al-buldān*, vol. 8, p. 405.
173 Zhōngguó had been used since the Shang Dynasty (r. ca. 1600 BCE–1046 BCE) in a number of different related manners including a name for the capital and royal domains, the centre of civilization, and the central states of the empire. Luke S.K. Kwong, 'What's in a Name: Zhongguo (or "Middle Kingdom") Reconsidered', *The Historical Journal* 58 (2015), pp. 781–804.

Chapter 4

1 Balādhūrī, p. 415; *Origins*, vol. 2, p. 179; Ya'qūbī, *Tārīkh*, vol. 2, p. 271; Ṭabarī, vol. 2, pp. 831–3; *The History of al-Ṭabarī*, vol. 21, pp. 209–10; Bal'amī, vol. 4, pp. 113–14; Ibn al-Athīr, vol. 4, pp. 175–6.
2 Ṭabarī, vol. 2, p. 1145; *The History of al-Ṭabarī*, vol. 23, p. 90.
3 Ṭabarī, vol. 2, p. 1146; *The History of al-Ṭabarī*, vol. 23, pp. 90–1; Ibn al-Athīr, vol. 4, p. 252.
4 Ṭabarī, vol. 2, pp. 1146–7; *The History of al-Ṭabarī*, vol. 23, p. 91; Ibn al-Athīr, vol. 4, pp. 252–3.
5 Ṭabarī, vol. 2, p. 1147; *The History of al-Ṭabarī*, vol. 23, pp. 91–2; Ibn al-Athīr, vol. 4, p. 253.
6 Ibn al-Athīr omits the *dihqān* but includes the rest of the narrative. Ṭabarī, vol. 2, pp. 114–8; *The History of al-Ṭabarī*, vol. 23, pp. 92–3; Ibn al-Athīr, vol. 4, p. 253.
7 For an older discussion of the Second Fitna (and the Battle of Marj Rāhiṭ (684) specifically) as the origins of the tribal strife, Wellhausen, *The Arab Kingdom and Its Fall*, pp. 180–2.
8 For an overview of the arguments for and against viewing these tribal confederacies as political parties, Patricia Crone, 'Were the Qays and Yemen of the Umayyad Period Political Parties?', *Der Islam* 71 (1994), pp. 1–57.
9 The Second Fitna involved multiple challenges to Umayyad authority from multiple opponents, including proto-Shi'ites supporting Ḥusayn b. 'Alī (626–80) who was defeated and killed at Karbalā' and then by the counter-caliph 'Abdallāh b. al-Zubayr (r. 680–92) who successfully seized control of half the empire. The most complete overview of the Second Fitna remains Gernot Rotter, *Die Umayyaden und der zweite Bürgerkrieg (680-692)* (Mainz, 1982).
10 Ṭabarī, vol. 2, pp. 488–9; *The History of al-Ṭabarī*, vol. 20, pp. 70–1.
11 Ṭabarī, vol. 2, pp. 583–4; *The History of al-Ṭabarī*, vol. 20, pp. 166–8.
12 Ṭabarī, vol. 2, p. 489; *The History of al-Ṭabarī*, vol. 20, pp. 71–2; Bal'amī, vol. 4, pp. 63–4; Ibn al-Athīr, vol. 4, p. 80.
13 According to Balādhūrī, the Bakr b. Wā'il were associated with Qūhistān from the conquests up to his own time, Balādhūrī, p. 403; *Origins*, vol. 2, p. 160. Similarly, Ḥākim al-Nīsābūrī mentions Ibn Khāzim's governorship following its initial conquest but also says that descendants of Ibn Khāzim were still living in Nīshāpūr in his own time, Ḥākim al-Nīsābūrī, *The Histories of Nishapur*, folio 6b, 60–1; Ḥākim al-Nīsābūrī, *Ta'rīkh-i Nīshābūr*, pp. 71, 203.
14 Balādhūrī, p. 414; *Origins*, vol. 2, pp. 177–8.
15 Balādhūrī, p. 414; *Origins*, vol. 2, pp. 177–8; Ṭabarī, vol. 2, pp. 490–3; *The History of al-Ṭabarī*, vol. 20, pp. 72–5; Bal'amī, vol. 4, pp. 64–5; Ibn al-Athīr, vol. 4, pp. 106–7.
16 Agha, 'The Arab Population in Ḫurāsān during the Umayyad Period: Some Demographic Computations', p. 216, n. 15.
17 Balādhūrī, p. 415; *Origins*, vol. 2, p. 179; Abū 'Alī Ḥusayn Sallāmī, *Akhbār wulāt Khurāsān*, Mohammad Ali Kazembeyki [ed.] (Tehran, 2011), p. 92; Ṭabarī, vol. 2, pp. 593–5; *The History of al-Ṭabarī*, vol. 20, pp. 177–8; Ibn al-Athīr, vol. 4, pp. 106–7.
18 See the forthcoming article from May Shaddel, ''Abd Allāh b. al-Zubayr, Yazīd b. Mu'āwiya, and the Beginnings of the Second Civil War: A Reappraisal'.
19 This chart is based on similar charts found in Walker, A Catalogue of the Arab-Sassanian Coins, p. l; Rotter, Die Umayyaden und der zweite Bürgerkrieg (680–692), p. 89. New information has been added based upon Album and Goodwin, Sylloge of Islamic Coins in the Ashmolean, I, p. 22–4.

20 The coin of Salm b. Ziyād struck in Marw and dated 68AH is peculiar, including two Arabic inscriptions, the typical bism Allāh and the unique for its date Allāh akbar. Album and Goodwin, Sylloge of Islamic Coins in the Ashmolean, I, p. 22.
21 Album and Goodwin, *Sylloge of Islamic Coins in the Ashmolean, I*, pp. 19–20.
22 Walker, *A Catalogue of the Arab-Sassanian Coins*, pp. 74, 78–80, 82–3 and ANS 1941.55.12, 1957.84.29, 1971.31.8, 1971.316.1285, 1975.238.8, 1990.41.2.
23 Walker, *A Catalogue of the Arab-Sassanian Coins*, pp. 90–1 and ANS 1917.215.3332, 1917.215.3333.
24 Ṭabarī, vol. 2, p. 488; *The History of al-Ṭabarī*, vol. 20, p. 70.
25 Ṭabarī does imply that Ibn Khāzim faced at least some challenges holding Marw. For example, after killing Ibn Khāzim's son Muḥammad at Herat, the Banū Tamīm are described as fleeing to Marw for safety. Ṭabarī, vol. 2, p. 595; *The History of al-Ṭabarī*, vol. 20, p. 178.
26 Walker, *A Catalogue of the Arab-Sassanian Coins*, pp. 87–8 and ANS 1954.119.70, 1975.238.7, 1984.196.5, 1993.40.4.
27 Balādhūrī, p. 415; *Origins*, vol. 2, p. 179; Ṭabarī, vol. 2, pp. 831–2; *The History of al-Ṭabarī*, vol. 21, p. 209; Ibn al-Athīr, vol. 4, pp. 175–6.
28 Walker, *A Catalogue of the Arab-Sassanian Coins*, pp. 76–7, 83; Album and Goodwin, *Sylloge of Islamic Coins in the Ashmolean, I*, p. 22 and ANS 1990.41.1.
29 Album and Goodwin, *Sylloge of Islamic Coins in the Ashmolean, I*, p. 22.
30 Walker, *A Catalogue of the Arab-Sassanian Coins*, p. 95.
31 Yaʿqūbī, *Tārīkh*, vol. 2, p. 252; Balādhūrī, p. 414; *Origins*, vol. 2, p. 178; Ṭabarī, vol. 2, p. 493; *The History of al-Ṭabarī*, vol. 20, p. 76. Ṭabarī tells us this raid occurred at Qaṣr Asfād which was east of Nīshāpūr while other sources simply say the raids came close to Nīshāpūr. See G.R. Hawting's comments in his translation of Ṭabarī. For Qaṣr Asfād, Guy Le Strange, *The Lands of the Eastern Caliphate* (Cambridge, 1905), p. 388; Rotter, *Die Umayyaden und der zweite Bürgerkrieg (680-692)*, p. 92.
32 On the Arab–Hephthalite coins, Walker, *A Catalogue of the Arab-Sassanian Coins*, pp. 76–7, 83; Göbl, *Dokumente zur Geschichte der iranischen Hunnen in Baktrien und Indien*, vol. 1, pp. 185–93; Album and Goodwin, *Sylloge of Islamic Coins in the Ashmolean, I*, pp. 40–1; Nicholas Sims-Williams, 'The Arab-Sasanian and Arab-Hephthalite Coinage: A View from the East', in Étienne de la Vaissière [ed.], *Islamisation de l'Asie centrale: processus locaux d'acculturation du VIIe au XIe siècle* (Paris, 2008), pp. 116–22.
33 Album and Goodwin, *Sylloge of Islamic Coins in the Ashmolean, I*, p. 24.
34 We do have a coin minted at Marw in Salm's name during this period, but it is an oddity and, at the very least represents a divergence from standard minting practices. Ibid., p. 22.
35 Album and Goodwin, *Sylloge of Islamic Coins in the Ashmolean, I*, p. 41.
36 Balādhūrī, p. 415; *Origins*, vol. 2, p. 179; Yaʿqūbī, *Tārīkh*, vol. 2, p. 271; Ṭabarī, vol. 2, pp. 831–3; *The History of al-Ṭabarī*, vol. 21, pp. 209–10; Balʿamī, vol. 4, pp. 113–14; Ibn al-Athīr, vol. 4, pp. 175–6.
37 Ṭabarī, vol. 2, p. 862; *The History of al-Ṭabarī*, vol. 22, p. 11. It is likely that the territories granted to the Bakr b. Wā'il – namely Marw al-Rūd and Herat – were the limits of Muslim authority in the 680s. The occasional coin minted at Balkh between 686 and 688 and accounts of the Bakr hiding in the desert outposts of Ṭālaqān are the only evidence for a presence in Ṭukhāristān during the fitna.
38 According to Ṭabarī, Ghudānī found himself in debtors' prison owing 20,000 dirhams. Ṭabarī, vol. 2, pp. 1022–3; *The History of al-Ṭabarī*, vol. 22, pp. 165–6; Ibn al-Athīr, vol. 4, p. 224. Balādhūrī says Bukayr raided in Ṭukhāristān and Transoxiana before revolting against Umayya while Yaʿqūbī only says that Bukayr revolted when Umayya

arrived; neither mention his indebtedness. Balādhūrī, pp. 416–7; *Origins*, vol. 2, p. 181; Ya'qūbī, *Tārīkh*, vol. 2, p. 271.

39 de la Vaissière, *Sogdian Traders*, pp. 273–5.

40 Mark Luce, 'Frontier as Process,' p. 225; Gardīzī, *Ta'rīkh-i Gardīzī*, p. 227.

41 For more details on Ibn al-Ash'ath and the Peacock Army, C. E. Bosworth, *Sīstān under the Arabs* (Rome, 1968), pp. 52–63. Khalīfa b. Khayyāṭ, *Ta'rīkh*, p. 284; Khalīfa b. Khayyāṭ, *Khalifa Ibn Khayyat's History on the Umayyad Dynasty (660-750)*, p. 149; Balādhūrī, p. 417; *Origins*, vol. 2, p. 182; Ṭabarī, vol. 2, pp. 1106–9; *The History of al-Ṭabarī*, vol. 23, pp. 53–6; Ibn al-Athīr, vol. 4, p. 243.

42 For Muhallab's campaign in Kish, Ṭabarī, vol. 2, pp. 1040–2, 1080–2; *The History of al-Ṭabarī*, vol. 22, pp. 188–90, vol. 23, pp. 29–31.

43 Ṭabarī, vol. 2, pp. 1106–9; *The History of al-Ṭabarī*, vol. 23, pp. 53–6; Bal'amī, vol. 4, pp. 143–4.

44 Shaban, *The 'Abbāsid Revolution*, p. 57.

45 When Muhallab quit his siege of Kish, he left Ḥurayth to collect the tribute with orders that he should not release any of the hostages until he returned to Balkh. Instead, Ḥurayth traded the hostages for the tribute before leaving Kish. Muhallab had Ḥurayth flogged causing the *mawlā* to lash out. Ṭabarī, vol. 2, pp. 1080–2; *The History of al-Ṭabarī*, vol. 23, pp. 29–31; Ibn al-Athīr, vol. 4, pp. 237–8.

46 Ṭabarī, vol. 2, p. 1027; *The History of al-Ṭabarī*, vol. 22, p. 170.

47 Balādhūrī, p. 418; *Origins*, vol. 2, pp. 183–4; Ṭabarī, vol. 2, pp. 1152–3; *The History of al-Ṭabarī*, vol. 23, 96–7; Ibn al-Athīr, vol. 4, pp. 254–5.

48 Gibb, *The Arab Conquests in Central Asia*, p. 26.

49 Balādhūrī, pp. 418–19; *Origins*, vol. 2, p. 184; Ṭabarī, vol. 2, pp.1152–3; *The History of al-Ṭabarī*, vol. 23, pp. 96–7; Ibn al-Athīr, vol. 4, p. 254.

50 Ṭabarī, vol. 2, p. 1024; *The History of al-Ṭabarī*, vol. 22, p. 167; Ibn al-Athīr, vol. 4, p. 224.

51 Recent work on the Seljuq frontier in Anatolia and the interaction between Seljuq, Armenian, Byzantine and Mongol authorities and the movement of elites between these polities may be a useful point of comparison. Sara Nur Yildiz, 'Reconceptualizing the Seljuk-Cilician Frontier: Armenians, Latins, and Turks in Conflict and Alliance during the Early Thirteenth Century', in Florin Curta [ed.], *Borders, Barriers, and Ethnogenesis: Frontier in Late Antiquity and the Middle Ages* (Turnhout, Belgium, 2005), pp. 91–120.

Chapter 5

1 Ṭabarī, vol. 2, p. 1229; *The History of al-Ṭabarī*, vol. 23, p. 176. On the documentary evidence for Ghūrak's coup, Richard Frye, 'Ṭarxūn-Türxūn and Central Asian History', pp. 121–5.

2 Ya'qūbī, *Tārīkh*, vol. 2, p. 287; Ṭabarī, vol. 2, pp. 1229–30; *The History of al-Ṭabarī*, vol. 23, pp. 176–7.

3 Ṭabarī, vol. 2, p. 1249; *The History of al-Ṭabarī*, vol. 23, p. 196.

4 Ṭabarī, vol. 2, p. 1205; *The History of al-Ṭabarī*, vol. 23, p. 153; Bal'amī, vol. 4, p. 167.

5 The details of the tribute vary from source to source with some saying 2,000 slaves were collected while others say as high as 100,000 slaves. The number 30,000 appears most often. Khalīfa b. Khayyāṭ, *Ta'rīkh*, p. 305; Khalīfa b. Khayyāṭ, *Khalifa Ibn Khayyat's History on the Umayyad Dynasty (660-750)*, pp. 177–8; Balādhūrī, p. 421; *Origins*, vol. 2, pp. 188–9; Ya'qūbī, *Tārīkh*, vol. 2, p. 287; Sallāmī, *Akhbār wulāt*

Khurāsān, pp. 106–8; Ṭabarī, vol. 2, pp. 1241–50; *The History of al-Ṭabarī*, vol. 23, pp. 189–98; Ibn Aʿtham, *al-Futūḥ*, vol. 3, pp. 122–9; Balʿamī, vol. 4, pp. 173, 177–82; Ibn al-Athīr, vol. 4, pp. 274–5, 283–5.

6 Balādhūrī, p. 421; *Origins*, vol. 2, p. 189.

7 Ṭabarī, vol. 2, p. 1246; *The History of al-Ṭabarī*, vol. 23, p. 194.

8 Ṭabarī, vol. 2, p. 1252; *The History of al-Ṭabarī*, vol. 23, p. 199. Sealing the hands and more often necks of conquered people was a sign of humiliation. Chase Robinson, 'Neck-Sealing in Early Islam', *Journal of the Economic and Social History of the Orient* 48 (2005), pp. 412–17.

9 Bartold, *Turkestan Down to the Mongol Invasion*, p. 95.

10 Balādhūrī, p. 422; *Origins*, vol. 2, p. 190.

11 In 711–12, the Khwārazmshāh's brother Khurrazādh usurped the throne and the king requested Qutayba's help in regaining it, in some accounts paying him 10,000 slaves along with gold and other goods. The Arabs defeated Khurrazādh and made a spectacle of killing 4,000 prisoners. In one account, Qutayba sat upon the throne of Khwarazm while 1,000 prisoners were executed to each side of him. After the Khwārazmshāh was restored, the people revolted and killed him. In response, Qutayba placed his brother ʿUbaydallāh in charge before the Arabs marched on towards Samarqand. Khalīfa b. Khayyāṭ, *Ta'rīkh*, p. 304; Khalīfa b. Khayyāṭ, *Khalifa Ibn Khayyat's History on the Umayyad Dynasty (660-750)*, p. 177; Balādhūrī, pp. 420–2; *Origins*, vol. 2, pp. 187–8; Yaʿqūbī, *Tārīkh*, vol. 2, p. 287; Sallāmī, *Akhbār wulāt Khurāsān*, p. 106; Ṭabarī, vol. 2, pp. 1236–41; *The History of al-Ṭabarī*, vol. 23, pp. 185–9; Ibn Aʿtham, *al-Futūḥ*, vol. 3, pp. 119–21; Balʿamī, vol. 4, pp. 175–7; Ibn al-Athīr, vol. 4, p. 283.

12 Ṭabarī, vol. 2, pp. 1250–1; *The History of al-Ṭabarī*, vol. 23, p. 198; Ibn al-Athīr, vol. 4, p. 285.

13 Blankinship, *The End of the Jihād State*, p. 29.

14 Salamah b. Muslim al-ʿAwtabī, *An Early Islamic Family from Oman: Al-ʿAwtabī's Account of the Muhallabids*, Martin Hinds (trans.) (Manchester, 1991), p. 28.

15 Ibn Aʿtham, *al-Futūḥ*, vol. 3, p. 93; al-ʿAwtabī, *An Early Islamic Family from Oman*, pp. 60–1.

16 For the Zunbīl, Wink, *Al-Hind*, vol. 1, pp. 112–28.

17 Ḥayyān's background is not clear except that he was a *mawlā* of Maṣqalah b. Hubayrah al-Shaybānī who had been governor of Ardashīrkhurrah (a district of Fārs) during the caliphate of ʿAlī. According to Ṭabarī, some say Ḥayyān was a Daylamite while others say he was Khurāsānī, but he was called the Nabatean because of his pronunciation of Arabic. He is said to have led a force of 7,000 *mawālī*. Balādhūrī, p. 337; *Origins*, vol. 2, p. 1180; Ṭabarī, vol. 2, p. 1291; *The History of al-Ṭabarī*, vol. 24, p. 14; Ibn Aʿtham, *al-Futūḥ*, vol. 3, p. 167.

18 Khalīfa b. Khayyāṭ, *Ta'rīkh*, p. 291; Khalīfa b. Khayyāṭ, *Khalifa Ibn Khayyat's History on the Umayyad Dynasty (660-750)*, p. 159; Balādhūrī, pp. 419–20; *Origins*, vol. 2, p. 186; Sallāmī, *Akhbār wulāt Khurāsān*, p. 104; Ṭabarī, vol. 2, p. 1180; *The History of al-Ṭabarī*, vol. 23, pp. 127–8; Ibn Aʿtham, *al-Futūḥ*, vol. 3, p. 104; Balʿamī, vol. 4, p. 153; Balkhī, *Faḍā'īl-i Balkh*, pp. 31–2; Ibn al-Athīr, vol. 4, p. 261. On the location of Akharūn and Shūmān, C. E. Bosworth, 'The Rulers of Chaghāniyān in Early Islamic Times', *Iran* 19 (1981), p. 1.

19 Sulaym's background is unknown but, in a later interaction, the Nīzak accuses the *mawlā* of abandoning him, presumably for Qutayba, which may imply that Sulaym had been an adviser to the Nīzak prior to Qutayba's arrival and may have been a

Hephthalite himself. Khalīfa b. Khayyāṭ, *Ta'rīkh*, p. 300; Khalīfa b. Khayyāṭ, *Khalifa Ibn Khayyat's History on the Umayyad Dynasty (660-750)*, p. 171; Balādhūrī, p. 420; *Origins*, vol. 2, p. 187; Ya'qūbī, *Tārīkh*, vol. 2, p. 286; Ṭabarī, vol. 2, pp. 1184–5; *The History of al-Ṭabarī*, vol. 23, p. 133; Ibn A'tham, *al-Futūḥ*, vol. 3, p. 102; Bal'amī, vol. 4, pp. 155–6; Balkhī, *Faḍā'īl-i Balkh*, p. 32; Ibn al-Athīr, vol. 4, p. 262.

20 Many have attempted to untangle the political situation in Bukhara in the late seventh and early eighth centuries. Both Khātūn, meaning 'lady' or 'wife of the lord' in Sogdian, and Ṭughshāda, from the Sogdian title shād also adopted by the Turks, are titles rather than proper names. Aleksandr Naymark has an overview of previous attempts to outline the political history of Bukhara. Aleksandr Naymark, 'Sogdiana, Its Christians and Byzantium: A Study of Artistic and Cultural Connections in Late Antiquity and Early Middle Ages' (PhD, Indiana University, 2001), pp. 257 ff. On the title shād, A. Bombaci, 'On the Ancient Turkish Title «Šaδ»', in *Gururajamañjarika: Studi in Onare Di Giuseppe Tucci* (Naples, 1974), pp. 168–93. Naymark has made a convincing argument based on numismatic evidence that Kh.n.k is the name of the Vardānkhudāh who was also the true ruler of Bukhara at the time of Qutayba's arrival. Aleksandr Naymark, 'Drachms of Bukhār Khudā Khunak', *Journal of Inner Asian Art and Archaeology* 5 (2010), pp. 7–32; Naymark, 'Sogdiana, Its Christians and Byzantium: A Study of Artistic and Cultural Connections in Late Antiquity and Early Middle Ages', pp. 274–8.

21 Narshakhī, pp. 44–5; *The History of Bukhara*, pp. 31–2.

22 Sören Stark has recently published a reassessment of Qutayba's conquests of Bukhara. Unfortunately, too recently to be incorporated into this discussion. Sören Stark, 'The Arab Conquest of Bukhārā: Reconsidering Qutayba b. Muslim's Campaigns 87-90 H/706-709 CE', *Der Islam* 95 (2018), pp. 367–400.

23 Khalīfa b. Khayyāṭ, *Ta'rīkh*, p. 300; Khalīfa b. Khayyāṭ, *Khalifa Ibn Khayyat's History on the Umayyad Dynasty (660-750)*, p. 171; Balādhūrī, p. 420; *Origins*, vol. 2, p. 187; Ya'qūbī, *Tārīkh*, vol. 2, pp. 285–6; Sallāmī, *Akhbār wulāt Khurāsān*, pp. 104–5; Ṭabarī, vol. 2, pp. 1186–9; *The History of al-Ṭabarī*, vol. 23, pp. 137–7; Ibn A'tham, *al-Futūḥ*, vol. 3, pp. 104–7; Narshakhī, pp. 61–2; *The History of Bukhara*, pp. 43–5; Bal'amī, vol. 4, pp. 156–8; Ibn al-Athīr, vol. 4, p. 263. Some of these accounts collapse several campaigns into one, including the arrival of an army of Turks, Sogdians and *barqash* who may be Hephthalites (Sallāmī and Ibn al-Athīr both call the Nīzak Ṭarkhān Nīzak al-Buzqashī in their accounts of the conquest of Paykand) who surrounded Qutayba and his army for two months, blocking off communications with Ḥajjāj causing him concern about the progress of the campaign.

24 De la Vaissière, *Sogdian Traders*, pp. 268–70.

25 Narshakhī, p. 62; *The History of Bukhara*, pp. 44–5.

26 Chavannes, *Documents sur les Tou-Kiue (Turcs) occidentaux*, p. 289; Khalīfa b. Khayyāṭ, *Ta'rīkh*, p. 301; Khalīfa b. Khayyāṭ, *Khalifa Ibn Khayyat's History on the Umayyad Dynasty (660-750)*, p. 172; Ṭabarī, vol. 2, p. 1195; *The History of al-Ṭabarī*, vol. 23, pp. 143–4; Ibn A'tham, *al-Futūḥ*, vol. 3, p. 109; Narshakhī, pp. 63–5; *The History of Bukhara*, pp. 45–7; Bal'amī, vol. 4, pp. 162–3; Ibn al-Athīr, vol. 4, p. 265.

27 Khalīfa b. Khayyāṭ, *Ta'rīkh*, p. 302; Khalīfa b. Khayyāṭ, *Khalifa Ibn Khayyat's History on the Umayyad Dynasty (660-750)*, p. 173; Ṭabarī, vol. 2, p. 1199; *The History of al-Ṭabarī*, vol. 23, p. 147; Bal'amī, vol. 4, p. 164; Ibn al-Athīr, vol. 4, p. 266.

28 Ṭabarī, vol. 2, pp. 1198–9; *The History of al-Ṭabarī*, vol. 23, pp. 146–7; Bal'amī, vol. 4, p. 164; Ibn al-Athīr, vol. 4, p. 266. Nasafī includes a variant of this on the authority of Ziyād b. Ṣāliḥ. 'Tie up Zamm (*zamma bi-Zamm*) and hasten to Amul (*malmala*

bi-Amul) and raze Nasaf (*ansifa Nasaf*) and reduce Kish (*kis bi-Kiss*) and confound Chāch (*shawasha al-Shāsh*) and empty Ferghana (*fargha Farghāna*) and fortify Samarqand (*taḥaṣṣana bi-Samarqand*).' Nasafī, *al-Qand fī dhikr ʿulamāʾ Samarqand*, pp. 64–5, 169.

29 Khalīfa b. Khayyāṭ, *Taʾrīkh*, p. 303; Khalīfa b. Khayyāṭ, *Khalifa Ibn Khayyat's History on the Umayyad Dynasty (660-750)*, p. 174; Ṭabarī, vol. 2, pp. 1201–4; *The History of al-Ṭabarī*, vol. 23, pp. 150–2; Narshakhī, p. 63; *The History of Bukhara*, p. 45; Balʿamī, vol. 4, pp. 164–6; Ibn al-Athīr, vol. 4, p. 269.

30 Narshakhī, pp. 66, 73; *The History of Bukhara*, pp. 48, 53.

31 Narshakhī specifies that they had not been *dahāqīn*, rather they were foreign nobles (*va īshān āz dihqānān nabūdand ghurabāʾ būdand aṣīl*). Narshakhī, p. 42; *The History of Bukhara*, p. 30.

32 For a general overview of the changing geography of Bukhara, see Hugh Kennedy, 'The Coming of Islam to Bukhara', in Yasir Suleiman (ed.), *Living Islamic History: Studies in Honor of Professor Carole Hillenbrand* (Edinburgh, 2010), pp. 77–91.

33 For a discussion of this process with regards to land tenure in Iran, see Ann K.S. Lambton, *Landlord and Peasant in Persia: A Study of Land Tenure and Land Revenue Administration* (London, 1991), pp. 17ff.

34 Balādhūrī, pp. 421–2; *Origins*, vol. 2, p. 189; Ṭabarī, vol. 2, pp. 1364–5; *The History of al-Ṭabarī*, vol. 24, pp. 94–5; Ibn al-Athīr, vol. 5, p. 31.

35 Narshakhī, pp. 74–5; *The History of Bukhara*, pp. 53–4.

36 de la Vaissière, *Sogdian Traders*, pp. 273–9; Haug, 'The Gate of Iron', pp. 279–81.

37 Shaban, *The ʿAbbāsid Revolution*, pp. 98–9.

38 See Payne, 'The Silk Road and the Iranian political economy in late antiquity', for a discussion of the role steppe empires played in securing and encouraging Silk Road trade.

39 Sallāmī, *Akhbār wulāt Khurāsān*, p. 109; Ṭabarī, vol. 2, pp. 1276–7; *The History of al-Ṭabarī*, vol. 23, pp. 223–4; Ibn Aʿtham, *al-Futūḥ*, vol. 3, p. 133; Balʿamī, vol. 4, p. 198; Ibn al-Athīr, vol. 5, p. 5. For a critical overview of the evidence related to this unlikely campaign, H. A. R. Gibb, 'The Arab Invasion of Kashgar in A.D. 715', *Bulletin of the School of Oriental Studies* 2 (1922), pp. 467–74.

40 Ṭabarī, vol. 2, pp. 1277–9; *The History of al-Ṭabarī*, vol. 23, pp. 225–8; Balʿamī, vol. 4, pp. 196–200; Ibn al-Athīr, vol. 5, pp. 5–6.

41 Bielenstein, *Diplomacy and Trade in the Chinese World, 589-1276*, p. 357.

42 Gibb, 'The Arab Invasion of Kashgar in A.D. 715', p. 473.

43 It was not unusual to build a mosque inside a city's fortifications. Haug, 'The Gate of Iron', pp. 109–10.

44 Narshakhī, p. 67; *The History of Bukhara*, p. 48.

45 Narshakhī, pp. 67–8; *The History of Bukhara*, p. 49.

46 Narshakhī, p. 43; *The History of Bukhara*, p. 31. Étienne de la Vaissière thinks these were the gates that were placed in the mosque and sees the Kashkatha as a resistance party. De la Vaissière, *Sogdian Traders*, p. 278.

47 Nasafī, *al-Qand fī dhikr ʿulamāʾ Samarqand*, pp. 201–2.

48 Ṭabarī, vol. 2, pp. 1129–31, 1144; *The History of al-Ṭabarī*, vol. 23, pp. 74–6, 88–9; Balʿamī, vol. 4, pp. 148, 150–1; Ibn al-Athīr, vol. 4, pp. 249, 252.

49 Ṭabarī, vol. 2, pp. 1130–1; *The History of al-Ṭabarī*, vol. 23, pp. 74–6.

50 Yaʿqūbī, *Tārīkh*, vol. 2, p. 286; Ṭabarī, vol. 2, pp. 1205–6; *The History of al-Ṭabarī*, vol. 23, pp. 153–4; Balʿamī, vol. 4, pp. 167–8; Ibn al-Athīr, vol. 4, p. 270. On the geography of his escape and the movement of his baggage train, Étienne de la

Vaissière, 'The Last Bactrian Kings', in Michael Alram, Deborah E. Klimburg-Salter, Minoru Inaba and Matthias Pfisterer (eds.), *Coins, Art and Chronology II: The First Millennium C.E. in the Indo-Iranian Borderlands* (Vienna, 2010), pp. 216–17.

51 Ṭabarī, vol. 2, p. 1206; *The History of al-Ṭabarī*, vol. 23, pp. 154–5; Balʿamī, vol. 4, p. 168; Ibn al-Athīr, vol. 4, p. 270.

52 Balādhūrī, p. 423; *Origins*, vol. 2, p. 193; Ṭabarī, vol. 2, pp. 1290–1; *The History of al-Ṭabarī*, vol. 24, p. 14; Ibn Aʿtham, *al-Futūḥ*, vol. 3, p. 148; Ibn al-Athīr, vol. 5, p. 10. The accounting of the troops during Qutayba's fateful final campaign puts the total at 47,000 but we know that more than 7,000 of those only arrived in Khurāsān after 714. The account also adds 7,000 from the *mawālī*. It is interesting to note that the number of Arabs in Khurāsān had actually shrunk slightly since the garrison was first established at Marw in 671. Shaban, *The ʿAbbāsid Revolution*, p. 64.

53 Ṭabarī, vol. 2, pp. 1206–7; *The History of al-Ṭabarī*, vol. 23, pp. 155–6; Balʿamī, vol. 4, p. 168; Ibn al-Athīr, vol. 4, p. 270.

54 Ṭabarī says Bādhān fled to Furs, which makes no sense. Marquart has proposed this should read *bilād al-Gharsh* or Gharshistān. See Martin Hinds' note in his translation. Sallāmī, *Akhbār wulāt Khurāsān*, p. 105; Ṭabarī, vol. 2, p. 1218; *The History of al-Ṭabarī*, vol. 23, p. 165; Balʿamī, vol. 4, p. 168. According to Ibn Aʿtham, Bādhān stayed to fight and was killed along with his sons. Ibn Aʿtham, *al-Futūḥ*, vol. 3, p. 116.

55 Sallāmī, *Akhbār wulāt Khurāsān*, p. 105; Ṭabarī, vol. 2, pp. 1207, 1218; *The History of al-Ṭabarī*, vol. 23, pp. 155, 165; Ibn Aʿtham, *al-Futūḥ*, vol. 3, p. 116; Balʿamī, vol. 4, p. 168; Ibn al-Athīr, vol. 4, pp. 270, 272. On mass crucifixions including that at Ṭālaqān in the Umayyad period, Sean W. Anthony, *Crucifixion and Death as Spectacle: Umayyad Crucifixion in Its Late Antique Context* (New Haven, CT, 2014), p. 66.

56 Sallāmī, *Akhbār wulāt Khurāsān*, p. 105; Ṭabarī, vol. 2, p. 1218; *The History of al-Ṭabarī*, vol. 23, p. 165; Ibn Aʿtham, *al-Futūḥ*, vol. 3, pp. 116–17; Ibn al-Athīr, vol. 4, p. 272. The relationship between the king of Gūzgān and the rulers of Ambīr known from the Arab–Hephthalite coins discussed in Chapter 4 is unclear. There appears to be at least one later reference to these rulers in the Bactrian documents dated to 722. Nicholas Sims-Williams, 'Bactrian Legal Documents from 7th- and 8th-Century Guzgan', *Bulletin of the Asia Institute* 15 (2001), pp. 20–1; Sims-Williams, 'The Arab-Sasanian and Arab-Hephthalite Coinage', p. 118.

57 Yaʿqūbī, *Tārīkh*, vol. 2, p. 286; Ṭabarī, vol. 2, pp. 1219–22; *The History of al-Ṭabarī*, vol. 23, pp. 165–9; Ibn Aʿtham, *al-Futūḥ*, vol. 3, pp. 111–12; Balʿamī, vol. 4, pp. 168–71; Ibn al-Athīr, vol. 4, pp. 272–3.

58 Balādhūrī gives a very short version of these events on the authority of Abū ʿUbayda Maʿmar b. al-Muthannā in which immediately after conquering Paykand Qutayba attacked Ṣughd or Samarqand and then went to Ṭukhāristān where he killed and crucified the Nīzak. Qutayba then conquered Kish and Nasaf. Balādhūrī, p. 420; *Origins*, vol. 2, p. 187. Yaʿqūbī's account is also truncated. Nīzak asks to return to Ṭukhāristān where he gathers together the 'Persians' (*al-aʿājim*) and revolts against Qutayba. Qutayba sends Sulaym the Counsellor to trick the Nīzak into surrendering. Once he does, Qutayba beheads the Nīzak and his nephew and sends their heads to Ḥajjāj. Yaʿqūbī, *Tārīkh*, vol. 2, p. 286.

59 For the use of 'military archipelago', Agha, *The Revolution Which Toppled the Umayyads*, pp. 185–6.

60 Khalīfa b. Khayyāṭ, *Taʾrīkh*, p. 313; Khalīfa b. Khayyāṭ, *Khalifa Ibn Khayyat's History on the Umayyad Dynasty (660-750)*, p. 188; Balādhūrī, pp. 422–4; *Origins*, vol. 2,

pp. 191–4; Ya῾qūbī, *Tārīkh*, vol. 2, pp. 295–6; Sallāmī, *Akhbār wulāt Khurāsān*, pp. 109–15; Ṭabarī, vol. 2, pp. 1284–1304; *The History of al-Ṭabarī*, vol. 24, pp. 6–28; Ibn A῾tham, *al-Futūḥ*, vol. 3, pp. 135–55; Narshakhī, p. 81; *The History of Bukhara*, pp. 58–9; Bal῾amī, vol. 4, pp. 201–17; Gardīzī, *Ta'rīkh-i Gardīzī*, pp. 249–50; Balkhī, *Faḍā'īl-i Balkh*, pp. 18, 34; Ibn al-Athīr, vol. 5, pp. 8–12.

61 Chavannes, *Documents sur les Tou-Kiue (Turcs) Occidentaux*, p. 148, n. 3; Karev, *Samarqand et le Sughd à l'époque ῾abbāsside*, p. 63.

62 On the fate of the wall and the establishment of the Turkish lord of Ṣūl in Dihistān, Pourshariati, *Decline and Fall of the Sasanian Empire*, pp. 253–4; Sauer, Rekzavandi, Wilkinson, and Nokandeh, *Persia's Imperial Power in Late Antiquity*, pp. 600–1.

63 Balādhūrī, p. 336; *Origins*, vol. 2, p. 42; Ṭabarī, vol. 2, pp. 1322, 1327; *The History of al-Ṭabarī*, vol. 24, pp. 46–7, 52; Ibn A῾tham, *al-Futūḥ*, vol. 3, p. 164; Bal῾amī, vol. 4, pp. 225–6; Ibn Isfandiyār, *Tārīkh-i Ṭabaristān*, pp. 161–2; Bahā' al-Dīn Muḥammad Ibn Isfandiyār, *An Abridged Translation of the History of Ṭabaristān*, Edward G. Browne (trans.) (Leiden, 1905), p. 105; Ibn al-Athīr, vol. 5, pp. 16, 17.

64 Balādhūrī, pp. 335–6; *Origins*, vol. 2, p. 41; Ṭabarī, vol. 2, p. 1318; *The History of al-Ṭabarī*, vol. 24, p. 43; Ibn A῾tham, *al-Futūḥ*, vol. 3, p. 164; Bal῾amī, vol. 4, p. 227; Ibn Isfandiyār, *Tārīkh-i Ṭabaristān*, p. 162; Ibn Isfandiyār, *An Abridged Translation of the History of Ṭabaristān*, p. 105; Ibn al-Athīr, vol. 5, p. 16.

65 Ṭabarī, vol. 2, p. 1331; *The History of al-Ṭabarī*, vol. 24, p. 55. On the *čākir* and their relationship to slave soldiers, de la Vaissière, *Samarcande et Samarra*, pp. 59–88.

66 This campaign is barely mentioned in ῾Awtabī's history of the Muhallabites. He reports only that Yazīd went to Gorgān and spent lavishly and then became governor of Khurāsān. al-῾Awtabī, *An Early Islamic Family from Oman*, p. 65.

67 Balādhūrī, p. 336; *Origins*, vol. 2, p. 41; Ṭabarī, vol. 2, pp. 1320, 1325; *The History of al-Ṭabarī*, vol. 24, pp. 46, 53; Bal῾amī, vol. 4, p. 228; Ibn al-Athīr, vol. 5, pp. 16, 18.

68 Khalīfa b. Khayyāṭ, *Ta'rīkh*, p. 315; Khalīfa b. Khayyāṭ, *Khalifa Ibn Khayyat's History on the Umayyad Dynasty (660-750)*, p. 191; Balādhūrī, pp. 337–8; *Origins*, vol. 2, pp. 43–4; Sallāmī, *Akhbār wulāt Khurāsān*, p. 120; Ṭabarī, vol. 2, pp. 1321, 1328, 1332–4; *The History of al-Ṭabarī*, vol. 24, pp. 46, 53, 57–8; Ibn A῾tham, *al-Futūḥ*, vol. 3, pp. 167, 171; Bal῾amī, vol. 4, pp. 229, 232–3; Gardīzī, *Ta'rīkh-i Gardīzī*, p. 251; Ibn Isfandiyār, *Tārīkh-i Ṭabaristān*, p. 164; Ibn Isfandiyār, *An Abridged Translation of the History of Ṭabaristān*, p. 108; Ibn al-Athīr, vol. 5, pp. 17, 19.

69 Khalīfa b. Khayyāṭ, *Ta'rīkh*, p. 320; Khalīfa b. Khayyāṭ, *Khalifa Ibn Khayyat's History on the Umayyad Dynasty (660-750)*, p. 197. This was not just ῾Umar's policy in the east. He also ordered withdrawals from newly captured territories in Spain and along the Arab–Byzantine frontier as well.

70 Paradigmatic of this attitude is M. A. Shaban who sees these differing attitudes as central to understanding the outbreak of the Abbasid Revolution. Shaban, *The ῾Abbāsid Revolution*. For a critique of Shaban's analysis, see the discussion in the following chapter as well as Patricia Crone, 'Were the Qays and Yemen of the Umayyad Period Political Parties?', pp. 1–57.

71 This anecdote begins with ῾Umar writing to Sulaymān and ordering him to build *khānāt* or inns in his lands so that he could provide any Muslim traveller with accommodations for up to two days and two nights. One may presume that new infrastructure was needed as merchants increasingly shifted their attention towards Iran and the west from China and the east following the Arab–Muslim conquests of Sogdiana. Balādhūrī, pp. 421–2; *Origins*, vol. 2, p. 189; Ṭabarī, vol. 2, p. 1364; *The History of al-Ṭabarī*, vol. 24, p. 94; Ibn al-Athīr, vol. 5, p. 31. According to a report

in Ibn Isfandiyār's *Tārīkh-i Ṭabaristān*, ʿUmar had generally invited anyone with a grievance against the Umayyads to come to him asking for compensation. Ibn Isfandiyār, *Tārīkh-i Ṭabaristān*, p. 53; Ibn Isfandiyār, *An Abridged Translation of the History of Ṭabaristān*, p. 12.

72 Ṭabarī, vol. 2, pp. 1364–5; *The History of al-Ṭabarī*, vol. 24, p. 94; Ibn al-Athīr, vol. 5, p. 31.

73 Ṭabarī, vol. 2, p. 1365; *The History of al-Ṭabarī*, vol. 24, pp. 94–5; Ibn al-Athīr, vol. 5, p. 31.

74 Yaʿqūbī, *Tārīkh*, vol. 2, p. 1365; Ṭabarī, vol. 2, p. 1365; *The History of al-Ṭabarī*, vol. 24, p. 95.

75 Balādhūrī, p. 426; *Origins*, vol. 2, p. 197; Yaʿqūbī, *Tārīkh*, vol. 2, p. 302; Ṭabarī, vol. 2, pp. 1354–5; *The History of al-Ṭabarī*, vol. 24, pp. 83–4; Ibn al-Athīr, vol. 5, p. 27.

76 Ṭabarī, vol. 2, p. 1509; *The History of al-Ṭabarī*, vol. 25, p. 48.

77 Daniel Clement Dennett, Jr., *Conversion and the Poll Tax in Early Islam* (Cambridge, MA, 1950), p. 128; Abd al-Aziz Duri, *Early Islamic Institutions: Administration and Taxation from the Caliphate to the Umayyads and ʿAbbāsids*, Razia Ali (trans.) (London, 2011), pp. 117–20.

78 Ṭabarī, vol. 2, p. 1354; *The History of al-Ṭabarī*, vol. 24, p. 83.

79 G.R. Hawting, *The First Dynasty of Islam: The Umayyad Caliphate AD 661-750* (Carbondale, IL, 1987), p. 89, n. 14.

80 Ṭabarī, vol. 2, p. 1508; *The History of al-Ṭabarī*, vol. 25, p. 47.

81 Dennett, Jr., *Conversion and the Poll Tax in Early Islam*, pp. 104–13.

82 Hawting, *The First Dynasty of Islam*, pp. 80–1.

83 His nickname was more reflective of a general opinion that he was weak and ineffectual with some accounts reporting that it originated among Arab soldiers and was connected with his failure to pursue the Türgesh vigorously. Balādhūrī, p. 427; *Origins*, vol. 2, p. 198; Ṭabarī, vol. 2, pp. 1417–18, 1421; *The History of al-Ṭabarī*, vol. 24, pp. 149, 152; Ibn al-Athīr, vol. 5, p. 45. In one account, Saʿīd explains his nickname is the result of his refusal to kill Yamanī Arabs and perpetuate tribal factionalism. Ṭabarī, vol. 2, p. 1867; *The History of al-Ṭabarī*, vol. 26, p. 235.

84 Ṭabarī, vol. 2, pp. 1418–20; *The History of al-Ṭabarī*, vol. 24, pp. 150–1; Ibn al-Athīr, vol. 5, p. 45.

85 Ṭabarī, vol. 2, pp. 1460–1; *The History of al-Ṭabarī*, vol. 24, pp. 190–1.

86 Chavannes, *Documents sur les Tou-Kiue (Turcs) occidentaux*, pp. 203–5; Gibb, *The Arab Conquests in Central Asia*, p. 60; Bielenstein, *Diplomacy and Trade in the Chinese World, 589-1276*, pp. 329, 334.

87 Gibb, *The Arab Conquests in Central Asia*, pp. 61–2.

88 Ṭabarī, vol. 2, pp. 1440–1; *The History of al-Ṭabarī*, vol. 24, pp. 169–71. On Bārkath, the text reads Bayārkath but no place with that name is known. Earlier in the passage it seems that Bayārkath is the name of one of the generals, so it may be a personal name. The *dihqān* of Buzmājan is said to accompany this army and we know that Buzmājan was the capital of the region of Sogdiana called Bārkath.

89 Khalīfa b. Khayyāṭ, *Taʾrīkh*, p. 328; Khalīfa b. Khayyāṭ, *Khalifa Ibn Khayyat's History on the Umayyad Dynasty (660-750)*, p. 207; Balādhūrī, p. 427; *Origins*, vol. 2, p. 199; Yaʿqūbī, *Tārīkh*, vol. 2, p. 311; Ṭabarī, vol. 2, pp. 1439–46; *The History of al-Ṭabarī*, vol. 24, pp. 169–77; Ibn Aʿtham, *al-Futūḥ*, vol. 3, pp. 214–15; Ibn al-Athīr, vol. 5, pp. 51–3.

90 Khalīfa b. Khayyāṭ, *Taʾrīkh*, p. 328; Khalīfa b. Khayyāṭ, *Khalifa Ibn Khayyat's History on the Umayyad Dynasty (660-750)*, p. 207.

91 Ṭabarī, vol. 2, p. 1445; *The History of al-Ṭabarī*, vol. 24, p. 176.
92 De la Vaissière, *Sogdian Traders*, p. 278.
93 Ṭabarī, vol. 2, p. 1441; *The History of al-Ṭabarī*, vol. 24, p. 171.
94 These documents have been collected and edited by V.A. Livshits, *Sogdiiskie dokumenty s Gory Mug. Chtenie, perevod, kommentarii, II: luridicheskie dokumentry i pis'ma* (Moscow, 1962).
95 Grenet and de la Vaissière, 'The Last Days of Panjikent'.
96 Frye, 'Ṭarxūn-Türxūn and Central Asian History', pp. 108–12.
97 Ṭabarī, vol. 2, p. 1446; *The History of al-Ṭabarī*, vol. 24, p. 177.
98 Grenet and de la Vaissière, 'The Last Days of Panjikent', p. 158.
99 Guitty Azarpay, *Sogdian Painting: The Pictorial Epic in Oriental Art* (Berkeley, CA, 1981), pp. 64–7.
100 Grenet and de la Vaissière, 'The Last Days of Panjikent', pp. 159–60.
101 Ibid., pp. 167–9.
102 Ṭabarī, vol. 2, p. 1447; *The History of al-Ṭabarī*, vol. 24, pp. 177–8; Ibn al-Athīr, vol. 5, p. 54.
103 Ṭabarī, vol. 2, p. 1448; *The History of al-Ṭabarī*, vol. 24, p. 178; Ibn al-Athīr, vol. 5, p. 54.
104 Grenet and de la Vaissière, 'The Last Days of Panjikent', p. 178.
105 Anthony, *Crucifixion and Death as Spectacle*, p. 67.
106 Ṭabarī, vol. 2, pp. 1448–9; *The History of al-Ṭabarī*, vol. 24, p. 179; Ibn al-Athīr, vol. 5, p. 54.
107 Ṭabarī, vol. 2, p. 1449; *The History of al-Ṭabarī*, vol. 24, p. 179.
108 Ṭabarī, vol. 2, p. 1453–7; *The History of al-Ṭabarī*, vol. 24, pp. 183–7; Ibn al-Athīr, vol. 5, pp. 56–7.
109 Balādhūrī, p. 428; *Origins*, vol. 2, p. 199; Yaʿqūbī, *Tārīkh*, vol. 2, p. 312; Ṭabarī, vol. 2, pp. 1473–7; *The History of al-Ṭabarī*, vol. 25, pp. 10–14.
110 Khalīfa b. Khayyāṭ, *Ta'rīkh*, p. 336; Khalīfa b. Khayyāṭ, *Khalifa Ibn Khayyat's History on the Umayyad Dynasty (660-750)*, p. 217; Balādhūrī, p. 428; *Origins*, vol. 2, pp. 199–200; Ṭabarī, vol. 2, pp. 1477–81; *The History of al-Ṭabarī*, vol. 25, pp. 14–17; Ibn al-Athīr, vol. 5, pp. 62–3. The Day of Thirst resonated long among the Muslims. When Naṣr b. Sayyār captured the Turkish prince Kūrṣūl in 739, he refused to ransom him after he declared that he had been present at that battle. Ṭabarī, vol. 2, pp. 1690–1; *The History of al-Ṭabarī*, vol. 26, pp. 26–7.
111 Khalīfa b. Khayyāṭ, *Ta'rīkh*, p. 337; Khalīfa b. Khayyāṭ, *Khalifa Ibn Khayyat's History on the Umayyad Dynasty (660-750)*, p. 219; Balādhūrī, p. 428; *Origins*, vol. 2, p. 200; Ṭabarī, vol. 2, p. 1489; *The History of al-Ṭabarī*, vol. 25, p. 25; Ibn al-Athīr, vol. 5, p. 66.
112 Khalīfa b. Khayyāṭ, *Ta'rīkh*, p. 338; Khalīfa b. Khayyāṭ, *Khalifa Ibn Khayyat's History on the Umayyad Dynasty (660-750)*, p. 220; Ṭabarī, vol. 2, pp. 1489–90; *The History of al-Ṭabarī*, vol. 25, p. 26. Ibn Aʿtham makes a vague reference to a campaign against Turks in their mountains and passes without naming a specific location. Ibn Aʿtham, *al-Futūḥ*, vol. 3, p. 273.
113 Iṣṭakhrī, *al-Masālik wa'l-mamālik*, p. 157; Ibn Ḥawqal, *Kitāb ṣūrat al-ard*, p. 444.
114 Balādhūrī, p. 428; *Origins*, vol. 2, p. 200; Ṭabarī, vol. 2, p. 1492–4; *The History of al-Ṭabarī*, vol. 25, pp. 30–2
115 Chavannes, *Documents sur les Tou-Kiue (Turcs) occidentaux*, pp. 206–8.
116 Balādhūrī, pp. 428–9; *Origins*, vol. 2, pp. 200–1; Ṭabarī, vol. 2, p. 1508; *The History of al-Ṭabarī*, vol. 25, pp. 46–7; Ibn al-Athīr, vol. 5, pp. 70–1.

117 Narshakhī, p. 82; *The History of Bukhara*, pp. 59–60.
118 Ṭabarī, vol. 2, pp. 1508–10; *The History of al-Ṭabarī*, vol. 25, pp. 47–8; Ibn al-Athīr, vol. 5, p. 71.
119 This nomenclature appears on coins in 111 and 112 AH (729–31 CE). Michael G. Klat, *Catalogue of the Post Reform Dirhams: The Umayyad Dynasty* (London, 2002), p. 84.
120 For an overview of the Türgesh, Golden, *An Introduction to the History the Turkic Peoples*, pp. 139–41.
121 Ṭabarī, vol. 2, pp. 1421–2; *The History of al-Ṭabarī*, vol. 24, pp. 153–4; Ibn al-Athīr, vol. 5, p. 46.
122 Ṭabarī, vol. 2, pp. 1423–5; *The History of al-Ṭabarī*, vol. 24, pp. 155–7; Ibn al-Athīr, vol. 5, pp. 46–7.
123 Ṭabarī, vol. 2, p. 1430; *The History of al-Ṭabarī*, vol. 24, pp. 160–1.
124 Ṭabarī, vol. 2, p. 1504; *The History of al-Ṭabarī*, vol. 25, pp. 42–3. *Rābiṭa* have in some contexts been seen as a forerunner to the *ribāṭ*. See Albrecht Noth, *Heiliger Krieg und heiliger Kampf in Islam und Christentum* (Bonn, 1966), pp. 66–87; Jacqueline Chabbi, 'Ribāṭ', *EI*[2]; Wheatley, *The Places Where Men Pray Together*, p. 256; Antoine Borrut and Christoph Picard, 'Râbata, ribât, râbita: une institution reconsidérer', in P. Sénac and N. Prouteau (eds.), *Chrétiens et Musulmans en Méditerranéee médiévale (VIIIe–XIIIe s.): échanges et contacts* (Pointiers, 2003), pp. 33–65; Étienne de la Vaissière, 'Le ribāṭ d'Asie centrale', in Étienne de la Vaissière (ed.), *Islamisation de l'Asie centrale: processus locaux d'acculturation du VIIe au XIe siècle* (Paris, 2008), pp. 71–94; Haug, 'The Gate of Iron', pp. 134–45; A. Asa Eger, 'Ḥiṣn, Ribāṭ, Thaghr or Qaṣr? Semantics and Systems of Frontier Fortifications in the Early Islamic Period', pp. 427–55.
125 Ṭabarī, vol. 2, pp. 1512–13; *The History of al-Ṭabarī*, vol. 25, pp. 50–1; Ibn al-Athīr, vol. 5, p. 71.
126 Ṭabarī, vol. 2, pp. 1513–16; *The History of al-Ṭabarī*, vol. 25, pp. 51–4; Ibn Aʿtham, *al-Futūḥ*, vol. 3, pp. 273–4; Ibn al-Athīr, vol. 5, pp. 71–2.
127 Ṭabarī, vol. 2, pp. 1516–25; *The History of al-Ṭabarī*, vol. 25, pp. 54–62; Ibn al-Athīr, vol. 5, pp. 72–3.
128 Ṭabarī, vol. 2, p. 1518; *The History of al-Ṭabarī*, vol. 25, p. 56; Ibn al-Athīr, vol. 5, p. 72.
129 Ṭabarī, vol. 2, p. 1518; *The History of al-Ṭabarī*, vol. 25, p. 56; Ibn al-Athīr, vol. 5, p. 72.
130 Ṭabarī, vol. 2, pp. 1527–9; *The History of al-Ṭabarī*, vol. 25, pp. 65–7; Balʿamī, vol. 4, p. 294; Ibn al-Athīr,vol. 5, p. 74.
131 For a succinct overview of the Battle of the Pass, Saleh Said Agha, 'The "Battle of the Pass": Two Consequential Readings', *Bulletin of the School of Oriental and African Studies* 63 (2000), pp. 342–4. Accounts of the battle appear in Khalīfa b. Khayyāṭ, *Ta'rīkh*, p. 344; Khalīfa b. Khayyāṭ, *Khalifa Ibn Khayyat's History on the Umayyad Dynasty (660-750)*, pp. 228–9; Ṭabarī, vol. 2, pp. 1532–50; *The History of al-Ṭabarī*, vol. 25, pp. 71–87; Ibn Aʿtham, *al-Futūḥ*, vol. 3, pp. 274–9; Balʿamī, vol. 4, pp. 295–6; Ibn al-Athīr, vol. 5, pp. 77–80; Nasafī, *al-Qand fī dhikr ʿulamāʾ Samarqand*, p. 115.
132 See Agha's computations. Agha, 'The "Battle of the Pass"', pp. 347–8.
133 Ṭabarī, vol. 2, pp. 1548–52; *The History of al-Ṭabarī*, vol. 25, pp. 85–9; Ibn al-Athīr, vol. 5, pp. 80–1. Of all these events, Balādhurī only discusses the arrival of the reinforcements. Balādhurī, p. 429; *Origins*, vol. 2, p. 201.

134 The first attempt to retake Samarqand did not occur until 735 when Asad al-Qasrī led a force against the polytheists of Samarqand, but he was only able to divert their water supply and not capture the city itself. Ṭabarī, vol. 2, pp. 1585–6; *The History of al-Ṭabarī*, vol. 25, pp. 121–2.
135 Blankinship, *The End of the Jihād State*, pp. 158–9.
136 Ṭabarī, vol. 2, pp. 1554–6; *The History of al-Ṭabarī*, vol. 25, pp. 90–2.
137 Ṭabarī, vol. 2, pp. 1593–1602; *The History of al-Ṭabarī*, vol. 25, pp. 131–9; Ibn al-Athīr, vol. 5, pp. 94–5.
138 Ṭabarī, vol. 2, p. 1594; *The History of al-Ṭabarī*, vol. 25, p. 132.
139 Khalīfa b. Khayyāṭ, *Ta'rīkh*, pp. 347–8; Khalīfa b. Khayyāṭ, *Khalifa Ibn Khayyat's History on the Umayyad Dynasty (660-750)*, p. 233; Ṭabarī, vol. 2, pp. 1604–12; *The History of al-Ṭabarī*, vol. 25, pp. 140–7; Ibn al-Athīr, vol. 5, pp. 95–7.
140 Ṭabarī, vol. 2, pp. 1613–14; *The History of al-Ṭabarī*, vol. 25, p. 148; Ibn al-Athīr, vol. 5, pp. 96–7.
141 Ṭabarī, vol. 2, pp. 1614–18; *The History of al-Ṭabarī*, vol. 25, pp. 149–52; Ibn al-Athīr, vol. 5, p. 97.
142 Ṭabarī, vol. 2, p. 1637; *The History of al-Ṭabarī*, vol. 25, pp. 168–9; Ibn al-Athīr, vol. 5, p. 102.
143 Ṭabarī, vol. 2, p. 1507; *The History of al-Ṭabarī*, vol. 25, p. 46. Patricia Crone believes this Rabīʿ to be a son of ʿImrān b. al-Faḍl al-Bujumī who participated in the conquest of Khurāsān and was one of the Arab nobles of Baṣra. Crone, *Slaves on Horses*, p. 114.

Chapter 6

1 Ṭabarī, vol. 2, p. 1568; *The History of al-Ṭabarī*, vol. 25, p. 106; Ibn al-Athīr, vol. 5, p. 86. The association of Sulaymān b. ʿAbdallāh with the Banū Tamīm should be a reminder of just how flexible tribal alliances were despite the narrative of Qays/Muḍar versus Yaman. As discussed in Chapter 4, ʿAbdallāh b. Khāzim had led a violent purge against the Banū Tamīm, who then joined forces with his son Mūsā and later Sulaymān.
2 Khalīfa b. Khayyāṭ, *Ta'rīkh*, p. 346; Khalīfa b. Khayyāṭ, *Khalifa Ibn Khayyat's History on the Umayyad Dynasty (660-750)*, p. 231; Ṭabarī, vol. 2, p. 1569; *The History of al-Ṭabarī*, vol. 25, pp. 107–8; Ibn Aʿtham, *al-Futūḥ*, vol. 3, p. 279; Balʿamī, vol. 4, p. 297; Gardīzī, *Ta'rīkh-i Gardīzī*, pp. 257–8; Ibn al-Athīr, vol. 5, p. 88.
3 Ṭabarī, vol. 2, p. 1570; *The History of al-Ṭabarī*, vol. 25, p. 108.
4 Ṭabarī, vol. 2, p. 1571; *The History of al-Ṭabarī*, vol. 25, p. 109.
5 On the murder of Ḥayyān, Ṭabarī, vol. 2, pp. 1430–1; *The History of al-Ṭabarī*, vol. 24, pp. 160–1.
6 As modern scholars understand the movement, Murji'ism emphasized the postponement of judgement, arguing that only God may judge one's sins. This was a welcoming position for new converts, especially those who maintained certain aspects of their pre-Islamic culture and identity or had not learnt Arabic. For an examination of Ḥārith b. Surayj in the context of Murji'ism and Hanafism in Greater Khurāsān, Wilferd Madelung, 'The Early Murjiʿa in Khurāsān and Transoxiana and the Spread of Hanafism', *Der Islam* 59 (1982), pp. 33–5. Salih Said Agha uses the appeal of a revolt with strong religious overtones as evidence of widespread

conversion among the populations of Khurāsān in the early eighth century. Agha, *The Revolution Which Toppled the Umayyads*, pp. 154–5.

7 For a more recent critique of the idea that Ḥārith enjoyed particularly strong support from the *mawālī* or had a message that was especially directed towards them, Elizabeth Urban, 'The Early Islamic Mawali: A Window onto Processes of Identity Construction and Social Change' (PhD, University of Chicago, 2012), pp. 128–35.

8 For Naṣr's poem, Ṭabarī, vol. 2, pp. 1575–6; *The History of al-Ṭabarī*, vol. 25, pp. 113–14.

9 Stuart D. Sears, 'The Revolt of al-Ḥārith Ibn Surayj and the Countermarking of Umayyad Dirhams in Early Eighth Century CE Khurāsān', in Paul M. Cobb [ed.], *The Lineaments of Islam: Studies in Honor of Fred McGraw Donner* (Leiden, 2012), p. 395. The coin appears in Klat, *Catalogue of the Post Reform Dirhams*, p. 86.

10 For Jahm b. Ṣafwān's background and theology, Joseph Van Ess, 'Jahm b. Ṣafwān', *EIr*.

11 Ṭabarī, vol. 2, p. 1582; *The History of al-Ṭabarī*, vol. 25, p. 119.

12 Ṭabarī, vol. 2, pp. 1576–7; *The History of al-Ṭabarī*, vol. 25, p. 115; Ibn al-Athīr, vol. 5, pp. 86–7.

13 Gibb, *The Arab Conquests in Central Asia*, p. 78.

14 Khalīfa b. Khayyāṭ, *Ta'rīkh*, p. 346; Khalīfa b. Khayyāṭ, *Khalifa Ibn Khayyat's History on the Umayyad Dynasty (660-750)*, pp. 231–2; Ṭabarī, vol. 2, pp. 1583–5, 1589–91, 1603; *The History of al-Ṭabarī*, vol. 25, pp. 120–1, 126–8, 139; Ibn Aʿtham, *al-Futūḥ*, vol. 3, pp. 279–80; Balʿamī, vol. 4, p. 297; Ibn al-Athīr, vol. 5, pp. 89, 93.

15 Ṭabarī includes an account of Asad feasting with and praising the *dahāqīn* during a celebration of the Zoroastrian harvest festival of Mihrijān. Ṭabarī, vol. 2, pp. 1635–8; *The History of al-Ṭabarī*, vol. 25, pp. 167–70.

16 Ṭabarī, vol. 2, p. 1603; *The History of al-Ṭabarī*, vol. 25, p. 139.

17 Ṭabarī, vol. 2, p. 1924; *The History of al-Ṭabarī*, vol. 27, p. 35.

18 Ṭabarī, vol. 2, pp. 1609–10; *The History of al-Ṭabarī*, vol. 25, p. 145; Ibn al-Athīr, vol. 5, p. 96.

19 Ṭabarī, vol. 2, p. 1611; *The History of al-Ṭabarī*, vol. 25, p. 146; Ibn al-Athīr, vol. 5, p. 96.

20 Turner, 'The Significance of the Frontier in American History', pp. 1–38.

21 Pourshariati, 'Iranian Tradition in Ṭūs and the Arab Presence in Khurāsān', p. 83.

22 Gerlof Van Vloten, *Récherches sur la domination arabe, le chiitisme et les croyances messianiques sous le khalifat des Omayades* (Amsterdam, 1894), p. 1.

23 Wellhausen, *The Arab Kingdom and Its Fall*, pp. 397, 558.

24 Dennett, Jr., *Conversion and the Poll Tax in Early Islam*, p. 128.

25 Duri, *Early Islamic Institutions*, pp. 117–20.

26 Shaban, *The ʿAbbāsid Revolution*, pp. 156–7.

27 Richard Bulliet, *Conversion to Islam in the Medieval Period: An Essay in Quantitative History* (Cambridge, MA, 1979), see Chapter 3 for the patterns of conversion in Iran.

28 For example, as mentioned in the previous chapter, both the Caliph ʿUmar II's governor Jarrāḥ b. ʿAbdallāh al-Ḥakamī and the Caliph Hishām's governor Ashras b. ʿAbdallāh al-Sulamī found it necessary to institute tests of circumcision on converts seeking tax relief. Ṭabarī, vol. 2, pp. 1354, 1508; *The History of al-Ṭabarī*, vol. 24, p. 83; vol. 25, p. 47.

29 Agha, 'The Arab Population in Ḫurāsān during the Umayyad Period', pp. 211–29; Agha, *The Revolution Which Toppled the Umayyads*, pp. 173–219.

30 Ṭabarī, vol. 2, p. 1660–5; *The History of al-Ṭabarī*, vol. 25, p. 188–92.

31 Ṭabarī, vol. 2, pp. 1664–5; *The History of al-Ṭabarī*, vol. 25, p. 192.

32 More precisely, Crone called it 'so faulty that it should have been generally dismissed' and wrote her response nearly a quarter century after the original publication of Shaban's work because 'it is tedious to explain its shortcomings year in and year out'. Crone, 'Were the Qays and Yemen of the Umayyad Period Political Parties?' p. 1.
33 Ibid., p. 32.
34 Urban, 'The Early Islamic Mawali.' See Chapter 3 for Urban's analysis of the *mawālī* during the period of Arab factionalism.
35 Kevin van Bladel, 'Ibn al-Muqaffaʿ on the Bactrian Language among the ʿAbbāsid Armies' (Annual Meeting of the American Oriental Society, Boston, MA, 2016).
36 On Daniel's use of the term 'feudal', Elton L. Daniel, *The Political and Social History of Khurasan under Abbasid Rule, 747-820* (Minneapolis, 1979), pp. 18–19.
37 Ṭabarī, vol. 2, p. 1563; *The History of al-Ṭabarī*, vol. 25, pp. 100–1.
38 Daniel, *The Political and Social History of Khurasan under Abbasid Rule*, pp. 20–1.
39 Ibid., p. 22.
40 For the central role of Marw and its impact on the historiography of the revolution, Farouk Omar, *The Abbasid Caliphate: 132/750-170/786* (Baghdad, 1969), p. 58; Shaban, *The ʿAbbāsid Revolution*, p. 152; Jacob Lassner, *The Shaping of ʿAbbāsid Rule* (Princeton, NJ, 1980), p. 276; Moshe Sharon, *Black Banners from the East: The Establishment of the ʿAbbāsid State: Incubation of a Revolt* (Leiden, 1983), pp. 196–7; Pourshariati, 'Iranian Tradition in Ṭūs and the Arab Presence in Khurāsān', pp. 153–60.
41 Agha, *The Revolution Which Toppled the Umayyads*, pp. 185–6. See also the chart on page 189.
42 Karev, *Samarqand et le Sughd à l'époque ʿAbbāsside*, pp. 45–7.
43 Kennedy, *The Armies of the Caliphs*, pp. 42–4.
44 When Naṣr first appears in our sources, he is already in his forties, campaigning alongside Qutayba's brother Ṣāliḥ and earning for himself a village called Tinjāna whose location remains a mystery. Ṭabarī, vol. 2, p. 1180; *The History of al-Ṭabarī*, vol. 23, p. 128.
45 Wellhausen, *The Arab Kingdom and Its Fall*, p. 73, n. 1.
46 Ṭabarī, vol. 2, pp. 1691–2, 1694–5; *The History of al-Ṭabarī*, vol. 26, pp. 28, 31; Ibn al-Athīr, vol. 5, p. 112.
47 Naṣr and Ḥārith were related by marriage. Naṣr's wife was of the Banū Tamīm, as was Ḥārith, and both relied on Tamīm as an important source of manpower. Ṭabarī, vol. 2, pp. 1867–8; *The History of al-Ṭabarī*, vol. 26, pp. 235–7; Ibn al-Athīr, vol. 5, p. 145.
48 Ṭabarī, vol. 2, pp. 1888–90, 1919; *The History of al-Ṭabarī*, vol. 26, pp. 263–5, vol. 27, pp. 30–1; Ibn al-Athīr, vol. 5, pp. 154, 162.
49 Ṭabarī, vol. 2, pp. 1932–3; *The History of al-Ṭabarī*, vol. 27, p. 43; Ibn al-Athīr, vol. 5, p. 163.
50 Ṭabarī places these all under a single year (121 AH/738–9 CE), but they probably occurred in three consecutive years – 739, 740 and 741 – as suggested by Carole Hillenbrand in her translation. Ṭabarī, vol. 2, p. 1688; *The History of al-Ṭabarī*, vol. 26, p. 23.
51 Ṭabarī, vol. 2, pp. 1689–91; *The History of al-Ṭabarī*, vol. 26, pp. 25–7; Ibn al-Athīr, vol. 5, pp. 111–12.
52 In her translation, Carole Hillenbrand translates *ṣāḥib* as friend, but in this context he is clearly the master of either Turkish slaves or a band of Turkish warriors. Ṭabarī, vol. 2, p. 1719; *The History of al-Ṭabarī*, vol. 26, p. 58.
53 Ṭabarī, vol. 2, p. 1767; *The History of al-Ṭabarī*, vol. 26, p. 118.

54 Ṭabarī, vol. 2, p. 1765; *The History of al-Ṭabarī*, vol. 26, p. 116.

55 C. E. Bosworth, 'Abū Ḥafṣ ʿUmar al-Kirmānī and the Rise of the Barmakids', *Bulletin of the School of Oriental and African Studies* 57 (1994), pp. 273–4.

56 de la Vaissière, *Samarcande et Samarra*, pp. 143–5.

57 For the general picture of declining frontier warfare, Blankinship, *The End of the Jihād State* (Albany, NY, 1994).

58 Ṭabarī, vol. 2, pp. 1717–18; *The History of al-Ṭabarī*, vol. 26, pp. 56–7; Ibn al-Athīr, vol. 5, p. 118.

59 Ṭabarī, vol. 2, pp. 1693–4; *The History of al-Ṭabarī*, vol. 26, pp. 29–31; Narshakhī, pp. 84–5; *The History of Bukhara*, pp. 61–2.

60 Ṭabarī, vol. 2, p. 1767; *The History of al-Ṭabarī*, vol. 26, pp. 117–18; Ibn al-Athīr, vol. 5, p. 126. By some accounts, Naṣr made these preparations to revolt on the encouragement of astrologers who foresaw *fitna* in Khurāsān.

61 Yūsuf b. ʿUmar was caught up in the civil war and was killed on the orders of Sulaymān b. Hishām in 744–5.

62 Dīnawarī, pp. 351–2; Yaʿqūbī, *Tārīkh*, vol. 2, p. 333; Ṭabarī, vol. 2, pp. 1859–63; *The History of al-Ṭabarī*, vol. 26, pp. 226–30; Ibn Aʿtham, *al-Futūḥ*, vol. 3, p. 314; Ibn al-Athīr, vol. 5, pp. 143–5.

63 Ṭabarī, vol. 2, p. 1865; *The History of al-Ṭabarī*, vol. 26, p. 233.

64 On the attempts to build an anti-Abbasid alliance, Moshe Sharon, *Revolt: The Social and Military Aspects of the ʿAbbāsid Revolution* (Jerusalem, 1990), pp. 107 ff.

65 Khalīfa b. Khayyāṭ, *Taʾrīkh*, p. 388; Khalīfa b. Khayyāṭ, *Khalifa Ibn Khayyat's History on the Umayyad Dynasty (660-750)*, p. 286; Dīnawarī, p. 361; Yaʿqūbī, *Tārīkh*, vol. 2, p. 341; Ṭabarī, vol. 2, pp. 1975–6; *The History of al-Ṭabarī*, vol. 27, pp. 84–5; Ibn Aʿtham, *al-Futūḥ*, vol. 3, p. 327; Balʿamī, vol. 4, p. 328; Ibn al-Athīr, vol. 5, pp. 171–2.

66 Ṭabarī, vol. 2, pp. 1997–8; *The History of al-Ṭabarī*, vol. 27, p. 105; Ibn al-Athīr, vol. 5, p. 181.

67 On Sharīk's *nisba*, some sources state it is Mahrī which would then, according to Saleh Said Agha, tie him to the Mahrā sub-tribe of the Quḍāʿa tribe of Yaman while others say Fihrī which Yury Karev has argued would tie him to the lineage of Fihr b. Mālik b. Naḍr b. Kināna. Agha, *The Revolution Which Toppled the Umayyads*, p. 371; Karev, *Samarqand et le Sughd à l'époque ʿAbbāsside*, pp. 54–5.

68 Yaʿqūbī, *Tārīkh*, vol. 2, p. 354; Ṭabarī, vol. 3, p. 74; *The History of al-Ṭabarī*, vol. 27, p. 197; Narshakhī, pp. 86–9; *The History of Bukhara*, pp. 62–5; Muṭahhar b. Ṭāhir Maqdisī, *Le livre de la création et de l'histoire de Motahhar Ben Tāhir El-Maqdisī, attribué à Abou-Zeid Ahmed Ben Sahr El-Balhī*, Clément Huart [trans.] (Paris, 1916), vol. 6, p. 74; Gardīzī, *Taʾrīkh-i Gardīzī*, pp. 268–9; Ibn al-Athīr, vol. 5, p. 212.

69 Crone, *The Nativist Prophets of Early Islamic Iran*, p. 118; Karev, *Samarqand et le Sughd à l'époque ʿAbbāsside*, p. 56.

70 Narshakhī, p. 14; *The History of Bukhara*, p. 11.

71 Narshakhī, p. 15; *The History of Bukhara*, p. 10.

72 It was not the Battle of Ṭarāz alone that caused China's retreat from Central Asia. The revolt of the Sogdian general An Lushan in 755 was much more damaging. For An Lushan, E. G. Pulleyblank, *The Background of the Rebellion of An Lu-Shan* (London, 1955).

73 Karev, *Samarqand et le Sughd à l'époque ʿAbbāsside*, p. 62. This runs counter to the argument made by Shinji Maejima, who argues that the Battle of Ṭarāz was an accidental meeting of two forces and mostly inconsequential. As cited by Minoru Inaba, 'Arab Soldiers in China at the Time of the An-Shi Rebellion', *The Memoirs of*

the Toyo Bunko 68 (2010), p. 40. Cited in Crone, *The Nativist Prophets of Early Islamic Iran*, p. 115, n. 57.

74 On Gao Xianzhi's campaigns, Beckwith, *The Tibetan Empire in Central Asia*, pp. 130–3.

75 Chavannes, *Documents sur les Tou-Kiue (Turcs) occidentaux*, pp. 45, 83, 143; Karev, *Samarqand et le Sughd à l'époque ʿAbbāsside*, p. 64. As discussed in Chapter 3, a similar campaign had brought Sūyāb under Tang control over fifty years prior.

76 Embassies from Chāch appeared at the Tang court in every year between 740, when the king of Chāch was given the title King Who Obeys Righteousness, and 749 except for 748. In 746 a prince from Chāch had been given the title King Who Cherishes Civilization by the Tang emperor. Bielenstein, *Diplomacy and Trade in the Chinese World, 589-1276*, p. 326.

77 Ibn al-Athīr, vol. 5, p. 212; Chavannes, *Documents sur les Tou-Kiue (Turcs) occidentaux*, pp. 82, 142; Karev, *Samarqand et le Sughd à l'époque ʿAbbāsside*, pp. 64–7.

78 Ibn al-Athīr, vol. 5, p. 212. It is important to note that contemporary Muslim sources were practically silent on the topic of the Battle of Ṭarāz. Karev, *Samarqand et le Sughd à l'époque ʿAbbāsside*, p. 77.

79 It is likely Abū Muslim first set a reconnaissance force under Saʿīd b. Ḥumayd and then organized a larger force at Samarqand once word was received that the Chinese were amassing at Ṭarāz. Karev, *Samarqand et le Sughd à l'époque ʿAbbāsside*, pp. 71–2.

80 For an overview of the Battle of Ṭarāz, Ibid., pp. 62–78; Beckwith, *The Tibetan Empire in Central Asia*, pp. 138–40.

81 Karev, *Samarqand et le Sughd à l'époque ʿAbbāsside*, p. 72.

82 Narshakhī, p. 89; *The History of Bukhara*, p. 65.

83 Ṭabarī, vol. 3, p. 80; *The History of al-Ṭabarī*, vol. 27, pp. 202–3; Ibn al-Athīr, vol. 5, p. 214.

84 Maqdisī, *Le livre de la création et de l'histoire de Motahhar Ben Tāhir El-Maqdisī*, vol. 6, pp. 74–5.

85 Karev, *Samarqand et le Sughd à l'époque ʿAbbāsside*, p. 81.

86 Ṭabarī, vol. 3, p. 74; *The History of al-Ṭabarī*, vol. 27, p. 197; Ibn al-Athīr, vol. 5, p. 212.

87 Bielenstein, *Diplomacy and Trade in the Chinese World, 589-1276*, p. 339; Karev, *Samarqand et le Sughd à l'époque ʿAbbāsside*, p. 79.

88 Ṭabarī, vol. 3, pp. 79–80; *The History of al-Ṭabarī*, vol. 27, p. 202; Ibn al-Athīr, vol. 5, p. 214.

89 In contrast to Abbasid issues, the coins of Ikhrīd do not include Qur'anic or other religious inscriptions. Stephen Album, *Checklist of Islamic Coins* (Santa Rosa, CA, 2011), p. 47. See Zeno-14025 at www.zeno.ru for samples of these rare coins.

90 Bielenstein, *Diplomacy and Trade in the Chinese World, 589-1276*, p. 331; Chavannes, *Documents sur les Tou-Kiue (Turcs) Occidentaux*, p. 140.

91 Karev, *Samarqand et le Sughd à l'époque ʿAbbāsside*, p. 84.

92 Nasafī, *al-Qand fī dhikr ʿulamā' Samarqand*, p. 64.

93 Crone, *The Nativist Prophets of Early Islamic Iran*, p. 156.

94 Yaʿqūbī, *Kitāb al-buldān*, pp. 248–9.

95 C. E. Bosworth, 'The City of Tarsus and the Arab-Byzantine Frontier in Early and Middle ʿAbbasid Times', *Oriens* 33 (1992), pp. 271–2.

96 Nasafī, *al-Qand fī dhikr ʿulamāʾ Samarqand*, p. 225; Karev, *Samarqand et le Sughd à l'époque ʿAbbāsside*, pp. 111–13. Portions of the wall have still been preserved. Ibid., p. 114.
97 Ṭabarī, vol. 3, p. 80; *The History of al-Ṭabarī*, vol. 27, p. 203; Ibn al-Athīr, vol. 5, p. 214; Yury Karev, 'Un palais Islamique du VIIIe siècle à Samarkand', *Studia Iranica* 29 (2000), pp. 273–96. On Abū Muslim's projects in Marw, Iṣṭakhrī, *al-Masālik wa'l-mamālik*, p. 147; Ibn Ḥawqal, *Kitāb ṣūrat al-ard*, p. 434.
98 Karev, 'Un palais Islamique du VIIIe siècle à Samarkand', pp. 292–3.
99 Ṭabarī, vol. 3, p. 83; *The History of al-Ṭabarī*, vol. 27, p. 207.
100 Luke Treadwell, 'The Monetary History of the Bukharkhuda dirham ("black dirham") in Samanid Transoxiana (204-395/819-1005)', *Oriental Numismatic Society Journal* 193 (2007), p. 26. Similar issues are found in Ṭabaristān from 763 until 793 where the names of Abbasid governors are found on Sasanian style coins featuring Pahlavi inscriptions, dates in the post-Yazdgird III era and images of Khusrow II. Hodge Mehid Malek, *The Dābūyid Ispahbads and Early ʿAbbāsid Governors of Ṭabaristān: History and Numismatics* (London, 2000).
101 The uniformity of the coins over time and lack of inscriptions has resulted in a wide range of potential dates. Treadwell, 'The monetary history of the Bukharkhuda dirham ('black dirham') in Samanid Transoxiana (204-395/819-1005)', p. 24.
102 Vladimir Nastich, 'A Survey of the Abbasid Copper Coinage of Transoxiana', http://www.academia.edu/3734886/A_Survey_of_the _Abbasid_Copper_Coinage_of_Transoxiana, pp. 13–18; Karev, *Samarqand et le Sughd à l'époque ʿAbbāsside*, pp. 150–1. It should be noted that the copper coins of Bukhara and Samarqand are the first recorded instances of the use of the title Mahdī by the future caliph and then governor of Khurāsān Muḥammad b. Manṣūr. Michael L. Bates, 'Khurāsānī Revolutionaries and al-Mahdī's Title', in Farhad Daftary and Josef W. Meri [eds.], *Culture and Memory in Medieval Islam: Essays in Honour of Wilferd Madelung* (London, 2003), p. 293.
103 See the chart of various inscriptions provided by Bates, 'Khurāsānī Revolutionaries and al-Mahdī's Title', pp. 298–302.
104 Ṭabarī, vol. 3, pp. 81–4; *The History of al-Ṭabarī*, vol. 27, pp. 205–8; Ibn al-Athīr, vol. 5, p. 215.
105 Ṭabarī, vol. 3, p. 107; *The History of al-Ṭabarī*, vol. 28, pp. 29–30; Balʿamī, vol. 4, pp. 328–9; Ibn al-Athīr, vol. 5, p. 223.
106 For a study of these revolts and the religious ideologies that developed around the figure of Abū Muslim, Crone, *The Nativist Prophets of Early Islamic Iran*.
107 There is no evidence of an organized attack by the Turks at this time other than ʿAbd al-Jabbār's claim.
108 Yaʿqūbī, *Tārīkh*, vol. 2, p. 371; Ṭabarī, vol. 3, pp. 134–5; *The History of al-Ṭabarī*, vol. 28, pp. 69–70; Balʿamī, vol. 4, pp. 377–80; Ibn al-Athīr, vol. 5, pp. 237–8.
109 He was a pretender on multiple levels, first in that he claimed the caliphate for himself and second in that he claimed to be an ʿAlid but was an impostor. Gardīzī, *Ta'rīkh-i Gardīzī*, pp. 274–5; Crone, *The Nativist Prophets of Early Islamic Iran*, p. 109.
110 Ibid., pp. 109–10. Muḥammad 'the Pure Soul' would openly revolt in Medina in 672.
111 Karev, *Samarqand et le Sughd à l'époque ʿAbbāsside*, p. 145.
112 Bates, 'Khurāsānī Revolutionaries and al-Mahdī's Title', p. 293; Nastich, 'A Survey of the Abbasid Copper Coinage of Transoxiana', pp. 16–17.
113 Nastich, 'A Survey of the Abbasid Copper Coinage of Transoxiana', p. 18.
114 Jere L. Bacharach, 'Laqab for a Future Caliph: The Case of the Abbasid al-Mahdī', *Journal of the American Oriental Society* 113 (1993), p. 273.

115 Narshakhī, p. 90; *The History of Bukhara*, pp. 65–6. Elton Daniel, with confirmation from Patricia Crone, has argued that this passage refers to Muqanna' and not his father as others have interpreted Narshakhī's passage. Daniel, *The Political and Social History of Khurasan under Abbasid Rule*, p. 138; Patricia Crone and Masoud Jafari Jazi, 'The Muqanna' Narrative in the Tārīkhnāma: Part II, Commentary and Analysis', *Bulletin of the School of Oriental and African Studies* 73 (2010), p. 411; Crone, *The Nativist Prophets of Early Islamic Iran*, pp. 106–7.

116 For Muqanna''s religious doctrine, Crone, *The Nativist Prophets of Early Islamic Iran*, pp. 128–35.

117 The reverse also includes a religious inscription, 'God ordered fidelity and justice.' B. Kochnev, 'Les Monnaies de Muqanna'', *Studia Iranica* 30 (2001), pp. 143–50; Aleksandr Naymark and Luke Treadwell, 'An Arab-Sogdian Coin of AH 160: An Ikhshid in Ishtihan?', *The Numismatic Chronicle* 171 (2011), pp. 360–2.

118 Narshakhī, p. 92; *The History of Bukhara*, p. 67.

119 Narshakhī, p. 93; *The History of Bukhara*, p. 67; Patricia Crone and Masoud Jafari Jazi, 'The Muqanna' Narrative in the Tārīkhnāma: Part I, Introduction, Edition and Translation', *Bulletin of the School of Oriental and African Studies* 73 (2010), p. 175; Gardīzī, *Ta'rīkh-i Gardīzī*, p. 278; Ibn al-Athīr, vol. 6, p. 19.

120 On Muqanna''s campaigns into Chaghāniyān, Crone and Jafari Jazi, 'The Muqanna' Narrative in the Tārīkhnāma: Part I', p. 172.

121 For a survey of these two revolts, Crone, *The Nativist Prophets of Early Islamic Iran*, pp. 151–7.

122 Crone and Jafari Jazi, 'The Muqanna' Narrative in the Tārīkhnāma: Part I', pp. 170–3; Gardīzī, *Ta'rīkh-i Gardīzī*, p. 279.

123 The duration of Muqanna''s revolt is typically listed at seventeen years from his declaration of prophethood to death. Ṭabarī, vol. 3, p. 494; *The History of al-Ṭabarī*, vol. 29, p. 209; Narshakhī, pp. 101–2; *The History of Bukhara*, pp. 74–5; Crone and Jafari Jazi, 'The Muqanna' Narrative in the Tārīkhnāma: Part I', p. 177; Ibn al-Athīr, vol. 6, pp. 24–5. It should be noted that this is not the same Sa'īd al-Ḥarashī who had violently suppressed the Sogdians in 722, see the previous chapter. This Sa'īd al-Ḥarashī was the son of a Turkish slave and the maternal aunt of the king of Ṭabaristān and had been the Amir of Herat according to Bal'amī. See Hugh Kennedy's comments in the Ṭabarī translation, *The History of al-Ṭabarī*, vol. 29, p. 196, n. 637. Both Narshakhī and Bal'amī include a story, perhaps rooted in Ḥarashī's Turkish background, in which he brought a herd of 10,000 sheep with him while campaigning against Muqanna' and they are captured by Turkish raiders. Narshakhī, p. 98; *The History of Bukhara*, p. 72; Crone and Jafari Jazi, 'The Muqanna' Narrative in the Tārīkhnāma: Part I', p. 174.

124 Narshakhī, p. 92; *The History of Bukhara*, p. 67.

125 Bal'amī writes of the *dahāqīn* of Ḥajdān named Nāwan and Nīra/Nabra. Crone and Jafari Jazi, 'The Muqanna' Narrative in the Tārīkhnāma: Part I', pp. 171, 173. The latter may be Niyāza, a village between Kish and Nakhshab. Bartold, *Turkestan Down to the Mongol Invasion*, p. 140; Karev, *Samarqand et le Sughd à l'époque 'Abbāsside*, p. 187.

126 Narshakhī, p. 93–5; *The History of Bukhara*, p. 68–9; Ibn al-Athīr, vol. 6, p. 19.

127 In a well-known passage, the geographer Muqaddasī, writing 200 years after these events, says that in the Bukhara oasis only the capital Numūjkath had a mosque because the people adhered to the Ḥanafī *madhhab* or legal school which states that congregational prayers may only occur in a place where legal penalties may be

administered, but the people of Paykand worked hard to receive one. Such a situation would tie Islam to the reach of the governor and would act as evidence that neither reached far to the villages. Muqaddasī, *Aḥsan al-taqāsīm fī ma'rafa al-aqālīm*, p. 282; Muqaddasī, *The Best Division for Knowledge of the Regions*, p. 251.

128 Narshakhī, p. 98; *The History of Bukhara*, p. 71; Crone and Jafari Jazi, 'The Muqanna' Narrative in the Tārīkhnāma: Part I', 174.

129 Crone and Jafari Jazi, 'The Muqanna' Narrative in the Tārīkhnāma: Part I', pp. 172–3.

130 Ibid., p. 176.

131 Karev, *Samarqand et le Sughd à l'époque 'Abbāsside*, pp. 209–10.

132 Bunyāt's execution is described in dramatic fashion. A group of horsemen rode up to the palace of Varakhshā, stormed into Bunyāt's chambers, decapitated him and then rode off. Narshakhī, pp. 14–15; *The History of Bukhara*, pp. 10–11.

133 Naymark and Treadwell, 'An Arab-Sogdian Coin of AH 160', pp. 359–60.

134 Karev, *Samarqand et le Sughd à l'époque 'Abbāsside*, pp. 208–9.

135 Ya'qūbī, *Tārīkh*, vol. 2, pp. 397–8.

136 Narshakhī, p. 94; *The History of Bukhara*, p. 68; Crone, *The Nativist Prophets of Early Islamic Iran*, pp. 138–9.

137 Tor, *Violent Order*.

138 Narshakhī, pp. 97–8; *The History of Bukhara*, p. 71.

139 Narshakhī, p. 93; *The History of Bukhara*, p. 68; Ibn al-Athīr, vol. 6, p. 19.

140 Crone and Jafari Jazi, 'The Muqanna' Narrative in the Tārīkhnāma: Part I', p. 173.

141 Narshakhī, pp. 98 ff.; *The History of Bukhara*, pp. 71 ff.

142 Crone, *The Nativist Prophets of Early Islamic Iran*, p. 139.

143 Narshakhī, p. 47; *The History of Bukhara*, pp. 33–4.

144 Gardīzī, *Ta'rīkh-i Gardīzī*, p. 286.

145 Gardīzī, *Ta'rīkh-i Gardīzī*, p. 279; Crone and Jafari Jazi, 'The Muqanna' Narrative in the Tārīkhnāma: Part I', p. p. 173; Ibn al-Athīr, vol. 6, p. 19.

146 Gardīzī, *Ta'rīkh-i Gardīzī*, pp. 283–4.

147 Ṭabarī, vol. 3, p. 517; *The History of al-Ṭabarī*, vol. 29, p. 234; Gardīzī, *Ta'rīkh-i Gardīzī*, pp. 274, 282.

148 Ṭabarī, vol. 3, p. 631; *The History of al-Ṭabarī*, vol. 30, p. 143; Ibn al-Athīr, vol. 6, p. 67.

149 Ṭabarī, vol. 3, p. 631; *The History of al-Ṭabarī*, vol. 30, pp. 143–4; Muḥammad b. 'Abdūs Jahshiyārī, *Kitāb al-wuzarā' wa'l-kuttāb*, Muṣṭafā Saqā, Ibrāhīm Abyārī, and 'Abd al-Ḥafīẓ Shiblī [ed.] (Cairo, 1938), p. 191.

150 Karev, *Samarqand et le Sughd à l'époque 'Abbāsside*, pp. 258–9.

151 Ṭabarī, vol. 3, p. 631; *The History of al-Ṭabarī*, vol. 30, p. 143; Gardīzī, *Ta'rīkh-i Gardīzī*, p. 287; Ibn al-Athīr, vol. 6, p. 67.

152 Ya'qūbī, *Kitāb al-buldān*, pp. 290–1; Ṭabarī, vol. 3, p. 634; *The History of al-Ṭabarī*, vol. 30, p. 147. Interestingly, in his history, Ya'qūbī credits Faḍl with a campaign against Ṭālaqān that had entered into rebellion and then a campaign against an unnamed master of the Turks without reference to the campaign against Kabul that he included in his geography. Ya'qūbī, *Tārīkh*, vol. 2, p. 407.

153 On 'Īsā b. Māhān, Crone, *Slaves on Horses*, p. 178. In 799–800, Hārūn al-Rashīd became suspicious that 'Alī b. 'Īsā was preparing a rebellion. In response, Ibn 'Īsā went to the caliph and gave him an immense sum of money. Hārūn responded by sending Ibn 'Īsā back to Khurāsān with his son Ma'mūn. Ṭabarī, vol. 3, pp. 648–9, 702–4; *The History of al-Ṭabarī*, vol. 30, pp. 171–2, 250–4; Bal'amī, vol. 4, p. 470; Abū al-Ḥasan 'Alī ibn Zayd Bayhaqī, *Tārīkh-i Bayhaq*, Qāsim Ghanī and 'Alī Akbar Fayyāḍ [eds.] (Tehran, 1970), pp. 416–19; Ibn al-Athīr, vol. 6, p. 75.

Chapter 7

1 Vladimir Minorsky, *Studies in Caucasian History* (London, 1953), p. 110.

2 These nationalist ideologies are associated primarily with the Ṣaffārid and Sāmānid dynasties and the rise of New Persian literature. The Ṭāhirids, who were culturally Arabized, receive somewhat less attention in this regard. For a sampling of these arguments, Yahya Armajani, 'The Saffarids: A Study in Iranian Nationalism', in B.G. Gafurov [ed.], *Trudy XXV. Mezhdunarodogo Kongressa Vostokovedov, Moskva 9-16 Avgusta 1960* (Moscow, 1963), pp. 168–73; S.M. Stern, 'Yaʿqūb the Coppersmith and Persian National Sentiment', in C. E. Bosworth [ed.], *Iran and Islam: In Memory of the Late Vladimir Minorsky* (Edinburgh, 1971), pp. 536–9; Lutz Richter-Bernburg, 'Linguistic Shuʿubiya and Early Neo-Persian Prose', *Journal of the American Oriental Society* 94 (1974), pp. 55–64; Richard Frye, 'The Sāmānids', in *CHIr4*, pp. 135–61; Richard Frye, *The Golden Age of Persia: The Arabs in the East* (London, 1975), pp. 200–7; Gilbert Lazard, 'The Rise of the New Persian Language', in *CHIr4*, pp. 606–32; Marilyn Robinson Waldman, *Towards a Theory of Historical Narrative: A Case Study of Perso-Islamicate Historiography* (Columbus, OH, 1980); Frye, *Bukhara*, pp. 60–9, 94–110; Julie Scott Meisami, *Persian Historiography to the End of the Twefth Century* (Edinburgh, 1999), pp. 15–46; James E. Montgomery, 'Ibn Rusta's Lack of "Eloquence", the Rus, and Samanid Cosmography', *Edebiyat* 12 (2001): 73–93.

3 Rocco Rante, '"Khorasan Proper" and "Greater Khorasan" within a Politico-Cultural Framework', in Rocco Rante [ed.], *Greater Khorasan* (Berlin, 2015), pp. 13–14.

4 This process was not entirely unique to Khurāsān and similar relationships were built in the late eighth and early ninth centuries between the caliphs and the local lords of other remote provinces such as Ṭabaristān. See my forthcoming article Robert Haug 'Local, Regional, and Imperial Politics: Ṭabaristān and the Early Empire, Struggle and Integration on Multiple Levels', in Stefan Heidemann [ed.], *The Reach of Empire* (Berlin, forthcoming).

5 For an overview of the origins of the Ṭāhirid family, Mongi Kaabi, 'Les Ṭāhirides: étude historico-littéraire de la dynastie des Banū Ṭāhir b. al-Ḥusayn au Ḫurāsān et en Iraq au IIIème s. de l'Hégire/IXème s. J.-C.' (Université de Paris-Sorbonne, 1971), pp. 62–79; Mongi Kaabi, 'Les origines ṭāhirides dans la daʿwa ʿabbāside', *Arabica* 19 (1972), pp. 145–64; C. E. Bosworth, 'The Ṭāhirids and Ṣaffārids', in *CHIr Vol. 4* (Cambridge, 1975), pp. 91–2.

6 Kaabi, 'Les origines ṭāhirides dans la daʿwa ʿabbāside', pp. 146–7. Ṭabarī makes one reference to Ruzayq participating in raids with Muhallab b. Abī Ṣufra. Ṭabarī, vol. 2, p. 1988; *The History of al-Ṭabarī*, vol. 27, p. 97.

7 Descent from the Banū Khuzāʿa is one of three lineages Ṭāhir b. al-Ḥusayn is accused of claiming (some members of his family employed the *nisba* Khuzāʿī). According to an elegy for Ṭāhir by Diʿbil b. ʿAlī al-Khuzāʿī (d. 860), he also claimed Quraysh through the Khuzāʿa and the Sasanian shahanshahs, though all three were mocked. Di'bil b. 'Alī Khuzā'ī, *Di'bil b. 'Alī, the Life and Writings of an Early 'Abbāsid Poet*, L. Zolondek [trans.] (Lexington, 1961), pp. 74–5, 118.

8 Ṭabarī, vol. 2, pp. 1987–8; *The History of al-Ṭabarī*, vol. 27, pp. 96–7.

9 Ibn al-Athīr, vol. 6, p. 21.

10 Crone, *Slaves on Horses*, pp. 67–8.

11 Yaʿqūbī, *Tārīkh*, vol. 2, p. 387.

12 Yaʿqūbī, *Kitāb al-buldān*, p. 304; Yaʿqūbī, *Tārīkh*, vol. 2, p. 398; Ṭabarī, vol. 3, p. 484; *The History of al-Ṭabarī*, vol. 29, p. 196. There are disagreements as to whether this is Layth b. Naṣr or Layth b. Ṭarīf, a *mawlā* of Mahdī and his governor in Sind. Bartold argues the former while Crone the latter. Bartold, *Turkestan Down to the Mongol Invasion*, p. 200; Crone, *Slaves on Horses*, p. 192.

13 Gardīzī, *Ta'rīkh-i Gardīzī*, p. 279; Crone and Jazi, 'The Muqannaʿ Narrative in the Tārīkhnāma: Part I, Introduction, Edition and Translation', p. 173; Ibn al-Athīr, vol. 6, p. 19.

14 As Yury Karev suggested, Sogdiana is, after all, far from the centres of Abbasid authority. Karev, *Samarqand et le Sughd à l'époque ʿAbbāsside*, p. 273.

15 Ṭabarī, vol. 3, pp. 707–8; *The History of al-Ṭabarī*, vol. 30, pp. 259–61; Balʿamī, vol. 4, pp. 471–2; Ibn al-Athīr, vol. 6, p. 89. For a more detailed examination of the Qārinids and their relationship to the Abbasid Caliphs, see Haug, 'Local, Regional, and Imperial Politics'.

16 Ṭabarī, vol. 3, p. 708; *The History of al-Ṭabarī*, vol. 30, pp. 260–1; Balʿamī, vol. 4, p. 472.

17 Ṭabarī, vol. 3, p. 712; *The History of al-Ṭabarī*, vol. 30, p. 267, On the status of the *ṣāḥib* of Chāch and his Turks, Karev, *Samarqand et le Sughd à l'époque ʿAbbāsside*, p. 281.

18 Ṭabarī, vol. 3, p. 719; *The History of al-Ṭabarī*, vol. 30, pp. 268–9; Ibn al-Athīr, vol. 6, p. 92.

19 For Harthama b. Aʿyan's *bona fides*, Crone, *Slaves on Horses*, p. 177.

20 Ṭabarī, vol. 3, pp. 716–18; *The History of al-Ṭabarī*, vol. 30, pp. 272–6; Balʿamī, vol. 4, p. 473.

21 Ṭabarī, vol. 3, pp. 724, 727; *The History of al-Ṭabarī*, vol. 30, pp. 283–4, 286–7.

22 Ṭabarī, vol. 3, p. 734; *The History of al-Ṭabarī*, vol. 30, p. 297; Balʿamī, vol. 4, p. 477.

23 On the Meccan Protocol, Tayeb El-Hibri, 'Harun Al-Rashid and the Mecca Protocol of 802: A Plan for Division or Succession?', *International Journal of Middle East Studies* 24 (1992).

24 The second was Hishām b. Farr-Khusraw, likely a local poet identified by C. E. Bosworth. Ṭabarī, vol. 3, pp. 713–15; *The History of al-Ṭabarī*, vol. 30, pp. 269–72; Ibn al-Athīr, vol. 6, p. 93.

25 Kaabi, 'Les origines ṭāhirides dans la daʿwa ʿabbāside', pp. 159–62.

26 Ibid. pp. 162–3.

27 Ṭabarī, vol. 3, p. 777; *The History of al-Ṭabarī*, vol. 31, p. 24; Gardīzī, *Ta'rīkh-i Gardīzī*, p. 292; Ibn al-Athīr, vol. 6, p. 105.

28 Narshakhī, pp. 104–5; *The History of Bukhara*, p. 76.

29 Yaʿqūbī, *Tārīkh*, vol. 2, pp. 435–6. Narshakhī also writes that Rāfiʿ fortified Samarqand. Narshakhī, p. 104; *The History of Bukhara*, p. 76.

30 Yaʿqūbī, *Tārīkh*, vol. 2, p. 436; Ṭabarī, vol. 3, p. 775; *The History of al-Ṭabarī*, vol. 31, p. 19; Ibn al-Athīr, vol. 6, p. 103.

31 Yaʿqūbī, *Tārīkh*, vol. 2, p. 436; Ṭabarī, vol. 3, p. 777; *The History of al-Ṭabarī*, vol. 31, p. 24; Ibn al-Athīr, vol. 6, p. 103.

32 Gardīzī, *Ta'rīkh-i Gardīzī*, p. 293.

33 Amikam Elad, 'The Armies of Al-Ma'mūn in Khurāsān (193–202/809–17–18): Recruitment of Its Contingents and Their Social-Ethnic Composition', *Oriens* 38 (2010), pp. 39–40.

34 The precise identification of the *abnā' al-dawla* is perpetually up for debate. For an overview of previous arguments as well as an important thesis emphasizing the late construction of their identity as a reaction to the civil war and Ma'mūn's employment

of Iranian Khurāsānīs, John P. Turner, 'The *abnā' al-dawla*: The Definition and Legitimation of Identity in Response to the Fourth Fitna', *Journal of Oriental and African Studies* 124 (2004), pp. 1–22.

35 A similar transformation was attempted regarding the Abbasid family itself, the largest portion of which had also sided with Amīn. In the aftermath of his victory Ma'mūn faced revolts from his relatives, most notably his uncle Ibrāhīm b. Mahdī (779–839), and attempted to designate the Shi'ite Imam ʿAlī al-Riḍa (766–818) as his successor, a plan which ultimately failed and may have ended with Ma'mūn assassinating ʿAlī in Ṭūs. For an overview of Ma'mūn's conflict with the Abbasid family, John A. Nawas, 'All in the Family? Al-Muʿtaṣim's Succession to the Caliphate as Denouement to the Lifelong Feud between Al-Ma'mūn and His ʿAbbasid Family', *Oriens* 38 (2010), pp. 77–88.

36 Balādhūrī, p. 430; *Origins*, vol. 2, pp. 203–4; Yaʿqūbī, *Tārīkh*, vol. 2, pp. 436–7; Ṭabarī, vol. 3, pp. 815-16; *The History of al-Ṭabarī*, vol. 31, pp. 71–2.

37 Ṭabarī, vol. 3, pp. 852, 859–60; *The History of al-Ṭabarī*, vol. 31, pp. 115, 124.

38 Ṭabarī, vol. 3, pp. 1044–5; *The History of al-Ṭabarī*, vol. 32, p. 108.

39 Narshakhī, pp. 104–5; *The History of Bukhara*, p. 76; Luke Treadwell, 'The Political History of the Sāmānid State' (University of Oxford, 1991), p. 77.

40 For details on Ma'mūnī, Crone, *Slaves on Horses*, p. 257, n. 599.

41 Bosworth, 'The Ṭāhirids and Ṣaffārids', p. 95.

42 Ṭabarī, vol. 3, pp. 1046–62; *The History of al-Ṭabarī*, vol. 32, pp. 110–29. For a study of the letter including a translation of the text, C. E. Bosworth, 'An Early Arabic Mirror for Princes: Ṭāhir Dhū l-Yamīnain's Epistle to His Son ʿAbdallāh (206/821)', *Journal of Near Eastern Studies* 29 (1970), pp. 25–41.

43 An example of such a coin is found in the collection of the American Numismatic Society, ANS 1972.79.675. Robert Haug, 'The Gate of Iron', pp. 168–9.

44 Dominique Sourdel, 'Les circonstances de la mort de Ṭāhir Ier Au Ḫurāsān en 207/822', *Arabica* 5 (1958): 66–9.

45 Hugh Kennedy, *The Prophet and the Age of the Caliphates*, second edition (Harlow, 2004), p. 160.

46 Ṭabarī, vol. 3, p. 1065; *The History of al-Ṭabarī*, vol. 32, p. 134. It is not clear if this is the same Sallām al-Abrash who was the previous owner of the Turkish slave general Ītākh and employed him as a cook. Matthew Gordon, *The Breaking of a Thousand Swords: A History of the Turkish Military of Samarra (A.H. 200-275/815-889 C.E.)* (Albany, NY, 2001), p. 19.

47 Balādhūrī, pp. 430–1; *Origins*, vol. 2, pp. 204–5; Ṭabarī, vol. 3, pp. 1065–6; *The History of al-Ṭabarī*, vol. 32, p. 135; Ibn al-Athīr, vol. 6, p. 178.

48 Ṭabarī, vol. 3, p. 1102; *The History of al-Ṭabarī*, vol. 32, p. 182.

49 Ṭabarī, vol. 3, p. 1268; *The History of al-Ṭabarī*, vol. 33, p. 136.

50 Yaʿqūbī, *Tārīkh*, vol. 2, pp. 476–7; Ṭabarī, vol. 3, p. 1298; *The History of al-Ṭabarī*, vol. 33, p. 172; Ibn Isfandiyār, *Tārīkh-i Ṭabaristān*, pp. 205–7; Ibn Isfandiyār, *An Abridged Translation of the History of Ṭabaristān*, pp. 145–7.

51 Ṭabarī, vol. 3, p. 1268; *The History of al-Ṭabarī*, vol. 33, pp. 136–7.

52 Yaʿqūbī, *Tārīkh*, vol. 2, p. 477; Ṭabarī, vol. 3, pp. 1268–9; *The History of al-Ṭabarī*, vol. 33, pp. 137–8; Masʿūdī, *Les Prairies d'or*, vol. 7, p. 138; Ibn Isfandiyār, *Tārīkh-i Ṭabaristān*, pp. 220–1; Ibn Isfandiyār, *An Abridged Translation of the History of Ṭabaristān*, p. 155.

53 Balādhūrī, p. 340; *Origins*, vol. 2, pp. 47–8; Yaʿqūbī, *Tārīkh*, vol. 2, p. 477; Ṭabarī, vol. 3, pp. 1303, 1311–12; *The History of al-Ṭabarī*, vol. 33, pp. 179–80, 190–1; Masʿūdī,

Les Prairies d'or, vol. 7, p. 137–8; Ibn Isfandiyār, *Tārīkh-i Ṭabaristān*, pp. 218–19; Ibn Isfandiyār, *An Abridged Translation of the History of Ṭabaristān*, p. 154–6.

54 For Bābak's revolt, Crone, *The Nativist Prophets of Early Islamic Iran*, pp. 46–76. The dual punishment of Māzyār and Bābak is a common trope. The Seljuq vizier Niẓām al-Mulk (d. 1092) includes a story in his *Siyāsatnāma* in which Muʿtaṣim raped the captured daughters of Bābak, Māzyār and the Byzantine Emperor Theophilos (r. 829–42) in a single hour as a sign of his victory and masculinity. Niẓām al-Mulk, *Siyar al-Mulūk*, Hubert Darke [ed.], second edition (Tehran, 1985), p. 243.

55 For the history of the Bāvandids, Wilferd Madelung, 'Āl-e Bāvand', *EIr*.

56 For an overview of these narratives, Treadwell, 'The Political History of the Sāmānid State', pp. 64–74.

57 Narshakhī, p. 81; *The History of Bukhara*, p. 59.

58 Abū Saʿīd ʿAbd al-Ḥayy Gardīzī, *Zayn al-akhbār*, ʿAbd al-Ḥayy Ḥabībī [ed.] (Tehran, 1968), p. 146.

59 Treadwell, 'The Political History of the Sāmānid State', pp. 65–7.

60 On these claims, Ibid., pp. 68–9.

61 Narshakhī, p. 105; *The History of Bukhara*, p. 76; Gardīzī, *Ta'rīkh-i Gardīzī*, p. 322; Ibn al-Athīr, vol. 6, p. 279.

62 For a full discussion of these coins, Haug, 'The Gate of Iron', pp. 171–3.

63 For rough outlines of mints and dates, Album, *Checklist of Islamic Coins*, pp. 152–3.

64 *Tārīkh-i Sīstān*, pp. 177–8, 183, 187–8; *The Tārikh-e Sīstan*, pp. 141, 145, 149.

65 Yaʿqūbī, *Tārīkh*, vol. 2, p. 461.

66 Deborah Tor, 'The Islamization of Central Asia in the Sāmānid Era and the Reshaping of the Muslim World', *Bulletin of the School of Oriental and African Studies* 72 (2009), p. 292.

67 Iṣṭakhrī, *al-Masālik wa'l-mamālik*, p. 291.

68 Muqaddasī, *Aḥsan al-taqāsīm fī maʿrafa al-aqālīm*, p. 283; Muqaddasī, *The Best Division for Knowledge of the Regions*, p. 252.

69 Iṣṭakhrī, *al-Masālik wa'l-mamālik*, p. 291; Ibn Ḥawqal, *Kitāb ṣūrat al-ard*, p. 471.

70 Paul, *The State and the Military*, pp. 8–10.

71 Treadwell, 'The Political History of the Sāmānid State', p. 97.

72 Narshakhī, pp. 15–16; *The History of Bukhara*, pp. 11–12.

73 Narshakhī, pp. 24–5; *The History of Bukhara*, pp. 17–18. On the identification of Aḥmad with Manṣūr, Treadwell, 'The Political History of the Sāmānid State', p. 226, n. 66.

74 Muqaddasī, *Aḥsan al-taqāsīm fī maʿrafa al-aqālīm*, p. 282; Muqaddasī, *The Best Division for Knowledge of the Regions*, p. 251.

75 Ibn al-Athīr, vol. 6, p. 237.

76 Ṭabarī, vol. 3, pp. 1307–8; *The History of al-Ṭabarī*, vol. 33, p. 185.

77 Balādhūrī, p. 431; *Origins*, vol. 2, pp. 205–6.

78 For an overview of the Turkish military of Sāmarrā', Gordon, *The Breaking of a Thousand Swords*.

79 'Appendix A: Retainer Forces in Early Islamic History', in Gordon, *The Breaking of a Thousand Swords*; ʿAthamina, 'Non-Arab Regiments and Private Militias during the Umayyād Period', pp. 347–78.

80 Gordon, *The Breaking of a Thousand Swords*, p. 35.

81 Ibn Khurradādhbih, *Kitāb al-masālik wa'l-mamālik*, p. 37.

82 Yaʿqūbī, *Kitāb al-buldān*, pp. 255–6.

83 Masʿūdī, *Les prairies d'or*, vol. 7, p. 281.

84 Ṭabarī, vol. 3, p. 1326; *The History of al-Ṭabarī*, vol. 33, p. 212.

85 Treadwell, 'The Political History of the Sāmānid State', pp. 287–8.
86 For the history of the Ṣaffārids, C. E. Bosworth, *The History of the Saffarids of Sistan and the Maliks of Nimruz* (Costa Mesa, CA, 1994); Tor, *Violent Order*.
87 Haug, 'Frontiers and the State in the Medieval Islamic World', pp. 637–40.
88 Tor, 'The Islamization of Central Asia in the Sāmānid Era and the Reshaping of the Muslim World', p. 280.
89 Bonner, *Aristocratic Violence and Holy War*.
90 Iṣṭakhrī, *al-Masālik wa'l-mamālik*, p. 163.
91 Ṭabarī, vol. 3, p. 2138; *The History of al-Ṭabarī*, vol. 38, p. 11; Narshakhī, p. 118; *The History of Bukhara*, pp. 86–7; Ibn al-Athīr, vol. 7, p. 216.
92 Narshakhī, p. 119–26; *The History of Bukhara*, pp. 87–92; *Tārīkh-i Sīstān* , pp. 255–6; *The Tārikh-e Sīstan*, pp. 201–3.
93 Paul, *The State and the Military*, p. 14, n. 49.
94 For a detailed discussion of *ribāṭāt* in Transoxiana as found in the geographers of the ninth and tenth centuries, Haug, 'The Gate of Iron', pp. 133–44.
95 Iṣṭakhrī, *al-Masālik wa'l-mamālik*, p. 163.
96 Narshakhī, p. 21; *The History of Bukhara*, p. 15.
97 Muqaddasī, *Aḥsan al-taqāsīm fī ma'rafa al-aqālīm*, pp. 273–4; Muqaddasī, *The Best Division for Knowledge of the Regions*, pp. 244–5.
98 Muḥammad Qazvīnī, '*Muqaddamah qadīm Shāhnāmah*', in Muḥammad Amīn Rīyāḥī [ed.], *Hazāra-i Firdausī* (Tehran, 2010), p. 190; Minorsky, 'The Older Preface to the Shāh-Nāma', p. 168. It may be important to note here, as Maʿmarī gathered his sources, the emphasis on Khurāsān is important. As it is currently understood, the *Shāhnāma* tradition is eastern in its origins, capturing not just the stories of the Sasanian heartland in Fārs or the political centre in Iraq but also the stories from Khurāsān, Sīstān and Ṭukhāristān. Rezakhani, *ReOrienting the Sasanians*, pp. 194–8.
99 Qazvīnī, '*Muqaddamah qadīm Shāhnāmah*', p. 189; Minorsky, 'The Older Preface to the Shāh-Nāma', p. 167.
100 Qazvīnī, '*Muqaddamah qadīm Shāhnāmah*', pp. 189–90; Minorsky, 'The Older Preface to the Shāh-Nāma', pp. 167–8.
101 It is important to highlight here, as in most known translations into New Persian, the text returned to Persian from an Arabic translation, not Pahlavi.
102 On Balʿamī's *Tārīkhnāma*, Peacock, *Mediaeval Islamic Historiography and Political Legitimacy*.
103 Qazvīnī, '*Muqaddamah qadīm Shāhnāmah*', p. 190; Minorsky, 'The Older Preface to the Shāh-Nāma', p. 168.
104 Julie Scott Meisami, 'The Past in Service of the Present: Two Views of History in Medieval Persia', *Poetics Today* 14 (1993), p. 253.
105 Minorsky, 'The Older Preface to the Shāh-Nāma', pp. 171–3.
106 Qazvīnī, '*Muqaddamah qadīm Shāhnāmah*', pp. 196–8; Minorsky, 'The Older Preface to the Shāh-Nāma', pp. 174–5.
107 Julie Scott Meisami has suggested that Firdawsī was imagining the beginning of a new cycle that combined Islamic and Iranian kingship under the Turk Maḥmūd of Ghazna. Julie Scott Meisami, 'Why Write History in Persian? Historical Writing in the Samanid Period', in Carole Hillenbrand [ed.], *Studies in Honour of Clifford Edmund Bosworth Volume II* (Leiden, 2000), pp. 361–2.
108 Qazvīnī, '*Muqaddamah qadīm Shāhnāmah*', pp. 198–200; Minorsky, 'The Older Preface to the Shāh-Nāma', pp. 175–6.

109 Qazvīnī, '*Muqaddamah qadīm Shāhnāmah*', pp. 200–1; Minorsky, 'The Older Preface to the Shāh-Nāma', pp. 177–8.
110 Qazvīnī, '*Muqaddamah qadīm Shāhnāmah*', pp. 201–2; Minorsky, 'The Older Preface to the Shāh-Nāma', p. 178.
111 Qazvīnī, '*Muqaddamah qadīm Shāhnāmah*', p. 202; Minorsky, 'The Older Preface to the Shāh-Nāma', p. 179.
112 Pourshariati, *Decline and Fall of the Sasanian Empire*, pp. 448–50; Crone, *The Nativist Prophets of Early Islamic Iran*, pp. 33–4.
113 For an overview of the Muḥtājids, Bosworth, 'The Rulers of Chaghāniyān in Early Islamic Times', pp.1–20.
114 Tor, 'The Islamization of Central Asia in the Sāmānid Era and the Reshaping of the Muslim World', pp. 293–4.
115 Treadwell, 'The Political History of the Sāmānid State', pp. 168–9.
116 Paul, *The State and the Military*, pp. 27–8.
117 Gardīzī, *Zayn al-akhbār*, pp. 152–3.
118 Ibid., p. 153.
119 Ibid., pp. 153–4; Ibn Isfandiyār, *An Abridged Translation of the History of Ṭabaristān*, pp. 218–19; Ibn al-Athīr, vol. 8, p. 170.
120 Bosworth, 'The Rulers of Chaghāniyān in Early Islamic Times', p. 5.
121 Ibid., p. 6.
122 On the competing accounts of Abū ʿAlī's revolt, representing different sides of the conflict, Bosworth, 'The Rulers of Chaghāniyān in Early Islamic Times', pp. 7–8; Treadwell, 'The Political History of the Sāmānid State', pp. 213–19.
123 Ibn al-Athīr, vol. 8, p. 223; Bosworth, 'The Rulers of Chaghāniyān in Early Islamic Times', p. 8; Treadwell, 'The Political History of the Sāmānid State', p. 218.
124 Gardīzī, *Zayn al-akhbār*, p. 158; Ibn al-Athīr, vol. 8, p. 234.
125 Treadwell, 'The Political History of the Sāmānid State', p. 8.
126 Gardīzī, *Zayn al-akhbār*, p. 160; Ibn Isfandiyār, *An Abridged Translation of the History of Ṭabaristān*, p. 224; Ibn al-Athīr, vol. 8, pp. 243–4.
127 Gardīzī, *Zayn al-akhbār*, p. 161.
128 Ibid., p. 162.
129 According to Gardīzī, Vushmgīr had Abū Manṣūr poisoned, leaving him in a weakened state when he entered the battle against the Sāmānids. Ibid., p. 162.
130 Richter-Bernburg, 'Linguistic Shuʿubiya and Early Neo-Persian Prose', p. 55.
131 For the situation at the Sāmānid court, see Luke Treadwell's detailed survey. Treadwell, 'The Political History of the Sāmānid State', pp. 170–85.
132 Ibid., pp. 233–5.
133 Tor, 'The Islamization of Central Asia in the Sāmānid Era and the Reshaping of the Muslim World', pp. 291–2.
134 Abū Naṣr ʿUtbī, *Kitāb al-yamīnī fī akhbār dawlat al-Malik Yamīn al-Dawla Abī l'Qāsim Maḥmūd b. Nāṣir al-Dawla Abī Manṣūr b. Sabuktakīn*, Yūsuf Hādī [ed.] (Tehran, 2008), p. 163f.
135 Ibid.
136 Ibid., p. 169.
137 Ibid., p. 174.
138 Treadwell, 'The Political History of the Sāmānid State', pp. 262–3.
139 Paul, *The State and the Military*, pp. 32–3.

BIBLIOGRAPHY

Abū al-Fidā'. *Kitāb Taqwīm Al-Buldān*. Edited by Joseph Toussaint Reinaud and William McGuckin de Slane. Paris: Imprimerie Royale, 1840.

Agathias. *The Histories*. Translated by Joseph D. Frendo. Berlin: Walter de Gruyter, 1975.

Agha, Saleh Said. 'The Arab Population in Ḫurāsān during the Umayyad Period: Some Demographic Computations'. *Arabica* 46 (1999): 211–29.

Agha, Saleh Said. 'The "Battle of the Pass": Two Consequential Readings'. *Bulletin of the School of Oriental and African Studies* 63 (2000): 340–55.

Agha, Saleh Said. *The Revolution Which Toppled the Umayyads: Neither Arab nor 'Abbāsid*. Leiden: Brill, 2003.

Agostini, Domenico and Sören Stark. 'Zāwulistān, Kāwulistān and the Land Bosi – On the Question of a Sasanian Court-in-Exile in the Southern Hindukush'. *Studia Iranica* 45 (2016): 17–38.

Ágoston, Gábor. 'A Flexible Empire: Authority and Its Limits on the Ottoman Frontiers'. *International Journal of Turkish Studies* 9 (2003): 15–31.

Album, Stephen. *Checklist of Islamic Coins*. Third edition. Santa Rosa, CA: Stephen Album Rare Coins, 2011.

Album, Stephen and Tony Goodwin. *Sylloge of Islamic Coins in the Ashmolean, I: The Pre-Reform Coinage of the Early Islamic Period*. Oxford: Ashmolean Museum, 2002.

Alram, Michael. 'Alchon und Nēzak. zur Geschichte der Iranischen Hunen in Mittleasien'. In *La Persia e l'Asia centrale da Alessandro al X secolo*, edited by Istituto italiano per il Medio ed Estremo Oriente and Accademia nazionale dei Lincei, 517–54. Rome: Accademia Nazionale dei Lincei, 1996.

Alram, Michael. 'Ardashir's Eastern Campaign and the Numismatic Evidence'. In *After Alexander: Central Asia before Islam*, edited by Joe Cribb and Georgina Herrmann, 227–42. Oxford: Oxford University Press, 2007.

Alram, Michael and Matthias Pfisterer. 'Alkhan and Hephthalite Coinage'. In *Coins, Art and Chronology II: The First Millennium C.E. in the Indo-Iranian Borderlands*, edited by Michael Alram, Deborah E. Klimburg-Salter, Minoru Inaba and Matthias Pfisterer, 13–38. Vienna: Verlag der Österreichischen Akademie der Wissenschaften, 2010.

Anthony, Sean W. *Crucifixion and Death as Spectacle: Umayyad Crucifixion in Its Late Antique Context*. New Haven, CT: American Oriental Society, 2014.

Antrim, Zayde. *Routes & Realms: The Power of Place in the Early Islamic World*. Oxford: Oxford University Press, 2012.

Arlinghaus, Joseph. 'The Transformation of Afghan Tribal Society, Tribal Expansion, Mughal Imperialism and the Roshaniyaa Insurrection 1450-1600'. PhD, Duke University, 1988.

Armajani, Yahya. 'The Saffarids: A Study in Iranian Nationalism'. In *Trudy XXV. Mezhdunarodogo Kongressa Vostokovedov, Moskva 9-16 Avgusta 1960*, edited by B.G. Gafurov, 168–73, Moscow: Izd-zo vostochnoi lit-ry, 1963.

Arrian. *Alexander the Great: The Anabasis and the Indica*. Translated by Martin Hammond. Oxford: Oxford University Press, 2013.

ʿAthamina, Khalil. 'Non-Arab Regiments and Private Militias during the Umayyād Period'. *Arabica* 45 (1998): 347–78.

al-ʿAwtabī, Salama b. Muslim. *An Early Islamic Family from Oman: Al-ʿAwtabī's Account of the Muhallabids*. Translated by Martin Hinds. Manchester: University of Manchester Press, 1991.

Azad, Arezou. *Sacred Landscape in Medieval Afghanistan: Revisiting the Faḍā'il-i Balkh*. Oxford: Oxford University Press, 2013.

Azarpay, Guitty. *Sogdian Painting: The Pictorial Epic in Oriental Art*. Berkeley, CA: University of California Press, 1981.

Bābur, Ẓahīr al-Dīn Muḥammad. *Bāburnāma: Chaghatay Turkish Text with Abdul-Rahim Khnkhanan's Persian Translation*. Translated by Wheeler Thackston. Cambridge, MA: The Department of Near Eastern Languages and Civilizations, Harvard University, 1993.

Bacharach, Jere L. 'Laqab for a Future Caliph: The Case of the Abbasid al-Mahdī'. *Journal of the American Oriental Society* 113 (1993): 271–4.

Baghbidi, Hassan Rezai. 'New Light on the Middle Persian-Chinese Bilingual Inscription from Xi'an'. In *The Persian Language in History*, edited by Mauro Maggi and Paola Orsatti, 105–15. Wiesbaden: Dr. Ludwig Reichert Verlag, 2011.

Balādhūrī, Aḥmad b. Yaḥyā. *Kitāb Futūḥ Al-Buldān*. Edited by M.J. de Goeje. Leiden: Brill, 1866.

Balādhūrī, Aḥmad b. Yaḥyā. *The Origins of the Islamic State*. Translated by Philip K. Hitti and Francis Clark Murgotten. New York: Columbia University Press, 1916.

Balʿamī, Abū ʿAlī Muḥammad. *Chronique de Abou-Djafar-Mohammed-ben Djarir-ben-Yezid Tabari, traduite sur la version persane d'Abou ʿAli Mohammed ben Belʿami*. Translated by Hermann Zotenberg. Paris: Oriental Translation Fund, 1867.

Balkhī, Abū Bakr ʿAbdallāh b. ʿUmar Wāʿiẓ. *Faḍā'īl-i Balkh*. Edited by ʿAbd al-Ḥayy Ḥabībī. Tehran: Bunyād-i Farhang-i Irān, 1350.

Barfield, Thomas. *Afghanistan: A Cultural and Political History*. Princeton, NJ: Princeton University Press, 2010.

Bartlett, Robert. *The Making of Europe: Conquest, Colonization, and Cultural Change, 950-1350*. Princeton, NJ: Princeton University Press, 1993.

Bartold, Vasily. 'Mā warā' al-nahr'. In *Encyclopaedia of Islam*. Second edition. Leiden: Brill, 1960–2009.

Bartold, Vasily. *Turkestan Down to the Mongol Invasion*. Fourth edition. Oxford: Oxbow Books, 1977.

Bartov, Omer and Eric D. Weitz, eds. *Shatterzone of Empires: Coexistence and Violence in the German, Habsburg, Russian, and Ottoman Borderlands*. Bloomington, IN: Indiana University Press, 2013.

Bates, Michael L. 'Khurāsānī Revolutionaries and al-Mahdī's Title'. In *Culture and Memory in Medieval Islam: Essays in Honour of Wilferd Madelung*, edited by Farhad Daftary and Josef W. Meri, 279–317. London: I.B. Tauris, 2003.

Baud, Michiel and Willem van Schendel. 'Toward a Comparative History of Borderlands'. *Journal of World History* 8 (1997): 211–42.

Baum, Wilhelm and Dietmar W. Winkler. *The Church of the East: A Concise History*. London: Routledge Curzon, 2003.

Bayhaqī, Abū al-Ḥasan ʿAlī ibn Zayd. *Tārīkh-i Bayhaq*. Edited by Qāsim Ghanī and ʿAlī Akbar Fayyāḍ. Tehran: Intishārāt-i Gām va Amīn, 1970.

Beckwith, Christopher. *The Tibetan Empire in Central Asia*. Princeton, NJ: Princeton University Press, 1987.

Bielenstein, Hans. *Diplomacy and Trade in the Chinese World, 589–1276*. Leiden: Brill, 2005.

Bivar, A.D.H. 'Hāritī and the Chronology of the Kuṣaṇas'. *Bulletin of the School of Oriental and African Studies* 33 (1970): 10–21.

Bivar, A.D.H. 'Hephthalites'. In *Encyclopædia Iranica*, New York: The Encyclopaedia Iranica Foundation, 2003.

Bivar, A.D.H. 'Kushan Dynasty i. Dynastic History'. In *Encyclopædia Iranica*, New York: The Encyclopaedia Iranica Foundation, 2009.

Blankinship, Khalid Yahya. *The End of the Jihād State: The Reign of Hishām Ibn ʿAbd Al-Malik and the Collapse of the Umayyads*. Albany, NY: State University of New York Press, 1994.

Blockley, Roger. 'Subsidies and Diplomacy: Rome and Persia in Late Antiquity'. *Phoenix* 39 (1985): 62–74.

Blockley, Roger. *The Fragmentary Classicising Historians of the Later Roman Empire: Eunapius, Olympiodorus, Priscus and Malchus*. Liverpool: Francis Cairns, 1983.

Bogue, Allan G. *Frederick Jackson Turner, Strange Roads Going Down*. Norman, OK: University of Oklahoma Press, 1998.

Bol'shakov, O.G. *Istorija Xalifata, III*. Moscow: Nauka., 1998.

Bombaci, A. 'On the Ancient Turkish Title «Šaδ»'. In *Gururajamañjarika: Studi in Onare Di Giuseppe Tucci*, edited by Instituto Universitario Orientale, 168–93. Naples: Istituto Universitario Orientale, 1974.

Bonner, Michael. *Aristocratic Violence and Holy War: Studies in the Jihad and the Arab-Byzantine Frontier*. New Haven, CT: American Oriental Society, 1996.

Bonner, Michael. *Jihad in Islamic History: Doctrines and Practices*. Princeton, NJ: Princeton University Press, 2006.

Bonner, Michael. 'The Naming of the Frontier: ʿAwāṣim, Thughūr, and the Arab Geographers'. *Bulletin of the School of Oriental and African Studies* 57 (1994): 17–24.

Borrut, Antoine and Christoph Picard. 'Râbata, Ribât, Râbita: une Institution reconsidérer'. In *Chrétiens et Musulmans en Méditerranéee Médiévale (VIIIe–XIIIe s.): Échanges et contacts*, edited by P. Sénac and N. Prouteau, 33–65. Pointiers: Université de Poitiers, Centre d'études supérieures de civilization médiévale, 2003.

Bosworth, C.E. 'Abū Ḥafṣ ʿUmar al-Kirmānī and the Rise of the Barmakids'. *Bulletin of the School of Oriental and African Studies* 57 (1994): 268–82.

Bosworth, C.E. 'An Early Arabic Mirror for Princes: Ṭāhir Dhū l-Yamīnain's Epistle to His Son ʿAbdallāh (206/821)'. *Journal of Near Eastern Studies* 29 (1970): 25–41.

Bosworth, C.E. 'The City of Tarsus and the Arab-Byzantine Frontier in Early and Middle ʿAbbasid Times'. *Oriens* 33 (1992): 268–86.

Bosworth, C.E. *The History of the Saffarids of Sistan and the Maliks of Nimruz*. Costa Mesa, CA: Mazda Publishers, 1994.

Bosworth, C.E. 'The Rulers of Chaghāniyān in Early Islamic Times'. *Iran* 19 (1981): 1–20.

Bosworth, C.E. Sīstān *Under the Arabs*. Rome: Istituto italiano per il Medio ed Estremo Oriente, 1968.

Bosworth, C.E. 'The Ṭāhirids and Ṣaffārids'. In *The Cambridge History of Iran, Vol. 4, The Period from the Arab Invasion to the Saljuqs*, edited by R.N. Frye, 90–135. Cambridge: Cambridge University Press, 1975.

Bosworth, C.E. 'Ṭukhāristān'. In *Encyclopaedia of Islam*. Second edition. Leiden: Brill, 1960–2009.

Brauer, Ralph W. 'Boundaries and Frontiers in Medieval Muslim Geography'. *Transactions of the American Philosophical Society*, New Series, 85, no. 6 (1995): 1–73.

Brunner, C.J. 'Abrāz'. In *Encyclopædia Iranica*, New York: The Encyclopaedia Iranica Foundation, 1983.
Bulliet, Richard. *Conversion to Islam in the Medieval Period: An Essay in Quantitative History*. Cambridge, MA: Harvard University Press, 1979.
Bulliet, Richard. *Cotton, Climate, and Camels in Early Islamic Iran: A Moment in World History*. New York: Columbia University Press, 2009.
Bulliet, Richard. *Islam: The View from the Edge*. New York: Columbia University Press, 1995.
Bulliet, Richard. 'Medieval Nishapur: A Topograhic and Demographic Reconstruction'. *Studia Iranica* 5 (1976): 67–89.
Bulliet, Richard. 'Naw Bahār and the Survival of Iranian Buddhism'. *Iran* 14 (1976): 140–5.
Carra de Vaux, B. 'Ḥadd'. In *Encyclopaedia of Islam*. Second edition. Leiden: Brill, 1960-2009.
Chabbi, Jacqueline. 'Ribāṭ'. In *Encyclopaedia of Islam*. Second edition. Leiden: Brill, 1960-2009.
Ch'ang, Li Chi. 'The Travels of Ch'ang Ch'un to the West, 1220-1223'. In *Mediaeval Researches from Eastern Asiatic Sources*, edited and translated by E. Bretschneider, 37–108. New York: Barnes & Noble, 1888.
Chavannes, Édouard. *Documents sur les Tou-Kiue (Turcs) occidentaux*. Paris: Librairie d'Amérique et d'Orient Adrien Maisonneuve, 1903.
Christensen, Peter. *Decline of Iranshahr: Irrigation and Environment in the Middle East, 500 B.C. - A.D. 1500*. London: I.B. Tauris, 2016.
Clavijo, Ruy González de. *Embassy to Tamerlane, 1403-1406*. Translated by Guy Le Strange. New York: Harper & Brothers, 1928.
Clavijo, Ruy González de. *Historia del Gran Tamorlan, e Itinerario y Enarracion del Viage*. Madrid: En la Imprenta de Don Antonio de Sancha, 1782.
Compareti, Matteo. 'Chinese-Iranian Relations xv. The Last Sasanians in China'. In *Encyclopædia Iranica*, New York: The Encyclopaedia Iranica Foundation, 2009.
Compareti, Matteo. 'The Last Sasanians in China'. *Eurasian Studies* 2 (2003): 197–213.
Conrad, Lawrence. 'The Quṣūr of Medieval Islam: Some Implications for the Social History of the Near East'. *Al-Abhāth* 29 (1981): 7–23.
Cribb, Joe. 'Numismatic Evidence for Kushano-Sasanian Chronology'. *Studia Iranica* 19 (1990): 151–93.
Crone, Patricia. *God's Rule: Government and Islam*. New York: Columbia University Press, 2004.
Crone, Patricia. 'Kavād's Heresy and Mazdak's Revolt'. *Iran* 29 (1991): 21–42.
Crone, Patricia. *The Nativist Prophets of Early Islamic Iran: Rural Revolt and Local Zoroastrianism*. Cambridge: Cambridge University Press, 2012.
Crone, Patricia. *Slaves on Horses: The Evolution of the Islamic Polity*. Cambridge: Cambridge University Press, 1980.
Crone, Patricia. 'Were the Qays and Yemen of the Umayyad Period Political Parties?'. *Der Islam* 71 (1994): 1–57.
Crone, Patricia and Masoud Jafari Jazi. 'The Muqannaʿ Narrative in the Tārīkhnāma: Part I, Introduction, Edition and Translation'. *Bulletin of the School of Oriental and African Studies* 73 (2010): 157–77.
Crone, Patricia and Masoud Jafari Jazi. 'The Muqannaʿ Narrative in the Tārīkhnāma: Part II, Commentary and Analysis'. *Bulletin of the School of Oriental and African Studies* 73 (2010): 381–413.

Cronon, William. 'Revisiting the Vanishing Frontier: The Legacy of Frederick Jackson Turner'. *The Western Historical Quarterly* 18 (1987): 157–76.

Dani, A.H. and B.A. Litvinsky. 'The Kushano-Sasanian Kingdom'. In *History of Civilizations of Central Asia, Vol. III, The Crossroads of Civilizations: A.D. 250 to 750*, edited by B.A. Litvinsky, Zhang Guang-da, and R. Shabani Samghabadi, 107–22. Paris: UNESCO, 1996.

Daniel, Elton L. *The Political and Social History of Khurasan under Abbasid Rule, 747–820*. Minneapolis, MN: Bibliotheca Islamica, 1979.

Darling, Linda. 'Contested Territory: Ottoman Holy War in Comparative Context'. *Studia Islamica* 91 (2000): 133–69.

Daryaee, Touraj. 'If These Walls Could Speak: The Barrier of Alexander, Wall of Darband and Other Defensive Moats'. In *Borders: Itineraries on the Edges of Iran*, edited by Stefano Pellò, 79–88. Venice: Edizioni Ca' Foscari, 2016.

Daryaee, Touraj. *Šahrestānīhā ī Ērānšahr: A Middle Persian Text on Late Antique Geography, Epic and History*. Costa Mesa, CA: Mazda Publishers, 2002.

Daryaee, Touraj. 'Wahrām Čōbīn the Rebel General and the Militarization of the Sasanian Empire'. In *Studies on the Iranian World I: Before Islam*, edited by Anna Krasnowolska and Renata Rusek-Kowalska, 193–202. Krakow: Jagiellonian University Press, 2015.

Davis, Dick. 'The Problems of Ferdowsī's Sources'. *Journal of the American Oriental Society* 116 (1996): 48–57.

Dennett, Jr., Daniel Clement. *Conversion and the Poll Tax in Early Islam*. Cambridge, MA: Harvard University Press, 1950.

Di Cosmo, Nicola. *Ancient China and Its Enemies: The Rise of Nomadic Power in East Asian History*. Cambridge: Cambridge University Press, 2002.

Dīnawarī, Abū Ḥanīfa Aḥmad b. Dāwud. *Kitāb al-akhbār al-ṭiwāl*. Edited by Vladimir Guirgass and Ignatius Kratchkovsky. Leiden: Brill, 1888.

Donner, Fred McGraw. 'Book Review: Robert Hoyland, In God's Path: The Arab Conquests and the Creation of an Islamic Empire'. *Al-ʿUṣūr Al-Wusṭā* 23 (2015): 134–40.

Donner, Fred McGraw. *The Early Islamic Conquests*. Princeton, NJ: Princeton University Press, 1981.

Dūghlāt, Mīrzā Haydar. *Ta'rīkh-i Rashīdī*. Edited by Wheeler Thackston. Cambridge, MA: The Department of Near Eastern Languages and Civilizations, Harvard University, 1996.

Duri, Abd al-Aziz. *Early Islamic Institutions: Administration and Taxation from the Caliphate to the Umayyads and ʿAbbāsids*. Translated by Razia Ali. London: I.B. Tauris, 2011.

Eger, A. Asa. 'Ḥiṣn, Ribāṭ, Thaghr or Qaṣr? Semantics and Systems of Frontier Fortifications in the Early Islamic Period'. In *The Lineaments of Islam: Studies in Honor of Fred McGraw Donner*, edited by Paul M. Cobb, 427–55. Leiden: Brill, 2012.

Eger, A. Asa. *The Islamic-Byzantine Frontier: Interaction and Exchange among Muslim and Christian Communities*. London: I.B. Tauris, 2015.

Eger, A. Asa. *The Spaces Between the Teeth: A Gazetteer of Towns on the Islamic-Byzantine Frontier*. Istanbul: Ege Yayınları, 2012.

Elad, Amikam. 'The Armies of Al-Ma'mūn in Khurāsān (193–202/809–17–18): Recruitment of Its Contingents and Their Social–Ethnic Composition'. *Oriens* 38 (2010): 35–76.

El-Hibri, Tayeb. 'Harun Al-Rashid and the Mecca Protocol of 802: A Plan for Division or Succession?' *International Journal of Middle East Studies* 24 (1992): 461–80.

Ełišē. *History of Vardan and the Armenian War*. Translated by Robert W. Thomson. Cambridge, MA: Harvard University Press, 1982.
Esin, E. 'Tarkhan Nīzak or Tarkhan Tirek? An Enquiry Concerning the Prince of Bādhghīs Who in A.H. 91/A.D. 709-710 Opposed the 'Omayyad Conquest of Central Asia'. *Journal of the American Oriental Society* 97 (1977): 323–32.
Euripides. *Bacchae, Iphigenia at Aulis. Rhesus*. Translated by David Kovacs. Cambridge, MA: Harvard University Press, 2003.
Eutropius, Flavius. 'Abridgment of Roman History'. In *Justin, Cornelius Nepos, and Eutropius, Literally Translated*, translated by Rev. John Selby Watson, 401–535. London: George Bell and Sons, 1886.
Falk, H. 'Kushan Dynasty iii. Chronology of the Kushans'. In *Encyclopædia Iranica*, New York: The Encyclopaedia Iranica Foundation, 2014.
Fancy, Hussein. *The Mercenary Mediterranean: Sovereignty, Religion, and Violence in the Medieval Crown of Aragon*. Chicago, IL: University of Chicago Press, 2016.
Fawcett, Charles Bungay. *Frontiers: A Study in Political Geography*. Oxford: Clarendon Press, 1918.
Febvre, Lucien. *La terre et l'évolution humaine; introduction géographique à l'histoire*. Paris: Renaissance du livre, 1922.
Felix, Wolfgang. 'Chionites'. In *Encyclopædia Iranica*, New York: The Encyclopaedia Iranica Foundation, 1991.
Firdawsī, Abū 'l-Qāsim. *Shāhnāma*. Edited by Y.A. Birtils. Moscow: Idārah-i Intishārāt-i Adabīyat-i Khavar, 1960.
Firdawsī, Abū 'l-Qāsim. *The Shāhnāma of Firdausī*. Translated by Arthur George Warner and Edmond Warner. London: K. Paul, Trench, and Trübner & Co. Ltd., 1905.
Forte, Antonino. 'On the So-Called Abraham from Persia: A Case of Mistaken Identity'. In *L'inscription Nestorienne de Si-Ngan-Fou*, edited by Paul Pelliot and Antonino Forte, 375–428. Kyoto and Paris: Italian School of East Asian Studies and Collège de France, 1996.
Fragner, Bert G. 'The Concept of Regionalism in Historical Research on Central Asia and Iran (A Macro-Historical Interpretation)'. In *Studies on Central Asian History*. In Honor of Yuri Bregel, edited by Devin DeWeese, 345–53. Bloomington, IN: Indiana University Press, 2001.
Frankopan, Peter. *The Silk Roads: A New History of the World*. New York: Vintage Books, 2015.
Frye, Richard. *Bukhara: The Medieval Achievement*. Second edition. Costa Mesa, CA: Mazda Publishers, 1996.
Frye, Richard. 'Dar-i Āhanīn'. In *Encyclopaedia of Islam*. Second edition. Leiden: Brill, 1960-2009.
Frye, Richard. 'Feudalism in Sasanian and Early Islamic Iran'. *Jerusalem Studies in Arabic and Islam* 9 (1987): 13–18.
Frye, Richard. *The Golden Age of Persia: The Arabs in the East*. London: Weidenfeld and Nicolson, 1975.
Frye, Richard. 'Kushans and Other Iranians in Central Asia'. In *Reşid Rahmeti Arat İçin*, 244–7. Ankara: Türk Kültürünü Araştirma Enstitüsü, 1966.
Frye, Richard. *Notes on the Early Coinage of Transoxiana*. New York: American Numismatic Society, 1949.
Frye, Richard. 'The Persepolis Middle Persian Inscriptions from the Time of Shapur II'. *Acta Orientalia* 30 (1966): 83–93.

Frye, Richard. 'The Political History of Iran under the Sasanians'. In *The Cambridge History of Iran, Vol. 3(1): The Seleucid, Parthian, and Sasanian Periods, Part 1*, edited by Ehsan Yarshater, 116–80. Cambridge: Cambridge University Press, 1983.

Frye, Richard. 'The Sāmānids'. In *The Cambridge History of Iran, Vol. 4, The Period from the Arab Invasions to the Saljuqs*, edited by R.N. Frye, 135–61. Cambridge: Cambridge University Press, 1975.

Frye, Richard. 'The Sasanian System of Walls for Defense'. In *Studies in Memory of Gaston Wiet*, edited by M. Rosen-Ayalon, 7–15. Jerusalem: Hebrew University of Jerusalem, 1977.

Frye, Richard. 'Ṭarxūn-Türxün and Central Asian History'. *Harvard Journal of Asiatic Studies* 14 (1951): 105–29.

Gardīzī, Abū Sa῾īd ῾Abd al-Ḥayy. *Ta'rīkh-i Gardīzī*. Edited by ῾Abd al-Ḥayy Ḥabībī. Tehran: Dunyā-yi Kitāb, 1984.

Gardīzī, Abū Sa῾īd ῾Abd al-Ḥayy. *Zayn al-akhbār*. Edited by ῾Abd al-Ḥayy Ḥabībī. Tehran: Bunyād-i Farhang-i Irān, 1968.

Gellner, Ernest. 'Tribalism and State Formation in the Middle East'. In *Tribes and State Formation in the Middle East*, edited by Philip S. Khoury and Joseph Kostiner, 109–27. Berkeley, CA: University of California Press, 1990.

Gerth, H.H. and C. Wright Mills. 'Introduction: The Man and His Work'. In *From Max Weber: Essays in Sociology*, 3–74. Oxford: Oxford University Press, 1946.

Ghirshman, Roman. *Iran: From the Earliest Times to the Islamic Conquest*. Harmondsworth: Penguin, 1954.

Ghirshman, Roman. *Les Chionites-Hephtalites*. Cairo: Imprimerie de l'Institut français d'archéologie orientale, 1948.

Gibb, H.A.R. *The Arab Conquests in Central Asia*. London: The Royal Asiatic Society, 1923.

Gibb, H.A.R. 'The Arab Invasion of Kashgar in A.D. 715'. *Bulletin of the School of Oriental Studies* 2 (1922): 467–74.

Gibb, H.A.R. 'The Evolution of Government in Early Islam'. *Studia Islamica* 4 (1955): 5–17.

Gignoux, Philippe. 'Les inscriptions en moyen-perse de Bandiān'. *Studia Iranica* 27 (1998): 251–8.

Gignoux, Philippe. 'L'organisation administrative sasanide: Le cas du marzbān'. *Jerusalem Studies in Arabic and Islam* 4 (1984): 1–29.

Gignoux, Philippe. 'Le site de Bandiān revisité'. *Studia Iranica* 37 (2008): 163–74.

Gillman, Ian and Hans-Joachim Klimkeit. *Christians in Asia before 1500*. Ann Arbor, MI: University of Michigan Press, 1999.

Göbl, Robert. *Dokumente zur geschichte der iranischen Hunnen in Baktrien und Indien*. Wiesbaden: Harrassowitz, 1967.

Göbl, Robert. *Sasanian Numismatics*. Translated by Paul Severin. Braunschweig: Klinkhardt & Biermann, 1971.

Goffart, Walter. *Barbarian Tides: The Migration Age and the Later Roman Empire*. Philadelphia: University of Pennsylvanian Press, 2006.

Golden, Peter B. *An Introduction to the History the Turkic Peoples: Ethnogenesis and State Formation in Medieval and Early Modern Eurasia and the Middle East*. Wiesbaden: Harrassowitz, 1992.

Golden, Peter B. 'Ṭarkhān'. In *Encyclopaedia of Islam*. Second edition. Leiden: Brill, 1960-2009.

Gommans, Jos. 'The Silent Frontier of South Asia, C. A.D. 1100-1800'. *Journal of World History* 9 (1998): 1–23.

Gordon, Matthew. *The Breaking of a Thousand Swords: A History Fo the Turkish Military of Samarra (A.H. 200-275/815-889 C.E.).* Albany, NY: State University of New York Press, 2001.

Graff, David A. 'Strategy and Contingency in the Tang Defeat of the Eastern Turks, 629-630'. In *Warfare in Inner Asian History (500-1800)*, edited by Nicola Di Cosmo, 33–71. Leiden: Brill, 2002.

Greenwood, Timothy William. 'Sasanian Echoes and Apocalyptic Expectations: A Re-Evaluation of the Armenian History Attributed to Sebeos'. *Le Muséon* 115 (2002): 323–97.

Greenwood, Timothy William. 'Sasanian Reflections in Armenian Sources'. *E-Sasanika* 3 (2008): 1–28.

Grenet, Frantz. 'Crise et sortie de crise en bactriane-sogdiane au IVe-Ve siècles: de l'héritage antique a l'adoption de modèles sassanides'. In *La Persia e l'Asia centrale da Alessandro al X secolo*, edited by Istituto italiano per il Medio ed Estremo Oriente and Accademia nazionale dei Lincei, 367–90. Rome: Accademia Nazionale dei Lincei, 1996.

Grenet, Frantz. 'Kidarites'. In *Encyclopædia Iranica*, New York: The Encyclopaedia Iranica Foundation, 2005.

Grenet, Frantz. 'Nēzak'. In *Encyclopædia Iranica*, New York: The Encyclopaedia Iranica Foundation, 2002.

Grenet, Frantz. 'Regional Interaction in Central Asia and Northwest India in the Kidarite and Hephthalite Periods'. In *Indo-Iranian Languages and Peoples*, edited by Nicholas Sims-Williams, 203–24. Oxford: Oxford University Press, 2002.

Grenet, Frantz and Étienne de la Vaissière. 'The Last Days of Panjikent'. *Silk Road Art and Archaeology* 8 (2002): 155–96.

Grenet, Frantz, Jonathan Lee, Philippe Martinez and François Ory. 'The Sasanian Relief at Rag-i Bibi (Northern Afghanistan)'. In *After Alexander: Central Asia before Islam*, edited by Joe Cribb and Georgina Herrmann, 243–67. Oxford: Oxford University Press, 2007.

Gutas, Dimitri. *Greek Thought, Arabic Culture: The Greco-Arabic Translation Movement in Baghdad and Early ʿAbbāsid Society (2nd-4th/8th-10th Centuries).* London: Routledge, 1998.

Gyselen, Rika. *The Four Generals of the Sasanian Empire: Some Sigillographic Evidence.* Rome: Instituta italiano per l'Africa e l'Oriente, 2001.

Gyselen, Rika. *La géographie administrative de l'empire Sassanide: Les témoignages sigillographiques.* Paris: Groupe pour l'étude de la civilization du moyen-orient, 1989.

Gyselen, Rika. 'La reconquête de l'est Iranien par l'empire Sassanide au VIe s. d'après les sources «iraniennes»'. *Arts Asiatiques* 58 (2003): 162–7.

Gyselen, Rika. 'Le Kadag-Xwadāy Sassanide: Quelques réflexions à partir de nouvelles données sigillographiques'. *Studia Iranica* 31 (2002): 61–9.

Gyselen, Rika. 'Realia for Sasanian History: Mint Networks'. In *Studies on the Iranian World I: Before Islam*, edited by Anna Krasnowolska and Renata Rusek-Kowalska, 211–22. Krakow: Jagiellonian University Press, 2015.

Ḥākim al-Nīsābūrī, Muḥammad b. ʿAbdallāh. *Taʾrīkh-i Nīshābūr.* Edited by Muḥammad Riẓā Shafīʿī Kadkanī. Tehran: Āgāh, 1996.

Ḥākim al-Nīsābūrī, Muḥammad b. ʿAbdallāh. *The Histories of Nishapur.* Edited by Richard Frye. Cambridge, MA: Harvard University Press, 1965.

Harmatta, János. 'Chionitae, Euseni, Gelani'. *Acta Antiqua Academiae Scientiarum Hungaricae* 31 (1985–8): 43–51.

Harmatta, János. 'Minor Bactrian Inscriptions'. *Acta Antiqua Academiae Scientiarum Hungaricae* 13 (1965): 149–205.
Harmatta, János. 'The Wall of Alexander the Great and the Limes Sasanicus'. *Bulletin of the Asia Institute*, New Series 10 (1996): 79–84.
Haug, Robert. 'Frontiers and the State in the Medieval Islamic World: Jihād Between Caliphs and Volunteers'. *History Compass* 9, no. 8 (2011): 634–43.
Haug, Robert. 'The Gate of Iron: The Making of the Eastern Frontier'. PhD, University of Michigan, 2010.
Haug, Robert. 'Local, Regional, and Imperial Politics: Ṭabaristān and the Early Empire, Struggle and Integration on Multiple Levels'. In *The Reach of Empire*, edited by Stefan Heidemann. Berlin: De Gruyter, forthcoming.
Hawting, G.R. *The First Dynasty of Islam: The Umayyad Caliphate AD 661-750*. Carbondale, IL: Southern Illinois University Press, 1987.
Heck, Paul. *The Construction of Knowledge in Islamic Civilization: Qudāma b. Jaʿfar and His Kitāb al-kharāj wa-ṣināʿat al-kitāba*. Leiden: Brill, 2002.
Hensel, Paul R. and Paul F. Diehl. 'Testing Empirical Propositions about Shatterbelts, 1945-76'. *Political Geography* 13 (1994): 33–51.
Herzfeld, Ernst. 'New Light on Persian History from the Pahlavi Inscriptions'. *Journal of the K.R. Cama Institute* 7 (1926): 103–14.
Hill, Donald R. *The Termination of Hostilities in the Early Arab Conquests, A.D. 634-656*. London: Luzac, 1971.
Hinnebusch, Raymond. *International Politics of the Middle East*. Manchester: Manchester University Press, 2003.
Hinz, W. 'Farsakh'. In *Encyclopaedia of Islam*, Second edition. Leiden: Brill, 1960-2009.
Honeychurch, William. 'The Nomad as State Builder: Historical Theory and Material Evidence from Mongolia'. *Journal of World Prehistory* 26 (2013): 283–321.
Howard Johnston, James. 'The Late Sasanian Army'. In *Late Antiquity: Eastern Perspectives*, edited by Teresa Bernheimer and Adam Silverstein, 87–127. Exeter: E.J.W. Gibb Memorial Trust, 2012.
Howard Johnston, James. 'The Two Great Powers of Late Antiquity: A Comparison'. In *The Byzantine and Early Islamic Near East, Vol. 3: States, Resources and Armies*, edited by Averil Cameron. Princeton, NJ: Darwin Press, 1995.
Hoyland, Robert G. *In God's Path: The Arab Conquests and the Creation of an Islamic Empire*. Oxford: Oxford University Press, 2014.
Hsüsan-tsang. *Si-Yu-Ki: Buddhist Records of the Western World*. Translated by Samuel Beal. London: Trübner, 1884.
Ḥudūd al-ʿālam. Edited by Manūchihr Sutūdih. Tehran: Chāpkhānah-i Danīshgāh-i Tehran, 1962.
Ḥudūd al-ʿālam: 'The Regions of the World'. Translated by Vladimir Minorsky. Edited by C.E. Bosworth. Second edition. Cambridge: E.J.W. Gibb Memorial Trust, 1970.
Humbach, Helmet and Pods Skjærvø. *The Sassanian Inscription of Paikuli: Part 3.1: Restored Text and Translation*. Munich: Dr. Ludwig Reichert Verlag Wiesbaden, 1983.
Huyse, Philip. *Die dreisprachige Inschrift Šābuhrs I. an der Kaʿba-i Zardušt (ŠKZ)*. London: School of Oriental and African Studies, 1999.
Ibn al-ʿAdīm, Kamāl al-Dīn ʿUmar b. Aḥmad. *Zubda al-ḥalab min tārīkh Ḥalab*. Edited by Khalīl Manṣūr. Beirut: Dār al-kutub al-ʿilmiyya, 1996.
Ibn Aʿtham, Aḥmad. *Al-Futūḥ*. Edited by Suhayl Zakkār. Beirut: Dār al-Fikr lil-Ṭibāʿah wa-al-Nashr wa-al-Tawzīʿ, 1992.

Ibn al-Athīr, ʿIzz al-Dīn Abū al-Ḥassan. *al-Kāmil fī 'l-ta'rīkh*. Edited by Samīr Shams. Beirut: Dār Ṣādr, 2009.
Ibn al-Faqīh, Abū Bakr Aḥmad. *Mukhtaṣar kitāb al-buldān*. Edited by M.J. de Goeje. Bibliotheca Geographorum Arabicorum 5. Leiden: Brill, 1885.
Ibn Ḥawqal, Abū al-Qāsim. *Kitāb ṣūrat al-ard*. Edited by J.H. Kramers. Bibliotheca Geographorum Arabicorum 2. Leiden: Brill, 1939.
Ibn Isfandiyār, Bahā' al-Dīn Muḥammad. *Tārīkh-i Ṭabaristān*. Edited by ʿAbbās Iqbāl. Tehran: Kitābkhānah-i Khāvar, 1320.
Ibn Isfandiyār, Bahā' al-Dīn Muḥammad. *An Abridged Translation of the History of Ṭabaristān*. Translated by Edward G. Browne. Leiden: Brill, 1905.
Ibn Khurradādhbih, ʿUbayd Allāh b. ʿAbdullāh. *Kitāb al-masālik wa'l-mamālik*. Edited by M.J. de Goeje. Bibliotheca Geographorum Arabicorum 6. Leiden: Brill, 1889.
Ibn Qutayba, Abū Muḥammad ʿAbdallāh b. Muslim. *Kitāb al-maʿārif*. Edited by Saroite Okacha. Cairo: Faculte des Lettres et Sciences Humaines de l'Université de Paris, 1960.
Ibn Rusta, Aḥmad. *Kitāb al-a'lāq al-nafīsa*. Edited by M.J. de Goeje. Bibliotheca Geographorum Arabicorum 7. Leiden: Brill, 1882.
Imber, Colin. 'What Does "Ghazi" Actually Mean?' In *The Balance of Truth: Essays in Honor of Professor Geoffrey Lewis*, edited by Çiğdem Balim-Harding and Colin Imber, 165–78. Istanbul: ISIS Press, 2000.
Inaba, Minoru. 'Arab Soldiers in China at the Time of the An-Shi Rebellion'. *The Memoirs of the Toyo Bunko* 68 (2010): 35–61.
Iṣṭakhrī, Abū Isḥāq. *al-Masālik wa'l-mamālik*. Edited by Muḥammad Jābir ʿAbd al-ʿĀl al-Ḥīnī. Cairo: Turāthunā, 1961.
Jackson Bonner, Michael Richard. *al-Dīnawarī's Kitāb al-aḫbār al-ṭiwāl: An Historiographical Study of Sasanian Iran*. Res Orientales 23. Leuven: Peeters, 2015.
Jackson Bonner, Michael Richard. *Three Neglected Sources of Sasanian History in the Reign of Khusraw Anushirvan*. Cahiers de Studia Iranica 46. Leuven: Peeters, 2011.
Jagchid, Sechen. 'Patterns of Trade and Conflict between China and the Nomadic Peoples of Mongolia'. *Zentralasiatische Studien* 11 (1977): 177–204.
Jagchid, Sechen and Van Jay Symons. *Peace, War and Trade along the Great Wall*. Bloomington, IN: Indiana University Press, 1989.
Jahshiyārī, Muḥammad b. ʿAbdūs. *Kitāb al-wuzarā' wa'l-kuttāb*. Edited by Muṣṭafā Saqā, Ibrāhīm Abyārī, and ʿAbd al-Ḥafīẓ Shiblī. Cairo: Muṣṭafā al-Bābī al-Ḥalabī wa Awlāduhu, 1938.
Jongeward, David, Joe Cribb and Peter Donovan. *Kushan, Kushano-Sasanian, and Kidarite Coins: A Catalogue of Coins from the American Numismatic Society*. New York: American Numismatic Society, 2015.
Joshua the Stylite. *The Chronicle of Pseudo-Joshua the Stylite*. Translated by Frank R. Trombley and John W. Watt. Liverpool: Liverpool University Press, 2000.
Justinus, Marcus Junianus. *Epitome of the Philippic History of Pompeius Trogus*. Translated by Rev. John Selby Watson. London: Henry G. Bohn, 1853.
Kaabi, Mongi. 'Les Origines Ṭāhirides dans la Daʿwa ʿabbāside'. *Arabica* 19 (1972): 145–64.
Kaabi, Mongi. 'Les Ṭāhirides: Étude historico-littéraire de la dynastie des Banū Ṭāhir b. Al-Ḥusayn au Ḫurāsān et en Iraq au IIIème s. de l'Hégire/IXème s. J.-C'. PhD, Université de Paris-Sorbonne, 1971.
Kałankatuąci, Moses. *The History of the Caucasian Albanians by Movsēs Dasxuranci*. Translated by C.J.F. Dowsett. London: Oxford University Press, 1961.

Kaldellis, Anthony. *Ethnography after Antiquity: Foreign Lands and Peoples in Byzantine Literature*. Philadelphia, PA: University of Pennsylvanian Press, 2013.

Karev, Yury. *Samarqand et le Sughd à l'époque ʿAbbāsside: Historie politique et sociale*. Paris: Association pour l'avancement des études iraniennes, 2015.

Karev, Yury. 'Un palais Islamique du VIIIe siècle à Samarkand'. *Studia Iranica* 29 (2000): 273–96.

Kennedy, Hugh. *The Armies of the Caliphs: Military and Society in the Early Islamic State*. Abingdon: Routledge, 2001.

Kennedy, Hugh. 'The Coming of Islam to Bukhara'. In *Living Islamic History: Studies in Honor of Professor Carole Hillenbrand*, edited by Yasir Suleiman, 77–91. Edinburgh: Edinburgh University Press, 2010.

Kennedy, Hugh. *The Great Arab Conquests: How the Spread of Islam Changed the World We Live In*. Philadelphia, PA: Da Capo Press, 2007.

Kennedy, Hugh. *The Prophet and the Age of the Caliphates*. Second edition. Harlow: Pearson-Longman, 2004.

Khalidi, Tarif. *Arabic Historical Thought in the Classical Period*. Cambridge: Cambridge University Press, 1994.

Khalīfa b. Khayyāṭ. *Khalifa Ibn Khayyat's History on the Umayyad Dynasty (660-750)*. Translated by Carl Wurtzel. Liverpool: Liverpool University Press, 2015.

Khalīfa b. Khayyāṭ. *Ta'rīkh*. Edited by Akram Ḍiyā' ʿUmarī. Damascus: Dār al-qalam, 1977.

Khazanov, Anatoly M. *Nomads and the Outside World*. Translated by Julia Crookenden. Cambridge: Cambridge University Press, 1984.

Khuzāʿī, Diʿbil b. ʿAlī. *Diʿbil b. ʿAlī, the Life and Writings of an Early ʿAbbāsid Poet*. Translated by L. Zolondek. Lexington, 1961.

Klat, Michael G. *Catalogue of the Post Reform Dirhams: The Umayyad Dynasty*. London: Spink & Sons LTD, 2002.

Kochnev, B. 'Les Monnaies de Muqannaʿ'. *Studia Iranica* 30 (2001): 143–50.

Kopytoff, Igor. 'The Internal African Frontier: The Making of African Political Culture'. In *The African Frontier: The Reproduction of Traditional African Societies*, edited by Igor Kopytoff, 3–84. Bloomington, IN: Indiana University Press, 1987.

Kuwayama, Shoshin. 'Historical Notes on Kāpiśī Kābul in the Sixth-Eighth Centuries'. *Zinbun* 34 (1999): 25–77.

Kuwayama, Shoshin. 'The Hephthalites in Tokharistan and Gandhara'. In *Across the Hindukush of the First Millenium: A Collection of Papers*, 107–39. Kyoto: Institute for Research in Humanities, Kyoto University, 2002.

Kwong, Luke S.K. 'What's in a Name: Zhongguo (or "Middle Kingdom") Reconsidered'. *The Historical Journal* 58 (2015): 781–804.

Lambton, Ann K.S. *Landlord and Peasant in Persia: A Study of Land Tenure and Land Revenue Administration*. London: I.B. Tauris, 1991.

Lambton, Ann K.S. *State and Government in Medieval Islam*. Oxford: Oxford University Press, 1981.

Landau-Tasseron, Ella. 'Sayf Ibn ʿUmar in Medieval and Modern Scholarship'. *Der Islam* 67 (1990): 1–26.

Lassner, Jacob. *The Shaping of ʿAbbāsid Rule*. Princeton, NJ: Princeton University Press, 1980.

Latham, J.D., and C.E. Bosworth. 'Thughūr'. In *Encyclopaedia of Islam*. Second edition. Leiden: Brill, 1960–2009.

Lattimore, Owen. *Inner Asian Frontiers of China*. New York: American Geographical Society, 1940.
Lazard, Gilbert. 'The Rise of the New Persian Language'. In *Cambridge History of Iran, Vol. 4. The Period Form the Arab Invasion Ot the Saljuqs*, edited by Richard Frye. Cambridge: Cambridge University Press, 1975.
Le Strange, Guy. *The Lands of the Eastern Caliphate*. Cambridge: Cambridge University Press, 1905.
Lerner, Judith and Nicholas Sims-Williams. *Seals, Sealings and Tokens from Bactria to Gandhara (4th to 8th Century CE)*. Vienna: Verlag der Österreichischen Akademie der Wissenschaften, 2011.
Lindner, Rudi Paul. *Explorations in Ottoman Prehistory*. Ann Arbor, MI: University of Michigan Press, 2007.
Lindner, Rudi Paul. 'What Was a Nomadic Tribe?' *Comparative Studies in Society and History* 4 (1982): 689–711.
Litvinsky, B.A. 'The Hephthalite Empire'. In *History of Civilizations of Central Asia: Vol. III The Crossroads of Civilizations: A.D. 250 to 750*, edited by B.A. Litvinsky, Zhang Guang-da, and R. Shabani Samghabadi, 136–65. Paris: UNESCO, 1996.
Litvinsky, B.A. and Zhang Guang-da. 'Central Asia: The Crossroads of Civilizations'. In *History of Civilizations of Central Asia: Vol. III The Crossroads of Civilizations: A.D. 250 to 750*, edited by B.A. Litvinsky, 469–87. Paris: UNESCO, 1996.
Livshits, V.A. Sogdiiskie *Dokumenty s Gory Mug. Chtenie, Perevod, Kommentarii, II: Iuridicheskie Dokumentry i Pis'ma*. Moscow: Izd-vo Vostochnoi Lit-ry, 1962.
Lovell, Julia. *The Great Wall: China against the World, 1000 BC-AD 2000*. New York: Grove Press, 2006.
Luce, Mark. 'Frontier as Process: Umayyad Khurāsān'. PhD, University of Chicago, 2009.
Macuch, Maria. 'Barda and Barda-Dāri ii. In the Sasanian Period'. In *Encyclopædia Iranica*, New York: The Encyclopaedia Iranica Foundation, 1988.
Madelung, Wilferd. 'Āl-e Bāvand'. In *Encyclopædia Iranica*, New York: The Encyclopaedia Iranica Foundation, 1984.
Madelung, Wilferd. 'The Early Murjiʿa in Khurāsān and Transoxiana and the Spread of Hanifism'. *Der Islam* 59 (1982): 32–9.
Malek, Hodge Mehdi. *The Dābūyid Ispahbads and Early ʿAbbāsid Governors of Ṭabaristān: History and Numismatics*. London: The Royal Numismatic Society, 2000.
Maqdisī, Muṭahhar b. Ṭāhir. *Le livre de la création et de l'histoire de Motahhar Ben Tāhir El-Maqdisī, attribué à Abou-Zeid Ahmed Ben Sahr El-Balhī*. Translated by Clément Huart. Paris: Éditions Ernest Leroux, 1916–19.
Marçais, G. 'Bustān'. In *Encyclopaedia of Islam*. Second edition. Leiden: Brill, 1960-2009.
Marcellinus, Ammianus. *The Roman History*. Translated by C.D. Yonge. London: George Bell and Sons, 1894.
Mashkour, Marjan, Roya Khazaeli, Homa Fathi, Sarieh Amiri, Delphine Decruyenaere, Azadeh Mohaseb, Hossein Davoudi, Shiva Sheikhi and Eberhard W. Sauer. 'Animal Exploitation and Subsistence on the Borders of the Sasanian Empire: From the Gorgan Wall (Iran) to the Gates of the Alans (Georgia)'. In *Sasanian Persia: Between Rome and the Steppes of Eurasia*, edited by Eberhard W. Sauer, 74–95. Edinburgh: Edinburgh University Press, 2017.
Masʿūdī, Abū al-Ḥasan ʿAlī b. al-Ḥusayn. *Kitāb al-tanbiyya wa'l-āshrāf*. Edited by M.J. de Goeje. Bibliotheca Geographorum Arabicorum 8. Leiden: Brill, 1893.
Masʿūdī, Abū al-Ḥasan ʿAlī b. al-Ḥusayn. *Les prairies d'or*. Translated by C. Barbier de Meynard and A. Pavet de Courteille. Paris: Imprimerie Nationale, 1861.

McDonough, Scott. 'The "Warrior of the Lords": Smbat Bagratuni at the Center and Periphery of Late Sasanian Iran'. *Iranian Studies* 49 (2016): 233–45.

Meisami, Julie Scott. *Persian Historiography to the End of the Twefth Century*. Edinburgh: Edinburgh University Press, 1999.

Meisami, Julie Scott. 'The Past in Service of the Present: Two Views of History in Medieval Persia'. *Poetics Today* 14 (1993): 247–75.

Meisami, Julie Scott. 'Why Write History in Persian? Historical Writing in the Samanid Period'. In *Studies in Honour of Clifford Edmund Bosworth Volume II*, edited by Carole Hillenbrand, 348–74. Leiden: Brill, 2000.

Menander Protector. *The History of Menander the Guardsman*. Translated by Roger Blockley. Liverpool: Francis Cairns, 1985.

Minorsky, Vladimir. *Studies in Caucasian History*. London: Taylor's Foreign Press, 1953.

Minorsky, Vladimir. 'The Older Preface to the Shāh-Nāma'. In *Studi Orientalistici in Onore Di Giorgio Levi Della Vida*, Vol. 2, 159–79. Rome: Istituto per l'Oriente, 1956.

Minqarī, Naṣr b. Muzāḥim. *Waqʿat Ṣiffīn*. Edited by ʿAbd al-Salām Muḥammad Hārūn. Qum: Manshūrāt maktaba Aya Allāh al-ʿUẓmā al-Marʿashī al-Najafī, 1962.

Miquel, André. *La géographie humaine du monde musulman jusqu'au milieu du 11e siècle: Géographie et géographie humaine dans la littérature arabe des origins à 1050*. Paris: Mouton, 1967.

Montgomery, James E. 'Ibn Rusta's Lack of "Eloquence," the Rus, and Samanid Cosmography'. *Edebiyat* 12 (2001): 73–93.

Morony, Michael G. *Iraq after the Muslim Conquest*. Princeton, NJ: Princeton University Press, 1984.

Mukhtarov, Akhror. *Balkh in the Late Middle Ages*. Translated by R.D. McChesney. Papers on Inner Asia 25. Bloomington, IN: Indiana University Research Institute for Inner Asian Studies, 1993.

Muqaddasī, Shams al-Dīn Abū ʿAbdallāh Muḥammad. *Aḥsan al-taqāsīm fī maʿrafa al-aqālīm*. Edited by M.J. de Goeje. Bibliotheca Geographorum Arabicorum 3. Leiden: Brill, 1906.

Muqaddasī, Shams al-Dīn Abū ʿAbdallāh Muḥammad. *The Best Division for Knowledge of the Regions*. Translated by Basil Anthony Collins. The Great Books of Islamic Civilization. Reading: Garnet Publishing, 1994.

Narain, A.K. 'Indo-Europeans in Inner Asia'. In *The Cambridge History of Early Inner Asia*, edited by Denis Sinor, 159–73. Cambridge: Cambridge University Press, 1990.

Narshakhī, Abū Bakr. *Ta'rīkh-i Bukhārā*. Edited by Mudarris Raẓavī. Tehran: Intishārāt-i Ṭūs, 1984.

Narshakhī, Abū Bakr. *The History of Bukhara*. Translated by Richard Frye. Cambridge, MA: The Mediaeval Academy of America, 1954.

Nasafī, ʿUmar b. Muḥammad. *al-Qand fī dhikr ʿulamā' Samarqand*. Edited by Naẓar Muḥammad Fāryābī. Riyad: Maktabat Kawthar, 1991.

Nastich, Vladimir. 'A Survey of the Abbasid Copper Coinage of Transoxiana'. https://www.academia.edu/3734886/A_Survey_of_the_Abbasid_Copper_Coinage_of_Transoxiana.

Nawas, John A. 'All in the Family? Al-Muʿtaṣim's Succession to the Caliphate as Denouement to the Lifelong Feud between Al-Ma'mūn and His ʿAbbasid Family'. *Oriens* 38 (2010): 77–88.

Naymark, Aleksandr. 'Coins of Bukharan King Kunak/Khanuk'. In *From Nisa to Niya: Studies in Silk Road Art and Archaeology*, edited by Madhuvanti Ghose and Lilla Russel-Smith. London: Safron, 2004.

Naymark, Aleksandr. 'Drachms of Bukhār Khudā Khunak'. *Journal of Inner Asian Art and Archaeology* 5 (2010): 7–32.
Naymark, Aleksandr. 'Sogdiana, Its Christians and Byzantium: A Study of Artistic and Cultural Connections in Late Antiquity and Early Middle Ages'. PhD, Indiana University, 2001.
Naymark, Aleksandr and Luke Treadwell. 'An Arab-Sogdian Coin of AH 160: An Ikhshid in Ishtihan?' *The Numismatic Chronicle* 171 (2011): 359–66.
Nerazik, E.E. 'Khwarizm: Part One: History and Culture of Khwarizm'. In *History of Civilizations of Central Asia, Vol. III, The Crossroads of Civilizations: A.D. 250 to 750*, edited by B.A. Litvinsky, Zhang Guang-da and R. Shabani Samghabadi, 212–26. Paris: UNESCO, 1996.
Nikitin, Alexander. 'Notes on the Chronology of the Kushano-Sasanian Kingdom'. In *Coins, Art, and Chronology: Essays on Pre-Islamic History of the Indo-Iranian Borderlands*, edited by Michael Alram and Deborah E. Klimburg-Salter, 259–63. Wien: Verlag der Österreichischen Akademie der Wissenschaften, 1999.
Nixon, C.E.V. and Barbara Saylor Rodgers. *In Praise of Later Roman Emperors: The Panegyrici Latini*. Berkeley, CA: University of California Press, 1994.
Niẓām al-Mulk. *Siyar Al-Mulūk*. Edited by Hubert Darke. Second edition. Tehran: Shirkat-i Intishārat-i ʿIlmī va Farhangī, 1985.
Noelle-Karimi, Christine. *The Pearl in Its Midst: Herat and the Mapping of Khurāsān (15th-19th Centuries)*. Vienna: Verlag der Österreichischen Akademie der Wissenschaften, 2014.
Nokandeh, Jebrael, Eberhard W. Sauer, Hamid Omrani Rekavandi, Tony J. Wilkinson, Ghorban Ali Abbasi, Jean-Luc Schwenninger, Majid Mahmoudi, David Parker, Morteza Fattahi, Lucian Stephen Usher-Wilsom, Mohammad Ershadi, James Ratcliffe and Rowena Gale. 'Linear Barrier of Northern Iran: The Great Wall of Gorgan and the Wall of Tammishe'. *Iran* 44 (2006): 121–73.
Nöldeke, Theodor. *The Iranian National Epic*. Translated by L. Bogdanov. Philadelphia, PA: Porcupine Press, 1979.
Noth, Albrecht. *The Early Arabic Historical Tradition: A Source-Critical Study*. Translated by Michael Bonner. Princeton, NJ: Darwin Press, 1994.
Noth, Albrecht. *Heiliger Krieg und heiliger Kampf in Islam und Christentum*. Bonn: Ludwig Rohrscheid Verlag, 1966.
Nyberg, S.H. *AManual of Pahlavi, Part I: Texts*. Wiesbaden: Harrassowitz, 1964.
Oikonomidès, Nicolas. 'Silk Trade and Production in Byzantium from the Sixth to the Ninth Century: The Seals of Kommerkiarioi'. *Dumbarton Oaks Papers* 40 (1986): 33–53.
Olbrycht, Marek J. 'Dynastic Connections in the Arsacid Empire and the Origins of the House of Sāsān'. In *The Parthian and Early Sasanian Empires: Adaptation and Expansion*, edited by Vesta Sarkhosh Curtis, Elizabeth Pendelton, Michael Alram, and Touraj Daryaee, 23–35. Oxford: Oxbow Books, 2016.
Omar, Farouk. *The Abbasid Caliphate: 132/750-170/786*. Baghdad: National Printing and Publishing Company, 1969.
Papaconstantinou, Arietta. 'Between Umma and Dhimma. The Christians of the Middle East under the Umayyads'. *Annales Islamologiques* 42 (2008): 127–56.
Parkin, Frank. *Max Weber*. Revised. London: Routledge, 2002.
Pʿarpecʿi, Łazar. *The History of Łazar Pʿarpecʿi*. Translated by Robert W. Thomson. Atlanta, GA: Scholars Press, 1991.

Paul, Jürgen. *Herrscher, Gemeinwesen, Vermittler: Ostiran und Transoxanien in vormongolischer Zeit*. Beirut: Franz Steiner Verlag, Stuttgart, 1996.
Paul, Jürgen. *Lokale und imperiale Herrschaft im Iran des 12. jahrhunderts: Herrschaftspraxis und konzepte*. Wiesbaden: Reichert Verlag, 2016.
Paul, Jürgen. *The State and the Military: The Samanid Case*. Bloomington, IN: Indiana University Research Institute for Inner Asian Studies, 1994.
P'awstos, Buzandats'i. *The Epic Histories Attributed to P'awstos Buzand*. Translated by Nina G. Garsoïan. Cambridge, MA: The Department of Near Eastern Languages and Civilizations, Harvard University, 1989.
Payne, Richard. 'The Making of Turan: The Fall and Transformation of the Iranian East in Late Antiquity'. *Journal of Late Antiquity* 9 (2016): 4–41.
Payne, Richard. 'The Silk Road and the Iranian Political Economy in Late Antiquity: Iran, the Silk Road, and the Problem of Aristocratic Empire'. *Bulletin of SOAS* 81 (2018): 227–50.
Peacock, A. C. S. *Mediaeval Islamic Historiography and Political Legitimacy: Bal'amī's Tārīkhnāma*. London: Routledge, 2007.
Perdue, Peter. 'From Turfan to Taiwan: Trade and War on Two Chinese Frontiers'. In *Untaming the Frontier in Anthropology, Archaeology, and History*, edited by Bradley J. Parker and Lars Rodseth, 27–51. Tucson, AZ: University of Arizona Press, 2005.
Perikhanian, Anahit. 'Iranian Society and Law'. In *The Cambridge History of Iran, Vol. 3(2): The Seleucid, Parthian, and Sasanian Periods, Part 2*, edited by Ehsan Yarshater, 627–80. Cambridge: Cambridge University Press, 1983.
Potts, Daniel T. *Nomadism in Iran: From Antiquity to the Modern Era*. Oxford: Oxford University Press, 2014.
Potts, Daniel T. 'Sasanian Iran and Its Northeastern Frontier: Offense, Defense, and Diplomatic Entente'. In *Empires and Exchanges in Eurasian Late Antiquity: Rome, China, Iran, and the Steppe, ca. 250-750*, edited by Nicola Di Cosmo and Michael Maas, 287–301. Cambridge: Cambridge University Press, 2018.
Pourshariati, Parvaneh. *Decline and Fall of the Sasanian Empire: The Sasanian-Parthian Confederacy and the Arab Conquest of Iran*. London: I.B. Tauris, 2008.
Pourshariati, Parvaneh. 'Iranian Tradition in Ṭūs and the Arab Presence in Khurāsān'. Unpublished PhD dissertation, Columbia University, 1995.
Procopius. *History of the Wars*. Translated by H.B. Dewing. London: William Heinemann, 1914.
Pulleyblank, E.G. *The Background of the Rebellion of An Lu-Shan*. London: Oxford University Press, 1955.
Puschnigg, Gabriele. *Ceramics of the Merv Oasis: Recycling the City*. Walnut Creek, CA: Left Coast Press, 2006.
Qazvīnī, Muḥammad. 'Muqaddamah Qadīm Shāhnāmah'. In *Hazāra-i Firdausī*, edited by Muḥammad Amīn Rīyāḥī. 177–202. Tehran: Mu'assasa-i Muṭāla'āt-i Islāmī-i Dānishgāh-i Tihrān, 2010.
Qudāma. *Kitāb al-kharāj wa-ṣinā'at al-kitāba*. Edited by Muḥammad Ḥusayn al-Zubaydī. Baghdad: Dār al-rashīd li-l-nashr, 1981.
Rahbar, Mohammad. 'Découverte de panneaux de stucs sassanides'. *Dossiers d'Archólogie* 243 (1992): 62–5.
Rahbar, Mohammad. 'Découverte d'un monument d'époque sassanide à Bandian, Dargaz (Nord Khorassan): Fouilles 1994 et 1995'. *Studia Iranica* 27 (1998): 213–50.

Rahbar, Mohammad. 'The Discovery of a Sasanian Period Fire Temple at Bandiyān, Dargaz'. In *Current Research in Sasanian Archaeology, Art and History*, edited by D. Kennet and P. Luft, 15–40. Oxford: Archaeopress, 2008.

Rante, Rocco. '"Khorasan Proper" and "Greater Khorasan" within a Politico-Cultural Framework'. In *Greater Khorasan*, edited by Rocco Rante, 9–25. Berlin: De Gruyter, 2015.

Rante, Rocco, and Annabelle Collinet. *Nishapur Revisited: Stratigraphy and Ceramics of the Qohandez*. Oxford: Oxbow Books, 2013.

Rante, Rocco, and Abdisabur Raimkulov. 'Les fouilles de Paykend: Nouveaux éléments'. *Cahiers d'Asie Centrale* 21/22 (2013): 237–58.

Rapin, Claude. 'Les Portes de Fer près de Derbent: Sur la route de Bactres à Samarkand'. UMR8546 CNRS/ENS-Paris, archéologie & philologie Orient & Occident. http://www.archeo.ens.fr/spip.php?article374&lang=fr.

Rapin, Claude. 'On the Way to Roxane: The Route of Alexander the Great in Bactria and Sogdiana (328-327 BC)'. In *Zwischen Ost Und West: Neue Forschungenzum Antiken Zentralasien*, edited by Gunvor Lindströn, Svend Hansen, and Alfried Wieczorek, 43–82. Darmstadt: Verlag Philipp von Zabern, 2013.

Rapin, Claude, Aymon Baud, Frantz Grenet, and Sh. A. Rakhmanov. 'Les Recherches Sur La Region Des Portes de Fer de Sogdiane: Bref État Des Questions En 2005'. *Istorija Material'noj Kul'tury Uzbekistana (IMKU, The History of Material Culture of Uzbekistan)* 35 (2006): 91–112.

Rapp Jr., Stephen H. *The Sasanian World through Georgian Eyes: Caucasia and the Iranian Commonwealth in Late Antique Georgian Literature*. Surrey: Ashgate, 2014.

Ratzel, Friedrich. *Politische Geographie*. Second edition. Munich and Berlin: Verlag von R. Oldenbourg, 1903.

Rezakhani, Khodadad. 'The Bactrian Collection: An Important Source for Sasanian Economic History'. *E-Sasanika* 13 (2008): 1–14.

Rezakhani, Khodadad. 'From the "Cleavage" of Central Asia to Greater Khurasan: History and Historiography of Late Antique East Iran'. *Iranian Studies* 49 (2016): 205–15.

Rezakhani, Khodadad. 'Mazdakism, Manichaeism and Zoroastrianism: In Search of Orthodoxy and Heterodoxy in Late Antique Iran'. *Iranian Studies* 48 (2015): 55–70.

Rezakhani, Khodadad. *Re Orienting the Sasanians: East Iran in Late Antiquity*. Edinburgh: Edinburgh University Press, 2017.

Richter-Bernburg, Lutz. 'Linguistic Shuʿubiya and Early Neo-Persian Prose'. *Journal of the American Oriental Society* 94 (1974): 55–64.

Rieber, Alfred J. *The Struggle for the Eurasian Borderlands: From the Rise of Early Modern Empires to the End of the First World War*. Cambridge: Cambridge University Press, 2014.

Robinson, Chase. 'The Conquest of Khūzistān: A Historiographical Reassessment'. *Bulletin of the School of Oriental and African Studies* 67 (2004): 14–39.

Robinson, Chase. *Empire and Elites after the Muslim Conquest: The Transformation of Northern Mesopotamia*. Cambridge: Cambridge University Press, 2000.

Robinson, Chase. *Islamic Historiography*. Cambridge: Cambridge University Press, 2003.

Robinson, Chase. 'Neck-Sealing in Early Islam'. *Journal of the Economic and Social History of the Orient* 48 (2005): 401–41.

Rogers, J. Daniel. 'Inner Asian States and Empires: Theories and Synthesis'. *Journal of Archaeological Research* 20 (2012): 205–56.

Rojas, Carlos. *The Great Wall: A Cultural History*. Cambridge, MA: Harvard University Press, 2010.

Ross, E. Denison, and Vilhelm Thomsen. 'The Orkhon Inscriptions: Being a Translation of Professor Thomsen's Final Danish Rendering'. *Bulletin of the School of Oriental Studies* 5 (1930): 861–76.
Rotter, Gernot. *Die Umayyaden und der zweite Bürgerkrieg (680–692)*. Mainz: Deutsche Morgenländische Gesellschaft, 1982.
Rubin, Zeev. 'K̲osrow I ii. Reforms'. In *Encyclopædia Iranica*, New York: The Encyclopaedia Iranica Foundation, 2009.
Rubin, Zeev. 'The Reforms of Khusro Anushirwān'. In *The Byzantine and Early Islamic Near East III. States, Resources, and Armies*, edited by Averil Cameron, 225–97. Princeton, NJ: Darwin Press, 1995.
Sallāmī. *Akbār wulāt Khurāsān*. Edited by Mohammad Ali Kazembeyki. Tehran: Miras-e Maktoob, 2011.
Sauer, Eberhard W., Hamid Omrani Rekavandi, Tony J. Wilkinson and Jebrael Nokandeh. *Persia's Imperial Power in Late Antiquity: The Great Wall of Gorgān and Frontier Landscapes of Sasanian Iran*. Oxford: Oxbow Books, 2013.
Schafer, E. H. 'Iranian Merchants in T'ang Dynasty Tales'. In *Semitic and Oriental Studies*, edited by Walter Joseph Fischel, 403–22. Berkeley, CA: University of California Press, 1951.
Scher, Addaï, ed. 'Histoire Nestorienne (Chronique de Séert), premiere partie, fasc. 2'. *Patrologia Orientalis* 5 (1910): 217–344.
Scher, Addaï, ed. 'Histoire Nestorienne (Chronique de Séert), seconde partie, fasc. 1'. *Patrologia Orientalis* 7 (1911): 95–203.
Scher, Addaï, and Robert Griveau. 'Histoire Nestorienne (Chronique de Séert), seconde partie, fasc. 2'. *Patrologia Orientalis* 13 (1919): 433–639.
Schindel, Nikolaus. *Sylloge Nummorum Sasanidarum: Paris-Berlin-Wien: Band III/1L Shapur II-Kawad I/2. Regierung*. Wien: Verlag der Österreichischen Akademie der Wissenschaften, 2004.
Schindel, Nikolaus. 'The 3rd-Century "Marw Shah" Bronze Coins Reconsidered'. In *Commutatio et Contentio: Studies in the Late Roman, Sasanian, and Early Islamic Near East, in Memory of Zeev Rubin*, edited by Henning Börm and Josef Wiesehöfer, 23–32. Düsseldorf: Wellem, 2010.
Schindel, Nikolaus. 'The Beginning of Kushano-Sasanian Coinage'. In *Sylloge Nummorum Sasanidarum Paris-Berlin-Wien. Band II: Ohrmazd I. - Ohrmazd II*, edited by Michael Alram and Rika Gyselen, 65–73. Wien: Verlag der Österreichischen Akademie der Wissenschaften, 2012.
Scott, James C. *The Art of Not Being Governed: An Anarchist History of Upland South Asia*. New Haven, CT: Yale University Press, 2009.
Sears, Stuart. 'The Revolt of al-Ḥarith Ibn Surayj and the Countermarking of Umayyad Dirhams in Early Eighth Center CE Khurāsān'. In *The Lineaments of Islam: Studies in Honor of Fred McGraw Donner*, edited by Paul M. Cobb, 379–405. Leiden: Brill, 2012.
Sebēos. *The Armenian History Attributed to Sebeos*. Translated by Robert W. Thomson. Liverpool: Liverpool University Press, 1999.
Sen, Tansen. *Buddhism, Diplomacy, and Trade: The Realignment of Sino-Indian Relations, 600-1400*. Honolulu, HI: Association for Asian Studies and University of Hawai'i Press, 2003.
Shaban, M.A. *The ʿAbbāsid Revolution*. Cambridge: Cambridge University Press, 1970.
Shahbazi, A. Shahpur. 'Hormozd Kušānšāh'. In *Encyclopædia Iranica*, New York: The Encyclopaedia Iranica Foundation, 2004.
Shahbazi, A. Shahpur. 'On the Xwadāy-Nāmag'. *Acta Iranica* 16 (1990): 208–29.

Shahīd, Irfan. *Byzantium and the Arabs in the Sixth Century, Vol. 2, Part 1*. Washington, DC: Dumbarton Oaks, 2002.

Sharon, Moshe. *Black Banners from the East: The Establishment of the ʿAbbāsid State: Incubation of a Revolt*. Leiden: Brill, 1983.

Sharon, Moshe. *Revolt: The Social and Military Aspects of the ʿAbbāsid Revolution*. Jerusalem: The Max Schloessinger Memorial Fund, the Hebrew University, 1990.

Shayegan, M. Rahim. *Arsacids and Sasanians: Political Ideology in Post-Hellenic and Late Antique Persia*. Cambridge: Cambridge University Press, 2011.

Shoshan, Boaz. *The Arabic Historical Tradition and the Early Islamic Conquests: Folklore, Tribal Lore, Holy War*. Abingdon: Routledge, 2015.

Siegman, Henry. 'The State and the Individual in Sunni Islam'. *The Muslim World* 54 (1964): 14–26.

Simpson, St John. 'Sasanian Cities: Archaeological Perspectives on the Urban Economy and Built Environment of an Empire'. In *Sasanian Persia: Between Rome and the Steppes of Eurasia*, edited by Eberhard W. Sauer, 21–50. Edinburgh: Edinburgh University Press, 2017.

Sims-Williams, N. 'The Arab-Sasanian and Arab-Hephthalite Coinage: A View from the East'. In *Islamisation de l'Asie centrale: processus locaux d'acculturation du VIIe au XIe siècle*, edited by Étienne de la Vaissière, 115–30. Paris: Association pour l'avancement des études iraniennes, 2008.

Sims-Williams, N. *Bactrian Documents from Northern Afghanistan, I*. Oxford: Oxford University Press, 2001.

Sims-Williams, N. *Bactrian Documents from Northern Afghanistan, II*. Oxford: Oxford University Press, 2007.

Sims-Williams, N. 'Bactrian Language'. In *Encyclopædia Iranica*, New York: The Encyclopaedia Iranica Foundation, 1996.

Sims-Williams, N. 'Bactrian Legal Documents from 7th- and 8th-Century Guzgan'. *Bulletin of the Asia Institute* 15 (2001): 9–29.

Sims-Williams, N. 'From the Kushan-Shahs to the Arabs: New Bactrian Documents Dated in the Era of the Tochi Inscriptions'. In *Coins, Art and Chronology: Essays on the Pre-Islamic History of the Indo-Iranian Borderland*, edited by Michael Alram and Deborah E. Klimburg-Salter, 245–58. Vienna: Verlag der Österreichischen Akademie der Wissenschaften, 1999.

Sims-Williams, N. 'The Sasanians in the East: A Bactrian Archive from Northern Afghanistan'. In *The Sasanian Era*, edited by Vesta Sarkhosh Curtis and Sarah Stewart, 88–102. London: I.B. Tauris, 2008.

Sinor, Denis. 'The Establishment and Dissolution of the Türk Empire'. In *The Cambridge History of Early Inner Asia*, edited by Denis Sinor, 285–316. Cambridge: Cambridge University Press, 1990.

Sinor, Denis. 'The First Türk Empire'. In *History of Civilizations of Central Asia: Vol. III The Crossroads of Civilizations: A.D. 250 to 750*, edited by B.A. Litvinsky, Zhang Guang-da, and R. Shabani Samghabadi, 322–30. Paris: UNESCO, 1996.

Skaff, Jonathan Karam. 'Survival in the Frontier Zone: Comparative Perspectives on Identity and Political Allegiance in China's Inner Asian Borderlands during the Sui-Tang Dynastic Transition (617-630)'. *Journal of World History* 15 (2004): 117–53.

Skaff, Jonathan Karam. 'Western Turk Rule of Turkestan's Oases in the Sixth through Eighth Centuries'. In *The Turks*, edited by Halil Inalcik, 364–72. Ankara: Yeni Türkiye, 2002.

Sneath, David. *The Headless State: Aristocratic Orders, Kinship Society, & Misrepresentations of Nomadic Inner Asia*. New York: Columbia University Press, 2007.

Sourdel, Dominique. 'Les circonstances de la mort de Ṭāhir Ier au Ḫurāsān en 207/822'. *Arabica* 5 (1958): 66–9.
Stark, Sören. *Die Alttürkenzeit in Mittel- Und Zentralasien: Archäologische Und Historische Studien*. Wiesbaden: Dr. Ludwig Reichert Verlag, 2008.
Stark, Sören, 'The Arab Conquest of Bukhārā: Reconsidering Qutayba b. Muslim's Campaigns 87-90 H/706-709 CE', *Der Islam* 95 (2018): 367–400.
Stark, Sören. 'Mercenaries and City Rulers: Early Turks in Pre-Muslim Mawarannahr'. In *Social Orders and Social Landscapes*, edited by Laura M. Popova, Charles W. Hartley, and Adam T. Smith, 307–34. Newcastle: Cambridge Scholars, 2007.
Starr, S. Frederick. *Lost Enlightenment: Central Asia's Golden Age from the Arab Conquest to Tamerlane*. Princeton, NJ: Princeton University Press, 2013.
Stern, S.M. 'Yaʿqūb the Coppersmith and Persian National Sentiment'. In *Iran and Islam: In Memory of the Late Vladimir Minorsky*, edited by C.E. Bosworth, 535–55. Edinburgh: Edinburgh University Press, 1971.
Strabo. *The Geography*. Translated by H.L. Jones. Cambridge, MA: Harvard University Press, 1932.
Ṭabarī, Abū Jaʿfar Muḥammad b. Jarīr. *Taʾrīkh al-rusul waʾl-mulūk*. Edited by M.J. de Goeje. Leiden: Brill, 1879.
Ṭabarī, Abū Jaʿfar Muḥammad b. Jarīr. *ʿAbbasid Authority Affirmed*. Translated by Jane Dammen McAuliffe. The History of Ṭabarī 28. Albany, NY: State University of New York Press, 1995.
Ṭabarī, Abū Jaʿfar Muḥammad b. Jarīr. *The ʿAbbasid Caliphate in Equilibrium*. Translated by C.E. Bosworth. The History of Ṭabarī 30. Albany, NY: State University of New York Press, 1989.
Ṭabarī, Abū Jaʿfar Muḥammad b. Jarīr. *The ʿAbbasid Revolution*. Translated by John Alden Williams. The History of Ṭabarī 27. Albany, NY: State University of New York Press, 1985.
Ṭabarī, Abū Jaʿfar Muḥammad b. Jarīr. *Between the Civil Wars*. Translated by Michael G. Morony. The History of Ṭabarī 18. Albany, NY: State University of New York Press, 1986.
Ṭabarī, Abū Jaʿfar Muḥammad b. Jarīr. *The Caliphate of Yazid b. Muʿawiyah A.D. 680-683/A.H. 60-64*. Translated by I.K.A. Howard. The History of Ṭabarī 19. Albany, NY: State University of New York Press, 1991.
Ṭabarī, Abū Jaʿfar Muḥammad b. Jarīr. *The Collapse of Sufyanid Authority and the Coming of the Marwanids*. Translated by G.R. Hawting. The History of Ṭabarī 20. Albany, NY: State University of New York Press, 1989.
Ṭabarī, Abū Jaʿfar Muḥammad b. Jarīr. *The Community Divided*. Translated by Adrian Brockett. The History of Ṭabarī 16. Albany, NY: State University of New York Press, 1996.
Ṭabarī, Abū Jaʿfar Muḥammad b. Jarīr. *The Conquest of Iran A.D. 641-643/A.H. 21-23*. Translated by G. Rex Smith. The History of Ṭabarī, 14. Albany, NY: State University of New York Press, 1994.
Ṭabarī, Abū Jaʿfar Muḥammad b. Jarīr. *The Conquest of Iraq, Southwestern Persia, and Egypt*. Translated by Gautier H.A. Juynboll. The History of Ṭabarī 13. Albany, NY: State University of New York Press, 1989.
Ṭabarī, Abū Jaʿfar Muḥammad b. Jarīr. *The Crisis of the Early Caliphate*. Translated by R. Stephen Humphreys. The History of Ṭabarī, 15. Albany, NY: State University of New York Press, 1987.
Ṭabarī, Abū Jaʿfar Muḥammad b. Jarīr. *The Empire in Transition*. Translated by David Stephen Powers. The History of Ṭabarī 24. Albany, NY: State University of New York Press, 1989.

Ṭabarī, Abū Jaʿfar Muḥammad b. Jarīr. *The End of Expansion*. Translated by Khalid Yahya Blankinship. The History of Ṭabarī 25. Albany, NY: State University of New York Press, 1989.

Ṭabarī, Abū Jaʿfar Muḥammad b. Jarīr. *The First Civil War*. Translated by G.R. Hawting. The History of Ṭabarī 17. Albany, NY: State University of New York Press, 1996.

Ṭabarī, Abū Jaʿfar Muḥammad b. Jarīr. *al-Manṣūr and al-Mahdī A.D. 763-786/A.H. 146-169*. Translated by Hugh Kennedy. The History of Ṭabarī 29. Albany, NY: State University of New York Press, 1990.

Ṭabarī, Abū Jaʿfar Muḥammad b. Jarīr. *The Marwanid Restoration*. Translated by Everett K. Rowson. The History of Ṭabarī 22. Albany, NY: State University of New York Press, 1987.

Ṭabarī, Abū Jaʿfar Muḥammad b. Jarīr. *The Reunification of the ʿAbbasid Caliphate*. Translated by C.E. Bosworth. The History of Ṭabarī 32. Albany, NY: State University of New York Press, 1987.

Ṭabarī, Abū Jaʿfar Muḥammad b. Jarīr. *The Sāsānids, the Byzantines, the Lakhmids, and Yemen*. Translated by C.E. Bosworth. The History of Ṭabarī, 5. Albany, NY: State University of New York Press, 1999.

Ṭabarī, Abū Jaʿfar Muḥammad b. Jarīr. *Storm and Stress along the Northern Frontier of the ʿAbbāsid Caliphate*. Translated by C.E. Bosworth. The History of Ṭabarī 33. Albany, NY: State University of New York Press, 1991.

Ṭabarī, Abū Jaʿfar Muḥammad b. Jarīr. *The Victory of the Marwanids*. Translated by Michael Fishbein. The History of Ṭabarī 21. Albany, NY: State University of New York Press, 1990.

Ṭabarī, Abū Jaʿfar Muḥammad b. Jarīr. *The Waning of the Umayyad Caliphate*. Translated by Carole Hillenbrand. The History of Ṭabarī, 26. Albany, NY: State University of New York Press, 1989.

Ṭabarī, Abū Jaʿfar Muḥammad b. Jarīr. *The War between Brothers*. Translated by Michael Fishbein. The History of Ṭabarī 31. Albany, NY: State University of New York Press, 1992.

Ṭabarī, Abū Jaʿfar Muḥammad b. Jarīr. *The Zenith of the Marwānid House*. Translated by Martin Hinds. The History of Ṭabarī, 23. Albany, NY: State University of New York Press, 1990.

Ṭabarī, Abū Jaʿfar Muḥammad b. Jarīr, and Franz Rosenthal. *The Return of the Caliphate to Baghdad*. The History of Ṭabarī 38. Albany, NY: State University of New York Press, 1985.

Taʾrīkh-i Sīstān. Edited by Mudarris Ṣādiqī, Jaʿfar. Tehran: Nashr-i Markaz, 1994.

The Tārikh-e Sīstan. Translated by Milton Gold. Rome: Istituto italiano per il Medio ed Estremo Oriente, 1976.

Thaʿālibī, Abū Manṣūr ʿAbd al-Malik. *Ghurar akhbār mulūk al-furs wa sīyarihim*. Edited by Hermann Zotenberg. Paris: Imrimerie Nationale, 1900.

Tibbetts, Gerald R. 'The Balkhī School of Geographers'. In *The History of Cartography, Vol. 2, Book 1: Cartography in the Traditional Islamic and South Asian Societies*, edited by J.B. Harley and David Woodward, 108–36. Chicago, IL: University of Chicago Press, 1992.

Tor, Deborah. 'The Islamization of Central Asia in the Sāmānid Era and the Reshaping of the Muslim World'. *Bulletin of the School of Oriental and African Studies* 72 (2009): 279–99.

Tor, Deborah. 'Privatized Jihad and Public Order in the Pre-Seljuq Period: The Role of the Mutatawwiʿa'. *Iranian Studies* 38 (2005): 555–73.

Tor, Deborah. *Violent Order: Religion Warfare, Chivalry, and the 'ayyār Phenomenon in the Medieval Islamic World*. Würzburg: Ergon Verlag, 2007.

Toumanoff, Cyril. *Studies in Christian Caucasian History*. Washington, DC: Georgetown University Press, 1963.

Treadwell, Luke. 'The Monetary History of the Bukharkhuda dirham ("black dirham") in Samanid Transoxiana (204-395/819-1005)'. *Oriental Numismatic Society Journal* 193 (2007): 24–39.

Treadwell, Luke. 'The Political History of the Sāmānid State'. PhD thesis, University of Oxford, 1991.

Turner, Frederick Jackson. 'The Significance of the Frontier in American History'. In *The Frontier in American History*, 1–38. New York: Henry Holt and Company, 1953.

Turner, John P. 'The Abnā' al-Dawla: The Definition and Legitimation of Identity in Response to the Fourth Fitna'. *Journal of Oriental and African Studies* 124 (2004): 1–22.

Urban, Elizabeth, 'The Early Islamic Mawali: A Window onto Processes of Identity Construction and Social Change'. Ph.D., University of Chicago, 2012.

ʿUtbī, Abū Naṣr. *Kitāb Al-Yamīnī Fī Akhbār Dawlat Al-Malik Yamīn Al-Dawla Abī l'Qāsim Maḥmūd b. Nāṣir Al-Dawla Abī Manṣūr b. Sabuktakīn*. Edited by Yūsuf Hādī. Tehran, 2008.

Vacca, Alison. *Non-Muslim Provinces under Early Islam: Islamic Rule and Iranian Legitimacy in Armenia and Caucasian Albania*. Cambridge: Cambridge University Press, 2017.

Vacca, Alison. 'Past the Mediterranean and Iran: A Comparative Study of Armenia as an Islamic Frontier, First/Seventh to Fifth/Eleventh Centuries'. In *An Armenian Mediterranean: Words and Worlds in Motion*, edited by Kathryn Babayan and Michael Pifer, 39–58. Cham, Switzerland: Palgrave Macmillan, 2018.

Vaissière, Étienne de la. 'Historiens arabes et manuscrits d'Asie centrale: Quelques recoupements'. *Revue des Mondes Musulmans et de la Méditerranée* 129 (2011). http://remmm.revues.org/7112.

Vaissière, Étienne de la. 'Huns et Xiongnu'. *Central Asiatic Journal* 49 (2005): 3–26.

Vaissière, Étienne de la. 'The Last Bactrian Kings'. In *Coins, Art and Chronology II: The First Millennium C.E. in the Indo-Iranian Borderlands*, edited by Michael Alram, Deborah E. Klimburg-Salter, Minoru Inaba and Matthias Pfisterer, 213–18. Vienna: Verlag der Österreichischen Akademie der Wissenschaften, 2010.

Vaissière, Étienne de la. 'Le Ribāṭ d'Asie centrale'. In *Islamisation de l'Asie centrale: Processus locaux d'acculturation du VIIe au XIe siècle*, edited by Étienne de la Vaissière, 71–94. Paris: Association pour l'avancement des études iraniennes, 2008.

Vaissière, Étienne de la. 'The Rise of Sogdian Merchants and the Role of the Huns: The Historical Importance of the Sogdian Ancient Letters'. In *The Silk Road: Trade, Travel, War, and Faith*, edited by Susan Whitfield and Ursula Sims-Williams, 19–23. Chicago, IL: Serindia Publications, 2004.

Vaissière, Étienne de la. *Samarcande et Samarra: Élites d'Asie centrale dans l'empire abbasside*. Paris: Association pour l'avancement des études iraniennes, 2007.

Vaissière, Étienne de la. *Sogdian Traders: A History*. Translated by James Ward. Leiden: Brill, 2005.

Vaissière, Étienne de la, and Éric Trombert. 'Des Chinois et des Hu: Migrations et intégration des Iraniens orientaux en milieu Chinois durant le Haut Moyen Âge'. *Annales. Histoire, Sciences Sociales* 59 (2004): 931–69.

Van Bladel, Kevin. 'The Bactrian Background of the Barmakids'. In *Islam and Tibet - Interactions along the Musk Routes*, edited by Anna Akasoy, Charles Burnett, and Ronit Yoeli-Tlalim, 43–88. Surrey: Ashgate, 2011.
Van Bladel, Kevin. 'Ibn al-Muqaffaʿ on the Bactrian Language among the ʿAbbāsid Armies'. In *Annual Meeting of the American Oriental Society*. Boston, MA, 18 March 2016.
Van Donzel, Emeri, and Andrea Schmidt. *Gog and Magog in Early Christian and Islamic Sources: Sallam's Quest for Alexander's Wall*. Leiden: Brill, 2010.
Van Ess, Joseph. 'Jahm b. Ṣafwān'. In *Encyclopædia Iranica*. New York: The Encyclopaedia Iranica Foundation, 2008.
Van Staël, J.P. 'Ḳaṣr'. In *Encyclopaedia of Islam*. Second edition. Leiden: Brill, 1960-2009.
Van Vloten, Gerlof. *Récherches sur la domination arabe, le chiitisme et les croyances messianiques sous le khalifat des Omayades*. Amsterdam: J. Müller, 1894.
Vondrovec, Klaus. *Coinage of the Iranian Huns and Their Successors from Bactria to Gandhara: 4th to 8th Century CE*. Vienna: Verlag der Österreichischen Akademie der Wissenschaften, 2014.
Vondrovec, Klaus. 'Coinage of the Nezak'. In *Coins, Art and Chronology II: The First Millennium C.E. in the Indo-Iranian Borderlands*, edited by Michael Alram, Deborah E. Klimburg-Salter, Minoru Inaba, and Matthias Pfisterer, 169–90. Wien: Verlag der Österreichischen Akademie der Wissenschaften, 2010.
Vopiscus, Flavius. *Scriptores Historia Augusta*. Translated by David Magie. Vol. 3. Cambridge, MA: Harvard University Press, 1961.
Waldman, Marilyn Robinson. *Towards a Theory of Historical Narrative: A Case Study of Perso-Islamicate Historiography*. Columbus, OH: The Ohio State University Press, 1980.
Waldron, Arthur. *The Great Wall of China: From History to Myth*. Cambridge: Cambridge University Press, 1990.
Walker, John. *A Catalogue of the Arab-Sassanian Coins*. Reprint. Oxford: Oxford University Press, 1967.
Wan, Xiang. 'A Study of the Kidarites: Reexamination of Documentary Sources'. *Archivum Eurasiae Medii Aevi* 19 (2012): 243–301.
Webb, Walter Prescott. *The Great Frontier*. Boston, MA: Houghton Mifflin, 1952.
Weber, Ursula. 'Wahrām II., König der Könige von Ērān und Anērān'. *Iranica Antiqua* 44 (2009): 559–643.
Weber, Ursula, and Josef Wiesehöfer. 'Der aufstand des Ormies und die Thronfolge im frühen Sasanidenreich'. In *Monumentum et Instrumentum Inscriptum: Beschrifete Objekte aus Kaiserzeit und Spätantike als Historische Zeugnisse: Festschrift für Peter Weiss*, edited by Henning Börm, Norbert Ehrhardt, and Josef Wiesehöfer, 217–25. Stuttgart: Franz Steiner, 2008.
Wellhausen, Julius. *The Arab Kingdom and Its Fall*. Translated by Margaret Graham Weir. Calcutta: University of Calcutta, 1927.
Wheatley, Paul. *The Places Where Men Pray Together*. Chicago, IL: University of Chicago Press, 2001.
Widengren, G. 'Sources of Parthian and Sasanian History'. In *The Cambridge History of Iran, Vol. 3(2): The Seleucid, Parthian, and Sasanian Periods, Part 2*, edited by Ehsan Yarshater, 1259–83. Cambridge: Cambridge University Press, 1983.
Wiet, Gaston. 'L'Empire Néo-Byzantin des Omeyyades et l'empire Néo-Sassanide des Abbasides'. *Cahiers d'Histoire Mondiale* 9 (1953): 63–71.

Wilde, Andreas. *What Is Beyond the River? Power, Authority, and Social Order in Transoxania (18th-19th Centuries) Volume 1*. Vienna: Verlag der Österreichischen Akademie der Wissenschaften, 2016.

Williams, A.V. 'Zoroastrians and Christians in Sasanian Iran'. *Bulletin John Rylands Library* 78 (1996): 37–53.

Wink, André. *Al-Hind: The Making of the Indo-Islamic World*. Leiden: Brill, 1990.

Wittek, Paul. *The Rise of the Ottoman Empire*. London: Royal Asiatic Society, 1938.

Yamamoto, Kumiko. *The Oral Background of Persian Epics: Storytelling and Poetry*. Leiden: Brill, 2003.

Yaʿqūbī, Aḥmad b. Abī Yaʿqūb. *Kitāb al-buldān*. Edited by M.J. de Goeje. Bibliotheca Geographorum Arabicorum 7. Leiden: Brill, 1892.

Yaʿqūbī, Aḥmad b. Abī Yaʿqūb. *Tārīkh al-Yaʿqūbī*. Beirut: Dār Ṣādr, 2010.

Yāqūt. *Muʿjam al-buldān*. Edited by Muḥammad ʿAbd al-Raḥman al-Murʿashlī. 8 vols. Beirut: Dār iḥayā' al-turāth al-ʿarabī, 1997.

Yarshater, Ehsan. 'Iranian National History'. In *The Cambridge History of Iran, Vol. 3(1): The Seleucid, Parthian, and Sasanian Periods, Part 1*, edited by Ehsan Yarshater, 359–477. Cambridge: Cambridge University Press, 1983.

Yazdī, Sharaf al-Dīn. *Ẓafarnāma*. Edited by M. ʿAbbāsī. Tehran: Amīr Kabīr, 1957.

Yihong, Pan. *Son of Heaven and Heavenly Qaghan: Sui-Tang China and Its Neighbors*. Bellingham, WA: Western Washington University Press, 1997.

Yildiz, Sara Nur. 'Reconceptualizing the Seljuk-Cilician Frontier: Armenians, Latins, and Turks in Conflict and Alliance during the Early Thirteenth Century'. In *Borders, Barriers, and Ethnogenesis: Frontier in Late Antiquity and the Middle Ages*, edited by Florin Curta, 91–120. Turnhout, Belgium: Brepols, 2005.

Zadeh, Travis. *Mapping Frontiers across Medieval Islam: Geography, Translation, and the ʿAbbāsid Empire*. London: I.B. Tauris, 2011.

Zakeri, Mohsen. *Sāsānid Soldiers in Early Muslim Society: The Origins of ʿayyārān and Futuwwa*. Wiesbaden: Harrassowitz, 1995.

Zeimal, E.V. 'The Kidarite Kingdom in Central Asia'. In *History of Civilizations of Central Asia, Vol. III, The Crossroads of Civilizations: A.D. 250 to 750*, edited by B.A. Litvinsky, Zhang Guang-da, and R. Shabani Samghabadi, 123–37. Paris: UNESCO, 1996.

Zonaras, John. *The History of Zonaras: From Alexander Severus to the Death of Theodosious the Great*. Translated by Thomas M. Banchich and Eugene N. Lane. London: Routledge, 2009.

INDEX

Abarshahr 51, 83, 104, 107. *See also* Nīshāpūr
  Abarshahrshāh 49
ʿAbbās b. Bukhārkhudā, Bukharan noble (early ninth century) 176
Abbasid Caliphate (r. 750–1258) 19, 28–9, 155, 158, 161, 163–5
  coinage 157, 159
  connections to royal family 164–5, 171–2, 174, 176, 178, 193–4
  and descendants of Umayyad officials 163, 172
  frontiers 18, 22, 40, 152, 154, 157, 165, 183
  as heirs of the Sasanians 73, 76, 97
  and local dynasties 4–5, 121, 153, 155–6, 167, 169–70, 176–8, 180, 182, 187, 189, 194
  military 134, 150, 154, 156–7, 162–4, 181, 194
  Revolution (747–50) 113, 137, 139, 151, 166
    and Arab settlement 147
    and frontiers 6
    historiography 142–3, 148
    Iranian participants 144–6
    and other revolutionary movements 142, 149
    and tribal feuds 143–4, 152
  slavery 181–2, 194
ʿAbbāsiyya 164
ʿAbd al-ʿAzīz b. Walīd I, Umayyad prince (d. 728–9) 122
ʿAbd al-Jabbār b. ʿAbd al-Raḥmān al-Azdī, Abbasid governor of Khurāsān (r. 757–8) 158–9, 163–4, 166
ʿAbdallāh b. al-Zubayr, counter-caliph (r. 680–92) 99, 102, 105–6, 108, 114
ʿAbdallāh b. ʿĀmir, governor of Baṣra (r. 649–56, 661–4) 76, 78, 82, 101, 108, 187
ʿAbdallāh b. Khāzm al-Sulamī, military adventurer (d. 691–2) 88, 99–106, 108, 110
ʿAbdallāh b. Ṭāhir, Ṭāhird governor (r. 828–45) 29, 32, 177–82, 194, 223–4 n.5
ʿAbd al-Malik, Umayyad caliph (r. 685–705) 79, 99, 102, 106–8, 114
ʿAbd al-Malik b. Nūḥ I, Sāmānid amir (r. 954–61) 190
ʿAbd al-Raḥmān b. Muḥammad b. al-Ashʿath, rebel (d. 704) 108, 114
ʿAbd al-Raḥmān b. Nuʿaym al-Ghāmidī, Umayyad governor of Khurāsān (r. 719–20) 125
ʿAbd al-Raḥmān b. Samura, governor of Sīstān (d. 670) 93
ʿAbd Shams, Arab tribe 78
Abīward 82, 120
abnāʾ al-dawla (sons of the dynasty) 165, 173, 175–6
Abū ʿAlī Chaghānī, Aḥmad b. Muḥammad, Muḥtājid ruler (d. 955) 187–92, 194
Abū ʿAlī Simjūrī, Simjūrid governor (d. 997) 193
Abū al-Ṣaydāʾ Ṣāliḥ b. Ṭarīf (early eighth century) 125, 136, 146
Abū Bakr Muḥammd b. Muẓaffar Chaghānī, Muḥtājid ruler (d. 941) 188–9, 192
Abū Dāwud Khālid b. Ibrāhīm, Abbasid governor of Khurāsān (r. 755–7) 155, 157–8
Abū Manṣūr Muḥammad b. ʿAbd al-Razzāq Ṭūsī (d. 961) 185–92, 194, 197

Abū Muslim, Abbasid general and governor of Khurāsān (ca. 718–755) 144, 147, 151–60, 162, 165–6, 171, 187
Ādur-Gushnasp 57
Afshīn (hereditary title of the ruler of Usrūshana) 11, 155–6, 165, 176–9, 181–2
Aḥmad b. Abī Khālid, Abbasid vizier (d. 823) 177
Aḥmad b. Asad b. Sāmānkhudā, Sāmānid amir (d. 864) 174, 179–80
Aḥnaf b. Qays, general (d. 686) 71–3, 75, 77–8, 80, 84–5, 87–9, 120
Akharūn 115, 127
Akhshunwār, Hephthalite king (late fifth century) 43–6, 62
Alai Mountains 11, 22
Alburz Mountains 12, 27, 59, 101
Alexander the Great (r. 356–23 BCE) 3, 24, 50, 59
ʿAlī b. Abī Ṭālib, caliph (r. 656–61) 78, 93, 160
ʿAlī b. ʿĪsā b. Māhān, Abbasid general (r. 796–808) 165, 172–5
Alkhan Huns 55, 59, 202 n.32
Alptigīn, Sāmānid general (d. 963) 190–1
Amida 53, 63
Amīn, Abbasid caliph (r. 809–13) 170–3, 175
Ammianus Marcellinus, Roman historian (330–95) 52–3, 55
ʿAmr b. Layth, Ṣaffārid amir (r. 879–901) 181, 184
Amū Darya. *See* Oxus, River
Āmul 56–7, 90–1, 100, 115, 132, 141, 150
Anastasian War (502–6) 63
Anbīr 105–6
Anda/Andarhaz, River 123
An Lushan Revolt (755–6) 93, 248 n.72
Antiochus I, Seleucid king (r. 281–61 BCE) 38
Anxi 95, 154
Arab–Byzantine Frontier 6–7, 20, 33, 40, 78, 241 n.69
 eastern fighters along 156, 173, 178, 192
Arab–Hephthalite coins 105
Arabic language 47, 105, 161, 185–6, 191–2
Arab–Muslim Conquests 4, 6, 33, 69–74
 'capture-rebellion-recapture' 73–4, 77, 97
 futūḥ narratives and historiography 72, 74–7, 79–80, 84–5
 negotiation with locals 71–4, 80–4, 97
 organization 77–8, 98
 raiding 71, 74, 78, 90–2
 resistance to 75, 78–9, 82–5, 88, 90–1, 93, 96–7, 115, 118, 120–1
 rules of conquest 117
 terminology 224 n.8
Arabs 67, 78–9, 90, 98, 100, 118, 145, 199
 alliances with non-Arabs 107–9
 anti-Arab attitudes 190–1
 settlement 39, 78–9, 84, 89, 92, 100–1, 104, 111, 113, 115–18, 120–1, 124, 133, 143–5, 147
 tribal divisions 101, 103, 110, 123–4, 129–30, 137, 145–6, 149, 151–2, 166, 199
Arab–Sasanian coins 78, 101, 103, 105, 157
Ardashīr I, Sasanian shahanshah (r. 224–41) 44, 49, 51
Area Commands 92, 95–6
Armenia 44, 49, 51–2, 63, 67, 176
Armenians 57
Armenian sources 45, 47
Asad b. ʿAbdallāh al-Qasrī, Umayyad governor of Khurāsān (r. 725–7, 735–8) 33, 129–32, 134–5, 141–2, 147–8, 179
Asad b. Sāmānkhudā, Sāmānid patriarch 174, 176, 179
asāwira (Iranian cavalry) 72, 78, 171
Ashʿath b. Yaḥyā al-Ṭāʾī, Abbasid governor of Ishtīkhan (r. ca. 757–62) 159
Ashina Ho-lu, Turkish khāqān (r. ca. 649–57) 95
Ashras b. ʿAbdallāh al-Sulāmī, Umayyad governor of Khurāsān (r. 727–30) 125–6, 130–2, 136

ʿĀṣim b. ʿAbdallāh al-Hilālī, Umayyad governor of Khurāsān (r. 734–5) 140–1
ʿayyār (errant warrior) 9, 162, 183
Azd, Arab tribe 102, 114, 119, 129–30, 140, 142, 144, 151, 153
Azerbaijan 57, 178

Bābak Khurramdīn, rebel (795–838) 177–8
Bāb al-Abwāb 59, 65
Bāb al-Ḥadīd. *See* Gate of Iron
Bactria 11, 38, 50
Bactrian documents 47, 53, 59, 63, 65, 67, 121
Bactrian language 11, 15, 53, 105, 146
Badakhshan 11, 59
Bādhām, Sasanian governor of Yemen (d. ca. 632) 72–3
Bādhān, *marzbān* of Marw al-Rūd (late seventh century) 72–5, 80, 87, 120, 187
Bādhghīs 13, 67, 82, 86–9, 106, 109, 112, 115, 119–20, 160, 174, 176
Baghdad 156, 165, 172–8, 181–3, 186
Bāhila, Arab tribe 114, 126
Bahrām I, Sasanian shahanshah (r. 271–4) 49
Bahrām II, Sasanian shahanshah (r. 274–93) 52
Bahrām III, Sasanian shahanshah (r. 293) 52
Bahrām Chōbīn, Parthian rebel (d. 591) 67–70, 81, 85, 179, 211 n.5
Bahrām V Gūr, Sasanian shahanshah (r. 420–38) 44–6, 56–8, 90, 157
Baisun-Tau Mountains 24, 26
Bakr b. Wāʾil, Arab tribe 102–6
Balādhūrī, historian (d. 892) 72–3, 76, 79, 82–3, 87, 91–2, 102, 112, 181
Balʿamī, Abū ʿAlī, Sāmānid vizier and historian (d. ca. 992–7) 77, 87, 160–1, 163, 186–7
Balʿamī, Abū Faḍl, Sāmānid vizier (d. 940) 186
Balkh 11, 13, 21, 23, 50, 68–9, 88, 90, 104, 115, 120–1, 129, 131, 134, 140–2, 149–50, 157, 164, 173–4, 198–9, 210 n.119. *See also* Naw Bahār
  Arab–Muslim conquest 77, 85–6, 89
  Asad b. ʿAbdallāh al-Qasrī's capital 135, 142, 147–8, 179
  Kidarite capital 55, 58–9
  pilgrimage site 12, 97
  Sasanian rule 51, 65, 67
  walls 36–7, 39, 41
Bāmān, Sasanian princess (mid seventh century) 93
Bāmiyān 12, 32, 35, 165
Bandiyān 57
Bānījurids, rulers of Ṭukhāristān 176
Barāz (Hephthalite title) 82, 86–7
Bārkath 127, 156
Barmak, title of the guardian of the Naw Bahār monastery 86, 97, 150
Barmakids, family from Balkh 86, 164–5, 174
Baṣra 65, 78, 89–91, 101–2, 108, 114, 123, 176, 182
Battle of Ṭalās (751) 154–5, 157
Battle of the Pass (731) 132–4
Bīdūn, Bukhārkhudā (mid seventh century) 90
Bīlāsh, Sasanian shahanshah (r. 484–8) 62
Bilgä, Turkish khāqān (r. 716–34) 25
border 2–4, 7, 14, 19–23, 28–30, 32, 34, 39–41, 44–6. *See also* ḥadd
  borderland 22–3, 198
Borzūya, Sasanian physician (early sixth century) 185–6
Bosi, Chinese province of Persia 92, 95
Buddhism 51, 53–4, 143, 159, 228 n.84
  pilgrims 12
Bughrākhān Abū Mūsā Hārūn b. Īlak, Qarākhānid ruler (d. 992) 193
Bukayr b. Wishāḥ al-Saʿdī, rebel (d. 696–7) 99, 106–9, 117
Bukhara 10, 23, 44, 65, 100, 109, 122, 130, 150–1, 153, 155–7, 161, 172–4, 180–1, 188, 210 n.119
  Arab settlement 116–18
  conquest 90–2, 94, 111–12, 115–16, 118, 136
  conversion to Islam 118–19, 126, 131
  geography 91
  and Muqannaʿ 159–61

Sāmānid capital 180, 193–4
Türgesh attacks 124, 132–3
walls 36–9, 41
Bukhāriyya 90, 134, 182
Bukhārkhudā 37, 90, 94, 100, 115–16, 136, 150–1, 153, 156–7, 164, 180, 184
Bumïn, Turkish khāqān (d. 552) 25, 64
Bunyāt b. Ṭughshāda, Bukhārkhudā (r. ca. 751–ca. 779) 153, 161
Būshanj 82, 86–7, 160, 171
Būyids (r. 934–1062) 189–92
Byzantine Empire (r. 330–1453) 44, 57, 59–60, 63, 66–8, 70, 158, 187
Byzantine sources 45, 47

čākira (personal bodyguard) 108, 123, 134, 150, 155, 182
Caspian Sea 9, 12–13, 25, 34, 38, 59–61, 65, 123, 198
Caucasus 25, 65–6, 69, 165, 177
Chāch (Tashkent) 1, 11, 25, 28–9, 38, 65, 67, 122, 128, 130, 132, 134, 149, 154, 156, 170, 173–4, 179, 182
Cháng'ān 93, 95–6
Chaghāniyān 11, 17, 22, 28, 40, 62, 65, 75, 84, 109, 115, 127, 129–30, 133, 157, 160, 164, 174, 180, 187–8, 190
Chargh 184
China 11–12, 27, 51, 54, 66, 68, 92–3, 95–8, 128, 154–5, 162
frontiers 13, 23, 28–30, 40, 95
Great Wall 60, 65
trade 51, 56, 62, 96, 116–18, 127–8
Chinese sources 47–8
Chionite Huns 52, 55–6, 58
Christensen, Arthur 46–7, 81
thesis 46
Christianity 57, 159, 184
Cilicia. *See* Ṭarsūs
de Clavijo, Ruy González (d. 1412) 25, 197
'crossroads of civilization' 27
crucifixion 121, 123, 129, 149
Ctesiphon 45, 52, 55, 67

Damascus 112–13, 122, 149–50
Dār al-Ḥarb (Abode of War) 2, 20–1, 31, 40
Dār al-Islām (Abode of Islam) 20–1, 31, 33, 40, 183, 192
Dār al-Jihād (Abode of Jihad) 2
Dar-i Āhanīn. *See* Gate of Iron
Dār Kufr (Abode of the Infidels) 33, 130
Dāwūd b. Bānījur, Bānījurid ruler 176
Day of Thirst 1, 130, 132
Dihistān 52, 123
dihqān (pl. *dahāqīn*, petty landed gentry) 35, 74, 78, 80–4, 86, 91, 97, 100, 115–17, 119, 125–6, 128–9, 131, 135, 140, 142, 144, 147–8, 150–1, 155–6, 160–1, 165, 180, 185, 193
Dīnawarī, historian (815–96) 87, 93, 147
Dīwāshtīch, Sogdian ruler (d. 722) 128–9, 132
'dynasticism' 49

Egypt 68, 173, 177, 180
empires 2–5, 45, 105, 198–200
centralization 18, 46–8
conquest 27
imperial cosmography 97–8
reach of 35–6, 39–40, 96
Euripides, playwright (480–406 BCE) 38

Faḍl b. Kāwūs b. Khārākhara, Transoxianan prince (early ninth century) 177
Faḍl b. Sahl b. Zādānfarūkh, Abbasid vizier (d. 818) 174, 176
Faḍl b. Sulaymān al-Ṭūsī, Abū al-ʿAbbās, Abbasid governor of Khurāsān (r. 782–7) 37, 163–4, 166
Faḍl b. Yaḥyā b. Khālid b. Barmak, Abbasid governor of Khurāsān (d. 808) 17–19, 21, 26, 35, 40, 46, 164–6, 177
Fā'iq Khāṣṣa, Sāmānid general (d. 999) 193
Farighūnids, rulers of Gūzgān 192
Farrukhzād, Sasanian general of the Ispahbudān Parthian family (d. 665) 82–3
Fārs 48, 101
farsakh, definition 203 n.3
Fāryāb 75, 84, 102, 120–1, 140, 149, 151

Ferghana Valley 1, 29, 65, 92, 118, 122–3, 127, 129–30, 133, 136, 154–5, 157, 163, 172–4, 179, 181, 188, 192–3, 229 n.106
description 11
'feudalism' 43, 46, 48–9, 53, 146, 180
Firdawsī, Iranian poet (940–1019 or 1025) 47, 87, 185–6, 191, 197
fitna (civil war) 95
First Fitna (656–61) 78–9, 92, 102
Second Fitna (680–92) 92, 98–9, 101–10, 113–14, 116, 199
Third Fitna (744–7) 151
frontiers 5, 13–14, 20–1, 26, 32, 45, 126–7, 140, 151, 183–5, 192, 194, 197–200. *See also thughūr*
eastern, geography 2, 9ff.
process 2, 6, 32, 34–5, 109, 137, 139, 143, 170–1
studies 5–9
thesis 6, 34 (*see also* Turner, Frederick Jackson)
zone 22, 40, 110, 135–6, 143, 185
futūḥ. *See* Arab–Muslim Conquests

Gandhāra 53, 55, 59
Gao Xianzhi, Tang general (d. 756) 154–6
Gāozōng, Tang emperor (r. 650–83) 93
Gardīzī, Iranian historian (d. ca. 1061) 164, 179, 192
Gate of Iron 23–6, 28, 30, 40, 95, 115, 149, 160, 197
Gēlānī 52, 55
Geli. *See* Gēlānī
Gharjistān. *See* Gharshistān
Gharshistān 11, 32, 86, 120, 130
Ghassān b. ʿAbbād, Abbasid governor of Khurāsān (r. 817–21) 176, 179
Ghazi (holy warrior) 7, 34, 184
Ghazna 190, 193
Ghaznavid Sultanate (r. 977–1186) 190, 193
Ghifārī, Ḥakam b. ʿAmr, companion of the Prophet Muhammad (d. 670) 89
Ghiṭrīf b. ʿAṭā al-Jurashī, Abbasid governor of Khurāsān (r. 792–3) 163
Ghūr 32–5, 40, 130
Ghūrak, king of Samarqand (r. 710–38) 111–12, 119, 127–8, 131, 133
Gog and Magog 204 n.7
Gorgān 12, 29, 51–2, 56, 59–61, 66, 101, 123, 129, 151, 189–90
Great Wall 12, 29, 38, 59, 61, 65, 68–70, 123, 199
Gurambad, Chionite king (mid fourth century) 55
Gushnāspdād, Kanārang (d. 488) 62–3
Gūzgān 11, 13, 32, 75, 84–5, 102, 105–6, 120–1, 135, 140, 160, 192

ḥadd (pl. *ḥudūd*) 19–21, 28, 30, 44, 205 n.28
Ḥajjāj b. Yūsuf al-Thaqafī, Umayyad governor of Iraq (r. 694–714) 108, 110, 112, 114–16, 122, 149
Hamadān 54, 151, 178
Ḥanash b. Subul, king of Khuttal (mid eighth century) 155
Ḥarashī . *See* Saʿīd b. ʿAmr al-Ḥarashī
Ḥarith b. Surayj, rebel (d. 746) 134, 139–44, 146, 148–9, 151, 156, 160, 162, 166
Harthama b. Aʿyan, Abbasid governor of Khurāsān (d. 816–17) 173–5
Hārūn al-Rashīd, Abbasid caliph (r. 786–809) 156, 164–5, 171–4, 183
Ḥasan b. Abī al-ʿAmarraṭah al-Kindī, Umayyad governor of Khurāsān (r. ca. 724–9) 1–2, 192
Ḥasan b. ʿAlī, Shi'ite Imam (624–70) 93, 159
Ḥasan b. ʿAlī al-Ma'mūnī, Abbasid governor of Armenia 176
Ḥasan b. Ḥaydar b. Kāwūs, prince of Usrūshana (ninth century) 181
Ḥasan b. Qaḥṭaba al-Ṭā'ī, Abbasid general (d. 797) 157
Hāshim b. Ḥākim al-Jāḥiẓ. *See* Muqanna'
Ḥaydar b. Kāwūs al-Afshīn, ruler of Usrūshana (d. 841) 165, 177–8, 182
Ḥayyān al-Nabaṭī, *mawlā* general (d. 720–1) 115, 136
Helmand, River 12, 54

Hephthalites 27, 58, 70, 75, 119–20, 179, 187, 198
alliances within Sasanian Empire 43, 57–8, 62–3, 80, 87–8, 92–3
and Arab-Muslim conquest 84–6
during the Second Fitna 105–6
imperial 63–4
mercenaries 80
vassals of Turks 65, 67–9
war against Pīrūz 43–5, 59–62
Herat 3, 10, 13, 43, 52, 56, 58, 67–8, 71, 82, 84, 86–9, 102–8, 120, 133, 157, 171, 179, 185, 199
Hindu Kush 9, 11–12, 27, 34, 51, 86, 94–5, 115, 165, 183, 193, 198
Hishām, Umayyad caliph (r. 724–43) 129–30, 132–5, 141, 145, 149–51
Hissar Mountains 11
Hormozd III, Sasanian shahanshah (r. 457–9) 43, 57, 59
Hormozd IV, Sasanian shahanshah (r. 579–90) 67, 69
Hormozd Kushānshāh (r. ca. 270–ca. 300) 51–3
Ḥudūd al-ʿālam 19–20, 32, 35, 37, 192
Ḥumayd b. Qaḥṭaba al-Ṭāʾī, Abbasid governor of Khurāsān (r. 769–75) 160, 187
Huns 53–4, 57, 60, 63–4, 66
Ḥurayth b. Quṭba, Sogdian official (d. 704) 108–9
Ḥusayn b. Muʿādh, Abbasid amir of Bukhara (r. ca. 770s) 161
Ḥusayn b. Muṣʿab b. Ruzayq, father of Ṭāhir (late eight–early ninth century) 174

Ibn al-Athīr, historian (1160–1233) 77, 154, 179, 181, 192
Ibn al-Faqīh, geographer (d. after 902) 17, 25, 30, 37, 86, 93
Ibn al-Muqaffaʿ, translator (721–56) 47, 146, 186
Ibn Ḥawqal, geographer (d. 973) 2, 20–1, 23, 25, 32–3, 35–6, 38, 130
Ibn Khurradādhbih, geographer and Abbasid bureaucrat (d. 911) 17, 25, 28–30, 32, 37, 74, 82, 86, 94, 182
Ibn Rusta, geographer (wrote before 912) 21–2
Ibrāhīm b. Jibrīl b. Yaḥyā al-Bajalī, Abbasid general (late eighth century) 35, 165
Ibrāhīm b. Khālid b. Bunyāt, Bukhārkhudā (late ninth century) 180
Ibrāhīm b. Simjūr, Abū Isḥāq, Simjūrid governor (d. 948) 189
Ikhrīd, king of Kish (d. 751–2) 155
Ikhshīd, Sogdian royal title 11, 91, 100, 111, 119, 127–8, 154, 159, 161–2
Īlaq 11, 25
Ilyās b. Asad b. Sāmānkhudā, Sāmānid amir (d. 856) 174, 179–81
Ilyās b. Isḥāq, Sāmānid prince (early tenth century) 188
India 12, 21, 25, 27, 51, 53–4, 66, 97, 185, 192
Iranian Intermezzo 169, 171, 188, 193
Iraq 81, 95, 107–8, 114–15, 122, 124, 130, 133, 151, 166, 174, 194
distance from Khurāsān 12, 99, 101, 106, 110, 123
as imperial center 2, 4, 116, 152, 170, 199
Ṭāhirids in 172, 176–7
taxes sent to 126–7, 172–3, 182, 198
warriors returning to 71, 74, 77–8, 86, 97
Isfahan 68–9, 103, 152
Isfījāb 25, 28, 32, 156–7, 181, 184
Ishtīkhan 112, 127, 159, 161
Islam 140–3, 159, 181, 183, 185
conversion to 73, 97, 118, 125–6, 131, 136, 145, 177–9
Islamization 8
Ismāʿīl b. Aḥmad b. Asad, Sāmānid amir (r. 892–907) 180–1, 183–4, 188
Ispahbudān Parthian family 82–3
Iṣṭakhrī, geographer (writing ca. 951) 2, 20–1, 23, 32–3, 35–6, 38, 130, 180, 184
Istämi, Turkish khāqān (r. 553–75) 64–6

Jahm b. Ṣafwān, Murji'ite theologian (d. 746) 141
Jarrāḥ b. ʿAbdallāh al-Ḥakamī, Umayyad governor of Khurāsān (r. 717–19) 125, 128
Jaxartes, River 3, 10, 30, 34, 111, 114, 122, 127, 130, 146, 149, 156, 166, 181, 198
Jayḥūn, River. *See* Oxus, River
Jibra'īl b. Yaḥyā al-Bajalī, Abbasid general (late eighth century) 162
jihad 2, 6–7, 9, 182–4, 192
jimi fuzhou ('loose-rein' prefectures) 95–8
jizya (poll tax) 78, 125–7, 131, 144, 147
Judayʿ b. Alī al-Kirmānī, chief of the Banū Azd (d. 747) 142, 144, 146, 149, 151–2
Junayd b. ʿAbd al-Raḥmān al-Murrī, Umayyad governor of Khurāsān (r. 730–4) 132–3, 146
Jurjān. *See* Gorgān
Justin, Roman historian (ca. second century CE) 50
Jūzjān. *See* Gūzgān

Kaʿaba-i Zardusht 49, 51
Kaʿb b. Maʿdān al-Ashqarī, poet 119
Kabul 12, 51, 53, 55, 65, 92–3, 97, 156, 182
Kābulistān 94
Kābulshāhs 12, 35, 120, 165, 176, 233 n.163
Kadag/Kadagistān 59, 63, 65
Kadra-i Khīna, Bukharan *dihqān* (mid eighth century) 117
Kalīla wa dimna, translation 185–6
Kamarja 132
Kanārang 83, 185, 187, 189
Kanārangiyān Parthian family 62, 83, 187
Kāpiśā 86, 233 n.163
Karmīniyya 116, 133
Kashgar 95, 118, 172, 188
Kashkatha 116, 119
Kaṣrī Bās 28–9
Kāwūs b. Khārākhara al-Afshīn, ruler of Usrūshana (d. after 822) 177
Khākhsar 128
Khalaj Turks 28. *See also* Turks
Khālid b. ʿAbdallāh al-Qasrī, Umayyad governor of Iraq (r. 724–38) 130
kharāj (land tax) 32, 109, 125–6, 144, 147, 164, 178
Khārākhara al-Afshīn, ruler of Usrūshana (late eighth century) 165
Kharākharāf, Sāmānid military commander (tenth century) 184
Kharijites 102, 144, 151, 180, 183
Khātūn, queen of Bukhara (late seventh century) 90–1, 115–16
Khazars 67, 92
Khīna, Bukharan *dihqān* (early eighth century) 117
Kh.n.k Vardānkhudā, ruler of Vardān (early eighth century) 115
Khudhayna. *See* Saʿīd b. ʿAbd al-ʿAzīz al-Khudhayna
Khujanda 127–9, 174
Khulayd b. ʿAbdallāh al-Ḥanfī, Arab commander (mid seventh century) 88
Khulayd b. Qurra al-Yarbūʿī, Arab governor of Khurāsān (r. ca. 657–9) 78, 93
Khulm 67, 121, 135
Khurāsān passim
  description 10
  Greater Khurāsān 4, 9, 12, 73–4, 169–71, 177–8, 194–5, 197, 200
  'Inner' Khurāsān 10, 179
  kings of 74
  'Outer' Khurāsān 10, 81, 84, 179
Khūrtegīn 29
Khusrow I Anūshīrwān, Sasanian shahanshah (r. 531–79) 10, 61, 64–6, 69–70, 185–6
  reforms 74, 80–1, 180
Khusrow II Parvīz, Sasanian shahanshah (r. 590, 591–628) 67–9, 72–3, 83, 115, 179, 187, 211 n.5
Khusrow b. Pīrūz b. Yazdgird III, Sasanian prince in exile (early eighth century) 132
Khuttal 21–22, 109, 130, 132, 134, 155, 174, 176
Khuzāʿa, Arab tribe 108, 171, 174

Khuzār 129
Khwādaynāma (*Book of Kings*) 47, 80–1, 185–6
Khwarazm 11, 51–2, 56, 85, 91, 104, 112, 122, 129, 157, 164, 174
Kidarites 44–5, 55–61, 64, 69–70, 90
Kīmāk Turks 29, 37. *See also* Turks
Kināna, Arab tribe 145
Kirmān 12, 101
Kirmānī, Abū Ḥafṣ ʿUmar b. al-Azraq, historian (d. ca. mid-ninth century) 85–6, 96, 150
Kish 65, 91, 100, 108, 116, 129, 132, 155, 160–1
Kūfa 78, 93, 114, 123, 152
Kumād 21–2, 127
Kunkhas, Kidarite king (mid fifth century) 59
Kūrbaghānūn al-Turkī , Turkish commander (early eighth century) 96, 116
Kūrṣūl, Türgesh khāqān (r. 738–9) 135, 149, 154, 243 n.110
Kushan Empire (ca. 30–ca. 375) 11, 25, 45, 49–52, 69
Kushano-Sasanian Kingdom (ca. 230–ca. 360) 45, 51–5, 58, 69
Kushānshahr 11, 51, 53
Kyzyl-Kum Desert 11, 91
Kyzyl-Suu. *See* Wakhsh, River

Layth b. Naṣr b. Sayyār, son of Umayyad governor (mid eighth century) 163, 172
Łazar P'arpecʿi, Armenian historian (late fifth century) 60
Leo I, Byzantine emperor (r. 457–74) 60
limes sasanicus 65
'loose-rein" prefectures. *See jimi fuzhou*

Madā'inī, historian (d. 843) 71, 76, 79, 85, 88, 91, 112–13, 118
Māhawayh, *marzbān* or Marw (mid seventh century) 78, 82–3, 87–9, 93, 97
Mahdī, Abbasid caliph (r. 775–85) 37, 156–9, 161–2, 164–5, 170, 172, 175, 194
Maḥmūd of Ghazna, Ghaznavid sultan (r. 998–1030) 193, 197
Makrān 27, 49, 51–2
Makrān-Pāmir Shatterzone 27
Maʿmarī, Abū Manṣūr, minister and historian (d. 961) 185–7, 190–2, 201 n.8
mamlūk. *See* slaves
Ma'mūn, Abbasid caliph (r. 813–33) 157, 169–77, 179, 186, 194
Manṣūr, Abbasid caliph (r. 754–775) 35, 117, 156, 158–60, 165–6, 172, 187
Manṣūr b. Nūḥ, Sāmānid amir (r. 961-76) 181, 186, 190–1
Manṣūr b. Qarātigīn, Turkish general (d. 952) 189–90
Marājil, mother of the caliph Ma'mūn (late eighth century) 174
Mardāvīj b. Ziyār, Ziyārid ruler (r. 930–5) 189
Marw 3, 10, 12, 17, 43–4, 51, 56–8, 69–71, 78, 99, 106, 109, 115, 123, 126, 140–2, 149, 156, 160, 164, 174–5, 179, 189, 199
  Abbasid Revolution 144, 147, 151–2, 166, 171
  Arab settlement 78, 89–92, 100, 104, 125, 144, 147
  conquest 76
  death of Yazdgird III 82–4, 87, 92
  Marwshāh 49
  mint 51, 53, 68, 78–9, 104–6
  Sogdians in 107–8, 118
Marw al-Rūd 3, 10, 13, 43, 58, 69, 102–3, 120, 140, 160, 199
  conquest 71–3, 75, 80, 82–4, 87
  foundation 57, 70
  mint 104–5
marzbān (frontier governor) 57, 71, 73–4, 80, 82–4, 86–8, 120, 187
Mashriq (the East) 9, 74, 210 n.119
Masʿūdī, geographer and historian (896–959) 37, 65
Maurice, Byzantine emperor (r. 582–602) 67
Mā warā' al-nahr. *See* Transoxiana
mawlā (pl. *mawālī*) (clients) 97–8, 108, 112, 115, 117, 120, 123–6, 128,

130–1, 135–6, 140–1, 145–6, 150–2, 165–6, 171–2, 174, 176–8
mawlā amir al-mu'minīn 171, 178, 193
Mazdak, heretical Zoroastrian priest (d. 528) 62
Māzyār b. Qārin, Ispahbad of Ṭabaristān (d. 840) 178, 194
Mecca 114, 173–4
Medina 78, 86, 88, 91
Merw. *See* Marw
Mesopotamia 43–5, 48, 55, 63, 65, 78, 141, 175
Mēyam, king of Kadag (fifth century) 59
Mihragān, Zoroastrian Autumn festival 85, 135
Mihrānid Parthian family 62, 67, 81
Mongolia 58, 64, 94
Mongols 23, 30
mosques 112, 118–19, 150, 157, 161, 164, 181
Mount Mugh 128
Muʿādh b. Muslim, Abbasid governor of Khurāsān (r. ca. 777) 161, 172
Muʿāwiya I, Umayyad caliph (r. 661–80) 89, 91, 102, 149
Muʿāwiya II, Umayyad caliph (r. 683–4) 102, 104
Muḍar. *See* Qays/Muḍar
Mufaḍḍal b. al-Muhallab, Umayyad governor of Khurāsān (d. 720) 89, 119
Muhallab b. Abī Ṣufra , Arab governor of Khurāsān (d. 702) 102, 108, 114, 171
Muhallabids, family of governors 108–10, 114–15, 119
Muhammad, Prophet (571–632) 72–3, 85, 125–6, 159–60
Muḥammad b. ʿAbdallāh b. Khāzim (late seventh century) 104, 106–7
Muḥammad b. Ibrāhīm b. Simjur, Sāmānid governor and general (r. 957–60) 190–1
Muḥammad b. Naṣr b. Sayyār , son of Umayyad governor (mid eighth century) 163, 172
Muḥammad b. Sulaym al-Nāṣiḥ, Umayyad governor of Ṭukhāristān (early eighth century) 120
Muḥammad Nafs al-Zakiyya (the Pure Soul), Shi'ite rebel (d. 762) 158–9
Muḥtājids, rulers of Chaghāniyān 188–90, 192
Mujashshir b. Muzāhim al-Sulāmī, Arab soldier (early eighth century) 132
Muqaddasī, geographer (ca. 945–1000) 2, 9, 23, 32, 37, 39, 180–1, 184, 232 n.148, 251–2 n.127
Muqanna', Hāshim b. Ḥākim al-Jāḥiẓ, rebel (d. ca. 783) 159–63, 165–6, 172, 187
Muqātil b. ʿAlī al-Sughdī, Umayyad military commander (mid eighth century) 149–50
Muqātil b. Ḥayyān al-Nabaṭī, Umayyad military commander (early eighth century) 140, 151
Murghāb, River 3, 10–11, 13, 55, 57–8, 69–71, 75, 84–5, 88, 140, 199
Murji'ites 140–1
Mūsā b. ʿAbdallāh b. Khāzim, ruler of Termez (d. 704–5) 99–100, 106–10, 140
Muṣʿab b. Ruzayq, Abbasid secretary (mid eighth century) 171
Musayyab b. Bishar al-Riyāḥī , Arab warrior (early eighth century) 131
Musayyab b. Zuhayr al-Ḍabbī, Abbasid governor of Khurāsān (r. 780–2) 164
Muslim b. Saʿīd al-Kilābī, Umayyad governor of Khurāsān (r. 722–4) 1, 129–30
Muʿtaḍid, Abbasid caliph (r. 892–902) 181, 184
Muʿtaṣim, Abbasid caliph (r. 833–42) 178, 181–2
mutaṭawwiʿa (volunteer fighters) 7, 123
Mutawakkil, Abbasid caliph (r. 847–61) 182
Muzāḥim b. Bisṭām, conqueror of Bāmiyān (mid eighth century) 35

Nakshshab. *See* Nasaf
Namrūn, king of Gharshistān (early eighth century) 130
Narseh, Sasanian shahanshah (r. 293–302) 49, 52–3
Narseh b. Pīrūz b Yazdgird III, Sasanian prince in-exile (d. after 709) 93, 96, 109
Narshakh 161–2
Narshakhī, local historian (ca. 899–959) 37–8, 90–1, 94, 115–18, 131, 150, 153, 159–62, 174, 176, 179–80, 188
Nasā 82–3, 86
Nasaf 65, 91, 116, 160–1, 173
Nasafī, historian and biographer (1067–1142) 119, 156, 184
Naṣr II b. Aḥmad, Sāmānid amir (r. 914–43) 186, 188–9, 191
Naṣr b. Sayyār, Umayyad governor of Khurāsān (r. 738–48) 25, 129, 133, 141–2, 144–7, 149–52, 156, 163, 166, 171–2, 243 n.110
Nawākit 160
Naw Bahār monastery 54, 86, 96–7, 150, 164
Nīshāpūr 10, 43, 57–8, 61, 68, 71, 78, 93, 102, 105–6, 120, 141, 151–2, 185, 189–90, 199. *See also* Abarshahr
  ʿAbdallāh b. Khāzim and 104, 107
  conquest 82–4, 88, 187
  mint 90, 104
  Shāpūr II's construction projects 56, 70
  Ṭāhirid capital 170, 178–9, 183
Nīzak Ṭarkhān, Hephthalite ruler of Bādhghīs (late seventh–early eighth century) 75, 82, 86, 89, 106, 109, 115, 129, 136
  and the death of Yazdgird III 87–8, 92, 97
  rebellion 112, 119–21
nomads 3, 9, 13–14, 23, 147, 197
  mercenaries 81, 90
  raids 5, 14, 20
  settlement and state formation 14, 43, 54, 63, 66, 70
Nūḥ I b. Naṣr II, Sāmānid amir (r. 943–54) 189–91
Nūḥ II b. Manṣūr, Sāmānid amir (r. 976–97) 193
Nūḥ b. Asad b. Sāmānkhudā, Sāmānid amir (d. 842) 174, 179–82
Numijkat 36–7, 160–1, 210 n.119
numismatics 45, 48, 52, 55, 65, 67, 86, 89–90, 103–6, 141, 155, 157, 159–60, 170, 172, 176–7, 179
Nūshajān 28–30, 33–4, 39
  Lower (*al-suflī*) 28–30, 32
  Upper (*al-aʿlā*) 28–32, 34, 40

Oghuz Turks 37, 181. *See also* Turks
Orkhon inscriptions 25
Oxus, River *passim*
  as border 3–4, 10–11, 65, 69–70, 193

Pahlavi 47, 53, 105, 185–6
Pāmir 21–2, 28, 40
Pāmir Knot 27
Pāmir Mountains 9, 11
Panj, River 22
Panjhīr 206 n.41
Panjikant 128–9, 131
Parthians 46, 49, 52, 59, 62, 74, 80–1, 83, 87, 88, 97, 106, 179, 187.
Paykand 37, 56, 67, 90, 100, 115–18, 124, 132, 136, 161 n.127
Peacock Army 108, 114
Pei Xingjian, Tang minister (d. ca. 682) 93, 96
Persian language 4, 47, 118, 136, 169, 185–8, 190–2, 197. *See also* Pahlavi
Pīrūz, Sasanian shahanshah (r. 459–84) 43–6, 57–62, 64–5, 69–70, 80
Pīrūz b. Yazdgird III, Sasanian prince in-exile (d. 679) 78, 92–3, 95–6
Pīrūzdukht, daughter of Pīrūz (late fifth century) 62
Procopius, Byzantine historian (ca. 500–ca. 554) 60–1, 63

Qā'in-Birjand Mountains 12
qanat 48–9
Qarākhānids (eleventh to thirteenth century) 157, 188, 192–4, 197

Qara-Qum Desert 11
Qarātagīn, Sāmānid military commander (d. 932) 184
Qārinid Parthian family 52, 62, 83, 88–9, 97, 178. *See also* Parthians
Qārlūq Turks 22, 28–9, 154, 156, 161–3, 174–6, 184. *See also* Turks
Qarshi. *See* Nasaf
qaṣr (pl. *quṣūr*, fortified estate) 38
Qaṣr Bāhiliyya 126, 131
Qays/Muḍar, Arab tribal confederations 101–3, 105, 114, 123–4, 126, 129–30, 132, 137, 140–3, 145–7, 149–51
Qubād I, Sasanian shahansshah (r. 486–96, 498–531) 44, 61–5, 80, 232 n.148
Qubād II Shirūy, Sasanian shahanshah (r. 628) 94
Qudāma b. Jaʿfar al-Kātib, Abbasid bureaucrat and writer (d. before 948) 17, 29–30, 32, 37
Qūhistān 12, 27, 88, 101–2, 104, 106
Qundūz 22, 86, 92–3, 95
Qutayba b. Muslim, Umayyad governor of Khurāsān (r. 705–15) 25, 73, 96, 110, 113–15, 123–4, 131, 136, 150–1, 166–7
  and China 118
  conquest of Bukhara 94, 111, 115–19
  conquest of Samarqand 111–13, 117
  fall and death 122–3
  legacy 124–5, 127, 153
  and Narseh b. Pīrūz 93
  and Nīzak Ṭarkhān 89, 112, 119–21
Qutayba b. Ṭughshāda, Bukhārkhudā (d. before 755) 38, 151, 153, 155

Rabīʿa, Arab tribal confederation 101–2, 129, 145, 151
Rabīʿ b. ʿImrān al-Tamīmī, Arab interpreter (early eighth century) 136
Rabīʿ b. Ziyād al-Ḥārithī, Umayyad governor of Khurāsān (d. 673) 89
Rāḍī, Abbasid caliph (r. 934–40) 189
Rāfiʿ b. Layth b. Naṣr, rebel (early ninth century) 163, 165–6, 171–6
Rāg-i Bībī 51
Rāmithān 90
Rāshidūn Caliphate (r. 632–61) 77, 169, 225 n.20
Rāsht 17–19, 21–3, 26, 28, 30, 40, 46, 164
Rayy 69, 82, 165, 172–3, 175, 189–90, 192
ribāṭ (pl. *ribāṭāt*) (frontier forts) 37–8, 164, 183–4, 244 n.125
Rōb 47, 53, 121
Roman Empire (r. 27 BCE–395 CE) 44, 51, 58, 87
Róurán Khāqānat (r. ca. 330–555) 64
Rūdakī, Persian poet (858–941) 186
Rukn al-Dawla, Buyid amir (r. 947–77) 189–90
Ruzayq, Ṭāhirid ancestor (late seventh century) 171

Sabal, ruler of Khutaal (early eighth century) 109
Saffāḥ, Abbasid caliph (r. 749–54) 153, 158
Ṣaffārids (r. 861–1003) 8, 181–2, 184, 194
Saʿīd al-Ḥarashī, Abbasid military commander (late eighth century) 160–1
Saʿīd b. ʿAbd al-ʿAzīz al-Khudhayna, Umayyad governor of Khurāsān (r. 720–1) 126–7, 131, 140
Saʿīd b. ʿAmr al-Ḥarashī, Umayyad governor of Khurāsān (r. 721–2) 127–9
Saʿīd b. ʿUthmān, Arab governor of Khurāsān (d. ca. 678) 91, 112
Sakā. *See* Scythians
Sakānshāh 49, 51–2, 57
Sakāstān 49, 68. *See also* Sīstān
Sallām al-Abrash, eunuch serving the Ṭāhirids (early ninth century) 177
Sallāmī, Ḥusayn b. Aḥmad, Sāmānid historian (d. ca. 961) 175, 190, 192
Salm b. Ziyād b. Abīhi, Umayyad governor of Khurāsān (r. 680–3) 91–2, 102–6

Sāmānids (r. 819–999) 5, 174, 176, 179–80, 188–90, 192–5, 200
and the Bukhārkhudās 180–1
and the frontier 170, 181–5, 192
and Greater Khurāsān 4, 169–70, 194
and Iranian kingship 169–70, 191
patronage of Persian literature 186, 191
Sāmānkhudā 179
slaves 181–2
Samarqand 1, 10, 25, 28, 62, 65, 100, 155, 157, 179–81, 188, 197, 210 n.119, 229–30 n.106
conquest 91–2, 111–13, 116–17, 122
mint 67, 157, 159, 179
and Muqanna' 160–2
and Rāfiʿ b. Layth 163, 172–5
rebellion 127, 131
settlement 124–5
and the Türgesh 131–4, 149, 166
walls 37–8, 157
Samarra' 178, 181–2
Sarakhs 82, 120
Sasanian Empire (r. 224–651) Chapter Two passim., 71, 125, 169–70, 180, 199
conquest 73–4, 81–4, 97
frontier 4, 11, 28, 43–4, 54–8, 65, 69–70, 85
historiography 46–8
in-exile 74–5, 78–9, 92–6, 109, 115, 132
organization 10, 45–6, 48–9, 52–3, 58, 61, 69, 74, 80–1
Sāvah Shāh. *See* Shābah
Sawra b. al-Ḥurr, Umayyad commander in Samarqand (d. 731) 133
Sayf b. ʿUmar, Arab historical traditionist (d. 796) 77, 84
Sayḥūn, River. *See* Jaxartes, River
Sāyrām. *See* Isfījāb
Scythians 12, 50, 52
Seljuqs (r. 1040–1194) 30, 169, 236 n.51
Shābah , Turkish khāqān (late sixth century) 67
Shāhfirind bt. Narseh, Sasanian princess and mother of Yazīd III (early eighth century) 93
Shahr-i Sabaz. *See* Kish
Shāpūr I, Sasanian shahanshah (r. 241–72) 49, 51
Shāpūr II, Sasanian shahanshah (r. 309–79) 52–3, 55–7, 65
Shāpūr III, Sasanian shahanshah (r. 383–8) 56
Shāpūr Sakānshāh 52
Sharʿabī al-Ṭā'ī, Arab poet (early eighth century) 134
Sharīk b. Shaykh al-Mahrī, Shi'ite rebel (d. ca. 751) 153, 155, 159, 161, 163, 166
Shāsh. *See* Chāch
shatterzone 23, 26–8, 31, 35–6, 40–1, 43, 45, 71, 73, 88, 97, 110, 136, 147, 180, 197–200
Shaʿyā b. Farighūn, Iranian encyclopedist (tenth century) 192
Shaybān b. Salama, Kharijite rebel (d. 747–8) 144, 151
Shi'ism 144, 147, 153, 158–60, 166
shīr (of Bāmiyān) 35, 41, 165
Shūmān 115, 129
Sijistān. *See* Sīstān
silk 66
'Silk Road' 10–12, 27, 51, 56, 118
Silziboulos. *See* Istämi
Simjūrids (10th century) 193
Sind 49, 52
Sinjibū Khāqān. *See* Istämi
Sīstān 9, 27, 50–3, 56, 61, 92–3, 95, 108, 114–15, 171, 177, 180–1, 183, 185
description 12
slaves 48, 91, 97, 112, 134, 150, 155, 173, 181–2
soldiers 123, 134, 149–50, 180–2, 188, 194
Smbat IV Bagratuni, Armenian prince (d. 617) 68–70, 85
Sogdiana passim
conquest 71, 73–4, 79, 89–92, 107, 111, 113–16, 135–6
description 10–11
language 15, 118, 128
merchants 10–11, 51, 56, 66, 90, 128, 198
alliances with the Arabs 107, 117–18

revolts 124, 127–9
taxation 125–7, 131, 136–7, 145, 150
Turco-Sogdian alliance 66–9, 71, 74, 90–1, 116, 127, 131–2
steppes 3, 9, 13–14, 23, 43, 58, 181, 193
confederacies 1, 27, 45, 54, 64, 68–9, 102, 134
empires 59–60
Strabo, Roman historian (63 BCE–23 CE) 38, 50
Suhrab, prince of Ṭālaqān (early 8th century) 140
Sūkhrā, Parthian minister (d. 493) 62
Sulaym, Arab tribe 102
Sulaym al-Nāṣiḥ (the Counselor), *mawlā* advisor (early 8th century) 115, 120–1
Sulaymān, Umayyad caliph (r. 715–17) 114–15, 122–3
Sulaymān b. Abī al-Sārī, Umayyad official (early 8th century) 117, 124–5, 129, 137
Sulaymān b. Kathīr al-Khuzāʿī, Abbasid propagandist (d. ca. 750) 171
Sulaymān b. Marthad, leader of the Banū Bakr b. Wā'il in Khurāsān (d. ca. 683–4) 102–3
Suluk, Türgesh khāqān (r. 716–38) 130–5, 142, 154
Sūren Parthian family 52
Surkhāb, River. *See* Wakhsh, River
Surkh Kōtal 51, 86
Sūyāb (Ak-Beshim, Kyrgyzstan) 93, 96, 154
'Swiss cheese' model 31, 39–40, 121, 147, 199
Syr Darya. *See* Jaxartes, River
Syria 44, 68, 78, 102, 104, 109, 112, 121, 142, 151, 175, 177, 199

Ṭabarī, historian (839–923) 1, 44–5, 47, 49, 57, 65, 67, 71–3, 76–7, 79, 81, 83, 87–9, 92, 104, 126, 128–30, 132, 135, 149, 155, 157, 164, 172–4, 177, 181, 184, 186–7, 200
Ṭabaristān 12–13, 82–3, 123, 162, 177–8, 189
Ṭāhir I b. al-Ḥusayn, Abbasid general and governor, founder of Ṭāhirid dynasty (ca. 776–822) 169, 171, 174–7
Ṭāhir II b. ʿAbdallāh, Ṭāhirid governor (r. 844–62) 181
Ṭāhirids (r. 821–73) 4, 37, 169–72, 174, 176–84, 194
Ṭālaqān 11, 13, 43, 57, 75, 84, 102–3, 120–1, 133, 140, 160
Ṭalās. *See* Ṭarāz
Ṭalḥa b. ʿAbdallāh al-Khuzāʿī, Arab governor of Sīstān (d. 685) 171
Ṭalḥa b. Ruzayq, Abbasid secretary (mid eighth century) 171
Ṭalḥa b. Ṭāhir, Ṭāhirid governor (r. 822–8) 177
Tamīm, Arab tribe 77–8, 103–7, 132, 139–41, 145, 223 n.3
Tang Empire (r. 618–907) 71, 75, 95–7, 97–8, 116, 135–6, 154–6
and the Arabs 28, 118, 123, 127, 154–6, 229–30 n.106
and the Sasanians 92–6, 229–30 n.106
and the Turks 68, 90, 94–5, 130–1, 154–6
Ṭār, king of Ferghana (early eighth century) 127
Ṭarāz 28–30, 154–5, 157, 184. *See also* Battle of Ṭarāz
Tardu b. Istämi, Turkish khāqān (r. 575–603) 68
Tarim Basin 11–12, 51, 63, 93, 95, 118, 154, 172
Ṭarkhūn, king of Samarqand (d. 710) 91, 100, 108–9, 111–12, 116, 119, 121, 128
Ṭarsūs 156, 164
Tashkent. *See* Chāch
Tawāwīs 37, 133
taxation 72, 80–1, 85, 108, 117, 119, 125–8, 130–1, 134–7, 144–5, 147, 150, 164–5, 173, 178, 183, 187, 194, 197–8. *See also* *jizya*; *kharāj*
Termez 17–18, 22–6, 91, 100, 106, 108–10, 140–1, 157, 179

Thābit b. Quṭba, Sogdian official (d. 704) 108–9
thughūr (sing. *thaghr*) 7, 20–1, 75. *See also* frontier
thughūrology 7
Tiānshān Mountains 9, 11, 30
Tibet 12, 29, 93, 96, 100, 154, 174
Tīmūr (r. 1370–1405) 25, 197
Tirmidh. *See* Termez
Tish al-Aʿwar, king of Chaghāniyān (early eighth century) 115, 127
Tŏng Yabghu Khāqān, Turkish khāqān (r. 619–30) 94
Transoxiana passim. *See also* Sogdiana
description 10–11
Ṭughshāda b. Bīdūn, Bukhārkhudā (d. 739) 90, 115–16, 121, 127, 131, 136, 150
Tughuzghuz Turks 29–30, 174. *See also* Turks
Ṭukhāristān passim
description 11
Tūrān 49, 52
Türgesh Turks 1, 29, 96, 118, 126, 130, 131–5, 141–3, 146, 148–52, 154, 156, 162. *See also* Turks
origins 131
and Sogdian revolts 124, 127–8, 131, 136, 166
Tūrghar b. Ghūrak, king of Samarqand (d. ca. 751) 155
Türk Khāqānate (r. 552–659) 1, 3, 25, 27–8, 64–70, 90, 94–6, 98, 131. *See also* Turks
alliance with Byzantines 66–7
Eastern 66, 94
organization 64, 66, 68
origins 64
Turco-Sogdian alliance 66
Western 1, 64–6, 68, 92, 94–5, 98, 103, 130
Türkmenabat. *See* Āmul
Turks 1, 54, 63, 92–3, 96, 101, 116, 121, 123–4, 129–30, 136, 140, 145, 156, 158, 162–3, 193, 197. *See also* Khalaj; Kīmāk; Oghuz; Qārlūq; Tughuzghuz; Türgesh; Türk Khāqānate
conversion to Islam 32, 175, 192–3
Land of the Turks 21–2, 28–30
in the lands of Islam 32
origins 64
pastoralism 30–1
raiding 17–19, 21, 36, 163–4, 181
slaves 134, 149–50, 180–2, 188
soldiers and mercenaries 87, 149–50, 160, 173, 181, 187–91, 193–4, 197, 200
sources 47–8
as term for all nomadic peoples 86, 88
Turner, Frederick Jackson, American historian (1861–1932) 2, 6, 20, 34–5, 109, 113, 137, 143
Ṭūs 62, 82–3, 173, 185, 187, 189–91

ʿUbaydallāh b. Ziyād, Umayyad governor of Khurāsān (r. 673–83) 89–91
ulema 6–7, 183
ʿUmar II, Umayyad caliph (r. 717–20) 85, 117, 123–6
ʿUmar b. al-Khaṭṭāb, caliph (r. 634–44) 77, 84
ʿUmar b. Hubayra al-Fazārī, Umayyad governor of Iraq (r. 721–4) 126, 129
ʿUmar Sūbakhī, rebel (ca. 770s) 160
Umayya b. ʿAbdallāh b. Khālid b. Asīd, Umayyad governor of Khurāsān (r. ca. 693–7) 107–9
Umayyad Caliphate (r. 661–750) 1–3, 91, 110–11, 113–14, 123–4, 139, 142–5, 149, 151–2, 164, 166, 169, 198–9
and local lords 115–16, 118–21, 136
Marwānids (r. 684–750) 73, 107, 114, 129, 140–1
rebellious governors 99–101, 106–9, 122–3, 151
and Sogdians 125–6, 131, 135–7, 150
Sufyānids (r. 661–84) 77, 102, 105
Umm Muḥammad bt. ʿAbdallāh al-Thaqafī, wife of Salm b. Ziyād (late seventh century) 91–2
Usrūshana 11, 128, 134, 155–6, 174, 176–7, 179, 181
Ustādhsīs, rebel (active 764–8) 160
ʿUthmān b. ʿAffān, caliph (r. 644–56) 6, 76–8, 88, 102, 187

ʿUwāfah, Arab tribe 117

Varahrān Kushānshāh (r. ca. 325–ca. 360) 53, 55
Varakhsha 37, 117, 153, 180–1
Vardānkhudā 94, 115–16, 136
Vushmgīr b. Ziyār, Ziyārid ruler (r. 935–67) 189

Wakhsh, River 22, 28, 40, 86, 129
Wakhshāb, River. *See* Wakhsh, River
Walīd I, Umayyad caliph (r. 705–15) 79, 93, 112, 114, 122
Walīd II, Umayyad caliph (r. 743–4) 151
walls 25, 36–9, 46, 60–1, 65, 70, 157, 163, 183
Wang Minyuan, Tang official (late seventh century) 96
Waraghsar 131
Wāshjird 17, 22
Wāṣil b. ʿAmr al-Qaysī, Umayyad lieutenant in Bukhara (d. 739) 150
'White-Clothed-Ones' 160–3, 172
Wǔ, Tang empress (r. 684–705) 93

Xiōngnú 51, 54, 63–4
Xuanzang, Buddhist pilgrim (ca. 602–64) 24–5, 233 n.164
Xuánzōng, Tang emperor (r. 712–56) 118, 156

Yabghu 92–5, 120–1, 127, 130, 134, 175–6
Yaḥyā b. Asad b. Sāmānkhudā, Sāmānid amir (d. 855) 174, 179–80
Yaḥyā b. Khālid b. Barmak, Abbasid vizier (d. 806) 165
Yaman, Arab tribal confederacy 101–2, 105, 123–4, 129–30, 137, 141, 143, 145–7, 149–51
Yaʿqūb b. Layth, Ṣaffārid amir (r. 861–79) 183, 194
Yaʿqūbī, historian and geographer (d. after 905) 21, 23, 35–6, 76, 91, 156, 162, 172, 174–5
Yāqūt, biographer and geographer (d. 1229) 17–19, 21, 30, 86
Yazdgird II, Sasanian shahanshah (r. 438–57) 43, 57–8
Yazdgird III, Sasanian shahanshah (r. 632–51) 47, 77–8, 82–3, 87, 92, 94, 185
Yazīd I, Umayyad caliph (r. 680–3) 102, 104
Yazīd II, Umayyad caliph (r. 720–4) 123, 126, 129
Yazīd III, Umayyad caliph (r. 744) 93
Yazīd b. al-Muhallab, Umayyad governor of Khurāsān (672–720) 89, 108–9, 114, 119, 122–3, 126
Yazīd b. Ghūrak, king of Samarqand (ca. 751–after 776) 155, 161–2
Yemen 66, 72
Yuèzhī 11, 51
Yūsuf al-Barm , rebel (active ca. 768–76) 160, 171
Yūsuf b. ʿUmar al-Thaqafī, Umayyad governor of Iraq (r. 738–44) 149, 151

Zābulistān 12, 65, 94, 233 n.163
Zāmāsp, Sasanian shahanshah (r. 496–8) 62
Zarāfshān, River 10, 13, 38, 70, 90–1, 113, 116, 128–9, 155
Zaranj 12, 92–3, 183
Zarmihr b. Sūkhrā, Parthian nobleman of Qārinid family (d. 558) 62
Zeno, Byzantine emperor (r. 474–5, 476–91) 60
Zhōngguó (Middle Kingdom) 98
Zhulād Gūzgān, king of Ghar (late seventh century) 105
Ziyād b. Abīhi, Umayyad governor of Iraq (d. 673) 89
Ziyād b. Ṣāliḥ, lieutenant to Abū Muslim (d. 752–3) 153, 155–6, 158
Zoroastrianism 12, 53, 62, 85, 119, 135, 143, 159, 174, 185
Zubayrids 105
Zunbīl 12, 115, 183, 233 n.163